Regional Integration: Theory and Research

Regional Integration

Theory and Research

Edited by Leon N. Lindberg and Stuart A. Scheingold

Harvard University Press, Cambridge, Massachusetts   1971

Distributed in Great Britain by Oxford University Press, London

Library of Congress Catalog Card Number 77-139717

The essays in this volume originally appeared in a special issue of
International Organization entitled "Regional Integration: Theory and
Research," Vol. XXIV, No. 4 (Autumn 1970).

Printed in the United States of America

To Madeleine, our primary source

Contents

Preface ix

I. Retrospection and Evaluation

1. Ernst B. Haas. The Study of Regional Integration:
   Reflections on the Joy and Anguish of Pretheorizing 3

II. Elaborations of Conceptual and Causal Paradigms

2. Leon N. Lindberg. Political Integration as a Multidimensional
   Phenomenon Requiring Multivariate Measurement 45
3. Donald J. Puchala. International Transactions and Regional Integration 128
4. Ronald Inglehart. Public Opinion and Regional Integration 160
5. J. S. Nye. Comparing Common Markets: A Revised
   Neo-Functionalist Model 192
6. Philippe C. Schmitter. A Revised Theory of Regional Integration 232
7. Hayward R. Alker, Jr. Integration Logics: A Review,
   Extension, and Critique 265

III. New Areas for Investigation

8. Fred M. Hayward. Continuities and Discontinuities between
   Studies of National and International Political Integration:
   Some Implications for Future Research Efforts 313
9. Andrzej Korbonski. Theory and Practice of Regional
   Integration: The Case of Comecon 338
10. Stuart A. Scheingold. Domestic and International
    Consequences of Regional Integration 374

Selected Bibliography 399

Index 417

PREFACE

In April 1969 a group of scholars concerned with research problems in the field of regional integration met in Madison, Wisconsin. The Conference on Regional Integration was held under the auspices of the World Peace Foundation and the International Studies Program at the University of Wisconsin. The papers in this volume were initially presented, albeit in embryo form, at the Madison conference. While the participants represented a number of approaches to the study of regional integration, they had a good deal in common. Most clearly, they shared an interest in the inquiry launched in 1958 by the publication of *The Uniting of Europe: Political, Social, and Economic Forces, 1950–1957* by Ernst B. Haas and a determination to evaluate the progress made since that initial work. Several of the participants had been students of Ernie Haas, and the guidance and support which he provided at the conference was only the most recent chapter in a longer story. Almost all of the participants knew one another and had worked together for some years either directly or with each other's ideas. We were, in other words, drawn together as friends as well as intellectual coconspirators in search of an increasingly elusive dependent variable. The Madison conference was convened, then, to take stock of the past and to look ahead to the future. We were not seeking a single blueprint for research but we were hoping to develop the broad contours of a research strategy to which we and our students might consciously relate in the years ahead.

These aspirations called for a spirit of collective synthesis at the conference as well as a list of topics which not only "covered" the field of integration studies as it is presently constituted but which reached beyond the present boundaries. Our research frontier was defined with various goals in mind: the development of a more sophisticated theory and methodology, the acceleration of comparative regional integration analysis, and the exploration of inchoate links to the problems of nation building and political change. To encourage synthesis the conference was built around a series of research memoranda followed by a rather elaborate process of editorial critique and revision.

The research memoranda were intended to serve as invitations to a colloquy. They were circulated prior to the conference and became the focal point for group discussions. We assumed that these memoranda would be preferable to formal papers in that the participants would be less constrained by pride of authorship and, thus, better prepared to take a critical look at what they had written in light of exchanges in the panels. In retrospect this seems to have been a good idea. The discussions were lively, uninhibited, and constructive. All of us learned much about the way in which our individual contributions related to the joint enterprise. Moreover, in the period since the conference the participants have been uniformly responsive to a long editorial process in which many papers have been drastically revised once and often twice in an effort to enhance the integrity of the collection. If this volume has been integrated, then, it is due primarily to the determination of the contributors to make this a collective effort: We cannot but feel that this community spirit was nurtured by the warmth of Madison's welcome and the gourmet spell cast over the proceedings by our wives, Beatrice and Leanora.

In a sense we see this volume as ringing down the curtain on the first act of integration studies. Our hope is that these essays answer some questions about where we have been and what we have accomplished. Certainly, one of our goals was the evaluation of more than a decade of intellectual effort by the contributors to this volume as well as many others who have pioneered in the study of integration. But we are really more interested in raising questions than in answering them. We look back only in order to look ahead, to prepare for the second act. Let us, then, consider briefly the unifying themes which lead us to see these ten separate essays as the individual parts of a common inquiry.

The opening article by Ernst B. Haas carries the main burden of overall retrospection and evaluation of the state of the field and serves as a general introduction to this volume. Haas characterizes and evaluates the contributions of the several "schools" of integration study, summarizes the empirical generalizations they have given us about the integration phenomenon, and identifies what remains to be done if we want to move beyond past efforts.

The articles in the second part of this volume represent variations on the themes announced by Haas. The pieces cohere in that each author seeks to develop logical or methodological elaborations of the main conceptual and causal paradigms with which integration students have worked. Leon N. Lindberg's article deals with the concept of political integration itself. He offers a definition and a conceptual paradigm which identify political integration as a multidimensional phenomenon requiring multivariate measurement. He goes into some detail in proposing operationalization strategies so that static and dynamic measurement, aggregated and nonaggregated, will be possible. Donald J. Puchala systematically surveys the character and utility of the various techniques for measuring integration provided by transaction flow analysis. He introduces some new procedures for generating and transforming data on political transactions. The substantial descriptive potential of transaction analysis is then illustrated with data from Western Europe. Ronald Inglehart focuses on one relatively poorly understood causal linkage in integration processes, that between the preferences of mass publics and the pro- or anti-integrative decisions taken by elites. He draws extensively on recent European public opinion data in order to specify what this might suggest for future prospects of European integration. Both Joseph S. Nye and Philippe C. Schmitter go well beyond a concern for definition and measurement or the specification of a single causal linkage. Each author seeks to develop a comprehensive causal paradigm for the comparative study of integration processes. Both depart from a "neo-functionalist" position but try to introduce insights and variables from other approaches as they deem necessary. Hayward R. Alker, Jr., focuses on "integration logics" and casts a critical eye on the efforts of students of integration to develop adequate measurements and explanatory theory. He explores at length the contributions that might be made in both areas by a greater attention to mathematical formalization.

The articles in the third part of this volume are distinctive in that each author seeks to broaden the scope of analysis beyond the standard paradigms now in use. Fred M. Hayward considers the concepts, methodologies, and data used by students of national political integration and seeks to demonstrate their potential relevance for the analysis of international integration. Andrzej Korbonski examines the economic integration phenomenon among the planned economies of Eastern Europe and finds that it cannot be adequately understood within the terms set by the standard causal paradigms. Finally, Stuart A. Scheingold draws attention to the fact that the preoccupation of scholars with the processes of integration has led them to neglect the question, "What difference does it make?" He proposes that more attention be devoted to studies of the consequences of integration, suggests some of the ends to be served by such studies, and indicates some research strategies which are likely to be fruitful.

As the work of ten different authors, who are at least as individualistic as independent scholars are typically wont to be, this volume will not reveal the true synthesis which can perhaps issue only from a single mind but rather a very substantial degree of convergence. The authors have worked hard to respond to each other as well as to their other critics. They have reached a wide area of agreement as to what is good and what is not so good in integration studies, the tasks that lie ahead, and the paths toward their completion. Indeed, several authors (Alker, Haas, Nye, Schmitter, Lindberg) are presently working together to design a series of computer simulations of integration processes. But a richness and diversity of approach is still evident in these articles. Integration studies have clearly not yet passed beyond their "Hundred Flowers" period. On the other hand, these articles are continuous with one another theoretically and methodologically, and they all lead in the same directions. The authors hope that this volume will stimulate other scholars to join them in the excitement of exploring these future paths.

Madison, Wisconsin   LEON N. LINDBERG
June 1970   STUART A. SCHEINGOLD

I

RETROSPECTION AND EVALUATION

1

The Study of Regional Integration:

Reflections on the Joy and Anguish of Pretheorizing

ERNST B. HAAS

I. WHY STUDY REGIONAL INTEGRATION?

WHY have we been studying something we call "regional integration" for about fifteen years? We were stimulated by two otherwise unrelated trends: the flowering in the United States of systematic social science and the blooming in Europe of political efforts to build a united continent, to "integrate" Western Europe at least.[1] But the story of integration encompassed a mixed bag of heroes ranging from such regional "integrators" as Napoleon Bonaparte and Simón Bolívar to nation-building statesmen such as Otto von Bismarck and Camillo Cavour. Some saw even in Adolf Hitler and Hideki Tojo certain characteristics of the political actor who seeks to integrate nations into a regional unit. Are we then studying *any* kind of political unification?

Often one gets the impression that the study of regional integration is the same as the study of regional cooperation, of regional organizations, of regional systems and subsystems, or of regionalism. All these terms are widely used. They compound the general uncertainty of whether regional conquerors and nation builders are also actors on the stage of regional integration. To delimit the field, therefore, it must be stressed that the study of regional inte-

ERNST B. HAAS is professor of political science at the University of California at Berkeley. This article owes an unquantifiable debt to many years of intensive collaboration, literal and spiritual, with the contributors to this volume as well as to Ivan Vallier, Stuart Fagan, Aaron Segal, Isebill Gruhn, Francis Beer, and Mario Barrera. This essay resulted from the project "Studies in International Integration," Institute of International Studies, University of California, Berkeley.

[1] I consider the pioneering work in this field to be Karl W. Deutsch's *Political Community at the International Level: Problems of Definition and Measurement* (Garden City, N.Y: Doubleday & Co., 1954). Deutsch raised all the major questions and introduced many of the concepts that still preoccupy and guide the research effort.

gration is unique and discrete from all previous systematic studies of political unification because it limits itself to *noncoercive* efforts. The study of federalism, national unification, nation and empire building is necessarily replete with attention to the use of force by the federalizer or the catalytic agent—external colonizing elite, military conqueror, or hegemony-seeking state. Our task is to explain integration among nations without recourse to these historical agents not because they have not been important but because they make the explanation too simple and too time-bound. The dominant desire of modern students of regional integration is to explain the tendency toward the voluntary creation of larger political units each of which self-consciously eschews the use of force in the relations between the participating units and groups.

The main reason for studying regional integration is thus normative: The units and actions studied provide a living laboratory for observing the peaceful creation of possible new types of human communities at a very high level of organization and of the processes which may lead to such conditions. The study of regional integration is concerned with tasks, transactions, perceptions, and learning, not with sovereignty, military capability, and balances of power. It refuses to dichotomize the behavior of actors between "high" political and "low" functional concerns; it is preoccupied with all concerns of actors insofar as they can be used for sketching processes of adaptation and learning free from coercion.

This central reason should not obscure other normative uses to which the study of regional integration can also be put; they are in fact suggested by the overarching concern just stated. We can discover whether regional peacekeeping machinery is more effective than United Nations procedures, an important lesson for future modes of conflict resolution. We can also discover when and where regional processes are merely a facade for the hegemony of one member state. We can get more information about which elite learns from whom in the interactions triggered by regional processes, discover what is learned, and trace the use to which the new insight is put. Again we can contrast this with similar events at the global level. We can discover whether regional common markets are really better for industrialization and effective welfare policies than is a global division of labor, whether they lead to redistribution and the equitable sharing of scarce resources—or to more competition for such spoils.

All this should be self evident. But it has been hidden by the concern of some students of integration for the canons of social science and its language. Nor is this to be regretted. Apart from and beyond the normative importance of these studies the empirical theory of international relations is advanced by clearly delineating and establishing recurrent practices. Moreover, the study of regional integration makes it possible to use the comparative study of foreign policy, even of domestic policies, and connect it with the study of international processes. In short, the field of "linkage politics"—as a conceptual bridge between theories of the international system and theories of national behavior—can be given real life if the empty boxes of its matrices can be filled with the interactions studied in the process of regional integration.[2]

In the following pages I shall attempt an evaluation of fifteen years of research on regional integration. I should like to confess at the outset that while inferences about learning, adaptation, and the evolution of shared tasks among nations have provided the foci for research, the normative uses to which the findings could be put have not received the attention they deserve. Nor has the field been systematically pressed into the service of theory building in the area of comparative foreign policy studies. This must be our first evaluative finding. But the effort at evaluation forces us to pose some other questions as well. They constitute a grab bag of nagging doubts and uncertainties rather than a methodologically satisfying scheme of analysis. Moreover these questions do not rest on a consensus as to what the field *should* yield, and therefore they are far from constituting a paradigm against which a variety of ongoing work can be judged. They are, in short, just questions which guided the effort of evaluation.[3]

1) I shall inquire whether these studies have yielded a set of generalizations of empirically founded truths about integration. 2) Further, I wish to know whether these truths are equally "true" everywhere. This necessitates further questions as to whether these generalizations apply to all regional efforts or only to selected geographical locales, to all conditions of modernization or social organization or only to some. 3) I wish to know whether these generalizations are applicable at identical levels of meaning or abstraction; that is, do they talk about facts or about descriptive variables unequivocally identified with appropriate indicators, or can they be grouped into more abstract concepts endowed with greater explanatory or predictive sweep? 4) I wish to ascertain the degree of methodological and epistemological rigor which characterizes the work of establishing generalizations and abstractions. 5) Most

[2] For an identification of highly or closely linked national polities with the notion of "integrated international system" see Michael K. O'Leary, "Linkages Between Domestic and International Politics in Underdeveloped Nations," in James Rosenau (ed.), *Linkage Politics: Essays on the Convergence of National and International Systems* (New York: The Free Press, 1969), pp. 324–346. See also the argument of W. F. Hanrieder to the effect that regional integration movements provide a key way of isolating linkages. Wolfram F. Hanrieder, "Compatibility and Consensus: A Proposal for the Conceptual Linkage of External and Internal Dimensions of Foreign Policy," *American Political Science Review*, December 1967 (Vol. 61, No. 4), pp. 972–973.

This approach is rejected by James N. Rosenau, "Compatibility, Consensus, and an Emerging Political Science of Adaptation," *American Political Science Review*, December 1967 (Vol. 61, No. 4), pp. 983–988. He argues that the questions addressed in integration frameworks of study cannot be combined with questions which hinge on adaptation. This is a more restrictive definition of adaptation and of integration than is necessary or desirable.

[3] I wish to acknowledge my great debt to Ivan Vallier in seeking to come to grips with these issues even though I fall short of attaining his ideal.

importantly, I wish to know whether the theories with which we have been working actually possess any substantial power.

Power to do what? Theories can and should be evaluated in a variety of ways. We would wish to know 1) whether a theory adequately *describes* what happens. Does it contain variables sufficient to account for what appears to be going on in a given regional integration process or is it sufficient for comparing several such processes? Does it identify the sequence, or the stages, through which such processes appear to pass? 2) We also wish to know whether the theory adequately *explains* why the stages occur. This is a matter of being able to recount how the variables interact so as to produce a given outcome. 3) Finally, we wish to know how well a given theory *predicts* future outcomes, whether it tells us which conditions must prevail in order to enable us to say, "If a certain number of variables are present in sufficient strength, then integration in area X will occur." No cat is being let out of any intellectual bag if I reveal at this stage that none of the theories used in integration studies fully meets any of these criteria.

A final preliminary step is essential. Semantic confusion about "integration" must be limited even if it cannot be eliminated. The study of regional integration is often confounded with overlapping and cognate activities which, however, usually address somewhat different problems. Unless care is taken to exclude these pursuits from the discussion, the search for evaluative clarity will prove fruitless. Specifically, it is necessary to distinguish between "regional integration" and such competing terms as regionalism, regional cooperation, regional organization, regional movements, regional systems, or regional subsystems of a global system.[4]

The study of regional integration is concerned with explaining how and why states cease to be wholly sovereign, how and why they voluntarily mingle, merge, and mix with their neighbors so as to lose the factual attributes of sovereignty while acquiring new techniques for resolving conflict between themselves. Regional cooperation, organization, systems, and subsystems may help describe steps on the way; but they should not be confused with the resulting condition.[5]

Even fifteen years of work have not quite sufficed to create a consensus on a clear delimitation. Amitai Etzioni treats "integration" as the terminal condition, not as the process of getting there. Philip Jacob and Henry Teune regard integration both as a process and as a terminal condition, a condition

---

[4] For a representative agenda of topics and articles illustrating the rubrics regionalism, regional cooperation, regional organization, regional systems, etc., see Joseph S. Nye, Jr. (ed.), *International Regionalism: Readings* (Boston: Little, Brown and Co., 1968).

[5] This stab at a definition differs appreciably from the working definition of integration involving a shift in the loyalties of political actors with which I had worked previously. In abandoning the earlier definition I am expressing my agreement with the criticism Nye leveled at my own and at Deutsch's definitions. See Joseph S. Nye, "Comparative Regional Integration: Concept and Measurement," *International Organization*, Autumn 1968 (Vol. 22, No. 4), pp. 856–858.

achieved when an unspecified threshold is passed by an unspecified mix of ten process variables (independent or intervening?). Karl Deutsch speaks of integration as a process leading to the creation of security communities; I consider it a process for the creation of political communities defined in institutional and attitudinal terms, a condition also described by Jacob and Teune. Federalists, finally, see the end of the integration process in the growth of a federal union among the constituent nations.[6]

Hence anything which contributes to a better understanding of integration, as provisionally defined above, provides valuable data or a relevant variable. But the study of regionalism or regional cooperation or regional organizations furnishes simply materials on important activities of actors or on their beliefs. The study of regional integration is concerned with the *outcomes* or *consequences* of such activities in terms of a "new deal" for the region in question even though these activities could of course be analyzed for other purposes as well.

The study of regional cooperation, for instance, may be considered as a part of the study of regional integration or as a separate interest. Regional cooperation is a vague term covering any interstate activity with less than universal participation designed to meet some commonly experienced need. Such activities often contain lessons and data for the study of regional integration. But judgments as to whether cooperation is "successful" must be based on criteria very different from those appropriate to the study of integration. The study of regional organizations sums up activities of interstate cooperative enterprises and links to these activities observations concerning institutional evolution. Integration studies derive much of their information from the activities of international organizations including nongovernmental groupings. Some integration theorists even prefer to use measures of organizational tasks and institutionalization as indicators of integration or disintegration. Still, the study of organizations seeks to pinpoint the "success" of such entities in terms which make the organizations the centers of concern rather than to focus on their impact on the members.[7] Integration studies must rely on the study of comparative politics and economics because the regional organizations through which integrative/disintegrative activity is carried on are properly

---

[6] These definitions are too well known to require extensive recapitulation. For discussions see Amitai Etzioni, *Political Unification: A Comparative Study of Leaders and Forces* (New York: Holt, Rinehart and Winston, 1965), chapter 1; the process of "political unification" is described in chapter 2. Philip E. Jacob and James V. Toscano (ed.), *The Integration of Political Communities* (Philadelphia: Lippincott, 1964), chapter 1; chapters 2 and 3 of this volume contain an admirable summary by Karl Deutsch of the communications-transactions approach to integration. The federalist case is made in a sophisticated fashion by Dusan Sidjanski, *Dimensions européennes de la science politique: Questions méthodologiques et programme de recherches* (Paris: Librairie générale de droit et de jurisprudence, 1963).

[7] Philippe C. Schmitter, "La dinámica de contradicciones y la conducción de crisis en la integración centroamericana," *Revista de la integración*, November 1969 (No. 5), pp. 140–147, offers the notion of self-encapsulation which highlights the problem of identifying organizational success with progressive integration.

considered intervening variables which help explain our real concern, the
attainment of the possible later conditions in which the region may find itself.

Some writers refer to regional subsystems and regional systems. If they mean
an especially intense network of international links within a defined geographi-
ical compass, they are talking about regional cooperation, transactions, or organizations though at a higher level of abstraction. A "regional system" is no
more than a figure of speech summing up and describing such interactions. To
be useful for dealing with the essentially dynamic concerns of the student of
integration the portrait of the totality as a "system" must yield to the analysis
of the separate strands of which the system is made up.[8] Regional "subsystems"
involve descriptions of the particularly intense interactions in a given locale,
e.g., the Middle East, explained largely in terms of the inputs of the "system"
(i.e., the global network of international relations). Regional subsystems,
then, are devices for explaining the interdependence between local ties and
concerns and the larger world which constrain them.[9] This may be terribly
important in helping to explain why regional integration efforts do or do not
progress; but since the basic concern is not the explication of integration, the
concepts and measures appropriate in one realm do not carry over into the
other. Further, the phenomenon of "regionalism" is sometimes equated with
the study of regional integration. Regionalism can be a political slogan; if so,
it is ideological data that the student of integration must use. Regionalism can
also be an analytical device suggesting what the world's "natural" regions are
(or ought to be?).[10] As such it has so far not helped students of the processes
of regional integration or disintegration because the actors who make integrative decisions do not always worry about the naturalness of their region.

With these preliminaries out of the way we can now turn to the actual work

[8] Discussion of the "Inter-American system," for instance, usually includes descriptions of all regional
organizations, programs, and commitments of the member states of the Organization of American States
(OAS) as well as of the relations between separate organizations. The "European system" is sometimes
taken as a descriptive term for the totality of Western European organizations and programs without
regard to any impact on the reciprocal integration of the member nations.

> The level of political integration is the main characteristic that distinguishes political commu-
> nities from other political systems. *System* is the more encompassing concept, indicating that
> changes in the action of one (or more) unit(s) affect actions in one (or more) other units, and
> that these latter changes in turn have repercussions on the unit or units in which or from which
> the change was initiated. . . . In short, units of systems are interdependent; members of communi-
> ties are integrated. [Etzioni, p. 6.]

To confuse matters further the notion of "system" is sometimes assimilated into that of a "model," a
recurrent and/or typical way in which integration is thought to go forward. This usage is reserved for
the discussion of how variables are to be organized, not for the delimitation of the field.

[9] Leonard Binder, "The Middle East as a Subordinate International System," *World Politics*, April
1958 (Vol. 10, No. 3), pp. 408–429. Michel Brecher, "International Relations and Asian Studies: The
Subordinate State System of Southern Asia," *World Politics*, January 1963 (Vol. 15, No. 2), pp. 213–
235.

[10] This is shown in Bruce M. Russett, *International Regions and the International System: A Study in
Political Ecology* (Chicago: Rand McNally & Co., 1967). See the comment on such treatments of region-
alism in Oran R. Young, "Professor Russett: Industrious Tailor to a Naked Emperor," *World Politics*,
April 1969 (Vol. 21, No. 3), pp. 486–511.

of evaluation. We shall, in turn, seek to establish the number and character of empirical generalizations which studies of regional integration have given us, locate these on a ladder of abstraction, and seek to group them under some kind of master variables. We shall discover that these variables are dependent on assumptions drawn from three well-known theories of regional integration, and we must therefore summarize and evaluate the power of these theories. Having done so, we shall discover that the theories are lamentably unspecific and inconsistent as to the dependent variable to which they address themselves. Nor are they clear with respect to the key independent variables which, in combination, are to result in the eventual condition which is described by the dependent variable. The evaluation completed, we can then propose some ways of doing better in the future.

II. EMPIRICAL GENERALIZATIONS AND THEIR LIMITS

We are now in a position to summarize some things which the study of regional integration seems to have established. Enormous quantities of information have been uncovered about common markets, parliamentarians, regional interest groups, trade and mail flows, attitudes of masses, self-definitions of interest by elites, career patterns of civil servants, role perceptions, relations between various kinds of economic tasks, links between economic, political, and military tasks, and the influence of extrasystemic actors. Moreover, this is by no means randomly collected information. Few of the studies undertaken are so primitively empirical as to ignore hypotheses drawn from a variety of sources and models. One major achievement is the willingness to use comparative analysis as a test of the generality of the empirical findings instead of withdrawing into the safe shell of geographical uniqueness and complacently noting that "things are different in Pago Pago." Comparative analysis has been more than a drive for higher-level generalizations; it is also a device for finding and explaining intraphenomenal variation.[11] True, as of now our empirical

[11] The list of studies dealing with aspects of law, economics, military strategy, current diplomacy, and ideology is immense. For an excellent selection of recent studies see Nye, pp. 73–74, 145–146, 282–283, 428–429. For Europe in particular also see European Community Institute for University Studies (Brussels), *University Studies on European Integration*, 1969 (No. 5). For an exhaustive list of documents relating to economic cooperation in the third world see Miguel S. Wionczek (ed.), *Economic Cooperation in Latin America, Africa, and Asia* (Cambridge, Mass: M.I.T. Press, 1969). The following studies, in addition to the ones included in these bibliographies, are highly relevant to the conclusions here reported: Carl J. Friedrich (ed.), *Politische Dimensionen der europäischen Gemeinschaftsbildung* (Cologne: Westdeutscher Verlag, 1968); Gerda Zellentin (ed.), *Formen der Willensbildung in den europäischen Organisationen* (Frankfurt: Athenäum Verlag, 1965); Kai Ewerlöf Hammerich, *L'union des industries de la Communauté européenne dans le Marché commun* (Stockholm: Federation of Swedish Industries, 1969); Werner Feld, *The European Common Market and the World* (Englewood Cliffs, N.J.: Prentice-Hall, 1967); Study Group of the Graduate Institute of International Studies (Geneva), *The European Free Trade Association and the Crisis of European Integration* (London: Michael Joseph, 1968); Henry G. Aubrey, *Atlantic Economic Cooperation* (New York: Frederick A. Praeger, 1967); Robert W. Gregg (ed.), *International Organization in the Western Hemisphere* (Syracuse, N.Y.: Syracuse University Press, 1968); Dusan Sidjanski, *Dimensiones institucionales de la integración latino-*

generalizations are strongest when they simply sum up the experiences of discrete regional groupings. But some findings of general relevance also emerge.

The generalizations which follow are untidy and often unclear with respect to the level of abstraction at which they are supposed to operate. Some appear to be of universal validity; others are conditional. Some sum up discrete facts; others seem to order groups of facts under some concept which is not encountered "in nature." All of these statements, in some sense, are verified hypotheses. But the phenomena summed up under these hypotheses exist at various levels of meaning. How does one cope with such a mixed bag if we lack an accepted hierarchy of key terms, concepts, and constructs?

I shall suggest one which I have found useful in coping with the imperfect pretheories that have guided the work of regional integration studies, imperfect precisely because each pretheory has its own internal hierarchy. The facts sought so diligently by all scholars constitute the first level in the hierarchy. But which facts do they select? We treat as facts the items which we call our independent variables, i.e., events, conditions, attitudes, behaviors, considered to be of causative significance in explaining the condition or the outcome which preoccupies us. Items grouped and arranged in such a fashion as to lend themselves to explanation are facts categorized as variables. Groups of variables so related to each other as to explain successfully some outcome *but not justified in terms of some more comprehensive intellectual structure* we call empirical generalizations. The findings of regional integration studies, insofar as they are understood and accepted by all students, are thus no more than empirical generalizations. They are "true," i.e., they are verified hypotheses. But their distance from the primitive facts of behavior is unclear, and hence their theoretical status is doubtful because their relationship to still other variables and their relative weight in a group of potentially important variables is not specified. Nor is their position in a recurring sequence of trends or events spelled out.

Empirical Generalizations: Global

1) Members of regional groupings perceive themselves as being increasingly interdependent as the volume and rate of transactions between them rises as compared to third countries. This remains true despite debate as to the most appropriate statistical techniques and indices.

2) a) Actors will evaluate interdependence as negative if they feel their re-

americana (Buenos Aires: Instituto para la Integración de América Latina, 1967); Armando Pruque, *Siete años de acción de la ALALC* (Buenos Aires: Instituto para la Integración de América Latina, 1968); Francisco Villagrán Kramer, *Integración económica centroamericana: Aspectos sociales y políticos* (Estudios Universitarios, Vol. 4) (Guatemala City: University of San Carlos, 1967); Roger D. Hansen, *Central America: Regional Integration and Economic Development* (National Planning Association Studies in Development Progress, No. 1) (Washington: National Planning Association, 1967); Donald Rothchild (ed.), *Politics of Integration: An East African Documentary* (EAPH Political Studies 4) (Nairobi: East African Publishing House, 1968).

gional partners profit more than they; negative evaluations can be predicted in common markets and free trade areas of less developed countries. b) Actors will evaluate interdependence as positive if they feel they benefit equally with their partners in *some* issue area though not necessarily in all or in all simultaneously; such a pattern can be predicted in economic arrangements between industrialized countries.

3) The relative size of the member states in a regional grouping is not a good overall predictor of the success of integration. Inequality may spur integration in some economic and military task settings if the "core area" can provide special payoffs. Inequality is certain to hinder integration, however, when such payoffs are not provided, e.g., the role of the Union of Soviet Socialist Republics in the Council for Mutual Economic Assistance (COMECON), of Argentina, Brazil, and Mexico in the Latin American Free Trade Association (LAFTA), or of the United States since 1963 in the North Atlantic Treaty Organization (NATO). Differentials in size may advance the integration of diplomatic groupings when one purpose is perceived as the control of the "core area" by the smaller partners, as in the Organization of American States (OAS).

4) The proliferation of organizational channels in a region (both governmental and private) stimulates interdependence among the members as they increasingly resort to these channels for the resolution of conflicts. However, a positive evaluation of such interdependence on the part of the actors cannot be predicted, e.g., the reactions of the Federal Republic of Germany in the European Economic Community (EEC) and of Nicaragua in the Central American Common Market (CACM).

5) A critical mass composed of integrative activities in a number of issue areas likely to result in a culmination of de facto or de jure political union is difficult to identify and hazardous to predict. Many fields of potentially integrative activity, after successful accomplishments, result in "self-encapsulation" organizationally and attitudinally and therefore may not contribute to the evolution of new demands by actors. Other areas of perceived interdependence result in the creation of rival organizations whose activities may or may not contribute to overall integration, leading to the "spill-around" situation which defies political centralization. Self-encapsulation has been observed especially in activities relating to telecommunications, transportation, the protection of human rights, military strategy and procurement, and public health.[12]

[12] This distinction was first clearly elaborated by Schmitter in the article cited in footnote 7. It may be observed also in Africa and in Eastern Europe. For a European example see Robert L. Pfaltzgraff and James L. Deghand, "European Technological Collaboration: The Experience of the European Launcher Development Organization (ELDO)," *Journal of Common Market Studies,* September 1968, (Vol. 7, No. 1), pp. 22–34.

6) Of all issues and policy areas the commitment to create a common market is the most conducive to rapid regional integration and the maximization of a spillover. Military alliances, even if equipped with far-ranging competences and standing organs, have triggered very little permanent integrative consequences.[13] Arrangements limited to the setting up of common technical and scientific services tend toward self-encapsulation.[14] Regional arrangements for the protection of human rights (confined to Western Europe and to the Western Hemisphere) have so far not contributed to the integration of values and attitudes and have generated few new institutions.[15] Organizations with an economic mandate short of creating a common market or a free trade area have great difficulty in influencing the policies of their members.

Hence new hypotheses concerning future regional integration had best be formulated in the context of common markets. This is the richest fund of data and the most powerful stimulus to actors and provides the largest sample of ongoing efforts from almost all portions of the globe. Much richer findings, moreover, can be culled from the literature dealing with specific regions and regional economic efforts. It is hardly surprising that the empirical generalizations that can be uncovered seem to fall into three groups: findings specific to the Western European setting, conclusions and lessons highly specific to socialist countries, and a large mass of heterogeneous generalizations that seem to characterize the late developing nations and their efforts.

Empirical Generalizations: Socialist Groupings

7) Mutual interdependence and dependence on the regional "core area" is

---

[13] The definitive study probing the ability of NATO to trigger integrative results outside the narrow military field is Francis A. Beer, *Integration and Disintegration in NATO: Processes of Alliance Cohesion and Prospects for Atlantic Community* (Columbus: Ohio State University Press, 1969). Modelski makes the same point about SEATO and Slater about the OAS (see Nye for full citation). See also Andrzej Korbonski, "The Warsaw Pact," *International Conciliation*, May 1969 (No. 573), and Korbonski's contribution to this volume.

[14] Isebill Gruhn, *Functionalism in Africa: Scientific and Technical Cooperation* (unpublished Ph.D. dissertation, University of California, Berkeley, 1967). W. R. Derrick Sewell and Gilbert F. White, "The Lower Mekong," *International Conciliation*, May 1966 (No. 558); Carl G. Rosberg, Jr., with Aaron Segal, "An East African Federation," *International Conciliation*, May 1963 (No. 543). Abdul A. Jalloh, *The Politics and Economics of Regional Political Integration in Central Africa* (unpublished Ph.D. dissertation, University of California, Berkeley, 1969).

[15] In Western Europe the Greek response to the strong condemnation on the part of the Council of Europe's organs confirms this finding. A. B. McNulty, "Stock-Taking on the European Convention on Human Rights," Council of Europe document DH(68)7, 1968. The Inter-American Commission on Human Rights has been active and innovating in the face of governmental indifference and is now presenting the OAS Council with a final draft for a stronger and more permanent hemispheric machinery. L. Ronald Scheman, "The Inter-American Commission on Human Rights," *American Journal of International Law*, April 1965 (Vol. 59, No. 2), pp. 335–343; José A. Cabranes, "The Protection of Human Rights by the Organization of American States," *American Journal of International Law*, October 1968 (Vol. 62, No. 4), pp. 889–908.

a disintegrative force because the smaller nations resent it with varying degrees of intensity and consistency.

a) The differences in the national economic planning systems of the member nations of COMECON hinder the definition of a regional economic policy.

b) Resources do no flow readily because of differences in national plans and the absence of a regional price and monetary system accepted by all as fair.

c) Ideological differences between Communist parties make themselves felt in trade and investment policy and impede regional efforts.

d) Differences in the level of industrialization sharply influence expectations of regional action and make the less developed eager to minimize dependence on the more developed. The same is true among non-socialist developing nations.

Empirical Generalizations: Industrialized-Pluralistic Nations

8) Economic integration in Western Europe displays these regularities:

a) Self-interest among governments and private groups has sufficed to weave webs and expectations of interdependence and mutual benefits. However, with shifts in economic conditions or in the political climate these expectations are capable of being reversed and reevaluated by the actors. Instrumental motives are not necessarily strongly or permanently tied to the EEC.

b) Collective decisions—from coal to steel, to tariffs on refrigerators, to chickens, and to cheese, and from there to company law, turnover taxes, and the control of the business cycle—were made incrementally, based often on consequences not initially intended by the actors (governments and important interest groups). This tendency is summed up in the phrase "spillover in the scope of collective action."[16]

c) Spillover in scope is confined to decisions and objectives relating to the realization of full benefits from an existing common market. It has not operated markedly in free trade areas; nor has it been true of all policy or decision sectors in common markets (e.g., energy policy, transport).

d) There has been very little spillover in the "level" of action, i.e., little progressive penetration from supranational institutions into the lower reaches of decisionmaking at the national and local levels (with the exception of the mining and agricultural sectors).

e) Nevertheless, groups, contacts, and organizations (trade unions, trade

[16] The distinction between "scope" and "level" in the discussion of the spillover mechanism is first made by Philippe C. Schmitter in "Three Neo-Functional Hypotheses about International Integration," *International Organization*, Winter 1969 (Vol. 23, No. 1), pp. 161–166.

associations, working parties of civil servants, parliamentarians, students, professions) grow and prosper across frontiers.

f) The style of bargaining is incremental, subdued, and unemotional and seeks reciprocity of benefits, unanimous agreement, and package deals among issue areas. French behavior to the contrary has not been accepted as legitimate and has not remained fixed or final.

g) Collective decisions with an economic substance tend to exhibit most spillover characteristics when they are mediated by a group of actors with overt or tacit federalist objectives. The pace of integration slows down when this group is lacking, i.e., the EEC after 1963, the European Free Trade Association (EFTA).

h) Young people in Europe are consistently more favorable to the intensification of the integration process than are older people in part because they are self-consciously "nonnationalistic."

i) The higher educated and professional layers of the population, of all ages, are consistently in favor of intensified integration. Those most satisfied with their standard of living also tend to be prointegration. In short, prointegration attitudes characterize the most successful and most "modern" segments of the population.[17]

j) A region of great cultural/linguistic homogeneity, even though its members easily create new ties between themselves, does not necessarily proceed easily to the making of integrative collective decisions when the issues perceived as being most salient by actors involve interdependence with countries outside the region. Hence self-encapsulation easily sets in with respect to practices and organs created previously (e.g., the Nordic Council and the network of Nordic cooperation).

Empirical Generalizations: Late Developing Nations

9) Integration in Africa has been largely symbolic; joint policymaking with economic objectives does not follow the European pattern:

a) Actor expectations are prematurely politicized, thus preventing incremental bargaining on relatively noncontroversial shared objectives.

b) Bargaining with reciprocal benefits, especially where payoffs have to be deferred, is all but impossible because of the limits on resources. Since issues cannot be kept separate easily, national differences in size and power become divisive.

c) The absence of pluralism makes the formation of voluntary groups on

17 See especially Ronald Inglehart, "An End to European Integration?" *American Political Science Review,* March 1967 (Vol. 61, No. 1), pp. 91–105. Inglehart's analysis received powerful confirmation from a poll of French opinion conducted in 1968; see "Les Français et l'unification politique de l'Europe d'après un sondage de la SOFRES," *Revue française de science politique,* February 1969 (Vol. 19, No. 1), pp. 145–170.

a regional basis very difficult. Ideological ties between leaders, where they exist, are helpful to integration; ideological cleavages are most divisive and cannot be overcome by shared economic aims.

d) Countries which are poorly integrated internally make poor partners in a regional integration process because of the reluctance of leaders to further undermine their control at home.

10) While noneconomic integration in Latin America has been largely symbolic, economic integration efforts share many characteristics with the European pattern:

a) Countries confident that their size and resource base make them relatively independent of regional partners take a very slight interest in regional integration. Under these specific conditions size and power differentials, therefore, inhibit integration.

b) Differential rates of economic and social development inhibit the evolution of regional elite responsiveness (LAFTA). But similarity of rates favors elite complementarity and responsiveness (CACM and the Andean Group).

c) Administrative and organizational diffuseness at the national level in a setting of poor local integration and weak nationalism facilitates regional integration dominated by technocrats (CACM). Strong central government and strong nationalism permit little leeway to technocrats (LAFTA).[18]

d) The incremental decisionmaking logic and the spillover tendency can operate even among late developing countries which are poorly integrated nationally despite a persistent aura of economic crisis (CACM). This is explained by propositions 10) c) and 11) a).

---

[18] For examples see Gustavo Lagos, "The Political Role of Regional Economic Organizations in Latin America," *Journal of Common Market Studies,* June 1968 (Vol. 6, No. 4), pp. 291–309.

For an argument that distribution crises (in East Africa and Central America) must be expected to arise in such settings, thus inevitably politicizing negotiations and institutions dealing with economic welfare, see Roger D. Hansen, "Regional Integration: Reflections on a Decade of Theoretical Efforts," *World Politics,* January 1969 (Vol. 21, No. 2), pp. 257–270. This feature, among others, leads Hansen to conclude that the neo-functional approach cannot be used for the analysis of regional integration among less developed countries. Hansen finds the tendency toward distribution crises to be an instance of "instant politicization" even though in Central America it did not occur until the integration process had gone on for seven years. In Europe such a development was avoided, he says, because the dominance of the hidden hand of automatic market forces assured more or less equitable distribution of benefits (an argument also made by Lawrence Krause, *European Economic Integration and the United States* [Washington: Brookings Institution, 1967]). The makers of monetary policy, those who fashion subsidies for miners, railroads, and farmers, and the businessmen who conclude specialization agreements would be interested to learn this! On the contrary, serious distribution crises were avoided because of a consistent bargaining style stressing package deals permitting the continuation of special benefits *not* to be expected if an automatic and general free market were to operate. While Hansen is quite right in calling attention to the limits on the spillover from economic policymaking into political unification (see proposition 5 above), he carries the criticism much too far by downgrading the importance of "expansive" bargaining styles and the institutions in which the styles take shape, whether supranational or not.

Empirical Generalizations: The External World

Relations between the regional system (subsystem) and the external world (either an important extrasystem state or a larger regional system of which the subsystem being studied is a part) can be of immense importance in explaining integration.[19] But various configurations—quite distinct in impact—of "the exogenous variable" must be made explicit. 1) The "global system" within which the region perceives itself as struggling may be the major concern of actors, as in the case of economic unions among late developing countries. 2) A single state (or its elite) may be perceived as the extraregional force which aids or hinders integration. 3) A regional countersystem may be the extraregional force which explains integration or disintegration. Thus:

11) Perceptions of being victimized by the global system tend to spur integration as a way of "getting out from under."

a) Economic unions among late developing countries are designed to change a situation in which prosperity depends on commodity exports to developed nations (LAFTA, East African Common Market [EACM]).

b) But perceptions of dependence on a larger system may be so pervasive as to be a disincentive to regional efforts (Nordic Common Market, efforts at economic union in Asia).

12) The role of extraregional single states (or their elites) is indeterminate in explaining regional integration.

a) A hegemonic extraregional actor can use his payoff capacity to undermine the will to integrate, as has been alleged of the United States in dealings with LAFTA and CACM.

b) But economic unions among late developing countries sometimes survive largely as a result of support from an exogenous actor (Union douanière et économique de l'Afrique centrale [UDEAC], Conseil de l'entente, and occasionally CACM).

13) Extraregional counterunions are a definite—but temporary—aid to integration.

a) Regional groupings with a military purpose survive only as long as they face a rival external grouping. The same is true of diplomatic groupings which do not take the form of an alliance.

19 Karl Kaiser, "The U.S. and the EEC in the Atlantic System: The Problem of Theory," *Journal of Common Market Studies*, June 1967 (Vol. 5, No. 4), pp. 388–425, and Karl Kaiser, "The Interaction of Regional Subsystems: Some Preliminary Notes on Recurrent Patterns and the Role of Superpowers," *World Politics*, October 1968 (Vol. 21, No. 1), pp. 84–107. See Etzioni, pp. 44–50, for a related treatment of "external elites." Robert E. Denham, "The Role of the U.S. as an External Actor in the Integration of Latin America," *Journal of Common Market Studies*, March 1969 (Vol. 7, No. 3), pp. 199–216. Nils Andrén, "Nordic Integration," *Cooperation and Conflict*, 1967 (Vol. 1), pp. 1–25.

b) Economic unions among industrialized countries may survive only because they seek united strength in dealing with another such union (EFTA).

Much ink has been spilled in debates between students of integration as to whether the exogenous variable is really *the* most salient one: For scholars still attached to some version of Friedrich Meinecke's dictum on the *Primat der Aussenpolitik* the military and diplomatic force of the larger system should always be considered as the weightiest influence on the fortunes of the regional subsystem. The failure of the EEC to spill over into political union among the six is explained sometimes in this fashion.[20] The resolution of this conundrum —an entirely unnecessary one conceptually and empirically—is linked to the discussion of "high" as against "low" politics. This takes us, more generally, to a consideration of conceptual problems which remain ill defined and unresolved in the study of regional integration despite the wealth of empirical generalizations which have been generated.

Gaps and Problems Remaining

It is clear by now that the truth conveyed by these summary statements is, to say the least, multilayered in meaning and implication. Only a few of these propositions rise above the level of verifying simple hypotheses based on readily observed behavior or trends rendered in terms of variables. Some, however, do: The propositions dealing with various kinds of spillover involve an act of conceptual evaluation on the part of the observer which is several steps removed from the actual variables. Conclusions about what spills over into which institutional vessel are *analytical:* They are deduced from facts arranged into variables, paired in the form of hypotheses. I am arguing that such analytical steps are highly desirable, if not imperative, if we wish to avoid simple empiricism. But from where do we get the leading ideas, the metaphors, the inspiration for such a summing up at a higher level of abstraction?

One of the major problems implicit in this list of findings is the dependence of most propositions on a number of explicit and implicit assumptions made prior to the initiation of research; there is a theoretical basis to the mere listing of relevant variables. The findings are as strong as the assumptions, and the assumptions cannot be made evident without looking at the theories which inspired them. The same is true of the measures and indicators embedded in various assumptions.

[20] For the classic statements of this position see Stanley Hoffmann, "Discord in Community: The North Atlantic Area as a Partial International System," *International Organization*, Summer 1963 (Vol. 17, No. 3), pp. 521–549, and Stanley Hoffmann, "Obstinate or Obsolete? The Fate of the Nation-State and the Case of Western Europe," *Daedalus*, Summer 1966 (Vol. 95, Nos. 3–4), pp. 862–916. Hansen treats the exogenous variable in this fashion, considering it the most "compelling" of all and using it as the most salient for predicting a reasonably rosy future for economic unions of less developed countries. He also explicitly accepts the dichotomy of "high" versus "low" politics, treating economic welfare issues in the third world as an instance of "high" politics. Hansen, *World Politics*, Vol. 21, No. 2, pp. 268–271, 246–250.

Another problem with this list is the indefinite nature of the end state or the terminal condition to which regional integration is supposed to lead. Integration appears to be both a process and an outcome. This confusion between process and outcome, appealing though it may be because it sidesteps the definitional problem, simply will not help us unless we know which mix of which variables results in a qualitatively new state of affairs. It is not only a question of whether we wish to explain the process, necessarily stressing a time dimension, whereby relationships change between nations and actors or to describe the terminal condition (which could be conceived in static terms) to which the process is likely to lead. The job is to do both; but the task of selecting and justifying variables and explaining their hypothesized interdependence cannot be accomplished without an agreement as to possible conditions to which the process is expected to lead. In short, we need a dependent variable. The list alone is insufficient for systematic explanation because it merely describes interregional variation in the importance attributable to single independent variables. It says little about the mix of variables to be considered optimal in general or optimal for specific regional settings.

Finally, I shall list four major gaps in factual and conceptual knowledge which began to oppress me after working with the findings I considered established. These gaps involve measurement, assumptions, theories, and a concern with the future on normative grounds. 1) Do variables explaining the initiation of a union also explain its maintenance, as we seem to have assumed? 2) Must we assume—as we have—that decisionmaking styles at the national level must be congruent with those at the regional level? What if the two styles evolve at different rates? 3) Are processes of integration in the underdeveloped world so different from those in the West that we need two different theories or models? This raises the important issue of the relative weight to be given to the variables in each geographical setting. 4) How do actors learn? Do perceptions of benefits from changing transactions affect the definition of interests? Is there some other process of socialization at work? Answers to each of these will have tremendous importance in the construction of a more adequate theory of regional integration, especially if the relative weight of each variable and process can be specified with respect to *each* of various postulated outcomes in *each* major geographical or cultural setting.

III. THREE PRETHEORIES OF REGIONAL INTEGRATION

The task of clarification of findings and filling of gaps bears some of the burdens of the fifteen years of work already done. Three separate theoretical conventions—federalism, the communications approach, and neo-functionalism—have not only shaped the fuzzy conceptions of the outcome of integration but have also been influential in defining independent variables. Students within each convention have postulated causative links between variables. Furthermore, each convention has brought its own methodology into the fray, illustrated especially by the heavy reliance on aggregate and survey data on the part of the communications school and on conceptually focused case studies of integrative efforts on the part of the neo-functionalists. Hence an agreement on a common research strategy or a new focus of study cannot be a matter of choosing between rival approaches or of simply adding them. Variables bear the burden of their ancestry, as do methods, measures, and indicators. Before an agreement on a set of dependent variables can be ratified in terms of a common agenda on hypothesized causes, modal action paths, and a common methodology, the main contours of these "theories" must be thrown into relief and their contributions summarized.

Generous borrowing from other disciplines and subject matters inspired and informed the three theoretical approaches which I shall call "pretheories" because they do not now provide an explanation of a recurring series of events made up of dimensions of activity causally linked to one another. Some pretheorists used as basic building blocks certain assumptions which are relationships demonstrated to be true empirically in the contexts from which they were borrowed; other pretheorists proceeded on the basis of knowledge taken to be self-evidently "true" though based on intuition rather than cognition. In any event, the status of these theories is of tremendous importance because it is they rather than the nature of things which lead students to postulate the relationships between variables; it is they, not the nature of things, which lead us to the specification of what is an independent and a dependent variable.

The *federal* approach assumes the identity of political postulates concerning common purpose and common need among actors irrespective of level of action. It also assumes the transferability, again on the basis of identical postulates, of institutions from the national to the regional level. The *communications* approach proceeds on the basis of the logic of isomorphisms. It transposes laws from cybernetic theory to the relations between groups of people, using the volume of transaction as its major indicator. All social processes are assumed to follow identical laws borrowed from cybernetics; these laws are applied isomorphically by expecting that the logic of the causal pattern is replicated in relations between nations and regions. The *neo-functional* approach rests its claim to fame on an extended analogy rather than relying on isomorphisms or identities between phenomena. It borrows the postulates of actor perception and behavior which are said to explain the character of a pluralistically organized national state; it notes that certain of these seem to coincide with behavior at the regional level and therefore holds that the rest of the behavior is also explicable in terms of the pluralistic national model. The major point requiring emphasis is that these pretheories are located at varying levels of abstraction, thus giving rise to behavioral postulates which are not symmetrically related. This alone should give rise to doubts as to whether the postulates are additive in terms of a unified theory.

The Federalist Approach

Federalist theorists actually can be divided into two quite distinct groups: an ideological group concerned with developing a theory of action designed to realize a regional federation (mostly in Western Europe but to some extent in Africa immediately before and after the attainment of independence by most African states and in the Malaysian nexus) as opposed to a group concerned with tracing and observing patterns of federal integration. The second group, however, has also been active in the drafting of constitutions for potential federal unions.[21] The two groups agree on many things. They share a concern with the primary importance of institutions and institution building; hence the efforts devoted to the writing of constitutions and to research on the actual history of such federal entities as the United States, Switzerland, and West Germany. They are preoccupied with the merits of rival methods of representation and elections; they devote much attention to the proper division of powers between the federal, the "national," and the local authorities; and they are concerned with checks and balances between organs of government. Moreover, they are both inspired by the dual character of federalism: It can be used to unite hitherto separate jurisdictions but it can also be applied to breaking up overly centralized national governments. Federalism, in short, seeks simultaneously to meet the need for more effective governmental action in some domains (through centralization) and the democratic postulate of local control and local autonomy (through decentralization).

The style of the activist group has been more consistently ideological. The major component of its theory is the imputed need of peoples and nations; these needs will (must, ought to?) result in a federal regime. In short, it is not always clear whether the assertions are normative or descriptive. They are certainly not explanatory. Granting these basic building blocks the theory provides (at least in the words of its major European and African spokesmen) descriptive postulates about necessary strategies and requisite behavior patterns for building regional institutions and solidarities. The main building blocks are normative assertions based on the faith of the asserters. The remainder is illustrative material chosen from the historical experience of federal nations. Undoubtedly it is this feature which has stimulated a recent commentator to consider neofunctional and federal theorizing as next-of-kin.[22] Events since 1954 in Europe

---

21 Illustrative of this practice is the massive work by Robert R. Bowie and Carl J. Friedrich (ed.), *Studies in Federalism* (Boston: Little, Brown and Co., 1954), which contains research and theorizing done on behalf of the then functioning European ad hoc Parliamentary Assembly.

22 Paul Taylor, "Concept of Community and the European Integration Process," *Journal of Common Market Studies*, December 1968 (Vol. 7, No. 2), pp. 83–101. This argument misses the essential distinctions between ends and means and between activist/actor and theorist/observer. To illustrate: Jean Mon-

and since 1960 in Africa have effectively contradicted these federalists' descriptions, explanations, and predictions. This approach, in its pure form, is probably discredited.[23]

Even though they stress the importance of institutional and constitutional questions somewhat more than do neo-functionalists, the theorist/observers among the federalists have tended to lose their identity as a clear-cut approach to questions of regional integration. First, federalist theorists do not share the activists' cavalier assumptions about popular needs or imminent and necessary events. Even though attached to federalism for normative reasons they do not push their preoccupation to the extreme of equating all of society's ills with dispersion or concentration of power and of identifying the federal formula as the royal remedy. Therefore, they are less inclined to talk about popular needs than about an optimal distribution of tasks among units of government in a setting of growing popular participation. Second, federalist theorists have shown more and more interest in questions of process, leading the main federalist theorist, Carl J. Friedrich, to speak of the "federalizing process" in terms difficult to distinguish from the medley of demands, expectations, rational bargaining, and ad hoc growth of institutions which neo-functionalists seek to trace.[24]

---

net and Walter Hallstein are "federalists" in the sense that they hope to create a united Europe with more or less federal institutions; they are "functionalists" in the sense that they do not believe in constitutional conventions and elaborate institutional schemes because they prefer to initiate common policies and arouse new client groups which will *eventually* result in a federal regime. Federalist theorists believe in the federal end but may be willing to use functional means; federalist activists despise the recourse to functional means. Neo-functionalist theorists are concerned with the end postulated by the actors only to the extent that they are preoccupied with understanding why and how actual integrative outcomes occur. Neo-functional theory and federal theory, therefore, are by no means similar.

[23] As examples of ideological federalists we cite the names of Denis de Rougemont, Hans Nord, Henri Brugmans. See also Alexandre Marc, *Europe: Terre décisive* (Paris: La Colombe, 1959). Another group of federal activists, in disappointment, has turned to a species of neo-functionalism for ideological sustenance; see Bino Olivi, *L'Europa difficile* (Milan: Edizioni di Communitá, 1964), and Altiero Spinelli, *The Eurocrats: Conflict and Crisis in the European Community* (Baltimore: Johns Hopkins Press, 1968). A new twist is given to this complex relationship by the emergence of a young group of federalists anxious to work with functional institutions to achieve the radical democratization of European society. They publish the monthly journal *Agenor*.

[24] This passage from Friedrich's most recent work speaks for itself:

> The review of selected issues in contemporary federal relations has . . . shown that federalism is more fully understood if it is seen as a process, an evolving pattern of changing relationships, rather than a static design regulated by firm and unalterable rules. This finding ought not to be misunderstood as meaning that the rules are insignificant; far from it. What it does mean is that any federal relationship requires effective and built-in arrangements through which these rules can be recurrently changed upon the initiative and with the consent of the federated entities. In a sense, what this means is that the development (historical) dimension of federal relationships has become a primary focal point, as contrasted with the distribution and fixation of jurisdictions (the legal aspect). In keeping with recent trends in political science, the main question is: What function does a federal relationship have?—rather than: What structure?

Carl J. Friedrich, *Trends of Federalism in Theory and Practice* (New York: Frederick A. Praeger, 1968), p. 173). For a similar treatment of federalism in Africa, Malaysia, and the West Indies see Thomas M. Franck (ed.), *Why Federations Fail* (New York: New York University Press, 1968).

The Communications Approach

Communications theory suggests—it does not assert or prove—that an intensive pattern of communication between national units will result in a closer "community" among the units if loads and capabilities remain in balance. Associated with this suggestion are a number of familiar additional postulates regarding trust, friendship, complementarity, and responsiveness. The units being considered by this theory are nations and only incidentally physical persons or groups. It should be made clear that the character of the suggestions takes the form of very specific hypotheses. "If the rate of transaction is such and so, under conditions of balanced loads and capabilities, then elite responsiveness increases. If elite responsiveness increases then a security community will arise. . . . " The hypotheses are certainly falsifiable. But even if they are found to correlate positively with the emergence of a security community, can we then assign causes that are clearly associated with human perceptions and motives? Communications theorizing rests content with the demonstration of covariance among variables at the systemic level. It hypothesizes that certain relationships between relationships, ratios between ratios in the case of some clusters of variables, result in a terminal condition, i.e., a security community. The systemic approach thus assumes either of the following: It may assume that transactions *measure* some human quality, a human perception of self-interest, and that the change in the magnitude of the measure records a change in the human behavior to be measured; in this case the indicator becomes a proxy variable for perception that leads to behavior. Alternatively the systemic approach assumes that transactions *are* a type of behavior summing up more mundane, humanly experienced facts and making it unnecessary for the investigator to concern himself with the human element. In brief, are factor scores of ecological variables really measures of actor behavior?[25] It is as if theorists of the balance of power need only worry about the application of the principles of mechanics to international politics and need not worry about how foreign ministers perceive themselves in this supergame.

The communications approach has sought to explain retroactively rather than to predict. The approach does not tell us the content of the messages and their imputed relationship to the evolution of capacity on the part of regional institutions. It does not explain when and how trust and responsiveness among actors, elites as well as masses, are to occur. Who are, or what is, to handle the load? Politics, in the sense of demands, negotiations, institutionalization, evolution of tasks, is not really part of the approach since the content of messages is not always treated. Deutsch suggested that future Western European integration is in doubt because of an ebbing in the increase of rates of trans-

---

[25] The work of Donald Puchala, as represented by his contribution to this volume, though part of this approach, is not based on all of these assumptions and makes a number of allowances to the judgments expressed here.

action, as measured by trade, mail, and tourist flow indicators and by the rate of supranational group formation.[26] Only certainty on the *causative* significance of these indicators can justify such a conclusion.

Yet the suspicion remains that transactions *must* have something to do with expectations and therefore with actor behavior. The successful prediction of the neo-functionalists with respect to negotiating behavior in the EEC can be fully explained only on the basis of the transactionalist's finding concerning trade. But whether the resulting ties are based on trust or greed remains an open question. Is the effect of transactions similar in late developing regions? Certainly there is a very good correlation between nontrade and noncommunity formation in LAFTA and an equally good one between the relative success of CACM and the spectacular increases in regional trade. In Africa, on the other hand, UDEAC continues to exist despite the absence of trade increases between the members while the East African Common Market was endangered because the high level of trade betwen the members was not associated, in their minds, with equitably distributed benefits. But then, perhaps, it is not trade or other kinds of transactions that are crucial in our judgment so much as the *perception* of present and future benefits in the minds of the actors. In that case this type of data is not a good indicator unless it is reinterpreted in terms of actor perceptions.

The Neo-Functional Approach

Neo-functionalists have their own troubles. True, neo-functional theorizing is consistently phenomenological; it avoids normative assertion and systemic generalization. Neo-functionalism stresses the instrumental motives of actors; it looks for the adaptability of elites in line with specialization of roles; neo-functionalism takes self-interest for granted and relies on it for delineating actor perceptions. Moreover, neo-functionalists rely on the primacy of incremental decisionmaking over grand designs, arguing that most political actors are incapable of long-range purposive behavior because they stumble from one set of decisions into the next as a result of not having been able to foresee many of the implications and consequences of the earlier decisions. Ever more controversial (and thus system-transforming) policies emerge, starting from a common initial concern over substantively narrow but highly salient issues. A new central authority may emerge as an unintended consequence of incremental earlier steps. Most neo-functionalists have not explicitly recognized, however, the crucial question of whether even this incremental style is not "foreseen" and manipulated by certain heroic actors (Jean Monnet, Sicco Mansholt, Walter Hallstein, Raúl Prebisch)—and eventually checked by certain equally prescient national actors (Charles de Gaulle).

[26] See Karl W. Deutsch, and others, *France, Germany and the Western Alliance: A Study of Elite Attitudes on European Intetgration and World Politics* (New York: Charles Scribner's Sons, 1967), especially p. 218.

The neo-functional theory is therefore a highly contingent one. One limitation is embedded in the source of the approach—the modern pluralistic-industrial democratic polity. That source offers a rationale for linking the separate variables found in the neo-functional model in Western Europe; but application to the third world has so far sufficed only to accurately predict difficulties and failures in regional integration while in the European case some successful positive prediction has been achieved. Another limitation, however, involves the very question of what constitutes a successful prediction. Neo-functionalist practitioners have difficulty achieving closure on a given case of regional integration because the terminal condition being observed is uncertain: Neo-functionalists do not agree on a dependent variable and therefore differ with each other on the point in time at which a judgment of "how much successful integration" is to be made. Thus, specific processes, specific cases of spillover, specific styles of accommodation and increasing mutual responsiveness among actors have been successfully predicted. But whether this adds up to achieving closure or the attainment of some kind of "community" in the region remains a matter of how we define the dependent variable. As of now the theory has not been falsified in the sense that a successful community has been achieved by virtue of processes not contained in the theory; if East Africa or the Association of Southeast Asian Nations (ASEAN) were to attain functioning supranational communities in their respective regions, such an event would falsify the theory. Nor has the theory been fully validated as long as it cannot explain how and why a postulated condition is attained.

Overlap between Communications and Neo-Functional Approaches

Both approaches share a commitment to a certain number of independent variables considered of great salience: regional transactions and the gains or losses associated with them by actors; verbal and symbolic communications between crucial elites; mutual expectations of elites; mutual responsiveness between elites; the adequacy of institutions to handle the transactional and communicational load. But they differ in the way in which they treat the load: Communications theorists consider all types of transactions equally salient and therefore measure whatever the statistics permit to be measured; neo-functionalists, however, argue that welfare-related and foreign or defense policy issues are most salient for actors. The load related to such transactions thus becomes crucial for studying particularly salient regional "tasks." Hence neo-functionalists prefer to observe bargaining styles and strategies as their basic data rather than to stress the volume and rate of transactions or the ebb and flow of public opinion. Moreover, they prefer to study cases of organizational growth or decay rather than the aggregate data preferred by the followers of the communications approach. In both cases data and measures are determined by initial theoretical assumptions. So are crucial organizing concepts for the data, such as the notions of responsiveness and spillover. The strength of communications theory is its generality, its systemic character. The strength of neo-functional theory is its closeness to the actors. But individual strength may turn out to be collective weakness when propositions derived from one fly like eagles through the ethereal heights of systems while those derived from the other burrow like moles through the mud of experience.

None of the major pretheories is very strong. True, only the federal approach has been falsified in the sense that none of its assertions-predictions have proven to be true. The neo-functional and communications theories have neither been falsified nor have they demonstrated positive predictive prowess outside Western Europe: They have been better in predicting failures. Moreover, they cannot be easily compared or added since they address different levels of abstraction. The looseness of the axioms of which they are made up does not help matters. What is clear and crisp at the national level comes close to assumption, or assertion, in the regional context to which the neo-functional theory seeks application. What is a simple hypothesis of great plausibility in the communications theory becomes question-begging when the assumptions underlying the hypotheses are made explicit.

Both theories have been accused of neglecting "high politics," especially in the form of hiding such obviously important matters as international power and prestige, war and peace, arms and alliances under such mundane labels as "interaction," "task expansion," or "welfare maximization." The thrust of world politics and of the superpowers on regional unions is sometimes mentioned as some special instance of "high politics" that cannot be treated or accommodated by either theory. Those who stress the unique qualities of high politics provide an important critical qualifier to both theories without advancing a theory of their own. They hold that all political decisions are either important or routine, that propositions seeking to relate political activity with economic or social objectives err intrinsically by assuming that human conduct in both spheres is identical. The devotees of high politics are thus forced to conclude that while common markets may flourish because of some men's grubby and greedy minds, such mundane arrangements will never lead to political union because that status demands that the pride and fury associated with nationalism be eliminated first. This, clearly, is argument by definition alone.[27] In neo-functional theorizing the existence of special "high political" motives can be discovered by studying the perceptions of actors when they react to external pressures and threats or when they link (or fail to link) extra-

---

[27] See the suggestion by Karl Kaiser that the distinction has relevance only to the attitudes of actors, not to the intrinsic character of the issue area or policy. Actors can shift back and forth as to the importance they attribute to any given issue area—with obvious implications for integration theory. The empirical problem for us is to be able to specify when and how such attitudinal shifts occur, an aspect of a theory of "learning" we shall discuss below. This is quite different from the eternally mystic qualities Hoffmann sees in these distinctions. Kaiser, *Journal of Common Market Studies*, Vol. 5, No. 3, pp. 401–402.

regional ambitions with regional decisionmaking. Whether "politics" is more important than "economics" is an empirical question, not a dichotomy given by nature. In communications theorizing the potency of high politics would be suggested when events take a turn sharply counter to what is indicated by the trends of growing interdependence. But General de Gaulle—not "France" —remains the only exception that has amended, but hardly destroyed, the consensus among students of integration that what we analyze are trends and decisions—without defining which are the most important and without arguing that economic questions are "routine."

IV. Toward a Dependent Variable

Our reflections have led us to two somber conclusions: First, the lessons we have learned from the study of regional integration have been imperfectly "integrated" because they coexist at several levels of abstraction, thus making it difficult to engage in conceptually focused evaluation and projection; moreover, a primary cause of imperfect conceptual integration is the nonadditive character of the pretheories which have inspired our research. Second, one major reason for the lack of fit between the major theories is disagreement on what constitutes the dependent variable. A giant step on the road toward an integrated theory of regional integration, therefore, would be taken if we could clarify the matter of what we propose to explain and/or predict.

Ideal Types and Terminal Conditions

Federalist theory has been the least ambiguous in telling which end product it seeks to explain or predict: The terminal condition of the process of integration is the achievement of a federal union among the units being studied, nation-states. Communications theorizing has used the construct of a security community as its terminal condition, recognizing the possibility that such a condition may be of the "amalgamated" or the "pluralistic" variety. This terminal condition, of course, is wider in scope than the federalists' though it is able to subsume the notion of a federal union. Neo-functionalists have worked with the idea of a political community or a political union, a concept which also subsumes a federal union but is less sweeping than a security community because it makes specific assumptions about central institutions and the progressive centralization of decisionmaking among the members. One of the more bothersome aspects of these efforts at specifying a dependent variable was the tendency to mix its imputed characteristics with those of independent and intervening variables.[28]

[28] But we have learned, too. Scholars are less prone to circular definitions between independent and dependent variables than they were a decade ago when a "community" was held to require a "sense of community" as a precondition and an integrating region was thought to demand a preexisting propensity to integrate. Still there are more indeterminate variables now than desirable. We certainly should discourage the tendency to add "fudge variables" whenever the standard ones do not seem to do the

The nagging thought persists that we lack clear dependent variables because we have followed the practice of erecting these terminal states by treating them as ideal types reconstructed from our historical experience at the national level and then of observing the types of behavior that contribute—or fail to contribute—to the attainment of that condition. These ideal types are not true dependent variables since they cannot yet be observed or measured in nature: The postulated conditions have not yet come about anywhere, at least in the contemporary world. At best we have a putative dependent variable.[29]

It is sobering to take a glance at some real-life dependent variables. The European Economic Community in 1962 seemed on the point of a breakthrough to a political community de facto because of an attempted expansion in the scope and level of its decisionmaking capacity; instead it settled down into the uneasy equilibrium state of continuing its established role until 1969. The East African Community moved from healthy exuberance to near-death between 1960 and 1965 only to revive, phoenixlike, after 1967; the Central American Common Market slips from one major crisis into another, always on the point of seeming collapse, but in the aggregate seems to do better than retain a state of equilibrium. The examples could be multiplied. They suggest that the variety of possible outcomes is considerable, that unions may settle down into a stable system without reaching any of the stages we defined in the earlier phases of our research. Yet these stages still represent higher degrees of "integration" than was true of the member states at an earlier point in time.

Scales as Dependent Variables

But why the insistence on a single ideal type as the terminal condition? The terminal condition envisaged could very well be more than a pluralistic security community and less than a political community, defined as the successful pluralistic-democratic state writ large; in fact, this is likely to be the case. Hence I suggest that we follow the approach of deliberately positing end states that could reflect extensive system transformation leading toward centralization *or* decentralization *or* the achievement of a new integrative plateau. The verbally defined single terminal conditions with which we have worked in the past— political community, security community, political union, federal union—are inadequate because they foreclose real-life developmental possibilities.

Efforts have indeed been made to get away from the ideal typical definition of end states. They have taken the form, predominantly, of specifying separate dimensions or conditions which would constitute a higher degree of integration as compared to a previous point in time. In addition, scales are provided

explanatory trick. This means that we ought to stop talking about "functional equivalents," "catalysts," "federalizers," "compellingness," "high politics," and similar mythical animals.

[29] Possible exceptions are the (mostly unsuccessful) noncoercive unions of new states attempted in the last two decades, as analyzed in Franck and in Etzioni. At best, these experiences help to falsify certain theoretical postulates without explaining how a successful federal union can be achieved.

in some instances to observe and measure how far a given union has moved along the specified dimension. The end state, then, is a quantitatively specified "point" on a scale; when several scales are used for several salient dimensions, the end state is a specified convergence of separate curves.[30]

But the quantitatively phrased multidimensional definition—usually rendered as an "integrated community"—also presents problems. It suggests that if the union being studied scores "high" on a number of salient dimensions, particularly if it scores progressively "higher" over time, some theoretically relevant outcome is being attained; yet the total shape of the outcome is not given. This approach has the virtue of papering over the disagreement over the appropriate mix of independent and intervening variables that are embedded in the various theoretical approaches to regional integration studies. It recognizes that we do not know what the mix is, nor whether it is the same for all situations. But it stresses simple observation for the careful development of hypotheses justifying and linking various independent variables—which in turn requires some kind of theory. Nor does this approach overcome the difficulty of foreclosing the future to a variety of possible integrative outcomes since it posits progressively "higher" scores instead of making a disciplined effort at imagining various future conditions. In short, the quantitative definition of progressive integrative developments is best seen as a methodological help in making accurate observations and at limiting recourse to overly restrictive verbal definitions; but it cannot alone provide the dependent variable. Scales of separate dimensions of integration are useful descriptively because they capture a process; but without hypothetically linked variables they are not explanatory of an outcome which, itself, remains unspecified.[31] When used in

[30] For examples of such efforts see Nye, *International Organization*, Vol. 22, No. 4; Philip Jacob and Henry Teune, "The Integrative Process: Guidelines for Analysis of the Basis of Political Community," in Jacob and Toscano, pp. 1–45.

A similar approach is suggested in the quantification of twelve independent variables, which in the aggregate are expected to yield an outcome called "automatic politicization," that could be considered a proxy variable for political community. See Mario Barrera and Ernst B. Haas, "The Operationalization of Some Variables Related to Regional Integration: A Research Note," *International Organization*, Winter 1969 (Vol. 23, No. 1), pp. 150–160; also the response by Philippe C. Schmitter, "Further Notes on Operationalizing Some Variables Related to Regional Integration," in *International Organization*, Spring 1969 (Vol. 23, No. 2), pp. 327–336. How politicization is sequentially linked to other developments during the integration process is set forth by Schmitter, *International Organization*, Vol. 23, No. 1, pp. 161–166. If interdependence along some highly salient dimension is considered a proxy variable for the outcome, the work of Reinton is most suggestive. See Per Olav Reinton, "International Structure and International Integration," *Journal of Peace Research*, 1967 (No. 4), pp. 334–365.

[31] See Nye, *International Organization*, Vol. 22, No. 4, pp. 864–875. I disagree with Nye's argument that the notion of integration ought to be "disaggregated" into economic, social, and political components without making any premature judgments as to how these separate ranges relate to each other causally. To avoid making causal assumptions and positing hypotheses merely sidesteps once more the difficulty of finding a dependent variable. Political integration, if that is what we are concerned about, is more important than economic and social trends; these are important because we think they are causally connected with political integration. Disaggregation helps in the attainment of operational accuracy but it hinders the removal of fuzzy dependent variables unless orders of causal priority are thought through. Humpty-Dumpty must be put together again, too, as it is in Nye's contribution to this volume.

lieu of descriptive or schematic images of end states they substitute premature operationalization for theory and vision.

This truth is firmly recognized by Leon Lindberg and Stuart Scheingold. They posit three possible outcomes: The *fulfillment* of a postulated task on the part of practices and/or institutions created for integrative purposes; the *retraction* of such a task (i.e., disintegration); and the *extension* of such a task into spheres of action not previously anticipated by the actors. Models are provided for explaining the sequence of action made up of events created by actors. These three terms sum up and interpret independent variables into recurrent patterns yielding one of the three possible outcomes.[32]

In their treatment Lindberg and Scheingold make these outcomes specific to the European community and the stipulations of the treaties establishing the EEC and the European Atomic Energy Community (Euratom). To avoid EECentricity the same scheme of analysis could be applied to the collectivity of organizations and transactions characterizing the links between a given group of nations though one particular salient organization (such as the EEC) could be taken as the nucleus of the analysis. In the case of Europe one would then bring in the work of the Council of Europe, NATO, the Organization of Economic Cooperation and Development (OECD), the European Launcher Development Organization (ELDO), etc., with respect to the fulfillment, retraction, or extension produced in relations between the six members of the EEC. To get a total picture one would have to strike a balance among all these issues and issue areas because retraction may have occurred in one and fulfillment in others. In short, one would need a master concept under which all the various functionally specific issues and tasks can be grouped and summed up. This master concept, moreover, would have to provide scores so that we could recognize whether overall fulfillment or retraction has taken place.

Such a master concept is the notion of "authority-legitimacy transfer" or "sharing," a formulation I would myself prefer to the stress put on elite loyalties in my own earlier formulations. Specific indicators for both authority and legitimacy could be provided; these have the advantage of being *ex hypothesi* relevant to all geographical settings. One such measure is the notion of "institutionalization." It could be considered a proxy variable for the notion of political community, and some have so used it. It would be more defensible to elaborate the items and dimensions considered involved in "institutionalization"

---

[32] Leon Lindberg and Stuart Scheingold, *Europe's Would-Be Polity: Patterns of Change in the European Community* (Englewood Cliffs, N.J.: Prentice-Hall, 1970), chapter 4. For a most complete and perceptive list of possible measures and indicators of progress toward the achievement of any one of these three conditions (or of regress) see Lindberg's contribution to this volume. It should be stressed, however, that these specifications still do not add up to the definition of one or several dependent variables in the sense of my argument. They have the enormous merit of providing measures specifically related to a series of independent and intervening variables while being pinpointed in one causative direction. In short, these measures do *not* substitute disaggregation of a fuzzy dependent variable for more sophisticated reaggregation.

and define them as indicators of authority and legitimacy transfers, as summed up from activity in specific functional and organizational sectors and as observed in elite and mass perceptions.

Multiple Dependent Variables

We appear to be approaching a dependent variable through a series of evasive movements, laterally rather than frontally. We need a definition which avoids the overly simplistic ideal typical of past efforts while aiming at a more sophisticated goal than measurement alone. The terms "fulfillment," "retraction," "equilibrium," and "authority-legitimacy transfer" introduced above do not constitute a definition of a dependent variable either; they are merely concepts evaluating a process at a somewhat higher level of abstraction than that of verified hypotheses. Without the help of such concepts we can hope neither to combine and make intelligible the separate lessons we have learned about integration nor to fill the gaps in knowledge which have been uncovered.

I am using the master concept "authority-legitimacy transfer" as an evaluative tool, much as Joseph Nye uses the term "political integration." We ought to be clear that indicators of political integration are *not* conceptually and sequentially on the same level of abstraction as are indicators of economic and social integration because these ought to refer to earlier points on the action paths. Political integration is simply another evaluative term for observing progress along a path of action—leading toward what?

I should like to propose three different dependent variables, all of which are heuristic in the sense that they do not have any real-life counterparts. They provide orienting terminal conditions on which our thoughts and efforts can focus. Nor are they really "terminal"; we can posit them as provisional points in the future on which we fix our analytical attention. But as students of political life we know that even if the postulated conditions are attained, they are unlikely to remain terminal for very long. Nor are the three dependent variables exhaustive of possibilities. They provide rather an invitation to imagine still different outcomes which involve a higher degree of unity among the participating units than existed at a previous time. In short they are *illustrations of possible temporary results* of the processes we sum up under the label regional integration, so designed as to stretch our imagination of what the future may hold. I shall label the three "regional state," "regional commune," and "asymmetrical regional overlap." The processes associated with all of our pretheories could, in principle, result in the attainment of any of these terminal conditions.[33] Minimally, they all must meet the attributes of a security com-

[33] These types were suggested by, and correspond to, certain constructs in organization theory, particularly by the literature on organizational complexity. Moreover, each type is derived from set theory and is capable of mathematical manipulation, thereby perhaps contributing to possibilities of computer simulation. Thus, regional state corresponds to a set-theory tree, regional commune to a full matrix, and asymmetrical overlap to a semilattice. I am greatly indebted for these ideas to Todd LaPorte and John Ruggie.

munity. The three differ in how the main resource—legitimate authority—is diffused. Hence normative questions of some moment are implied.

A regional state is a hierarchically ordered arrangement resembling states familiar to us. Political authority is concentrated at the center; resources are marshalled and distributed from it. The centralized authority is legitimate in the eyes of the citizens, voluntary groups, and subordinate structures. To the extent that the political culture of the region is "participant" in character the legitimacy bestowed upon the central authority represents a sense of "regional nationalism."

There is nothing unfamiliar about this construct. But its opposite, a regional commune, is a much stranger beast. It assumes the kind of interdependence among the participating units which does not permit the identification of a single center of authority or perhaps of any clear center. It is an anarchoid image of a myriad of units which are so highly differentiated in function as to be forced into interdependence. Authority is involved primarily in the sense of having been taken away from previous centers without having found a new single locus. Legitimacy, however it can be imagined, would not take the form of a loyalty akin to nationalism.

Asymmetrical overlapping involves a much more complex arrangement. Many units depend on many others but the pattern of interdependence is asymmetrical: For some purposes all may be equally interdependent, but for others a few of the units cohere closely with a few others while for still other purposes the pattern may again be different without involving all units equally. In short, while authority is certainly withdrawn from the preexisting units, it is not proportionately or symmetrically vested in a new center; instead it is distributed asymmetrically among several centers, among which no single dominant one may emerge, though one might imagine subtypes of this dependent variable involving various degrees of centralized authority. The ensemble would enjoy legitimacy in the eyes of its citizens though it would be difficult to pinpoint the focus of the legitimacy in a single authority center; rather, the image of infinitely tiered multiple loyalties might be the appropriate one. Perhaps the now existing Western European pattern approaches this image.

What about the vexing question of dependence on extraregional centers of influence, if not authority? How significant is it to talk about such end states of regional integration processes when the resulting structure may be autonomous in a rather fictitious sense? It is possible to describe a variant of each type which locates the regional cluster within a larger system and specifies the degree of subservience to it. Moreover, other variants or subtypes will readily come to mind. I emphasize again that nothing exhaustive is being attempted at this stage: My concern is to provide some generalized images of outcomes before we get lost in operationalization.

One final advantage of using heuristic multiple variables is the emancipation thereby provided from our pretheories. Neo-functional efforts stress case studies of decisionmaking within a region and in regional organizations, an interest justified by the neo-functionalist assumption that decisionmakers are the true heroes and villains of the integration process. Transactionalists counter that a great deal of relevant activity goes on outside of organizations and decisional encounters, an argument based on the assumption that anybody who "transacts" or "communicates" anything is potentially relevant to the creation of integrative/disintegrative trends. Obviously, these two approaches are far from mutually exclusive. Linking them, however, requires articulate hypotheses about presumed relationships between decisional outcomes and communication patterns. Since the multiply defined dependent variable, in turn, implies different scopes of collective decisionmaking and varying strength of interunit dependence, such hypotheses can be usefully linked with the presumed attainment of one or the other of these outcomes. This, in turn, requires a specification of what mix of which independent variables is likely to lead to a given outcome—something clearly not achieved by our pretheories or our empirical generalizations—and raises questions as to what kinds of studies ought to be tackled next.

V. Toward a Theory?

A Plethora of Independent Variables and How to Link Them

What yardstick is there for choosing and justifying ways to explain the arrival of various degrees of regional unity? One extreme is to list every conceivable variable, from the length of the shoreline of the member nations to the proportion of the national budget devoted to veterans' pensions, so that the resulting list of 250 can be reduced by factor analysis. Such a generous and comprehensive approach really implies that we do not know enough on the basis of common sense and immersion in the factual details of regional integration to select variables more economically. It also begs the old question of whether the variable exists "autonomously" at the systemic level or is reflected in the cognitive processes of actors, i.e., whether it merely acts as an indicator (of what?) or accounts for behavior.

Moreover, there is an enormous difference between codifying empirical findings—as I sought to do above—and assessing the significance of specific variables as explanations of outcomes. The empirical generalizations discussed above do not tell us which of several independent variables is the more (or the most) powerful in propelling a given unit toward a specified end state. Nor does the possibility of positively correlating certain trends with an independently assessed growth in integrative institutions settle the question of causation or explanation. In short, several things remain to be done before we even approach an inductive theory. The independent variables with which we propose to work must be specified and operationalized. The hypotheses linking them must be made explicit. And a way must be found to evaluate conceptually the significance of the verified hypotheses in terms of their contribution to explaining an outcome.

The specification of independent variables, their operationalization, and the establishment of clear links between them is advancing rapidly. Several contributors to this volume are engaged in this process; I therefore need only call attention to their work. Nye's list is comprehensive and well chosen in reflecting what we already know about the experiences of various regional efforts on the basis of descriptive case studies. Philippe Schmitter's list, though somewhat different in inspiration, is equally comprehensive, and it self-consciously incorporates presumed links between variables and explicit hypotheses, equally general in their inspiration and mindful of research already completed. Donald Puchala is careful to specify expected correlations between transactional and conflict-resolution data, thus linking the communications and the neo-functional strands as well as jumping the gap between approaches relying on aggregate data and the behavior of elites. Variables are most explicitly specified and justified.

But one cannot *link* independent variables into some kind of explanatory scheme without recourse to concepts or ideas at a higher level of abstraction than the variables themselves, the facts they comprehend, and the empirical generalizations which sum them up. In short, an external source for *linked* variables is necessary; pretheories do have the virtue of providing such sources. Still, we do not wish to accept pretheories as final; we wish to do better than simply arrive at more empirical generalizations of the type summarized above. Hence we must draw our inspiration for identifying and linking variables from some intellectual constructs that command general acceptance for their utility without being fully validated and without having found a clear and final niche in some as yet to be formulated theory.

I label such constructs evaluative concepts. Appropriately scored concepts associated with the explanation of one of our postulated outcomes constitute an "action path." We expect the recurrence of particular relations between independent variables. In order to explain a sequence of events, say from background to the initiation, maintenance, slow growth, and eventual stabilization of a federal state, one would examine and score such variables as elite complementarity, perceived benefits from transactions, the role of external pressure, the substitution of one type of leadership for another, and the creation of new groups of actors, especially nongovernmental ones. We would sum up the particular experience by talking about such things as spillover, spill-around, learning, socialization, elite responsiveness, or institutionalization. In short, these terms are empirically grounded evaluations, not simple facts. They can be inferred from observed variables if one is clear about how and why variables are linked. But once they have been inferred, they can be used to sum up many ranges of activities and interconnected variables in many places. If our objective is the sketching of action paths leading to one of our postulated outcomes, we must evaluate patterned events with concepts summing up processes.[34]

We are now in a position to summarize and rearrange the various strands of the argument. The act of judging whether a concrete regional set of trends and decisions approaches one or the other of the three terminal conditions involves a series of evaluative steps on the part of the observer. After specifying the independent variables he expects to be important, observing their operation over time, and after verifying hypotheses involving these variables, several valuations then become necessary:

1)   What is the mix of recurrent behaviors which accounts for a given trend in a given sector? This involves the use of such evaluative concepts as spillover, elite responsiveness, and bargaining style.

2)   What is the mix of all integrative and disintegrative trends in all sectors for the region (or the sum of the separate organizational and transactional experiences)? This calls for the application of the evaluative concepts we labeled fulfillment, extension, and retraction. We could discover, for instance, that fulfillment occurred in the field of agriculture, extension tariff negotiations with third countries, and retraction in defense policy, as associated with differential patterns of spillover, elite responsiveness, and bargaining styles in each.

3)   What is the sum of all the processes described under these labels? This calls for the application to the region as a whole of the master concept we have called authority-legitimacy transfer.

The multiple dependent variable we have devised enables us to specify to whom the authority and legitimacy have been transferred. The indicators of institutionalization described elsewhere in this volume would facilitate the evaluation.

[34] This way of seeing concepts and data involves a change in perspective on my part as to what constitutes a variable and a method of linking variables, as distinguished from a validated summary of a recurring process expressed by a conceptual label such as "spillover." In short, I no longer accept as sufficiently well-explicated and "placed" the "variables" that appear in Ernst B. Haas and Philippe C. Schmitter, "Economics and Differential Patterns of Political Integration: Projections about Unity in Latin America," *International Organization*, Autumn 1964 (Vol. 18, No. 4), pp. 705–737, and in Barrera and Haas, *International Organization*, Vol. 23, No. 1, pp. 150–160.

A given action path is characterized by a certain kind of learning, a certain pattern of responsiveness, a certain degree of spillover, whether in scope or level. Michel Crozier has suggested a new term which seems appropriate for summing up the kind of process that we ought to use more as a device for linking variables: *apprentissage institutionnel*. It can be used to light up the interconnections between a pattern of transaction, disappointment, declining responsiveness, bargaining, and the eventual redefinition of common or converging interests.

Action Paths and Some Unsolved Problems

When we evaluated the empirical generalizations offered earlier, we noted four major gaps in our knowledge which were in no sense resolved even if we assumed the descriptive accuracy and modest analytical significance of our generalizations. The questions were: 1) Can forces which explain the initiation of a movement toward regional union also be used to explain the maintenance of progress of that union? 2) Is it useful and defensible to use a political model in the study of regional integration which postulates the congruence of national and regional political styles? 3) Is it necessary or desirable to have a special model in the study of regional integration applicable to late developing countries? 4) What should we know about social learning as a way to link various variables? I now wish to reexamine these questions in the light of our discussion regarding dependent variables and the notion of action paths linking independent variables and tying them sequentially to the attainment of a terminal condition. This reexamination should serve the dual purpose of illustrating the notion of action paths and give a few indications of some useful next steps to be taken in research. If regularly observed—and properly evaluated—processes can act as organizing and explanatory concepts for further empirical observations, we ought to be in a position to incorporate them into new research efforts and thus to advance theorizing.

Initiation versus Maintenance of Integration

Actors change their minds, redefine their interests, see new opportunities, and respond to new institutions at home and regionally. Many of these new stimuli arise as a predicted result of what goes on in the integration process and can be evaluated conceptually without introducing new variables at a later point in an integrative/disintegrative sequence. This would argue in favor of assuming the constancy of the explanatory power of a set of variables over time. On the other hand, one could also argue that either of two sets of possibilities can upset this assumption. First, political or social forces internal to the union or common market may arise after initiation and deflect (or strengthen) the initial forces without having been included in the explanation of the origin. This is discussed further when we turn to congruence of national and regional processes. Second, the international environment may change after the initiation of the process and produce an external stimulus for (or against) continued integration not included in the explanation of origin. In either case the assumed linearity between initially programmed impulses and eventual outcome is disturbed.

If we accept the formulation of the dependent variable(s) offered above, a solution to this problem seems possible. Our task is to specify the action paths, i.e., the particular combination of independent variables that most accurately describe the attainment of any one of the postulated outcomes *and* the sequence describing which combination comes to prevail. The list of variables will then remain constant; but the score of each variable will not. The plotting of an action path can then take the form of a scale of progress toward each outcome, made up of the same variables scored differently at various points in time. And the recognized fact of possibly simultaneous integration and disintegration in the same region—depending on task and issue—can then be captured by adding negative and positive scores. Note, however, that such a procedure would still call for the revision of the initial list of independent variables to account for the possibility of the later introduction of the deflecting forces sketched above. This requires the kind of hindsight on the part of the observer which can only arise as a result of assimilating the lessons learned from a considerable number of descriptive case studies of given regional integration experiences. The standard list of conceptually linked variables provided by Joseph Nye and Philippe Schmitter is particularly useful for enabling us to specify which forces remain of equal importance during the early and the later phases of the integration process and which forces drop out of the picture as the process goes forward.

National-Regional Congruence

We would do better if, in our tailoring of empirical generalizations to selected dependent variables, we kept our minds open to a neglected possibility: Rates of change at the national and regional levels may not be congruent. The Western European model has assumed that changes making for pluralism, incrementalism, and instrumental behavior at the nationl level are wholly congruent with the same characteristics at the regional level. Neo-functionalists use an implicit congruence model to select and link variables. Efforts in the Latin American and African settings, by contrast, have relied on the lack of congruence between national and regional structures as an important organizing concept. There impatience with immobilisme at the national level was treated as a positive expectation with respect to regional movement. Both perspectives are time-bound.

A congruence model suggests a different set of intervariable links than a noncongruence model does. Furthermore, a strong case could be made that the notion of noncongruence should in the future inspire the search for links between variables no matter which terminal condition we seek to explore. Some of us have assumed that in the initial period of a union the causal influence would run from the nations to the central institutions and in the subsequent period in the reverse direction—national outputs would dominate first, regional outputs later. The example of the EEC since 1965 suggests that this pattern is unwarranted as a general inspiration. Certain national outputs continue to dominate—very strikingly!—but in other issue areas the regional outputs assert their potency as well. National systems are changing at a different rate than the regional system; new national stimuli stressing demands for change with a consummatory quality strike Brussels while the national arena continues to be struck with EEC outputs that correspond to the earlier incremental-instrumental style. National actors and political styles are being re-ideologized, but the regional system holds its pragmatic own; it maintains itself, though stagnating in terms of earlier ambitious objectives. By focusing on a noncongruence model of national-regional interaction we capture this seemingly paradoxical reality; we sensitize ourselves to a two-way flow of inputs and outputs, and we keep in mind that the environmental conditions that made a given pattern possible initially keep changing and therefore produce new—and perhaps qualitatively different—inputs. Evaluative concepts which sum up such trends realistically are thus useful in pinpointing *different* action paths toward a postulated outcome.

Donald Puchala's contribution to this volume is particularly useful in establishing this perspective for future studies of regional integration. He shows why the communicational hypotheses create a presumption in favor of increasing elite responsiveness as a result of increasing transactions. If, therefore, a *lack* of responsiveness on some ranges of interdependence is shown to be correlated with growing transactions and more favorable attitudes toward one's partners, a sharply noncongruent feature will be thrown into relief. This would force us to alter a number of poorly validated propositions. Such linked variables as the Nye and Schmitter lists contain could then be pressed into service to explain the lack of congruence and thus give us propositions explaining one of the postulated outcomes. For example, the list contains linked variables which suggest:

> initial converging but instrumental actor motives→ disappointment→ exogenously furnished rewards (or threats)→ revalued actor motives→ larger task and increasing institutionalization of decisionmaking power

An investigation sensitive to noncongruence, however, could detect and explain why increasing institutionalization might *not* occur because, for example, the exogenous impulses are so powerful and so diverse as to inhibit revaluation within the region by turning the attention of the actors to arenas outside.

A Special Model for the Third World?

The pretheoretical efforts have mostly started with a set of universal assumptions and hypotheses which had to be shored up and rescued by recourse to various extraparadigmatic devices. The corrective for this practice is not to reify it by claiming a special status for the exogenous variable and turning it into a deus ex machina capable of reviving a floundering common market in Pago Pago. Nor should we expect a charismatic leader or an ideology with

consummatory qualities to ride to the rescue.[35] Rather, the answer is to make
the range of independent variables broad, keep in mind the possible variations
of their mix depending on which outcome is being investigated, and experiment with weights for each variable that seem appropriate for given regional
settings. But as long as political actors are sufficiently rational to calculate their
interests and seek accommodations on that basis, our ingenuity ought to be
great enough to devise observational techniques, concepts, and indicators to
catch the interregional variation in their modes of calculation. What matters
most for the task of systematic study is that there be reasonable agreement on
which variables are considered causatively important and on their links with
other variables. The specification of action paths leading to each of several
postulated outcomes is a capping device for keeping the theory "whole" while
recognizing various roads to salvation within it.

Transactions, Attitude Change, and Learning

How can we link variables that describe the rate of transaction between
units with variables that describe the attitudes of masses and members of the
elites? Some causal link must be imputed or established if the transactional
approach to integration is to be blended with generalizations about attitudes.
Further, how can the empirical generalizations we have established with respect to changing bargaining patterns and styles, institutional evolution, and
the predictable resolution of conflicts between actors be linked with data on
transactions and on attitudes? We can say that only when actors perceive and
evaluate the events that are summed up by such findings as "changes in the
rate of transaction" and "evolution of attitudes" is such a link established causally. But before the cause is established it would be useful to know what the
sheer statistical relationship between the three rates of change might be.

In other words, even the magic of action paths will not suffice to tell us
how different types of actor experiences combine to produce a given trend.
The linking of independent variables through articulate hypotheses, even if
we allow for the points raised under our discussion of noncongruence and the
addition of new forces after the initiation of a trend, will not quite do the
trick of adequate explanation. Action paths toward each of the postulated
terminal conditions would also have to include explanations of who learns
from whom in producing elite responsiveness, how institutions induce or re-
tard learning, and who communicates what to whom when channels of contact
open up. It is not good enough simply to note that various independent vari-

---

[35] Etzioni, Nye, Haas, and Schmitter have all indulged in this practice. It is raised to a point
of faith in Hansen, *World Politics,* Vol. 21, No. 2, pp. 270–271. To those who argue that comparative
studies of integration could still proceed if we had one model for industrialized and one for underdeveloped regions it must be pointed out that our findings suggest a different mix of variables at work in
explaining the maintenance of regional economic arrangements in Central America, South America, East
Africa, and Equatorial Africa, not to mention Eastern Europe.

ables are associated in a given mix in a given action path toward a federal state or an asymmetrically overlapping system.

One very major link would be the notion of social learning. The enterprise of regional integration studies would be improved enormously if we knew when, how, and why actors "learn" to behave differently than they did in the past—either in an integrative or a disintegrative direction. Is it a function of cross-national contact and familiarity, as the psychotherapist would have us believe? Is it the result of ever more complex patterns of intergroup loyalties and of social roles that require a single individual to cater to many patterns simultaneously? Is it related to education and informal socialization practices? Some scholars link interpersonal trust and responsiveness, as a hypothesis, with progressively rewarding experiences derived from the activities of common markets. Thus:

progressively rewarding experiences→ learning→ trust

Others seek to press simple stimulus-response theory into service in suggesting that the intensity and the frequency of the regional interaction pattern will explain a given integrative outcome. Still others assume a more cognitive style of social learning for explaining the kinds of increasing responsiveness in which we are interested and therefore prefer the lessons of formal decision and coalition theory to discover how and when actors redefine their utilities in bargaining with each other. This approach, of course, differs sharply from the study of emotive forces, affect, and the manipulation of symbols as agents of social learning.[36]

The truth is that we simply do not know enough about the forces and processes which mediate between the various independent variables we consider salient. Moreover, we do not yet know how to conceptualize—or ask questions of—the forces which presumably do the mediating. I suggest as a high order of priority that the notion of social learning be included in new studies of integration in order to make our action paths more than highly intercorrelated scores. Such studies should include not only the investigation of who "learns"

[36] Donald J. Puchala, "The Pattern of Contemporary Regional Integration," *International Studies Quarterly*, March 1968 (Vol. 12, No. 1), pp. 38–64. Among social psychologists there are exceedingly few whose assumptions and methods can be readily related to the study of social learning as mediated through experiences in bargaining, defining, and redefining interests because the bulk of the psychological literature is organized around the trust-love-friendship-peace versus distrust-hate-enmity-war dichotomy. For notable and important exceptions see Daniel Katz, "Nationalism and Strategies of International Conflict Resolution," in Herbert C. Kelman (ed.), *International Behavior: A Social-Psychological Analysis* (New York: Holt, Rinehart and Winston [for the Society for the Psychological Study of Social Issues], 1965), as well as Kelman's own work, as summarized by himself in ibid., chapter 16. For a discussion of stimulus-response theory in this context see Henry Teune, "The Learning of Integrative Habits," in Jacob and Toscano, pp. 247–282. The work of Chadwick Alger on United Nations diplomats illustrates the same set of assumptions. Fred Iklé with Nathan Leites discusses the modification of actor utilities in "Political Negotiations as a Process of Modifying Utilities," *Journal of Conflict Resolution*, March 1962 (Vol. 6, No. 1), pp. 19–28. In purely game-theory term the work of John Harsanyi is the most suggestive with respect to the exploration of this area.

what from whom. It must include the meaning of the messages sent through the expanding channels of communication, i.e., with what results in terms of attitude change. Moreover, studies of social learning can easily be linked with the investigation of organizational dynamics in terms tracing the evolution of institutionalized behavior for defining goals, resolving conflict, and persuading actors to live up to their commitments. More abstractly, the application of organization theory to integration studies can tell us more about how the perception by actors of an increasingly complex environment leads them to redefine goals and mechanisms of accommodation so as to increase either adaptiveness or the capacity to control the environment. My own preference in the study of social learning is the application of decision and coalition theory so as to trace modal patterns of redefinition of utilities by actors and the inclusion of this kind of material in the elaboration of a given action path.

The Next Steps

The main utility of the studies of regional integration completed so far has been the systematic investigation of certain potentially crucial independent variables and the search for verification of the assumptions embedded in the pretheories which led to the positing of the independent variables in the first place. Thus, the accumulation of figures on major trends in transaction and communication has served to map important ties between nations and their evolution over time. The completion of a modest number of decisional case studies has taught us a lot about the limits on the cognitive abilities of leaders and elites to define their own and their colleagues' interests. But I suspect that the utility of these types of studies has been exhausted. We now have our list of major independent variables, and we know enough to correct earlier false assumptions about congruence and the linear projection of variables found to have been causatively significant at the beginning of a given regional integrative process. We must now do systematic comparisons of regional experiences and national behavior patterns clustering around the evaluative concepts posited above in order to delineate the action paths which presumably recur.

Computer simulation is one of the most exciting possibilities open to students of regional integration. It forces them to reduce their multilayered and nonadditive generalizations to a common denominator, to agree on likely—but verifiable and testable—sequences of action. The possibility of simulation has both a sobering and an intellectually explosive impact: sobering because of the standardization of variables, of links between variables, and of measures that is demanded; intellectually explosive because the standardization also requires subordination to concepts which seem to summarize observed processes and which can thus become branching points on the flow chart. Finally, the most exciting possibility inherent in computer simulation is the chance it affords to go beyond the very limited number of actual historical cases from which our pretheorizing has sprung. While seeking to replicate these cases, the practice of simulation can also imagine new combinations of concepts and variables which have not yet occurred "in nature" and play them out. In short, computer simulation can show us action paths which have not yet been followed or imagined. But it is made more powerful by the availability of heuristic end states.

Concurrently, the possibility of simulation further enhances the need for a methodological synthesis and gives it a special urgency. If the simulators wish to replicate known decision sequences of organizations and groups active in regional integration, they must find ways of grouping and summing the variables from which concepts summarizing recurring processes are deduced. If they wish to replicate and predict integrative outcomes with the help of ecological and/or attitudinal variables, they must achieve agreement on their definition and on the imputed causal links between them. This would incidentally compel students of integration to settle the question of which weights ought to be attached to such variables. In short, progress in theorizing depends on the acceptance of the discipline which computer simulation implies; but computer simulation, in turn, depends on further progress along the lines of resolving the four issues raised by the gaps in our knowledge.

But why do we need a theory? Why can we not continue to follow our individual inclinations and study the phenomenon of regional integration according to the predilections implicit in the existing pretheories? Because the stakes are too high! The systematic links demanded by computer simulation add up to a whole which at least resembles a theory. And simulation can help us explore the question of a future world order.

Mankind may well be taking steps which could lead to a more multi-layered, more complex, less "integrated" world that would permit much local violence but bar global conflict because of its very fragmentation. But regional integration may lead to a future world made up of fewer and fewer units, each a unit with all the power and will to self-assertion that we associate with classical nationalism. The future, then, may be such as to force us to equate peace with nonintegration and associate the likelihood of major war with successful regional integration.

This is possible, not certain, and perhaps not likely. But we ought to inquire about the degree of possibility or likelihood. In short, one major normative utility of the study of regional integration is its contribution as a conceptual, empirical, and methodological link between work on the future of the international system and the future of the nation-states whose interrelationships make up the system. Suppose that local national movements in Wales, Scotland, Bavaria, Brittany, Nagaland, West Irian, Biafra, the Ogaden desert, Quebec, and in dozens of other ethnically complex places succeed in obtaining cultural and linguistic—and much political—autonomy. Suppose further that the same states enter into tighter economic relationships with their regional neighbors. Suppose further still that they ally themselves militarily and diplomatically with states other than their economic partners. Not only will the state decline as an autonomous decisionmaker, but the power to make decisions will be given to many other units, some smaller and some larger than the present state. This, I believe, would be a wholesome development for world peace whereas the concentration of all power in a few regional units would endanger it. Simulation would be enormously helpful in enabling us to play out the possible trends at the subnational, the national, the regional, and the global levels of political action. Simulation would truly stretch, if not blow, our minds and give us a purchase on the future. But such an adventure first demands a more systematic theory. Our groping has enabled us to ask the questions that the theory should answer; it has also given us some concepts for refining the questions. But much work needs to be done to realize the potential of these achievements.

II

ELABORATION OF CONCEPTUAL AND CAUSAL PARADIGMS

2

Political Integration as a Multidimensional Phenomenon Requiring Multivariate Measurement

I. Introduction

I view international political integration as a distinctive aspect of the more inclusive process (international integration, generally) whereby larger groupings emerge or are created among nations without the use of violence. Such groupings can be said to exist at a variety of different analytical levels. At each level we can conceive of a number of nations linked to each other in certain salient ways. For example, their populations may be linked by *feelings* of mutual amity, confidence, and identification. Or their leaders may hold more or less reliable *expectations,* which may or may not be shared by the populations, that common problems will be resolved without recourse to large-scale violence. Or a grouping might be defined as an area which is characterized by intense concentrations of economic *exchange* or the free *circulation* of productive factors (labor, capital, services). In describing these phenomena we speak of social community, security community, and of economic union. Political integration can be said to occur when the linkage consists of joint participation in regularized, ongoing decisionmaking. The perspective taken here is that international political integration involves a

LEON N. LINDBERG, a member of the Board of Editors, is professor of political science at the University of Wisconsin, Madison.

The author began working on the subject of this article several years ago when he was a research associate at the Center for International Affairs, Harvard University. A major reworking and rethinking was accomplished during the summer of 1969 when he was a participant in a workshop on the formal analysis of international systems at the Center for Advanced Study in the Behavioral Sciences, Palo Alto, California. In between he benefited greatly from the constructive criticisms of his students; most particularly he wants to thank Peter Beckman, Brian Silver, Peter Cocks, William Fisher, Robert Weisberg, Jefferey Obler, and Keith Billingsley. Among the numerous colleagues in this country and in Europe who have commented on the previous versions of this article the author expresses a special debt of gratitude to Hayward Alker, Joseph S. Nye, Jr., Richard Brody, and Jack Dennis.

group of nations coming to regularly make and implement binding public decisions by means of collective institutions and/or processes rather than by formally autonomous national means. Political integration implies that a number of governments begin to create and to use common resources to be committed in the pursuit of certain common objectives and that they do so by foregoing some of the factual attributes of sovereignty and decisionmaking autonomy, in contrast to more classical modes of cooperation such as alliances or international organizations.

Political integration can thus be defined as the evolution over time of a collective decisionmaking system among nations. If the collective arena becomes the focus of certain kinds of decisionmaking activity, national actors will in that measure be constrained from independent action. It is the task of students of political integration to seek to document the emergence of collective decisionmaking institutions and processes among given clusters of nations, to explain how and why such efforts are made and how and why they succeed or fail, and to build causal theory about the nature of political integration as a process and its relationship to other aspects of the overall integration phenomenon (i.e., to social community, security community, economic integration, etc.). The progress, or lack thereof, made in these directions has been examined at length in a number of recent publications and in the other articles in this volume. One of the most serious shortcomings in the field, as Joseph S. Nye[1] and Ernst B. Haas[2] have pointed out, has been the failure to achieve conceptual clarity with regard to the dependent variable(s) that is (are) the putative object(s) of analysis. Nye's signal contribution was to separate out the various ways in which the concept of "integration" has been defined and measured, but this sort of disaggregation is only a first step in the right direction, as he clearly recognizes.

It will be my purpose in this article to propose an analytic paradigm, derived from systems analysis and decision theory, that conceives of the study of political integration as what Hayward Alker has called "the study of the emerging properties of complex open systems."[3] The paradigm identifies the multiple properties of collective decisionmaking systems, defines each property as a range of variation, and conceptualizes political integration as the buildup over time of a variety of such properties or of combinations among them. It will be argued that most studies of political integration have concentrated on one or another aspect of what I take to be an interactive multidimensional process; that is, they have described and analyzed only some of these properties. Partial descriptions have been generated and have served as the basis of causal expla-

---

[1] Joseph S. Nye, Jr., "Comparative Regional Integration," *International Organization*, Autumn 1968 (Vol. 22, No. 4), pp. 855–880.

[2] Ernst B. Haas in this volume.

[3] Hayward Alker, "Computer Simulations of Integration Processes," research memorandum prepared for the Conference on Regional Integration, University of Wisconsin, Madison, April 24–26, 1969.

nation and of predictions about the overall integrative process. But multidimensional phenomena require multivariate description. Our task is to describe the *multiple properties* of collective decisionmaking systems that emerge among nations. This is the foundation of the "interpretable comparisons" which are the necessary first step in theory building. It will not do to focus on single properties or characteristics of such systems in isolation from the others, for it is the nature of the interactions among all the properties that gives each its meaning and significance.

Closely related to the failure of students of integration to adequately conceptualize political integration is the equally serious failure to *fully operationalize* the several dependent and independent variables employed. A fully operational definition is one "which actually spell(s) out the procedures used in measurement" and which provides "a detailed set of instructions enabling one to classify . . . unambiguously."[4] Ideally, in order to permit more than nominal measurement these definitions should be specified as continua rather than as attributes.[5] Just as political integration cannot be adequately described in unidimensional terms, neither can it be adequately described in the dichotomous terms of achieving, or failing to achieve, certain conditions or attributes. Hence, once I have identified the multiple properties of a collective decisionmaking system and indicated how these relate to each other at any point in time, I will go into considerable detail in proposing a variety of operationalization strategies designed to make possible comprehensive multivariate description. These measures are presented in a clearly tentative fashion. They will need to be compared, tested, and evaluated for reliability and validity in a variety of empirical settings. Some are better worked out than others. Only a few have already been subjected to even preliminary testing with data. In due time most will be revised and yet others will be rejected in favor of new approaches. I offer them here in preliminary form as a stimulus to others to improve upon. Even in preliminary form these measures should serve as useful guides to future data gathering. They indicate in some detail the kind of data that is required if we are to make meaningful descriptive or causal statements about international political integration.

I will also address myself to the problem of how (or if) overall or aggregated measures might be achieved. How will it be possible to argue that one cluster of nations evinces a greater degree of political integration than another? If it is not enough simply to compare collective decisionmaking systems in their various individual properties over time and with each other (although this will

[4] Hubert M. Blalock, Jr., *Social Statistics* (New York: McGraw-Hill, 1960), p. 9:
>   The notion of reliability is thus built into this conception of the operational definition. The definition should be sufficiently precise that all persons using the procedure will achieve the same results.

[5] For a discussion of these problems and of the advantages of continuous variables as compared with attributes see Hubert M. Blalock, Jr., *Causal Inferences in Nonexperimental Research* (Chapel Hill: University of North Carolina Press, 1961), pp. 30–38.

be interesting and useful), on what bases can aggregate measurement be made? I will argue that at this level theory building and measurement go hand in hand, for in my view the key to aggregate measurement and comparison of the properties of collective decisionmaking systems is to be found in concepts such as "autonomy-subordination," "performance in the face of stress," and "decisionmaking capability." To measure (or predict) the autonomy, performance, or capability of a collective decisionmaking system implies that one fully understands the nature of the causal interrelationships between its diverse properties and between them and exogenous factors. The paradigm will be again useful in this regard, for it suggests the general form of the interrelationships that must be established by empirical research if autonomy, performance, or capability are to be ascertained.

The article thus will offer a rather complex set of concepts and an even more complex array of measurement strategies. I claim that these concepts will capture and integrate in a meaningful way what has too often been studied in isolation. The extensive efforts made to operationalize the concepts are a necessary prelude to systematic multivariate description and to the testing of empirical relationships. They should also be valuable as guides to the kinds of data that empirical case studies of collective decisionmaking systems among nations ought to gather. The paradigm and the measures together point the way toward the dynamic measurement of such salient aggregate properties of collective decisionmaking systems as autonomy, performance, and capability.

II. THE PROPERTIES OF A COLLECTIVE DECISIONMAKING SYSTEM

The essence of political integration is the emergence or creation over time of collective decisionmaking processes, i.e., political institutions to which governments delegate decisionmaking authority and/or through which they decide jointly via more familiar intergovernmental negotiation. Collective decisionmaking processes are complex; they have multiple properties; hence we view the political integration process as the gradual buildup over time of a variety of such properties. *These properties bear a systematic relationship to each other at any given point in time and, as will be seen later, over time as well.* Systems analysis seems a particularly useful tool in eliciting what these properties might be and in suggesting the nature of their dynamic interrelationships.

Systems analysts like David Easton focus directly on what I have chosen to accept as the distinctively political, that is, that system of interactions through which binding or authoritative allocations are made and implemented.[6] Comprehensive and dynamically interrelated analytical categories are developed that, although they owe much to the nation-state as a model, explicitly seek

[6] David Easton, *A Systems Analysis of Political Life* (New York: John Wiley & Sons, 1965).

to isolate authoritative allocative processes in general, whatever types of system may exist—primitive and undifferentiated societies, complex industrialized pluralistic nation-states, or incipient multinational systems. Systems analysis thus sensitizes us to the possibility that other kinds of political systems than the nation-state have had decisionmaking capabilities, that there are other ways of responding to stress than the use of coercion (the essence of many definitions of a political system), that a political system can persist without the existence of a matching cultural or social system, and that political systems can be characterized by multiple levels of authority. Finally, systems analysis will guide us in our search for dynamic, aggregated measurement. For the systems analyst the most crucial problems for study are: How do systems of authoritative decisionmaking, whatever their type and characteristics, cope with stress from their environments? Do their efforts to do so bring about an expansion or contraction of those very decisionmaking activities and affect their capacity to persist through time? Furthermore, by organizing conceptually around the problem of persistence (and by inference, growth and decay) systems analysis points clearly to some of the ways in which group theory, decision theory, and coalition and game theory can be used to illuminate the political integration process. For my purposes it is useful to distinguish ten properties that a collective decisionmaking system will have. Each of these can be described as a range of variation, and these ranges can be clustered into three overall categories according to a systems paradigm, referring respectively to the level, animators, and consequences of a collective decisionmaking system. If we conceive of such a system at any point in time, we can first describe the level of collective decisionmaking activity, that is, the extent to which the constituent countries actually make decisions as a group. Level can in turn be described in terms of the *scope* of policy areas affected, the *range of stages* of the total decision process involved, and the degree to which collective decisions in any area or at any stage are the more *decisive* ones. The level of collective decisionmaking activity in any integration system at any time is essentially a product of past decisions in that system and past decisions made by appropriate authorities in the constituent states. The second set of properties, what I call activators, describes the energy available to the system at the time of analysis. A decisionmaking system is activated by the flow of demands for action to it from relevant political actors and by the behaviors of collective decisionmakers in response to these demands. How such demands are processed into decisions will be determined by the level of *resources* available to collective decisionmakers, the way in which leaders make use of them, and by the *propensity of national bargainers to "consume"* these resources for the maximization of collective as against individual interests. Finally, the *consequences* that collective decisions may have for the constituent systems can be described in terms of the degree to which the decisions *penetrate* the system, the degree to which the decisions are *complied with,* and the *distributive consequences* of the decisions.

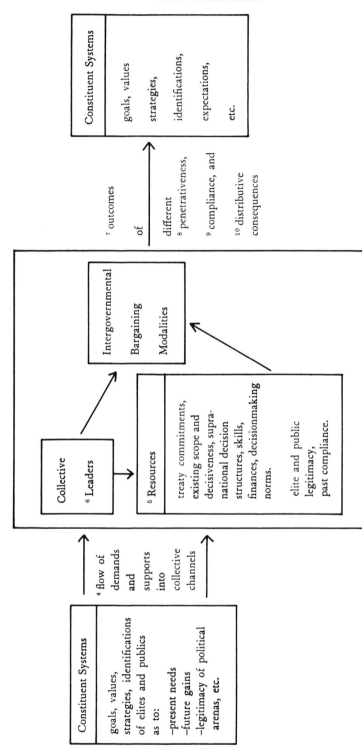

FIGURE 1. TEN PROPERTIES OF THE COLLECTIVE DECISIONMAKING PROCESS. Collective decisionmaking activity is described in terms of [1]scope, [2]stage of decision, and [3]decisiveness.

I have suggested that students of political integration have generally concentrated their attention on only one or a few of these properties (or the linkages between them) taking the property(ies) studied to be indications of the whole. They have thus failed to make explicit (or indeed to understand) how these properties interacted with each other and with the broader integrative process. In some cases, inferences about the state of an emerging collective decisionmaking system and efforts to account for that state have both been made using data on a single property or linkage. This would not be a serious problem if we could assume that variations along the different properties were likely to occur symmetrically. But empirical research has revealed that this is not the case. One collective decisionmaking system may show a wide, but superficial, policy coverage, be animated by few demands, and have only marginal consequences for the constituent nations. Another might touch relatively few policy areas, but for these matters it might have become the most decisive political arena. Similarly, in any given system some properties may be increasing, others decreasing, and others remaining stable at any point in time. Thus scholars might easily be led to opposite conclusions, both as to a description of what *is* and to *predictions* of the direction of change, by virtue of an exclusive concentration on one or a few properties. Some properties, it will be argued, are likely to be more salient both as descriptors of the overall system and as *predictors of future change in the system,* i.e., of political integration. As I go into greater detail in describing the paradigm I will try to indicate which properties and linkages have been most studied and which ones generally neglected. I hope it will also become clear how the paradigm can combine in a meaningful way what has hitherto been left disaggregated.

The Level of Collective Decisionmaking

The first task in describing a partially integrated collective decisionmaking system at any point in time will be to identify the contours of what David Easton calls "the political division of labor" that binds the constituent units together. The problem is to determine to what exent the constituent units are members of a group that shares a political structure as determined by their joint participation in the making of binding decisions. The focus is

> not on the form . . . of political processes but rather on the group of members who are drawn together by the fact that they participate in a common structure and set of processes, however tight or loose the ties may be.[7]

The constituent units need not "form a community in the sociological sense of a group of members who have a sense of community or a set of common traditions."[8] Similarly, the notion of a common division of political labor is

---

[7] Ibid., p. 177.
[8] Ibid.

distinct from the sentiments people may have about it (sense of political community or support for it).

It seems to me to be important to maintain these analytical distinctions between the division of political labor itself, sentiments about it (support), the specific forms it takes (e.g., supranationality), and sense of social-historical community. There is no necessary reason to assume that they must exist together or that they are causally interrelated in any standard and predictable fashion. In my paradigm, support for the existing division of political labor, institutional forms like supranationality, and social-emotional ties among peoples are treated as three of the several kinds of variable *resources* that a collectivity may have and that may be used to process demands into decisions. The role that each plays in the formation and the functioning of a given collective decisionmaking system should be a matter for empirical research. Too often scholars have seemed to treat them as either equivalent or as accurate indicators of each other, i.e., as if they were uniformly intercorrelated. For example, Karl Deutsch has asserted that the European integration movement was largely halted in 1957.[9] His evidence included 1) time-series data on the *mutual preferences* shown by members of the European Economic Community (EEC) for each other's trade, mail, tourism, and students and 2) opinion data on the sentiments European peoples and elites hold toward each other. In terms of the concepts in my paradigm Deutsch has data on the existence of social-emotional ties and on an aspect of support for a division of political labor. But no data at all was gathered on the extent to which these six countries in fact act together to make collective decisions. The implication is that no political integration of any consequence can exist if levels of social integration are low. But this is only an assumption and is never demonstrated. William Fisher has shown that in fact they do not appear to be closely correlated in the European case.[10]

Curiously we have made rather little progress in developing the concepts necessary to describe the political division of labor inherent in a collective decisionmaking system. We have extensive descriptions of the nature of bargaining in such systems but little in the way of systematic treatments of the scope and political significance of the decisions actually taken.[11]

[9] Karl W. Deutsch, "Integration and Arms Control in the European Political Environment," *American Political Science Review,* June 1966 (Vol. 60, No. 2), pp. 354–363. Karl W. Deutsch, and others, *France, Germany and the Western Alliance: A Study of Elite Attitudes on European Integration and World Politics* (New York: Charles Scribner's Sons, 1967), part 3.

[10] William E. Fisher, "An Analysis of the Deutsch Sociocausal Paradigm of Political Integration," *International Organization,* Spring 1969 (Vol. 23, No. 2), pp. 254–290.

[11] The lawyers and the economists have done somewhat better insofar as the legal and economic policy implications are concerned. For legal analyses of European community "legislation" see Gerard Bebr, *Judicial Control of the European Communities* (New York: Frederick A. Praeger, 1962); and Peter Hay, *Federalism and Supranational Organizations: Patterns for New Legal Structures* (Urbana: University of Illinois Press, 1966). For a very useful analysis of economic policy implications of European integration see Finn B. Jensen and Ingo Walter, *The Common Market: Economic Integration in Europe* (Philadelphia: J. B. Lippincott & Co., 1965).

The political division of labor that characterizes any given collective decisionmaking system can be specified in terms of three ranges of variation. First, the scope of collective decisionmaking may be generalized over many issue areas or be specialized to a few policy domains. Second, the range of participation in joint decisionmaking may be limited to predecisional stages of the process, i.e., to what Harold Lasswell[12] calls problem-recognition and information-gathering; or it may extend to the formulation of action alternatives, to choices among them, and to the administration and enforcement of the policies and rules that result. Finally, collective decision processes may be more or less decisive, compared to national processes, in determining public allocations at different stages of the process and in different issue areas.

Animators of Collective Decisionmaking Activity

The concepts of the scope, stages, and decisiveness of joint processes will give us a summary description of how extensive and intensive is the political division of labor that binds a group of countries in an integration system. They give only a static and a partial portrait, however, for they say nothing about those properties that describe the dynamics of activity within the system. Such a system functions in response to *demands for action* made by political actors. The flow of demands into collective channels may be large or small, increasing or decreasing, depending on the goals and strategies of politically relevant actors and their expectations as to what ought to be decided upon collectively. Demands for action typically enter the collective arena from the constituent systems and may originate with ultimate decisionmakers, high staff officials, technical experts, party leaders, or interest groups. In most cases national governments act as prime gatekeepers between demands welling up from elites or groups within constituent systems and the collective decisionmakers, although in some groupings, notably the European community, groups may press their demands directly upon community officials. Since governments pool decisionmaking activities out of some expectation that they may thereby more efficiently maximize certain of their goals, we may expect that the strength and homogeneity of demand flows from subunit systems will be important predictors of future states of the system as well as vital ingredients in depictions of the system at discrete points in time.

In order to process demands a system must possess both *resources,* which can affect the cost-benefit calculations of political actors, and *leaders* who use these resources to perform gatekeeping, demand aggregation, coalition formation, and compliance-inducing functions. Resources may consist of certain aspects of the system itself: the extent of prior agreement among the participat-

[12] Harold D. Lasswell, *The Decision Process: Seven Categories of Functional Analysis* (College Park, Md: Bureau of Government Research, College of Business and Public Administration, University of Maryland, 1956).

ing governments (in treaties or subsequent legislation) with regard to the
matters that can be handled collectively (regime values for Easton); the decision rules and norms (regime norms) that prevail among governments and
other collective decisionmakers and that define the procedures "that are expected and acceptable in the processing and implementation of demands";[13]
the extent to which supranational decision structures have been able to develop appropriate expertise and autonomy; and the extent to which the system is able to dispose of monetary resources (either by government allocation
or taxation). Collective leadership may also be able to call upon a variety of
resources that are analytically outside of the system and that enter it from the
constituent systems. These resources, which are akin to Easton's familiar concept of support, might include: 1) expectations of future gain or acceptable
outcomes on the part of elites or groups based on past experience with the
system (specific support) and 2) expectations that those to whom collective
outcomes are addressed will comply with them, either because they accept the
collective arena itself as legitimate (diffuse support) or because there is a high
level of mutual political identification among the populations of the constituent units.

The ways in which collective decisionmakers will respond to the flow of
demands will depend not only on the extent to which those playing leadership roles are able and willing to use the resources available but also on the
propensity of other actors in the system to consume proffered resources. According to John Harsanyi,[14] one must distinguish between the conditions under which the environment is ready to supply resources to an actor and the
utility function which determines his "demand" for them. One way of describing a collectivity's utility function is to identify the modal types of intergovernmental bargaining behaviors that characterize it, or, in other words, a
system's bargaining modalities. These modalities will reflect the kinds of
strategies pursued by actors seeking either to maximize their own interests or
to optimize the interests of the collectivity in collective decisionmaking situations. The strategies pursued are themselves reflective of the aims and expectations of the actors vis-à-vis each other and may range from the classic pure
conflict model, or a zero-sum game in which only one player wins and the
rest lose proportionally to his gain, to complex cooperative games in which
aims and expectations may be changed and everyone may gain, if only because the collectivity gains.

Consequences of Collective Decisions

The decisions of a collective decisionmaking system will be determined by
demands, resources, and bargaining modalities as they operate within a collec-

---

[13] Easton, p. 193.

[14] John Harsanyi, "Measurement of Social Power, Opportunity Costs, and the Theory of Two-Person Bargaining Games," in Martin Shubik (ed.), *Game Theory and Related Approaches to Social Behavior: Selections* (New York: John Wiley & Sons, 1964), p. 195.

tive arena of given scope, stages, and decisiveness. These decisions may themselves have a variety of consequences for the constituent systems, depending on the degree to which these decisions change the goals, values, strategies, identifications, and behaviors of those to whom they are addressed or whom the decisions influence indirectly. The properties of penetrativeness, compliance, and distributive consequences will describe how much change occurs at the national level as a consequence of collective decisions. They are clearly among the crucial descriptors of how much political integration there is. They will also be important predictors of the future; that is, how much political integration or disintegration there *will be.*

The extent to which change occurs in national systems as a consequence of collective decisions will depend first on how deeply decision outcomes actually penetrate into constituent systems—how much change in behavior is implied for how many people. In some cases the outcomes of collective decision processes will be bargains struck at the level of governmental negotiators and binding only on them for the next round in the bargaining process. Only their future bargaining behaviors in the area in question are affected or constrained by the decision. In other cases collective decisions will be binding on national governments per se but will commit them only to pursue common policy goals. How these goals are to be achieved and implemented is left to national decision processes, national laws, and enforcement procedures. Or collective decisions may be policies and rules that apply directly to whole categories of individuals (e.g., all farmers) and are directly enforceable by collective institutions and procedures (as with much of agricultural marketing policy in the European community).

The amount of change attributable to collective decisions will also vary with the extent of compliance with them. If noncompliance with collective decisions is as likely as compliance, it will be difficult to say that individuals have accepted these decisions as premises for their own behavior. Similarly, the knowledge that decisions or agreements have or have not been fulfilled or enforced may operate as a powerful inducement to future bargaining. Frequent evasion or violation of agreements is certainly not likely to increase or maintain the mutual trust and readiness to make the concessions that are a necessary ingredient of collective decisionmaking processes. Reliable expectations of compliance can also serve to enhance the authority or legitimacy of the collective arena in the eyes of other actors and of broader publics alike, and it may in fact stimulate the flow of demands into collective channels.

Finally, collective decisions can bring about changes at the national level by virtue of their differential consequences for the relative and absolute distribution of rewards and deprivations among nations and within nations in the issue areas affected. Depending on the penetrativeness of decisions and the degree of compliance with them, greater or lesser distributive consequences may be perceived by formal decisionmakers, by groups of elites (businessmen, traders), by social categories (workers, farmers), or by entire populations. It seems clear that the measurement and comparison across systems and over time of variations in actual allocations of value ought to be central to descriptive analysis. It is also likely to be a vital explanatory variable. In collective decisionmaking systems, grouping diverse nations with different interests and long histories of sovereign existence, memories of past gains or losses, may be the most instrumental factor in leading political actors either to continue to press demands in collective channels or to abandon them, or to induce political actors or broader publics to consider collective channels appropriate. There is ample evidence from the European community, from the East African Common Services Organization (EACSO), and from the Central American Common Market (CACM) to confirm that willingness to proceed with further political integration or to sustain the present level of integration is dependent upon some balance of returns among the participating units so that none seems to be disproportionately advantaged. Yet there is also evidence to support the notion that an integrative undertaking will not thrive and grow in scope unless it has (or is believed to have) significant distributive consequences for important actors.[15] Of course, there must be some overall balance over time among important distributive outcomes so that actors who lose or gain relatively little in one situation will be able to gain relatively more on some other issue. In other words, significant tangible or symbolic benefits must be perceived as available now or in the future in order for national political actors (or mass publics) to alter goals, values, strategies, identifications, and behaviors, so that they can participate in and support an ongoing collective decisionmaking process of any significant scope, decisiveness, etc. I would argue, for example, that the major reason for the very modest degree of political integration among the countries of Scandinavia—in spite of the fact that they have been a "security community" for a long time and that they score very high on most lists of background conditions and on measures of community formation—is that actors there have perceived very limited benefits resulting from pooled decisionmaking. The stakes involved have simply not been worth the investment of resources, the changes in habits, the partial loss of autonomy in their own affairs that political integration typically implies.

Let me summarize my argument thus far. The extent to which a group of nations engages in collective decisionmaking at any point in time can be described in terms of ten variable properties. We would like to know of any system:

1) Is its functional scope limited to a few issue areas or generalized over many?

---

[15] Leon N. Lindberg and Stuart A. Scheingold, *Europe's Would-Be Polity: Patterns of Change in the European Community* (Englewood Cliffs, N.J.: Prentice-Hall, 1970), pp. 178–180, 283.

2) Are collective processes invoked only at predecisional stages of the decisionmaking process or do they affect the whole range of decision stages, including policy choices and their implementation?

3) Are collective processes marginal or decisive in determining public allocations in given issue areas?

4) Are few demands and/or contradictory demands articulated into the collective arena, or is there a strong and homogeneous flow of demands for collective action?

5) Do collective decisionmakers have at their disposal resources that are meager and restricted in kind, or can they call on a wide range of ample resources?

6) Are efforts to provide leadership at the level of the collectivity ad hoc and spasmodic, or is leadership regularly offered via institutionalized and legitimated roles and norms?

7) Do the bargaining modalities of the system tend to maximize the individual interests of particular nations or those of the collectivity or a substantial portion of it?

8) Do collective decisions have a marginal effect on the behavior of a narrow range of individuals, or do they penetrate deeply, touching many people in many ranges of their behavior?

9) Are collective decisions generally ignored, or is there a high probability that they will be complied with?

10) Do collective decisions have minimal or important distributive consequences for constituent systems and for particular actors within them?

In general, we can say that the higher the score or ranking on any of the above properties, the more political integration there is. If the scores all increase over time we can speak of a process of political integration, and if they all decrease, of political disintegration. But what if some are high and others low, some increasing and others decreasing? How then do we determine whether integration or disintegration is occurring? Similarly, how shall we determine which of two collective decisionmaking systems that differ widely in their scores on these properties is the more integrated politically? We can simply admit that such comparisons will indeed be difficult because political integration is not a single thing but rather refers to a lot of different phenomena. There are sophisticated methodological techniques for handling such multiple-indicator problems, and we might experiment with some of these, e.g., vector analysis, multidimensional scaling, or unfolding analysis. Another possible approach would be to arbitrarily select out some property (or properties), such as scope (or the three descriptors of *level*), resources, or distributive consequences, and to consider variations on these to be what we mean by political integration-disintegration. More attractive to me, and I would argue much more useful, would be some form or forms of theory-based aggregate measurement; several types will be explored in the final section of this article. One of the keys to such aggregation has already been hinted at, namely, our suggestion that certain of the above properties are not only *descriptors* of how integrated the system is, but they have also been identified by students of integration to be powerful *predictors* of whether or not the system is likely to integrate further.

Before moving on to these issues of how to handle multivariate measurement of political integration we must first cope with the question of how the different properties can be operationally defined in actual research.

III. Toward Multivariate Description: Some Strategies of Operational Definition of Individual Properties and Subproperties

If the ten variable properties introduced earlier are to actually facilitate multivariate description of real-world integrating (or disintegrating) systems and thus set the scene for dynamic aggregate measurement and for theory building, each must be given precise operational meaning. This means simply that each concept must be defined so that it can have various values that imply increased integration and that the researcher can determine unambiguously, by means of actual observations on data, which value it has at a given point in time. In each case I will try to present a full formulation of my understanding of the concept (i.e., property). I have typically derived concepts from systems analysis and translated them into a verbal framework I take to be appropriate to the study of political integration. I will then identify those aspects of that description that seem to lend themselves to direct or indirect measurement and propose guides for making these measurements. In the case of some very complex properties (like scope or resources) a number of separate indicators may have to be combined into indices or else treated as vectors.

We are still in the early stages of development as far as the measurement of political integration is concerned, and the indicators and indices to be proposed will reflect the relatively primitive state of our thinking. The indicators suggested for each property or subproperty should be judged according to a number of criteria. First, there must be a plausible relationship between the concept being studied and that aspect of it that the indicator measures. Second, the indicators should be objective and reliable; that is, they should permit repeated measurements with similar results by independent researchers. Third, the indicators ought to be functionally equivalent for meaningful use in cross-system research. Finally, they should be subject to as precise quantitative measurement as is consistent with the other criteria. The closer one can get to interval and ratio scales, rather than ordinal or nominal measures, the better.

However, when it has seemed to me that I had to make a choice between *validity* and level of measurement, I have opted for the former. Hence, I have often settled for indicators permitting only ordinal measurement.

A. *Functional Scope of Collective Decisionmaking*

The essence of political integration is that governments begin to do together what they used to do individually; namely, they set up collective decision-making processes that in greater or lesser degree handle actions, engage in behaviors, and make allocations of goods or values that used to be done (or not done) autonomously by governments or their agencies. We want to know how extensive this collective activity is—how inclusive it is of the decisionmaking activities of the constituent political systems. Getting at this presumes some method of listing scopes of activity or functions performed by collective decisionmaking systems, tabulating these lists, and comparing them both over time and across systems. One way of proceeding is to draw up some sort of standardized list of the functions of government (or the political process or the social system). This is, of course, an inherently arbitrary process. There have been many efforts by social scientists to develop such lists,[16] but it would be difficult to argue that any of these seems to be clearly the most useful or the most widely accepted. Similarly, students of power and influence processes have considered the "scope of power," i.e., the classes of activities across which one individual or collectivity can affect the behavior of another, to be one of the central dimensions of their concept, but, as Dahl points out, they have not developed any "generally accepted way of defining and classifying different scopes."[17] Perhaps the most elaborate effort is that of Harold Lasswell and Abraham Kaplan who identify the following as the chief "values" allocated by social processes: power, respect, rectitude, affection, well-being, wealth, skill, enlightenment.[18]

Ultimately the researcher must be guided by his own judgment as to what sort of "check list" will best suit the purposes of his inquiry. In the present case what I have tried to develop is an exhaustive list of mutually exclusive decision or issue areas that will 1) permit a substantial disaggregation of governmental activities of different types in terms of behaviors that can be readily observed and classified by coders; 2) that will facilitate comparisons between

[16] See, for example, Gabriel Almond, "A Developmental Approach to Political Systems," *World Politics,* January 1965 (Vol. 17, No. 2), 183–214, and M. J. Levy, Jr., *The Structure of Society* (Princeton, N.J: Princeton University Press, 1952).

[17] *International Encyclopedia of the Social Sciences,* Vol. 12 (n.p: Macmillan Co. and Free Press, 1968), p. 408.

[18] Harold D. Lasswell and Abraham Kaplan, *Power and Society: A Framework for Political Inquiry* (New Haven, Conn: Yale University Press, 1950), pp. 55–56 and 72. For some research applications of this taxonomy see J. Zwi Namenwirth, "The Lasswell Value Dictionary," Yale University, January 1968. (Mimeographed.) J. Zwi Namenwirth and Harold Lasswell, *Cyclical Value Changes in American History: Essays in Social Dynamics* (forthcoming) and J. Zwi Namenwirth, "Wheels of Time and the Interdependence of Value Change," Yale University. (Mimeographed.)

integrating systems; 3) that will be demonstrably relevant to the concerns of the student of international relations or of comparative politics who will be interested in the scope of collective decisionmaking as an independent or intervening variable. The following list[19] seems to meet these criteria fairly well although there is certainly room for improvement:

External Relations Functions

1. Military security
2. Diplomatic influence and participation in world affairs
3. Economic and military aid to other polities
4. Commercial relations with other polities

Political-Constitutional Functions

5. Public health and safety and maintenance of order
6. Political participation (i.e., symbolic participation, voting, office-holding)
7. Access to legal-normative system (equity, civil rights, property rights)

Social-Cultural Functions

8. Cultural and recreational affairs
9. Education and research
10. Social welfare policies

Economic Functions

11. Counter-cyclical policy (government expenditures, price and wage controls, budgetary policy)
12. Regulation of economic competition and other government controls on prices and investments
13. Agricultural protection
14. Economic development and planning (including regional policies, aid to depressed industries, public finance, guarantees of investments, etc.)
15. Exploitation and protection of natural resources
16. Regulation and support of transportation
17. Regulation and support of mass media of communication (including post office, television, radio, etc.)
18. Labor-management relations
19. Fiscal policy
20. Balance-of-payments stability (exchange rates, lending and borrowing abroad, capital movements)
21. Domestic monetary policy (banking and finance, money supply)
22. Assurance of free movement of goods, services, and other factors of production (not including capital)

FIGURE 2. LIST OF ISSUE AREAS

[19] This list is a composite of the efforts of a number of scholars and has been refined and tested for cross-national validity in seminars at the University of Wisconsin. The list is derived from the results of William H. Riker, *Federalism: Origin, Operation, Significance* (Boston: Little, Brown and Co., 1964); E. S. Kirschen, and others, *Economic Policy in Our Time* (Amsterdam: North-Holland Publishing Co., 1964); and Jensen and Walter. For an earlier version of this effort to measure scope see Leon N. Lindberg, "The European Community as a Political System: Notes Toward the Construction of a Model," *Journal of Common Market Studies*, June 1967 (Vol. 5, No. 4), pp. 356–360.

The list emphasizes the economic sector both because economists have gone farther in devising useful classificatory schemes and because most contemporary integrative undertakings have taken the form of free trade areas, customs unions, or common markets. The list was originally developed for application to the European Communities and as a result there may be a bias in the direction of developed, industrialized, capitalistic, and pluralistic systems that could limit its utility when applied to developing countries or to communist and other nonpluralistic societies. I have revised the list to try to overcome these problems, while at the same time retaining its utility as applied to such systems as the European Communities, European Free Trade Association (EFTA), and to the Nordic area.

At the simplest level, we can measure scope by counting, at given time intervals, the number of issue areas in which collective decisionmaking takes place. Since we would propose using a scope measure in conjunction with indicators of the *range of decision stages* involved, we can set a relatively low threshold for inclusion (i.e., as problem-recognition, see below). For example, an issue area might be counted if: 1) a group of governments or their representatives had formally recognized that certain problems concerned the collectivity and that concerted, coordinated, or joint action might be desirable; 2) governments or their representatives had actually met together to discuss, or authorized collective institutions to discuss, the ways and means of concerting, coordinating, or deciding jointly; and 3) these discussions actually involved the gathering and exchange of information and the generation of alternative solutions or of specific proposals for action. It should not be difficult to make these judgments with the aid of official government documents, the publications of collective institutions, press releases, news reports, etc. Using the above list of issue areas and a somewhat more stringent threshold for inclusion (demanding actual collective choices among alternative solutions), Stuart Scheingold and I tabulated the number of issue areas that were subject to joint decisionmaking in the European Communities at selected intervals between 1950–1970. We found a substantial increase in functional scope over time: from 0 issue areas in 1950 to 7 in 1957, to 17 out of a list of 22 in 1968 and in 1970.[20] These results could also have been expressed in percentages.

Since it is clear that the individual issue areas are palpably unequal in importance, salience, or controversiality, we might prefer to divide issue areas into sublists containing roughly comparable items and tabulate separately. One method of doing so would be to distinguish, as is done in our list, between external relations, political-constitutional, social-cultural, and economic functions. Individual tabulations can be made and the scope score expressed as a set of separate numbers, i.e., as vectors.[21] Thus, using data from *Europe's*

[20] Lindberg and Scheingold, p. 74.
[21] Harsanyi, in Shubik, p. 186.

Would-Be Polity, we could describe the changing functional scope of the European Communities in vector terms, tabulating numbers respectively of external relations, political-constitutional, social-cultural, and economic functions.

TABLE I. A VECTOR REPRESENTATION OF THE FUNCTIONAL SCOPE OF THE EUROPEAN COMMUNITY, 1950–1970

Date	Number of Issue Areas Included
1950	0, 0, 0, 0
1957	0, 1, 1, 5
1968	3, 2, 2, 10
1970	3, 2, 2, 10

Alternatively, different weights could be assigned to each sublist or to individual issue areas on the basis of some criteria of importance or political salience. But setting up a valid and reliable weighting scheme is no mean task. It is difficult to find agreement on the determinants of saliency or controversiality. What is salient for one actor (or state) may not be salient for another. What is salient for any actor may vary over time in response to a whole host of factors like the presence or absence of an external military threat or the state of the economy.

Nye[22] has suggested that one might construct a salience measure based on the proportion of total governmental expenditures in the individual issue areas. There is a certain face validity to the notion that the importance of governmental activity is proportional to its cost; indeed, most quantitative analyses of governmental output are based on expenditure figures. Such an indicator is attractive because it is already in interval form and readily amenable to statistical manipulation, but a glance back at our list in Figure 2 should remind us that governmental action in issue areas not involving the provision of goods or services—such as maintaining balance-of-payments stability or regulating competition or the money supply, not to speak of political participation or access to the legal normative system—cannot be meaningfully scored for salience on such a basis.[23]

Another approach might be to work out formal criteria by means of which trained coders could assign salience weights to individual issue areas. This could be done individually for each nation involved and the scores averaged

[22] Nye, *International Organization,* Vol. 22, No. 4, p. 869.
[23] Nye suggests combining expenditure indicators with reputational rankings of ministries by experts.

somehow[24] to get an overall score for an issue area, or we could try to get overall judgments for all member states in a particular grouping. For example, we might assert that salience consists of three components: the intensity of preferences and feelings in a particular area; the power of the actors whose preferences are involved; and the nature of the deprivations that they anticipate—i.e., whether conflicts are perceived as zero-sum or subject to resolution with nobody losing very much of importance, as in Theodore Lowi's distinction between redistributive and distributive policies.[25] Expert judges might be able to assign dimensional scores using a five-point scale as follows:[26]

		1	2 3	4 5
Dimensions of Salience	*Intensity*	Stakes are low, no strong preferences or commitment to existing policies.	→	Feelings are intense, strong preferences are involved. Actors see most important issues involved.
	Power of the Actors	Those affected have no or very little political power.	→	Those affected represent the most potent political forces in the system.
	Anticipated Deprivation	Can be readily resolved with all gaining and nobody losing.	→	Can be resolved only on a zero-sum basis—only one wins, rest lose.

FIGURE 3. CODING FOR SALIENCE

The overall salience of an issue area could be computed on the basis of the average of the scores given by the judges for the individual dimensions. Lack-

24 The method chosen would depend on such things as the relative power of the nations vis-à-vis each other and on whether or not decisions require unanimity or majority assent. One convention could be to base aggregate issue-area scores on the highest salience found, on the assumption that most integration systems are structured in a way to make any issue as salient as the most concerned actors are prepared to make it.

25 Theodore Lowi, "The Public Philosophy: Interest-Group Liberalism," *American Political Science Review*, March 1967 (Vol. 61, No. 1), pp. 5–24.

26 It would, of course, be preferable if we could find objective quantitative indicators for each of these salience dimensions.

ing more objective criteria (and better indicators) we might weight each dimension equally and calculate the salience of an issue area as the product of the three average scores.[27] Functional scope might then be expressed as a series of vector products[28] or as an aggregate (or several aggregates if we subdivide the list) of the number of issue areas subject to collective decision *times* the sum of the salience scores for those areas. Such an aggregate scope score could also be expressed as a percentage of the sum of the salience scores of all issue areas on the list.

B. *Range of Decision Stages Involved*

The concept of functional scope describes a horizontal dimension—which of the totality of functions performed by constituent governments are pooled in an integration system. The concept of the range of decision stages is designed to direct our attention to what we can conceive of as a vertical dimension. That is, how many different kinds of decision activities are performed in the collective arena. As political scientists we know that to fully describe the decisionmaking process we must observe it at a variety of different stages. For example, Lasswell identified the stages of problem-recognition (intelligence), information (design), and choosing (choice).[29] These were subsequently elaborated to include intelligence, recommendation, prescription, invocation, application, appraisal, and termination.[30] Such a list then describes the typical steps through which established political systems pass as they process any given demand through to final allocations. But collective decisionmaking systems are only partially established or integrated since political actors usually entrust functions and activities to them on an incremental basis. Consequently, we must ask how far the activities of the collective system extend along this decision path in particular functional areas.

Integration systems differ widely as to the range of decision stages made subject to collective decisionmaking. These differences would seem to be vital not only in developing suitable descriptive profiles but also in explaining other differences between integration systems, such as their relative capacity for self-maintenance and self-generated growth and the impact they are likely to have

[27] A simpler approach would be to have a number of judges rank order issue areas for increasing salience, or classify them into sublists which could be ranked high, moderate, and low saliency, or to each of which we could assign a numerical measure. Alternatively, an arbitrary total score of perhaps 100 points might be assigned to each state (or group of states) and expert judges asked to divide up the 100 points among issue areas in terms of their relative saliency, using a variety of criteria, including some of the above. For a similar approach to a different weighting problem see Mario Barrera and Ernst B. Haas, "The Operationalization of Some Variables Related to Regional Integration: A Research Note," *International Organization*, Winter 1969 (Vol. 23, No. 1), pp. 152–154.

[28] On the uses of vectors see Hugh G. Campbell, *Matrices with Applications* (New York: Appleton-Century-Crofts, 1968).

[29] Harold D. Lasswell, "Current Studies of the Decision Process: Automation versus Creativity," *Western Political Quarterly*, September 1955 (Vol. 8, No. 3), pp. 381–399.

[30] Harold D. Lasswell, *The Decision Process*.

on the member states and on the general international system. Systems such as in the Nordic or Australia–New Zealand ones, where the bulk of collective activity occurs at the "prechoice" stages—that is, where problems are studied together, compatible or parallel solutions are developed, but governments then act independently to translate (or not) these into authoritative form[31]—are likely to have very different consequences insofar as creating new interdependencies, changing elite and public attitudes, expectations, identifications, etc., than are systems in which integration extends to the national and transnational coalition-formation and support mobilization processes involved in actually *choosing* a particular policy option together (as in the European Communities). The effect in the latter case may be to create a new regional political arena in which new interest groups form and old ones devise new strategies and new interest perceptions and expectations of collective gain develop, these in turn creating new demands and resources for the collective process. These things seem less likely to occur in the case of "prechoice" integration.

I would hypothesize that whether or not a group of governments will extend the range of stages involved will depend, first, on how close together (or far apart) the nations are initially in terms of indicators of interdependency, mass and elite community formation, economic development, types of political system, and the content of public policies; and, second, on the nature of the benefits that political actors can reasonably expect to flow from integration. In the case of "distance apart" I would expect the relationship to be curvilinear; both too much difference and too much similarity are likely to cause actors to limit the range of stages subject to collective decision. In the Nordic area the nations and populations already enjoy a high degree of social similarity. These countries are frequent reference groups for the citizens or policymakers in the others. Many of the goals that actors seek to advance via collective action can be achieved without the creation of extensive common institutions and processes.

On the other hand, the members of the European Communities could hardly have expected to overcome the legacy of past division, war, and enmity by pursuing a "Nordic" strategy. They were too far apart and felt too compelling a need for rapid action to settle for the piecemeal, step-by-step harmonization of policy in noncontroversial areas so characteristic of the Scandinavian ap-

---

[31] On the Nordic area see Nils Andrén, "Nordic Cooperation," *Cooperation and Conflict*, 1967 (No. 2); Barbara Haskell, "Is There an Unseen Spider?" *Cooperation and Conflict*, 1967 (No. 2), and Barbara G. Haskell, "External Events and Internal Appraisals: A Note on the Proposed Nordic Common Market," *International Organization*, Autumn 1969 (Vol. 23, No. 4), pp. 960–968; Stanley V. Anderson, *The Nordic Council: A Study of Scandinavian Regionalism* (Seattle: University of Washington Press, 1967). On Australia-New Zealand see Alan Robinson, "Trends in Australian-New Zealand Relations," *Australian Quarterly*, March 1969 (Vol. 41, No. 1), pp. 43–51, and Alan Robinson, *Towards a Tasman Community?* (Discussion Paper No. 5) (Wellington, New Zealand: Institute of Economic Research, 1965).

proach.[32] But integration research has also shown that countries that have vastly different social and political systems and few linkages in the economic or social spheres are unlikely candidates for integration.

As for benefits expected, I would posit a more linear relationship—that is, only if crucial elites develop expectations of major benefits to be achieved via integration, and perhaps only by that route (e.g., preventing another Franco-German war, competing with the Americans and the Russians, or transforming economic ruin to the promised prosperity of a market of continental scope), could the bolder European community approach be made possible. A less far-reaching political integration scheme was adopted by nations in Scandinavia largely because they were involved in few conflicts with each other, were relatively prosperous economically, and were dependent upon extraregional actors in political-security areas and because they therefore had relatively little to gain from more ambitious schemes. These states were already very much alike, already constituted a security community, and were already characterized by intensive community formation processes.

The ordinal scale in Figure 4 is proposed as a device to aid in the measurement of the range of stages of the decision process that is involved in collective decisionmaking. It can be used to score the range of collective activities actually engaged in by a group of states within any of the issue areas identified earlier. The scale is based on the distinction made by Lasswell between problem-recognition, decision, and application. *Problem-recognition* refers to those political activities involved in recognizing that problems confront the group as a whole, that some sort of concerted or coordinated or joint action is called for. It includes the gathering and exchange of information and the processes of generating alternative solutions or proposals for action. *Decision* refers to those activities involved in choosing between alternative solutions, i.e., the mobilization of support for one or another proposal, negotiation and bargaining among authorities, and the final authoritative prescription of general policies or rules. *Application* covers those activities involved in the implementation of policies and rules in reference to conduct and includes specifically administration, enforcement, the hearing of appeals, etc.

For each issue area listed in the scope of a given collective system we would keep a cumulative tally of the specific activities that had been turned over to the collective arena. Each collective act could then be scored as a 1–6 for range of decision stage and frequency distributions tabulated at regular intervals. If we assume only an ordinal level of measurement we could describe the resultant distributions in terms of the percentages of cases in each rank, the median or the mode. Were we to make interval assumptions, we could de-

[32] The successes and failure of the Organization for European Economic Cooperation (OEEC) and Council of Europe illustrated the limitations of the approach to the six countries that eventually went ahead to more far-reaching efforts; see Lindberg and Scheingold, pp. 11–21.

Range Score	Stage of Decision	Coding Instructions
1	Collective problem-recognition	Formal recognition by governments or their representatives that problems are common and that concerted, coordinated, or joint action might be desirable. Intergovernmental meetings are held or collective institutions meet to discuss ways and means of concerting, coordinating, or deciding jointly. Joint information gathering is initiated with object of concerting national policies as distinct from carrying out a service for one or more governments.
2	Specific action alternatives *defined* collectively	Some policy options are defined as acceptable, others as not. National decisionmakers agree to a range of *compatible* policies. Most politically relevant elites must be mobilized. Study sessions of civil servants are of little moment in fields where great interest group associations are dominant and decisive, unless their leadership is also engaged in the process. On the other hand, the relevant elite for monetary policy or for capital movements will be smaller and the role of governmental actors more decisive.
3	Collective decisions on policy guidelines	Intergovernmental bargaining and choice of a type of policy (e.g., anti-inflationary economic policy), leaving it up to national authorities to translate into policy (e.g., to hold government expenditures stable or freeze wages or prices).
4	Detailed collective goal-setting implementation by national rules	Choice of policy actually limits national authorities to passing legislation implementing a detailed collective decision. Some discretion due to interpretation.
5	Decisions on policies and rules *directly binding* on individuals	No national discretion since intergovernmental decision requires no translation into national law via national processes. Actual implementation and enforcement by national authorities.
6	Collective implementation and enforcement	Common institutions are created to administer and enforce detailed binding rules as adopted by collective decision.

FIGURE 4. RANGE OF DECISION STAGES

scribe decile scores, the mean, standard deviation, degree of skewness, etc. Such summary measures could give us a way of succinctly describing the extent to which collective activities in specific scopes encompass the hierarchy of stages involved in the authoritative allocative process. They can be combined in a number of suggestive ways with the aggregate or vector measures of functional scope that have been proposed above.

C. *The Relative Decisiveness of the Collective Arena*

The final step in delineating the extent to which a group of nations has become linked by virtue of joint participation in decisionmaking is to ascertain the relative roles of collective and autonomous national processes in determining overall public allocations in particular issue areas. One grouping may score impressively on functional scope, another on the modal or mean range of decision stages involved, but both may be limited to technical and noncontroversial matters that are marginal to basic public policy choices in the area in question. On the other hand, one can readily imagine cases (for example, the North Atlantic Treaty Organization [NATO] in the 1950's) where although only policy guidelines (range score of 3) were established in a few areas by means of collective processes, they covered the most central policy questions at stake in those areas. The continuum I envisage for each issue area would extend from a situation in which the collectivity processed only a few technical and noncontroversial matters to a situation in which collective activity encompassed the full sweep of the most central policy questions at stake.

Actually, there are two related aspects to this property of relative decisiveness. On the one hand, we are seeking a way of rank ordering the broad types of possible substantive governmental decisions within one of our issue areas in terms of their increasing preemptiveness vis-à-vis the policy latitudes or discretion available for other types. For example, agricultural economists typically argue that there are four types of public policy decisions in that issue area, namely, decisions on marketing policy (typically price levels, support arrangements, and the like), trade policy (duties, levies, quotas, export subsidies), social policy, and structural policy. Most would probably agree that the specific decisions taken in certain of these subareas will fundamentally limit the available policy options in others; e.g., setting and supporting high price levels for agricultural products will clearly foreclose some options and force others in trade and structural policy. And secondly, we are looking for ways to estimate the extent to which more or less preemptive decisions are taken in the collective arena. For example, we might ask about the European Communities if collective decisions setting price levels and support regulations for agricultural products include 30 percent, 60 percent, or 90 percent of the value of agricultural production in the constituent countries.

The measurement problems here will be similar to those encountered in our effort to develop objective indicators of salience, and it is difficult to see how we can avoid a similar reliance on subjective coding and ordinal measures. Scheingold and I sought to tap this dimension using a simple device to score what we called "the locus of decisionmaking" in the European Communities. We assigned one of the following five ordinal rankings to each issue area at four different times on the basis of our best expert judgment.

Low Integration

1) All policy decisions are made by individual governments by means of purely internal processes or are made in other nonnational settings (e.g., NATO).

2) Only the beginnings of European-level decision authority have appeared.

3) Substantial regular policymaking goes on at the European level, but most matters are still decided by purely domestic processes.

4) Most decisions must be taken jointly, but substantial decisions are still taken autonomously at the nation-state level.

5) All choices are subject to joint decision in the European system.

High Integration

FIGURE 5. LOCUS OF DECISIONMAKING. The figure above is adapted from pp. 68–69 of *Europe's Would-Be Polity*. For brief explanations of how the rankings were made see pp. 70–73 of that book.

We presented our findings for all issue areas in tabular form as follows:

TABLE 2. THE SCOPE OF THE EUROPEAN COMMUNITY SYSTEM, 1950–1970

	1950	1957	1968	1970
External Relations Functions				
1. Military security	I	I	I	I
2. Diplomatic influence and participation in world affairs	I	I	2	2
3. Economic and military aid to other polities	I	I	2	2
4. Commercial relations with other polities	I	I	3	4
Political-Constitutional Functions				
5. Public health and safety and maintenance of order	I	I	2	2
6. Political participation	I	I	I	I
7. Access to legal-normative system (civic authority)	I	2	3	3
Social-Cultural Functions				
8. Cultural and recreational affairs	I	I	I	I
9. Education and research	I	I	3	3
10. Social welfare policies	I	2	2	3
Economic Functions				
11. Counter-cyclical policy	I	I	2	3
12. Regulation of economic competition and other government controls on prices and investments	I	2	3	3
13. Agricultural protection	I	I	4	4
14. Economic development and planning	I	2	2	3
15. Exploitation and protection of natural resources	I	2	2	3
16. Regulation and support of transportation	I	2	2	3
17. Regulation and support of mass media of communication	I	I	I	I
18. Labor-management relations	I	I	I	I
19. Fiscal policy	I	I	3	3
20. Balance-of-payments stability	I	I	3	4
21. Domestic monetary policy	I	I	2	2
22. Movement of goods, services, and other factors of production within the customs union	I	2	4	4

SOURCE: Lindberg and Scheingold, *Europe's Would-Be Polity*.

NOTE: "Scope" combines what we have here called "functional scope" and "decisiveness." The "stages of decision" threshold for inclusion was set at actual choice behavior.

TABLE 3. OVERALL CHANGES IN THE DISTRIBUTION OF DECISION AREA SCORES, 1950–1970

Locus of Decision	1950	1957	1968	1970
1. All national	22	15	5	5
2. Only very beginning community	0	7	9	5
3. Both, national predominates	0	0	6	8
4. Both, community predominates	0	0	2	4
5. All community	0	0	0	0

SOURCE: Lindberg and Scheingold, Europe's Would-Be Polity, p. 74.

TABLE 4. CHANGES IN THE DISTRIBUTION OF DECISION AREA SCORES, BY FUNCTIONAL CATEGORY

Locus of Decision	External Relations				Political-Constitutional				Social-Cultural				Economic			
	1950	1957	1968	1970	1950	1957	1968	1970	1950	1957	1968	1970	1950	1957	1968	1970
1. All national	4	4	1	1	3	2	1	1	3	2	1	1	12	7	2	2
2. Only very beginning community	0	0	2	2	0	1	1	1	0	1	1	0	0	5	5	2
3. Both, national predominates	0	0	1	0	0	0	1	1	0	0	1	2	0	0	3	5
4. Both, community predominates	0	0	0	1	0	0	0	0	0	0	0	0	0	0	2	3
5. All community	0	0	0	0	0	0	0	0	0	0	0	0	0	0	0	0

SOURCE: Lindberg and Scheingold, Europe's Would-Be Polity, p. 74.

FIGURE 6. STAGE OF DECISION PROCESS. Issue areas were scored individually for the three decision stages.

Locus of Activity		Problem-Recognition	Decision	Application-Enforcement
All activity at the national level	0	No authoritative decision to study problems with a view to concerted action. No actor engagement.	No decision behavior in the collective system.	Governments have complete discretion in administration and experience all feedback. No collective administration of policy.
Preponderance at national level, some collective	1	A narrow range of problems is authoritatively accepted as common. Slight actor mobilization.	A narrow range of problems is carried to specific policies or rules. or A few important problem areas are involved but decision only to goals or general policies.	Very little direct administration by collective system. Governments have almost complete discretion, subject to some "coordination." There may be very little feedback.
Substantial activity at collective level, but national is dominant	2	A few important areas are seen as common and studied as such, but decisive issues are still subject to national processes. Substantial actor mobilization.	A few important problems carried to specific policies or rules. or As many decisive problems are dealt with at collective as national levels, but only to point of goals or general policy.	A few important policies are directly administered with limited government discretion. Some feedback activity likely in collectivity.
Roughly equal activity at both levels	3	Within a given issue area these problems dealt with collectively are equivalent in number or importance to those still subject to national systems alone.	Problems resolved in collective system to point of specific policy or rules are as important. or Most problems are subject to joint decision on goals and broad policy, but substantial autonomy to governments re specific policy and rules.	Government administrative discretion substantially limited for many decisive issues. Some feedback activity.

(Continued on next page)

Figure 6—Continued

Locus of Activity		Problem-Recognition	Decision	Application-Enforcement
Collective level is dominant, but substantial national activity	4	The most decisive problems are seen as common; data is gathered and alternatives generated in collective system. Important areas still subject to autonomous national activity.	The most decisive problems are decided upon in common to level of policies and rules. *or* Only a narrow range of problems is not involved, but decision activity reaches only to goals or broad policies.	Collective administration exists for most of the policies, only limited government discretion. Substantial feedback through European system.
Preponderance of activity at collective level, small national role	5	Only a narrow range of problems is viewed as solely of national scope. The great bulk of recognition, communication, and problem solving takes place in the European system.	Only a narrow range of problems is still decided upon in national systems autonomously. *or* All problems are dealt with authoritatively, but implementing policies and rules still subject to governmental discretion.	Very restricted governmental discretion in administration. Most feedback also through collectivity.
All activity is at the collective level	6	All basic problems are perceived as common by authorities and relevant actors and are dealt with as such. Distinction between internal policy and collective policy disappears.	All decision behavior down to implementing rules takes place in collectivity.	All administration and feedback is in collectivity.

Simple tabulations gave us a crude indicator of the extent to which the locus of decision had shifted over time in the direction of the community (see tables 3 and 4). We were also able to draw some general conclusions as to the type of decision that seemed to predominate (in this case regulative decisions rather than ones concerning allocations of goods and services) and to speculate about likely implications insofar as concerned the development of a "constituency" for European community decisions.[33]

Of course, as they stand, these specific categories and codes are clearly inadequate for use as a serious research tool. They were developed and used

[33] Ibid., pp. 75–80.

for heuristic and expository purposes alone. Nevertheless, they can be easily improved upon. The ways in which such an indicator might be used, once developed, is, however, suggested by the above examples.

In an earlier unpublished paper[34] I proposed a more elaborate set of coding instructions that combined the properties of relative decisiveness (or locus of activity) and range of decision stages.

This device was used by several expert judges in 1967 to code the European Communities and by graduate students in seminars in 1967–1968 to code activity in various other regional groupings, including the Central American Common Market, the Council for Mutual Economic Assistance (Comecon), the Council of Europe, Benelux, EFTA, the Nordic Council, and the Latin American Free Trade Association (LAFTA). The level of agreement on coding between the expert judges scoring the European Communities was high enough to warrant presenting the coding scheme here in substantially its original form.[35] However, the consensus among graduate student coders was that, given their level of competence in the other regions, the instructions were too vague or the data too scattered for them to make reliable judgments.[36] Clearly, more precision in definition is needed before such codes can become reliable research tools. Best of all might be to push further the development of a device for rank ordering different policy types such as the one suggested earlier for agricultural policy. We might ask a number of experts in different policy areas to identify the major types of public decisions in those areas and to arrange them in order of increasing decisiveness. If lists can be devised so that

[34] Leon N. Lindberg, "Europe as a Political System: Measuring Political Integration," Center for International Studies, Harvard University, April 1967. (Mimeographed.)

[35] Kendall's W, the "coefficient of concordance," a nonparametric measure of rank association, was calculated. This statistic is a form of analysis of variance and it expresses the average agreement between ranks on a scale from .00 to 1.00. The overall W for the expert judges was .899. For the formula and details on computation see Fred N. Kerlinger, *Foundations of Behavioral Research: Educational and Psychological Inquiry* (New York: Holt, Rinehart and Winston, 1965), p. 267.

[36] Some indication of the nature of these results and how they compare to my own 1966 ranking of the EEC is given by the following summary scores obtained by adding ranks across issue areas:

Grouping	Problem-Recognition	Decision	Application-Enforcement	Totals
European Economic Community (1966)	44	30	24	98
Organization for European Economic Cooperation (1958)	12	7	1	20
Organization for Economic Cooperation and Development (1965)	8	2	0	10
Council of Europe (1966)	30	15	8	53
Benelux (1965)	20	15	11	46
Nordic Area (1967)	50	1	1	52
Central American Common Market (1967)	27	14	10	51
Latin American Free Trade Association (1966)	6	6	4	16
Council for Mutual Economic Assistance (1965)	25	23	22	70

several judges agree within tolerable limits of error, then the ranks that they establish could serve as the basis for a quantitative index of decisiveness for that issue area.[37] Thus if ten types of decisions were found to characterize the issue area of fiscal policy and these were successfully rank ordered in terms of decisiveness, we could assign a rank score of from 1–10 to any given integration system that produced collective decisions on fiscal policy. One possible advantage of such a procedure would be that it might enable one to take account of the phenomenon that a given collective decision might effectively preempt national decisionmaking discretion in *lower ranked* areas even though those areas were still subject to formal national action.

The Level of Collective Decisionmaking: A Preliminary Note on Aggregation

We have sought to conceptualize and define operationally three distinct properties: functional scope, range of decision stages, and relative decisiveness—which taken together constitute an exhaustive description of the level of decisionmaking authority assigned to or acquired by an integrating system at a particular point in time. We can represent them schematically as follows:

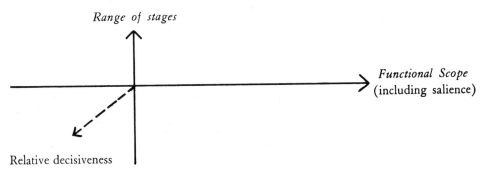

FIGURE 7. LEVEL OF COLLECTIVE DECISIONMAKING AUTHORITY

Each of these properties can vary more or less independently of the other, and it will be important to observe and explain the variations, both within a single system over time and between systems with different characteristics. We may also be interested in some questions that will require aggregating the three into a single number (vector, matrix). How this would be done would depend on whether vectors, weighted scores, or some combination of the two were used in the first place. For example, if we knew a system's scope,

---

[37] For procedures and details for a similar way of scaling see Lincoln E. Moses, and others, "Scaling Data on Inter-nation Action," in *Science*, May 26, 1967 (Vol. 156, No. 3778), pp. 1054–1059.

range, and relative decisiveness, we might be able to calculate the probability that a given policy question arising within the territory of the countries which are members of an integrating system will be referred to the collective arena.[38] It would be especially interesting to compare such probabilities over time.

D. *Demand Flow*

David Easton defines demand as

> an expression of opinion that an authoritative allocation with regard to a particular subject matter should or should not be made by those responsible for doing so.[39]

The demands made upon the authorities of a political system sum up a wide range of conditions and events that are transmitted to the system from its environment. Easton conceives of the flow of demand inputs in terms of *volume* and *variety* and observes that it is changes in the volume and variety of demands that represent the major source of stress flowing from changes in the environment. Demand flow is much more than the chief source of stress in integrating systems, however. In a fundamental sense it is the lifeblood of such systems, for the essence of the political integration process rests on the perception by political actors that it is the collective decisionmakers who have (or ought to have) the responsibility for acting in certain areas in the name of the group. Governments do not create a collective political arena unless political actors at some level (statesmen, *técnicos,* political parties, interest groups, elites) have come to articulate at least some of their expectations and aspirations in terms of the collectivity.

Thus, because we are interested in how and why such systems grow or decline over time, changes in the volume and variety of demands made for collective action do not just constitute a source of stress for us but represent the leading edge of the integration process. Such changes reflect events and changes in the environment, including, of course, the consequences of the past functioning of the integration system itself. Indeed, the role of demands in the integration process and the dynamics of demand change have been central foci of attention for students of political integration, especially those of the neo-functionalist persuasion. And we have accumulated a wealth of detailed empirical description which we have sought to relate in more or less impressionistic fashion to successes or failures of integration. We have generated hypotheses, but we have not succeeded in defining and operationalizing the concept of demand flow in such a way that these hypotheses could be systematically tested and refined. For example, the major summary indicator we have used to describe variations in the variety of demands—namely, the dis-

---

[38] This resembles Dahl's concept of "the amount of power"; see Robert A. Dahl, "The Concept of Power," *Behavioral Science,* July 1957 (Vol. 2, No. 3), pp. 203–205.

[39] Easton, p. 38.

tinction made between identical, convergent, or divergent actor interests or goals—has been used metaphorically rather than as a precise measure with clear and unambiguous empirical referents.

We might make a start in the direction of developing a more precise definition by returning to Easton's distinction between the *volume* and the *variety* of demands. Demand flow at any point in time can be conceptualized as a product or vector of these two components or forces. Each component could be expressed in terms of absolute values of appropriate indicators, rates of change in such values, subjective codings, scores on suitable indices, etc. The *volume of demands* made for collective action will be some function of the number of actors who develop demands relative to the collective arena, the power or influence or resources (usually in the constituent systems) of the authors of these demands, the intensity of their concern, and the extent to which they mobilize to press their case. The *variety of demands* will be determined both by the substantive policies desired and by the type of action being requested.

Choosing indicators and constructing indices will again pose challenging problems. In *Europe's Would-Be Polity* Scheingold and I made the following admittedly crude operationalizations.[40] As concerned the power, influence, or resources of actors making demands, we distinguished between dramatic-political and incremental-economic actors and between those whose responsibilities or constituencies or authority was system-wide rather than limited to a region, category, industry, or interest group. Intensity was estimated in terms of the extent to which actors anticipated redistributive benefits and in the political efforts expended in trying to influence the decisionmaking process, both at the national level and in the collective arena. As for variety of demand we distinguished between those demands that called for the extension of the functional scope of the system or the authority of its institutions, those that called for their maintenance at a status quo level, and those that called for their reduction. Total demand flow was then found to be a function of the extent to which five conditions were fulfilled.[41]

1. Political actors with system-wide power or with a substantial constituency (i.e., interest groups) within several member countries come to identify their interests with the creation of a Community decisionmaking capability, i.e., with an extension of the scope or capacities of the system.

2. Political actors in control of one or more governments perceive progress in a particular area or sector to be a central item on their agenda.

3. Political actors can anticipate redistributive benefits in the area of most concern to them as a result of the change to the Community arena.

4. The goals sought by actors are generally consistent with each other, i.e., the

40 Lindberg and Scheingold, pp. 121–128.
41 Ibid., pp. 283–284.

demand pattern is identical or convergent rather than conflictual. Growth will be a function of the *balance* between supporters, opponents, and "conservers," as well as of the kinds of actors (dramatic-political, incremental-economic, systemic, subgroup) that pursue these different kinds of goals. The likelihood that a prointegrative balance will emerge seems to vary as follows:

a. It will be *high* if:
  1. Systemic actors and subgroup actors with dramatic-political and incremental economic aims favor the measure, even if for different reasons
  2. If there is opposition only from some subgroup actors
b. It will be *moderate* (50/50) if:
  1. Systemic actors with incremental economic aims are opposed but they are offered side-payments, or subgroup actors are mobilized to support the measure, or systemic actors with dramatic-political goals are in favor
  2. If opposition can be isolated to one or two countries and to one level or type of aim (except systemic dramatic-political)
  3. Only incremental-economic elites are mobilized
c. It will be *low* if:
  1. Systemic actors with dramatic-political aims oppose the measure
  2. Systemic, dramatic-political actors favor integration but pursue inconsistent goals
  3. Both kinds of actors at both levels oppose
  4. Most kinds of actors in any one country oppose the measures
5. Intra- and intersectoral bargaining remains open enough to yield a rough equivalence of benefits (gains and losses as a result of integration) among the member countries.

Needless to say, more conceptual specification and more sophisticated indicators are needed. We can be much more precise in determining the extent to which the major relevant political actors within member states are attentive to the collective arena and develop expectations of it. This can be studied via surveys or by means of content analyses of interest group conferences and conventions, speeches and pronouncements of government officials, parliamentary debates, and tabulations of actual formal demands (including meetings called, days in session, etc.) put into the system in one way or another. Intensity and activity can also be more effectively measured in terms of such things as the ratio of influence attempts directed to collective channels over all influence attempts, weighting them equally, or in terms of their importance to the actor or the urgency of the wording. Techniques for coding interactions and influence attempts, using printed material such as news reports or news summaries have been developed by Charles McClelland in his World

Event/Interaction Survey Project.[42] One might also measure the rate at which new interest groups or political party organizations are set up at the level of the collectivity, the growth in their staffing and budgets, the absolute increases or decreases in the volume of their activity (formal statements and communications sent to collective institutions, meetings and exchanges of visits, etc.). Content analytic techniques can also be developed for a more sophisticated coding of the *variety of demands*. Tabulations on all of the above can be made within individual issue areas as well as for the system as a whole.

E. *Resources of Collective Decisionmakers*

The concept of "resources" is an important one in the social sciences. It has been particularly salient among students of power who have sought to explain one actor's ability to influence another's behavior in terms of the resources he possesses, including his economic assets, his formal or constitutional prerogatives, the military forces at his disposal, his popular prestige, and so forth. Among students of integration Amitai Etzioni has been the most comprehensive and self conscious in identifying the resources (he calls them assets) available to a union and in trying to use the concept systematically to help explain successful and unsuccessful unions. He distinguishes between *utilitarian, coercive,* and *identitive* assets.

> *Utilitarian* assets include economic possessions, technical and administrative capabilities, manpower, etc. . . .
>
> .   .   .   .
>
> *Coercive* assets are the weapons, installations, and manpower that the military, the police, or similar agencies command. . . .
>
> .   .   .   .
>
> The term *identitive* assets refers to the characteristics of a unit or units that might be used to build up an identitive power. These identitive potentials are usually values or symbols. . . . [43]

He then goes on to posit a series of propositions about the kind, distributions, and amounts of integrating power, defined as assets actually *used* to bring about some effect, needed for successful unification.[44] These are then "explored" in four case studies.[45] The analysis is highly suggestive but is somewhat marred by Etzioni's tendency to confuse assets, power, and outcomes

---

[42] See Barbara Fitzsimmons, and others, "World/Event/Interaction Survey, Handbook and Codebook," Department of International Relations, University of Southern California, January 1969; and Charles A. McClelland, "International Interaction Analysis: Basic Research and Some Practical Applications," Department of International Relations, University of Southern California, November 1968. (Mimeographed.)

[43] Amitai Etzioni, *Political Unification: A Comparative Study of Leaders and Forces* (New York: Holt, Rinehart and Winston, 1965), pp. 38–39.

[44] Ibid., pp. 94–96.

[45] United Arab Republic, Federation of the West Indies, Nordic Associational Web, and the European Economic Community.

and by his failure to operationalize or provide even crude measurement of either assets or power.

In the following pages I make some suggestions as to how the concept of resources can be further elaborated and how each component can be brought to life. At least ten such components or subproperties will be discussed:

1) Prior agreement on what can be decided collectively (existing level)
2) Decisionmaking norms
3) Supranational structures
    a) Supranational structural growth
    b) Resources of supranational structures
    c) National-supranational transactions
4) Financial resources
5) Support resources
    a) Expectations of future gain
    b) Belief in legitimacy
    c) Belief in a common interest
    d) Sense of mutual political identification

The significance of each in the integration process is likely to vary from one grouping to another and from one time period to another for any particular grouping. Some may be depleted with use, others replenished. Some systems will be able to create their own resources, others will be dependent on national systems for fresh supplies. In each case we will be identifying resources that may or may not be *available* to an integration system. Whether or not they are *used actively* is not dealt with here but rather in the next subsection on leadership.

I conceive of resources as varieties of means available to collective decision-makers that enable them to process demands. This involves preeminently the formation of coalitions, for by definition political integration is a voluntary process involving consensual decisions.

> The decisions that are finally made will thus represent the outcome of a long series of bargains, exchanges, concessions, and accommodations at both the national and Community levels. In order for a proposal or cluster of proposals [demands] to get all the way through the process, more and more supporters must be recruited and potential opponents neutralized, either by adjusting the proposal to meet additional demands, by eliminating objectionable portions, by promising other things in other areas or at future times, and so on.[46]

The chief problem for collective decisionmakers is then to induce political actors to join coalitions at different levels and stages of the decision process.

[46] Lindberg and Scheingold, p. 116.

They can do this by manipulating the incentives or opportunity costs of these actors. John Harsanyi[47] lists four main ways in which this can be done: 1) by providing unconditional advantages or disadvantages such as facilities, goods, and services, 2) by setting up rewards and punishments, that is, advantages and disadvantages that are conditional upon certain prescribed terms, 3) by supplying information on existing advantages and disadvantages, and 4) by relying on legitimate authority which makes other actors attach direct disutility to the act of not complying.

In the following review of the kinds of resources available to collective decisionmakers that might enable them to manipulate incentives and opportunity costs I have stopped short of any effort to propose procedures or devices for aggregating a total resource score. We do not know enough about the role played by each of these resources, or combinations of them, at the various stages of integration and in different regions to establish weights or composite indices. A vector approach may be once again the most appropriate.

1) PRIOR AGREEMENT ON WHAT CAN BE DECIDED COLLECTIVELY

The starting point for any system of decisionmaking is the shared understandings among the members of the system on what is appropriately within its sphere and what is outside. The most direct way of measuring governmental expectations is to refer to the *existing level of integration,* that is, to the cumulative effect on scopes, stages, and decisiveness of the original treaty obligations and of past decisions and their consequences. We are likely to be interested in particular in whether or not, in what ways, and at what rates the *level* of activity is increasing or decreasing. On the assumption that some types of expectations or commitments are likely to provide the collectivity with more resources than others we may also want to classify these formalized intergovernmental understandings in one way or another and compare frequency distributions. For example, Ernst Haas and Philippe Schmitter distinguish between "built-in" integration and negotiated integration and argue that "politicization" (growth, success?) is more likely if the former prevail rather than the latter.[48] They have several things in mind that must be considered separately if we are to assimilate their discussion to the purpose of measuring different levels of formalized intergovernmental agreement or understanding. They are listed here as attributes, but they could be redefined as continuous variables.

a) Are future actions self-executing, i.e., is there a firm agreed-to schedule according to which tariffs will be reduced or the construction of a new policy initiated, or does each step have to be negotiated anew?

[47] Harsanyi, in Shubik.

[48] Ernst B. Haas and Philippe C. Schmitter, "Economics and Differential Patterns of Political Integration: Projections about Unity in Latin America," *International Political Communities: An Anthology* (Garden City, N.Y: Doubleday & Co., 1966), pp. 259–300.

b) Are exemptions from established rules administered by the collectivity, or are they possible at the whim of any member government?

c) Does the scope of the enterprise extend to economic and welfare policy-making which are much more likely to generate spillover because "it is almost impossible to make isolated decisions in discrete economic sectors," or does it invlove simply a customs union or a free trade area?

d) Do independent bodies of uninstructed bureaucrats have initiating, advocacy, or policymaking powers, or are such bodies absent?

e) If such bodies exist, do they work in close collaboration with national governments and interest groups, or are they effectively isolated?

f) Are voting formulas based on majority decision based on weighting, or are they unanimous and nonweighted?

With the exception of d and e (which refer to a different kind of resource) all of these are relevant categories in terms of which one might measure different levels of shared understanding among the members of a collective decisionmaking system.

2) DECISIONMAKING NORMS

Another important resource in any decisionmaking system is the extent to which there is agreement on norms, rules, and conventions governing the *way in which* conflicts are to be resolved. If such agreement were nonexistent or minimal, the rules and aims of political interaction would be largely random and indeterminate.

> In that event, members of the system would have to argue about day-to-day actions and decisions at the same time as they questioned the fundamental assumptions about the way in which these daily differences should be settled or about the validity of the procedures that determined who was to have the major power and responsibility for negotiating differences and establishing authoritative and binding outcomes. They would argue about how to go about doing things that they want to get done as well as the things themselves; matters of basic procedure as well as substance would be intermingled.[49]

The existence of such a set of norms might be inferred by means of an adaptation of the McClelland/Puchala event/interaction analysis referred to earlier. We might code interactions within the collective decisionmaking system in terms of the extent to which they reflect conformity or nonconformity to some kind of collective "procedural code."[50] Thus certain kinds of acts could be weighted positively if they seem to involve active invocations of collective norms (e.g., threats to withdraw, rejection of services of suprana-

---

[49] Easton, p. 191.
[50] For an effort to delineate the content of such a procedural code or set of decision rules see Lindberg and Scheingold, pp. 95–97.

tional institutions, boycotts, nonnegotiable demands, etc.). On the basis of such codings we could both characterize the *content* of a set of decisionmaking norms and measure aggregate levels and changes over time in invocation and derogation. Another procedure using the same data base would be to simply tabulate the number of interactions (or days in meetings) that involve important conflicts over rules or procedures as a proportion of total interactions (or days in meetings). The higher the resulting number, the more the system could be said to approach randomness or indeterminacy as to norms.

3) SUPRANATIONAL STRUCTURES

Easton's concept of regime structures refers to the roles and positions of those through whose actions binding decisions can be taken in a polity and to the relationships between them. These structures at the same time condition and reflect the way in which power is distributed and used in the system. The emergence and subsequent "institutionalization" of such structures has been viewed as one of the fundamental aspects of the process of political development[51] and it seems at least suggestive for political integration as we are defining it. We can visualize a continuum running from a situation in which each collective decision is made and implemented by unique and ad hoc structures to one in which all decisions are made by completely regularized structures endowed with legitimate authority. Clearly, the capacity of a system to process demands and thereby to stimulate support is some function of the growth of regime structures; i.e., political institutions *are* fundamental resources of any political system. Any macro-level measurement of political integration must therefore include indices of the growth and regularization of collective political institutions. The indices that follow have been designed to meet this need and to help answer three questions. First, to what extent have "pure" system-level regime structures developed? Here I refer to institutions we conventionally describe as "supranational." Second, what resources do they have for influencing the behavior of governments in the collective arena?[52] Third, what is the general nature of the structural relationships between these "supranational" structures and the existing constituent structures (institutions of the nation-states), especially, though not exclusively, as they occur in system-level mixed institutions like councils of ministers, committees of permanent representatives, and the like? Is it cooperative or hostile, stable or unstable, dependent or autonomous?

We make these distinctions because collective decisionmaking systems can and do develop institutional resources in two different ways: first, through

---

[51] For example, see Samuel Huntington, "Political Development and Political Decay," *World Politics,* April 1965 (Vol. 18, No. 3), pp. 386–430.

[52] With regard to supranational institutional growth and resources we do not here seek to measure the extent to which they are actually used in the integrative process.

the processes whereby "supranational" institutions, formally independent of the governments, have been established and have built up their authority; second, through the processes and patterns of interaction between national structures and the supranational ones (and among the national structures of the participating countries). Although I have always argued that these developments have in the past complemented each other in promoting integration in the European case, it is important to have independent measures of each.[53] Furthermore, they may not always complement each other, or they may come to develop at radically different rates. In either case it would be of basic significance for the nature of the system.

a) SUPRANATIONAL STRUCTURAL GROWTH

Since supranational institutions seem to represent such an important resource, it is of special relevance to measure the growth, stagnation, or decline of such institutions over time as one aspect of systemic development. We may expect that the longer such structures go on performing important roles as they survive changes in internal leadership and external political climate, as they grow in size and complexity, and as they take on new functions, the more safely one can infer that they will continue to constitute a significant element in the overall regime structure and that their role in that structure has become stable and legitimate.

Several indicators may be taken to measure structural growth: size of the administrative staff and administrative budgets of collective institutions as a percentage of total national staff and administrative budget; number of organizational subunits; the number of meetings convened and chaired by the collective institutions as part of their independent responsibilities (including expert study groups, working parties, meetings with interest groups, etc.); and the number of action proposals made and the proportion acted upon by member governments individually or collectively. Most of these can be readily tabulated on a yearly basis for most integration systems, and, for some at least, tabulations could also be made for individual issue areas. Percentage change and rates of change over time could then be plotted. Experience with various of the measures should tell which areas or what combinations of them are likely to be the best indicators of structural change.

b) RESOURCES OF SUPRANATIONAL STRUCTURES

Distinct from structural change is the concept of the influence resources of these supranational structures. As Joseph Nye points out:

---

[53] There are, of course, many who consider the two patterns basically incompatible. For example, some see the integration of Europe as depending upon the rapid centralization of authority and decision in supranational institutions while others are partisans of a *"Europe des patries"* where integration is more a process of consultation between national authorities.

The budget and staff of many international organizations do not increase solely as a function of a growth in the importance of the organization's outputs or its internal coherence as an institution. . . . In other words, the resources of international organizations may grow because of diplomatic considerations, whether they be the political designs of a Great Power or the political awkwardness of firing rather than hiring a duplicate international bureaucrat.[54]

(Staff, budget, meetings, and proposals are also resources, but it is most useful for my purposes to conceive of them as system resources.) It has become standard to think of the influence resources of supranational institutions in terms of rather formal criteria such as the possession of clear decisionmaking jurisdiction and authority or the ability to impose sanctions. For example, Puchala uses indices of rulemaking competence and rule-enforcement authority as part of his measure of international institutionalization.[55] I am skeptical of these as valid indicators for the simple reason that few, if any, supranational institutions possess these resources in any important degree; and if they possess them, they have not been effectively employed.[56] At the same time it seems undeniable that some supranational institutions have played important roles in the decisionmaking process, participating actively at all stages and enjoying considerable success in having their policy preferences or goals accepted by the collectivity. Their ability to do so does not seem to be clearly related to whether or not they can issue binding rules or impose sanctions. Rather it depends on the ways in which they are able to interact with governmental officials and other national political actors by providing services and skills that are in demand.

Studies of the European Communities have indicated that three resources are primary to an effective decisionmaking role for supranational institutions: attributed prestige and legitimacy, a treaty granting "power" of initiative, and mastery of technical expertise.[57] The first of these has been perhaps the most important in the European case. The Commission of the European Communities has been able to speak as the only actor that could claim to represent the interests of all nations or of the collectivity. The commission is widely viewed by governmental officials, interest groups, and in opinion polls as indispensable and as a legitimate spokesman for "Europe."

[54] Nye, *International Organization*, Vol. 22, No. 4, p. 867.

[55] Rulemaking competence measures extent to which an international organization can control or regulate states through binding rules. Rule-enforcement authority measures the existence of sanctioning authority and coercive resources to ensure compliance. Donald J. Puchala, "Integration and Disintegration in Franco-German Relations, 1954–1965," *International Organization*, Spring 1970 (Vol. 24, No. 2), pp. 203–208; Nye, ibid., pp. 867–868.

[56] See, for example, Ernst B. Haas, *The Uniting of Europe: Political, Social, and Economic Forces, 1950–1967* (Stanford, Calif: Stanford University Press, 1958), pp. 486–527; and Leon N. Lindberg, *The Political Dynamics of European Economic Integration* (Stanford, Calif: Stanford University Press, 1963), pp. 49–93.

[57] Lindberg and Scheingold, chapter 4. See also chapter 5 for a classic case of maximum utilization of these resources.

This has made it possible for the commission to play an active advocacy role not only directly with government representatives but also with groups, elites, and publics within the member states. Furthermore, it is an essential determinant of its intergovernmental mediation and brokerage activities. Possession of a formal right to initiate most policy proposals, to be present as these are discussed by the governments, and to participate actively in the discussion, as well as the responsibility for reporting treaty violations, i.e., to act as watchdog of past obligations, have also been important resources. If political integration involves highly complex matters, as most cases of economic integration typically do, there may arise an increased need for technical expertise and information *at the level* of the collectivity and coming from a trusted, nonnational source.

Each of these notions could be readily operationalized in terms of concrete indicators, content analyses, or subjective codings. *Attributed prestige* can be measured on the basis of event/interaction analysis or content analysis of government statements or behaviors in the collective arena, in terms of governmental requests for assistance from or expressions of confidence in or reliance on supranational actors, because they have the best ideas, provide initiative and guidance, or are indispensable. On the other hand, governments may condemn these actors, attempt to restrict their role, exclude them from intergovernmental bargaining, or place restrictions on their publicity and advocacy activities. Similar analyses could be carried on for interest groups and political parties using content analysis or reports of meetings and for elites and mass publics using opinion surveys.[58] Each component could be measured separately, or a combined index of overall attributed prestige and legitimacy could be designed. Formal rights of initiative and participation can be deduced directly from treaties and subsequent legislation and practice or can be derived from the judgments of expert coders. Weights can be assigned on the basis of what prerogatives a supranational institution enjoys in how many issue areas, and some kind of overall score can be generated. Possession of technical expertise can perhaps be inferred from the data on the growth of administrative staff, especially in high-level and professional categories. We may want to consider the construction of a composite, weighted (or multiplicative) index of the influence resources of supranational institutions on the grounds that formal prerogatives and technical skill are of little moment if institutions and their activities are not considered legitimate.

[58] Some data could be gleaned from surveys such as the following investigations in Western Europe: Haas; Paul Kapteyn, *L'assemblé de la Communauté européenne du Charbon et de L'Acier* (Leyden: A. W. Sythoff, 1962); Jean Meynaud and Dusan Sidjanski, *Europe des affaires: Rôle et structure des groupes* (Paris: Payot, 1967): Werner Feld, "Political Aspects of Transnational Business Collaboration in the Common Market," *International Organization,* Spring 1970 (Vol. 24, No. 2), pp. 209–238; Ronald Inglehart in this volume.

c) NATIONAL-SUPRANATIONAL TRANSACTIONS

Another distinct subdimension of the structural resources of a trans-national collective decisionmaking system is the volume (and rates of change) of transactions or interactions between supranational institutions and collective authority structures on the one hand and national authority structures on the other. There is reason to believe that the capacity of a collective decisionmaking system to process demands, produce outputs, generate specific support, and maintain or increase the level of diffuse support or general legitimacy depends on the volume of such interactions. This is because:

—supranational institutions do not have, nor are they likely to develop, sufficient authority, skills, or personnel to develop and implement policy without constant and close collaboration with national-level institutions. Problem-recognition, decision, and application are activities implying a long-term relationship between the two.

—the impact of cleavage based on nationality is lessened by representative structures such as the councils, permanent representatives, etc., which engage the representatives of the governments in decision-making.

—the more intense and sustained are transactions, the more likely is it that norms of conflict resolution will develop, thus facilitating bargaining and joint problem solving.

—one of the basic ways in which diffuse support is built up is by means of socialization in the form of learned patterns of political interaction, new loyalties, and habits of communication developed as a result of participating in common political activities. Thus the greater the volume of transaction and the wider its extent, the more likely is such support to become pervasive on the part of the most important national actors.

—for most members of the mass public, support is and will long continue to be mediated through the national authorities and elites. Hence continued support for and participation in the system's structures on the part of national authorities and elites is important.

The volume of transactions between national and collective structures could be measured in terms of the following kinds of indicators; year-by-year tabulations can be made and patterns of change and rates of change calculated.

—the number and frequency with which national civil servants participate in collective activities of problem-recognition, decision, or application and enforcement.

—the flow of communications between national representatives to these activities and their home ministries in the form of phone calls, mail, or telex transmission.

—the number of administrative units in national bureaucracies directly engaged by collective decisionmaking activities.

—days spent in meetings of councils, committees of permanent representatives, or other high-level intergovernmental bodies, and in "low-level" expert groups convened by any of these.

4) FINANCIAL RESOURCES

One way in which decisionmakers respond to demands and induce compliance with and support for authoritative outcomes is by expending financial resources for the direct provision of public goods and services to the members of the system. Integration systems will differ widely in their ability to mobilize financial resources. Most have been so far limited to performing regulative or organizational functions and not directly providing goods and services. They may achieve impressive levels of integration and accrue capacity to resist stress on the basis of such functions although their "constituency" will probably remain small and their support base limited. To the extent that significant operational budgets are made available to collective decisionmakers they are more likely to attract more demands, to gain in their ability to process them satisfactorily, and to substantially broaden their support base beyond the level of governmental and interest group elites. Calculation of the financial resources made available to collective decisionmakers for operational purposes can be carried out on an annual basis and by issue area for some organizations. A collectivity's financial resources (and changes therein) could be expressed in terms of its operational budget as a percentage of the total operational budgets of the member states or of their aggregate gross national product (GNP). Thus if a collectivity's budget were increasing more rapidly over time than national budgets or GNP, we might infer that it was probably performing more and more valued functions, becoming a more salient political entity, and attracting more support.

5) SUPPORT RESOURCES

Another way in which political systems differ from one another is in the extent to which their authoritative decisionmakers are able to count on (and/or make effective use of) positive sentiments on the part of the population toward the collectivity as a whole and toward its institutions and leaders. Such "supports" are important as a resource in any political system but are most particularly vital in democratic or pluralist systems that are based to greater or lesser extent on the "consent of the governed." Analysis of the development over time of such attitudes and sentiments has been a primary research focus of students of political development and nation building. Scholars who approach the study of international integration from that general tradition (e.g., Karl Deutsch) have often tended to assume (or assert) that the development of such ties and supportive attitudes was a sine qua non of political integration. However, the available evidence does not seem to provide unambiguous support for this position. Fisher has shown that in the European Communities there was a sevenfold increase in supranational institutional decisionmaking and allocating authority between 1953 and 1964 even though social assimilation at the level of mass publics did not increase.[59] He argued that Deutsch's sociocausal paradigm of political integration was deficient primarily because it failed to specify the nature of the linkages between mass attitudes and elite behaviors, i.e., collective decisionmaking. Fisher observed that:

> In order to fully describe this linkage situation we must specify the variables involved—the substantive issue or problem, the relevant elite, the specific elite behavior, the distribution of mass opinion, the elites' perception of mass opinion, and the elites' attitudes; we must state the logically distinct models of opinion transmission; and finally we must test the separate models by various statistical techniques to determine which model best fits the observed system of variable interrelationships.[60]

Puchala,[61] in his study of Franco-German relations, also concluded that the data indicates that there is no *direct* relationship between "community formation" and political integration. He feels, however, they are somehow related and argues for further research with more complex research designs. He hypothesizes the existence of a three-cornered linkage between community bonds, governmental capabilities for cooperation, and political integration.

> Emotional and identitive affinities between peoples create conditions within which governments can work toward more positive international cooperation. Community ties between peoples tend to dampen international conflict by relieving domestic pressure for diplomatic adamance, consequently defusing questions of "face," and thereby making compromise and accommodation feasible. Community, in short, adds an "endurance" factor to political relations between governments, and, as such, it adds capabilities for weathering international political strains.[62]

Scheingold and I reached a somewhat similar conclusion. The data we examined indicated that there existed in Western Europe

> a "permissive consensus" among the general public and elite groups as far as the legitimacy of the Community and its institutions was concerned. This extended to a very wide range of economic and social functions and to a strong,

[59] Fisher, *International Organization*, Vol. 23, No. 2, pp. 285–286.
[60] Ibid., p. 288.
[61] Puchala, *International Organization*, Vol. 24, No. 2, pp. 183–208.
[62] Ibid., p. 199.

independent role for the supranational Commission. Within the parameters of this consensus national and Community decision-makers can expect to operate relatively freely without encountering significant opposition.[63]

The converse of this is that when such a permissive consensus exists, integration projects are probably less vulnerable to nationalist challenges. National leaders may thus find themselves constrained from overt forms of opposition to integration.[64] On the other hand, leaders of supranational institutions may be able to take advantage of such a generally supportive environment to cajole reluctant governments to go somewhat farther than they might otherwise do.[65]

But both of these formulations are far too general to be very satisfying. They do not begin to meet the criteria set forth by Fisher, namely, a clear specification of elite and mass attitudinal variables and the formulation and testing of competing models of opinion transmission. Clearly we have much work to do in this area. The system paradigm being used here is not much help in answering such questions. It can, however, be of utility in suggesting the kinds of supportive attitudes or behaviors that are likely to be politically most relevant.

In *Europe's Would-Be Polity* we developed a systems analysis-based classification of dimensions of support embodying a twofold distinction, on the one hand between links between individuals and links between individuals and political institutions and processes and, on the other hand, between support based on perceived and concrete utilitarian interests and support based on more diffuse and affective responses. These generate the following matrix and the resulting four general categories or dimensions of support as a political resource.

Level of Interaction

Basis of Response		Systemic	Identitive
	Utilitarian	Expectations of future gain as a result of past satisfactions.	Belief in a common interest.
	Affective	Belief in legitimacy, as basis of willingness to comply with authoritative outputs of system.	Sense of mutual political identification.

FIGURE 8. DIMENSIONS OF SUPPORT AS A POLITICAL RESOURCE

[63] Lindberg and Scheingold, p. 121.
[64] See Inglehart in this volume. See also Lindberg and Scheingold, pp. 252–257.
[65] For an illustration from the history of the European community see Lindberg and Scheingold, pp. 172–176.

Each of these can be operationalized for both mass publics and elites in a variety of ways using attitudinal data, either individual items or composite scales, and/or raw or transformed *behavioral* data. Most of the examples that follow are drawn from *Europe's Would-Be Polity* (pp. 38–63).

a) EXPECTATIONS OF FUTURE GAIN

One important way in which decisionmakers can maintain the authoritativeness of their activities or the legitimacy of political institutions is by producing actual or symbolic benefits or advantages for the public (and/or elites) or by inducing the public (and/or elites) to develop perceptions that such benefits or advantages are likely to be forthcoming. At the very least, it is desirable that people perceive decisions to be neutral with regard to their interests. Data on matters such as these may be difficult to come by. Unless one is able to generate his own survey data on the existence and distribution of satisfaction with past performance and on future expectations,[66] it may be necessary to make inferences about people's perceptions of the system as benign or threatening on the basis of more general expressed attitudes. For example, most of the European data we assembled on this dimension pertained to survey questions tapping approval or disapproval of the "common market idea," people's willingness to intensify common policymaking or to extend it to new issue areas, and people's willingness to accept further limitations on national sovereignty.[67] In most cases we had only indirect evidence that these sentiments were actually the result of specific satisfactions with how the system had functioned in the past or of expectations of future benefits from it.

b) BELIEF IN LEGITIMACY

David Easton points out that most political systems have found it helpful or necessary to create and strengthen

> the conviction on the part of the member that it is right and proper for him to accept and obey the authorities and to abide by the requirements of the regime.[68]

There are obviously other bases for compliance such as fear of force, habit, or expediency, but a sense of legitimacy is likely to be the most stable and dependable basis of support. It is probably true that most transnational collective decisionmaking systems have very limited resources of this type; and to the extent that they do, such convictions are unlikely to extend be-

---

[66] Ronald Inglehart, Stuart A. Scheingold, Jack Dennis, and I, working in collaboration with European Community Information Service, have been generating data on dimensions such as these for samples of youth and adults in seven Western European countries. For some early findings see Inglehart in this volume.

[67] Lindberg and Scheingold, pp. 55–61.

[68] Easton, p. 278.

yond a relatively limited circle of elites. Of course, it is often very difficult to determine the extent to which (or even if) a sense of legitimacy exists for a particular regime or set of authorities. This is especially difficut if their activities are not particularly salient. One can, of course, argue that the very fact that people acquiesce passively in the decisionmaking activities of a European community commission or council is ipso facto evidence of their legitimacy. One is on stronger ground if one can demonstrate that people's acceptant attitudes persist even though they perceive that their own interests may occasionally be negatively affected or that people are willing to accept that their own country may on occasion be overruled by a European-wide "government."[69]

Other indirect evidence of the existence of sentiments of legitimacy might include certain political actions taken in support of integration or against those who are perceived as endangering such goals. An example of the former would be the development by political parties, religious organizations, or interests groups of general prointegrative ideologies and action strategies; examples of the latter would include electoral campaigns directed against politicians for anti-integration activities. One could also content analyze the elite and mass circulation press, interest group and party conferences and publications, legislative debates, electoral campaign speeches, etc., for the relative frequency of the invocation of collective goals and symbols and for statements of the moral validity of collective institutions, processes, and authorities.

c) Belief in a Common Interest

In transnational systems the development of horizontal, identitive ties among elites, and perhaps mass publics, is likely to be an important political resource, especially if the system is to handle stressful issues. Such systems are particularly susceptible to the effects of nationality-based cleavages, for these may simultaneously introduce rigidities into the coalition structure available for processing demands, create hostilities among groups leading to threats or acts of secession, and offer competitive points of emotional attachment.[70] It would seem unlikely that an extensive or penetrative transnational decisionmaking system could emerge or long survive in the absence of some kinds of perceptions of a common stake in the present and the future. Such identitive ties may develop as a result of objective perceptions of shared or compatible utilitarian interests; that is, people may believe that certain important concrete benefits or advantages (like economic stability or military security) can be achieved (or retained) only in associa-

---

[69] For European data on these dimensions see Lindberg and Scheingold, chapters 2 and 8.

[70] Easton, pp. 240–242. See also Leon N. Lindberg, *Journal of Common Market Studies*, Vol. 5, No. 4, p. 378.

tion with other countries. In *Europe's Would-Be Polity* we sought to tap such sentiments indirectly by using trade data, both raw figures and those transformed by the index of relative acceptance, on the grounds that changes in trading patterns reflect changes in economic interest perceptions.[71] We also used survey items which directly asked elites and mass publics with what countries they felt their nation shared a common interest, who they would trust as allies, etc. Trade data and other indicators of economic integration may be the most reliable measures[72] and can be used in a variety of other ways to indicate the dimensions of what might be called the "rewards" of integration, e.g., indices of total trade, respective market shares, the relative acceptance of exports, etc.[73]

d) Sense of Mutual Political Identification

Horizontal identitive ties may be based less on perceptions of pragmatic interests in common and more on sometimes diffuse sentiments of sharing a common culture, of having similar or compatible values, of being able to predict each other's behavior, of being somehow part of an organic entity.[74] In pure form these are, of course, practically synonymous with the concept of nationalism. But it is not at all unreasonable to expect that transnational systems too will be characterized to some extent by the existence of affective identifications and that it will make a difference to decisionmakers how extensive and intensive these ties are. We might, for example, measure the extent to which elites or publics of different nationality think of each other with "good feelings," or as "having a way of life similar to our own," or as "having a great deal in common with us," etc. Or we might assess readiness to serve in military units under foreign command or to vote for politicians of another nationality, etc. Content analyses might also be carried out on parliamentary debates, party congresses, and party and interest group press. Behavioral data or actual individual transactions such as mail, tourism, and student travel may also be analyzed on the assumption that these are reflective of feelings of identification and good will.[75] Joint participation in strikes or demonstrations by workers or farmers of different nationalities would constitute another behavioral indicator.

Once again, our systems analytic paradigm suggests that these are four support dimensions that are likely to be relevant as resources to political decisionmakers. I have offered a kind of grab bag of examples of how each might be operationalized, but I have not proposed specific composite scales

[71] Lindberg and Scheingold, chapters 2 and 6.

[72] Lawrence B. Krause, *European Economic Integration and the United States* (Washington: Brookings Institution, 1968), especially pp. 20–25, 32–74, 94–109, 120–139, and appendices B and C.

[73] Puchala, *International Organization*, Vol. 24, No. 2, pp. 186–188.

[74] Karl W. Deutsch, and others. "Political Community and the North Atlantic Area," in *International Political Communities*, pp. 1–92.

[75] See Lindberg and Scheingold, chapter 2, and Deutsch, and others.

or measures largely because to do this effectively we must have theoretical propositions that more clearly specify the dimensions as well as link them to each other and to the broader process of political integration. At this point we are unfortunately not much beyond the stage of simply noting increases or decreases in discrete behavioral indicators or in the patterns of survey item responses.

F. *Collective Leadership*

The foregoing resources represent action potentials. They must be used by political leaders. They may be *available* to a greater or lesser extent in any given collective decisionmaking system, but they may or may not be invested wisely, or they may be used up and not replenished. It will be crucial for any political system that those playing leadership roles have the skills and abilities to make use of available resources in the pursuit of collective goals.

Leadership is important for any political system, but for integrating systems it is likely to be one of the most vital dimensions of the ability of such systems to persist or to grow over time. Whereas Easton can say that it is historically very unusual to have a situation in which nobody is seen as equal to the task of managing the affairs of a political system, it is not so difficult to imagine such a situation in an evolving integration system. A collective system-in-becoming from the voluntary activities of a number of preexisting, often highly self-conscious and warring systems whose elites and publics may still harbor mutual antagonisms, hatreds, and fears from the past and who find themselves in distinctly different "national situations" will surely encounter difficulties in agreeing on who is to rule or who is to lead. We know from studies of the experience of the first decade and a half of the European Communities (e.g., Haas, Lindberg) and from studies of other voluntary integration efforts (Deutsch, Etzioni) that "success" has depended on some elite or combination of elites asserting and justifying a leadership role, succeeding in making it acceptable to the others involved, and then cajoling, pushing, even dominating the process, all the while showing a fairly high degree of responsiveness to the needs and preoccupations of the others. It is thus important to ask of any collective decisionmaking system if there are system authorities who offer *leadership* and *direction* in the identification and solution of problems, who pay attention that differences are handled in acceptable ways, who evaluate output and store and retrieve information, who articulate goals for the collectivity and symbolize them effectively. Are they capable of building up support for the legitimacy of their own role through ideological appeals, through association with accepted norms or structures, or through their own personal qualities? Are they able to engineer the consent of other authorities and elites in the system by organizing bargaining and the exchange of concessions and the creation of output satisfactions? Are they able to stimulate a belief in a common interest and the conviction that *they* are its major spokesman?

In integration systems both national and supranational actors may aspire to or actually play leadership roles, making use of the various resources available to them—i.e., of prior agreements; of norms of conflict resolution; of supranational structures and their prestige, powers, and expertise; of financial resources; and of support in its several dimensions. Supranational actors may excel in providing task-oriented leadership—identifying common problems, supplying information and technical expertise, suggesting solutions; whereas national actors, although they also have access to such resources, may excel in their ability not only to invoke but to replenish both decisionmaking norms and supports.[76]

1) SUPRANATIONAL ACTORS

What appear to be the principal determinants of effective leadership or resource mobilization by supranational actors? Organizational skill, imagination, energy, and a sophisticated understanding of the limits and potentialities of the political situation come immediately to mind. But what kinds of skill and understanding and in what spheres? There is a growing body of literature on leadership in international organizations that can be of assistance here. In *Beyond the Nation-State*[77] Haas suggests that there are three critical determinants of effective leadership.

a) Definition of an *organizational ideology* which points to a few clear priority goals for the organization and which defines strategies for their attainment. Such an ideology must be responsive to the demands of constituents but avoid becoming only an accumulation of responses to outside pressures. It should be possible to develop methods of textual and content analysis of statements and proposals of supranational leaders, over time and as compared with the demands and preferences of national actors, that would enable one to judge the extent to which such an ideology is developed.

b) A bureaucracy must be built up that is committed to this ideology, i.e., to the goals and strategy of the leadership. As in all bureaucracies this will depend in part on how the leadership manages the internal workings of the organization. But for transnational bureaucracies recruitment procedures and career patterns are even more vital. If a cohesive and loyal staff is to be developed and maintained, it seems crucial that at least the top officials will identify themselves with the organization in terms of

[76] Lindberg and Scheingold, pp. 128–133.

[77] Ernst B. Haas, *Beyond the Nation-State: Functionalism and International Organization* (Stanford, Calif: Stanford University Press, 1964), pp. 87–125. See also Robert W. Cox, "The Executive Head: An Essay on Leadership in International Organization," *International Organization,* Spring 1969 (Vol. 23, No. 2), pp. 205–230.

career planning. Short-term secondment from regional administrations certainly has its virtues[78] and may suffice in homogeneous, limited-purpose organizations. But it does not appear to be conducive to the development of an identification with the transnational entity or to the ideology of its leadership. I am certainly not arguing for the development of a completely autonomous, apolitical internatonal civil service in which positions are distributed on the basis of individual merit and so forth. It is only realistic to expect (and I would argue, to prefer[79]) that most high officials will be initially recruited from national bureaucracies. Governments will typically seek to have equal representation in important posts and to send officials in whom they have confidence. But once recruited it would seem desirable that officials spend a substantial time in service during which they can be assimilated to the organization's goals.[80] We can get an operational measure of this mobilization resource by tabulating frequency distributions of the time-in-service of the occupants of top policymaking positions. This might be done either at a point in time or historically over the life of an organization to get a sense of the trend. The greater the proportion (or the trend toward) that entered on short-term secondment, the less likely would be the organization to develop the kind of cohesive staff necessary for effective leadership.

c) Supporting coalitions and alliances must be built among individuals, groups, and organizations in the member national systems, around the ideology and the specific action proposals of the supranational leadership.[81] This requires that the leaders have access to important national actors, that they have adequate information about their goals and perceptions, and that they are able to produce symbolic or concrete outcomes so that such actors will perceive identities of interest.[82]

> In order to be able to work in this way the executive head must have great political skill. He needs also a personal confidential intelligence network reaching into domestic politics of key countries. Of necessity these networks of contacts will be limited for any single individual to a very few countries; and taking this into account, the ideal executive head is one who is able to engage in political confrontation in those countries which at the particular time are crucial in the evolution of the organization.[83]

Studies of social background and previous career patterns of the head

---

[78] See Cox, ibid., pp. 215–218; and David Kay, "Secondment in the United Nations Secretariat: An Alternative View," *International Organization*, Winter 1966 (Vol. 20, No. 1), pp. 69–75.

[79] See Lindberg, pp. 286–287.

[80] Cox, *International Organization*, Vol. 23, No. 2, pp. 222–226.

[81] For extensive discussion of this leadership function in the European community see Lindberg and Scheingold, passim.

[82] Cox, *International Organization*, Vol. 23, No. 2, pp. 225–230.

[83] Ibid., p. 225.

or collective leadership of supranational organizations, as well as the types of and frequency of their political promotional activities vis-à-vis national actors since joining the organization, would be obvious ways of developing operational measures.

If we think of the exercise of leadership as the creative use of available resources in order to manipulate actor incentives and opportunity costs in the interests of a collective goal, then we might develop a crude measure of leadership *exercised* by simply tallying how many appropriate actions have indeed been taken by supranational leaders. Building on Haas's and Cox's analyses we might stipulate that supranational leaders will be likely to maximize their potential to the extent that they engage in the following activities:

Type of Activity	Specification
1. Goal articulation and advocacy	Articulates long-term goals for the collectivity, legitimated in terms of an organizational ideology or a belief in a common interest. Engages in public advocacy of specific proposals by invoking long-term goals so as to mobilize supporters and neutralize enemies.
2. Consultation, cooptation, and coalition building	Takes the initiative in identifying problems to be solved by joint or coordinated action and in making specific proposals. Proposals should be developed through intensive consultation and compromise with client groups and with the relevant national bureaucracies so as to assure full information and expertise, build a policy consensus and a coalition of supporters, and minimize resistance.
3. Recruitment and organization	Builds an effective organizational team by providing leadership and ideological rationales. Induces specialists to keep long-term goals of the organization to the fore and avoids "subgoal dominance." Recruits so as to maximize prior national contacts and experience, technical expertise, and, at higher levels, political position and prestige.
4. Redefine goals and expand scope	Is alert to the possibilities of convincing governments and present or potential client groups to redefine organizational goals and purposes "upward." Calls for new policies, new tasks, new powers for system authority structures, but justifies these in terms of their usefulness to the governments and their contribution to national goals. Avoids proposals that are unacceptable for doctrinal reasons.
5. Brokerage and package deals	Plays an active and constructive role in intragovernmental bargaining at all levels and stages of the decision process by fully understanding the positions of each government and the possibilities for movement and compromise; by defending and explaining its own proposals but by making changes where necessary to accommodate to specific demands; by acting the role of "honest broker" and by constantly seeking the package deal that optimizes joint gains.

FIGURE 9. COMPONENTS OF SUPRANATIONAL LEADERSHIP

For most integration systems it will be possible to rate supranational authorities on an issue area by issue-area basis as well as in the aggregate.[84] This might be done simply by tallying *how many* of the above enumerated activities were engaged in.

2) NATIONAL ACTORS

The ability of national leaders to invoke or replenish collective decision-making resources derives essentially from the fact that they occupy authoritative roles in both the collective and the national systems. At the national level it is typically national leaders who perform gatekeeping functions by aggregating and transmitting demands to the collective arena. To do this effectively requires some kind of relatively efficient information gathering and data-processing capabilities, e.g., bureaucratic organization and skills. National actors are also likely to serve as mediators of popular support for the collective system.[85] For example, Easton has written of the European Communities that:

> It is quite conceivable that the initial and major bonds among the relevant political systems of Europe, if a European political community, in our sense, finally succeeds in emerging, will depend upon the leadership rather than the general members of all cooperating national political units. A possible sequence would be simple to identify. Each unit would be tied to an emerging European political community through the fact, first, that the leadership of each unit has such sentiments; second, that the followers in each unit identify closely with their elite; and third, that support from the followers will continue to be available even if the policies of the leadership lead to the subordination of each political system to a European supra-system. In due course, however, we might anticipate that the continuation of a new political community might depend upon nurturing some direct bonds between the general members as individuals and the new political community.[86]

To be effective mediators of support, national leaders and their activities must themselves be authoritative and legitimate in the eyes of their populations. Thus, effective national leadership at this level seems, in part at least, dependent on both the degree and quality of bureaucratic organization and on the degree of belief in the legitimacy and authoritativeness of national leaders in the eyes of their own populations.

National actors also play an important role at the level of the collectivity. Research seems to indicate that little progress will take place unless at least one government shows a strong interest in pushing for something and is willing to mobilize resources in order to convince the others. The chief obstacle to assertions of such a leadership role seems to be nationality cleavage. This

---

[84] For an example of a study of differences in the availability of leadership from one issue area to another and of the consequence of that difference for success or failure, see Lindberg and Scheingold, chapter 5.

[85] On mediation of support see Easton, pp. 225–229.

[86] Ibid., pp. 228–229.

is, after all, an area which involves perhaps the greatest break with the past and which demands the most pervasive and far reaching attitude changes on the part of authorities, elites, and mass publics. Consequently we can expect at best only a gradual pattern of change. All concerned have to learn new rules, develop new identifications and new patterns of mutual trust and regard. National actors seeking to guide the collectivity in a particular area must learn how to make their efforts effective and acceptable. Actors in all the participating nations will have to accept that some among them are going to play leading and often determining roles in the evolution of policy in those areas where they have special interests or special resources (e.g., in the European Communities we would expect leadership by France in nuclear affairs, by the Federal Republic of Germany as a capital market, by the Netherlands in transportation, etc.).

We can measure national leadership made available in much the same way as was proposed for supranational leadership, i.e., by tallying and scoring activities engaged in. By means of what kinds of activities would we expect that national leaders might affect the incentives or opportunity cost calculations of other national actors? The following list seems an appropriate starting point.

Type of Activity	Specification
1. Assertion of a "natural" leadership role	Actively asserts a role of leadership of the group. Claims to be spokesman of "European common interests." Articulates long-term goals and purposes.
2. Expansive proposals	Makes specific proposals for action involving new tasks and new powers for the system. Seeks to persuade others by forming coalitions and making concessions.
3. Commitment to the system	Shows frequent and strong commitment to the system by stressing the expectation and desire that it persist, the rewards of membership, the benefits to be expected. Defends the group against external challenges. Does not threaten withdrawal.
4. Support and responsiveness	Shows support for other members of the system and attention and responsiveness to their interests, preoccupations, and goals. Avoids making unacceptable demands.
5. Bargaining activity	Plays an active role in intragovernmental bargaining, offering guidance and compromise solutions and promoting agreement in the interests of all.

FIGURE 10. COMPONENTS OF NATIONAL LEADERSHIP

We would be interested in the overall incidence of such activities if they were increasing or decreasing over time, if the efforts were symmetrical or asymmetrical with each other, and if leadership was being exercised by different national actors for different issue areas.

G. Bargaining Modalities

It seems to be generally true that the development of a political system is often closely related to the processes whereby new bargaining styles and new patterns of coalition behavior emerge. Indeed, many theorists of political development[87] see these as the key to the process whereby primordial loyalties are overcome and political linkages, programs, and a constitutional order are developed. Similarly, if an emergent transnational collective decisionmaking process is to thrive or resist stress or persist, we may expect to see some analogous development, i.e., new styles of bargaining based on mutual predictability, the perception of common interest, and a spirit of compromise. Earlier in this article we described these as constituting a kind of collective "utility function" which would in fact help determine the demands that decisionmakers representing the constituent nations would make on the resources made available to them, either by supranational actors or by national actors asserting a leadership role, as the latter sought to process the demands flowing into the collective arena. Thus we must try to identify the modal bargaining styles that characterize any given collective decisionmaking system at any point in time, overall and by issue area, and measure changes in these modalities over time.

Ernst B. Haas was the first to try to construct a measure of bargaining modalities or "modes of accommodation" as an indicator for "judging progress along the path of integration."[88] He distinguished between accommodation on the basis of the "minimum common denominator," "splitting the difference," and "upgrading common interests," each successive type being indicative of an increasing integration. He then used this crude scale to summarize the experience of eight European regional organizations. In my own study of the European Economic Community[89] I sought to use these categories to actually code decision sequences but found that I could not make them truly operational to complex bargaining processes largely because they are conceptualized in terms of comparisons of initial bargaining positions with the collective outcome, the distance moved by actors in the bargaining sequence, and the equivalence of concessions made and because the specifications combine in a somewhat confusing manner the concept of modes of accommodation with that of institutional forms or arenas.

In seeking to develop a more discriminate measure and one that might be more readily operationalized I have drawn in eclectic fashion on the litera-

---

[87] See, for example, David E. Apter, *The Politics of Modernization* (Chicago: University of Chicago Press, 1965), chapter 1.

[88] Ernst B. Haas, "International Integration: The European and the Universal Process," *International Organization*, Autumn 1961 (Vol. 15, No. 4), pp. 366–392.

[89] Lindberg, pp. 285–286.

ture on game theory and coalition theory.[90] Implicit in both is the same theme we found in the political development literature, namely, that the kind of games "played" (or coalitions formed) in a collectivity reflect the *kind of society* it is. What is further implicit here, although it cannot be derived directly from existing game theoretic formulations, is that there is a continuum from the nonintegrated to the highly integrated society (or the cooperative society). Anatol Rapoport[91] distinguishes between *fights,* involving only reactions and hostility, *games,* which imply calculation and estimation in the effort to maximize interests, and *debates,* in which viewpoints, intentions, and interests are changed and a perception of a common interest begins to emerge. Similarly, John Nash[92] contrasts "zero-sum rationality" with "cooperative rationality," suggesting that an ideal form of the latter implies the existence of a social contract between the members of a society. James Buchanan and Gordon Tullock[93] propose a continuum of games running from a simple model without "side payments" to what they call a "compex log-rolling model with unrestricted side payments," with the latter type possible only because of a particular set of underlying political and socioeconomic parameters.

Although it is clear that a whole host of subdimensions or components interact in these notions, the game theory analogy leads me to propose the following summary ordinal index of types or styles of bargaining as having at least an intuitive validity. With the aid of a device like this, one could score individual bargaining sequences and thus derive frequency distributions for individual issue areas or for the whole system within some standardized time period. These distributions could then be compared (e.g., in terms of the mode(s), median, area under the curve, the shape of the curve, etc.), system with system, issue area with issue area, high saliency areas with low saliency areas, and one time period with others. The higher the average or modal rank, the more integrated the system. In interpreting the result of this kind of measure we must recall that even in the cooperative society of the game theorist there will be instances of zero-sum bargaining, i.e., situations involving, as Buchanan and Tullock put it, "power maximizing" rather than "utility maximizing" behavior.[94] It is rather the *changes* over time in the form of our distributions of bargaining style in which we are interested and how these relate to other developments in the system and its parameters.

An obvious alternative to the above procedure would be to single out each

[90] For example, James M. Buchanan and Gordon Tullock, *The Calculus of Consent: Logical Foundations of Constitutional Democracy* (Ann Arbor: University of Michigan Press, 1962); William H. Riker, *The Theory of Political Coalitions* (New Haven, Conn: Yale University Press, 1962); Anatol Rapoport, *Fights, Games, and Debates* (Ann Arbor: University of Michigan Press, 1960); R. D. Luce and H. Raiffa, *Games and Decisions* (New York: John Wiley & Sons, 1957); and Martin Shubik.

[91] Rapoport, pp. 8–12.

[92] John Nash, "Two-Person Cooperative Games," *Econometrica,* January 1953 (Vol. 21, No. 1), pp. 128–140.

[93] Buchanan and Tullock, chapters 10 and 11.

[94] Ibid., pp. 297–306.

FIGURE 11. SCALE OF BARGAINING STYLES

Rank Number	Bargaining Style	Specification	Coding Instructions and Illustrations
1	Competitive zero-sum unit veto model	No possibility of increasing utilities through cooperation or collusion. Individual rationality tending to maximize the gain of a *single* player whose preference ordering must be accepted. Other players lose.	Little or no bargaining. Involves making of unacceptable demands, no changes of position. Free use of threats (including to leave the system), ultimata and faits accomplis. High hostility.
2	Competitive zero-sum minimum coalition model	Limited cooperation or collusion to maximize gain of a winning coalition. Only *their* benefits are increased, others lose. No side payments or important changes of position on part of members of winning coalition.	Same as above except that some cooperation or collusion takes place between members of the minimum winning coalition.
3	Cooperative constant-sum game simple logrolling model	All may reorder preferences and make limited sacrifices and trades in own interest. Some get more than others, but all get something, may approach "Paretan optimality." Involves compromise of present interests, the division of existing resources, or the ratification of existing arrangements. Involves more than minimum winning coalition. Side payments and exchanges of votes only on limited range of closely related issues.	All show willingness to reach limited agreements of mutual interest. Fewer threats and more exchange although threats and bluffs are still common. Concern is only to reorder existing resources in terms of unchanged goals and preference orderings. Package deals occur only within scope of closely related matters.
4	Cooperative variable-sum game complex logrolling model	Unrestricted side payments make possible extensive logrolling and trades over wide range of issues. Issues are not seen as separate and unrelated to each other but in context of a continuous process of decision. Compromise or rearranging of *existing* interests and resources and ratification of existing arrangements.	Similar to above except that package deals are of more unlimited scope. More exchanges and threat removal. Basic goal is still to reorder resources within existing definitions of goals and interests although there may be efforts to change the "images" of players.

(Continued on next page)

FIGURE 11—Continued

Rank Number	Bargaining Style	Specification	Coding Instructions and Illustrations
5	Cooperative variable-sum game complex logrolling model	Like number 4 except that players combine to create new resources and institutions. Players make sacrifices for mutual benefit.	Conversions to each other's view take place, as do changes in goals and images. Efforts are made to increase resources, create new policy innovations, also to expand the political division of labor or the powers of the system institutions. Exchange and threat removal. Frequent invocation of common interests. New standards for the *evaluation* of output begin to develop.
6	Cooperative variable-sum game general benefit. Progressive taxation model	Cooperation to optimize the interests of society itself. Acceptance of notion of an overriding collectivity interest distinct from maximization of individual utilities. Involves basic transformation of images and goals. Some accept losses to increase benefits of others.	Emergence of sense of common interests which may transcend individual actor interests.

of the subdimensions incorporated in the index (on the *presumption* that they covary), gather data individually, and then see if a homogeneous index or scale is still justified or if some are better measures than others. There are at least nine of these subdimensions, each of which, it could be argued, represents some kind of a continuum from low to high integration.

1) The extent to which players expect to increase their benefits or utilities by engaging in cooperative or collusive behavior—from not at all to general social gain.

2) The number of winners (or the size of the winning coalition)—from one to the collectivity.

3) The "efficiency" or "productivity" of the collective action—from low-level reordering of existing resources to creation of new ones.

4) The availability of side payments and hence the potential for logrolling and vote trading (package deals in the EEC). Side payments "improve the results" of bargaining not only because they increase the chances of reaching a settlement at all but also because, by making it possible to compensate play-

ers, one can get decisions which benefit fewer than all the members of the winning coalition, thus further maximizing net productivity. If unlimited side payments are possible (complex logrolling), that is, if players are willing to make bargains involving a wide range of heterogeneous issues, the system's productivity is still further increased. It also reflects the range and distribution of preferences and intensities in the society (its cleavage structure). The greater the incidence of bargaining involving complex logrolling, the more the system approximates a "market" situation in which cleavages are not cumulative[95] and in which there are relatively few barriers to the most efficient trades and exchanges in the mutual interest.

5) The intensity of communication between players and their "receptivity" to each other's messages.

6) The degree of socialization or learning as a result of participation in the bargaining system, including both "norm internalization" and also what James Coleman describes as "coming to see the long-term consequences to oneself of particular strategies of action, thus becoming more completely a rational, calculating man."

7) The way in which the following factors are taken into account by the players: the influence *everyone* should be conceded before bargaining begins, the weight to be given to individual actor preferences in the collective preference ranking, and the selection of preference dimensions as relevant to the case at hand.[96]

8) The tactics appropriate in bargaining. As we move down the scale, we expect that the incidence of the use of ultimata and faits accomplis would decline in favor of tactics of "exchange" and "threat removal" (Rapoport), i.e., conveying to the others that they have been heard, that their position is valid and legitimate, and that there is an "assumption of similarity," that all share things in common and can be believed and trusted.

9) The extent to which the players *change their images and goals* in the process—from not at all to redefinition in terms of a sense of a common interest.

Another quantifying procedure that could be readily adapted to the measurement of bargaining modalities is the technique devised by Donald J. Puchala to measure cooperative and competitive international interactions in Franco-German relations.[97] He identifies and assigns positive and negative

[95] Cleavages may be noncumulative (which increases the incentives for conciliation) because the distribution of most opinions is unimodal or because they are of low coincidence. See Robert A. Dahl (ed.), *Political Oppositions in Western Democracies* (New Haven, Conn: Yale University Press, 1966), pp. 367–371. See also the literature on "the end of ideology" and on "technocracy" and "plannism," e.g., Ernst B. Haas, in Stephen R. Graubard (ed.), *A New Europe?* (Boston: Beacon Press, 1963), pp. 62–87.

[96] See Hayward Alker, Jr., *Mathematics and Politics* (New York: Macmillan Company, 1965), chapter 7.

[97] Puchala, *International Organization*, Vol. 24, No. 2.

intensity weights to ten different kinds of cooperative actions and twelve different kinds of competitive actions.[98] On the basis of content analyses of a standardized news source, *Keesing's Contemporary Archives,* he identifies 700
discrete episodes of Franco-German interaction between 1954–1965, coding
each according to date, type of action, intensity, issue, and issue saliency. He
then computed episode scores for cooperative and competitive interactions,
averaging at three-year intervals, and used them to chart overall trends in
Franco-German political accommodation.

If we succeed in adopting Puchala's procedure or the McClelland event/in-
teraction analysis techniques, which it resembles, to our purpose of measuring
bargaining modalities, we would be able to compare interaction profiles of a
given group of nations (or subgroups among them) before and after they
join in forming a collective decisionmaking entity. One could also compare
them across issue areas and across time to see if there are significant variations
depending on the level of collective decisionmaking in the area. In so doing
we must somehow take account of the fact that there are subtle but important
differences between conflicts that occur within a system of rules and norms
and those that occur in the absence of such a system. This is particularly the
case when what one is coding are verbal or written statements or messages
rather than concrete behaviors. Actors within an ongoing consensual system
find themselves quite often in conflict, express strong hostility to each other,
and may even issue threats, ultimata, and the like, without it having the same
significance as if it characterized the behavior of two competing states.[99] The
language of diplomacy differs sharply from the rough-and-tumble of domestic
politics precisely because language has different meanings in different contexts.

We must furthermore keep in mind the related point that involvement in a
collective decisionmaking system, because it creates new interdependencies and
because it brings the parties into closer and closer contact on more and more
issues, may well *produce* or *crystallize* conflicts between member states and
between categories of political actors within them. Thus we must use great
care in tabulating and interpreting cooperation-competition scores lest we mis-
take the conflicts that can produce community for those that signal disintegration.

H. *The Penetrativeness of Collective Decisions*

Stuart A. Scheingold in his contribution to this volume has established the
point that we have by and large neglected to systematically analyze the domestic and international consequences of integration.[100] Certainly, we have

[98] *Cooperative* are: concurrences, formal treaty signings, assurances, goodwill gestures, support, praise,
deference, cooperative initiatives, policy convergences, joint cooperative initiatives.

    Competitive are: simple disagreement, slight, rebuttal, rebuff, criticism, concern, displeasure, uni-
lateral disruptive initiative, threat, warning, protest, impasse.

[99] See, for example, Lindberg, pp. 280–281, note 20 on p. 349.

[100] Stuart A. Scheingold in this volume.

no studies of the political consequences of the decision outcomes of collective decisionmaking systems comparable to the efforts of economists to analyze and measure economic consequences.[101] As Scheingold's essay makes clear, one can define the problem of analyzing, measuring, or evaluating consequences in a variety of ways. We might be concerned to evaluate outcomes in terms of the extent to which the actors' original goals are met, or one's own preferred values are served, or "objective" standards of sound policy content are met or in terms of their success or failure in reducing stress on national systems, on the transnational system, or on the wider international system. On the other hand, we may be interested in measuring the degree of change in the attitudes, values, and behaviors of individuals that can be attributed to collective decisionmaking activity or in precisely describing the extent to which the autonomy (range of choices and resources) of national decisionmakers is affected.

The general question posed by the concept of penetrativeness is "Whose behavior is changed, and how much, as a consequence of the existence and activities of a given collective decisionmaking system?" At this level it raises a veritable multitude of conceptual and methodological issues long familiar to students of power, influence, and the evaluation of public policies. For example, what classes of behaviors should we study, how do we measure change in overt and covert behaviors (i.e., in observed actions and in attitudes, beliefs, values, incentives), how do we differentiate the effects of one presumed causal factor (a particular public policy or a collective decision) from others, and what aspects of a public policy or collective decision are most important in inducing changes in behavior? It is the purpose of what follows to make some initial suggestions about how we might begin to think about this dimension of the political integration process.

We are, first of all, interested in the behavior of both individuals and collectivities, granted that with collectivities it is also individuals who act in the name of or on behalf of an interest group, political party, or a government. Governments may begin to change their public policies or aspects of their internal organization as a direct consequence of collective decisionmaking activity. Interest groups may alter their political strategies, turning for example to *transnational* lobbying activities. Farmers may change from one type of crop to another or be driven off the farm entirely because a particular transnational agricultural policy is adopted. Large numbers in the general public may develop awareness of and affective orientations toward the system and its works. We are also interested in both observable actions (actors not doing or

---

[101] See Krause; Ingo Walter, *The European Common Market: Growth and Patterns of Trade and Production* (New York: Frederick A. Praeger, 1967); Tibor Scitovsky, *Economic Theory and Western European Integration* (Stanford, Calif: Stanford University Press, 1958); A. Lamfalussy, *The United Kingdom and the Six: An Essay on Economic Growth in Western Europe* (London: Macmillan and Company, 1963).

doing something different than what they used to do) and in "in-the-mind" phenomena such as perceptions, attitudes, incentives, beliefs. Changes at both levels can feed back into the system and influence future collective decision-making. Collective outcomes may actually have the effect of disallowing behavior (discriminating against Germans in awarding licenses or selling land) or obliging people to do something (pay a tax or a special levy), with some sort of sanction attached (a fine or a lawsuit or a positive inducement available only to those who act appropriately). Or collective outcomes may positively reward or advantage some, i.e., increase their mobility, their security, their income, or their sense of well-being. In some cases outcomes may only change the range of policy options available to a decisionmaker or the content and flow of information upon which he bases his judgments.

Since our focus is on the processes of collective decisionmaking, we must also allow for the possibility of a flow of effects back into the system which are rooted less in the substantive decision outputs of the system than in the experience of actually participating in it at some stage of policy preparation, lobbying, advocacy, negotiation, decision, or administration. In *Europe's Would-Be Polity* we referred to this as "actor socialization."

> We can well imagine how participants engaged in an intensive on-going decision-making process, which may extend over several years and bring them into frequent and close personal contact, and which engages them in a joint problem-solving and policy-generating exercise, might develop a special orientation to that process and to those interactions, especially if they are rewarding. They may come to value the system and their roles within it, either for itself or for the concrete rewards and benefits it has produced or that it promises.
>
> For example, actors may gradually internalize the Community's decision-making and bargaining norms (its procedural code), and thus accept the constraints upon nonconsensual actions implied by those norms. This could increase the Community's institutional capacity in that it would likely make it more probable that these norms would be consistently applied in intra-governmental bargaining. Institutional capacity would also benefit if, as a result of working in the system, more and more governmental and interest group representatives were to come to expect, and to accept as legitimate, an active role by the Commission, as the representative of the nascent Community interest. These same actors might also be brought to a realization of an enlarged common interest, which can lead them to encourage their respective governments to allocate new tasks to the Community system.[102]

Similarly, mass publics or portions thereof may change values or beliefs or identifications or develop positive or negative attitudes toward the system (or toward other nationalities) largely on the basis of their attention to the policy-making *process* itself or some aspects of the "symbolic" performance of the system, rather than in response to the substance of actual decisions.

[102] Lindberg and Scheingold, p. 119.

Simply outlining the scope of what is involved in assessing penetrativeness suggests how complex the conceptual and measurement problems are. What we clearly require is more empirical research and conceptual clarification of these relationships between a system and those who are affected by it. It may be that at this stage detailed case studies will yield the greatest insights, for in spite of the centrality of notions of "adaptation" and "learning" in the integration literature they are typically used metaphorically, and we actually know very little about the consequences of integration at the national level or of the relationship between such consequences and future systemic development.

For purposes of macro-level measurement we seem inevitably to be forced to make sometimes dubious inferences, either that certain observed changes in behavior are due to the decision outcomes of a particular system or that certain categories of outcomes or activities are likely to have a greater impact on behavior than others.

1) DATA ON ATTITUDES AND BEHAVIORS. Survey data on public and elite awareness of, information about, and perceptions of the consequences of the activities of an integration system for their own lives can be used, when they are available, as crude indicators of penetrativeness. Or we might use data on changes in interest group and political party attention to and activity about integration issues. A more direct measure might be derived from analyses of the content of governmental foreign and domestic policies. Are they becoming more similar in areas in which there has been collective action? I know of no systematic effort to compare public policies and to develop measures of similarity although some have sought to measure the similarities between foreign policies in terms of increasing homogeneity of voting behavior in the United Nations. Nevertheless, it should not be an insuperable task if we turn our minds to it.

2) DATA ON OUTCOMES. Fisher's article is clearly the most sophisticated and extensive analysis of output performance in the literature. He calculated *total output performance scores* for the European community from 1953–1964 and then conducted a time-series analysis using a least squares linear regression model. The scores were derived by counting all official actions of the three communities each year and weighting each "so as to reflect the relative authority and scope of the different types of actions that could be taken."[103] Certain actions were scored as "three" because they were decisions that were formally binding and directly enforceable as law upon citizens or firms in the member states. Lower weights were assigned for decisions that, while binding on nation-states, only referred to the result to be achieved, not the ends or means to be used. Still lower weights were given to actions that were binding only on other community organizations or that were recommendatory.[104] One

[103] Fisher, *International Organization*, Vol. 23, No. 2, pp. 262–263.
[104] For a fuller discussion see ibid., p. 263.

might argue, although Fisher does not do so explicitly, that decisions that are directly binding within member states are more likely to change more behaviors than are other kinds of collective outcomes. A more elaborate system of weights might be developed on the basis of my decision stage scale (see Figure 4). The validity of inferences from such data could perhaps be improved if we were able to weight further by quantitative indices of the economic stakes involved in a particular decision area or by some measure of the size and political power of the potential "clientele" for different decisions (see my discussion of salience). Another approach might be to analyze the content of collective outcomes directly in terms of the *constraints* they imply on national level actors or the behavioral changes they seem to demand. It should be possible to develop some kind of scale, perhaps along the lines suggested earlier for the measurement of decisiveness, on the basis of which one could weight and classify outputs on a year-by-year basis.

I. *Compliance with Collective Decisions*

What is the likelihood that the formal decision outcomes of a collective decisionmaking system will be complied with by those to whom they are addressed? A measurement of penetrativeness tells us what sets of individuals or collectivities have had their behavior changed by collective outcomes, but it does not indicate whether or how often they accepted these outcomes as premises of their own subsequent behavior. The distinction is similar to that made in the literature on power between the *extension* of power (the set of individuals over whom an actor has power) and the *amount of power*. ("The net increase in the probability of B's actually performing some specific action X, due to A's using his means of power against B.")[105] Compliance is also related to the concept of authoritativeness. We may consider a decisionmaking system authoritative to the extent that there is a high probability that its rules and decisions will be complied with. The basis of compliance will, of course, vary: legitimacy of the collective system itself, mediated support via national authorities, self-interest, inertia and indifference, fear of coercion, etc.

It will be relevant for both descriptive profiles as well as comparative analytic purposes to be able to identify and measure different compliance probabilities over time, from one issue area to another, for different types of individuals or groups, for different member states, for different forms of collective outcomes, and for differing degrees of penetrativeness. Such probabilities would have to be calculated in different ways for different organizations, issue areas, etc. The kinds of indicators that one could use for this purpose might include tabulations of:

1) the number of rulings of national courts (or other authorities) challenging the validity of collective rules on the jurisdiction of collective institutions.

---

[105] Harsanyi, in Shubik, p. 184.

2) the number of complaints made or suits for treaty or rule violation filed by supranational actors or by national actors against other national actors.

3) the incidence of boycotts, meetings missed, etc.

4) the relative frequency with which governments or other national actors demand exceptions from collective rules or invoke "escape clauses."

5) the number of complaints or suits filed with collective institutions by governments and individuals seeking redress and invoking the authority of the system and its rules.

6) the number of requests by national legal authorities for interlocutory rulings by collective legal institutions (if they exist).

7) the number of published judgments of national courts or tribunals interpreting and/or confirming, wholly or in part, the rules of the collectivity or the rulings of collective decisionmakers.

J. *Distributive Consequences*

I have already noted that while various "learning theories" have been advanced as explanations of the integration process, these have seldom been expressed in operational terms so that they could be explored empirically. One theme that is central to most such theories is that when people have experienced a high level of transactions and when these tend to bring rewards rather than deprivations, they will come to like them.

> When these transactions are highly visible, easy to identify and differentiate, people may form images of the community or of the group involved in the transactions. If these transactions were rewarded, the image of a community may be strongly positive. Liking this kind of community, people may say: We belong together. In their favorable reaction to the community, they might then also say, I can see myself as a member of this community; I will call it "we" if I speak of a group. I will call it "home" if I speak of territory. . . . What is done to this . . . group or to its symbol . . . is done to me. I feel diminished or enlarged, depending on the diminution or enlargement of this country or this group.[106]

Other models of human behavior suggest that individuals tend to act rationally in choice situations on the basis of assessments of the "opportunity costs" or incentives associated with one decision as against another. Harsanyi[107] argues that it is crucial to the measurement of the power relationship between A and B to measure B's opportunity costs of refusing to do what A wants him to do, as these represent the strength of B's incentives for yielding to A's influence. These calculations can be manipulated by A in a variety of ways,

---

[106] Karl W. Deutsch, "Communication Theory and Political Integration," in Philip E. Jacob and James V. Toscano (ed.), *The Integration of Political Communities* (Philadelphia: J. B. Lippincott Co., 1964), p. 54.
[107] Harsanyi, in Shubik, pp. 189–192.

including the conditional or nonconditional provision of advantages or rewards (disadvantages or punishments). Thus, we may expect that future decisions to support an integration system, to process a demand through the new channels, or to comply with the decisions of new collective institutions will be some function of the perceptions that actors have of the system's past or potential future distributive consequences (their opportunity costs).

If we want to test and refine broad and general propositions such as these we must give more attention than we have to the problem of what we mean empirically and operationally by distributive consequences. It seems to me that there are at least three major questions involved. First, are *new* advantages, benefits, resources, or disadvantages created as a consequence of the system and its works? Second, if there are such new benefits (or costs), how are they distributed? Third, what is the impact of collective decisions on the overall distribution of benefits and costs in the member societies?[108] Clearly, these are extraordinarily complex issues, and I will be able here to merely sketch some general suggestions and guidelines for future research. I will rely heavily on the work of economists, who are by and large the only social scientists to have given these matters systematic thought.

In seeking to determine whether or not the total benefit "pie" has been increased as a consequence of integration we should first distinguish between increases in "private goods" and increases in "public goods."[109] By public goods is meant either services or functions from which nobody can be excluded and which are equally available to all or spillovers or externalities of other policies or activities; for example, education, social overhead capital, balance of payments, economic stabilization, etc. With the latter type it is not always possible to make a clear demarcation between public and private goods, for clearly some gain more than others at the same time that almost everybody benefits indirectly. It may well be that the chief impact of integration will be to increase the relative availability of such generalized and indivisible benefits as greater military security, increased growth rates and overall economic stability, a heightened sense of importance in the world, ability to travel more easily, greater product choice for the consumer, etc. Some of these, for example, greater military security, will be very difficult to operationalize. Economic growth and stability, travel and product choice are more readily measured, but it is always difficult to establish the precise causal effects of integration as against other factors. One can argue, for example, that everybody benefits to the extent that integration increases business investment, productivity, economic efficiency, or stimulates the growth rate in a given area, even if there are no direct income effects for most people.

---

[108] The problem of whether and how these distributive consequences are actually perceived will be taken up in the next section. The concern here is to establish methods of determining objective consequences.

[109] See Mancur Olson, Jr., *The Logic of Collective Action: Public Goods and the Theory of Groups* (Cambridge, Mass: Harvard University Press, 1965).

Increases in trade within the area can also be treated as a public good in the same sense as above, but here it may be relatively easier to identify those individuals, firms, economic sectors, regions, or countries that gain disproportionately. For example, Lawrence Krause's study of the EEC shows that while all countries increased the value of their intra-EEC exports between 1958–1959 and 1965, there were clear differences in their respective proportional shares of the total export market; i.e., West Germany increased its share relative to France and Italy, and the share of the Netherlands and Belgium–Luxembourg actually dropped.[110] The relative acceptance index developed by Karl Deutsch and I. Richard Savage[111] is another potentially useful tool for discerning *relative* differences in transaction flow fluctuations that can be attributed to integration. Most research using the relative acceptance index has used the nation-state as the unit of analysis, but it would seem possible to employ this and other techniques on regional units and perhaps on different economic sectors. What is needed are techniques which determine how the joint rewards and penalties of integration cut, whether by class, region, or nation.[112]

To the extent that the decisions of integration systems involve actual financial expenditures, investment decisions, or income transfers we get closer to the notion of private goods or benefits. For example, a recent European study developed an interesting method for analyzing cost-benefit ratios for all the financial contributions and receipts arising indirectly or directly from European integration between 1953 and 1963.[113] It showed a clear disparity in benefits received as compared with national budgetary contributions. In this case France, Italy, and Luxembourg were net gainers and Germany the net loser. Of course, it is no simple matter to interpret the significance of a particular pattern of distributive outcomes. For example, moral philosophers, welfare economists, and game theorists have long struggled with the problem of determining a group social-welfare function on the basis of which to determine the "fairness" of the division of benefits in a society.[114] One of the major problems seems to be that of determining "a single social ordering of alternative social choices which would correspond to individual orderings."[115] Some "solutions" of the problem suggest that no division of benefits is "rational" if any single individual suffers a decrease in his welfare no matter how substantial or widespread the gains of others may be (Paretan optimality). Others would award shares on the basis of the marginal utilities of the actors,

[110] Krause, p. 73 and p. 237.

[111] I. Richard Savage and Karl W. Deutsch, "A Statistical Model of the Gross Analysis of Transaction Flows," *Econometrica*, July 1960 (Vol. 28, No. 2), pp. 551–572. See also Donald J. Puchala in this volume.

[112] Deutsch, in Jacob and Toscano, p. 53.

[113] Bernard Heidelberger, "La ventilation des dépenses communautaires: Le juste retour" (unpublished manuscript), September 1968, as cited in Lindberg and Scheingold, p. 300.

[114] See Shubik, pp. 30–70.

[115] Daniel Bell, "Notes on the Post-Industrial Society (II)," *The Public Interest*, Spring 1967 (No. 7), p. 105.

i.e., whose preferences were strongest (classical utility theory). Unbalanced growth economists might argue that progress or efficiency is possible only if certain individuals or groups or industries or regions benefit more rapidly even if at the expense of others[116] on the grounds that there is little to distribute until productivity has been maximized and new resources or benefits created.

New collective benefits may be created by an integration system but at the expense of the preexisting overall distribution of benefits among the countries participating, and within individual countries, at the expense of certain regions, sectors, or classes. There are a number of suggestive themes in the economic literature that pertain to the problem of assessing overall consequences. A major preoccupation of the theory of customs unions has been with the problem of the trade diversion (as against trade creation) effects of economic integration. Participating countries may increase their trade with third countries, who may suffer relative losses in welfare. These losses may feed back into an integration system if increases in intracollectivity trade come at the expense of certain participating countries' trade with the outside.[117] Development economists have been concerned with what Gunnar Myrdal called the "spread-effects" and the "backwash-effects" of integration.[118] The general argument is that integration inevitably favors already developed regions (or countries) at the expense of backward regions (or countries).[119] Bela Balassa argues that these effects are not likely to be very important in the case of the European Communities because the members enjoy a relatively high stage of economic development in which spread-effects will be the more powerful.[120] On the other hand, in integration systems among developing countries the problem of regional imbalances is a major one.[121]

There have been very few efforts to systematically analyze possible changes in the distribution of political benefits, such as access to or influence over decisionmakers, political power, etc. André Gorz,[122] for example, argues that integration advantages those who are able to organize effectively and quickly at the transnational level (businessmen) at the expense of those

[116] See Albert O. Hirschman, *The Strategy of Economic Development* (New Haven, Conn: Yale University Press, 1958).

[117] Krause, pp. 70–72.

[118] Gunnar Myrdal, *Economic Theory and Under-Developed Regions* (London: Duckworth, 1957), chapter 3.

[119] See Herbert Giersch, "Economic Union between Nations and the Location of Industries," *Review of Economic Studies*, 1949–1950 (Vol. 17, No. 2), pp. 87–97; Maurice Byé, "Customs Unions and National Interests," *International Economic Papers* (No. 3), pp. 208–234; Francois Perroux, "Note sur la notion de 'pole de croissance'," *Economie appliquée*, January–June 1955 (Vol. 8, Nos. 1–2), pp. 307–320; André Gorz, *Strategy for Labor* (Boston: Beacon Press, 1964), pp. 154–160.

[120] Bela Balassa, *The Theory of Economic Integration* (London: George Allen & Unwin, 1961) pp. 203–205.

[121] Roger Hansen, "Regional Integration: Reflections on a Decade of Theoretical Effort," *World Politics*, January 1969 (Vol. 21, No. 2), pp. 242–271.

[122] Gorz, pp. 140–154.

groups whose power base is limited to the national level (trade unions). Others seek to demonstrate that national parliaments have lost power to executives and bureaucracies as a direct consequence of integration.[123] Hans Schmitt has argued that when economic integration goes beyond a certain point, political pressures will mount for capital market integration and currency unification. If these succeed, certain core-areas of highest economic growth will inevitably attract capital and become the effective financial center of the collectivity, with all the political and economic power that portends for the country in which the center is based.[124] Schmitt fears that when the members of the European Communities come face-to-face with the probability that such gains will accrue to West Germany, they may be sorely tempted to abandon the whole enterprise. Of course, an alternative course might be for "deficit" countries to bargain for countervailing benefits and advantages in other issue areas. Scheingold argues for more case-by-case empirical research on political consequences such as these. The need for this is clear. What we also need if we are to compare and to build theory is innovation in the invention or construction of operational indicators of such effects.

IV. The Multivariate Measurement of Political Integration

In what ways can I claim to have contributed to our thinking about the dependent variable problem that has so vexed students of integration? I have identified ten properties that represent the multifold effects of the various processes we speak of aggregatively as international (or regional) political integration, and I have suggested in varying detail how each of these might be operationalized so that it can be studied empirically and so that some kind of macro-level measurement will be possible. The image I will have conveyed is that the political integration phenomenon is enormously complex, even more so than has been suggested by Nye[125] or by Haas in his contribution to this volume.

I have argued that if we are interested in documenting the extent to which collective decisionmaking institutions and processes have emerged among groupings of nations and in explaining how and why they succeed or fail, we will have to begin with an awareness of the relevant dimensions of variation that may exist in that phenomenon. Collective decisionmaking systems will differ, first, in the extent to which they actually make decisions as a group, as described by differential functional scopes, ranges of decision stages, and relative policy decisiveness; second, in the energy levels that characterize the

---

[123] For a discussion see Alfred Grosser, "The Evolution of European Parliaments," *Daedalus*, Winter 1964 (Vol. 93, No. 1), pp. 173–176.

[124] Hans Schmitt, "Capital Markets and the Unification of Europe," *World Politics*, January 1968 (Vol. 20, No. 2), pp. 228–244.

[125] Nye, *International Organization*, Vol. 22, No. 4, passim.

system, as defined in terms of demand flow, resources available to collective leaders, the way in which they are manipulated, and bargaining modalities; and third, in the consequences collective decisions have for the constituent systems, as captured in the concepts of penetrativeness, compliance, and distributive consequences. We must keep the distinctions between these variable properties clearly in view not because they are discrete, autonomous dimensions—they are clearly related—nor because they are of equivalent descriptive or explanatory importance but because, even if they are of unequal importance and even if they are not independent of each other, they may occur in surprising juxtapositions and they may vary over time at different rates and in different directions. And these unanticipated combinations and differential rates and directions of change are likely to be vital to an understanding of the phenomenon. After all, these are incipient and unstable systems. The key to understanding them and to predicting their future paths may well be the asymmetries that occur among the various properties that we have here identified. On the other hand, "stability" in the sense of a relatively persistent balance among properties may also be achieved by such systems in surprising and unanticipated ways not at all resembling the nation-state or any other form of polity that has occurred empirically.

But in defining the dependent variable in this multifold fashion, have I not fallen into the error, described by Haas, of substituting "premature operationalization for theory and vision?"[126] Have I met his criterion of "a definition which avoids the overly simplistic ideal typical of past efforts while aiming at a more sophisticated goal than measurement alone?"[127] The answer will depend largely on what we now *do* with the properties as here operationalized. After all, my original point of departure was that students of integration have tended to look at the parts in isolation whereas they should have been looked at as they are interrelated, logically and functionally, *in time* (i.e., as level, activator, consequence) and causally *over time*. To separate out the individual properties and to suggest how data on each might be systematically gathered and aggregated for measurement purposes were simply the necessary first steps. Were we to conclude here, saying that political integration involves discrete variations on these ten dimensions, then Haas might be correct in arguing that we had not advanced very far in the direction of facilitating explanatory theory. The definitions and operations proposed might then be

> useful descriptively because they capture a process; but without hypothetically linked variables they are not explanatory of an outcome which, itself, remains unspecified.[128]

Haas urges us to seek ways and means of ascertaining the aggregate sum of

[126] Haas in this volume, p. 633.
[127] Ibid., p. 634.
[128] Ibid., p. 632.

all integrative and disintegrative processes in all issue areas and across all properties. What do they add up to, and toward what hypothetical end states do they appear to lead? However, it seems to me that premature aggregative visions and theories to explain them may be as much of a problem as premature operationalizations. By this I mean that we might be better off defining integration as ten ranges of variation, observing what patterns, balances, and imbalances among these properties occur in real-world systems and then setting out to explain such patterns, balances, and imbalances. Certainly, the student who is interested in accurate descriptive analysis and in short- and medium-term forecasts for any particular grouping—whether defined as a region (Western Europe) or as a particular organizational setting (EEC)—will want to obtain "readings" of the kinds we have proposed at regular time intervals. At the very least this would indicate trends and show if and in what ways the grouping had evolved a higher degree of integration than before. Comparisons of such readings for different issue areas and/or over time for any system and between different integration systems could also lead to the construction of clearer classifications and typologies as a basis for the kind of correlational analysis of background and process characteristics proposed by Nye and Schmitter in their contributions to this volume.

On the other hand, I do agree that some efforts at aggregation are also called for. Haas proposes a "master concept" of authority-legitimacy transfer and three heuristic types describing different kinds of such transfers (regional state, regional commune, asymmetrical regional overlap) as examples of appropriate aggregative concepts. It does not seem to me that these are really aggregative, although it is difficult to be certain since Haas provides neither nominal nor operational definitions for his master concept. I will argue that any meaningful aggregations must be theory-based and that the development of appropriate concepts and their operational definition can be greatly facilitated by the creative application of the panoply of concepts I have proposed in this article.

Thus, in the concluding pages I will briefly discuss two different approaches to the multidimensional measurement of political integration. I will first suggest what we might learn from measurements on individual properties and combinations of them without aggregation. Second, I will discuss some of the problems inherent in aggregation and make some suggestions as to the kinds of aggregative concepts which seem to me to be the most compelling. I will limit my discussion to fairly general suggestions as to what ought to be done, leaving it up to those with more sophisticated mathematical and statistical skills to work out the details of how to do it.

The Comparison of System Properties

Partially integrated decisionmaking systems among nations, captured at a particular time T, will possess in varying degree the ten properties I have identified. Measurements of the kinds proposed will describe how far a group of nations has moved away from individual autonomy in public decision-making—how linked they have become as a consequence of participation in collective decisionmaking—and will suggest the extent to which national actors are constrained by the collective arena. That distance is the greater, those links the stronger, the constraint the more pervasive:

1) the more issue areas of greater salience are affected by collective decisions;

2) the greater the average or modal number of decision stages affected;

3) the higher the average or modal rankings of relative decisiveness within particular issue areas;

4) the greater the volume of demands that enter the collective arena and the less their variety;

5) the greater and the more varied the resources at the disposal of collective decisionmakers for manipulating the opportunity costs of national actors;

6) the greater the number of appropriate strategies and actions engaged in by national and supranational actors seeking to play leadership roles;

7) the higher the modal bargaining style in the system along a continuum from competitive zero-sum to cooperative variable-sum models;

8) the greater the changes that take place in the behavior of the larger number of people as a consequence of collective decisions;

9) the higher the probability that collective decisions will be accepted as legitimate and complied with and/or enforced by national or collective agencies;

10) the greater, the more rewarding, and the more symmetrically shared are the distributive consequences of collective decisions.

If we obtain scores on all these multiple indicators we could in principle generate the following matrix of information for any collective decision-making system at one or a number of points in time.

	By Individual Properties (2–10)	Across All Properties
By Individual Issue Areas (each of 22)	22 x 9 measurements	22 measurements, expressed as vectors or summarized as in Guttman-Lingoes.
Across All 22 Issue Areas	9 measurements, expressed as vectors or weighted by salience of issue area or summarized as in Guttman-Lingoes scaling procedures.	one measurement somehow summarized.

FIGURE 12. MEASUREMENTS OBTAINABLE WITH THE PARADIGM

Individual measurements, or the changes in individual measurements from T to T+1, etc., or the rates of change can then be used as a basis for accurate description, for the construction of typologies, and for making the kinds of interpretable comparisons across systems and over time that are required if we are to build valid theory. The stage will thus be set for the following kinds of operations, to mention only a few of the many that are possible:

1) Profiles of the degrees to which a given grouping has become linked as a consequence of participation in collective decisionmaking activities.

2) Comparisons across groupings of such profiles and of individual properties.

3) The development of typologies based on selected properties or subsets of properties, for example, classifications of systems according to the following kinds of matrices:

Activators

	Low		High	
	Low Consequence	*High Consequence*	*Low Consequence*	*High Consequence*
Low				
High				
Level				

FIGURE 13-A.

Range of Stages

	Limited		Extensive	
	Low High		Low High	
	Decisiveness		*Decisiveness*	
Narrow				
Broad				

Functional Scope

FIGURE 13-B.

4) Profiles of amount and direction of change and/or rates of change across properties and issue-area scores for individual groupings (or for subsets of each), e.g:

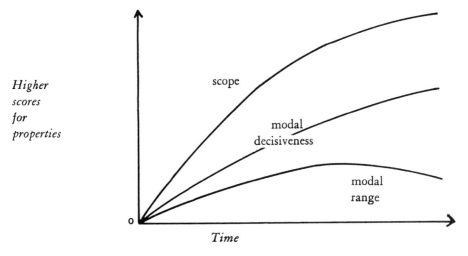

FIGURE 14-A

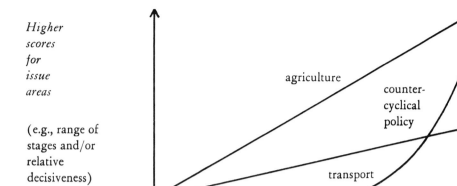

Higher scores for issue areas

(e.g., range of stages and/or relative decisiveness)

Time

FIGURE 14-B

5) Such profiles can be very valuable in facilitating within-system comparisons. We may, for example, observe if (and seek to explain why) some properties (or issue areas) score equally (differently), move in the same (or different) direction, at similar (or different) rates, etc.

6) We may compare across systems and/or time seeking to discover what correlations exist in level, direction, and rate of change for individual properties and issue areas, or for subsets or summaries of either.

7) We might construct typologies on the basis of both within-system and across-system comparisons of patterns and rates of change.

8) We might focus attention on the relationships between properties (or issue areas) or subsets of properties (or issue areas). For example, we may wish to explore the relationship between varying levels of resources (and kinds of resources) at T and subsequent compliance (or vice versa) or between distributive consequences at T and resources (e.g., support) at $T+1$.

9) The indicators should be useful in constructing and operationalizing *summary* concepts such as Haas's notion of authority-legitimacy transfer. It appears that Haas uses four criteria to develop his three ideal types of authority-legitimacy transfer (i.e., regional state, regional commune, and asymmetrical regional overlap).[129] They are: a) Where is authoritative decision-making concentrated, at the center, in a myriad of functionally specific units, or asymmetrically among several centers? (This factor can be operationalized

[129] Ibid.

in terms of indicators of scope, range of stages, and decisiveness.) b) Who marshals and distributes resources? (This factor can be measured in terms of the leadership activities and resources available to national and supranational actors.) c) Toward which structures do citizens and groups direct feelings of legitimacy? (This factor can be measured via indicators of belief in legitimacy and as willingness to comply as measured in behavior.) d) Do horizontal links in the form of a regional nationalism develop, or is there some kind of many-tiered system of multiple loyalties? (This factor is measurable via indicators of "belief in a common interest" and "sense of mutual political identification.") With the assistance of separate indicators for each of the dimensions of authority-legitimacy transfer we should be able to carry on a more discriminating analysis than if we are limited to Haas's threefold typology.

10) We might also wish to operationalize summary integration concepts akin to Robert A. Dahl's concept of the amount of power, i.e., "the net increase in the probability of B's actually performing some specific action X, due to A's using his means of power against B."[130] Integration analogues might be the net variation, from T to $T+1$, etc., in the probability of political actors (nations, officials, industries, citizens) actually *complying* with collective decisions in variable *scopes* as weighted by *salience* and *decisiveness,* and/or by the amount of *behavioral change* involved, and/or the size of the *distributive consequences.*

11) The suggestive concepts proposed by Alker in his contribution to this volume could also be given operational meaning; for example, his notion of "collective demand processing success"[131] which involves measuring the number and range of demands, as weighted by salience, that are satisfied (or coped with) by means of complied-with decisions, this as a proportion of the total number and range of demands made on the system.

Aggregate Measurement

The kinds of operations and combinations listed above do not give us concepts which are really aggregative in the sense that they sum up the *integral* meaning of all the property and issue-area measurements taken together. Since the individual properties are defined as parts of a *system,* we expect that they will be systematically interrelated and that it is in those interrelationships that we must seek their aggregate significance. All aggregation procedures make assumptions or are based on theories about how the differ-

---

[130] Harsanyi, in Shubik, p. 184.
[131] Hayward Alker in this volume.

ent variables or components are related to each other. Different vector scores can be aggregated in a number of ways, most simply according to the general formula:

$$v = \sqrt{x_1^2 + x_2^2 + x_3^2 + \ldots x_n^2},$$

but all these procedures assume equal or known weights for each dimension and assume a particular logical form to their interrelationship. The same is true of other standard aggregative techniques such as factor analysis and Guttman scaling.

The analytic systems perspective I have adopted suggests several ways in which we might proceed in developing theory-based aggregate measures of decisionmaking system properties. I will discuss two here under the headings of system autonomy-dependency and system capabilities.

1) SYSTEM AUTONOMY-DEPENDENCY

I remarked early in this article that one key to aggregation lay in the fact that some properties were not only descriptors of how integrated the system was at T but also powerful predictors of how integrated it was likely to be at T+1 and after. A central concept in systems analysis is "feedback." In our terms we ask in what ways the properties relate to each other over time so as to contribute to the further integration or disintegration of the system.

The capacity of any collective decisionmaking system to respond to stress—to persist, to grow, to decline—can be seen in part in terms of the effects that flow back into the system (either directly or via the constituent systems) as a consequence of collective decisionmaking activity and the impact of that activity. Future collective decisionmaking is in some sense then a function of past performance. The cumulation of past practices may broaden or narrow the scope of decisionmaking, increase or decrease decisiveness, the ranges of decision stages affected, and the strength and homogeneity of the flow of demands. Resources may be used up or replenished or new ones created. Bargaining modalities and the consequences of the decisions that are produced (in terms of their penetrativeness, degree of compliance, and distributive effects) will also change over time in dynamic fashion as in Figure 15.

Integration theorists have spoken broadly of these feedback effects, using such concepts as spillover, spill-back, or encapsulation to describe whether the cumulative effect of past decisions has increased, decreased, or stabilized the level of integration. But the precise cause and effect relations have seldom been specified in empirical research, in which it is clearly indicated what kinds of collective decisions have what kinds of consequences for which future properties and as a result of what causal processes (learning, socialization, identification, politicization, etc.). The paradigm I have proposed should

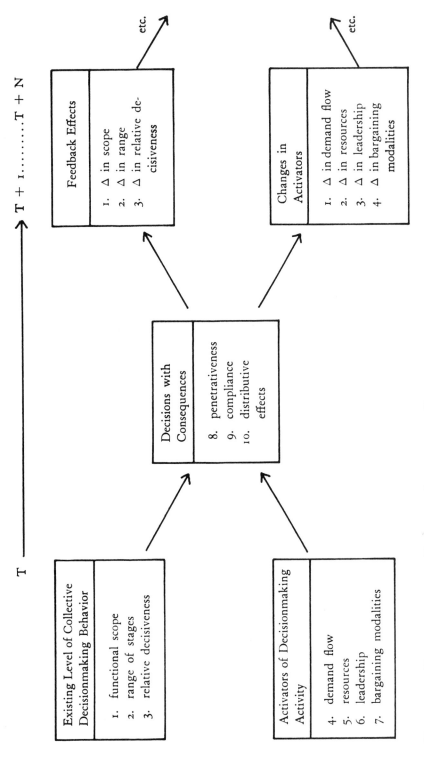

FIGURE 15. FEEDBACK IN THE POLITICAL INTEGRATION PROCESS

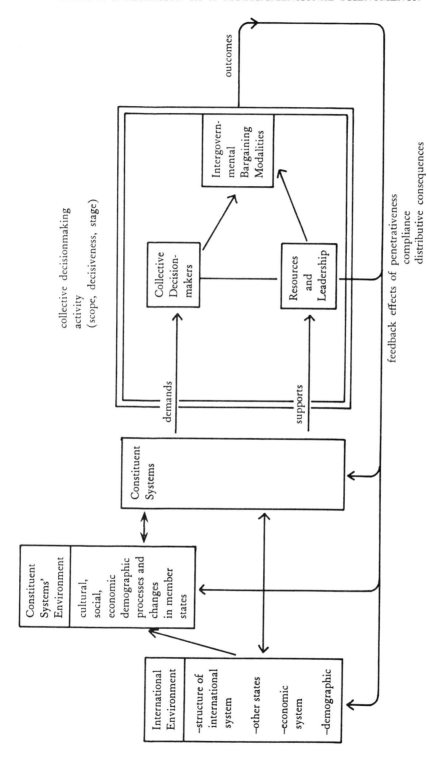

FIGURE 16. POLITICAL INTEGRATION PROCESS—EXOGENOUS LINKAGES

facilitate this kind of research. The simple paradigm I have been using up to now focuses on the interactions between constituent systems and the collectivity, on the one hand, and between the various properties of the collective decisionmaking process, on the other. We have so far left out of consideration the impact on collective decisionmaking, either of effects flowing from the international environment or of independent developments within the political, economic, cultural, and social systems of the constituent systems. But we need now to broaden our concerns to include such exogenous effects (see Figure 16).

Such exogenous factors can be treated as parameters of our system; we are interested in their effects on the system of behaviors we are analyzing, but it is not necessary to account for their dynamics. In other words, exogenous factors are treated as givens. Concepts and dynamic links can be provided so that these effects and the ways in which they are transmitted to the system can be observed and compared with the effects of systemic or endogenous variables.[132]

On the basis of a comparison of the effects of endogenously determined feedback and of "new" inputs from the constituent systems, it should in principle be possible for us to develop aggregate measures that will describe the relative contribution of endogenous and exogenous effects to the overall political integration process in particular groupings. Such an autonomy-dependency index would give us a measure of the capacity of any system for self-generated growth or for self-maintenance and would advance us far beyond sterile debates about *the* external variable or the *inevitable* dominance of the "national situation" or of "high political" concerns.

2) SYSTEM CAPABILITIES

A given system may be endogenously determined but still not "healthy" in the sense of being capable of withstanding crises or serious strains. One of the most fundamental aggregate properties of political systems will be their relative stress-response capabilities. Consequently, we would like to be able to measure (predict) what range of what intensity issues a particular system can cope with and with what costs as far as existing scopes, resources, modalities, etc. In order to do this we will have to be able to specify the conditions and determinants of *how* collective decisionmakers are able to respond to demands by transforming differential amounts of their resources into collective outcomes. Such a conception would be the direct analogue of Harsanyi's notion of "power in a schedule sense."

> [A] given individual's power can be described not only by stating the specific values of the five dimensions [scope, amount, extension, strength, and costs] of his power (whether as single numbers, or as vectors, or as lists of specific items), but also by specifying the mathematical *functions* or *schedules* that

[132] The broadened paradigm should also facilitate the work of those who would focus directly on the ways in which exogenous and endogenous variables (and processes) interact. For example, Puchala's interests in delineating the several dimensions of the "community formation process," seeing how they interact with each other and with what he terms "political amalgamation," would, it seems to me, benefit from a more complex delineation of the political integration process seen in the context of environmental and constituent system processes of greater or lesser independence. To the extent that community formation processes and political integration processes are related, it should be possible to specify the links with the aid of a model like the following:

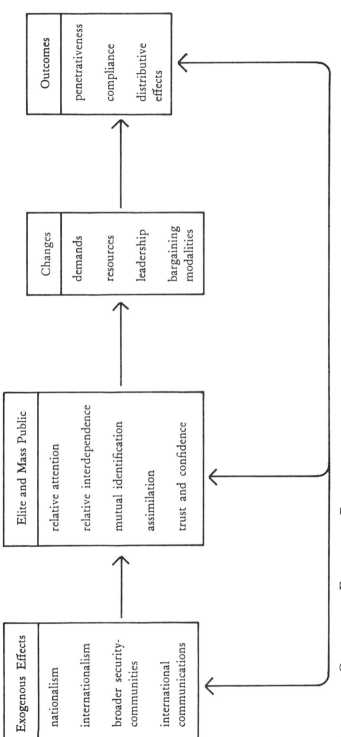

FIGURE 17. COMMUNITY FORMATION PROCESS

connect the costs of his power with the other four dimensions. . . . Power in a schedule sense can be regarded as a "production function" describing how a given individual can "transform" different amounts of his resources (of his working time, his money, his political rights, his popularity, etc.) into social power of various dimensions (of various strengths, scopes, amounts, and extensions). The commonsense notion of social power makes it an *ability* to achieve certain things. . . .[133]

Here again theory and method certainly go hand in hand. We will need empirically validated propositions (ideally in the form of mathematical equations) precisely defining the causal interrelations between the different properties and between them and exogenous effects if we are to construct aggregate measures of a system's stress response capabilities. One form that such a measure might take has been suggested by Alker in his formula for "collective demand processing success potential" (formula 29b).[134] Nye and Schmitter in their contributions to this volume point the way in which we must proceed in developing the *schedules* that will permit the development of such measures.

In fact, stress response capability gets us very close to one of the fundamental normative bases of international integration studies. It seems to me that we have been ultimately interested in integration efforts out of some concern for learning how one might overcome either the patently destructive effects of national rivalries or the economic, social, or political "inefficiencies" of the state system. If this is true, then our conception of integration must include a focus on the stressful issues that lie at the heart of internation rivalry and conflict. How politically integrated a grouping of nations is must in this sense be calculated in terms of its success in inventing voluntary political structures or procedures that are able to substitute cooperative and mutually beneficial (or minimally harmful) solutions for competitive zero-sum solutions. Such a conception might, of course, yield higher scores for high-stress systems with moderate performance _than for low-stress systems with high levels of performance.

Concepts such as "stress response capability" might well help "integrate" the subfields of international integration and international conflict studies. It is rather curious that although international integration has been generally recognized as having more than casual significance for both the external behavior and the internal political life of the constituent units, there has been by and large very little actual incorporation of integration theories or findings into either the dominant frame of reference in studies of international politics[135] or into that subfield that is in some ways the most advanced, i.e., em-

[133] Harsanyi, in Shubik, pp. 194–195.

[134] Alker in this volume.

[135] See Oran Young, "The Actors in World Politics," in James N. Roseman, Vincent Davis, and Maurice A. East (ed.), *The Analysis of International Politics* (forthcoming). See also Oran Young, "Interdependencies in World Politics," (forthcoming).

pirical studies of international conflict behavior. Part of the problem is that we have seldom made any explicit and systematic effort to develop definitions and measures of political integration that would be useful or compelling as independent and intervening variables in the analysis of state or individual behavior. In order to explain or predict changes in the international behavior of states an integration concept must be able to tell us what difference it makes that one or another level or type of integration exists within a particular grouping. Stress response capability may be one such concept.

3

International Transactions and Regional Integration

Donald J. Puchala

The relevance of transaction analysis to the study of regional integration has been the subject of controversy.[1] In dialectical fashion though, this controversy has produced improved understanding. Early exponents, who tended at times to overestimate the efficacy of the transaction approach, have accepted its limitations, and, by the same token, some early critics of transaction analysis have accepted its usefulness. Overall, we have come to recognize that regional integration is a multidimensional phenomenon, much more complex than initially imagined. Transaction approaches are appropriate and useful for investigating some aspects of regional integration; they are less useful for investigating others.

The purpose of this essay is to explore the strengths and limitations of transaction analysis in the context of a broad theoretical and methodological assault on the regional integration problem. Discussion below develops in several parts. After some definitional notes concerning the nature of international transactions, transaction flow analysis is set in the context of a descriptive model of regional integration. Next the relevance of the transaction approach is tested, first logically, then empirically. In all, it will be posited and demonstrated that, when handled properly, transaction flows provide reasonably reliable descriptive barometers for several social, economic, and political processes that

Donald J. Puchala is a research associate at the Institute of War and Peace Studies, Columbia University. This study was partially supported by the Social Science Research Council and the Institute of War and Peace Studies, Columbia University.

[1] For expositions on some of the issues in controversy see: Ronald Inglehart, "An End to European Integration," *American Political Science Review*, March 1967 (Vol. 59, No. 1), pp. 91–105; Stanley Hoffmann, "Discord in Community: The North Atlantic Area as a Partial International System," *International Organization*, Summer 1963 (Vol. 17, No. 3), pp. 521–549; Karl W. Deutsch, "Towards Western European Integration: An Interim Assessment," *Journal of International Affairs*, 1962 (Vol. 16, No. 1), pp. 89–101; Ernst B. Haas, "The Challenge of Regionalism," in Stanley Hoffmann (ed.), *Contemporary Theory in International Relations* (Englewood Cliffs, N.J: Prentice-Hall, 1960), pp. 223–240.

occur during regional integration. Whether transaction approaches can carry research in regional integration beyond description and toward causality is currently an open question. Aspects of this question are considered in concluding sections of this study.

ANALYTICAL AND OPERATIONAL ATTRIBUTES OF INTERNATIONAL TRANSACTIONS

Transactions are contacts or dealings. In international relations transactions have to do with contacts and dealings, both governmental and nongovernmental, between states. As such they have a number of analytical attributes. Transactions, for example, may be analyzed with respect to *substance*. Generally speaking, dealings between states may be of an economic or political nature, or they may concern social, cultural, or technical affairs or any number of specific matters included under these broader headings. On another analytical tack, transactions may be studied by placing emphasis upon the "whos," "whoms," and *directions* of international contacts. Different states exchange different volumes of different kinds of transactions at different periods in time. It will be shown later that continuities and shifts in transaction flows can reflect movement toward or away from regional integration. Similarly, but more broadly, just as directions of transaction flow vary under differing conditions, *intensities* of flow also vary. Most broadly speaking, permutations of substance, direction, intensity, and time define patterns of transaction flow, and these in turn describe structure and process in the international system.[2] Analyzing transaction flows then theoretically opens the way to observing and recording who is (was) dealing with whom, how or how much, about what, when.

Operationally, of course, it is impossible to observe the full range of transactions between states. Many varieties of international transactions are never recorded; transactions that are recorded are often stripped of substance in statistical reporting; some ranges of political transactions are kept secret. Analyzing international transaction flows therefore becomes a process of sampling in a rather biased way (i.e., one can use only data that can be located) and then using sampled data as indices of broader transaction ranges. By convention, transaction analysts have tended to use foreign trade data to index ranges of economic transactions, international mail deliveries and newspaper and periodical circulation to index information exchange or social communication, educational exchange to index cultural interaction, and diplomatic representation and activity to index political transaction.[3] There is nothing

---

[2] Steven J. Brams, "Transaction Flows in the International System," *American Political Science Review*, December 1966 (Vol. 60, No. 4), pp. 880–898.

[3] For a variety of transaction indices see: Hayward Alker, Jr., and Donald J. Puchala, "Trends in Economic Partnership: The North Atlantic Area, 1928–1963," in J. David Singer (ed.), *Quantitative International Politics: Insights and Evidence* (New York: Free Press, Collier-Macmillan, 1968), pp.

particularly sacred about the conventional transaction flow indices. They are used repeatedly because data is available and because this data comes in quantitative formats.[4] Moreover, there is nothing particularly misleading about the conventional indices as long as the analyst recognizes that each index studied in isolation reveals only a partial description of transactions between states. As a rule, depth in transaction flow analysis, especially as applied to regional integration problems, follows from monitoring multiple indices and following data series over extended periods in time.

While this essay is in no sense intended as a "cookbook" in transaction flow analytical techniques, it must nonetheless be noted that data for transaction analysis may, and should, be processed in a variety of ways, and the choice of a technique should follow from the nature of the transaction relationship sought. As the summary in Table 1 and the brief notes following suggest, different transformations of basic data become appropriate according to whether one is interested in measuring relative direction, relative intensity, dependence, interdependence, partnership, concentration, acceleration, and other quantities or qualities in transaction relationships.

287–316; Bruce M. Russett, *Community and Contention: Britain and America in the Twentieth Century* (Cambridge, Mass: M.I.T. Press, 1963), passim; Karl W. Deutsch, and others, *France, Germany and the Western Alliance: A Study of Elite Attitudes on European Integration and World Politics* (New York: Charles Scribner's Sons, 1967), passim; J. David Singer and Melvin Small, "The Composition and Status Ordering of the International System, 1815–1940," *World Politics,* January 1966 (Vol. 18, No. 2), pp. 236–282; Chadwick F. Alger and Steven J. Brams, "Patterns of Representation in National Capitals and Intergovernmental Organizations," *World Politics,* July 1967 (Vol. 19, No. 4), pp. 646–663; Zbigniew K. Brzezinski, *The Soviet Bloc: Unity and Conflict* (New York: Frederick A. Praeger, 1961), pp. 445–479; Michael Michaely, *Concentration in International Trade* (Contributions to Economic Analysis No. 28) (Amsterdam: North-Holland Publishing Co., 1962), pp. 133–142.

  [4] While it is clearly impossible to list all sources of transaction flow data in a short footnote, it is worth citing some of the standard sources. There are many sources of international trade data including the United Nations series, *Direction of International Trade,* and the World Bank series, *Direction of Trade,* both of which present reliable data in country-table formats especially convenient for transaction analysis. In addition, the OEEC/OECD series, *Foreign Trade: Overall Trade by Countries* provides reliable trade statistics for the North Atlantic area. For the period between the world wars the League of Nations series, *Memorandum on International Trade and Balance of Payments,* is an indispensable source. Michael G. Mulhall's, *The Dictionary of Statistics* (London: George Rutledge & Sons, 1892) provides fragmentary, though interesting, listings of trade statistics for the eighteenth and nineteenth centuries. Furthermore, most modern states publish their own trade figures in national yearbooks or statistical abstracts. The standard source for international mail figures is the Universal Postal Union's series, *Statistique des expéditions dans le service international,* which began in approximately 1890 and terminated in 1961. Figures on international tourism are generally of questionable reliability because of national inconsistencies in counting and reporting. Nevertheless the *United Nations Statistical Yearbook* intermittently lists tourist flow statistics. Two works also contribute figures for international tourism during the period between the world wars: A. J. Norval, *The Tourist Industry* (London: Pitman & Sons, 1936) and F. W. Ogilvie, *The Tourist Movement* (London: King & Sons, 1933). The standard source for data concerning international student exchanges is the UNESCO yearbook, *Study Abroad.* For fragmentary data on student exchanges during the interwar period one might consult the League of Nations, Institute for Intellectual Cooperation series, *Bulletin for University Relations.* Student flows into and out of the United States are reported in the *Annual Report* of the United States Immigration and Naturalization Service. International migration statistics are largely nonexistent except on a very fragmentary and highly unreliable basis. National yearbooks such as the *Annuario statistico italiano,* the *Statistisches Jahrbuch für die Bundesrepublik Deutschland,* the *Statistical Abstract of the United States,* etc., are the best sources, but differences in counting and reporting render international comparisons difficult.

1. ABSOLUTE TRANSACTION VOLUMES may be used to order transacting units according to "size" where "size" means immensity or littleness of output into the international system. Transaction "size" often correlates with other "size" measures such as territorial expansiveness, population, national income, and military capability. But, while the latter indices measure "power" in a general way, transaction volumes more accurately index "participation" in international affairs. Phenomena such as international isolationism and activism show in volumes of states' transactions, and these show even better when transaction behavior is compared with potential for such behavior reflected in standard "power" indices.

In an even more direct way, absolute volumes of transactions may be used to index international partnership and interdependence (i.e., high volume, two-way flows of transactions), and such use may contribute insight to transaction analysis that is sometimes blurred by sophisticated data transformations. Where percentages, proportions, and relative acceptance scores standardize for size, such standardization is not always analytically desirable. It may, for example, be interesting to know that in year "x" both the Federal Republic of Germany (West Germany) and the Netherlands shipped 15 percent of their exports to Italy. What might be more significant for assessing international interdependence, however, is the fact that in year "x" West Germany's exports to Italy amounted to 100 million dollars and the Netherlands' exports to Italy totaled five million dollars. As a rule of thumb the transaction analyst should use absolute transaction volumes as a check upon more sophisticated statistical manipulations. Computed measures are intended to aid in interpreting patterns and trends in absolute volume data. They should not, however, grossly distort the basic data.

2. PERCENTAGE AND PROPORTION TRANSFORMATIONS are performed on raw message counts (i.e., absolute volume data) first to standardize for "size," second to clarify patterns and trends, and third to eliminate nuisance in dealing with extremely large numbers (hundred-thousands, millions, and billions for the most part). When transacting units are of approximately the same "size" or when relative "size" is unimportant in the transaction analysis, conversions to percentages or proportions simplify interpretation and presentation. To take several examples: 1) *directions* in transaction flow may be expressed as proportions of total systemic message output moving in different bilateral or multilateral channels, 2) *intensities* of transaction preference may be measured as percentages of states' total transactions shared with other particular states (see "examples" in Table 1), 3) *partnership* or *interdependence* in transaction behavior might be indexed as proportions of partners' total transactions that are mutual transactions, or 4) *dependence* upon transactions with particular partners will show in the difference between two states' pro-

TABLE I. VARIETIES OF TRANSACTION INDICES

Index	Description	Utility
Absolute transaction volumes	Raw data used as presented in data source.	Best reflector of relative "size" of transacting units. Used to evaluate reasonableness of all computed measures.[a]
Percentage and proportion transformations	Relative transactions between pairs or groups of actors.	Standardizes for "size" of transacting units. Measures direction and intensity of actors' relative transaction preferences.
Relative acceptance transformation[c]	Actual transaction compared with predicted transactions in random or "null model" system.	Most concise measure of intensity of transaction flow standardized for relative "size" of transacting units. Distinguishes between bilateral and regional peculiarities in transaction behavior and world trends or patterns.
Michaely concentration index[d]	$$Gjx = 100\sqrt{\Sigma(Xsj/X.j)^2}$$ where, Xsj = j to s $X.j$ = total transactions for j	Measures intensity of geographic concentration of transaction behavior and therefore becomes an index of preference, partnership, interdependence, or dependence.
Foreign-to-domestic ratios[f]	External transactions/internal transactions.	Most appropriate measure of penetration, interpenetration, internationalism, and isolationism.
Rate measures	Percentage change in transaction volume over unit time.	Measures acceleration and deceleration in growth of transaction relationships. May be a basis for projection to hypothesized future patterns.

[a] "Reasonableness" as used here means intuitive validity. All computed measures distort raw data in some way. The analyst must therefore exercise caution to see that computed measures do not produce patterns or trends in transaction relationships that are unreal and result only because computations distorted data. A way to control against such artificial findings is to compare computed indices with raw data trends and to ask repeatedly whether the computed index is clarifying a pattern in the raw data or whether it is imposing a pattern upon this data that was not actually there before computation.

[b] "EEC" for the years prior to the establishment of the European Economic Community refers to the six countries that became members of the community in 1958.

[c] See I. Richard Savage and Karl W. Deutsch, "A Statistical Model of the Gross Analysis of Transaction Flows," *Econometrica*, July 1960 (Vol. 28, No. 3), pp. 551–572.

TABLE 1—Continued

Examples		
Trade with EEC[b]		
	France	Belgium-Luxembourg
1938	$ 462.8 million	$ 578.9 million
1954	1633.4 million	2023.5 million
1965	8135.1 million	7430.1 million
Trade with EEC as percentage of Total Trade		
	France	Belgium-Luxembourg
1938	21.1 percent	37.8 percent
1954	19.4 percent	41.9 percent
1965	39.9 percent	63.1 percent
National Relative Acceptance of EEC Exports		
	France	Belgium-Luxembourg
1938	.4	1.1
1954	.4	1.4
1965	.6	1.6
Regional Concentration of Trade[e]		
	France	Belgium-Luxembourg
1938	39.4	45.8
1954	41.6	49.0
1965	46.4	65.7
EEC Trade-to-GNP Ratios		
	France	Belgium-Luxembourg
1938	4.5	29.2
1954	4.9	30.4
1965	8.6	44.0
Average Annual Change in Trade with EEC[g]		
	France	Belgium-Luxembourg
1938–1954	25.2 percent per year	25.0 percent per year
1954–1965	22.8 percent per year	34.1 percent per year

[d] Michaely, pp. 6–25.

[e] The concentration measure as demonstrated here is used to examine EEC trade with France and Belgium-Luxembourg as compared with these countries' trade with nine other regions of the world—North America, Central America, South America, non-EEC Western Europe, Eastern Europe, the Middle East, Asia, Africa, and Oceania. Rising index scores indicate greater concentration within the EEC. A score of 100 would indicate that all trade was with this single region.

[f] Karl W. Deutsch, "The Propensity to International Transactions," *Political Studies,* June 1960 (Vol. 8, No. 2), pp. 147–155.

[g] The greatest proportion of the "1938–1954" increase occurred between 1948 and 1954.

portional transactions with each other. Despite the utility and widespread application of percentage and proportion transformations caution must be exercised when such computed indices are used to analyze transaction relationships between acting units grossly different in "size."

3. RELATIVE ACCEPTANCE TRANSFORMATIONS are similar to percentage and proportion conversions in that they standardize for "size," reduce cumbersome absolute figures to decimal indices, clarify patterns and trends in absolute data, and measure such factors as transaction *intensity* (high relative acceptance [RA] scores), *direction* (high RA scores in some channels, low ones in others), *partnership* or *interdependence* (high RA scores in both directions in bilateral channels), and *dependence* (high RA scores in one direction only). Moreover, the relative acceptance score has the further attractiveness of taking on both positive and negative values to show both communications links and communications gaps between actors. In addition, since the relative acceptance index can be computed only from a universal transaction matrix (total world or total regional), RA scores capture specific bilateral or multilateral shifts in transaction behavior while controlling for overall increases or decreases in transaction flows in the universal system. Then, too, the RA score may be tested directly for statistical significance.

Since the computation and interpretation of the relative acceptance score are fully explained in a number of works, let it suffice here to say that the index measures deviations from a "null model" system in which all transactions are permitted to flow in proportion to the relative "size" of transacting units. Hence, if a unit contributes 20 percent of the total transactions in a system, we expect, under the null model, that this unit will contribute 20 percent of the transactions for every other unit in the system. Actual flows may deviate from this expected 20 percent, and these deviations, positive or negative, large or small, become the basis for computing the relative acceptance measure. If two units share many more transactions than expected on the basis of their total transactions, RA scores will be positive and high (see "examples" in Table 1). If they share many fewer transactions than expected, scores will be negative and low. Since the computing formula for the RA index calls for dividing the difference between actual and expected transactions by expected transactions (RA = actual-expected ÷ expected) relative acceptance scores may take values ranging from −1.0 (no transactions at all) to 0.0 (transactions as expected) to infinity (a great many more transactions than expected).

While the relative acceptance index is attractive for reasons mentioned and while it is used widely in gross transaction flow analysis, some caution should be exercised in selecting this measure. First, unless transacting units are of approximately the same "size" (or again, if relative size is incidental to the analysis) relative acceptance computations should be avoided since RA scores can greatly distort patterns reflected by absolute flows. For example, under the RA computational scheme two very "small" but intensely interacting units may well score much higher in relative acceptance rating than two very "large" but less intensely interacting units, and this scoring would occur despite the fact that the large units, by actual message count, exchanged many more transactions than the smaller units.

4. THE MICHAELY CONCENTRATION INDEX measures tendencies toward geographic concentration in transactions. The measure shows the extent to which an actor's transactions are either distributed throughout the international system (low score on Michaely index), or concentrated with a small cluster of partners (high score on index), or shared with a single partner only (highest score on index). Dependence, interdependence, relative transaction preference, and partnership could all be operationalized in terms of the Michaely index.

Computing the Michaely index, as suggested in Table 1, is straightforward. The index derives basically from summing squared proportions of given actors' transactions with all other actors. It is clear from the formula (see table) that concentrated transactions (i.e., large proportions with few partners) would drive the index upward toward 100 while unconcentrated transactions would drive the index downward toward zero. The Michaely index has not been used outside of economics as yet. Nonetheless, aside from complexities in computation and the fact that this index, as others, distorts "size" the Michaely measure would serve most of the analytical purposes that percentages, proportions, and relative acceptance scores currently serve.

5. FOREIGN-TO-DOMESTIC RATIOS are the most frequently used measures of penetration, interpenetration, dependence, and interdependence. They compare transactions exchanged internally with transactions shared with international partners. High external to internal ratios (trade/gross national product, for example) may index "participation" in the international system or "dependence" upon the system. Similarly, high external to internal ratios for transactions with single partners may show such partners' penetration into one's own system and, hence, one's dependence (see Belgium-Luxembourg in Table 1). Or, mutually high external to internal transaction ratios in bilateral or multilateral channels may index the disappearance of distinctions between "foreign" and "domestic" transactions between particular states and, hence, the progress toward international community. While foreign-to-domestic ratios are most often computed to chart and evaluate economic relationships, they are equally useful applied to other varieties of transactions also.

6. RATE MEASURES help to evaluate the momentum of transaction trends over time. Rates of change are quotients of positive or negative increments

in transactions between earlier and later time periods divided by levels of transactions in the earlier periods (i.e., percentages of change over time). Among other uses rate measures show "growth" or "deterioration" in transaction relationships and "acceleration" or "deceleration" in forming partnerships. In addition, with caution and under specific assumptions rate measures can become the bases for projecting probable transaction patterns to hypothesized future time periods.

When all is said, the analyst selects or devises his indices according to their assumed accuracy in reflecting a particular quantity or quality of transaction behavior. As a rule, the closer he remains to his basic data, the more likely his analysis will turn out accurate and reasonable.

TRANSACTION PATTERNS AND REGIONAL INTEGRATION

Condensing an extensive body of theory into a relatively few words, it can be proposed that, descriptively at least, regional integration is a process of multidimensional merger. The regional integration phenomenon encompasses the merger of territories, governments, polities, economies, societies, and cultures. Empirically, merger in each of these dimensions, and subdimensions within each, can be indexed and charted, so that at the descriptive level we actually "watch" regional integration as it happens.[5]

Without losing sight of the multidimensionality of the phenomenon it is possible theoretically to collapse across dimensions, to abstract, and to construct a model wherein regional integration becomes essentially a two-phased occurrence. At this higher level of abstraction regional integration comes to involve either or both the merger of national communities (i.e., peoples) to form international communities (multinational societies) or the merger of national governments to form supranational governments. Hence, to borrow a page from Karl Deutsch, and others in *Political Community and the North Atlantic Area,* processes of regional integration may produce "integrated" systems, "amalgamated" systems, or "integrated and amalgamated" systems.[6] Integration (later called "community formation" here) and amalgamation as used in this article are taken as quantitative variables. It is assumed that there can be degrees of both "international community" and "supranational government" and hence a number of possible "termination states" for regional inte-

---

[5] For further discussion of dimensionality in the regional integration phenomenon see Joseph S. Nye, "Comparative Regional Integration: Concept and Measurement," *International Organization,* Autumn 1968 (Vol 22, No. 4), pp. 855–880; Mario Barrera and Ernst B. Haas, "The Operationalization of Some Variables Related to Regional Integration: A Research Note," *International Organization,* Winter 1969 (Vol. 23, No. 1), pp. 150–160; Donald J. Puchala, "Integration and Disintegration in Franco-German Relations, 1954–1965," *International Organization,* Spring 1970 (Vol. 24, No. 2), pp. 183–208.

[6] Karl W. Deutsch, and others, *Political Community and the North Atlantic Area: International Organization in the Light of Historical Experience* (Princeton, N.J.: Princeton University Press, 1957), pp. 5–8.

gration processes.[7] What is of particular interest in this article is that degrees of both international community and supranational government can be measured with instruments of transaction flow analysis.

Transaction Flows and Community Formation: The Nationalism Paradigm

Impressionistic similarities between the institution of marriage (i.e., twentieth-century Western), the evolution of nationalities, and the hypothetical emergence of "supranationalities" are not coincidental: marriage, nationalism, and international community formation are all community formation processes. Each starts with at least two separate human units (individuals or groups); each produces a state of affairs in which the initially separate units achieve mutual identification; each becomes subject, under conceptually similar conditions, to strains, deterioration, and divorce. Most important for purposes here, whether it binds two people in wedlock, two tribes in a nation, or two nations in an international community, community formation is reflected in characteristic transaction flow patterns.

A community, by definition, is a group of people who share certain attributes. Members of a community share values, preferences, and life-styles. They also share memories of common experiences. They aspire toward common ends, show deference or loyalty to common symbols, and sense common destinies. Most important, they identify with one another and distinguish between themselves and outsiders.[8]

Communities vary with regard to both intensity and expansiveness. Bonds of commonality may be numerous and highly salient for community members, in which case a strong and cohesive community results. Or, such bonds may be few and relatively unimportant for community members, with the result that the community is weak and possibly unstable. While national communities (nationalities) are probably best known and most studied by political scientists, groups that may meet the definition of community range from families to supranationalities.[9]

Theoretical and empirical linkages between transaction flows (i.e., communications patterns) and community were introduced into the literature of political science by Karl W. Deutsch. The thrust of Deutsch's earlier work

[7] Amitai Etzioni, *Political Unification: A Comparative Study of Leaders and Forces* (New York: Holt, Rinehart and Winston, 1965), pp. 60–66.

[8] This definition of "community" is my own though it follows directly from Deutsch's discussion of the concept. Cf. Karl W. Deutsch, *Nationalism and Social Communication: An Inquiry into the Foundations of Nationality* (1st ed: Cambridge, Mass: Technology Press; New York: John Wiley & Sons, 1953), pp. 60–81, especially pp. 61–67. Deutsch's development of the community concept reflects a synthesis of findings drawn from the history of nationalism, from cultural anthropology, and from the theory of communications.

[9] "Supranationality" as used here is a community of peoples of more than one nationality. A "European community" (in the sense that community is used here) would be a supranationality, just as the present-day "Canadian community" is a supranationality to the extent that "Canadianness" overarches or complements the Britishness or Frenchness of Canadian citizens.

was to postulate and then prove that it is empirically feasible to ascertain the existence of a community by observing people's communications behavior. In *Nationalism and Social Communication* (1953) Deutsch models the national community as a system of quantitatively intense and qualitatively rich and varied intragroup transactions.[10] Notwithstanding its theoretical and substantive interest, the important methodological contribution in *Nationalism and Social Communication* is Deutsch's proposition that characteristic transaction patterns both indicate the existence and define the "boundaries" of national communities.[11] More formally stated: Whenever it is the case that a population shares values, preferences, life-styles, common memories, aspirations, loyalties, and identifications, it is also the case that people within this population communicate with one another (i.e., transact) frequently, rapidly, clearly, and effectively, in balanced manner, over multiple ranges of social, economic, cultural, and political concerns. Furthermore, these people communicate between themselves much more frequently over a much broader range of concerns than they communicate with peoples of other communities, so the "boundaries" of their community are marked by relative discontinuities of transaction flow.[12]

In *Political Community at the International Level* (1954) Deutsch observes, upon impressionistic survey, that multinational (or international) communities have emerged intermittently in history. He further observes that their emergence and tenure frequently coincided with periods of stability within international federations and with periods of peace between states. Contrariwise, the deterioration of international communities appeared related to the collapse of federations and the outbreak of war between states.[13] From these observations Deutsch hypothesized that a more systematic study would show close relationships between the presence and strength of international communities and the stability of international federations and international peace. Drawing upon earlier findings from the study of national communities, Deutsch suggests in the operational sections of *Political Community at the International Level* that international community could be ascertained and measured by examining the volume, content, and scope of international transactions between hypothesized community members.[14]

---

[10] Deutsch, *Nationalism and Social Communication*, p. 75 and passim.

[11] Ibid., pp. 62–63, 20–21.

[12] This formulation is my restatement of the community-communications linkage. In effect, this is what I understand Deutsch to be saying in both *Nationalism and Social Communication* and in *Political Community at the International Level: Problems of Definition and Measurement* (Garden City, N.Y: Doubleday & Co., 1954). It should be noted that the first part of the proposition is not logically closed since saying that the presence of community implies the presence of intense communications is not the same as saying that the presence of intense communications implies the presence of community. The logical inconsistency does not, however, affect Deutsch's argument in *Nationalism and Social Communication* since in this work he posits a causal relationship between communication and community.

[13] Deutsch, *Political Community at the International Level*, pp. 3–32.

[14] In all, Deutsch lists fourteen operational tests for the existence of international community, with transaction analyses most prominent among these. Cf. *Political Community at the International*

Findings from the Princeton University project that produced *Political Community and the North Atlantic Area* (1957) not only validated Deutsch's hypothesis about community, federal stability, and international peace, but also revealed that the existence of reasonably strong community bonds between peoples or their elites constituted a precondition for federation.[15] Most important for this article, the methodology of the Princeton study established "unbroken links of social communication" over "a multiplicity of ranges" as indices of international community. It further established increasing and increasingly rich and varied international transactions as indices of international community formation.[16]

With theoretical and empirical linkages between communications and community thus exposed, the operational step into transaction analysis is uncomplicated. In transaction analysis applied to international community formation problems the analyst searches for patterns of communication that characterize community at the international level. As suggested in the discussion above, two such patterns are most prominent:

1. International community is indicated by high volumes of international transactions over multiple ranges of social, economic, cultural, and political concerns. International community formation, therefore, would be indicated by increasing volumes of multiple-ranged transactions between potential community members.

2. International community is indicated by differences in volumes and ranges of communications between hypothesized community members on the one hand and between themselves and "outsiders" on the other. Community formation, therefore, is indicated by increasingly marked discontinuities in transactions between members of an emerging community and surrounding "external" populations.

Operationally, then, if international community formation is in progress, one would expect to observe internal intensification and expansion of transaction flow patterns, matched by increasingly apparent external discontinuation of these patterns. Community formation and its characteristic transaction flow patterns can be readily demonstrated with data that reflects integration trends in Western Europe in the post-World War II era.

Level, pp. 46–64. What must be underlined in regard to Deutsch's tests of international community is that *indicators* cannot be confused with the *phenomenon indexed.* A system of intense transaction flows is not in and of itself a community. A community is a population sharing attributes as defined above. The system of intense transaction flows *indicates* the presence of a community. Other operational factors also indicate the presence of a community.

[15] This latter finding has generated controversy among students of regional integration. (Cf. Haas, in Hoffmann.) The question of preconditions for political amalgamation and the question of causal linkages between community and amalgamation remain without satisfactory answers. On the other hand there is no dispute about Deutsch's main finding that international community is a component of stable international federations.

[16] Deutsch, and others, pp. 46–59.

*Community Formation in Western Europe: Internal Intensification and the
Franco-German and Franco-British Cases*

The extent of international community formation in Western Europe during the two decades since the end of World War II is perhaps nowhere reflected more dramatically than in the Franco–West German relationship.
When polled concerning proposed West German rearmament in the fall of
1954, Frenchmen overwhelmingly rejected the idea of an independent German army, criticized West German participation in an integrated European army, and reacted very coolly to the idea of integrating West German
forces into the North Atlantic Treaty Organization (NATO).[17] Deeper prob-
ings of these French responses uncovered strong latent fears of renewed German militarism, visions of another Franco-German war, and general and
bitter anti-Germanism.[18] Other pollings conducted in France in the early
1950's revealed high levels of mistrust and widespread hostility toward Germans and Germany, relative French satisfaction with the division of Germany,
and strong French feelings about continuing rigid controls over West German
sovereignty.[19] While West German attitudes toward France and Frenchmen
during the early 1950's are not as specifically documented as French attitudes,
available poll data strongly suggests that ill feelings harbored in France were
reciprocated in West Germany.[20] Therefore, up to 1954 at least, Frenchmen
and West Germans remained deeply and mutually estranged.

Yet by 1968 (actually probably somewhat earlier) the same kinds of indices that marked Franco-German estrangement in the 1950's were registering
amity and confidence between the two peoples. Again the data is more specific on the French side. As Table 2 shows, the "unthinkability" of war had
come to characterize the Franco-German relationship, at least as far as Frenchmen were concerned. In addition, considerable international confidence had
also entered French thinking about Germans by 1968. Most fascinating of
all, part 3 in Table 2 exhibits evidence of mutual identification—i.e., some
hint of a "we feeling" was there! As a footnote to the more specific
data shown in the table it might be added that Frenchmen were about six
times more likely to express "good feelings" for Germans in 1965 than they
were in 1954.[21] On the West German side, data is less complete and detailed,
and we can note only general trends in international confidence and good
feeling. As concerned attitudes toward France and Frenchmen, these trends
in German public opinion moved sharply upward during the late 1950's and

[17] Richard L. Merritt and Donald J. Puchala (ed.), *Western European Perspectives on International
Affairs: Public Opinion Studies and Evaluations* (New York: Frederick A. Praeger, 1968), pp. 314–316.

[18] Donald J. Puchala, "The Pattern of Contemporary Regional Integration," *International Studies
Quarterly*, March 1968 (Vol. 12, No. 1), p. 54.

[19] Merritt and Puchala, p. 413.

[20] Ibid., p. 235.

[21] *International Survey XX–17* (Washington: United States Information Agency, 1965).

TABLE 2. FRENCH PUBLIC OPINION INDICES OF FRANCO-GERMAN COMMUNITY IN 1968

1. *Security Community and the "Unthinkability" of War*

"Wars between Germans and Frenchmen are now finished: it is time to forget the past."

Agree	74 percent
Disagree	17 percent
No Opinion	9 percent
	100

2. *Confidence/Predictability*

"The Germans are now sincere Europeans in whom one can have confidence."

Agree	53 percent
Disagree	25 percent
No Opinion	22 percent
	100

"The Germans are looking to profit from European political unity by dominating their neighbors."

Agree	24 percent
Disagree	45 percent
No Opinion	31 percent
	100

3. *Mutual Identification*

"Among the following peoples, which have a way of life most resembling that of the French?"

Germans	34 percent
Americans	4 percent
English	5 percent
Italians	28 percent
None	9 percent
Don't know	20 percent
	100

"And which have ways of life that least resemble those of Frenchmen?"

Germans	7 percent
Americans	42 percent
British	22 percent
Italians	8 percent
None	2 percent
Don't know	19 percent
	100

TABLE 2—Continued

3. *Mutual Identification* (Continued)

"If a European Union does come into existence one day, which countries, in your opinion, must participate?"

France	51 percent
Belgium	47 percent
Germany	45 percent
Italy	45 percent
Luxembourg	45 percent
Netherlands	44 percent
Switzerland	32 percent
Spain	21 percent
Sweden	21 percent
United Kingdom	33 percent

"The other countries of a European Political Union should help West Germany to gain reunification."

Agree	48 percent
Disagree	22 percent
No Opinion	30 percent
	100

SOURCE: "L'Europe et le nationalisme" (Paris: Société française d'enquêtes par sondage [SOFRES], 1968).

early 1960's.[22] Overall, with poll data indices as a guide, it can be concluded that a marked change in the attitudinal atmosphere surrounding relationships between Frenchmen and West Germans occurred during the years 1954–1965.

Public opinion indices reflecting positive changes in French and West German attitudes are substantively interesting in themselves. But the purpose in presenting them here is methodological. Most of these public opinion trends are indices of international community formation in that they reflect either the presence or the emergence of transnationally shared attributes described in the definition of "community" offered earlier. Perceptions of shared lifestyles are reflected in part 3 of Table 2, as is evidence of mutual identification —a key index of community. Perceptions of shared destiny are hinted at in answers to the question concerning the countries that "must participate" in a European union. Also contained in the public opinion data are three important indices of international community contained in Karl Deutsch's work: 1)

[22] Merritt and Puchala, p. 235; *International Survey XX–15, International Survey XX–16, International Survey XX–17* (Washington: United States Information Agency, 1963, 1964, 1965).

Mutual predictability of behavior is indexed in part 2 of Table 2; 2) mutual responsiveness is indexed in the "German reunification" question; and 3) "security community" is directly indexed in part 1 of Table 2.[23] In varying degrees all of these indices of international community show that community was increasingly evident in Franco-German relations in the 1960's.

What is important for this essay is that while Franco-German community formation was clearly indexed in attitudinal data, it was also unmistakably indexed in transaction flow data.[24] Transaction flow analysis shows that Franco-German transactions increased markedly in volume over multiple ranges during the 1950's and 1960's.

Data in extended time series, recording several ranges of Franco-German international transactions, is available in scattered statistical sources. Five data series are used for demonstration purposes here—1) international trade flows, 1938–1965; 2) international mail flows, 1937–1961; 3) international tourism, 1929–1961; 4) international student exchanges, 1925–1960, and 5) international migration, interwar, postwar, and recent.[25] All but the migration figures are transformed into percentages to show relative proportions of respective international transactions directed through Franco-German channels over time. If Franco-German international community formation were in progress during the postwar era, as the public opinion data suggests, then, according to our paradigm, we should expect to observe increasing Franco-German transactions over multiple ranges. Table 3 exhibits these increases with remarkable clarity.

In absolute value Franco-German trade increased more than 30 times over between 1938 and 1965, with greatest expansion between 1954 and 1965. Proportionally, French purchases of German products accounted for 4.4 percent of the German export market in 1938 but 13.1 percent in 1965. Even more impressively, German purchases in France accounted for 6.7 percent of the French export market in 1938 but 21.5 percent in 1965. Positive shifts in Franco-German mail flow were equally significant between the interwar and postwar periods: Absolute volumes more than quadrupled between 1937 and 1961, and proportional shares likewise increased considerably. Similarly, the tourist flow across the Franco-German border increased by a factor of ap-

---

[23] Cf. Deutsch, *Political Community at the International Level,* pp. 49–54.

[24] Helen Peak, "Problems of Objective Observation," in Leon Festinger and Daniel Katz (ed.), *Research Methods in the Behavioral Sciences* (New York: Dryden Press, 1953), pp. 243–299. Here Helen Peak explains index validation by comparison with an external criterion. The analogous procedure in this essay is to establish "community formation in progress" via public opinion indices and then to show transaction patterns coincident with this.

[25] It must be noted, in fairness to the reader, that the migration figures offered here are of questionable validity. First, migration data was largely nonexistent for periods of several years during test range. But, more than this, there were often great discrepancies in national reportings between emigrants departing and immigrants arriving (although, in actuality, these figures should be identical). To compound problems even further, definitions of "emigrant," and "immigrant" varied from country to country.

TABLE 3. TRENDS IN FRANCO-GERMAN INTERNATIONAL TRANSACTIONS

1. Economic Transactions (Trade Flow as Index)

Date	Total Trade ($ US)	French Exports to West Germany	German Exports to France	Percentage of French Exports to Germany	Percentage of German Exports to France
1938	148.3 million	56.4 million	91.9 million	6.7	4.4
1954	699.0	351.8	347.2	8.8	6.8
1957	1213.6	545.8	667.8	11.3	7.9
1965	3940.5	1990.8	1940.5	21.5	13.1

2. Information Flows (International First Class Mail as Index)

Date	Total Letters Exchanged	France to Germany	Germany to France	Percentage of French Letters Sent to Germany	Percentage of German Letters Sent to France
1937	11.5 million	6.2 million	5.3 million	4.6	4.7
1961	54.5	28.1	26.4	11.7	10.1

3. International Tourism

Date	Total French-German Tourists (000s)	France to Germany	Germany to France	Percentage of French Tourists to Germany	Percentage of German Tourists to France
1929	64.1	28.9	35.2	7.4	3.6
1961	1207.4	475.4	732.0	9.1	8.6

4. International Student Exchange

Date	Approximate Number of Students Exchanged[a]	France to Germany	Germany to France	Percentage of French to Germany	Percentage of Germans to France
1925	b	7	b	1.8	b
1952	608	75	533	5.8	14.4
1955	1151	308	843	27.4	17.5
1960	1545	360	1185	25.2	18.0

TABLE 3—Continued

5. *International Migratory Movements*

Date	Total Movement Across French-German Border	France to Germany	Germany to France
Circa 1934	152[c]	60	92[c]
Circa 1950	2542	682	1660
Circa 1960	14314	9850	4464

SOURCES: UN Document ST/STAT/SER.T *(Direction of International Trade)*, Universal Postal Union, United Nations *Statistical Yearbook*, OEEC, League of Natons, UNESCO, French and German national yearbooks.

[a] Complete records unavailable.

[b] No reliable reportings located for 1920's or 1930's.

[c] Early records of German migration to France are unavailable. However the *Statistisches Jahrbuch für das deutsche Reich* (Berlin: 1934, p. 51) lists 92 Germans going to "other European countries." According to omissions in the German list, this category could include Germans going to France. In any event the total number of Germans going to France in 1934 was less than 92. Therefore, total migratory movement was less than 152.

proximately twenty between 1929 and 1961, student exchanges more than doubled during the 1950's, and migrations increased from virtually zero in 1934 to over 14,000 in 1960. On the whole, Table 3 strongly suggests that the attitudinal changes indicative of emerging Franco-German community displayed in Table 2 were reflected during the 1950's in major absolute and proportional increases in the two peoples' transactions over multiple ranges.

Table 4 was compiled to control the experiment attempted in the compilation of Table 3. While the public opinion data for the 1950's and 1960's tends to evidence Franco-German community formation, the same is not true with regard to France and the United Kingdom. It would be misleading to label the relationship between Frenchmen and Britons as "estrangement" since levels of mutual amity and confidence have remained high throughout the postwar era.[26] But these levels have not been increasing generally, and in very recent years amity levels have begun to deteriorate. In addition, part 3 of Table 2 indicates that Frenchmen mutually identify with Britons only to a very limited extent. Scant evidence suggests reciprocal British coolness toward France and Frenchmen. In all, we might posit that the intensity of Franco-British international community has not increased in the postwar era, and, if anything, it may have deteriorated. This being the case, we would expect little

[26] Merritt and Puchala, pp. 236 and 241; also *International Survey XX–15, XX–16 and XX–17*.

TABLE 4. TRENDS IN FRANCO-BRITISH INTERNATIONAL TRANSACTIONS

1. *Economic Transactions* (Trade Flow as Index)

Date	Total Trade ($ US)	French Exports to UK	British Exports to France	Percentage of French Exports to UK	Percentage of British Exports to France
1938	196.0 million	103.4 million	92.6 million	12.4	4.6
1954	405.1	241.4	163.7	6.0	2.8
1957	510.9	279.6	231.3	5.7	2.6
1965	1005.5	463.9	541.6	4.9	4.7

2. *Information Flows* (International First Class Mail as Index)

Date	Total Letters Exchanged	France to Britain	Britain to France	Percentage of French Letters Sent to Britain	Percentage of British Letters Sent to France
1937	29.3 million	16.8 million	12.5 million	12.5	7.6
1961	35.1	21.2	13.9	8.5	4.3

3. *International Tourism*

Date	Total French-UK Tourists (000s)	France to Britain	Britain to France	Percentage of French Tourists to Britain	Percentage of British Tourists to France
1929	936.7	55.7	881.9	14.2	55.0
1961	939.7	219.7	720.0	5.1	18.5

4. *International Student Exchange*

Date	Approximate Number of Students Exchanged[a]	France to Britain	Britain to France	Percentage of French to Britain	Percentage of British to France
1925	781	42	739	9.9	28.5
1952	813	81	732	6.3	30.0
1957	711	88	623	7.2	27.0
1960	936	53	883	3.4	27.0

SOURCES: See Table 3.

[a] Complete records are unavailable.

increase in Franco-British international transactions over time and possibly some decrease. Table 4 paints the expected picture vividly.

While it is certainly true that total volumes of Franco-British transactions increased over time in several ranges, these increases tended to reflect general trends in the "shrinking of the world" rather than the emerging or intensifying of Franco-British community bonds. Significantly, and much in contrast to Franco-German trends, respective relative proportions of French and British shared transactions for the most part declined between the interwar and the postwar periods and in the postwar period itself. What this means is that Frenchmen and Britons have been paying increasingly less attention to each other over a fairly broad transaction range. Each people has apparently come to prefer the attentions of other partners. Therefore, it would appear again that the transaction flows meaningfully reflect the state of international community formation in a bilateral case. If the transaction trends are a guide, Franco-British community may be described as weak, and community formation should be reported "faltering."

Community Formation in Western Europe: Internal Intensification, External Discontinuity, and the Case of the "Six"

According to the paradigm sketched earlier, in charting community formation with transaction flow indices we should expect to observe not only increasing internalization of transactions but also more clearly marked external discontinuity. Table 3 evidences discontinuity by inference. Certainly if Frenchmen and Germans are paying more relative attention to each other, they must be paying less attention to other peoples. However, these "other peoples" are by and large not other peoples of the European Economic Community (EEC). In fact, both Frenchmen and West Germans have been "submerging" to an extent in the larger international community forming in the EEC region. Consequently, the most dramatic pattern of emerging discontinuities in transaction flow in Western Europe is not one that distinguishes France and West Germany from their immediate neighbors but rather one that distinguishes the EEC from its peripheral neighbors. Table 5 begins to display this pattern of discontinuities. The relative acceptance index is used in Table 5 because of this statistic's facility for concisely describing internal/external relationships within and between multistate transacting units.

Parts 1 and 2 of Table 5 test for, and essentially exhibit, increasing internalization of transactions among the "six." Very simply interpreted, the figures in these sections respond to the question, "How much more or less transaction was there between EEC members than might have been expected on the basis of these members' and the community's share of total world transactions?" In all cases, save Italy (interestingly), the answer is the same. Transactions with the community were increasing for each member over time,

TABLE 5. EMERGING EXTERNAL DISTINCTION OF THE "SIX" AS A TRANSACTION NETWORK

1. *Region-to-Country Relative Acceptance of Exports, 1938, 1954, 1963*

from the "Six" to:	1938	1954	1963
a. France	.2	·3	·7
b. Germany	·5	·9	·9
c. Belgium-Luxembourg	1.0	1.4	1.2
d. Netherlands	1.0	1.0	1.7
e. Italy	·7	·4	·3

2. *Country-to-Region Relative Acceptance of Exports, 1938, 1954, 1963*

from (Country) to "Six":	1938	1954	1963
a. France	·4	·4	.6
b. Germany	·5	·9	.8
c. Belgium-Luxembourg	1.0	1.4	1.0
d. Netherlands	·7	1.1	·9
e. Italy	·5	·3	·5

3. *Region-to-Periphery; Periphery-to-Region Relative Acceptance of Exports, 1938, 1954, 1963*

	1938	1954	1963
a. Six-to-Six	.6	.8	.8
b. Six-to-Scandinavia	·7	·7	.1
c. Scandinavia-to-Six	.2	.2	.1
d. Six-to-Anglo-American Area	−·5	−·5	−.6
e. Anglo-American Area-to-Six	−·5	−·4	−·5
f. Six-to-World beyond Atlantic Area	.1	−.1	−.1
g. World beyond Atlantic Area-to-Six	.0	−.1	−.1

4. *Region-to-Country Relative Acceptance of Mail, 1937, 1955, 1961*

from "Six" to:	1937	1955	1961
a. France	.2	·4	1·3
b. Germany	.1	.6	·3
c. Belgium-Luxembourg	1.1	1.1	·9
d. Netherlands	.6	·5	.6
e. Italy	.2	·7	·3

5. *Country-to-Region Relative Acceptance of Mail, 1937, 1955, 1961*

from (Country) to "Six":	1937	1955	1961
a. France	.1	·9	·5
b. Germany	−.1	·3	·4
c. Belgium-Luxembourg	1.4	1·3	1.2
d. Netherlands	.6	·5	.6
e. Italy	·3	.1	·5

TABLE 5—Continued

6. *Region-to-Periphery; Periphery-to-Region Relative Acceptance of Mail, 1937, 1955, 1961*

	1937	*1955*	*1961*
a. Six-to-Six	.3	.6	.9
b. Six-to-Scandinavia	.2	.0	.0
c. Scandinavia-to-Six	.0	.0	−.1
d. Six-to-United Kingdom	−.4	−.5	−.5
e. United Kingdom-to-Six	−.4	−.5	−.5
f. Six-to-World beyond Atlantic Area	.1	−.1	−.1
g. World beyond Atlantic Area-to-Six	.1	.0	.1

SOURCES: United Nations, *Direction of International Trade;* Universal Postal Union, *Statistique des expéditions dans le service international.*

sometimes dramatically. Note especially how West Germany actually *entered* Western Europe between 1938 and 1960!

Parts 3 and 4 of Table 5 test for, and exhibit, external discontinuities between the EEC and its periphery. In contrast to the intensifying transactions noted between the "six," levels of relative acceptance between the "six" and Scandinavia declined abruptly in the postwar period. Similarly, relative acceptance in Continental-British-American and in Continental-British channels has always been lower than expected, and here RA scores continue their decline in the postwar period. Broadening the perspective, transactions between the "six" (i.e., Europe) and the non-Western world never achieved very high levels, but, still, these levels were slightly higher than expected during the interwar period (when colonies were parts of European transaction systems). Most RA scores became negative, however, in transactions between the "six" and the "world beyond the Atlantic area" after World War II.

While Table 5 exhibits internal/external patterns in only two transaction ranges, trade and mail, trends exhibited strongly suggest a matching of increasing internal intensity and external discontinuity for the "six" in the postwar period. In short, the transaction trends suggest community formation in progress.

Transaction Analysis and Political Amalgamation

For all that might be said for the usefulness of transaction flow indices in the charting of international community formation, it must be remembered that "community formation" and "regional integration" are neither semantically synonymous, conceptually congruent, nor empirically inseparable. As noted and underlined, regional integration, most abstractly described, involves community formation *plus* political amalgamation. Hence, given the current level of understanding concerning the regional integration phenomenon, one

can get theoretically confused and empirically nowhere in trying to draw conclusions about overall regional integration or about political amalgamation
on the basis of community formation indices.[27] More directly to the point, the
kinds of transaction flow analyses that serve well in the study of international
community formation are, for the most part, inappropriate for the study of
international political amalgamation. As will be shown though, other kinds
of transaction flow analyses can be extremely useful in the study of international political amalgamation.

While models of nationalism guide transaction approaches to community
formation, "federal government" is the analytical prototype for the study of
political amalgamation.[28] That is, political amalgamation during regional integration may be thought of as movement toward a political system in which
initially separate units are linked under a central government. Subunit autonomy is curtailed in varying degrees under various federal arrangements.
Analytically the "federal" paradigm calls for 1) central political decisionmaking bodies with jurisdiction and authority that encompasses internal relations
among federated subunits and external relations with "third" parties and 2)
a politics of reward allocation at the federal level or, in structural-functional
terms, a full set of input and output functions performed in a supranational
arena.[29]

Political amalgamation during regional integration need not necessarily result in a political federation. Amalgamation processes may terminate at stages
of political development short of full federation. Nevertheless, in examining
political interactions during regional integration it is helpful to hold up the
federal model as an "ideal type," to treat federation as a set of quantitative
variables, and to evaluate amalgamation in terms of *degrees of federalism*
emergent and present in regional institutionalization and rulemaking processes.

The pathway into political amalgamation via transaction analysis follows
from the commonsense proposition that amalgamation has to do with the variety, quality, and directions of political dealings between merging political

[27] Ernst B. Haas, Philippe C. Schmitter, Karl W. Deutsch, Joseph S. Nye, Donald J. Puchala, and
others, have all attempted to isolate and explain relationships between community formation and political amalgamation during regional integration. Indefiniteness on the part of most of these authors,
and disagreement between them, however, underline the fact that theoretical understanding in this
area remains incomplete. Cf. Ernst B. Haas and Philippe C. Schmitter, "Economics and Differential Patterns of Political Integration: Projections about Unity in Latin America," *International Organization*, Autumn 1964 (Vol. 18, No. 4), pp. 705–737; Karl W. Deutsch, and others, *Political Community and the North Atlantic Area;* J. S. Nye, "Patterns and Catalysts in Regional Integration," in
Joseph S. Nye, Jr. (ed.), *International Regionalism: Readings* (Boston: Little, Brown and Co., 1968), pp.
333–349; Nye, *International Organization*, Vol. 22, No. 4, pp. 855–880; Donald J. Puchala, *International
Studies Quarterly*, Vol. 12, No. 1, pp. 38–64.

[28] K. C. Wheare, *Federal Government* (London: Oxford University Press [under the auspices of the
Royal Institute of International Affairs], 1946), passim.

[29] See, for example, Leon N. Lindberg, "Decision Making and Integration in the European Community," *International Organization*, Winter 1965 (Vol. 19, No. 1), pp. 56–80.

units and between central decisionmaking organizations and constituent subunits. To index and map the course of political amalgamation during regional
integration one assumes, and then searches for, indicative channels and patterns of *political* transaction. More specifically, one might assume and search
for:

1) *The initiation and expansion of central institutional channels for political transaction flow.* While the creation of regional institutions in itself indicates little concerning the volume or content of transactions that flow through
institutional channels, patterns of institutionalization do nonetheless reflect
the structure of emergent regional political systems. In short, who is likely
to be "in" and who is likely to be "out" of a possible federation is reflected
in patterns of "who shares how many institutional partnerships with whom."

2) *The channeling of widening ranges of international political transactions
through institutional networks.* Progress toward regional government is indexed by the degree to which merging units are able to initiate and use standardized procedures for cooperation, coordination, and conflict resolution.
Relatedly, and importantly, progress toward regional government is indexed
by the degree to which institutional channels actually facilitate cooperation,
coordination, and conflict resolution. In short, international organization
should represent a step away from the anarchy of international politics. Quantitatively, increased channeling through organizational networks would show
in increasing ratios of political transactions conducted within organizations
to political transactions conducted outside of them. Institutional functioning
in cooperation, coordination, and conflict resolution would show in relative
frequencies of cooperative and competitive outcomes from transactions directed through institutional channels. "Spillover," "spill-around," and "spill-
back" all have to do, descriptively, with the number and kinds of political
transactions channeled through international institutions over time. Numbers
can be counted, kinds can be identified, and trends in "spill" can be mapped
quantitatively.

3) *Qualitative and quantitative expansion of transnational transactions between nongovernmental political groups and increasing contacts between these
groups and regional rulemaking institutions.* Polity formation aspects of international political amalgamation have to do with the emergence and growth
of political interaction between groups in a supranational arena.[30] This being
the case, if political amalgamation is in progress, we may expect: 1) more contacts between national political groups across national lines (i.e., more meetings, conferences, coalitions, dialogues, debates, etc.); 2) increasing variety
in the substance of transnational political contacts between nongovernmental

---

[30] Ernst B. Haas, *The Uniting of Europe: Political, Social, and Economic Forces, 1950–1957* (Stanford,
Calif: Stanford University Press, 1958), passim; Leon N. Lindberg, *The Political Dynamics of European
Economic Integration* (Stanford, Calif: Stanford University Press, 1963), passim.

groups; 3) increasing contacts between nongovernmental groups and regional decisionmaking bodies; and 4) increasing variety in the substance of these contacts.

As alluded to earlier, techniques for studying international political amalgamation via transaction analysis differ from those used to index and chart community formation. Wheras data for community formation studies by and large comes "ready made" in the form of statistical reports published by national and international agencies, data appropriate for systematically studying amalgamation must for the most part be gleaned and "hardened" from historical documentary materials.[31] Through day-by-day scrutiny of the historical record the transaction analyst, focusing on political amalgamation, can reduce episodes in relations between states and between political groups to discrete political transactions of varying direction, substance, and tone. Once transactions have been isolated and separated, they can be analytically assembled in various ways to test different hypotheses concerning international political amalgamation.

The analysis offered below demonstrates transactional techniques applied to testing three hypotheses concerning political amalgamation in Western Europe. It must be noted that analysis here is not a comprehensive test of the federal paradigm since no data is shown that reflects communications patterns of subnational groups. Hence polity formation does not get tested.[32] Nevertheless the trends in institutionalization and diplomatic interaction are suggestive of the speed, direction, and extent of international amalgamation on the continent in recent years.

Transaction Analysis and Political Amalgamation in Western Europe

Entry into the current debate about the political future of Western Europe tends to be granted to analysts who can present evidence showing either that

---

[31] Notable progress in "data-making" concerning political interactions between states has been made under the auspices of the World Event/Interaction Study (WEIS) directed by Charles A. McClelland at the University of Southern California. Cf., for example, Charles A. McClelland, "Access to Berlin: The Quantity and Variety of Events, 1948–1963," in Singer, pp. 159–186. Also see Charles A. McClelland, "International Interaction Analysis: Basic Research and Some Practical Applications," Department of International Relations, University of Southern California, November 1968. (Mimeographed.) Relatedly, see Alvin Richman, *A Scale of Events along the Conflict-Cooperation Continuum* (Research Monograph Series No. 10) (Philadelphia: Foreign Policy Research Institute, University of Pennsylvania, 1967), and Lincoln E. Moses, and others, "Scaling Data on Inter-Nation Action," *Science*, May 26, 1967 (Vol. 156, No. 3778), pp. 1054–1059.

[32] Moreover untested are many hypotheses generated in the functionalist analysis of decisionmaking at the international level at which communications between subnational groups and between them and supranational executives become elements of the dynamics of international amalgamation. While the task of data collection would be enormous, data showing who communicates with whom, when, and about what at the level of subnational groups could be extremely enlightening. It is conceivable that such data could provide reliable indices for "spillover" and its variants for "task expansion" and other functional concepts. For Western Europe the *Yearbook of International Organizations* lists nongovernmental organizations and thereby gives a hint of the complexity of the regional polity. Beyond this, the *Bulletin* of the European Economic Community lists meetings, personnel flows, contact with the commission, etc. Still, the job of turning the *Bulletin* listings into systematic data series is formidable.

political amalgamation on the Continent has halted or, on the other hand, that political amalgamation has been making headway despite Gaullist, post-Gaullist, and other obstacles. Tables 6, 7, and 8 are entry tickets into this debate. The data in the tables is exhibited to test three hypotheses concerning political amalgamation between France and West Germany particularly but also between the "six" by implication. The hypotheses follow from the amalgamation paradigm already discussed:

1) If political amalgamation were in progress, this would be evidenced by the emergence and proliferation of institutional channels of political transaction;

2) If political amalgamation were in progress, this would be evidenced by the direction of increasing proportions of intraregional political transactions through regional institutional networks;

3) If political amalgamation were in progress, this would be evidenced by increasing cooperation and conflict resolution among states (and nongovernmental groups) facilitated via institutional channels.

1. POLITICAL AMALGAMATION AND PROLIFERATING CHANNELS OF INSTITUTIONAL TRANSACTION. Table 6 lends affirmation to hypothesis number one. By assembling data concerning joint memberships in regional organizations in matrix format and carrying the arrangement through time the proliferation of institutional channels politically interlinking the "six" stands out. Moreover, closely comparing the matrix for 1950 with the one for 1964 underlines especially the remarkable growth of Franco-German organizational links— from seven joint memberships in 1950 to 27 in 1964.[33] Hence, formal channels for routinized political transaction, for cooperation, and for conflict resolution opened steadily on the Continent between 1950 and 1964.

2. POLITICAL AMALGAMATION AND THE VOLUME OF INTRAINSTITUTIONAL TRANSACTION. Table 7 shows in a rather crude, but suggestive, way what exactly was passing through the Franco-German institutional network during the 1950's and early 1960's. For contrast, Table 8 exhibits patterns of Franco-British intrainstitutional and extrainstitutional transactions for the same period.

The "political transactions" recorded in the tables were isolated from the running chronology of world events reported in *Keesing's Contemporary Archives*. Recording followed the procedures of "event/interaction analysis."[34]

---

[33] Since a number of relationships in highly technical organizations were omitted from counting here, the total of 27 overlapping memberships in 1964 actually understates the extensiveness of Franco-German institutional ties.

[34] Very little material has thus far been published concerning techniques of "event/interaction analysis." The interested reader is advised to procure mimeographed materials currently available. See, for example, Charles A. McClelland, "International Interaction Analysis"; Donald J. Puchala, "Recording Diplomatic Interactions," paper prepared for the Workshop in Interaction Analysis at the annual convention of the American Political Science Association, New York, September 1969.

TABLE 6. FREQUENCY OF MUTUAL MEMBERSHIP IN REGIONAL ORGANIZATIONS

1950	United Kingdom	Belgium	Luxembourg	Netherlands	Germany	France	Italy	Switzerland	Sweden	Denmark	Norway	Iceland
United Kingdom		9	7	9	6	9	7	6	7	8	8	4
Belgium			10	11	7	11	8	7	6	7	7	4
Luxembourg				9	5	9	7	5	5	6	6	3
Netherlands					7	11	8	7	6	7	7	4
Germany						7	6	7	5	5	5	3
France							8	7	6	7	7	4
Italy								6	6	7	7	4
Switzerland									5	5	5	3
Sweden										7	7	3
Denmark											8	4
Norway												4
Iceland												

1964	United Kingdom	Belgium	Luxembourg	Netherlands	Germany	France	Italy	Switzerland	Sweden	Denmark	Norway	Iceland	Finland
United Kingdom		14	12	14	14	14	13	11	12	13	13	7	2
Belgium			25	26	24	24	22	12	12	13	13	8	2
Luxembourg				24	22	23	20	10	11	13	13	6	2
Netherlands					24	24	22	12	12	14	14	7	2
Germany						27	23	13	12	13	13	8	2
France							23	13	12	13	13	7	2
Italy								12	12	13	13	6	2
Switzerland									11	11	11	5	2
Sweden										16	16	8	4
Denmark											17	10	4
Norway												9	4
Iceland													3

SOURCE: *Yearbook of International Organizations* (Brussels: Union of International Association); A. H. Robertson, *European Institutions: Co-Operation: Integration: Unification* (New York: Frederick A. Praeger, 1958).

TABLE 7. INSTITUTIONALIZATION IN FRANCO-GERMAN POLITICAL TRANSACTIONS, 1952–1965

1. *Intrainstitutional and Extrainstitutional Political Transactions*

Period	Intrainstitutional		Extrainstitutional		Total	
	Number	Percentage	Number	Percentage	Number	Percentage
1952–1958	66	32.8	138	67.2	204	100
1959–1965	135	62.2	82	37.8	217	100

$$X^2 = 36.9$$
$$p = .001$$

2. *Intrainstitutional and Extrainstitutional Political Transactions—Expanded Frequency Distribution*

Period	Intrainstitutional		Extrainstitutional		Total	
	Number	Percentage	Number	Percentage	Number	Percentage
1952–1954	39	34	75	66	114	100
1955–1957	21	32	45	68	66	100
1958–1960	29	48	32	52	61	100
1961–1963	63	70	27	30	90	100
1964–1965	52	58	38	42	90	100

3. *The Proportional Distribution of Franco-German Organizational and Organization-Related Activity, 1952–1965*

Period	Establishment of Organizational Linkages		Internal Operations of Existing Organization		
	Cooperation	Conflict	Cooperation	Conflict	
	Percentage	Percentage	Percentage	Percentage	
1952–1954	41	38	21	0	100
1955–1957	65	13	13	9	100
1958–1960	14	0	86	0	100
1961–1963	24	1	40	35	100
1964–1965	8	4	26	62	100

TABLE 8. INSTITUTIONALIZATION IN FRANCO-BRITISH POLITICAL TRANSACTIONS, 1952–1965

1. Intrainstitutional and Extrainstitutional Political Transactions

Period	Intrainstitutional		Extrainstitutional		Total	
	Number	Percentage	Number	Percentage	Number	Percentage
1952–1958	81	43.5	105	56.5	186	100
1959–1965	77	52.1	70	47.9	147	100

$$X^2 = 5.2$$
Not Significant

2. Intrainstitutional and Extrainstitutional Political Transactions—Expanded Frequency Distribution

Period	Intrainstitutional		Extrainstitutional		Total	
	Number	Percentage	Number	Percentage	Number	Percentage
1952–1954	38	58	28	42	66	100
1955–1957	26	31	58	69	84	100
1958–1960	29	39	45	61	74	100
1961–1963	57	70	24	30	81	100
1964–1965	8	29	20	71	28	100

$$X^2 = 30.4$$
$$p = .001$$

Briefly, the "event/interaction" technique involves: 1) reducing international political transactions to elemental units of state behavior, 2) observing and recording attributes of behavioral units, and 3) tabulating and cross-tabulating behavior and attribute frequencies in order to define patterns of international political behavior. For purposes of this presentation each act of French, West German, and British international behavior reported in *Keesing's* between 1952 and 1965 was identified as one of 22 possible types of behavior—eleven *cooperative* and eleven *competitive*. Acts of cooperative behavior included statements or gestures of agreement, support, assurance, goodwill, praise, and other varieties. Competitive behavior included disruptive initiatives, rebuffs, rebuttals, threats, warnings, impasses, and other acts.[35] In addition to noting variety of action, each international exchange was coded with respect to its

---

[35] Operational definitions and coding procedures for this event/interaction analysis are described and discussed in the appendix to Puchala, *International Organization*, Vol. 24, No. 2, pp. 203–208.

date of occurrence, its initiator and its target, and its substance or issue of concern. The result of scrutinizing some fourteen years of day-to-day European diplomatic history was a *Western European Interaction Data Collection*[36] that includes several hundred records of political transactions in Franco-German, Franco-British, and Anglo-German channels.

The headings "intrainstitutional" and "extrainstitutional" used in tables 7 and 8 have specific meanings under the scheme of the *Western European Interaction Data Collection*. "Intrainstitutional" matters include all recorded transactions concerning the establishment (or proposed establishment) of the European Coal and Steel Community (ECSC), the European defense community, the European political community, the European Economic Community, the European Atomic Energy Community (EURATOM), the European free trade area, the European Free Trade Association (EFTA), and the Gaullist union of states. These matters also include transactions concerning the operations of the established institutions just listed, plus NATO and the Organization for European Economic Cooperation/Organization for Economic Cooperation and Development, plus the establishment and operations of a number of smaller technical organizations. "Extrainstitutional" matters concerned all issues between France and West Germany and France and the United Kingdom not related to the establishment or operations of institutions, and otherwise handled outside of institutional channels.

The general conclusion that follows from Table 7, buttressed by comparison with Table 8, is that steadily increasing proportions of Franco-German political transactions were channeled through the European organizational network over time. In fact, the ratio of intrainstitutional to extrainstitutional political transactions for France and West Germany reversed between 1952 and 1965. *The European institutional arena steadily became the prime arena for Franco-German political transaction.* Table 8 suggests that this was generally not the case as far as Franco-British transactions were concerned. Proportionally, there appears a slight movement toward increased Franco-British institutional transactions in the early 1960's, but this had to do mainly with the ill-fated British bid for entry into the EEC. Moreover, even with the flurry of activity surrounding the entry bid Franco-British institutional transactions never attained a level high enough to produce statistical significance in comparison with extrainstitutional transaction volumes.

Part 3 in Table 7 is the test of hypothesis number three cited earlier, in which increasing cooperation and conflict resolution via institutional channels were assumed to indicate political amalgamation in progress. If the hypothesis is true, then Table 7 reflects developing difficulty for Franco-German amalgamation beginning in the period 1961–1963 and continuing to the end of the data series of 1965. After a halcyon period between 1958 and 1960 in which

---

[36] Puchala, "Recording Diplomatic Interaction."

14 percent of Franco-German intrainstitutional transactions concerned cooperation in establishing new organizations and 86 percent concerned cooperation in operating established ones, a new period of difficulty developed wherein conflict concerning the operation of established institutions occupied increasing proportions of French and German political attention. In sum, the transaction evidence—at least up to 1965—suggests that regional institutions were faltering in facilitating Franco-German cooperation and conflict resolution in the early 1960's. This somewhat clouds any positive prognosis for political amalgamation on the Continent in the immediate future.

Transaction Analysis and the Causal Dynamics of Regional Integration

Emphasis in this article upon the *descriptive* utility of transaction approaches in the study of regional integration has been deliberate. While arguments and illustrations presented above are by no means definitive, they are suggestive of the usefulness of transaction techniques for monitoring the progress of regional integration in various dimensions. By and large, the transaction indices are as valid as the descriptive theories and models that prompt their introduction into analysis and as reliable as the data bases that permit their computation. If the "proof of the pudding" must be in the eating, this author is willing to posit that transaction flow patterns, uncovered in transaction analysis, tell the story of Western European integration rather well.[37]

However, it cannot be underlined too strongly that there is a major difference between *describing* regional integration and *explaining* it. More directly to the point, transaction flows reflect regional integration. Heightened and broadened levels of transactions between governments, political groups, and populations are parts of regional integration. *But transaction flows do not cause regional integration.* Moreover, since it is not entirely clear, either theoretically or empirically, exactly what causes, accelerates, or reverses transaction flows, there is some risk in using transaction analysis *predictively* in integration studies.

Still, if use is cautious and critical and when care is taken to maintain conceptual distinctions between indices and phenomena indexed, transaction flow analysis may shed light upon the causal dyamics of regional integration:

First, several of the questions currently outstanding in regional integration theory concern patterns of priority and precondition in the process of multidimensional merger. What comes before or after what with respect to community formation, political amalgamation, and subprocesses included under these headings constitutes one set of puzzles for current research. What *must*

---

[37] Donald J. Puchala, "Western European Integration: Progress and Prospects" (Ph.D. dissertation, Department of Political Science, Yale University, 1966).

happen before something else happens in regional integration constitutes a second set of related problems. Since it is possible to operationalize and quantitatively trace several different theoretical dimensions of regional integration with different transaction flow indices, it may become possible to isolate patterns of priority by comparing various transaction trends. Was the upswing in Franco-German community formation registered in the indices before or after the upswing in institutionalization, or was there a "feedback" effect? Furthermore, it may also become possible, through comparative case studies, each developed from transaction approaches, to ultimately answer questions about preconditions during regional integration.

Second, if it becomes possible to say a great deal more about the substance of international transactions in a systematic way and if more is uncovered concerning transnational impacts of transactions, a way may be opened to testing and possibly proving the validity of social and cultural learning theories that have been advanced to explain regional integration.[38] If stimuli and responses could be operationalized in terms of transaction indicators and flow patterns, it may become empirically possible to detect relationships between input and output among societal and governmental systems, and in so doing to discern the accuracy of learning theoretical explanations of these input-output linkages.

In sum, research in regional integration over several years has accomplished a great deal in the descriptive realm. Part of this accomplishment is to be credited to the application of transaction flow analysis to regional integration problems. At present, most of those primarily concerned with regional integration are asking causal questions. There is strong reason to believe that transaction flow analysis can and will contribute to answering these questions.

[38] Henry Teune, "The Learning of Integrative Habits," in Philip E. Jacob and James V. Toscano (ed.), *The Integration of Political Communities* (Philadelphia: J. B. Lippincott, 1964), pp. 247–282.

4

Public Opinion and Regional Integration

RONALD INGLEHART

I. PUBLIC PREFERENCES AND NATIONAL DECISIONMAKING

For the time being, at least, survey data is relevant to the study of regional integration chiefly insofar as it gives an indication of the influence of the public (and various elite groups) on the decisions of the respective national governments—and vice versa. As integration progresses in given regions our focus may change, and we may become primarily interested in the degree to which given groups direct support or demands toward supranational institutions. But for the present the basic question seems to be:

> To what extent do public preferences constitute an effective influence on a given set of national decisionmakers, encouraging them to make decisions which increase (or diminish) regional integration?

In attempting to answer this basic question we are led to examine the nature of elite-mass linkages and to attempt to specify the conditions under which public opinion is likely to play a relatively important, or relatively insignificant, role. In regard to our basic question one might even ask, "Does the public have *any* influence on foreign policy decisions?" It seems to us that the answer is "yes" although the degree of influence can vary widely. To the extent that a given polity permits free elections, referenda, and demonstrations in the streets, the public can exert pressure on their decisionmakers. It seems reasonably evident, for example, that the American public had a significant influence on the 1968 decision to halt the bombing in the Democratic Republic of Vietnam (North Vietnam) and on President Lyndon Johnson's decision not to seek reelection. Similarly, one of the burning questions in British politics recently was whether public opinion would cause Prime Minister Harold Wilson to reverse his stand in favor of entry into the European Economic Community (EEC). The sudden decision to hold general elections in the spring of 1970 diminished the immediacy of this pressure, but by no means excludes it as a factor bearing on the negotiations. Even in an extreme situa-

RONALD INGLEHART is assistant professor of political science at the University of Michigan, Ann Arbor.

tion, such as that of the Czechoslovak Socialist Republic today, occupied by foreign troops, it would appear that the Czech public is able to effect at least a slight modification in the behavior of their decisionmakers through such techniques as work slowdowns. The vital question, then, is the empirical one, "How much influence—and under what conditions?" This question is by no means easy to answer.

For one thing, the direction of causality is not usually clear. If it is true that public preferences can generally exert at least some degree of pressure on national decisionmakers, it seems equally evident that opinion leaders can often influence public opinion. Thus, the Labor Party's reversal of position regarding entry into the Common Market seems to have led a number of members of the Labor electorate to modify their views (at least temporarily): Prior to this decision Labor supporters were less favorable to entry than was the Conservative electorate; afterward, they were relatively *more* favorable. Conversely, Charles de Gaulle's opposition to supranational European integration during his last several years in power may have led his electorate to migrate from a position of one of the groups most favorable to European integration to a rank, in 1968, of least favorable. The change was only relative (a majority of Gaullists were still favorable) and was probably the result of his losing the support of a certain number of pro-European voters as well as a reflection of his personal influence. Nevertheless, one suspects that the phenomenon was at least partially a case of influence from the top down. We see the relationship between public preferences and political decisionmakers, then, in terms of a feedback model.[1] But the relative importance of the societal input is conditioned by at least three main factors:

1) *The structure of the national decisionmaking institutions:* Are they pluralistic or monolithic? To the extent that there is institutionalized competition between alternative groups of decisionmakers they are likely to bid against each other for societal support. In the Union of Soviet Socialist Republics, for example, during succession struggles various members of a collective leadership have frequently tried to mobilize support from lower levels of the party hierarchy or from the broader public in order to strengthen their position; with the consolidation of power in the hands of a given leader, fewer concessions seem to be made to the preferences of societal groups and a harder line may be taken behind a single policy.

   The norms and perceptions of elite decisionmakers are also important. A closed, hierarchical decision structure seems likely to be reinforced by norms which play down the importance and legitimacy of independent inputs from the public: Mass demonstrations of support may be encour-

[1] See David Easton, *A Systems Analysis of Political Life* (New York: John Wiley & Sons, 1967), for a discussion of some basic concepts underlying our analysis.

aged, but this represents manipulation of the public more than influence by the public. To the extent that the leaders of such a system are guided by an explicit or implicit political ideology, deference to public preferences is of secondary importance since the leaders already *know* what is best for the public. Their appraisal of the public interest may be correct; in any case, it is formed more in reference to the ideologues' internalized values and perceptions than on the basis of an investigation of the distribution of preferences in the society. Public opinion polling techniques are likely to be viewed as of little value.

The same tendency seems to apply to political systems having institutionalized competition, provided the elite groups can maintain cohesion on a given issue: As long as no genuine alternative is offered to the public, its influence can be minor. Thus, in the face of overwhelming public support for a return to capital punishment British political party leaders maintained a more or less solid front in rejecting it recently; similarly, as long as all three leading parties remain committed to entry into the Common Market, none of them risks paying a political price for their stand. The situation would be quite different if one of them broke the cartel.

2) *The distribution of political skills within the society.* In virtually all modern societies there exists a stratum of individuals who play a largely passive role in the national decisionmaking process. One indication of the existence of this group is the presence, in public opinion survey results, of respondents who consistently give no opinion about national issues and who seem likely to be nonvoters. The relative size of this stratum apparently varies considerably from one society to another; within Western Europe, for example, it tends to be larger among samples of the Italian public than among the French public and smaller still among the British public. Within given nations it may vary from region to region: The "no opinion" stratum seems to be larger in southern Italy and the islands than in the rest of Italy. In regard to given issues this stratum could be seen as consisting of those individuals who lack interest in, and knowledge about, the given topic. One might distinguish between the uninformed public and the informed public—or the "attentive public," to use James Rosenau's term.[2] This could be a short-term distinction, the parameters of which might be changed substantially by an information campaign. But this stratum may also reflect a long-term difference: an absence of basic political skills which enable an individual to participate effectively in the politics of an extensive polity. Perhaps the most basic of these skills is literacy—but it is also

[2] See James N. Rosenau, *Public Opinion and Foreign Policy: An Operational Formulation* (New York: Random-House, 1961).

a matter of a whole group of formative experiences which provide the habits and knowledge needed to cope with the bureaucratic organizations which make most of the national-level decisions in modern societies. Karl Deutsch's distinction between the "politically relevant"[3] and "politically irrelevant" segments of society is useful to describe the long-term situation. In settings where most of the public remains "parochial"[4] in its skills and orientation public opinion data is of little significance to the study of regional integration (although surveys of elite attitudes may be useful). It would seem that decisionmaking in regard to regional integration in East Africa, for example, remains the province of a very restricted elite.[5] In Western Europe, by comparison, public opinion seems to have a greater potential influence.

3) *The degree to which the given decision relates to deep-seated values among the public or evokes only relatively superficial feelings.* Here again, we must attempt to distinguish between a feedback relationship based on short-term and long-term effects. There is substantial evidence that certain aspects of an individual's political orientations tend to be formed relatively early in life and to persist thereafter with a relatively low probability of change. Specific age cohorts whose basic orientations are formed under conditions differing from those shaping the socialization of other cohorts may therefore retain a distinctive outlook over a period of years. The formation of political party identification seems to fit this pattern: Levels of support for a given party may fluctuate, but there is an underlying tendency for given individuals to prefer a given party consistently over time. Angus Campbell, Philip Converse, Warren Miller, and Donald Stokes, for example, have pointed to the existence of certain age cohorts which have tended to show a relatively high proportion of vote for the Democratic Party over time; they explain this in terms of formative experiences associated with the New Deal.[6] David Butler and Donald Stokes find evidence of a somewhat similar phenomenon among the British Labor Party electorate which they attribute to the lasting effect of formative experiences associated with World War II.[7]

An individual's sense of national identity also seems to have a tendency to be formed early and to persist through later life. Jean Piaget

[3] See Karl Deutsch, "Social Mobilization and Political Development," *American Political Science Review*, June 1961 (Vol. 55, No. 2), pp. 497–502; cf. Deutsch, *Nationalism and Social Communication: An Inquiry Into the Foundations of Nationality* (Cambridge, Mass: M.I.T. Press, 1966).

[4] See Daniel Lerner, *The Passing of Traditional Society: Modernizing the Middle East* (New York: Free Press of Glencoe, 1958).

[5] See Joseph Nye in this volume.

[6] See Angus Campbell, and others, *The American Voter* (New York: John Wiley & Sons [for the Survey Research Center, Institute for Social Research, University of Michigan], 1960), chapter 7.

[7] See David Butler and Donald Stokes, *Political Change in Britain: Forces Shaping Electoral Choice* (London: Macmillan Co., 1969), chapter 5.

found that Swiss children had generally formed a sense of nationality by the age of twelve.[8] Applying this line of reasoning to the study of regional integration, it has been argued that changes in the conditions governing the socialization of different European age cohorts would lead us to expect differences in the degree of support for European integration: The older cohorts, who received their basic socialization in the nationalistic atmosphere prevailing in most Western European countries up through World War I, would retain a relatively nationalistic basic attitude which would tend to work against the acceptance of supranational integration. The cohorts who received their basic socialization in the period after World War II—an atmosphere in which traditional nationalism had recently been discredited and European community institutions existed and were widely regarded as beneficial—would lack these underlying reservations and would more readily support proposals for European integration. Preliminary evidence seemed to support this interpretation.[9] To the extent that a sense of national (or supranational) identity does represent an early instilled and relatively deep-seated orientation it is resistant to short-term manipulation; it is an input into the political decisionmaking process which the decisionmakers can modify only marginally and gradually—largely through the socialization of new cohorts. We would expect a substantial time lag between changes in the conditions governing socialization of a given age cohort and the impact of these changes, through recruitment into political relevance (and, eventually, into decisionmaking roles) of these individuals.

Let us sum up these hypotheses about the impact of mass and elite preferences on political decisionmaking. To do so we will make use of two diagrams. The first illustrates the short-term relationship between society and decisionmakers and consists of a familiar input-output diagram supplemented by a decision funnel or pyramid to emphasize the different roles played by different groups in the society (see Figure 1). The decisionmakers themselves play the central role, but outside this limited circle there are a variety of groups having various degrees of influence: Far out on the periphery we find individuals who may be unaware, or only vaguely aware, of the decision being made and who have little or no influence on it;[10] close to the decisionmaking

[8] See Jean Piaget with Anne-Marie Weil, "The Development in Children of the Idea of the Homeland and Relations with Other Countries," *International Social Science Bulletin,* Autumn 1951 (Vol. 3, No. 3), pp. 561–578. Cf. Gustav Johoda, "The Development of Children's Ideas about Country and Nationality," *The British Journal of Educational Psychology,* 1963 (Vol. 33, Nos. 1 and 2), pp. 47–60; 143–153.

[9] See Ronald Inglehart, "An End to European Integration?" *American Political Science Review,* March 1967 (Vol. 61, No. 1), pp. 91–105.

[10] An individual may be located on the periphery for a variety of reasons: In a short-term sense he may be there in regard to a given decision simply because he is not interested or informed on the topic. In a long-term sense he may be there because he has not attained cognitive mobilization, is below the age of political relevance, or belongs to a category which is coercively excluded from participating in the decisionmaking process.

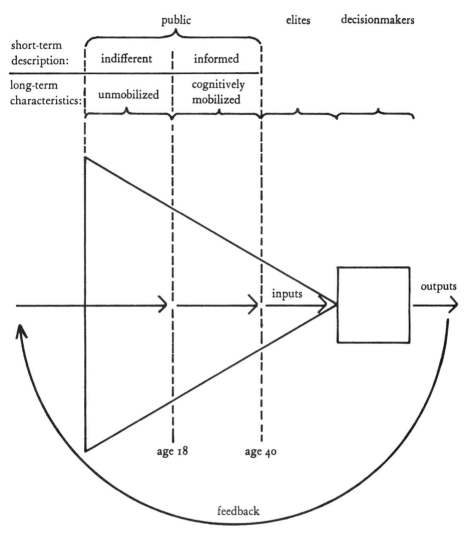

FIGURE 1. FEEDBACK PROCESS: SHORT-TERM RELATIONSHIP BETWEEN PUBLIC, ELITES, AND DECISIONMAKERS

center we find individuals playing elite roles, possessing information, skills, and contacts which enable them to exert a relatively strong influence on the decisionmakers themselves. The results of public opinion surveys then provide a potential means of analyzing the importance of societal pressures favorable or unfavorable to integrative decisions—but the data cannot be interpreted in an undifferentiated way. The preferences of certain individuals are likely to have much greater weight than the preferences of others. Moreover, the impact of public preferences can be blocked at various levels: Thus (in Figure 1) we indicate the inputs to the decisionmaking process by a line which is broken at the frontier between the mobilized and the unmobilized public; at the level of influential elites;[11] and at the level of the national decisionmakers. "Blockage" occurs when a set of values prevailing among the public is not transmitted into political decisions. The most common case, perhaps, is one in which a given issue is of low salience at a given time—and hence potentially relevant values are not perceived by decisionmakers. Such cases are trivial to the extent that a deep-seated value is not relevant and the prevailing preference may be easily changed. Blockage at the elite and decisionmaking levels can more readily occur to the extent that the decision-making structure tends to be monolithic rather than pluralistic. In a totalitarian system a tightly disciplined decision hierarchy acts on behalf of a set of values already internalized at the top, inhibiting the communication of information about noncompatible values at lower levels. Figure 2 illustrates the long-term relationship between society and decisionmakers, emphasizing the time lag between formation of basic skills and values and their role as political input—and the implicit possibility of intergenerational differentiation linked with the tendency toward persistence which presumably characterizes these aspects of an individual's character.

The first type of feedback relationship is likely to apply to the more or less rational assessment of immediate advantages or disadvantages resulting from political outputs—what Stanley Hoffmann has called "low politics." Probably the most important example would be economic conditions. Political decisions on this level can produce relatively rapid changes in public support.

The second type of feedback relationship describes the less rational level of "high politics"; the legitimacy of a given regime would be an example. If decisionmakers have relatively less short-term leeway in changing the underlying values themselves, they can attempt to change the terms of reference of a given decision—reinterpreting it to emphasize its congruence with already instilled values. Much of the controversy in France over the European defense community, for example, was based on whether the individual saw it primarily as a means to defend *la patrie*—or as the rearming of an ancient enemy.

It will be noted that our analysis tends to associate stable preferences with early instilled ones. Strictly speaking, this is not necessarily the case. Some individuals may well form deep and lasting political orientations relatively late in life. Nevertheless it seems that by the time they have reached adulthood, most politically relevant citizens have already formed a basic set of

---

[11] For our purposes defined as individuals who normally transmit the preferences of the unorganized public to the actual decisionmakers and as such occupy positions of above-average influence—especially elected representatives and governmental officials but also leaders of labor, business, agricultural, scientific, military, and other groups.

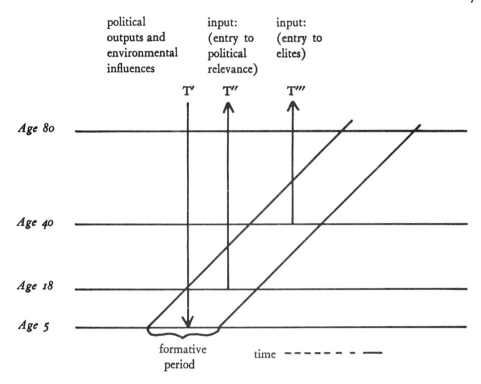

political   input: input:
outputs and   (entry to   (entry to
environmental   political   elites)
influences   relevance)

FIGURE 2. FEEDBACK PROCESS: LONG-TERM RELATIONSHIP BETWEEN PUBLIC, ELITES, AND DECISIONMAKERS

value priorities; later learning will take place in reference to these values, and it is probably more difficult to unlearn an existing set of orientations than to learn a new outlook from the start. We have suggested elsewhere that a certain degree of "structural commitment" impedes changes in an individual's outlook once basic socialization has taken place.[12] An analogy might be seen in the relative ease with which young people learn foreign languages; it is relatively rare (although not impossible) that an adult learns to speak a new language with perfect fluency and without a foreign accent.

Finally, we must distinguish between salience and stability of opinion. The two may tend to go together but they are certainly not identical. Under given conditions a previously unimportant issue may become the object of heated public feelings. Our hypothesis is that, except to the extent that such feelings reflect relatively early instilled attitudes, they probably cannot be regarded as

[12] See Inglehart, *American Political Science Review*, Vol. 61, No. 1; cf. Paul Abramson and Ronald Inglehart, "The Development of Systemic Support in Four Western Democracies," *Comparative Political Studies*, January 1970 (Vol. 2, No. 4); and Richard Merelman, "Learning and Legitimacy," *American Political Science Review*, September 1966 (Vol. 60, No. 3), pp. 548–561.

an independent input to the political process as much as the reflection of current political outputs and environmental influences.

Public opinion survey responses at any given time represent a mixture of these two types of feedback, and it is difficult to separate the two elements. But insofar as we are dealing with the former, public opinion is probably more largely a reflection of elite decisions than an influence on them. To the extent that a decision evokes deep-seated values decisionmakers must deal with something they cannot change quickly; they may have to accept certain limits to their policies or pay the political costs of public disaffection (which, of course, vary from system to system).

We have suggested a set of conditions under which societal opinion is likely to be an important factor relating to regional integration. Our ideas are drawn from impressionistic evidence; they remain to be validated empirically. They suggest a research strategy: Ideally, we should measure the preferences of elite and mass samples, representing each of the structural levels of the decision process; furthermore, we must attempt to distinguish between deeply internalized values and relatively superficial preferences. We would need to make such measurements at a series of points in time in order to analyze the relationship between societal preferences and integrative (or disintegrative) decisional outputs.[13] The latter could, perhaps, best be measured by an expert-rating system similar to that suggested by Leon Lindberg and Stuart Scheingold.[14] An extensive series of these measurements would be necessary in order to enable us to control for the effect of environmental variables—changes in economic conditions, trade flows, external threats, etc. Public opinion may be an important influence on the decision process, but it is almost certainly only one of several major factors.

Clearly, this would necessitate a costly research effort continuing over many years. It seems, however, that any definitive conclusions about the role of public/elite preferences in foreign policy decisions would have to be based on a data base of this kind. Properly done, such an analysis could enable us to begin to move toward making predictive statements about the probable outcome of integrative processes.

While we still have a long way to go, a fair amount of time-series data on the topic of European integration does already exist. What is needed is a more continuous effort with greater attention to achieving comparability in the data gathered and a clearer knowledge of the degree to which given survey items tap relatively basic attitudes.

---

[13] Another interesting (and related) line of investigation lies in the analysis of monochronic correlations between public opinion and the perceptions, preferences, and behavior of elite representatives. This approach clarifies only part of the process—the elite-mass linkage—but has the advantage of immediate feasibility. For an example see Warren Miller and Donald Stokes, "Constituency Influences in Congress," in Angus Campbell, and others, *Elections and the Political Order* (New York: John Wiley & Sons [for the Survey Research Center, Institute for Social Research, University of Michigan], 1966).

[14] See Leon Lindberg and Stuart Scheingold, *Europe's Would-Be Polity: Patterns in the European Community* (Englewood Cliffs, N.J.: Prentice-Hall, 1970).

In the meantime, we can only draw some tentative conclusions about the impact of societal preferences on regional integration based on fragmentary evidence. It may be worthwhile to do so by way of indicating progress to date and some problems still to be solved. Our observations will be limited to integration in Western Europe—the only region for which a substantial data base exists.

II. European Opinion and Decision Structures: A Permissive Consensus?

For many years what might be called a "permissive consensus"[15] seems to have existed among the Western European publics regarding European integration. There was a favorable prevailing attitude toward the subject, but it was generally of low salience as a political issue—leaving national decision-makers free to take steps favorable to integration if they wished but also leaving them a wide liberty of choice. It seems, for example, that the Schuman Plan was launched by a small elite working in almost conspiratorial fashion and able to maneuver swiftly and effectively in part *because* of the lack of public involvement. This margin may be growing narrower as time goes by.

Since the early 1950's majorities of the public in the Federal Republic of Germany (West Germany), France, Italy, and the United Kingdom, have supported the general idea of uniting Western Europe. In response to a question concerning "efforts to unify Western Europe," support dropped below the 50 percent level only twice during the 1952–1962 decade: in France in 1955 (the year after the defeat of the European defense community and in the United Kingdom in 1962 (the year of public controversy over the Conservative Party's decision to try to enter Europe). Apart from these special cases a majority of the French public has consistently supported the general idea of "unification," with only about 12 percent in declared opposition (a sizable group giving no opinion). The favorable majority in West Germany has generally been above 70 percent (dropping to a low of 69 percent in 1955); in Italy it has been at least 55 percent (the low point, again, being 1955); and in the United Kingdom it has remained at least 58 percent, with the exception noted.[16] Despite these fluctuations the relative positions of the various national

---

[15] The term is from Lindberg and Scheingold.

[16] This data is from United States Information Agency (USIA) surveys of 1952 through 1962, reported in Richard L. Merritt and Donald J. Puchala, *Western European Perspectives on International Affairs: Public Opinion Studies and Evaluation* (New York: Frederick A. Praeger, 1968), pp. 283–285. This book contains a rich collection of additional background data on the subject. The above remarks are also based on supplementary data from a 1962 survey (using the same item) sponsored by the European Communities Information Service and similar data from the 1964 USIA surveys, tabulated by myself. For additional evidence concerning the development of public support for European political integration over the past ten years see Jacques-René Rabier, *L'opinion publique et l'Europe* (Brussels: Institute of Sociology, University of Brussels, 1966); *Deutschland und die Europäischen Gemeinschaft* (Allensbach: Institüt für Demoskopie, 1967); and Jacqueline Bissery, *L'opinion des français sur le Marché commun et l'unification européenne* (Paris: L'Institute français d'opinion publique, 1968).

publics nearly always have been rather consistent, the Germans (with the Dutch, when data is available) nearly always ranking as most pro-European. In all four countries a low point was reached in the aftermath of the defeat of the projected European defense community. The decline associated with this crisis was especially marked in France—the country in which the European defense community debate had been sharpest. Somewhat similarly, the British public registered a sharply depressed level of support for European unification during the 1962 debate over British entry into the Common Market. After a subsequent recovery of British support, this phenomenon seems to be repeating itself at present when another possible leap into the unknown looms before the British public. Since de Gaulle's first veto of British entry into the Common Market, levels of public support for European integration in all four countries have been below their peak level of the 1950's—if we use this very general question as our indicator.

This item concerning "efforts toward unifying Western Europe" has the advantage of having been used in an exceptionally long time series. It has the disadvantage, however, of having what might be called a "floating referent": It does not ask whether an individual is for or against a specific measure (such as a European army) but tends to refer to whatever topics are currently salient in the public eye. Consequently it probably does not reflect more specific developments going on in public opinion. Among the most important of these developments seems to be a convergence of opinion within the European community in support of measures which would have been considered unfeasible a decade or so ago and the development of a European public within which nationality is a variable of secondary importance (ranking behind such variables as formal education, age, social class, and sex as a predictor of attitude).[17] This emerging European consensus seems to support supranational political integration—it apparently is ready for a "United States of Europe." The homogenization of opinion seems to have been achieved by a process in which the slow pace may have disappointed German expectations but gave the French a chance to catch up. In 1955 a two-thirds majority of the German public already favored building a "United States of Europe." This figure rose to a peak of 81 percent by 1961 in the early days of the Common Market. By 1967 it had declined to 78 percent, fell to 73 percent in 1968, and was only slightly above its 1955 level (with 69 percent in favor) in early 1970.[18] Available data for France is only very roughly comparable, but it ap-

---

[17] A tree analysis of predictors of pro-European attitudes based on survey data from Britain, France, Germany, and Italy gathered in 1963 and in 1968 bears this out while suggesting the growing importance of a cleavage between the publics of the United Kingdom and the European community. See Ronald Inglehart, "Cognitive Mobilization and European Identity," *Comparative Politics*, October 1970 (Vol. 3, No. 1), pp. 47–72.

[18] The 1955–1967 figures are from *Deutschland und die Europäischen Gemeinschaft*, Table 10; 1967 figures are from *Die Einstellung der deutschen Jugend zur Vereinigung Europas* (Allensbach: Institut für Demoskopie, 1967); 1968 figures are from a cross-national pilot survey undertaken by Leon Lind-

pears that as of 1957 only 35 percent of the French public were in favor of a "federation of Western Europe." This figure rose gradually to 38 percent (1962), 42 percent (1964), and 55 percent (1966). Approximately the same percentage (57 percent) was favorable to a "United States of Europe" in 1968 —a level which rose to 67 percent in 1970.[19]

For a dozen years the publics of the six European community countries have lived under common institutions having limited but real powers. They have shared a certain set of experiences and they seem to be taking on a common perspective. But while this development has been going on, there is evidence of a growing differentiation across community borders: specifically, between the publics of the six and the British. Although in the 1950's and early 1960's the British public appeared to be about as pro-European as the French, there was an extraordinary reversal of opinion at the time of the second veto of British admission in late 1967, followed by a downward trend continuing to the present. Thus, in early 1970 a survey of the adult publics of the United Kingdom and the five largest members of the six obtained the following responses to a series of proposals for European integration (Table 1): Perhaps the most striking aspect of Table 1 is the contrast between the Europeanism of the British and the European community publics. Equally important, however, is the high level of support among the publics of Europe for certain proposals which imply far-reaching supranational political integration. These are not simply "motherhood and virtue"-type items with which one must inevitably agree: It is possible for a reasonable man to reject them (and heavy majorities of the British do). The breadth of the majority which supports them within the community, then, is all the more impressive—as is the relative homogeneity of the European consensus.

As we move farther up the decision pyramid, we find results which are consistent with the public preferences indicated above. In a group of elite interviews conducted in 1964 Karl Deutsch found that among a sample of French elites 83 percent were at least conditionally in favor of further limitations on national sovereignty, as compared with 13 percent who were opposed. Among a sample of German elites the respective figures were 91 percent in favor and 4 percent against.[20]

As is true at the mass level, the French—and especially the German elites—

berg, Stuart Scheingold, and myself; 1970 figures are from a cross-national survey sponsored by the European Communities Information Service.

[19] Data for 1957 is calculated from tables in Merritt and Puchala; 1962–1966 data appears in Rabier, p. 24; 1968 and 1970 figures are from the respective sources cited in the preceding footnote.

[20] See Karl Deutsch, and others, *France, Germany and the Western Alliance: A Study of Elite Attitudes on European Integration and World Politics* (New York: Charles Scribner's Sons, 1967), p. 280; cf. Karl Deutsch, *Arms Control and the Atlantic Alliance: Europe Faces Coming Policy Decisions* (New York: John Wiley & Sons, 1967). Deutsch's samples consisted of leaders in the fields of business, politics, administration, journalism, and academic life—men who, while not the actual decisionmakers themselves, were reputedly influential in the national political system.

TABLE 1. LEVELS OF SUPPORT FOR FIVE EUROPEAN INTEGRATION PROPOSALS
(Percentage responses by country, February 1970)

1. *"United States of Europe."*

	For	Undecided	Against	N
Germany	69	22	9	(1731)
Netherlands	64	19	17	(1482)
France	67	22	11	(2130)
Belgium	60	30	10	(1155)
Italy	60	33	7	(1941)
United Kingdom	30	22	48	(2147)

2. *British entry into Common Market.*

Germany	69	24	7
Netherlands	79	13	8
France	66	23	11
Belgium	63	29	8
Italy	51	40	9
United Kingdom	19	18	63

3. *Election of European Parliament.*

Germany	66	25	9
Netherlands	59	20	21
France	59	26	15
Belgium	56	34	11
Italy	55	39	6
United Kingdom	25	20	55

4. *Supranational European government with common defense, foreign, and economic policies.*

Germany	57	24	19
Netherlands	50	18	32
France	49	23	28
Belgium	51	30	19
Italy	51	39	11
United Kingdom	22	18	60

5. *Would vote for president of "United States of Europe" from a country other than respondent's own.*

Germany	69	19	12
Netherlands	63	19	18
France	61	17	22
Belgium	52	24	24
Italy	45	36	19
United Kingdom	39	20	41

SOURCE: Survey sponsored by European Communities Information Service, with collaboration of the author.

find support for European integration compatible with support for integration with another region:

> When asked to choose between policies of strengthening mainly European institutions, such as EEC, and strengthening NATO, 40% of the 124 articulate French respondents prefer EEC, whereas only 4% favor NATO. . . . [Among the German respondents] a 72% majority refuses to choose and insists on supporting both—a middle way favored also by a French plurality of 49%.[21]

A series of elite interviews carried out in 1956, 1959, 1961, and 1965 in France, Germany, and the United Kingdom yield similar results. In reporting their findings Daniel Lerner and Morton Gorden place heavy emphasis on the emergence of a pragmatic consensus among West European elites—overriding time-honored cleavages between left and right and between nationalities. The consensus was especially strong regarding European *economic* integration:

> By 1965, two-thirds of all panels even believed that European integration had passed the "point of no return." At worst, they believed that delays might occur. But essentially, time was on the side of European integration.[22]

At the elite level the evidence seems to demonstrate the existence of a consensus favorable to at least a limited measure of further integration—even in France (and even among Gaullist elites). But when we examine the political outputs of recent years, we find another story.

Major attempts to broaden and strengthen the European community have met with failure over the last several years[23]—and the European esprit has suffered severely. Negotiations for British admission have twice ended in a unilateral veto; a far-reaching set of proposals to strengthen the role of the Commission of the European Communities was stalemated in early 1966 after a demoralizing six-month boycott of the European community by the French government.

Despite the prevailing consensus in favor of broadening and strengthening the community why has policymaking not followed the path indicated by these underlying pressures? To answer this question we must move to another level of analysis—that of personality. In this case we must examine the personality of General de Gaulle. It appears that in regard to certain issues prevailing pressures within the French (and hence the European) decision structure were, for a limited time, successfully blocked at the very top level—by a strategically located individual.

[21] Ibid., p. 27. Deutsch reports that only 7 percent of the French and 3 percent of the German elites indicated that they did not wish to strengthen *either* European or NATO institutions (ibid., p. 122).

[22] Daniel Lerner and Morton Gorden, *Euratlantica: Changing Perspectives of the European Elites* (Cambridge, Mass: M.I.T. Press, 1969), chapter 5. These elite samples are drawn from approximately the same groups as those interviewed by Deutsch, and others.

[23] We should not, however, ignore indications of a gradual expansion of the scope of European decisionmaking activities: See Leon Lindberg and Stuart Scheingold.

It seems almost too simple to explain major historical events in terms of the influence of one man: Surely there are "deeper" causes—causes to be found, for example, in the socioeconomic structure of the society. As a general rule this view is probably correct; only in rare cases do individual actors have a major influence on shaping events. Fred Greenstein has summarized the circumstances under which this can happen.[24] According to him, it depends on:

1) location of the actor in a given environment. A limiting case would be that of a dictator in a totalitarian system; here there is a tendency for political machinery to become "a conduit of the dictatorial personality."[25] While certainly more limited in his powers than a totalitarian dictator, de Gaulle had the advantages of a seven-year term, plenary emergency powers, and a reserved domain in foreign affairs—reinforced by a widespread belief that he was indispensable to France. In the realm of foreign policy de Gaulle alone was in effective control of France.

2) the degree to which action admits of restructuring—in this case, *can* an individual in effective control of French policy contrive to block European political integration? As long as the European decision system is based on international unanimity, open to unilateral vetoes, the answer is yes.

3) personal strengths (or weaknesses) of the actor. De Gaulle's strengths —his skill as a politician and as an actor in the theatrical sense—were exceptional. "Strength of character" is another important aspect: His insensitivity to personal popularity constituted a great strength from this viewpoint. To an extraordinary degree de Gaulle was a man who acted on the base of internalized values rather than in response to external stimuli.[26]

Thus, survey data by itself can predict political outcomes only to a limited extent; both mass and elite preferences can be overruled by a tiny minority or even a single individual within given decision structures.

But, to the extent that the analysis of survey data delineates the existence and character of given political generations it may even aid us in interpreting such apparently unpredictable factors as a de Gaulle. De Gaulle tended to act on the basis of deeply internalized values. In 1940 this trait redounded to his great honor, and in a great many respects his unique role after 1958 was highly positive. In certain of his decisions relating to European integration he may have represented an extreme case of delayed feedback into the political system—imposing a perspective which lagged behind current realities of French and European society. For in 1963, as in 1940, he acted in a way which was

---

[24] Fred I. Greenstein, "The Impact of Personality on Politics: An Attempt to Clear Away Underbrush," *American Political Science Review*, September 1967 (Vol. 61, No. 3), pp. 629–641.

[25] The phrase is from Robert C. Tucker, *The Soviet Political Mind: Studies in Stalinism and Post-Stalin Change* (Praeger Publications in Russian History and World Communism) (New York: Frederick A. Praeger, 1963), cited in ibid, p. 634.

[26] This corresponds approximately to Karl Deutsch's definition of "will": the closure of a communications network against new messages. See Deutsch, *The Nerves of Government: Models of Political Communication and Control* (New York: Free Press, 1963).

faithful to his early formation—that of a member of the French bourgeosie, trained as a military officer, who came to maturity in the intensely national-istic period preceding World War I. It is not surprising, then, that de Gaulle was strongly committed to a balance-of-power view of the world, one which reacted chiefly according to concepts of domination/subordination, rather than perceiving the possibility that integration could represent cooperation among equals.

As a result of his exceptional situation de Gaulle was able—for a limited number of years—to make foreign policy decisions almost without reference to the prevailing trends in French mass and elite opinion. This applied to a number of issues apart from those of European integration. Deutsch found, for example, that "the idea of a *national nuclear deterrent* is unpopular among the elites of France, where it is official government policy. . . . "[27] Similarly, his withdrawal from NATO, his gestures in support of *Québec libre,* his anti-Israeli posture during the Six-Day War of June 1967 were apparently received with a mixture of chagrin and astonishment by the bulk of the French people.

Lerner and Gorden provide some quantitative evidence on this score: They selected approximately twenty questions each from their 1961 and 1965 sur-veys of elite opinion in France, Germany, and the United Kingdom. Ques-tions were selected for which a clear government policy had been enunciated (and agreed upon by a panel of judges). They then examined the degree of congruence between official policy and elite opinion as reflected in their sur-veys. (See Table 2.)

TABLE 2. ELITE-GOVERNMENT-POLICY CONGRUENCE

	United Kingdom		France		Germany	
	1961 n = 19	1965 n = 19	1961 n = 21	1965 n = 21	1961 n = 23	1965 n = 18
Degree of Congruence	79 percent	89 percent	61 percent	48 percent	83 percent	82 percent

SOURCE: Lerner and Gorden, appendix 4; adapted from a working paper by John Child, Jr. The num-ber of issues rated is shown for each year and country.

The results show a consistently high level of congruence between elite pref-erences and government policy in both Germany and the United Kingdom—and, by contrast, a low and declining level of congruence in France. Indeed, by 1965 congruence existed between the French government and the French elite sample on less than half of the items rated!

We hypothesized that the role of public opinion tends to be minor when the political institutions of a given country do not present genuine alterna-

[27] Deutsch, *Arms Control,* p. 58.

tives. In a special sense this situation describes France under de Gaulle. To be sure, the institutions of competitive political parties and other independent organizations existed. But France had known a long series of political crises, leading up to the revolt which toppled the Fourth Republic in 1958, followed by a series of abortive revolts continuing until the achievement of Algerian independence in 1962. Despite divergences between himself and prevailing societal preferences on the European issue and other questions during the mid-1960's, de Gaulle was widely regarded as indispensable—the one man who could provide something valued even more highly: domestic political and economic stability. He was thus, to a certain degree, insulated from the pressures of public opinion on lesser issues. Nevertheless, it would be inaccurate to conclude that the European issue could not impose certain political costs; the December 1965 French presidential election seems to indicate the contrary. This election was held during de Gaulle's boycott of the European Communities, and the European question became the central issue, with both of the general's leading opponents taking pro-European stands. A specifically European candidate, Jean Lecanuet, was launched by the Center, competing directly for the votes of socioeconomic groups which in the recent past had supported de Gaulle. Lecanuet—almost unknown previously—succeeded in winning a considerable segment of these votes in the first round. French farmers seem to have reacted particularly sharply to the charge that de Gaulle was anti-European and to the fact that he was boycotting the Common Market, but the bulk of the Lecanuet vote seems to have been from the middle class.

To be sure, de Gaulle polled 45 percent of the vote on the first round against Lecanuet's 16 percent. But this left de Gaulle with a level of support far below what he had won in previous referenda and forced him into the humiliation of a runoff election. His claim to speak for all of France was made less plausible. Upon his elimination from the race, Lecanuet announced, "The question of Europe will be the determining factor in the choice I and my friends of the Democratic Center will make on December 19" (the date of the runoff election). On the basis of this issue he threw his support to de Gaulle's opponent, François Mitterrand, and a good half of his voters followed him. These voters—who moved across the chasm which normally prevents partisans of the French Center (or Right) from voting for a candidate who has Communist support—may well have been largely motivated by the European issue. While a minority of the electorate, they nevertheless constituted a significant bloc. Furthermore, the campaign may have contributed to a polarization according to age-group which was to become increasingly important: The vote in 1965 was age-related to an unprecedented degree. A survey made by l'Institut français d'opinion publique (IFOP) shortly before the election found that in the 21–34-year-old age-group, among those voters who had made up their minds, only 35 percent had decided in favor of de Gaulle, while 21 percent chose Lecanuet. If the franchise had been limited to this age-group, de Gaulle might have lost the election in the second round.

It would seem, then, that de Gaulle paid a certain price for his boycott of Europe: It did not cost him his job, but it did tend to undermine his prestige. His relative immunity, however, was due to an exceptional position which an eventual successor would be unlikely to maintain.

On the basis of an analysis of the elite and mass opinion data cited above (and an examination of transaction flow data) we concluded in 1967 that de Gaulle's successor would probably need to conciliate the Center; this *tendance* appeared to be the most strongly pro-European of the French political families, at both elite and mass levels. Consequently, we conjectured that:

> De Gaulle is likely to remain in power through 1972 at the latest. From that point on . . . the various underlying pressures which have been discussed here should again begin to be reflected in elite-level political activity. Other things being equal, we would expect that:
>
> 1) The United Kingdom will be admitted to the European Community.
> 2) The movement toward supranational organization of Europe will be resumed.
> 3) French anti-American and anti-Canadian politics will diminish.[28]

Certainly, we failed to foresee the substantial shift in British public opinion which began later that year—and which may yet prevent British entry into the European community. But in its application to French politics our analysis appears to have been accurate. Let us examine the series of events leading up to what some observers have called the European *relance* at the Hague in December 1969.

The revolt of May–June 1968 had a critical impact on the French national decision structure. The strength of de Gaulle's position, we have argued, was based on a widespread feeling that he was the only man who could provide political and economic stability for France. The events of May demonstrated that not even he could provide it—and that an alternative existed. By comparison with de Gaulle (who sometimes seemed to be losing his grip) the premier, Georges Pompidou, performed very coolly during the crisis, emerging with a prestige within the government which rivaled de Gaulle's own and a popularity (as reflected in public opinion polls) which was even higher than de Gaulle's. From the general's viewpoint the solution was clear: Pompidou had to go. He was dismissed shortly after the Gaullist legislative electoral victory which he had largely engineered. Nevertheless, a certain alternative now existed. And it seems likely that the April 1969 referendum, on which De Gaulle gratuitously staked his presidency, was held, in part, be-

---

[28] Ronald Inglehart, "Trends and Non-Trends in the Western Alliance: A Review," *Journal of Conflict Resolution*, March 1968 (Vol. 12, No. 1), p. 128.

cause he hoped to reestablish his position as the paramount national leader independent of Pompidou. The referendum was voted down for a variety of reasons. Among the most important, it seems, was the fact that Pompidou now was waiting in the wings, a discreet but distinctly available candidate for the succession, and the fact that once again a not widely known centrist (this time Alain Poher) came forward to campaign against the referendum, introducing the European issue as one of his major themes. It appears that it was the erosion of support from the centrist constituency which brought about de Gaulle's defeat in the referendum, leading to his immediate resignation.[29]

In the presidential campaign which followed Pompidou made great efforts to appear at least as European as his leading rival, Poher. One of his first steps was to conciliate the Independent Republican leader, Valéry Giscard d'Estaing (who had worked against the referendum): Converted, Giscard campaigned with posters of himself plastered all over France bearing the words: "Liberal and European, I support the candidacy of G. Pompidou." After a face-to-face radio interview in which he gave the right answers to the European question Pompidou won over another leading European, Jacques Duhamel; in doing so, he succeeded in splitting the centrist electorate with which both Poher and Duhamel were linked. In the first round Pompidou got 44 percent of the vote to Poher's 23 percent (the rest was split among four candidates of a seriously divided Left). Pompidou won the runoff by a comfortable margin due (in part) to the fact that the Communists abstained massively. His new government included leading Europeans in several key positions (including the ministries of agriculture, economy and finance, and foreign affairs).

There are indications that the current regime is relatively sensitive to public opinion, including, specifically, the results of public opinion polls (which predicted the defeat of the 1969 referendum). It may be significant, for example, that shortly before the Hague conference (December 1969) French survey results showing high levels of support for supranational integration were commented on in prominent articles in *Le monde, L'express,* and *Paris match;* in all three cases the findings were interpreted in a context which took for granted that President Pompidou would not only be aware of them but would be influenced by them in his actions at the Hague.

Pompidou's role there was far from simple: He had to avoid the risk of an open break with the orthodox Gaullist faction in his own party, preserving the appearance of continuity with the general's foreign policy (to which he gave lip service) while accepting major revisions. At that conference and in subsequent negotiations the leaders of the six agreed to form a European economic

---

[29] See Alain Lancelot, "Comment ont voté les français le 27 avril et les 1er et 15 juin 1969," *Projet,* September–October 1969 (No. 39), pp. 926–947.

and monetary union; to reopen negotiations on British entry by mid-1970; and to provide the European institutions with their own financial resources, independent of contributions from the national governments. These resources, for the immediate future, are very modest in size, but the principle involved represents one of the essential first steps toward the creation of an autonomous supranational government and reverses an important aspect of the stand taken by de Gaulle in his 1965–1966 boycott. Moreover, in requiring approval of the budget at Strasbourg the agreements give a measure of real power to the European Parliament. Europe has a very long way to go, but it is possible that it has begun moving again. And it seems that within the community the public consensus in favor of European integration is becoming increasingly capable of influencing that movement.

III. Cognitive Mobilization: The Changing Balance of Political Skills

Some evidence has been presented that public opinion is becoming increasingly important in relation to decisions concerning European integration. We pointed to various fragments of evidence which suggest the presence of an increasingly favorable distribution of values as well as recent structural changes which tend to produce a greater openness to societal inputs in France. But there are other reasons to believe that, as a long-term trend, the role of public opinion is becoming increasingly significant in Western Europe. One of these reasons relates to the changing distribution of political skills in these countries. To explain this we will briefly trace a certain broad historical development.

In the small traditional polity, based on word-of-mouth messages and face-to-face loyalties, political communication was accessible to all, as far as possession of the relevant skills was concerned. Hence, an equalitarian decision process is frequently found within the tribe or peasant village, based on a consensus reached by all mature males (and, sometimes, all mature females). Such a process is rarely or never found in the more complex and extensive traditional monarchies or bureaucratic empires. With the development of an extensive political community fundamental changes necessarily take place in the making and executing of political decisions: It becomes a question of making decisions involving millions, rather than hundreds or thousands, of people and of coordinating the activities of a geographically scattered population rather than a group assembled in one place. New techniques of communication and control must be developed, and, increasingly, an elite must be differentiated which possesses specialized skills. Personal loyalties no longer suffice; a system of legitimacy must be developed which is based on impersonal roles to at least some extent. Word-of-mouth communications no longer suffice; records must be kept based on abstract symbols. Perhaps the most significant of the new skills is literacy; but others are also important: skills in bookkeeping, the ability to conceptualize authority relations at a distance and over long periods of time. To sum up these skills in one general concept we might view them as the ability to manipulate political abstractions. We will refer to the process by which these skills become increasingly widely distributed as "cognitive mobilization."

In a subsistence economy it is very unlikely that the entire population will have sufficient leisure time to develop these skills. They tend to become the monopoly of a differentiated minority: royal officials, a priestly caste, mandarins, etc. The differentiation of such an elite, in a sense, is a great leap forward in political development. It permits the formation of extensive polities, maintaining order over large areas, based on the resources of relatively large numbers of people. But the resulting shift in the relative distribution of political skill implies, almost inevitably, a diminution of popular control and participation. During this phase the politics of the political community tend to move out of the ken of the common man and become the sphere of a relatively skilled and cosmopolitan elite. By comparison the great bulk of the population of traditional monarchies or bureaucratic empires is parochial.[30] Likely to have a low level of awareness and comprehension of national-level politics, the majority finds it difficult to project themselves into the role of a distant political authority. As a consequence they tend to be politically inert.

With increasing economic and technological development resources become available which make it possible to begin to readjust the balance of political skills between elite and mass. It is probably not by sheer coincidence that, in the political development of European nations, expansion of the electorate tended to be linked with expansion of public education: A literate citizenry could keep in touch with national-level politics via the printed mass media.

Although they attained widespread literacy decades ago, the great majority of the publics of Western European countries still have no more than a primary education. By contrast, the bulk of government officials at a policymaking level have university educations; a citizen with a primary school education is scarcely on an even footing. The bureaucrat operates at a level of abstraction which is scarcely comprehensible to the average citizen; it is unlikely that the latter will be able to articulate his grievance effectively— quite possibly he will not even be able to figure out which official he ought to contact.

The massive expansion of higher education in recent years has tended to equalize this balance of political skills at least among the younger cohorts. Increased student activism may represent, in part, the type of input described in Figure 2: the attainment of political relevance by cohorts which possess

---

[30] Our use of the terms "parochial" and "cosmopolitan" is based on Daniel Lerner's classic work cited above.

relatively high levels of political skills and, in some respects, different basic value priorities from those of older cohorts.

On the whole, increasing cognitive mobilization seems to favor European integration. It is perfectly conceivable that it could be associated with rising feelings of nationalism; indeed, this pattern seems to have characterized an earlier stage of the process in nineteenth-century Europe. Cognitive mobilization increases an individual's capacity to receive and process messages relating to remote political objects: The effect of exposure to such messages depends, in large part, on the *content* of the messages. In the Western European environment since World War II the content of communications relating to European integration seems to have been predominantly favorable. Hence, we would expect individuals with high skill levels to take a relatively favorable position. There are additional reasons why we might expect this. Increasing familiarity with European-level politics may make them seem less remote, more familiar. For the less sophisticated public the Brussels institution may remain dimly understood, perhaps somewhat threatening.

Survey evidence bears out this expectation. If we take formal education as an indicator of cognitive mobilization, we find a consistent tendency for the more educated to give a higher level of support to proposals for European integration. In part this is because the more educated are notably more likely to have an opinion on the subject. But even controlling for this effect we find a general tendency for the more educated to be relatively pro-European (see Table 3). It might be argued that the linkage between education and Euro-

TABLE 3. PERCENTAGE "FOR" SUPRANATIONAL EUROPEAN GOVERNMENT, BY EDUCATION AMONG THOSE GIVING AN OPINION (FRANCE AND GERMANY, 1968)

Educational Level	France	Germany
Primary School Only	52 percent (500)	50 percent (946)
Beyond Primary School	71 percent (598)	69 percent (471)

peanness is spurious—that it simply reflects an association between higher education and higher social class, higher income level or distinctive political party preferences. In fact the correlation between education and Europeanness tends to be stronger than the correlation between Europeanness and these other variables; it may be more plausible to view part of the linkage between higher income and Europeanism as resulting from the effect of education rather than the other way around.[31]

Again, our evidence is not conclusive. But there are indications of a long-

[31] See Inglehart, *Comparative Politics*, Vol. 3, No. 1, pp. 47–72.

term trend toward an increasingly active role for public opinion in Western Europe, and there is reason to believe that this more active public is relatively favorable to European integration.

IV. Internalized Values: A Delayed Feedback into the Political System

In a previous article we hypothesized that certain basic political orientations tend to become crystallized during an individual's preadult years and are relatively unlikely to change greatly during the remainder of the individual's life.[32] It follows from this hypothesis that when substantially different conditions govern the political formation of two or more respective age cohorts, these differences should be reflected in the attitudes of the age-groups in later life. One's sense of national identity, we argued, is one of these basic orientations. If this is true, then those Western European age cohorts which were formed in the intensely nationalistic period preceding World War I, for example, should show a relatively nationalistic response pattern even today, by contrast with the cohorts formed after World War II—in an atmosphere in which traditional nationalism had recently been discredited and influenced by the existence of supranational European institutions and by the absence of violent hostilities between Western European nations.

On the basis of these assumptions we predicted (and found) age-group differences in the indicated direction in response to a series of proposals for European integration which presumably tapped a basic nationalism/internationalism dimension. We would, furthermore, except the magnitude of these age-group differences to vary according to the recent historical experience of the given country. Among the four which we analyzed, age-group differences were largest in Germany which had undergone cataclysmic changes from the chauvinism of the Kaiserzeit to the antinationalistic reaction following the defeat of Adolph Hitler. Age-group differences were smallest in the Netherlands, already characterized by a relatively internationalistic outlook in the pre-1918 period, with France and the United Kingdom falling between these two extremes.

In Table 4 we replicate the previous age-group comparison, using data gathered in 1970.[33] (See Table 4.) The expected age-group differences appear and

[32] See Inglehart, *American Political Science Review*, Vol. 61, No. 3. This article was based on secondary analysis of cross-national public opinion surveys carried out in 1962 (sponsored by the European Communities Information Service) and in 1963 (sponsored by the Reader's Digest Association). For descriptions of this data and a presentation of some findings see, respectively, *Journal of Common Market Studies*, November 1963 (Vol. 2, No. 4), and *Products and Peoples* (London: Reader's Digest Association, 1963).

[33] The items asked were: 1) "Are you in favour of, or against, Britain joining the Common Market?" 2) "Assuming (in these next four questions) that Britain *did* join, would you be for or against the evolution of the Common Market towards the political formation of a United States of Europe?" 3) "Would you be in favour of, or against, the election of a European parliament by direct universal suffrage; that is, a parliament elected by all the voters in the member countries?" 4) "Would you be

TABLE 4. PERCENTAGE "FOR" FOUR PROPOSALS FOR SUPRANATIONAL INTEGRATION, BY COUNTRY AND AGE-GROUP: 1970

For "United States of Europe":

Age-Group	Germany	Netherlands	France	Belgium	Italy	United Kingdom
21–34	75	69	71	67	66	33
35–49	75	61	66	67	63	30
50–64	64	65	71	61	57	30
65+	57	60	60	42	42	24
Age spread:	+18	+9	+11	+25	+24	+9

For British entry in to Common Market:

Age-Group	Germany	Netherlands	France	Belgium	Italy	United Kingdom
21–34	75	80	69	60	58	23
35–49	73	78	64	71	54	20
50–64	65	80	65	59	49	17
65+	59	73	66	57	36	14
Age spread:	+16	+7	+3	+3	+22	+9

For European Parliament:

Age-Group	Germany	Netherlands	France	Belgium	Italy	United Kingdom
21–34	73	64	64	54	60	30
35–49	70	57	56	61	60	25
50–64	62	61	63	57	51	23
65+	55	54	50	43	38	19
Age spread:	+18	+10	+14	+11	+22	+11

For supranational European government, responsible for foreign affairs, defense, and economy:

Age-Group	Germany	Netherlands	France	Belgium	Italy	United Kingdom
21–34	66	54	53	52	57	28
35–49	60	49	51	60	53	22
50–64	53	51	51	51	49	21
65+	42	45	40	37	33	14
Age spread:	+24	+9	+13	+15	+24	+14

Would vote for president of a "United States of Europe" from another country:

Age-Group	Germany	Netherlands	France	Belgium	Italy	United Kingdom
21–34	81	73	73	58	59	54
35–49	71	67	63	60	45	42
50–64	61	57	59	51	40	34
65+	54	47	46	33	25	20
Age spread:	+27	+26	+26	+25	+34	+34

willing to accept, over and above the British Government, a European Government responsible for a common policy in foreign affairs, defence and the economy?" 5) "If a President of a United States of Europe were being elected by popular vote, would you be willing to vote for a candidate *not* of your own country, if his personality and programme corresponded more closely to your ideas than those of the candidates from your own country?"

in the predicted direction (younger cohorts showing a rather consistent tendency to give higher levels of support for supranational European integration). Moreover, the *relative* magnitude of the age-group differences again conforms to our expectations: Among the four countries examined previously the differences are greatest in Germany and smallest in the Netherlands, with France and the United Kingdom again falling into intermediate positions. An Italian sample has been added to our analysis this time, and it proves to have the largest age-group differences of all. In part this reflects unusually high nonresponse rates among the older Italian cohorts (which we would interpret as indicating relatively low levels of cognitive mobilization). However, we cannot uniformly discount nonresponse as simple absence of opinion: There is reason to believe that among certain individuals it reflects reticent opposition, an intermediate position between outright opposition and outright support.[34]

We would view the Italian historical experience as parallel to that of Germany in several respects: The older Italian cohorts (like the Germans) were formed in what might be called a period of nascent nationalism after a relatively recent struggle for unification. Basic socialization of the younger cohorts, on the other hand, took place in an atmosphere influenced (as in Germany) by the fact that an aggressively nationalistic regime had been discredited by defeat in World War II. The relative magnitude of the Belgian age-group differences presents few problems, but the internal pattern shows certain anomalies: For one, the youngest age-group shows no sign of being more European than the next oldest, if anything, it seems less so. Has the recent renewal of intensity of Belgium's traditional linguistic conflicts tended to shift the focus of political identification toward a narrower, rather than a broader, community? For the time being we will sidestep this question.[35]

Our cross-sectional analysis has possible cross-temporal implications. We interpret the findings as indicating a process of gradual political change: If

[34] Evidence exists that those who take a minority position in regard to prevailing norms are relatively likely to give "no response" to relevant survey items. Thus, for example, support for the French Communist party is consistently and substantially underrepresented in surveys as compared with its actual vote in elections. For a theoretical treatment see James McCroskey, and others, "The Significance of the Neutral Point on Semantic Differential Scales," *Public Opinion Quarterly*, Winter 1967–1968 (Vol. 31, No. 4), pp. 642–645. In previous research we found that the older cohorts who give a relatively high nonresponse rate on European integration proposals seem relatively likely to shift from support to neutrality or from neutrality into opposition in the face of events which weaken overall support (and hence, the strength of the majoritarian norm). This finding seems consistent with our interpretation, according to which these older cohorts have underlying orientations less supportive of European integration: In a relative sense they tend to be "fair-weather friends." See Inglehart, *American Political Science Review*, Vol. 61, No. 1, pp. 91–105.

[35] Similarly, the importance of this internal conflict may have reduced the pressure on the oldest age-group (the presumed "fair-weather friends" of internationalism) to conform to post-World War II internationalist norms—which might account for the surprisingly large gap between them and the next younger age-group. Our data, which has just become available, permits certain more detailed analyses which might shed light on this question (as well as the nonresponse problem); we have not yet undertaken these analyses. Nevertheless, we felt it would be interesting to present at least the broad outlines of the most recent cross-national survey on the subject.

our hypothesis is correct concerning the relative stability of these attitudes, then as new age cohorts are recruited into the electorate (and eventually into the decisionmaking elite) one would expect to find increasing support for European integration. This interpretation, however, raises important methodological questions:

1) Are the differences due to life-cycle changes rather than intergenerational change?

2) Are the given age-groups really comparable?

3) Are the differences stable?

We will deal briefly with each of these problems. In regard to the first the cross-national pattern of age-group differences gives us some reassurance that the differences are not simply inherent in the process of aging: They tend to correspond to the historical experience of the given nations in a reasonably orderly way.[36] And a recent analysis of American survey data seems to support the hypothesis that such age-cohort differences can persist over long periods of time. In an analysis of twenty national sample surveys, carried out at five-year intervals over the period 1946–1966, Neal E. Cutler examined the deviations among attitudes within both age-cohort and life-stage groups. Analyzing the results of polynomial regressions on foreign policy attitudes of each of the respective groups, Cutler concludes that both the aging process and the generational interpretation explain part of the observed differences in public opinion; the generational cohorts, however, provide a relatively stronger explanation than do life-cycle groups: Foreign policy has relatively higher salience for the younger American cohorts and given cohorts have maintained their relative position over a period of decades.[37]

The question remains: "Are the age-groups in our European data really comparable?" In theory a representative national sample should contain a number of respondents in their early twenties proportionate to their distribution in the total population and approximately similar to the rest of the sample in social background factors other than age. In fact, this youngest adult group is very often undersampled: It is less likely to be found at home. To cope with this problem we adopted a technique which permits us to examine the problem of intergenerational change in a different fashion. We asked the adults sampled in our 1968 pilot study whether they had any children in certain specified age categories (15–16 and 19–20).[38] In case of affirmative re-

[36] Nor are youth necessarily more internationalistic: In the mid-1950's the youngest adult cohort gave only moderately favorable responses, at least in France; only in the 1960's—when the post-World War II cohorts began to reach maturity—did the youngest age-group begin to show the highest level of Europeanness. See Bissery, pp. 43–45.

[37] See Neal E. Cutler, *The Alternative Effects of Generations and Aging Upon Political Behavior: A Cohort Analysis of American Attitudes toward Foreign Policy, 1946–1966* (Oak Ridge, Tenn: Oak Ridge National Laboratory, 1968).

[38] Cross-sectional analysis of these three national samples also revealed age-group differences in the predicted direction. See Ronald Inglehart, "Regional Integration, Political Development and Public Opinion," paper presented at Conference on Regional Integration, Madison, Wisconsin, April 24–26, 1969.

sponse we recorded names and addresses of those children—who were interviewed the following year in a survey carried out by the European Communities Information Service. In this way we obtained responses to three items concerning European integration from parent-child pairs.[39] While this technique has the disadvantage of being relatively costly in relation to the number of responses obtained, it has certain advantages: The two age-groups being compared are from *precisely* the same households—exerting automatic controls for ethnicity, region, religion, and family background. The results of this direct intergenerational comparison are presented in Table 5.

TABLE 5. PARENT-CHILD COMPARISONS: 1968–1969 SURVEYS

	Germany		France		United Kingdom	
	Parents	*Youth*	*Parents*	*Youth*	*Parents*	*Youth*
"United States of Europe"						
For	71 percent	92 percent	65 percent	83 percent	31 percent	76 percent
Neutral	21 percent	5 percent	26 percent	15 percent	22 percent	10 percent
Against	8 percent	3 percent	9 percent	2 percent	48 percent	15 percent
European army						
For	54 percent	72 percent	47 percent	57 percent	32 percent	47 percent
Neutral	26 percent	16 percent	35 percent	25 percent	18 percent	11 percent
Against	20 percent	11 percent	18 percent	18 percent	50 percent	42 percent
European government						
For	37 percent	50 percent	46 percent	48 percent	21 percent	45 percent
Neutral	31 percent	20 percent	31 percent	17 percent	12 percent	7 percent
Against	31 percent	30 percent	24 percent	35 percent	67 percent	48 percent

NOTE: Respective numbers of parent-child pairs are: 80, 98, 166.

A rather striking set of intergenerational differences appears: In every case the youth give a higher level of positive response than their parents—sometimes by 30 percentage points or more. Indeed, the differences here are greater than those which would be expected on the basis of a cross-sectional analysis of the adult survey. It is possible that our cross-sectional analysis tends to *under*estimate the degree of intergenerational change. This would be the case if, for example, there were a systematic tendency to undersample a more mobile, and more European oriented, type of youth.

[39] Text of questions: 1) "If a United States of Europe were being established, would you be for or against having Britain become a part of it?" 2) "Would you be for or against having the British army become part of one unified European army?" 3) "Do you think that the government of a United States of Europe should have the right to overrule the government of Great Britain on some important matters?"

The question of the stability of the age-group differences found in our European data cannot be resolved conclusively: To do so would require a longitudinal study lasting several decades. Nevertheless, the presumption that they are indicative of long-term factors gains a certain amount of support from the fact that the predicted differences have been found in cross-sectional analyses of a substantial number of national samples carried out over the past several years as well as in the comparison of parent-child pairs just cited.

The interpretation of these findings depends on the extent to which a given item tends to tap short-term reactions (of the type depicted in Figure 1) or basic early instilled orientations (the long-term feedback depicted in Figure 2). Our problem is complicated by the fact that the former pattern is likely to be superimposed on the latter. To the extent that a given item referring to European integration does tap a basic sense of national-supranational identity we would expect overall response levels to that item to change only gradually over time, largely as a result of the recruitment of new cohorts into a given population.

Most of the European-integration items for which we have time-series data seem to conform to this latter criteria reasonably well although support levels *do* fluctuate, apparently in response to important national and international events. The decline in support for a series of European integration items from 1962 to 1963 is an example,[40] the key event presumably being the first veto of British admission (see Table 6). But a notable exception exists to this rule of

TABLE 6. MEAN PERCENTAGE "FOR" FOUR KEY MEASURES,
1962 AND 1963, BY COUNTRY

	1962	1963	CHANGE
The Netherlands	78.5 percent	73.0 percent	−5.5
West Germany	68.2 percent	61.8 percent	−6.4
Belgium	67.0 percent	60.0 percent	−7.0
Italy	62.0 percent	60.8 percent	−1.2
France	58.8 percent	54.4 percent	−4.4
(United Kingdom)		(56.5) percent	

NOTE: These proposals concerned abolition of tariffs, free movement of workers and businesses, a common foreign policy, and use of national taxes to aid poorer countries of Europe.

limited fluctuation; it concerns the attitudes of the British public toward entry into the Common Market. In this case the recent shift is so sudden, and its magnitude so extreme, as to make it dubious that this item taps a basic

[40] See Merritt and Puchala for additional evidence.

sense of national identity—one might even ask whether such an orientation exists. We cannot exclude the possibility that it does not.

We can, however, point to similar phenomena in the realm of electoral behavior where sharp swings are known to take place and yet where the bulk of the evidence points to the persistence of a long-term sense of political party identification among significant numbers of people. In the two most recent American presidential elections, for example, there was a shift from the landslide victory of the Democratic Party in 1964 (when it won 61 percent of the votes cast) to that party's defeat in 1968 (when it polled 42 percent of the vote). Yet during that period the percentage of those reporting that they considered themselves Democrats, or closer to the Democrats, changed only slightly—indeed, these figures had changed very little since 1952.[41] The changes in vote seem largely due to public shifts on given issues and especially in assessment of the various candidates.

Does a measure of political party identification have any value if it does not necessarily correspond to the way a person votes in a given election? It is widely conceded that it does: 1) Despite a certain amount of slippage it is a good indicator of how an individual will actually vote (much of the shift seems to come from those who have a weak or nonexistent sense of partisan identification); 2) the measure is of value in analyzing long-term trends.

There is evidence that a sense of political party identification is often instilled in one's family of orientation and tends to persist through adult life.[42] We would think that a sense of national identity is likely to be at least equally early instilled and long lasting. Our problem is to find items which effectively tap this underlying orientation. We would expect such items to show 1) relative stability over time; and 2) in the contemporary Western European setting these items would be expected to show relatively great age-group differences, the old being more nationalistic.

Early in this article we hypothesized that short-term attitudinal shifts are relatively likely to be influenced by conscious, rational considerations; the type of feedback shown in Figure 1 is likely to be shaped by an assessment of immediate economic consequences, for example. Long-term feedback (illustrated in Figure 2) is more likely to reflect prerational considerations—one's reaction to symbols of national prestige or sovereignty, for example.

At any given time the two types of effects may be superimposed on each other, but it would seem that the British public today reacts to the question of Common Market membership largely in terms of what it will do to the cost of living. In a survey carried out in late 1969, 67 percent of the British public expressed the fear that if Britain joins the community, prices will go

---

[41] See marginals from Survey Research Center surveys, 1952–1968.

[42] See Angus Campbell, and others, *The American Voter*, chapter 7; cf. Philip Converse and Georges Dupeux, "Politicization of the Electorate in the US and France," in Angus Campbell, and others, *Elections*.

up (by comparison, only 11 percent gave this response in 1961).[43] Fears of loss of political identity were mentioned by only 10 percent (about the same level as in 1961).[44]

We appear to have a problem of measurement: If the item about Common Market entry does not tap one's basic sense of national identity, do any items exist which do? Perhaps the answer is "yes": In the survey just cited the same British respondents were asked about "closer political relations with Europe"; 55 percent said that they would be a "good thing"[45]—a figure close to the long-term level of support for other European integration proposals.

In our more recent survey we find something similar: While the British public opposed entry into the Common Market by a 3:1 margin, the same respondents—despite the possible effect of response set[46]—divide almost evenly on the question about a foreign president of Europe. Could it be that the latter item is a relatively accurate indicator of a long-term sense of national identity? To the extent that the size of age-group differences (shown in Table 4) reflects the persistence of long-term orientations this latter item appears to tap the relevant dimensions more effectively. The age-group difference associated with it is greater than those found with the other items; among the British public it is nearly four times as great as those associated with the item concerning entry into the Common Market (a difference of 34 percentage points as compared with a difference of 9 points). This does not seem to be accidental; the age-group differences produced by this item are consistently the largest among any of the five items within all six national samples. The item itself seems to tap something which older cohorts find harder to accept than younger ones. We suggest that, prior to 1967, items concerning British entry into the Common Market did tend to be answered by the British (as they still are by the European community publics) in terms of an underlying nationalism/internationalism. Levels of support for this and other European integration proposals were roughly comparable, and responses to the various items tended to have relatively strong positive correlations. An analysis of data gathered in 1964–1965 among youth in France, Germany, the Netherlands, and the United Kingdom indicated that for respondents from the three European community countries a relatively well-defined structure of attitudes toward European integration existed. Among the British respondents attitudes favoring European integration were more loosely structured and less distinct from a general internationalism; however, responses to an item concerning British entry into the Common Market was at the heart of this general clus-

[43] If this is the case, further analysis should show two relatively distinct dimensions appearing in British responses, corresponding to these two sets of orientations.

[44] See *Gallup Political Index* (London), December 1969 (No. 116).

[45] Ibid. Only 13 percent said it would be bad.

[46] The latter item was asked only a minute or two after the one concerning entry into the Common Market.

ter.[47] At that time attitudes toward British entry served as a fairly good predictor of this group's attitudes toward other aspects of European integration.

Since 1967 levels of support for British entry have begun to diverge from the levels of support for other European integration items, and it is possible that the former question now tends to tap a different dimension from the nationalist/internationalist orientation. The shock of a second failure, in late 1967, brought about a profound negative reaction in British public opinion (see Table 7). By December 1967 a strong plurality was already opposed to

TABLE 7. TRENDS IN BRITISH PUBLIC OPINION REGARDING ENTRY
INTO EUROPEAN COMMUNITY

	February 1965	February 1966	February 1967	December 1967	June 1968	November 1969	February 1970
For	59 percent	59 percent	59 percent	38 percent	36 percent	36 percent	19 percent
Don't know / No answer	22 percent	22 percent	21 percent	12 percent	21 percent	19 percent	18 percent
Against	19 percent	19 percent	20 percent	50 percent	43 percent	45 percent	63 percent

entry: Having twice proposed marriage and twice been refused, they tended to dissociate themselves from Europe, perhaps as a matter of ego defense. This prepared the ground for widespread acceptance of negative economic arguments which became widely disseminated thereafter and gave a reassuring rationale for not wanting to go in: The woman who had jilted you wasn't so lovely after all. Thus, the frame of reference for the EEC-entry item may have shifted after 1967 from a basic nationalism/internationalism to a skeptical assessment of immediate economic effects.[48]

Ironically, then, the British public is now predominantly unfavorable to joining Europe at the very time when entry has at last become possible. And it seems that this public now reacts to entry into the Common Market on the basis of a negative evaluation of its immediate economic consequences; they react relatively favorably to the idea of political integration—which may tap an underlying nationalism/internationalism dimension to a greater degree. Current opposition to Common Market membership, then, may be relatively responsive to short-term factors; it may decline as rapidly as it rose.

Life would be much simpler if a given item always tapped the same underlying orientation. Unfortunately, this may be an unrealistic expectation. There

[47] See Ronald Inglehart, "The New Europeans: Inward or Outward Looking?" *International Organization*, Winter 1970 (Vol. 24, No. 1), pp. 129–139.

[48] The economic arguments are less than persuasive: In October 1969, 81 percent of a sample of 92 British financiers and bankers—a group presumably well informed on the probable long-term economic effects—were favorable to British entry. See *Grand Bretagne et Marché commun* (Paris: Agence économique et financière, March 1970).

is no guarantee that the question about British entry to the Common Market ever did tap a deeply instilled orientation of the British public. The relatively close correlation found earlier between responses to this item and a variety of Europeanism and internationalism items suggests that up to 1967 perhaps it did; the subsequent instability of response levels, as well as the apparent bifurcation between responses involving economic, as compared with political integration, indicates that after 1967 it did not.

This item, then, may give a poor basis for comparison of the basic nationalism or Europeanism of the British, as compared with the European, publics: The two are probably closer together than it would indicate. Nevertheless, the situation appears very serious from the perspective of European integration. There are indications of convergence toward a European consensus supporting supranational integration among the public of the community. At the same time the British public seems to be moving in the opposite direction. If British entry does not take place in the immediate future (despite public preferences) it may become an increasingly remote possibility at any future time.

Conclusions

We have argued that the role of public opinion in regional integration must be examined in the light of three types of conditioning factors: institutional structure, the distribution of skills, and the internalization of values among the public. We have discussed some available evidence about how these three factors have influenced the relationship between public opinion and European integration. Recent changes in the French national decision structure seem to have led to a somewhat greater openness to societal preferences (*"ouverture en continuité,"* as Pompidou has put it). The increasingly wide distribution of politically relevant skills also appears likely to enhance the role of public opinion in Western Europe. Finally—apart from the possible exception concerning British attitudes toward entering the EEC—there are indications that public attitudes toward European integration tend to reflect long-term orientations. Taken together, these findings suggest that public preferences are likely to constitute an increasingly effective long-term influence on political decisionmakers, an influence which (in the community, at least) is basically favorable to supranational integration.

5

Comparing Common Markets:

A Revised Neo-Functionalist Model

J. S. NYE

THERE are several approaches to regional integration, both in actor's strategies and in academic analysis. One of the pioneering political science efforts at providing a causal model of regional integration was developed under the stimulus of events in Western Europe in the late 1950's and not surprisingly it reflects these origins. We will refer to it as academic neo-functionalism.[1]

The neo-functional approach is more suited to the analysis of cases such as common markets in which significant institutions have been created or market forces released than it is to the analysis of loosely structured relationships.[2] Not all regional economic organizations involve significant institutional or liberalization forces. The "common market" schemes that enjoy such popularity today are more common than market. But in cases in which important market forces are released or institutional forces created by a group of states can we find regularities in the ensuing political behavior? Is it true, as is commonly said, that common markets must progress to political union or else slip backward into disintegration? What, in short, are their political dynamics?

In *The Uniting of Europe: Political, Social, and Economic Forces, 1950–1957*

J. S. NYE, a member of the Board of Editors of *International Organization,* is an associate professor in the Government Department at Harvard University, Cambridge, Massachusetts. The author is grateful to Hayward Alker, Lawrence Finkelstein, Ernst Haas, Stanley Hoffmann, Harold Jacobson, Peter Katzenstein, Robert Keohane, Uwe Kitzinger, Leon Lindberg, Stuart Scheingold, Philippe Schmitter, and Robert van Schaik for their comments on an earlier version of this paper.

[1] A pioneering work of the same period which gave rise to the broader "transactional" approach was Karl W. Deutsch, and others, *Political Community and the North Atlantic Area: International Organization in the Light of Historical Experience* (Princeton, N.J: Princeton University Press, 1957). For the differences between federal, functional, and neo-functional strategies see J. S. Nye, *Peace In Parts* (Boston: Little, Brown and Co., forthcoming), chapter 2.

[2] Nor is it well suited for the analysis of hegemonic (e.g., France-Monaco) and coercive integration (e.g., nineteenth-century Germany) in which the preferences of one partner tend to determine the process. We deal with the ambiguities of symmetry in some detail below.

Ernst B. Haas took the partially articulated strategy of the neo-functional statesmen, related it more clearly to party and group interests, and put it in theoretical terms that have been enormously fruitful in generating further studies both in Europe and in other areas.[3] Haas, Leon Lindberg, and others have subsequently refined the original academic neo-functionalist formulations and concepts as applied to Europe; Haas and Philippe Schmitter have elaborated the approach still further in developing what is probably the most widely accepted paradigm for comparative analysis.[4]

Despite these refinements, however, the neo-functional approach still embodies a number of faults that reflect its origins in the 1950's. For this reason the approach has been subject to considerable criticism (including criticism by its authors) and to questions about its usefulness as a framework for comparative analysis both in the changed European context and in relation to less developed areas.[5] Nonetheless, the academic neo-functionalist approach has a number of virtues. It has been developed out of the theoretically sophisticated field work of able scholars; it specifies many of the most important variables expressed in an economical way; useful work has begun to be done on operationalizing its variables;[6] and it has gained a certain acceptance among scholars interested in a comparative approach to the politics of common markets.

The neo-functional approach can be modified so that it is not too Europocentric to be useful as a framework for comparative analysis if the following revisions are made: 1) the dependent variable is stated less ambiguously, 2) the idea of a single path from quasi-technical tasks to political union by means of spillover is dropped and other potential process forces and paths are included; 3) more political actors are added; and 4) the list of integration conditions is reformulated in the light of comparative work that has been done on integration processes in less developed areas.

I. The Dependent Variable

The ambiguities of the terms used in the study of integration are well known, and "automatic politicization," the dependent variable of the Haas-

[3] Ernst B. Haas, *The Uniting of Europe: Political, Social, and Economic Forces, 1950–1957* (Stanford, Calif: Stanford University Press, 1958).

[4] Leon N. Lindberg, *The Political Dynamics of European Economic Integration* (Stanford, Calif: Stanford University Press, 1963); Ernst B. Haas and Philippe C. Schmitter, "Economics and Differential Patterns of Political Integration: Projections about Unity in Latin America," *International Organization*, Autumn 1964 (Vol. 18, No. 4), pp. 705–737.

[5] See, for example, J. S. Nye, "Patterns and Catalysts in Regional Integration," *International Organization*, Autumn 1965 (Vol. 19, No. 4), pp. 870–884; Stanley Hoffmann, "Obstinate or Obsolete? The Fate of the Nation-State and the Case of Western Europe," *Daedalus*, Summer 1966 (Vol. 95, Nos. 3–4), pp. 862–916; Roger D. Hansen, "Regional Integration: Reflections on a Decade of Theoretical Efforts," *World Politics*, January 1969 (Vol. 21, No. 2), pp. 257–270.

[6] Mario Barrera and Ernst B. Haas, "The Operationalization of Some Variables Related to Regional Integration: A Research Note," *International Organization*, Winter 1969 (Vol. 23, No. 1), pp. 150–160, and Philippe C. Schmitter, "Further Notes on Operationalizing Some Variables Related to Regional Integration," *International Organization*, Spring 1969 (Vol. 23, No. 2), pp. 327–336.

Schmitter paradigm, is no exception.[7] In addition, the emphasis on whether "economic integration of a group of nations automatically trigger[s] political unity"[8] reflects the concerns of the European neo-functionalists a decade ago more than the interests of elites of less developed countries who enter into integration schemes. Skeptics might reply that the answer to the question posed by Haas and Schmitter is simply "no" and thus reject the paradigm as uninteresting.

The choice of a dependent variable is somewhat arbitrary, reflecting interests and values. People like J. J. Servan-Schreiber who believe that it is not enough for Europeans to live like Swiss or Swedes or who argue that a Europe capable of a common defense and foreign policy will contribute significantly to a peaceful world order might choose some fairly integrated form of political institution as the dependent variable and probably the development of supporting attitudes and loyalties as well.[9] Those more interested in economic benefits who argue that a high degree of economic interdependence between states can help to diminish their propensity for conflict might choose economic integration as the dependent variable.

Economic "liberals" restrict this operationally to what John Pinder calls "negative economic integration"[10]—the removal of discriminatory obstacles to free trade within a region. Skeptics of the liberal approach (as many economists are on the basis of the structural imperfections of markets in less developed countries) or those interested in a degree of economic interdependence which involves positive action because it costs governments some of their sovereignty or freedom of action will choose positive economic integration or economic union as the dependent variable and will measure it by the amount of shared services and degree of coordination of policies.[11] Our choice of collective decisionmaking in the policies involved in an economic union has the

[7] See Joseph S. Nye, "Comparative Regional Integration: Concept and Measurement," *International Organization*, Autumn 1968 (Vol. 22, No. 4), pp. 855–880. In several places below I refer to terms defined in the earlier article.

[8] Haas and Schmitter, *International Organization*, Vol. 18, No. 4, p. 705.

[9] J. J. Servan-Schreiber, *The American Challenge*, trans. by Ronald Steel (New York: Atheneum, 1969).

[10] John Pinder, "Problems of Economic Integration," in G. R. Denton (ed.), *Economic Integration in Europe* (London: Weidenfeld and Nicolson, 1969), p. 145.

[11] In practice this could be done by applying Leon Lindberg's scale of locus of decision (see Leon N. Lindberg, "The European Community as a Political System: Notes toward the Construction of a Model," *Journal of Common Market Studies*, June 1967 [Vol. 5, No. 4], p. 359) to the following policies which are regarded by Bela Balassa as part of economic union: 1) free trade (percentage of trade included); 2) customs union (percentage of imports covered by common external tariff); 3) degree of freedom of flow of labor and capital; 4) fiscal policy; 5) countercyclical policy; 6) monetary policy; 7) social policies. See Bela Balassa, *Theory of Economic Integration* (London: George Allen and Unwin, 1962), p. 1. Pinder would add: 1) industrial investment and location policy; 2) coordination of managed or regulated markets (e.g., agriculture, transport, energy); 3) scientific and technological research; 4) external commercial policy; 5) internal regional incomes equalization policy. This gives us a list of twelve economic policies (instead of Lindberg's more varied seventeen) for constructing an index of extent of economic policy coordination as a measure of our dependent variable.

virtue of closeness to the manifest motives and interests of the actors involved in integration schemes in less developed states as well as closeness to what seems to be the "neither fish nor fowl" institutional shape of the current integration process in Europe. Alternatively, a broad list of policy areas including more specifically political functions can be used.[12] In any case the dependent variable must be more carefully stated.

II. Actors and Intentions

In the original neo-functionalist model the important actors are integrationist-technocrats and various interest groups which get governments to create a regional economic integration organization for a variety of convergent aims. Once done and depending on the degree of initial commitment this action unleashes the new forces of sector imbalance or *engrenage,* increased flows of transactions, and involvement of an increasing number of social groups which gradually focus their activities at the regional level.

These process forces or mechanisms in turn lead to two outcomes: 1) National governmental decisionmakers, under the joint pressures of the inconvenience of sector integration and of groups eager to preserve their gains from sector integration, agree to increase the initial grant of power to the regional institutions and 2) group activities and eventually mass loyalties increasingly flow to the regional center as it answers more and more of the interests previously satisfied by the national governments. The net effect is a continuous and automatic process leading to political unions if there are: 1) certain "background" conditions of symmetry between the national units, social pluralism, high transaction flows, and elite complementarity; 2) initiation conditions mentioned above; and 3) process conditions of technocratic decision-making style ("supranationality in practice"), rising transactions, and adaptability on the part of governments. In diagramatic terms the model is presented in Figure 1.

The impact of Charles de Gaulle on the process of European integration led Haas to revise this theory and add another type of political actor—what he called the actor with "dramatic-political" aims.[13] Even in a setting like postwar Europe in which politics is highly bureaucratized and welfare is a predominant popular concern[14] a dramatic political leader was able to prevail over leaders with incremental economic aims and to divert the integration process from the predicted course.

[12] In his article in this issue Lindberg lists 22 external, political-constitutional, sociocultural, and economic issue areas. Twelve of the 22 are economic and very similar to my list. The two approaches are very similar. The broader list has the advantage of completeness but also raises more problems about weighting the issue areas.

[13] Ernst B. Haas, "The *Uniting of Europe* and the Uniting of Latin America," *Journal of Common Market Studies,* June 1967 (Vol. 5, No. 4), pp. 315–343.

[14] See Stephen Graubard (ed.), *A New Europe?* (Boston: Houghton Mifflin Co., 1964).

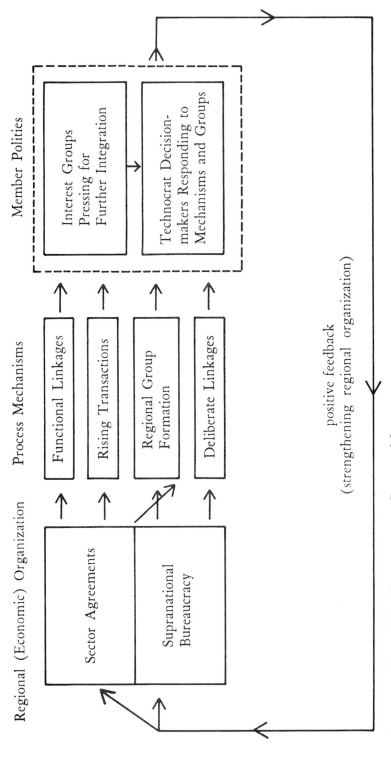

FIGURE 1. EARLY NEO-FUNCTIONALIST PROCESS MODEL

The problem of leadership in an integration process is not one of techno-crats versus politicians or administration versus politics. Nor does it always involve drama. It is more a question of the dominance of different styles of politics in different settings and at different times. The so-called technocrats who came from the planning offices and ministries of economy and who played such an influential role in the inauguration of the European Coal and Steel Community (ECSC), the Central American Common Market (CACM), and the Latin American Free Trade Association (LAFTA) were really quite heavily involved in politics.[15] Their political style, however, was that of the committee room and their power was based on reputation for expertise. This is quite different from the politician whose style is that of the market place (or the television studio) and whose power is based on his capacity to mobilize broad public support or the politician whose style is that of the officers' club or party office and whose power is based on capacity to mobilize the support of the elites of crucial military and political organizations. These latter types of electoral or "support" politicians tend to be guardians of the security and "pooled self-esteem" aspects of national life that Stanley Hoffmann has re-ferred to as "high politics."[16] They play an important function in legitimizing (or destroying the legitimacy of) various actions involved in regional integra-tion. The technocrat-politicians, on the other hand, play an important role in responding to the economic logic of integration and working out the com-promises necessary to make the process work.

Finally, the list of national actors should include not only groups which perceive themselves benefited by integration but also groups opposed to it and neutral groups that may be mobilized for either side. As Leon Lindberg and Stuart Scheingold point out, certain groups, by occupation or by region, may lag behind in the distribution of benefits associated with integration.[17] Al-though they may not be opposed to integration if they do not perceive the relationship of their problems to the common market, they represent a poten-tial problem. Finally, we should add the category of mass opinion leaders who create broad or narrow limits for the legitimacy of integrationist programs. In some cases, when integration becomes an electoral issue, opinion leaders create specific support or opposition to integrationist programs.[18]

In the original neo-functionalist model, developed at a time when many observers were noting the bureaucratization of politics, the decline of ideology,

[15] Joseph S. Nye, Jr., "Central American Regional Integration," *International Conciliation*, March 1967 (No. 562), p. 27. Christopher Mitchell, "The Role of Technocrats in Latin American Integration," *Inter-American Economic Affairs*, Summer 1967 (Vol. 21, No. 1), pp. 3–30.

[16] Stanley Hoffmann, "The European Process at Atlantic Crosspurposes," *Journal of Common Market Studies*, February 1965 (Vol. 3, No. 2), pp. 85–101.

[17] See Leon Lindberg and Stuart Scheingold, *Europe's Would-Be Polity: Patterns of Change in the European Community* (Englewood Cliffs, N.J: Prentice-Hall, 1970).

[18] Jacques-René Rabier, *L'Opinion publique et l'Europe* (Brussels: Institute of Sociology, University of Brussels, 1966).

and the growing popular concern for welfare and when foreign policies were held more closely in the vise of cold-war bipolarity, the national decisionmakers in the model were assumed to be economic incrementalists and thus be responsive to the economic logic of integration. It was thought that the technocrat-politicians could bypass the electoral or support politicians and forge links to the ever stronger regional organization until *engrenage* had proceeded so far that it was too late for anyone to change the pattern.

In this sense the neo-functionalists relied on "integration by stealth" and the positive role of popular ignorance. To a considerable extent this fit the early days of LAFTA and CACM. This picture is less accurate as a description of the *initiation* of European integration (Robert Schuman, Konrad Adenauer, and Alcide de Gaspari obviously played vital roles), but it is reasonably accurate for the workings of the ECSC. The protective cloak of noncontroversiality quickly wears out, however, as more sensitive interests are touched and as political heat generated by the integration process grows. Indeed there are some political climates in which economic issues are sufficiently highly politicized from the start that the cloak of noncontroversiality cannot be worn in the first place. Thus whatever the value of the simplified neo-functionalist model for explaining the early stages of integration in some settings, it quickly loses its explanatory value. By adding other categories of actors we make the model more complex and unwieldly, but we also extend its range of applicability.

Once we admit that (except for the early stages of integration in certain settings) important decisions affecting the integration process must be channeled through the political legitimizing leadership, we greatly enrich the model by admitting the possibility of negative as well as positive syndromes of responses resulting from the impact of the process forces upon the national decisionmakers. Actors can pull back from common tasks and institutions as well as increase their scope and authority.

There is also a third possible syndrome of responses to the impact of the process forces—the maintenance of the status quo. If the process forces are not too strong, the political leaders may prefer to tolerate the inconvenience of living with them rather than face what from their view are the political costs of negative or positive feedback. If group pressures are not too strong (a factor that will vary with the strength of pluralism) and if mass opinion is not intense in one direction or the other, the "normal" reaction of decisionmakers who are cast in the role of guardians of the security and identitive functions of the state would be the middle course of the status quo. In short, our hypothesized expectation is inertia.

If the above conditions do not hold, however, or if the political legitimizing leaders themselves have strong preferences for or against integration, there will be negative or positive feedback to the regional organization. Rapid or dramatic changes in leadership will have to be treated as an exogenous variable. In light of the European experience in which a French colonial crisis precipitated new leadership with a traditional view of the importance of the sovereign state we often think of such changes in association with political movements to the right. However, a leftist revolutionary movement that brought new leadership committed to the use of the state and of planning to restructure society could also have a very nationalistic effect.

III. PROCESS MECHANISMS

A wide variety of reasons may be needed to account for the initial creation of a regional economic organization. Among the most important are the rise of a new reformist elite with incremental economic goals that is conscious of the welfare implications of existing market sizes[19] and events in the external environment that impress upon both mass opinion and political legitimizing leaders the political cogency or usefulness of asserting their regional identity in an institutional form. Our model, however, is not designed to account for initiation. We want to discover the forces that follow from the creation of a new organization and exert pressure on decisionmakers for integrative or disintegrative responses. What are the process mechanisms that exist after the creation of a regional economic organization?

As we have seen, the early neo-functionalist model gave essentially four process mechanisms that follow the creation of a common market: 1) the inherent functional linkages of tasks; 2) increasing flows or transactions; 3) deliberate linkages and coalitions; and 4) economic pressure groups, including at a later state the formation of groups at the regional level. Subsequent work by other scholars has suggested at least three other process mechanisms that may arise or be enhanced by the creation of a regional economic organization; 5) involvement of external actors; 6) regional ideology and intensification of regional identity; and 7) elite socialization.

These process mechanisms can be divided into those which follow from the liberalization or removal of state barriers to the free flow of goods and factors and those which are created by the establishment of administrative institutions. Whether political decisionmakers can ignore the pressures for decisions that the process mechanisms create or whether they will be forced into integrative or disintegrative decisions will depend upon the strength of the process mechanisms and upon conditions to be outlined below. In short, as we shall show in each case below, depending on certain conditions, process mechanisms that generate strong pressures can have negative rather than positive effects on an integration process.

---

[19] Deutsch found a close association between the rise of a new elite and integration in the historical cases in Deutsch, and others.

The stronger the initial commitment as expressed in treaty commitments on liberalization (timetables, lack of escape clauses, etc.) and in the institutions that are established (both in resources and jurisdiction), the stronger the process mechanisms that are created. In addition, the mechanisms interact with each other in such a way as to enhance or diminish their net impact on political decisionmakers. For instance, rising transactions and inherent linkages are likely to increase elite socialization and deliberate linkages. On the other hand, high involvement of external actors may sometimes diminish the ideological-identitive appeal.

A. *Functional Linkage of Tasks*

The concept of "spillover" has frequently been misapplied to cover any sign of increased cooperation, thus robbing it of its explanatory value. Even its original formulation was somewhat ambiguous. Haas used the term to cover both perceived linkages between problems arising out of their inherent technical characteristics and linkages deliberately created or overstated by political actors (what might be called "cultivated spillover"). Despite these problems and the lesser effectiveness of the force than was originally believed to be the case, the perception that imbalances created by the functional interdependence or inherent linkages of tasks can press political actors to redefine their common tasks remains an important insight In Walter Hallstein's words, "the material logic of the facts of integration urges us relentlessly on from one step to the next, from one field to another."[20]

For example, after tariff barriers were reduced in the European Economic Community (EEC), profit margins of firms and their competitive positions were more strongly affected by different systems of taxation, and this fact led to the adoption by the EEC countries of a common system of calculating tax on value added.[21] When French costs began to increase relative to those of the Federal Republic of Germany (West Germany) by about 3 percent a year (i.e., inflation was higher in France than in West Germany), the initial result was the monetary crisis of November 1968 and French imposition of measures to restrain trade in order to protect its balance of payments. The longer term impact was to persuade the governments to accept a plan proposed by the Commission of the European Communities for coordination of short- and medium-term economic policies. In agriculture the surpluses generated by the common pricing system pressed the governments toward a common structural policy.

In Central America once the governments had reduced tariff barriers, they found themselves compelled (though not without delaying action and resistance by some) to adopt a common policy on the incentives they offered to

---

[20] *European Community*, June 1967 (No. 103), p. 11.
[21] The crisis-torn Italian government delayed in following this course.

attract foreign industry to their particular parts of the larger market. In East Africa the existence of a common railroad service led the three countries to coordinate studies of road transport. Such forces work in planned economies as well. According to Frederick Pryor, in the Council for Mutual Economic Assistance (CMEA) "the difficulties in achieving a consistent intra-Bloc trade pattern forced attention on the possibilities of a coordination of Bloc production" and resulted in an increasing scope of activities of CMEA.[22]

The redefinition of tasks need not mean an upgrading of common tasks. The response can also be negative. If the conditions to be spelled out below have not resulted in a positive experience for a major coalition of actors, the inconvenience created by the imbalance may be overcome by undoing the original linkage—for instance, the national solutions to the 1958 coal crisis in the ECSC,[23] the isolation of the French and West German agricultural market after the changes in currency values in 1969, or the breaking of the common currency in East Africa in 1966. If this linkage can cause spillover, it can also cause spill-back. When the little wheels mesh but the resistance of the big wheels is too great, they are either disengaged or broken.

B. *Rising Transactions*

If the initiation of a regional integration scheme gives rise to an unexpected response by societal forces that result in a large rise in transactions (trade, capital movements, communications), political actors may 1) be faced with the overburdening of the institutions they have established for dealing with such transactions and with the need to curtail the transactions; 2) try to deal with them through national measures; or 3) increase the capacity of the common institutions that they have established.

Strictly speaking this is somewhat different from spillover as defined above since the dynamic does not arise from the imbalance created by sector integration in a functionally interdependent system but is closer to Amitai Etzioni's image of having to increase the size of a pipe as volume of flow is increased.[24] In other words, rising transactions need not lead to a significant widening of the scope (range of tasks) of integration but may lead rather to the intensification of central institutional capacity to handle a particular task.

Whether the feedback from rising transactions has a positive or negative effect on further progress toward economic union depends, again, on changes in the conditions below. An example of a positive response has been the willingness of the Central American governments to nearly double their budgetary contributions to the integration institutions during a period (1965–1968) of

[22] Frederic L. Pryor, *The Communist Foreign Trade System* (Cambridge, Mass: M.I.T. Press, 1963), p. 199.

[23] There is an excellent account in Leon Lindberg's and Stuart Scheingold's book cited above.

[24] See Amitai Etzioni, *The Active Society: A Theory of Societal and Political Processes* (New York: Free Press, Collier-Macmillan, 1968), p. 564.

rapid growth of intraregional trade. On the other hand, given the tendency for agglomeration of industry and the backwash effects resulting from mere liberalization of trade among less developed states, increasing trade may also bring severely unbalanced benefits and actually have a negative effect. For example, a rapid rise in intra-East African trade from 1963 to 1965 (20 percent per year compared to 11 percent per year from 1959 to 1962) was followed by an abridgment of the common market and the imposition by Tanzania of quotas on 40 percent of the imports coming from Kenya.[25]

C. *Deliberate Linkages and Coalition Formation*

Coalition formation tends to be based on what we called "cultivated spill-over." In contrast to pure spillover in which the main force comes from a common perception of the degree to which problems are inextricably intertwined in a modern economy, problems are deliberately linked together into package deals not on the basis of technological necessity but on a basis of political and ideological projections and political possibilities. Some initiatives come from interest groups desiring to benefit from new opportunities. Other initiatives at coalition formation come from politicians concerned with the need to maintain a balance of benefits in the integration scheme.[26] International bureaucrats also play an important role in coalition formation both by presenting proposals that link issues and by acting as honest brokers during bargaining.

Two contrasting examples come from the EEC. A 1960 package deal hastened internal tariff cuts to satisfy those eager to advance the common market and simultaneously lowered the external tariff to satisfy those concerned about a loss of foreign trade. In contrast, in 1965 the Commission of the European Communities was unsuccessful with its proposed package deal of agricultural prices favorable to France, direct revenues for the EEC commission, and direct elections to the European Parliament.[27] The proposal touched off the 1965 EEC crisis, and there were no more successful large-scale package deals until the summit meeting at the Hague in December 1969. In other words, bureaucratic activism can also lead to bureaucratic slapdown in which packages are untied by politicians. But even deliberate linkage of problems and creation of coalitions by politicians can lead to the undoing of earlier integrated tasks if there are unfavorable changes in some of the conditions listed below that prevent members from meeting their commitments. Accusations of bad faith over partially fulfilled bargains were one of the major causes of the 1969 crisis in which Nicaragua threatened to leave the Central American Common Market.

[25] Peter Robson, *Economic Integration in Africa* (London: George Allen and Unwin, 1968), chapter 4, and Arthur Hazelwood, *African Integration and Disintegration* (London: Oxford University Press, 1967), chapter 3.

[26] Lindberg and Scheingold. See also Lindberg, *Journal of Common Market Studies*, Vol. 5, No. 4.

[27] See John Lambert, "The Constitutional Crisis 1965–66," *Journal of Common Market Studies*, May 1966 (Vol. 4, No. 3), pp. 195–228.

The nature of the coalition of supporting groups involved in a process can also cause problems. In less developed areas an integration scheme may result from the decisions of very few people. Nonetheless, once the regional organization is established, it can attract the support of specific groups through the benefits it offers them. For example, the Central American Common Market was created largely through the efforts of a small group of economist-politicians in spite of the suspicions of most Central American business interests. Subsequently, however, most business interests realized a benefit and became firm supporters of the program.

Regional bureaucrats and politicians may deliberately tailor programs and put together packages so as to broaden their coalition of specific support. Similarly they may try to convince parties or groups of the benefits to be gained by identification with the program; take, for example, Jean Monnet's formation of the Action Committee for a United States of Europe.[28] These efforts to build a coalition of specific support may have a negative effect, however, if the program becomes too closely identified with particular groups which subsequently decline in political fortune. Palace coups in Honduras and Guatemala have not affected the Central American Common Market, but a social revolution in one of the countries almost certainly would. Similarly, if an integration scheme is closely identified with support by a specific group (e.g., white business in East Africa) this may diminish its broader identitive appeal. Finally, dependence on a particular coalition of support may give that group a veto power over further steps toward economic union, particularly in circumstances of unfavorable integrative conditions.

D. *Elite Socialization*

The initiation of an integration scheme creates opportunities both for political decisionmakers attending meetings and bureaucrats seconded to regional institutions to develop personal ties and a possible corporate feeling. Leon Lindberg and Lawrence Scheinman have both focused attention on the increased contacts of politicians, national bureaucrats, and commission bureaucrats through the various meetings and institutions of the EEC.[29] Accounts of the workings of the permanent representatives and the council of the EEC as well as accounts of the meetings of the ministers of economy in Central America have pointed to the development of feelings of collective identity among the individuals taking part.

If the conditions listed below are not favorable or change in an unfavorable

---

[28] See Walter Yondorf, "Monnet and the Action Committee: The Formative Period of the European Communities," *International Organization*, Autumn 1965 (Vol. 19, No. 4), pp. 885–912. Monnet relied on center-left groups whose importance declined somewhat in the 1960's.

[29] See Lawrence Scheinman, "Some Preliminary Notes on Bureaucratic Relationships in the European Economic Community," *International Organization*, Autumn 1966 (Vol. 20, No. 4), pp. 750–773; and Lindberg and Scheingold, chapter 4.

direction, however, increased personal contact may enhance the potential acri-
mony (as it did, for example, in East Africa in 1963). Even if the contact results in socialization of political or bureaucratic decisionmakers into a system
perspective, if integrative conditions become worse this may merely result in
the isolation of the most prointegration actors from political effectiveness. Some
accounts of bureaucrats returning from Brussels to Paris and Bonn support
this view.[30] Moreover, it is possible that contacts that are positive from the
point of view of the individual can cause a negative response on the part of
insecure leaders who wish to keep their populations isolated.

One of the reasons that elite socialization is a particularly important potential process mechanism is that it touches one of the groups that is often most
resistant to loss of national control—the bureaucrats in the national governments who immediately feel the loss of power as tasks are shifted to the regional center. To the extent that these national bureaucrats are involved in the
regional process on committees or by secondment to the regional secretariat
they can "learn by doing" and the distinction between regional and national
bureaucrats is blurred.

Nonetheless, this is a force that works slowly. Although some 12,000 national bureaucrats were involved in 1,200 meetings of various committees in
the EEC system alone in 1964, the number of seconded personnel who have
returned to the national capitals is only a few hundred (a figure that must be
divided by six capitals with a score of ministries in each).[31] Ironically in view
of the public image, the French policy of sending personnel to Brussels for a
short period is more favorable to this process force than the more orthodox
Dutch view which insisted that a national civil servant cut his ties with the
home service after a year and become a pure Eurocrat.

One of the aims of the Economic Commission for Latin America (ECLA)
and subsequently of the Inter-American Development Bank and its Institute
for Latin American Integration has been the use of training programs to create
a strong group of national bureaucrats favorable to integration. Some estimates
of the size of this group of "graduates" is put at over 5,000. In Central America
a high official referred to an "integration mafia" of several hundred persons
who had at one time or another worked with the integration institutions.[32] On
the other hand, the importance of these contacts can be overestimated. It is
interesting that when the former secretary-general of ECLA and the former
executive secretary of LAFTA rejoined their national governments, they did
not succeed in creating more integrationist policies. In East Africa in 1969 an
important administrator who had once worked for the East African Common

---

[30] I am indebted to Andrew Taussig for this point.

[31] Stephen Holt, *The Common Market* (London: Hamish Hamilton, 1967), p. 60. See also David
Coombes, *Towards a European Civil Service* (European Series No. 7) (London: Chatham House, Political and Economic Planning, 1968).

[32] Interview with Jorge Viteri, UN official, June 1966; Nye, *International Conciliation*, No. 562, p. 45.

Services Organization (EACSO) and believed in East African cooperation freely admitted that he discouraged several economists who were thinking of joining the understaffed community because he needed them in his organization.[33]

E. *Regional Group Formation*

Once a regional integration scheme is established, it may serve as the stimulus for private groups to create various types of formal and informal nongovernmental regional organizations to reflect and protect their common interests at the regional level. In addition to representing a shift of political activity toward the regional level and a potential source of regional pressure on national governments these nongovernmental groupings themselves have elite socialization effects. By 1965 there were 231 regional offices of business and trade associations and 117 regional agricultural associations with offices in Brussels.[34] Similarly there has been a considerable growth of regional nongovernmental organizations in Central America since the formation of the Common Market. In the 1969 crisis the Federation of Chambers of Commerce and Industry of Central America issued statements defending the Common Market.

In general, however, these regional nongovernmental organizations remain a weak force.[35] In many cases the types of interests that are aggregated at the regional level tend to be very general, with more specific interests and structures remaining at the national level. For instance, despite the existence of regional trade union secretariats in Brussels, the idea of collective bargaining at the European level in response to the creation of a European market has not taken hold—in part because of the divisions in the labor movement but also because of the importance of national governmental power in collective bargaining.[36] Although the European commission has taken steps to encourage industrial and agricultural organizations like Union des industries de la Communauté européenne (UNICE) and the Comité des organisations professionelles agricoles (COPA) by formally consulting with them rather than with national organizations, the most important source of power for interest groups still remains at the national level.[37]

[33] Interview, Dar-es-Salaam, August 1969.

[34] Holt, p. 60.

[35] On European groups see Werner Feld, "National Economic Interest Groups and Policy Formation in the EEC," *Political Science Quarterly,* September 1966 (Vol. 81, No. 3), pp. 392–411; Jean Meynaud and Dusan Sidjanski, *Les groups de pression dans la Communauté européenne* (Montreal: University of Montreal Press, 1969), pp. 473–491; for East Africa see Joseph S. Nye, Jr., *Pan-Africanism and East African Integration* (Cambridge, Mass: Harvard University Press [under the auspices of the Center for International Affairs], 1965), chapter 1; for Central America see James D. Cochrane, *The Politics of Regional Integration: The Central American Case* (Tulane Studies in Political Science, Vol. 12) (New Orleans, La: Tulane University Press, 1969), chapter 4.

[36] See International Institute for Labor Studies, International Collective Bargaining Symposium held in Geneva, May 1969.

[37] Ironically, a 1968 demonstration in Brussels by 5,000 farmers (many of them French) against the EEC can be seen as a better tribute to power in that sector. *New York Times,* May 28, 1968.

The same configuration is true of Central America and East Africa. In the latter case the common services represented an important power at the regional level, but when the East African trade unions attempted to organize at the regional level, the governments became worried and discouraged the effort. With this process force as with the others it is possible to conceive of negative as well as positive feedbacks resulting from the pressures it might exert on decisionmakers in certain conditions to be defined below.

F. *Ideological-Identitive Appeal*

A taste shared by smaller groups to be identified as a larger group is frequently one of the factors that leads to initiation of regional integration schemes. Once established, a regional organization, by the symbol of its existence as well as by its actions (e.g., the efforts of the Hallstein commission, particularly before 1965), may heighten this sense of identitive appeal. The myth of permanence and inevitability is an important aspect of ideological-identitive appeal. The stronger the sense of permanence and the greater the identitive appeal, the less willing are opposition groups to attack an integration scheme frontally. For instance, Honduran and Costa Rican politicians cool to integration found it more expedient to attack the way the market was being run than the concept itself.[38]

In some cases a sense of permanence and strong identitive appeal can help groups or governments to tolerate short-term losses or sacrifices in the belief that they will be requited later.[39] Finally, the stronger the myth of permanence, the more likely are businessmen to invest on the basis of the larger market and thus to make the myth reality in the concrete form of new industrial investments—as happened in the early days of the EEC.[40] On the other hand, depending on the conditions listed below, the mere existence of the organization may serve as the token gratification of this weak popular taste, or actions of the organization under adverse conditions may actually heighten the competition from the sense of national identity as Charles Anderson and Ali Mazrui argue occurred as the result of economic contacts in LAFTA and the East African Common Market (EACM), respectively.[41] Finally, even if there is an impressive growth of identitive appeal, it may cause a negative response on the part of insecure or nationalistic leaders, particularly under unfavorable integrative conditions.[42]

---

[38] See Nye, *International Conciliation*, No. 562, p. 50.

[39] Lindberg and Scheingold.

[40] Alexandre Lamfalussy, "Europe's Progress: Due to the Common Market?" in Lawrence B. Krause (ed.), *The Common Market: Progress and Controversy* (Englewood Cliffs, N.J: Prentice-Hall, 1964), pp. 90–107.

[41] Charles W. Anderson, *Politics and Economic Change in Latin America* (Princeton, N.J: D. Van Nostrand, 1967), p. 61; Ali Mazrui, "Tanzania versus East Africa: A Case of Unwitting Federal Sabotage," *Journal of Commonwealth Political Studies*, November 1965 (Vol. 3, No. 3), pp. 209–225.

[42] For a distinction between symbolic, normative, and functional nationalism and their different pro-

G. *Involvement of External Actors in the Process*

The original neo-functionalist formulation paid insufficient attention to the role of external factors in integration processes perhaps in reaction to federalist theories that overstressed them, perhaps in the absence of change in this situation in Europe at the time of the formulation of the approach. When a variable does not change, we often fail to see it. We are now beyond the stage of the initial criticism when we can talk of "catalysts" or "external factors" in general terms.[43] Building upon the distinction between passive and active external factors[44] (those of a broad nature not affected by the process contrasted with those that represent deliberate action by external actors affected by the creation of a regional scheme), I include regional actor *perceptions* of the external situation as one of the integrative conditions that we will examine below and consider only *involvement* of external actors in the integration scheme as a process mechanism.

An integration process can involve various actors, including other governments, other international organizations, and nongovernmental actors such as international corporations. For example, the United States Agency for International Development and the United Nations Economic Commission for Latin America have both played important roles in the Central American Common Market. French governmental support has played an important role in organizations of ex-French African states: Joint African and Malagasy Organization (OCAM), Union douanière et économique de l'Afrique centrale (UDEAC), and Conseil de l'entente. Nonindigenous corporations have played important roles in taking advantage of the larger market opportunities created by both the EEC and LAFTA.[45]

Some external actors perceive their interests to be adversely affected by an integration process, and they become involved in a negative way.[46] This negative effect may be determined in part by some of the integrative conditions listed below, but by and large exogenous factors are probably the more important determinants. On the other hand, a large positive involvement of external actors can also produce a negative effect in cases in which this gives them a veto power on further integrative steps (for instance, United States attitudes toward the Central American industrial allocation scheme).[47] Finally, as we

pensities for international organization see John DeLamater, Daniel Katz, and Herbert C. Kelman, "On the Nature of National Involvement: A Preliminary Study," *Journal of Conflict Resolution*, September 1969 (Vol. 13, No. 3), pp. 321–357.

[43] Nye, *International Organization*, Vol. 19, No. 4, pp. 870–884.

[44] Nye, *International Conciliation*, No. 562.

[45] See Raymond Vernon, "The Role of U.S. Enterprise Abroad," *Daedalus*, Winter 1969 (Vol. 98, No. 1), p. 123.

[46] For an example concerning United States shipping interests see Miguel Wionczek, "Latin American Integration and United States Economic Policies," in Robert Gregg (ed.), *International Organization in the Western Hemisphere* (Syracuse, N.Y: Syracuse University Press, 1968), pp. 116–117.

[47] James D. Cochrane, "Central American Economic Integration: The 'Integrated Industries' Scheme," *Inter-American Economic Affairs*, Autumn 1965 (Vol. 19, No. 2), pp. 63–74.

mentioned earlier, too heavy an involvement of external actors in an integrative process may weaken its identitive appeal.

In summary, the response of political decisionmakers to the pressures generated by these process mechanisms will depend partly on the strength of the pressures—i.e., are they weak enough that the inconvenience they create is easier to tolerate than the political costs that might be incurred by a positive or negative response? The partially revised model is presented in Figure 2.

IV. Integrative Potential

The second determinant of the type of response is a set of conditions that we will refer to as the integrative potential of a region. These conditions are associated with positive responses to the pressures generated by the integrative mechanisms. They also affect the strength of initial commitment and thus the strength of the process mechanisms. The following list of conditions that constitute the integrative potential of a region is based on the Haas and Schmitter checklist but with certain omissions, additions, and restatements. The first amendment is to drop their categorization by stages (background, initiation, process) and replace it with a distinction between structural conditions which are conceived as relatively stable variables more determined by factors other than the integration process and perceptual conditions which are quite volatile during an integration process and are determined more by the integration process itself.

The conditions at the time of initiation do matter, but they matter because of the degree of commitment implied by the motives that are reflected in the institutions or treaty obligations. These remain important (and go up and down) during the whole process. Similarly, the categorization of certain conditions as belonging to the background is misleading if conceived of only as an early stage since the conditions continue to be important throughout the process and it is the effect of their variation over the process that we wish to observe. It is not clear, for example, why Haas and Schmitter singled out rate of transactions as the only background condition to be looked at over time. What happens to the other background conditions such as complementarity of elites, pluralism, and the symmetry ("size") of the units is equally important even though it is largely determined by exogenous factors.

As for transactions the rate of *initial* transactions is *not* an important background condition for economic integration among less developed countries. To single it out is to overemphasize a static analysis of existing trade patterns rather than potential trade in new (usually industrial) products which is a basic motivation for such schemes.[48] After all, intraregional trade was only 3 percent of

---

[48] See the comment by Raymond F. Mikesell on Robert Loring Allen, "Integration in Less Developed Areas," *Kyklos*, 1961 (Vol. 14, No. 3), p. 334, to the effect that large-scale import substitution under high protection is going to take place anyway, so the larger the market the better.

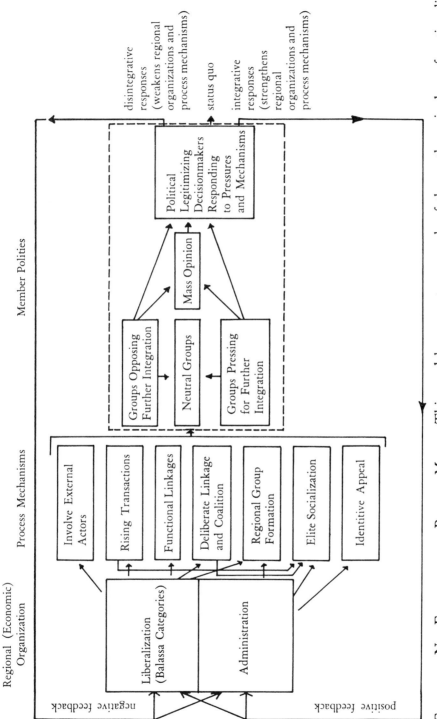

FIGURE 2. NEO-FUNCTIONALIST PROCESS MODEL. This model represents one cycle of the partly revised neo-functionalist process model.

Central American trade in the early 1950's but grew to over 20 percent in the 1960's. Thus, as indicated above we have treated changes in transactions as a process mechanism affected by the initiation of a scheme and capable of creating positive or negative feedback according to the integrative conditions.

A. *Structural Conditions*

The structural conditions that affect the nature of the initial commitment and the later impact of the process forces that follow the initiation of an economic integration scheme are as follows:

I. SYMMETRY OR ECONOMIC EQUALITY OF UNITS. This is restatement of Haas's and Schmitter's "size in the specific functional context of the union." At first glance it seems to contradict the proposition that "core areas" and unequal size may be helpful conditions for integration. Citing Karl Deutsch and Amitai Etzioni, Bruce Russett argues that there is no

> very convincing theory or evidence about international integration that indicates that the prospective members of a new unit should be the same size. (On the contrary, the idea of a powerful core area to provide centripetal force is rather more persuasive.)[49]

Yet others argue that economic integration cannot be successful between unequal partners. Given the tendency of industry to cluster to take advantage of the external economies available from the presence of other industries in more developed parts of a region, there is a danger that (in Gunnar Myrdal's terms) the "spread" effects of increased economic activity will be less important to the poorer areas than the "backwash" effect of the attraction of resources from the poorer to the richer areas. A case frequently cited is the deleterious effect of the unification of Italy upon southern Italy in the nineteenth century.

There are several points worth noting about this apparent theoretical dispute over the role of size in integration theory. First, it vanishes in the face of more precise formulation of what we mean by integration. What may be true of one type of integration (for example, trade) may not be of another (for example, political union). Problems of unequal size have plagued the Latin American Free Trade Association, but they did not stop the Sardinian leadership in the creation and maintenance of common institutions in Italy in the face of an elite sense of national identity and within the nineteenth century international system in which an aspect of coercion was acceptable. And it is worth remembering that Deutsch's original hypothesis about "cores" was formulated in relation to a number of historical cases of security community.[50] Etzioni's argu-

[49] Bruce M. Russett, *International Regions and the International System: A Study in Political Ecology* (Chicago: Rand McNally & Co., 1967), p. 21.

[50]

> Contrary to the "balance of power" theory, security-communities seem to develop most frequently around cores of strength. . . .

Deutsch, and others, p. 10.

ment that egalitarian unions tend to be less decisive than elite unions but more capable of generating commitments[51] may be true of unions concerned with low-level coordination of foreign policy (witness the difference between the Organization of American States [OAS] and Organization of African Unity [OAU]) but not of higher levels of economic union (for example, LAFTA versus CACM).

If inequality is interpreted not in simple terms of square miles, or even gross national product (GNP), but rather as a level of development with per capita GNP as the indicator, a simple scattergram quickly indicates a relationship between trade integration and level of development. The number of cases is few, but it seems roughly true that in nonhegemonial regional economic organizations the more equal the level of development (measured by per capita GNP), the higher the regional trade integration (intraregional exports as a percentage of total exports). (See Figure 3.) Moreover, no economic integration scheme (common market or free trade area) which does over 20 percent

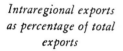

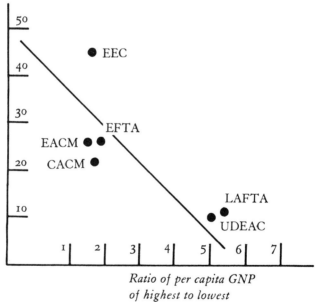

FIGURE 3. TRADE INTEGRATION AND EQUALITY OF DEVELOPMENT, MID-1960's. The coordinates are EEC, 1.7 and 44; EFTA (without Portugal), 1.9 and 25; EACM, 1.5 and 25; CACM, 1.7 and 22; LAFTA, 5.4 and 10; UDEAC, 5.0 and 6.

[51] Amitai Etzioni, *Political Unification: A Comparative Study of Leaders and Forces* (New York: Holt, Rinehart and Winston, 1965), p. 297.

of its trade intraregionally has more than a 2:1 ratio of difference in per capita incomes (Portugal, in EFTA, is the exception).

If inequality is interpreted not in terms of level of development but in terms of total size of the economy (measured in GNP), then size seems to have a very different effect in less developed than in developed areas. Relatively high degrees of trade integration have been achieved by integration schemes among developed countries in which the ratio of the largest to smallest economies (in GNP) is more than 5:1. Among less developed countries, however, the only schemes with trade integration over 20 percent have ratios of largest to smallest (in terms of GNP) of less than 2.5:1. It almost looks as if the lower the per capita income of the area, the greater the necessary homogeneity in size of economy.

While one must be cautious about using this evidence when the number of cases is so few, there are also intuitive grounds for believing that where income is lower and welfare is scarcer problems of its distribution are likely to be more strongly contested. In addition, it is more likely that backwash effects and clustering of industry to take advantage of external economies will be more politically apparent and difficult to resolve in smaller and poorer economies with fewer poles of growth.

While these measures of inequality based on GNP and per capita income have the virtue of simplicity, they may not be sufficiently refined to show changes over short periods. Politically sensitive indicators such as ratios of industrial production or differential rates of inflation may be more useful indicators. For instance, in East Africa industry accounted for some 11 percent of GNP in Kenya while the comparable figure for Uganda and Tanzania was only 5 percent. Or taking inflation, severe differentials between LAFTA countries not only have had adverse impacts on balance-of-payments positions and thus have created pressures for controls, but costs and competitive positions have been very unstable and difficult to calculate.[52] In short, the degree of favorability of the structural condition of symmetry may be strongly affected by the choice of indices.

Schmitter has suggested a further approach for studying changes in symmetry based on the hypothesis that the greater the rank incongruence measured by Kendall's coefficient of concordance (W) in "size-power" variables, the greater the chances of progression toward supranational political institutions (or economic union) because overall winning and losing statuses are harder to assign and package deals are easier to negotiate. He shows that the coefficient of concordance between GNP, per capita GNP, rate of growth, industry as a percentage of GNP, rate of inflation (inverted), governmental budget, military forces, and total surface area rose in Central America from .08 to .25 at the

[52] Sidney Dell, *A Latin American Common Market?* (London: Oxford University Press [under the auspices of the Royal Institute of International Affairs], 1966), p. 164ff.

same time that integrative decisions became more difficult.[53] Similarly, among the states of the European Communities Kendall's W rose from .16 in 1957 to .30 in 1961 and declined slightly to .25 in 1965.[54]

2. ELITE VALUE COMPLEMENTARITY. Whether corresponding elite groups do or do not think alike makes a difference; witness the effects of the addition of a Gaullist elite to the constellation of Christian-Democratic and Socialist decisionmakers in Europe in the mid-1950's. But which elites count and how much complementarity is necessary? For instance, military and democratically elected regimes have been able to cooperate in the Central American Common Market despite changes of government and military coups because the societal structure of power was not greatly affected.

On the other hand, the same elites that worked closely together at the time of East African independence have subsequently followed divergent paths of development with consequent occasional stress upon the East African Common Market. For our purpose it is the elites who control economic policy decisions that matter. These are not the same in all settings and may change over time with the politicization of a process as we shall see below. In general, the greater the complementarity of elites with effective power over economic policy as reflected in similar statements and policies toward the most salient political-economic issues in their region, the better the conditions for positive or integrative response to the pressure for decisions arising from the process mechanism.

3. PLURALISM (MODERN ASSOCIATIONAL GROUPS). Functionally specific, universalistic, achievement-oriented groups in all member states were important components of the neo-functional path in Europe. The relative absence or weakness of such groups in many less developed countries has been shown to make integration more difficult (though not impossible) by depriving regional bureaucrats of potential allies and by depriving governments of channels of information useful in the formation of realistic economic policy.[55]

Articles by Mario Barrera and Haas and by Schmitter have suggested ways to measure this condition.[56] While the absence of such groups does not make integration impossible—witness CMEA[57]—it does change the nature of the process and make it more difficult as we will see below. Our hypothesis is that the greater the pluralism in all member states, the better the conditions for an integrative response to the feedback from the process forces.

[53] Schmitter, *International Organization*, Vol. 23, No. 2, pp. 327–336.

[54] My calculation, leaving out military expenditure.

[55] See Anderson on the importance of modern groups as a feedback link that contributes to realistic rather than ideological formulation of economic policy.

[56] Barrera and Haas, and Schmitter, *International Organization*, Winter 1969 (Vol. 23, No. 1), pp. 150–160 and 161–166, respectively.

[57] See Andrzej Korbonski, "*COMECON*," *International Conciliation*, September 1964 (No. 549). Also Michael Kaser, *COMECON* (London: Oxford University Press, 1965), chapters 5 and 6.

4. CAPACITY OF MEMBER STATES TO ADAPT AND RESPOND. This is a slight adaptation of the Haas-Schmitter condition to include Deutsch's concept of "internal noise" which inhibits the capacity to respond.[58] Governments in less developed countries are notoriously weak in their capacity to commit their societies. As Miguel Wionczek has pointed out, presidential agreements in Latin America cannot always commit nationalized industries, much less governments or societies.[59] Even preferential legal treatment for Honduras in the CACM may not be sufficient to overcome the problems of fewer entrepreneurs, poor infrastructure, and governmental inefficiency that account for Honduran failure to benefit as much as its partners from the CACM. For instance, Honduras was granted priority in receiving loans from the Economic Integration Bank, but its government had difficulty in preparing sufficient fundable projects.[60]

Moreover, competing demands of internal instability (now perhaps in Europe as well as in less developed countries) on decisionmakers' attention may hinder the capacity of the more prosperous states to "hear" the messages from their weaker partners or to respond to them. On the other hand, internal noise is likely to have this effect only when it affects the key decisionmakers concerned with economic policy. In some situations, such as Central America in the 1950's, instability that absorbed the attention of the presidents but not the ministers of economy proved to be a beneficial condition.

Our hypothesis for this condition is that the greater the internal instability and other factors that diminish the capacity of the key decisionmakers in economic policy (both public and private) to adapt and respond to problems and crises, the more likely that feedback from the process mechanisms will have a negative effect.

The structural conditions constituting integrative potential tend to remain relatively constant during the course of an integration process. When they do change, they change primarily as a result of factors not closely related to integration (for example, violent overthrow of a government).

B. *Perceptual Conditions*

The following three perceptual conditions, on the other hand, are highly affected by the process of integration.

1. PERCEIVED EQUITY OF DISTRIBUTION OF BENEFITS. All students of comparative regional integration emphasize the importance of this condition. It differs from the structural condition of symmetry because it is based on perception by the actors. There is often a gap between the actual changes in economic

---

[58] See Karl Deutsch, "Communication Theory and Political Integration," in Philip Jacob and James Toscano (ed.), *The Integration of Political Communities* (Philadelphia: J. B. Lippincott Co., 1964), pp. 46–74.

[59] Wionczek, in Gregg.

[60] See Roger D. Hansen, *Central America: Regional Integration and Economic Development* (National Planning Association Studies in Development Progress, No. 1) (Washington: National Planning Association, 1967), p. 63.

symmetry in a region and the perception of equity among decisionmakers.

The politics of regional economic integration is not only the "politics of co-operation" but also the "politics of status" between states that have been traditional rivals. The cooperative or welfare aspect is more like a nonzero-sum game, and it is relevant (as economists have done) to use aggregate economic data to show that all states are better off or that even if a state like Honduras has not gained as much as El Salvador or Tanzania as much as Kenya, it is better off than it would have been without the common market.

The status aspect, however, is more like a zero-sum game. What matters is how decisionmakers perceive that they have gained or lost status or rank in relation to their neighbors. This is not always predictable from the hard data of economic changes. Rather it will be affected by the sensitivity of the traditional competition (such as the Franco-German rivalry) between the states and the personal predilections of particular decisionmakers. A great deal will depend on whether politicians make it a particular point to dramatize inequalities. For instance, despite survey evidence of Franco-German rapprochement some Gaullist supporters of Georges Pompidou in the 1969 French election accused the rival candidate, Alain Poher, of being the "German candidate" because of his more favorable views on European unity. The hypothesis accompanying this condition is of course that the higher the perceived equitable distribution in all countries, the better the conditions for further integration.

2. PERCEPTIONS OF EXTERNAL COGENCY. The way that regional decisionmakers perceive the nature of their external situation and the manner in which they should respond to it is an important condition determining agreement on further integration. There are a variety of relevant perceptions such as a sense of external threat from a giant neighbor, loss of status felt by Europeans and Latin Americans as a result of bipolarity and simple demonstration effects ("everybody's doing it").[61]

Roger Hansen and Philippe Schmitter have both suggested that the external dependence of less developed countries on traditional primary exports is a condition that accounts for their interest in regional integration, and Schmitter has suggested (among other measures) taking two main exports as a percentage of total exports as a measure of external dependence.[62] One problem with using such data alone is that it measures dependence, not perception of dependence by politically relevant elites. By this measure Latin American countries were even more dependent in the past, but it is only recently that they turned to regional integration. Though this perception of dependence usually exists today, its timing and intensity need to be explained.

Other aspects of external dependence might be operationalized by looking

[61] See Karl Kaiser, "The Interaction of Regional Subsystems: Some Preliminary Notes on Recurrent Patterns and the Role of Superpowers," *World Politics*, October 1968 (Vol. 21, No. 1), pp. 84–107

[62] Hansen, *World Politics*, Vol. 21, No. 2, pp. 257–270, and Schmitter, *International Organization*, Vol. 23, No. 1, pp. 161–166.

at economic and military aid and perhaps also at drawings on the International Monetary Fund (IMF), at alliances, and at organizational memberships. Again, however, the important question is the existence of common
perceptions of the cogency of such dependence, particularly when different
dependences pull in different directions—e.g., differing French and West
German perceptions of what to do about dependence on the United States
and the way these differences affected their policies toward European integration.[63] It is the common definition of the nature of the external situation
and the measures to be taken to deal (or not deal) with it that constitutes the
favorable condition for an integrative response to the process mechanisms.

3. LOW (OR EXPORTABLE) VISIBLE COSTS. A key tenet of neo-functional strategy is to make integration seem relatively costless by carefully choosing the
initial steps. Where visible costs are low it is easier to get agreement on the
first steps that will start the process of *engrenage*. Over time, of course, costs
are likely to become higher and more visible.

Finding low-cost situations is not always easy. For example, in Central
America, unlike much of South America, there had been little industrialization behind high tariff walls. Consequently in the former case there were
few vested interests that saw a cost in the reduction of intraregional tariffs.
In LAFTA, however, after the first rounds of tariff concessions cut the fat of
overprotection, a number of protected industries saw high costs in further
reductions.

Regional integration schemes usually involve a strong protectionist element,
whether it be European farmers or Central American manufacturers or nationalized industries in the LAFTA countries. Strickly speaking, this protection represents a real cost to consumers *inside* the region (compensated in the
long run perhaps if there are infant industries being protected, though this
is hardly the case in European coal and agriculture) as well as to foreigners
in terms of their trade that is diverted (which may not be fully compensated
by new trade created).[64]

Nonetheless, in accord with Harry Johnson's theory of economic nationalism the widely dispersed and less visible costs of protectionist subsidies are not
as politically influential as are the concrete benefits to the specific groups being
protected. Thus to the extent that it looks as though only outsiders are being
hurt and the visible costs can be "exported," agreement on integration policies
may be easier.[65]

Similarly among less developed countries if the solution to an integration
problem can be met largely through the provision of external aid, the costs
of the solution are exportable and it may be more likely to be adopted. This

[63] Hoffmann, *Journal of Common Market Studies,* Vol. 3, No. 4, pp. 85–101.

[64] Harry G. Johnson, *Economic Nationalism in Old and New States* (London: George Allen and
Unwin, 1968), chapter 1.

[65] Lindberg and Scheingold.

situation may help explain the recent popularity and role of regional development banks that attract outside funds. They often appear to represent relatively cost-free integration. In short, the greater the prospects for avoiding or exporting the visible costs of measures to cope with the feedback created by the process mechanisms, the more favorable the conditions for an integrative response.

In summary, our revised list of process mechanisms and integrative conditions looks as follows:

I. Process Mechanisms

    A. Functional linkage of tasks
    B. Rising transactions
    C. Deliberate linkage and coalition formation
    D. Elite socialization
    E. Regional group formation
    F. Ideological-identitive appeal
    G. Involvement of external factors

II. Integrative Potential

    A. Structural Conditions
        1. Symmetry of units
        2. Capacity of member states to adapt and respond
        3. Pluralism (modern associational groups)
        4. Elite value complementarity
    B. Perceptual Conditions
        5. Perceived equity of distribution of benefits
        6. Perceived external cogency
        7. Low (or exportable) visible costs

One way to illustrate the point of our analysis thus far is the rather arbitrary assessments of the strength of process forces and favorability of integrative conditions in six organizations given in Table 1. These aggregate judgments are not useful for any but illustrative purposes since they assume equal weighting of the variables, ignore interaction effects, and are based only on intuitive scoring by the author. Nonetheless, they help illustrate our central point about a balance between the strength of process mechanisms and the favorability of conditions.

For example, a reading for the East African Common Market in 1965 shows strong process mechanisms and only low to moderate favorability of integrative conditions. Thus we would have predicted disintegrative responses on the part of political legitimizing decisionmakers which in fact occurred with the rupture of the common currency, dissolution of some common services, and application of intraregional quotas on trade. These actions reduced the strength of the process mechanisms. At the same time outside pressures and suggestions increased the perceived cogency of the external situation, thus improving the favorability of integrative conditions. By the end of 1967 the East African leaders had agreed on a new institutional formula that seemed to have stabilized the situation.

TABLE I. PREDICTED OUTCOMES, SIX ORGANIZATIONS, MID-1960's

	Aggregate Judgment on Process Mechanisms	Aggregate Judgment on Conditions	Expected Responses
EEC	High-Moderate	Moderate-High	Integrative
EFTA	Low-Moderate	Moderate-High	Status Quo
CACM	Moderate-High	Moderate-High	Integrative
LAFTA	Low-Moderate	Low-Moderate	Status Quo
EACM	High-Moderate	Low-Moderate	Disintegrative
CMEA	Low-Moderate	Low-Moderate	Status Quo

V. PHASING AND CONSEQUENCES

Comparative readings of the strength of mechanisms or favorability of conditions between areas or in one region over time tells us only part of what we want to know. What is the likely sequence of interactions between forces, conditions, and actors over time? Do the relationships change during the course of a process? Is the process likely to be continuous, even assuming no major change in exogenous forces? Obviously, the sequences and phasing of integration process will vary with the politics of each region. Nonetheless, we can introduce some order into the study by formulating certain hypotheses about the likely shape of the integration process and try to establish the conditions under which those hypotheses are likely to be true.

We will hypothesize four conditions that are likely to characterize an integration process over time: 1) politicization; 2) redistribution; 3) reduction of alternatives; and 4) externalization. These conditions are abstracted from the experience of three major cases: the European Economic Community, the East African Common Market, and the Central American Common Market.

A. *Politicization*

If, over the course of time, positive responses to the process forces lead to higher levels of integration (stronger institutions and greater coordination of economic policy), we would expect the process to become more "political." By politics we mean the process by which conflicting visions of a common interest are agitated or settled.[66] In short, politics in this sense implies controversy and with growing controversy a broadening of the arena of participants.

At the other end of the continuum of controversy are technical procedures which involve the choice of "optimal" solutions by reputed experts by apparently "rational" criteria. It is worth noting, however, that a number of subjects that are apparently technical in the sense of depending on expertise may not be amenable to purely technical procedures. For example, European cooperation in the science and technology field has been highly politicized or controversial right from the outset perhaps because of its symbolic content and the difficulties of making precise calculations of benefits in a new field.[67] Similarly, economic issues which fall closer to the technical-administrative end of the continuum of controversialism in the European context are frequently highly politicized from the outset in African settings.

We would expect politicization to increase during the course of an integration process for several reasons. More groups become involved through the effects of rising transactions, inherent linkages, or deliberate coalition formation. The larger the numbers, the more likely the possible divergent interpretations of the common interest in integration. The growth of the powers of the central institutions not only makes them more visible to mass opinion but may also stimulate action by groups opposed to integration, including national bureaucrats jealous of incursion into their powers. The growth of ideological-identitive appeal and the involvement of external actors makes the integration process more salient both to mass opinion and to the dramatic-political decisionmakers. At the same time costs are likely to rise or become more visible as the effects of integration begin to work themselves out.

The greater the politicization of subjects, the less amenable they are to the quiet technocratic decisionmaking style that

> stresses the role of uninstructed experts who tend to agree among themselves with respect to the reasoning patterns and antecedent conditions relevant to a decision, *and* with respect to the outcome to be attained.[68]

This does not necessarily mean that further integration is impossible. It does mean, however, that reaching decisions may be more difficult and involve a wider range of forces.

Politicization is not necessarily bad for an integration process though it has

[66] E. C. Banfield, in *A Dictionary of the Social Sciences,* ed. by Julius Gould and William L. Kolb (Glencoe, Ill: Free Press [compiled under the auspices of the United Nations Educational, Scientific and Cultural Organization], 1964).

[67] See Robert L. Pfaltzgraff and James L. Deghand, "European Technological Collaboration: The Experience of the European Launcher Development Organization," *Journal of Common Market Studies,* September 1968 (Vol. 7, No. 1), pp. 22–34; Also Robert Gilpin, *France in the Age of the Scientific State* (Princeton, N.J.: Princeton University Press, 1968), chapter 12.

[68] Haas and Schmitter, *International Organization.* Vol. 18, No. 4, p. 715.

the effect of reducing the favorability of one of the integrative conditions, i.e., perceived low costs. It seems inevitable and probably useful for the stability of solutions achieved that political legitimizing decisionmakers and broad public opinion become more heavily involved as integration decisions make heavier incursions upon national sovereignty and the identitive functions of the states.

Whether politicization acts as a brake on further integration responses depends on the structure of political interests in the member countries, and this in turn may depend to a large extent on timing. The important question is whether mass opinion and the support of groups benefited grows quickly enough to overcome the opposition of other groups and the likely proclivities of many political decisionmakers toward inertia or hostility as their sense of sovereign control is increasingly infringed. The problem for further integration is not politicization but premature politicization before supportive attitudes have become intense and structured. As we will see below, this is particularly a problem in many less developed countries.

B. *Redistribution*

As economic integration progresses, it is likely to have an effect on the distribution of welfare, status, and power both among groups within the member states and between the member states themselves. Within states certain groups or areas are more likely than others to benefit from rising transactions, package deals and coalitions, or alliances with external actors. Certain political actors and bureaucrats will benefit more than others from their involvement in integration, particularly if public support for integration increases during the process.

Other groups, while not necessarily directly hurt by the process of integration, may lag behind in incomes and status relative to those more directly benefited by integration—for instance, shopkeepers and small farmers or some of the peripheral areas of the European market. What effect this has on integration depends on the power of the groups affected, but even "weak" groups may have an influence if they turn to anomic behavior that diminshes the capacities of the governments to adapt and respond.

Favorable location, a more skilled entrepreneurial group, a political system more attractive to outside capital, or a more advanced industrial sector may attract transactions or external investors in some countries more than others. As we saw earlier, even when all countries benefit in terms of welfare compared to their opportunity costs, there may be redistribution of status which will cause one or more of the countries to take disintegrative actions.

This problem is particularly acute in less developed areas. Better prospects for industrialization tend to be a major incentive for common markets, and each country is intensely concerned with industrialization for status as well as welfare reasons. At the same time there is a tendency for industry to cluster to take advantage of existing external economies. Where there is little industry or few poles of growth this tends to create serious imbalances in the distribution of industry. Moreover, in some circumstances there may even be what one economist has likened to a soap bubble effect with the largest bubble absorbing the smaller ones.[69]

Redistribution is not totally bad for an integration process though it has obviously unfavorable effects in a region. On the contrary, as Lindberg and Scheingold point out, in Europe the prospect of redistribution is a major incentive for actors to push for further progress in integration. Roy Blough and Jack Behrman have argued that one of the causes of stagnation in LAFTA is the existence of so many guarantees against redistribution that there are few incentives for integration.[70] A certain amount of redistribution is necessary whether it be a new technocratic elite increasing its power or an area or two within a market serving as leading points of growth.

A crucial question with redistribution is the phasing of the growth of the process forces flowing from liberalization compared to those coming from the common institutions. If the role of the common institutions is increased and agreement is reached on common approaches, for example, to regional incomes policy or industrial location policy, the most severe effects of redistribution may be controlled. However, such policies involve difficult political coordination (and a more consciously perceived sacrifice of sovereign control). In the short run, governments often find it politically easier to promote integration indirectly ("negative" integration) through liberalization of their respective trade policies than to agree upon common approaches and the consequences of liberalization ("positive" integration). The difficult details are then worked out by the hidden hand of market forces whereas common policies involve hard political decisions on details. Even in Europe increasing trade integration was not matched by institutional growth.[71] To the extent that governments take the apparently easy way and rely almost solely on market forces, redistribution may generate resistances that become a brake on the integration process.

C. *Reduction of Alternatives*

An early neo-functionalist hypothesis was that integration was automatic. Once *engrenage* took place, it would become increasingly difficult and costly

[69] A. J. Brown, "Economic Separatism versus a Common Market in Developing Countries," *Yorkshire Bulletin of Economic and Social Research,* May 1961 (Vol. 13, No. 1), pp. 38ff.

[70] Roy Blough and Jack N. Behrman, "Problems of Regional Integration in Latin America," (Committee for Economic Development, Supplementary Paper No. 22), in *Regional Integration and the Trade of Latin America* (New York: Committee for Economic Development, 1968), p. 31.

[71] Leon N. Lindberg, "Integration as a Source of Stress on the European Community System," in Joseph S. Nye, Jr. (ed.), *International Regionalism: Readings* (Boston: Little, Brown and Co., 1968), pp. 231–268.

and thus impossible for political leaders to disentangle their nations. Although the original formulation was oversimplified and therefore misleading, the notion of automaticity was based on a useful insight. The sovereign alternatives open to political decisionmakers are reduced as an integration process goes forward.

As transactions rise and more groups (including external actors) become involved, the pressures on decisionmakers are greater. Similarly, the stronger the ideological-identitive appeal becomes (particularly if the ideology involves a myth of permanence or irreversibility that discourages opposition groups and encourages others to greater commitment), the stronger the pressure on the political decisionmaker and the fewer his political alternatives. As more tasks become interrelated through inherent links or package deals the costs of disintegrative actions become greater because there is the danger of pulling the whole house of cards down.

While it would at first appear that reduced alternatives would have an unambiguously good effect over the course of the integrative process, higher costs do not necessarily determine the actions of all political decisionmakers. Having fewer alternatives is not the same as having no alternatives.

In some cases decisionmakers may not perceive or may deliberately ignore diminished alternatives and thus precipitate crises. In other cases the knowledge that other countries are equally ensnared by the diminished alternatives may be a positive incentive for the leader more willing to practice brinksmanship to provoke crises deliberately. Finally, the further integration progresses, the larger the crises are likely to become both because a greater degree of interdependence has been created and because the resistance of some political leaders may become more intense as integration approaches the security and identitive areas of greatest concern to them. In Hoffmann's image the process of integration diminishing sovereignty may be less like a salami to be sliced off in even parts than an artichoke in which the heart has a different consistency than the outer leaves.[72]

Crises, however, can be productive for integration processes. If changes of attitudes or willingness to make the effort to overcome inertia depend on the dramatization of the alternative to cooperation, the crisis may have a productive effect. Whether or not it is true that people learn more from frustration than from success or whether or not there is an alternative to crises as a means of getting people to focus attention on opportunity costs, it is quite possible that the larger crises that accompany decreasing alternatives may play a productive role if the perceived common interests are strong enough.

D. *Externalization*

Schmitter has argued that whatever the original intentions, as integration proceeds member states will be increasingly forced to hammer out a collec-

---

[72] Hoffmann, *Daedalus*, Vol. 95, Nos. 3–4, pp. 892–916.

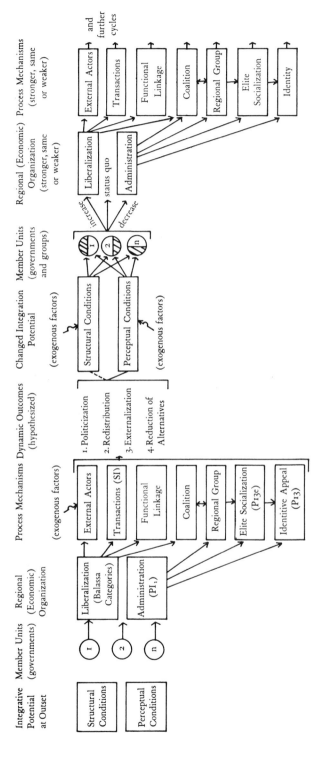

FIGURE 4. REGIONAL INTEGRATION PROCESS OVER TIME. Arrows indicate a strong relationship, broken arrows a weak relationship; shaded areas of circles indicate groups opposed, and open areas of circles indicate groups in favor.

tive external position vis-à-vis nonparticipant third parties because the further integration proceeds, the more third parties will react to it, either with support or hostility.[73]

Simultaneously as internal groups with vested interests in the process seek to protect themselves from external pressures or as mass opinion responds to the ideological-identitive appeal, there will be more pressure on decision-makers for agreement on external policy. In addition, political leaders may be tempted to use the integration process as an instrument for furthering their particular concerns with external relations. The inherent linkage of tasks is likely to touch external relations issues as the process reaches higher levels—for instance, the link between common external tariff, common commercial policy, and foreign policy (e.g., European trade treaties with Israel and the Union of Soviet Socialist Republics) or the link between free trade, monetary policy, international reserves, and a European position in the Group of Ten. Finally, in cases of success there may be overtures by other countries to join the union, and this presents a challenge to the existing structure of power.

While a sense of external identity is important in the early stages of the process and perhaps again at higher levels of integration, it seems that too great involvement in the problems of external policies in the middle stages of integration may have a braking effect. It diverts attention, raises antici-pated problems that make package deals and coalitions based on the existing structure of interests more difficult, and precipitates unnecessary crises. These in turn may stimulate opposition groups and speed up politicization through the involvement of political leaders and mass opinion in sensitive areas at too early a stage.

VI. Conclusions

What are the likely effects of the outcomes of an integration process over time? Other things (such as the external environment or generational change) being equal, the model would lead us to expect that integration pro-cesses would slow down rather than accelerate over time, particularly in less developed areas. First, in most settings the process of politicization means that low-cost integration and technocratic style decisionmaking procedures are unlikely to last very long and certainly not until a widespread popular support or a powerful coalition of intensely concerned interests have developed to the point at which they determine the decisions of political decision-makers.[74]

[73] Philippe C. Schmitter, "Three Neo-Functionalist Hypotheses about International Integration," *International Organization*, Winter 1969 (Vol. 23, No. 1), p. 165.

[74] In Etzioni's view the problem with high-level economic unions is that their need for consensus is out of balance with this capacity to generate it. Amitai Etzioni, "The Dialectics of Supranational Unification," *American Political Science Review*, December 1962 (Vol. 56, No. 4), p. 933.

Second, the ability to reach difficult political agreement on "positive integration" measures to cope with the problems created by redistribution is likely to lag behind the forces created by more easily agreed upon liberalization measures. Alternatively, in settings in which market forces are weak and liberalization cannot be agreed upon it seems likely that process forces will also be weak.

Third, the sense of reduced alternatives and the precipitation of larger crises will probably fail to have an integrative effect the closer the issues come to the security and identitive areas that are of greatest concern to popular political leaders. These are also the areas in which they are least likely to have the clear overriding common interests that make crises productive rather than destructive. Finally, the pressures both inside and outside the region for a common external policy are likely to develop more rapidly than popular or group support for a high degree of integration develops in these generally more controversial fields.[75]

In brief, unless the structure of incentives offered by the international system is seriously altered, the prospects for common markets or microregional economic organizations leading in the short run (of decades) to federation or some sort of political union capable of an independent defense and foreign policy do not seem very high. This does not mean, of course, that coordination of economic policies cannot help provide a basis for more coordination of foreign and defense policies as long as that is desired by the relevant political leaders. But this is a far cry from political union and single external policy.

If common markets do not lead to federation, does this mean that they must slip backward or fall apart? Is there no point of equilibrium in between? The belief that common markets must go forward or fall backward is widely accepted. Indeed, it was an essential part of the neo-functional myth. It has even been accepted by skeptics such as Stanley Hoffmann who has argued that "half-way attempts like supranational functionalism must either snowball or roll back."[76]

While this does seem to be the case when one looks at integration from the perspective of a simple neo-functionalist model, it no longer seems necessarily to be the case according to our revised model. Indeed our basic hypothesis is that most political decisionmakers will opt for the status quo at any level as long as the process forces or popular pressures are not strong enough to make this choice unbearable for them. If the process forces are too strong, political decisionmakers may downgrade commitment to a point at which they are tolerable, as we saw in the East African case. But though equilibrium may not be tolerable at a given level, it does not follow that the only equilib-

---

[75] This does not mean that minor coordination of foreign policies cannot be undertaken at low levels of integration—witness the Scandinavian states at the UN.

[76] Hoffmann, *Daedalus,* Vol. 95, Nos. 3–4, p. 915.

rium point is in the cellar of disintegration. On the contrary, a certain amount of economic integration, particularly if it can be handled by the hidden hand of market forces and thus not involve costly political decisions, may go part way to meet the concerns of those who argue that existing states are too small to provide adequate welfare. Half-measures may take the edge off the urgency of the situation and reduce the force of their demands.

Moreover, as Lawrence Krause and Leon Lindberg have pointed out and the case of EFTA shows, this type of market integration need not greatly strengthen the regional institutions.[77] In short, it seems most likely that under the current structure of international incentives dramatic-political decision-makers will find some point of equilibrium at which they would rather tolerate the inconvenience of the existing level of process forces than incur the greater political costs of full integration or disintegration.

Does this model hold for the politics of common markets among less developed countries as well as in the more familiar European case? Skeptics might object that it is impossible or misleading to develop a model of a regional integration process that covers both Europe and less developed areas because the political and economic contexts are so different. The European experience is not relevant and cannot be imitated in less developed areas.

A simple response to this objection is that an impressive level of integration has been created among the less developed country members of the East African and Central American common markets. Nonetheless, if the objection is stated in a less sweeping manner, it contains a great deal of truth. Considering the value of regional economic integration for less developed states and the frequent attempts to achieve it, there are remarkably few successful cases. And it is tautologously clear that the political and economic context in less developed countries is different.

It does not follow from this, however, that we cannot develop a model of an integration process for comparison of different contexts. The original neo-functionalist model was close to its origins in the strategies of European integrationists in the 1950's and thus might be seen as a tempting and misleading guide for policy in other areas. The revised neo-functionalist model is not something to be imitated but is simply a tool for making comparisons. We want to know what difference it makes if a group of states form a common market. Are new forces and procedures created that would otherwise not exist? How strong are they likely to be over time and under what conditions? These questions can be asked of less developed countries as well as of developed ones. Indeed, unless we ask common questions, we cannot really say to what extent integration in less developed areas *is* different.

There have been a great number of a priori and systematically unrelated

[77] Lindberg (note 71), pp. 231–268. Lawrence Krause, *European Economic Integration and the United States* (Washington: Brookings Institution, 1968).

statements about integration in the non-European context. For example we are told that integration is unlikely because existing levels of transactions are low or that integration is likely because many of the new states are not encumbered with the historical baggage of sovereignty as European states are. We are told that feelings of nationalism are too profound to tolerate integration and that regional integration is impossible until national integration has been accomplished first.

Yet, as we saw above, existing transactions are less important than potential transactions. On the other hand, leaders of new states that have been weak in their de facto sovereignty have spent great energies on trying to increase their sense of sovereign control, thus becoming more rather than less concerned with sovereignty. The lack of vested interests and pressure groups that should in principle free leaders to make integrative decisions has also deprived them of support and information for realistic economic policy formation and thus has led them to act more on the basis of ideology and insecurity—neither of which are sound foundations for economic integration.

Nationalism has often been profound not in the sense of a widespread feeling of national consciousness (such as exists in Europe) but in the lack thereof. The result tends to be a countervailing emphasis on nationalist ideology by insecure elites anxious to provide a better basis for their authority. Thus lack of national integration is a serious obstacle. On the other hand, Guatemala has played an important part in the Central American Common Market although half its population is very poorly integrated into the nation. In short, these ad hoc generalizations about integration among less developed countries add up to very little unless they are related to some model of an integration process.

Looked at from the perspective of our model, there are several reasons why the success of integration is limited in less developed areas. In the first place the economic structure of underdevelopment is likely to result in weaker process forces. Taking the forces resulting from liberalization—imperfect market mechanisms, lack of entrepreneurial resources, and inadequate infrastructure—all inhibit the rate at which transactions rise. Looser interdependence of economic sectors limits the pressures arising from inherent linkage of tasks. In addition, in many cases ideological biases against capitalist market mechanisms and nationalist reactions against external actors attracted by the prospects of a larger market lead to political inhibitions of the process forces resulting from liberalization.

Turning to the process forces resulting from the creation of new institutions, lack of administrative resources hampers regional bureaucracies. Premature politicization of economic issues greatly reduces the scope for bureaucratic initiative and quietly arranged package deals. In Arab countries "economic activity has a high political content"; in Southeast Asia, "matters that relate to the economy are subjects of high governmental priority"; and "experience in Latin America shows that a regional grouping quickly comes up against all kinds of problems calling for solutions at the highest political level."[78]

This is not to say that all economic issues are emotionally laden "high politics" in less developed countries and technically soluble "low politics" in developed settings. The salience of an issue area and its susceptibility to a consensual style of decision varies with each particular political context. There is greater monetary coordination in East Africa than in Europe (where it involves questions of Franco-German balance of power).[79] Labor migration is easy for the Nordic countries but not for Central America. On the question of a common external tariff the situation is reversed. The basic point, however, is that in many less developed areas a greater number of economic issue areas tend to become highly politicized than is the case in more developed settings.

Not only is it probable that process forces will be weaker in less developed areas but the integrative potential is likely to be lower. As we saw above, the lower the income and the lower the level of industrialization, the lower the tolerance to differences in symmetry and the more sensitive the problem of equitable distribution of benefits. Not only does the problem of redistribution require more coordination of positive policy and thus involve a greater sense of loss of sovereignty, but the resources available for compensating for redistribution are in shorter supply, and many of the lags result from problems of human resource and infrastructure that cannot be cured in the short run.[80]

Low levels of modern associational pluralism restrict the role of groups in the integration process at the same time that traditional pluralism and other problems of internal malintegration are likely to create a setting of internal noise that restricts the capacity of governments to adapt and respond. Finally, perceived external cogency is possibly higher for less developed countries because of their high dependence on a few commodities which often have sluggish growth rates and because of their vulnerability to penetration by outside actors. But where this vulnerability differs among member states and where dependence of member states is on different outside forces (e.g., British and French Africa and the situation in the Caribbean),[81] external cogency may not be perceived in the same way by all the potential partners.

[78] Robert W. MacDonald, *The League of Arab States: A Study in the Dynamics of Regional Organization* (Princton, N.J: Princeton University Press, 1965), p. 284; Bernard K. Gordon, *The Dimensions of Conflict in Southeast Asia* (Englewood Cliffs, N.J: Prentice-Hall, 1966), p. 142; Sidney Dell, "Regional Integration and the Industrialization of Less Developed Countries," *Development Digest,* October 1965 (Vol. 3, No. 3), p. 45.

[79] Hans O. Schmitt, "Capital Markets and the Unification of Europe," *World Politics,* January 1968 (Vol. 20, No. 2), pp. 228–244.

[80] Hansen, *World Politics,* Vol. 21, No. 2, pp. 257–270.

[81] See Aaron Segal, *The Politics of Caribbean Economic Integration* (Puerto Rico: Institute of Caribbean Studies, 1968).

These conditions do not make regional economic integration among less developed countries impossible—witness again the East African and Central American cases—but when seen in the context of our model, they do indicate why it is likely to be difficult. The early success of Central American integration can be attributed to a variety of rather exceptional factors—the existence of entrepreneurial resources, willingness to rely on liberalization and market mechanisms, favorable external actors such as the United States Agency for International Development and the active role of ECLA, common perceptions of their giant neighbor, the lack of previous industrialization which, in contrast to LAFTA, meant low costs in the early stages of the process, a fairly strong historical sense of regional identity, and, perhaps most important, a rather unique political culture in which economic development issues were not highly politicized.[82] Consequently the process forces were stronger and the integrative potential more favorable than is typical of less developed countries.

The East African states are more typical of less developed countries in their political culture and in many of the other characteristics sketched out above. A big difference, however, is the fact that they were, so to speak, born integrated. The basic structure of East African integration was created in the womb of British colonial rule. Even so, the degree of integration that existed upon independence was intolerable to the political leaders. After a failure to federate, their responses led to a series of disintegrative outcomes that reduced the strength of some of the process forces. The interesting point is that, under the pressure of crisis and commonly perceived external cogency, the three states seemed able to halt the process of disintegration by redistributing the headquarters of common services, allowing an internal "infant industry" tariff to be applied by the less industrialized states under carefully controlled circumstances, and creating a regional development bank which could attract outside funds and expand the possible pie to be divided. It is interesting that Kenya found it easier to sacrifice the opportunity costs of funds to be attracted from outside than to sacrifice revenues or rights to industrial activity as was attempted in previous solutions.[83]

In face of the difficulties that confront the formation of common markets or free trade areas among less developed countries a number of proponents of regional integration have turned to two other devices: regional development banks and partial integration schemes.[84] Since 1960 regional development banks have been established for Latin America (1960), Central America

---

[82] For details see Nye, *International Conciliation*, No. 562.

[83] Arthur Hazelwood, "Notes on the Treaty for East African Cooperation," *East African Economic Review*, December 1967 (Vol. 3, No. 2), pp. 63–80; also Robson.

[84] See I.M.D. Little, "Regional Integration Companies as an Approach to Economic Integration"; Jaroslav Vanek, "Payments Unions among the Less Developed Countries and their Economic Integration"; and Felipe Herrera, "The Inter-American Development Bank and the Latin American Integration Movement," all in *Journal of Common Market Studies*, December 1966 (Vol. 5, No. 2).

(1961), the Entente (1966), Africa (1966), Asia (1966), and East Africa (1967) and are projected for Central Africa, the Arab countries, the Andean countries, and the Caribbean.[85] Partial integration schemes include such devices as limited sector integration (not picked for their spillover potential), agreed specialization and allocation of market shares, joint services, and jointly owned public corporations. Regional Cooperation for Development (RCD) and the Maghreb Council are two such examples.[86] To the extent that one of the goals of such devices is integration it is useful to look at them from the perspective of our model.

The advantage of such schemes is that by restricting the scope of integration they restrict the area in which integration potential needs to be high. While it may not be high for entire economies, it may be high for a given sector. On the other hand, both banks and partial integration schemes tend to have modest effects in the process forces that they unleash. Rising transactions are likely to be low, and linkages with the rest of the economy are deliberately excluded or limited. In a narrow sector the number of groups likely to become involved and the breadth of the package deals and coalitions that can be worked out is likely to be very restricted.[87]

Two process forces that *are* released are socialization of elites brought into contact by the scheme and symbolic effects on the sense of regional identity, but both of these will also be limited. Perhaps the major process force will be the involvement of external actors, whether it be governments willing to be donors to the regional bank or outside corporations or governments willing to participate in the partial schemes. Limited forces are better than no forces, however, from the regionalist point of view. And even the skeptical outsider must admit that if one is interested in dampening potential conflict, a limited scheme is likely to have more effect (even though a slight one) than a grandiose scheme that fails.

In principle, many of the problems that face economic integration schemes in less developed areas could be resolved by regional planning, and appeals for regional planning are frequently heard. If planning is more than window dressing, however, it proves to be exceedingly difficult to carry out at a regional level since it involves a much higher and deliberate sacrifice of sovereignty than unplanned market integration does.

---

[85] See International Bank for Reconstruction and Development, "Multilateral Regional Financing Institutions," 1968 (mimeographed); and Manmohan Singh, "Regional Development Banks," *International Conciliation,* January 1970 (No. 576).

[86] See Organization for Economic Cooperation and Development, *International Economic Integration among Developing States* (CD/R/68.1), Paris, 1968, pp. 71–86. (Mimeographed.) Also William Culbert, *Regionalism in the Northern Tier: The Implications of RCD* (Washington: Foreign Service Institute, 1969).

[87] For an example of the restricted possibilities for coalition formation in a single sector approach see Lawrence Scheinman, "Euratom: Nuclear Integration in Europe," in Nye, *International Regionalism,* pp. 269–281.

The experience of CMEA is instructive in this regard. High levels of trade integration have been reached through bilateral arrangements but at the sacrifice of considerable welfare. National planners tend to want to exclude exogenous factors such as trade over which they have less control. While CMEA standing commissions have been able to reach a number of sectoral specialization agreements and a number of common services do exist, efforts to upgrade the role of the institutions and reach any serious coordination of plans have been defeated by governments unwilling to sacrifice sovereign control.[88]

As the Secretariat of the Economic Commission for Asia and the Far East (ECAFE) has noted of Asia,

> if planning is comprehensive, as it is in most of the Asian countries whether it is indicative or imperative, then comprehensive integration can be adopted only if the development plans of all the participating countries are fully harmonized.

The Secretariat has rather drily noted that "at the present time, this does not seem to be politically feasible in Asia."[89]

In short, we conclude that the skeptics are wrong if they overstate their argument that regional integration is restricted to Western Europe alone. But they are correct if they state that greater difficulties inhere in the creation of successful common markets in less developed areas. More important from an analytic point of view is our argument that it is both possible and imperative to study the politics of common markets in a comparative perspective and that the neo-functional model, suitably revised to free it of some of the characteristics that tied it rather too closely to the particular case of Europe in the 1950's, can serve as a useful process model for analyzing the comparative politics of common markets in a variety of settings.

---

[88] On the desire of the less developed Romanians to control their own planning see John Montias, "Background and Origins of the Rumanian Dispute with COMECON," *Soviet Studies*, October 1964 (Vol. 16, No. 2), pp. 125–151.

[89] See UN Document E/AC.54/L.35, March 20, 1969, p. 16.

6

A Revised Theory of Regional Integration

PHILIPPE C. SCHMITTER

THE study of regional integration, of how national units come to share part or all of their decisional authority with an emerging international organization, is one of the areas of political inquiry in which a cumulative research tradition has developed. Previous paradigms are scrutinized critically in new settings; replications are made and even encouraged; new concepts, hypotheses, and measures are suggested and incorporated without obliterating past work. Under these conditions theoretical formalization may play a particularly fruitful role.

The first attempt at the statement of a comprehensive, yet parsimonious, model of the political consequences of integration movements by Ernst Haas and myself[1] was, I think it fair to say, a successful failure. It was a failure in the sense that it has proven to be an inadequate and easily misunderstood theory. Variables were sloppily conceptualized; few operational referents were

PHILIPPE C. SCHMITTER, an assistant professor of political science at the University of Chicago, Chicago, Illinois, is currently a visiting fellow at the Center for International Affairs, Harvard University, Cambridge, Massachusetts.

The author acknowledges a major debt to the participants of the Conference on Regional Integration, April 24–26, 1969, many of whose articles appear in this volume. Joseph S. Nye, Jr., Larry Finkelstein, Leon Lindberg, and Hayward Alker, Jr. have offered detailed criticisms of an earlier draft which were found useful in the revision. The author also wishes to thank his colleagues at the Instituto para la Integración de América Latina (INTAL) in Buenos Aires who were so generous with their time and so helpful with their criticisms: José Maria Aragão, Natalio Botana, Jaime Campos, Ricardo Cappelletti, John Elac, Enrique Melchior, Felix Peña, Jaime Undurraga, Eduardo White and INTAL's director, Felipe Tami; of course, all of the above are absolved from any responsibility for the ensuing product.

Mr. Schmitter's research in Argentina was supported by an ACLS-SSRC grant and a generous leave of absence from the University of Chicago. In intellectual inspiration this article is part of the International Integration Studies project of the Institute of International Studies, University of California at Berkeley, directed by Ernst B. Haas.

[1] Ernst B. Haas and Philippe C. Schmitter, "Economics and Differential Patterns of Political Integration: Projections about Unity in Latin America," *International Organization*, Autumn 1964 (Vol. 18, No. 4), pp. 705–737.

suggested; little attention was paid to specifying relations between variables—to *process,* in other words; and, above all, no sensitivity was shown to the likelihood of different integration outcomes. It was a success in the sense that it proved to be an attractive target. Intelligent and constructive criticism was leveled at it; "respeculation" was inspired by it; some empirical analysis was conducted around it. This article offers an updated target—a revised formalization of the neo-functionalist or structuralist theory of the political consequences of regional integration with pretensions to general comparative relevance.

ASSUMPTIONS

This model involves an explicit research strategy and, with it, a set of unexamined meta-assumptions. If the following, deliberately parametric, conditions seem unacceptable or unrealistic for the specific case one is examining, the explanations the model proposes are very likely to prove inappropriate.

1) The integration of formally independent political entities engages—in the contemporary world—basically the same variables and processes. These can be specified by induction from existing empirical research and can be understood in a probabilistic sense by means of a single analytical model. Variable values will, of course, differ, as will outcomes; but the integration process is structurally similar in all such settings.

1a) This does not mean that in all contexts variables will produce the same effect, marginal or absolute. For example, see macrohypothesis number six below for speculation on the weighting or transformation of variables in lesser developed and more developed settings.

1b) Nor does it imply necessarily that the same variable will be equally effective throughout the integration process. See macrohypothesis number four (pp. 243–244 and the discussion on pp. 258–264) for suggestions concerning the relation between changes in national structures/values and regional subprocesses as the movement approaches the formation of a political community.

1c) The specification of operative variables in the form of a model does not mean that *only* these are relevant to understanding integration outcomes.

> Variation in other variables can also cause variation in the caused variable . . . without falsifying the causal law. Any given dependent variable may be involved in a large number of causal laws.[2]

Macrohypothesis number four also deals with the probable effect of error variables.

With these caveats protecting me I would, however, readily concede that *if the specified operative conditions were to prove irrelevant in a given integrative context* (for example, if transactions increased but were not associated

---

[2] Arthur L. Stinchcombe, *Constructing Social Theories* (New York: Harcourt, Brace and World, 1968), p. 32.

with any change in perceived inequalities or the formation of regional interest groups) or that *if actor strategies were to change significantly in the absence of variation in the specified variables* (such as would occur if regional institutions were permitted to augment their authoritative control over member policies without any prior variation in perceived inequalities, regional group activity, common identitive appeal, deliberate manipulative attempts by regional *técnicos,* or sensitivity to deterioration in international status), *something is very likely wrong with the model.*

The decision to limit the number of variables to those which seem to be operative in *all* contemporary contexts—taken partly to stimulate research on the comparative rather than idiosyncratic characteristics of integration processes and partly to ensure minimal potential manipulability—leaves the model open to the charge that some major, omnipresent variable has been left out. For example, I have accepted the critique leveled at the previous formalization that certain external conditions were everywhere relevant to reading probable outcomes, and I have, therefore, attempted to incorporate these conditions systematically in the present model.

2) The theory proposed herein is—like all social theories—composed of variables and hypotheses about variable relationships. A variable is

> a *concept* which can have various values and which is defined in such a way that one can tell by means of observations which value it has in a particular occurrence.[3]

As such, variables are observer-invented orderings of facts and perceptions, not the physical occurrences themselves. Nor are they necessarily the categories with which actors order and explain their behavior. Much of the previous "neo-functional" work on integration, especially that of Ernst Haas, has drawn a good deal of its explanatory strength from using concepts which are rather close to the categories used by decisionmakers, and it has often scored actor perceptions of facts rather than the facts themselves. This fact has, I believe, not only improved our capacity to observe process relations, such as learning, and to predict outcomes, but it has greatly facilitated direct communication with participants. Some of us have had the rather unnerving experience of hearing our special jargon spouted back at us by those whom we are studying. This model stays within this tradition and its successful operationalization would demand techniques of direct observation to measure not only what happened but also how relevant actors perceived what was happening.

Even more confusingly, these concepts are usually summations or aggregate evaluations of complex, interrelated behaviors. Such classifications, rankings, or scorings pose a major operational difficulty for this theory. Unclear

---

[3] Ibid., pp. 28–29.

definitions and failure to specify how the multiple observations are to be collapsed into a single assessment have plagued comparative research and made intersubjective reliability poor.

This article will contribute little to resolving these problems. I only hope that it will not add to them. Elsewhere Ernst Haas, Mario Barrera, and I have begun a discussion of some operational difficulties,[4] and Joseph Nye, Jr. has made some important definitional contributions.[5]

3) The basic causal imagery of the model is *functionalist*. As Arthur Stinchcombe has so cogently exposed, the structure of such an explanation is one in which "the *consequences* of some behavior or social arrangement are essential elements of the causes of that behavior."[6] In this conception of the integration process national units originally adopt strategies of action which converge in the establishment of some permanent regional institution(s) (RI₁) for the purpose of attaining certain common objectives (CO₁). The attainment of these objectives is made difficult by the presence of certain tensions or, better, contradictions. The latter are a specific set of *tension-producing conditions which are generated by the integration process itself*, i.e., by the collective at-

National actors adopt

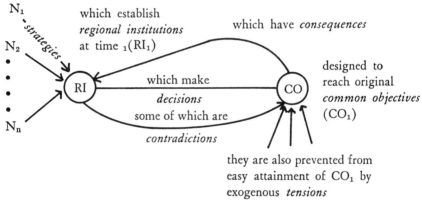

FIGURE 1. FUNCTIONALIST CAUSAL IMAGERY AND INTERNATIONAL INTEGRATION. This figure was inspired by Arthur Stinchcombe.

tempt to obtain CO₁. Summarizing (and hypothesizing), these basic contradictions are: a) uncertainty in regard to the capacity to guarantee relative

[4] Mario Barrera and Ernst B. Haas, "The Operationalization of Some Variables Related to Regional Integration: A Research Note," *International Organization*, Winter 1969 (Vol. 23, No. 1), pp. 150–160; Philippe C. Schmitter, "Further Notes on Operationalizing Some Variables Related to Regional Integration," *International Organization*, Spring 1969 (Vol. 23, No. 2), pp. 327–336.

[5] Joseph S. Nye, "Comparative Regional Integration: Concept and Measurement," *International Organization*, Autumn 1968 (Vol. 22, No. 4), pp. 855–880.

[6] Stinchcombe, p. 80.

equality of perceived benefits once new productive and distributive forces are unleashed *(equity)*; b) impossibility of maintaining prolonged separability of different issue areas in a complex, interdependent policy matrix *(engrenage)*; c) difficulty in isolating joint regional deliberations from a context of global socioeconomic dependence *(externalization)*; d) heightened sensitivity to the comparative performance of one's "partners" generated by higher transactions and available information *(envy)*.[7] The consequences produced by this "competition" between regional institutions and exogenous tensions or process-generated contradictions "feed back" to the regional institutions.

In the event that the policymaking forum originally established is sufficiently elaborate and flexible to handle the consequences and sustain satisfactory performance toward the attainment of CO_1, a self-maintaining international subsystem is likely to emerge. I have labeled this integrative outcome "encapsulation."[8] If, however, as a result of the consequences of trying to reach CO_1, the performance of RI_1 is inadequate, actors may be forced to revise their strategies and to consider alternative integrative obligations, i.e., they may reevaluate the level and/or scope of their commitment to regional institutions. In Figure 2 these successive redefinitions (RI_2, RI_3) lead to increases in the level of authority devolved upon joint institutions until at RI_4 the actors agree upon a manifestly new set of common objectives (CO_2). *Transcendence* has been accomplished in the exotic lexicon of this theory. This particular "success syndrome" is only one of several possible outcomes to be discussed herein and not a very probable one at that. I might just as well have diagrammed a "spill-back" syndrome whereby in response to tensions actors consequentially withdraw from their original objective, downgrading their commitment to mutual cooperation.

As was the case with meta-assumption two, this functionalist imagery can ultimately be falsified. For example, if RI_1 changes in the absence of a prior increase in tensions, it hardly seems warranted to classify it as a functional consequence. Or, if one or more of the contradictions listed should appear and there is forthcoming neither more "compensatory" activity from RI_1 nor some alternative search behavior, the basic functionalist assumption is false.

The above functionalist diagram should make clear one of the major strategic options of this theory: the selection of the dependent variable. *All its effort focuses upon an attempt to specify and predict the conditions under which the consequences generated by prior joint decisions will lead to redefinitions of actor strategies vis-à-vis the scope and level of regional decision-*

---

[7] This propensity of regional integration to heighten sensitivities to the relative performance of one's partners might be called "Anderson's paradox." See Charles W. Anderson, *Politics and Economic Change in Latin America: The Governing of Restless Nations* (Princeton, N.J.: D. Van Nostrand Co., 1967), p. 61.

[8] Philippe C. Schmitter, "La dinámica de contradicciones y la conducción de crisis en la integración centroamericana," *Revista de la integración*, November 1969 (No. 5), pp. 87–151.

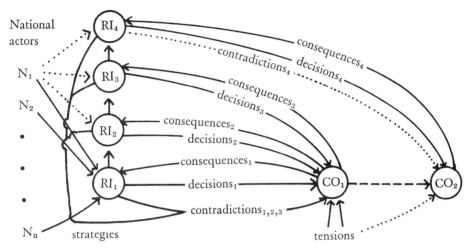

FIGURE 2. FUNCTIONALIST CAUSAL IMAGERY AND A DYNAMIC THEORY OF INTERNATIONAL INTEGRATION

making. Whether member states will expand or contract the type of issues to be resolved jointly *(scope)* or whether they will increase or decrease the authority for regional institutions to allocate values *(level)* are the two basic dimensions of the dependent variable, and, as we shall discuss, they are by no means always covariant. This, then, is an eminently *political* theory of integration which asks not whether "artificial" barriers to exchange are decreasing, resources being more efficiently distributed, or peoples growing to like each other more and more, but what kind of a strategy politically relevant actors are likely to adopt in a given context. These other conditions of economic and social integration do, of course, form important elements in the model but as independent and intervening, not dependent, variables.

4) Certain variables have been deliberately excluded. These have been historically operable in integration processes and, in fact, play a prominent role in other theoretical formulations.[9] Their presence I consider to be either unlikely in contemporary settings or so disturbing as to call for a very different conceptual formulation.

---

[9] For example, Karl Deutsch, and others, *Political Community and the North Atlantic Area: International Organization in the Light of Historical Experience* (Princeton, N.J: Princeton University Press, 1957); Amitai Etzioni, *Political Unification: A Comparative Study of Leaders and Forces* (New York: Holt, Rinehart and Winston, 1965).

4a) The first of these is the postulated or assumed absence of conquest or organized physical violence on the part of one member or group of members to enforce compliance with regional decisions or to compel changes in the strategy of other participants. This, in other words, is a model pertaining to the peaceful and voluntary transformation of international systems. It does not, of course, exclude the relevance of "bluff, bombast, and brinkmanship" in actor styles, but physical coercion *to enforce regional decisions* makes the model irrelevant.[10]

4b) "Irrational" postures or strategies, whether for dogmatic-ideological or personal-emotive reasons, are never absent from social action, even at the international level, but they are from this theory. They fit very uncomfortably within it. "Instant brotherhood" as a motive, "all or nothing" as a strategy, make its operation exceedingly difficult. Unless some policy area can initially be separated out as jointly manipulable and unless some possibility of subsequent compromise involving tradeoffs or side payments exists, international integration, as conceived herein, is not likely to occur. The model assumes that integration is basically (but not exclusively) a rational process whereby actors calculate anticipated returns from various alternative strategies of participation in joint decisionmaking structures. With the usual limitations imposed by incapacity to predict fully the consequences of one's own and others' actions, by restricted imagination, and by imperfection of information—*in other words, in a context of considerable uncertainty*—the actors will avoid the worst possible solution for either and generally not risk all on the intransigeant promotion of their own maximum interest, but will settle for some intermediate payoff. In short, the model works best where the opportunity for all to gain without harming anyone (Pareto's optimal gain) is greatest.

This does not exclude integration movements from "infringing" upon the symbolic and emotional areas of so-called "high politics." Nevertheless, as the Mitchells among others warn us, the margin for peaceful maneuverability in these "indivisible" arenas is very limited.[11] As we shall see below, most integration processes are likely to get encapsulated long before they reach such touchy issues.

CRISIS-INDUCED DECISIONAL CYCLES

The process whereby an emerging regional center gains or loses in the scope or level of its authority vis-à-vis preexistent national centers is best conceived as involving a series of crisis-provoked decisional cycles. These recurrent cy-

---

[10] *Nota bene* the caveat "to enforce regional decisions." International violence not directly related to integration issues doesn't "disprove" the theory and may not even make it irrelevant. See my article in *Revista de la integración*, No. 5 for a discussion of this in the context of the El Salvador-Honduras "Football War."

[11] Joyce M. Mitchell and William C. Mitchell, *Political Analysis and Public Policy: An Introduction to Political Science* (Chicago: Rand McNally, 1969), pp. 135–159, especially pp. 138–139.

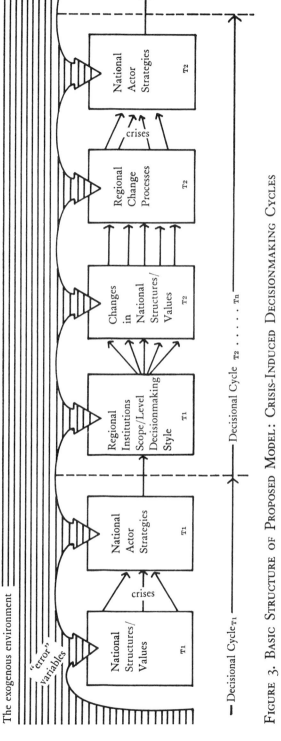

FIGURE 3. BASIC STRUCTURE OF PROPOSED MODEL: CRISIS-INDUCED DECISIONMAKING CYCLES

cles of activity, generated by indogenous contradictions and/or exogenous tensions, compel national and regional authorities to revise their respective strategies and, collectively, to determine whether the new joint institution(s) will expand or contract. The basic structure of the following model, therefore, consists not of a single continuum or even of a multitude of continua, nor does it involve any assumptions about cumulative and irreversible progress toward a single goal. Successive cycles of induced decisionmaking may involve complex movements "upward" and "downward" simultaneously in different issue areas. Various strategies, national and regional, may be adopted and various outcomes or endpoints are possible and even likely. Once, however, a given regional process fails to generate or respond to crises, it has disintegrated; if it responds by reasserting previous strategies, it has reached a state of stable self-maintenance *(encapsulation)*.

THE DEPENDENT VARIABLE: ACTOR INTEGRATION STRATEGIES

The proposed model focuses on predicting the policies adopted—in response to crisis-induced decisional cycles—by national actors[12] with regard to expanding or contracting the scope and/or level of regional authority.

One easy (?) way of visualizing the alternatives open to a given actor is to plot them in two-dimensional space. The vertical axis is defined by the degree of decisional authority conceded to, devolved upon, or taken away from regional institutions[13]; the horizontal axis is defined by the issue areas with which these institutions are permitted or not permitted to deal.[14] Each move-

---

[12] In the initial cycles of the model national actors are treated as unities—as national governmental authorities calculating a single strategy vis-à-vis the issue at hand. Subsequently, during the transforming cycles these national actors become differentiated into subnational groups each with its own integrative strategy. Both Joseph Nye and Leon Lindberg in their comments on the first draft of this article suggested that national actors lose their unity earlier in the process than I have hypothesized here. Lindberg, citing Ernst Haas's *The Uniting of Europe: Political, Social, and Economic Forces, 1950–1957* (Stanford, Calif: Stanford University Press, 1958) as evidence, even argued that in the initial cycles one is likely to find differentiated national strategies rather than a single, prior, elaborated position.

[13] I have sought to operationalize this dimension by means of a scalogram of some 44 dichotomized institutional characteristics measuring change in the four Parsonian functional domains. On the basis of a pretest which solicited evaluations from colleagues doing research in international organizations I have tentatively concluded that, while a reproducible and reliable scalogram does emerge, its utility is limited to gross, aggregate comparison across institutions. The measurement interval is too great to permit accurate, discrete measurement of the evolution of the authority of a single international organization over time. I hope to publish this preliminary analysis shortly. See my "International Organization Development: Measuring the Dependent Variable" (unpublished manuscript, University of Chicago, January 1969).

Leon Lindberg has been experimenting with a variety of 0–6 ranking techniques which may also prove useful for comparative purposes, although he draws a distinction between "stage of decision" and "degree of decisiveness" not made here. Cf. his contribution to this volume. For a related effort in the context of the United Nations see Robert O. Keohane, "Institutionalization in the United Nations General Assembly," *International Organization,* Autumn 1969 (Vol. 23, No. 4), pp. 859–896.

[14] Lindberg has proposed a checklist of some 22 issue areas covering external, economic, political-constitutional, and sociocultural issues. I would be much more inclined to begin with Joseph Nye's nomothetic suggestion and simply list "outward" governmental ministries, autonomous agencies, and

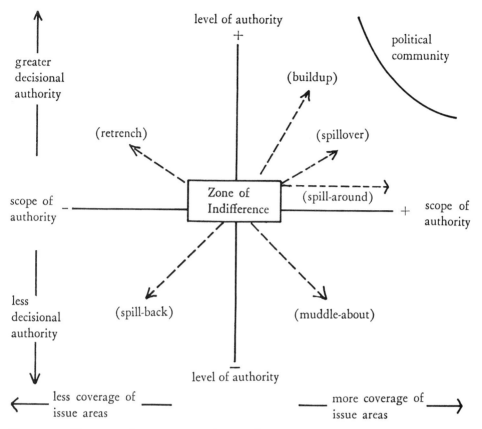

FIGURE 4. PLOT OF ALTERNATIVE ACTOR STRATEGIES

ment is surrounded at any given moment by a "zone of indifference" (Barnard), as defined by the ongoing convergence of actor purposes, within which the activities or absence thereof of regional actors go uncontested. As long as they restrict themselves to "doing their thing" and incur no new costs, they are tolerated. Moving outside this zone—which is what a dynamic political theory of integration should focus upon—does involve costs. Moving "downward" and/or "backward" involves forgoing some established payoffs from greater collaboration and the loss of "sunken costs" which went into the original establishment of the institutions.[15] Moving "upward" and/or "forward," of course, involves both greater uncertainty, the upsetting of established pat-

quasi-public institutes for each member state according to some inductive criteria of their "political distance" from the original joint policymaking areas. This technique has the added payoff of pointing out asymmetric organizational patterns and differential policy coverage of the integrating units. Cf. Joseph S. Nye, Jr., *International Organization*, Vol. 23, No. 4, p. 869.

[15] My emphasis on "sunken costs" in explaining organizational behavior was inspired by Arthur Stinchcombe, pp. 120–125.

terns of reward, and, probably, progressively greater controversiality (see macrohypothesis number three below). These "boundary" conditions help explain why I hypothesize that the maintenance of the institution within its zone of indifference or encapsulation is the most probable outcome (see macrohypothesis number two).

Typologizing crudely, the following seem to be the strategic options open to a given actor in a given context: 1) *spillover,* i.e., to increase both the scope and level of his commitment concomitantly; 2) *spill-around,* i.e., to increase only the scope while holding the level of authority constant or within the zone of indifference; 3) *buildup,* i.e., to agree to increase the decisional autonomy or capacity of joint institutions but deny them entrance into new issue areas; 4) *retrench,* i.e., to increase the level of joint deliberation but withdraw the institutions(s) from certain areas; 5) *muddle-about,* i.e., to let the regional bureaucrats debate, suggest, and expostulate on a wider variety of issues but decrease their actual capacity to allocate values; 6) *spill-back,* i.e., to retreat on both dimensions, possibly returning to the status quo ante initiation; 7) *encapsulate,* i.e., to respond to crisis by marginal modifications within the zone of indifference. (This alternative, as we shall see, is the one most likely to be chosen.)

Plotted over time, the evolution of a national integration policy or regional institution (the negotiated sum of national policies) is quite likely to be erratic and may well demonstrate no cumulative trend at all. Derived from the plot is, however, the hypothesis that the most *direct* route to political community (defined operationally as an integration movement which has attained a certain level of authority and covers a sufficient variety of concerns) is by way of successive spillovers or package deals involving new issues and new competences. Other routes may prove to be *quicker,* however. In the long run inconspicuous spill-around may avoid reaction-formation for some time, until a crisis forces a consolidation of disparate authorities; "built-up" institutions with an established reputation for efficiency and equity may be called upon suddenly to take over other, crisis-ridden domains. On the other hand, initially fast rising spillover movements may get trapped at stable, high levels of clientele satisfaction at which the risk of moving ahead into symbolic "indivisible" issues does not compensate for increased uncertainty over established payoffs and may find themselves occupying the same zone of indifference for protracted periods of time.

Macrohypotheses

Informing the model throughout are a series of macrohypotheses or major probabilistic assertions of relationship between variables which purport to be relevant to all decisional cycles. The first two of these are derived from the basic functionalist causal imagery discussed above.

1) Tensions from the global environment and/or contradictions generated by past performance give rise to unexpected performance in the pursuit of agreed-upon common objectives. These frustrations and/or dissatisfactions are likely to result in the search for alternative means for reaching the same goals, i.e., to induce actors to revise their respective strategies vis-à-vis the scope and level of regional decisionmaking. This is the basic functionalist proposition, called "the spillover hypothesis" by me in a previous article[16] and the "principle of equifinality" by Arthur Stinchcombe.[17]

2) In their search among alternatives national actors will tend to arrive at that institutional solution (in terms of scope and level) which will meet minimal common objectives despite prevailing tensions and will subsequently seek to seal the regional organization off as much as possible from its environment, thereby adopting a self-maintaining set of institutional norms. This "hypothesis of natural entropy" suggests that all integration processes will tend toward a state of rest or stagnation—unless disturbed by exceptional (i.e., unpredictable) or exogenous conditions not present in the original convergence or in the institutions themselves. Expressed in terms of strategies, the highest probability is that in any decisional cycle the actors will opt for encapsulation rather than spillover, spill-around, buildup, or spill-back.[18]

3) In those cases where strong exogenous tensions and/or powerful internal contradictions (the independent variables in the model seek to predict these conditions) force successive "upward" evaluations of strategy, i.e., tend to involve more national actors in an expanding variety of policy areas and increasing degree of joint decisionmaking, costs and resistances are likely to increase. The "politicization hypothesis" refers, then, initially to this process whereby the controversiality of joint decisionmaking goes up.

> This in turn is likely to lead to a widening of the audience or clientele interested and active in integration. Somewhere along the line, a manifest redefinition of mutual objectives will probably occur (transcendence). . . . Ultimately, one could hypothesize that, given the above, there will be a shift in actor expectations and loyalty toward the new regional center.[19]

Nevertheless, it seems worth repeating that only in exceptional, i.e., high scoring, circumstances is such a cumulative process to be anticipated. Normally, the response to higher costs and wider publics will be entropic.

4) The integration process begins with a large number of unspecified exogenous conditions which are very important in determining outcomes. Idio-

---

[16] Philippe C. Schmitter, "Three Neo-Functional Hypotheses about International Integration," *International Organization*, Winter 1969 (Vol. 23, No. 1), pp. 162–164.

[17] Stinchcombe, pp. 80–82.

[18] See pp. 256–264 for additional discussion of possible "motives" underlying this propensity for entropic solutions. For a discussion in the light of case study see my article in *Revista de la integración*, No. 5, pp. 141, 147–148.

[19] Schmitter, *International Organization*, Vol. 23, No. 4, p. 166.

syncratic and random variables play their most important roles before the consequences of regional decisions have begun to affect national structures and values and set off regional processes. The model is, therefore, a very poor predictor of the initiation of integration movements and of the consequences of its first decisional cycles. It does not purport to synthesize such sufficient causes. If, however, it has any analytical validity, the residual proportion of variance attributable to these idiosyncratic and random events should decline. In other words, predictability should increase with successive "upward-grading" cycles as the movement approaches a political community. I grant that when applied to integration schemes which encapsulate early and/or whose decisions are so limited in scope or ineffectual in authority that they have little or no impact upon changes at the national or regional level, the model may never prove very predictive of changes in actor strategy. One might call this speculation the "hypothesis of increasing mutual determination."

5) External conditions begin, as do all the independent "background" variables, as "givens." While the changes in national structures and values become at least partially predictable as consequences of regional decisions, the global dependence and client status of the member states and the region as a whole continue to be exogenously determined for a longer time. Nevertheless, integrating units will find themselves increasingly compelled—regardless of original intentions—to adopt common policies vis-à-vis nonparticipant third parties. This "externalization hypothesis" predicts that external conditions will become less exogenously determined if integrative rather than disintegrative strategies are commonly adopted.[20] The "independent" role of these conditions should decline as integration proceeds until joint negotiation vis-à-vis outsiders has become such an integral part of the decisional process that the international system accords the new unit full participant status.

6) At each decisional cycle actors will be induced to reconsider their respective strategies of participation. What influences (and predicts) the result of these "reconsiderations of policy" is a central concern of the model. Of equal interest are the questions of how these conditions combine and what sort of a formula is used in weighing their marginal contribution to the position finally adopted. As a first guess I would advance "the additive hypothesis"— namely, that actor perceptions of the impact of regional processes enter into their calculations of interest, as do variables in a stepwise multiple regression equation, one at a time with each successive one contributing (positively or negatively) to the prediction of a remaining portion of the variance. Frankly, I suspect this to be an excessive simplification in that the simultaneous presence of certain variables, e.g., great perceptions of inequality coupled with low rates of transnational group formation, is likely to have a *multiplicative* effect on the type of strategy chosen—in this case, to make it much more likely to opt for one of the disintegrative strategies.

[20] Ibid., p. 165.

By induction from existing empirical research we have discovered that the relative impact (*beta* weights, to continue the multiple regression analogy) of change processes differs in different macrosettings, especially among more developed and less developed units. Greater sensitivity to inequalities of return, activism on the part of regional *técnicos,* and awareness of international status considerations seem to characterize the latter. Attention paid to transnational interest articulation and the more effective and rapid emergence of common identitive appeal seem more relevant in the former setting. Of course, post-factum regressions on past decisions should pick up these distinctions and can then be projected forward for the prediction of future responses.[21]

7) One must never forget that international integration is an innovative and experimental process. It takes place in an ambiance of considerable uncertainty and trepidation in which negotiating actors can rarely be sure of the probable effect of their joint "solutions" on established interests and statuses. In some cases they are venturing into policy areas not previously handled at the national level; in all cases they are creating new channels of influence and new reward systems. Under these conditions even "good" performance, e.g., more transactions, greater equality, more internal pluralism, etc., can become upsetting when it outruns expectations and the capacity to absorb change gradually.

Another way of stating this is that the relationship between indicators of change at the national and regional level is likely to be *curvilinear* or, better, *parabolic.*[22] Up to a point the relation between change processes and integrative strategies is probably linear, e.g., increases in transactions are positively associated with increases in regional group formation or mutual identity. When, however, changes are so rapid and large in magnitude as to clog existing channels of communication or confound existing categories of evaluation, then actors are liable to react defensively, if not negatively. They are getting too much of a good thing but not knowing what to do with it or how to react to it. My field work on integration among less developed countries (LDCs) convinces me that the parabolic effect of independent and dependent variables is particularly crucial there, as the whole governing system has a very limited capacity for absorbing change, even "good" change. This "curvilinear hypothesis" complicates our model-building exercise but, I would argue, is a necessary concession to reality.

8) When I first presented these ideas at a seminar in Buenos Aires, one of my colleagues from the Instituto para la Integración de América Latina (INTAL), Felix Peña, raised a very cogent objection. He observed that the

---

[21] One case study which in effect tried this has concluded that the original Haas-Schmitter list of variables was both irrelevant and incomplete. See Abdul Aziz Jalloh, "Regional Political Integration in Africa: The Lessons of the Last Decade" (unpublished manuscript, Yale University, 1970).

[22] Cf. J. S. Nye's article in this volume for the original inspiration concerning curvilinearity.

stated bias of the model toward rational, "minimaximilizing" behavior on the part of national and regional strategists overlooked one crucial fact of the less developed country (and, to a lesser degree, of the more developed country) environment: the *global insecurity* of political decisionmakers. Uncertainty in calculation is not simply a function of imperfect information and incapacity to project consequences into the future but also an immediate product of the fact that negotiators cannot be sure that they will be around long enough to implement their commitments or that other actors will not be suddenly and unconstitutionally removed from office and that their successors will not deny responsibility for previously negotiated "solutions." "Peña's insecurity principle," if incorporated in a comprehensive model, acts more as a constant than a variable, generally increasing the likelihood that actors in such settings of global insecurity, however impelled by regional change processes, will adopt conservative strategies vis-à-vis long-range mutual commitments.

THE MODEL

The following specification of relationships constitutes an *open* system of explanation in the sense that antecedent conditions are not perfect or even exclusive predictors of succedent ones. Error variables—exogenous, partly random conditions—are present throughout the model although according to the "hypothesis of increasing mutual determination" these should decline with successive positive resolutions of decisional crises. For example, the model hypothesizes that the combined effect of changes in relative size/power, changes in the rate of transactions, and changes in internal pluralism and external factors "predicts" the perceived equity in the distribution of benefits. This "outcome" (or better, "throughcome"!!!) in turn helps predict probable changes in national actor strategy. In each case the prediction is probabilistic, i.e., it estimates the mean change in the dependent variable, and incomplete, i.e., it includes a large error variable. Another way of stating this is that each variable in the model is, to a degree, independent.

Variable definitions and operationalizations for the initiation cycle:

Relative size/power (RSP): degree of homogeneity or symmetry in relative capacity to control outcomes in the specific context of the regional institution. Operationalizations: for individual units, relative position in rankings or deviation from regional mean on a series of indicators of potential power; across the region, the rank incongruence between these independent indicators.[23]

Rates of transaction (ROT): extent of interdependence based on relative patterns of economic, social, and cultural exchange within, as contrasted to without, the region. Operationalizations: 1) intraregional trade/total foreign trade; 2) relative

---

[23] Cf. the Haas-Barrera and Schmitter articles on operationalization cited in footnote 4.

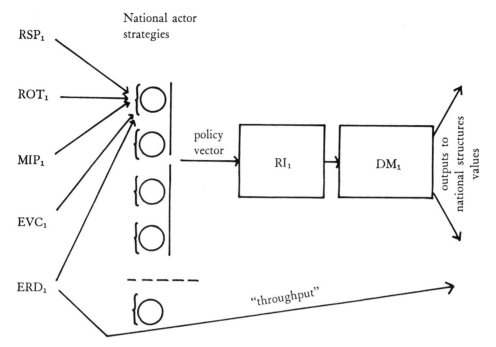

FIGURE 5. TIME₁: THE INITIATION CYCLE

acceptance ratio[24]; 3) "chooser-chosen" ratios[25]; 4) capital flow ratios of interpenetration in fixed investment; 5) labor flow ratios of exchanges of workers across national borders; 6) communications flow ratios of exchange of mail, telegrams, etc., within and without the region. All can be calculated for each member unit and also aggregated across the region for comparative purposes. Correlations between these indicators may be relatively high, but asynchronic patterns are common, especially among LDCs, and may be particularly significant for specific issue crises.

Member internal pluralism (MIP): extent to which functionally differentiated and formally organized groups within member states are organized and capable of articulating demands and influencing policy outcomes independent of control by authority groups. Operationalizations: for individual member, proportion of total population organized in representative associations (in practice, trade unions) multiplied by an index of freedom of expression or association; for the region as a whole, the standard deviation of the previous scores.[26]

Elite value complementarity (EVC): distribution of expectations and evaluations

---

[24] I. Richard Savage and Karl W. Deutsch, "A Statistical Model for the Gross Analysis of Transaction Flows," *Econometrica*, July 1960 (Vol. 28, No. 3), p. 551.

[25] Bruce M. Russett, " 'Regional' Trading Patterns: 1938–1963," *International Studies Quarterly*, December 1968 (Vol. 12, No. 4), pp. 360–379. For an excellent discussion of the utility of various transactional indicators see Donald Puchala in this volume.

[26] Again, see the Haas-Barrera and Schmitter articles cited in footnote 4.

(pro and con) vis-à-vis regional integration across national participant political groups. Operationalizations: panel-type survey data on nature and intensity of commitment to similar goals within and across integrating units relative initially to specific context of proposed regional collaboration. In the absence of such data,[27] content analysis of statements by elected representatives and self-appointed spokesmen about motives for participation and anticipated returns.

Extraregional dependence (ERD): extent to which member states and region as a whole are subjected to asymmetric economic and political relations which reduce their individual and collective capacity for independent decisionmaking without placing similar or mutual restrictions on extraregional hegemonic powers. Operationalizations: two not necessarily covariant dimensions should be distinguished. 1) the global network of economic weakness and dependence as measured by concentration of export earnings in few items, high international trade to gross national product ratios, persistent decline in terms of trade; 2) the specific policy network surrounding patron and client states as measured by such asymmetric exchanges as economic aid per capita, military aid as percentage of the total military budget, external debt as a percentage of gross national product, International Monetary Fund drawings per capita.[28]

National actor strategies: extent to which negotiating national actors promote and/or accept increases in the number and type of issues to be deliberated regionally (scope) and/or increases in the decisional autonomy of regional institutions (level). Operationalization: see above discussion on the dependent variable, especially Figure 4, p. 241.[29]

Policy vector: the concatenation of national actor strategies into a joint policy vis-à-vis the scope and/or level of regional institutions. Vector can be the result of 1) *identity* where all national strategies are the same; 2) *convergence* where they differ but within margins which tolerate a mutually acceptable institutional solution; 3) *divergence* where they differ so much as to cause the collapse of negotiations or the withdrawal of individual bargainers.

Level/scope of regional institutions (RI₁): the area or "zone of indifference" within which the global policy matrix treated by regional decisionmaking in terms of 1) the joint capacity at least to discuss a given issue or set of issues and 2) the degree of decisional authority to deal with the issue. Operationalization: see pp. 240–242 above, especially Figure 4 and footnotes 13 and 14.

Decisionmaking style (DM₁): within the formal institutional attributes as determined by scope and level above, the manner of jointly resolving disputes and allocating resources according to two independent dimensions: 1) the degree of autonomy enjoyed by national negotiators and 2) the degree of unanimity enforced in reaching decisions. Operationalization: classification according to a four-cell matrix based on dichotomized attributes mentioned below.

---

[27] Cf. articles by Donald Puchala and Ronald Inglehart in this volume.

[28] Schmitter, *International Organization,* Vol. 23, No. 2, pp. 334–336.

[29] See the caveat introduced in footnote 13, p. 240.

degree of enforced unanimity

		high	low
autonomy of national representation	low	*Lowest Common Denominator*	*Splitting the Difference*
	high	*Package Dealing*	*Upward-Grading*

FIGURE 6. DECISIONMAKING STYLES IN REGIONAL INSTITUTIONS. This figure is a result of personal communication with Ernst B. Haas.

BIVARIATE HYPOTHESES CONCERNING THE INITIATION CYCLE (Time$_1$)[30]

1) The greater the symmetry in potential size/power or, operationally, the greater the rank incongruence between indicators of potential power, the greater the probability of accepting and/or promoting positive integrative strategies.

2) The higher and more varied the initial rates of transaction, the greater the probability of adopting/supporting a positive integrative strategy.

3) The greater the extent of member internal pluralism, the greater the likelihood that actors will respond to tensions and contradictions by upgrading the authority of regional institutions and/or expanding the scope of regional deliberations.

4) The more similarly distributed (and, obviously, the more positive) the values held by respective national elites attentive to integration issues, the greater the probability that positive integrative strategies will be followed.

5) The greater the initial global dependence, the greater the likelihood that actors will accept the costs at the national level of widening the scope and heightening the level of regional deliberations.

6) The relation between the extent of patron-client policy dependence and prointegrative strategies is indeterminate since the major conditioning factor is the national interest perception of the hegemonic extraregional power—a variable exogenous to this model.

7) The greater the initial scope and/or level of regional institution(s), the greater the likelihood that the decisionmaking style will be expansive, i.e., tend toward "upward grading."

---

[30] All of these hypotheses, although stated in a linear fashion, are subject to the caveat introduced on p. 245 above, that beyond a certain threshold their predicted effect is likely to become curvilinear or even parabolic.

Multivariate Hypotheses concerning the Initiation Cycle (Time$_1$)

1) The more even the national scores in RSP$_1$, ROT$_1$, MIP$_1$, EVC$_1$, and ERD$_1$, the more likely the national actors will converge on some formula for establishing a regional institution or institutions.

2) The higher the overall scores on the above independent variables, the greater is likely to be the initial scope and level of regional institutions.

3) The greater the initial scope and level of regional institutions, the greater the consequent impact of regional decisions upon changes in national structures and values. This hypothesis could also be called the "functionalist paradox." The narrower, more separable, and hence more technical, the scope of "integrated policymaking," the easier it may be to get initial agreement but the less significant is likely to be the subsequent impact upon national structures/values and, indirectly, regional processes. This is not simply due to the segregation of the sector involved (lack of potential *engrenage* and *externalization*) and its low visibility (lack of *envy* and *equity* side effects), but only institutions with a multiplicity of objectives and a wide scope provide regional reform-mongers with an increased capacity for engaging in a style of decisionmaking which seems crucial to voluntaristic integration movements. Extending the number and variety of policies subject to collective deliberation (wider scope) enhances the possibilities for combining sacrifices and benefits in intersectorial "logrolls." It is hard to imagine how an integration scheme confined to a single, circumscribed task could expand beyond the desires of its most reluctant member (i.e., decisionmaking style would be confined to "lowest common denominator"). All things being equal, the more sectors potentially involved, the easier it will be to strike such a series of linked compromises.[31] The outputs from the previous decisional cycle enter from the left as inputs (with the exception of extraregional dependence [ERD] which is a direct "throughput" since the regional institutions have not yet acquired an independent capacity to affect these exogenous conditions). As a consequence of these decisions (and of an unspecified, but admittedly large, error variable) national structures and values begin to undergo changes. These in turn affect regional processes. Important (and critical) assumptions of the model are 1) that the impact of regional decisions upon regional process is mediated by changes at the national level (with one important exception) and 2) that the changes at the national level are, in turn, mediated by the regional processes in the definition and redefinition of national actor strategies. In short, I am postulating that the magnitude and type of change at the regional level is dependent (with one exception) upon prior changes in the member units and

---

[31] Schmitter, *International Organization*, Vol. 23, No. 4, pp. 162–163. For the case study from which this paradox is derived see Lawrence Scheinman, "Euratom: Nuclear Energy in Europe," *International Conciliation*, May 1967 (No. 563).

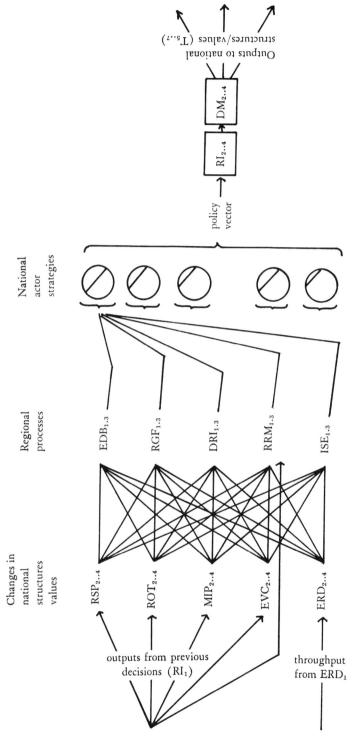

FIGURE 7. TIME$_{2..4}$: THE PRIMING CYCLE(s). The number of "priming cycles" is indeterminate. Three are suggested merely for convenience (T$_2$, T$_3$, T$_4$). A given regional integration process may go through many more or many less decisional crises until it either breaks through into the next qualitatively distinct cycle, encapsulates itself, or disintegrates.

that national actors in recalculating their respective strategies will use as relevant criteria primarily the effects of changes at the regional level.

Variable definitions and operationalizations for priming cycle(s):

Δ *Relative size/power* ($RSP_{2..4}$): changes in relative rankings or subsequent deviations from the regional mean for individual units; changes in overall rank incongruence across all units for the region.

Δ *Rates of transactions* ($ROT_{2..4}$): changes in indicators mentioned above (ROT_1).

Δ *Member internal pluralism* ($MIP_{2..4}$): changes either in the number and coverage of interest associations or in their freedom to articulate demands.

Δ *Elite value complementarity* ($EVC_{2..4}$): mobilization of interest on the part of newly affected groups and/or changes in the similarity of preinterested elites.

Δ *Extraregional dependence* ($ERD_{2..4}$): changes in previously mentioned indicators, especially emergence of insistence by extraregional hegemonic actor upon multilateral dealings.

Regional Processes:

Equitable distribution of benefits (EDB): extent to which benefits accruing from regionally induced transactions are *perceived* as being reciprocally distributed among participants. Operationalization: in addition to such "surrogate" indicators as balances of trade and payments, pattern of new industrial location and distribution of new employment, classification of responses of relevant elites as to their perceptions of payoff relative to that of others.

Regional group formation (RGF): formation and active participation of new nongovernmental or quasi-governmental organizations representing some or all members and designed explicitly to promote the interest of complementary groups at the regional and/or national levels. Operationalization: classification of data on sectorial coverage, membership, degrees of voluntary support and participation, organizational vitality, and demand articulating activities of regional nongovernmental organizations.

Development of regional identity (DRI): extent to which participants or observers in regional processes come to regard such activity as rewarding due to material inducements, emotional-fraternal-symbolic ties, status satisfactions, etc., and, thereby, acquire a larger sense of loyalty. Operationalization: panel survey research on selected samples exposed to intensive regional socialization; inference from single surveys on residual importance of regional contacts/level of information when controlled for other variables[32]; study of career patterns of participants and inferences from subsequent behavior and attitudes.[33]

[32] For a summary see the above cited articles by Donald Puchala and Ronald Inglehart. Also Richard Merritt and Donald J. Puchala, *Western European Perspectives on International Affairs* (New York: Frederick A. Praeger, 1968); Karl W. Deutsch, and others, *France, Germany and the Western Alliance: A Study of Elite Attitudes in European Integration and World Politics* (New York: Charles Scribner's Sons, 1967); Daniel Lerner and Morton Gordon, *Euratlantica: Changing Perspectives of the European Elites* (Cambridge, Mass: MIT Press, 1969).

[33] The research of Lawrence Scheinman is particularly relevant here. See his "Some Preliminary Notes on Bureaucratic Relationships in the European Economic Community," *International Organization*, Autumn 1966 (Vol. 20, No. 4), pp. 750–773.

Regional reform-mongering (RRM): degree to which actors employed by or closely associated with the new regional institutions engage actively and deliberately in the promotion of new policies by anticipation, i.e., on the basis of an intellectual or technical calculation before such measures are demanded or opposed by aroused interest representatives, or *políticos*. Operationalization: detailed case studies of issue initiation, conflict resolutions, organizational ideologies in the wrapping of package deals and the performance of brokerage and mediation roles by regional *técnicos*.

International status effect (ISE): extent to which the relative standing of individual countries or the region as a whole is perceived as dependent upon the performance of regional institutions. Operationalization: survey or content analytic evidence on perceived collective changes in status, especially vis-à-vis the successful operation of regional integration schemes elsewhere, or, more crudely, score inferred from changes in rankings on global modernization/development variables.

Δ *National actor strategies,* Δ *level and scope of regional institutions* $(RI_{2..4})$ Δ *decisionmaking style* $(DM_{2..4})$: changes in values of these variables according to previously discussed scoring procedures. For the first time, national actor strategies will become plural, with differentiation into subsets pursuing different objectives. Full, multiple differentiation with separate participation in regional decision-making is probably more characteristic of the next "transforming cycles."

BIVARIATE HYPOTHESES CONCERNING THE PRIMING CYCLE(S) $(Time_{2..4})$

1) The less change in the relative size and power of national actors (vis-à-vis each other), the more likely that perception of benefits will be equitable.

2) The greater and more varied the changes in rates of transaction, the higher is the likely rate of regional group formation and the more rapid is the development of a distinctive regional identity likely to be.

3) The greater the increase in internal pluralism within and across member states, the more likely are transnational groups to form and are regional identities to emerge.

4) The more complementary elites come to acquire similar expectations and attitudes toward the integration process, the easier it will be to form transnational associations and to accept regional identities. Similarly, their joint sensitivity to variations in international status is likely to be stronger.

5) The greater the previous scope and level of regional institutions and the more "upward-grading" their decisional style, the more likely are regional bureaucrats to engage in reform-mongering. This holds independently of changes in national srtuctures/values, but these anticipating *técnicos* may pick up important allies in the form of support from extraregional hegemonic powers and newly mobilized interest groups. Certain prior changes in elite values, e.g., attitudes toward planning, efficiency, etc., also make their task easier.

6) The effect of changes in extraregional dependence seems particularly paradoxical or parabolic. Both the marked rise or decline in global economic dependence may heighten sensitivity to international status. In the former case new regional institutions may come to be regarded as the only bulwark of defense against further deterioration; in the latter they may be at least partially credited with the relative success. Specific attempts by extraregional authorities to influence the integration process likewise may have a dual effect. As mentioned, their support may strengthen the hand of regional *técnicos;* on the other hand such overt attempts to control or guide regional outcomes may—by reaction-formation—stimulate resistance on the part of regional interest groups and promote a greater sense of mutual identity. I think it reasonable to hypothesize that extraregional policies which are indeterminate or undefined as regards the performance and objectives of regional institutions, e.g., symbolic statements of approval without financial inducements or negotiating concessions and refusals to deal with the region as a whole, are the least likely to provoke or promote changes at the regional level. Strong alterations in extraregional stands for and against the decisions forthcoming from regional organizations will have the greatest impact.

7) Actors who perceive their returns from integration as equitable—in line with anticipated returns and in proportion to those of others—will *not* reevaluate their integrative strategies (unless forced by less satisfied actors) and eventually will opt for encapsulation. Only actors dissatisfied with the equity of returns will promote or reconsider alternative strategies. Within a certain negative range the most likely response is a positive one—push the process into new areas or provide central decisionmakers with more resources or authority to redistribute returns. Beyond that negative range the response will probably be negative in either scope or level or both.

8) The greater the coverage, density, participation, vitality, and autonomy of regional interest associations, the greater the propensity for overcoming national resistance to expansions in scope and/or level.

9) The greater the development of a distinctive regional identity and the wider its distribution across classes and corporate groups, the more likely national actors will be able to build supportive coalitions for prointegrative strategies.

10) The greater the reform-mongering activism of regional bureaucrats, the greater the likelihood of prointegrative strategies being adopted. (However, see pp. 260–261 for a countervailing hypothesis.)

11) The greater the perceived effect of participation in a regional organization upon enhancing international status, the greater the propensity for devolving new obligations upon that organization.

These have been a selection of the most obvious and direct, *ceteris paribus,* bivariate relationships in the model during the priming cycle(s). All seem to me to be at least potentially falsifiable, and many I suspect would be falsified if one could examine them in such a discrete, bivariate setting. Since the limited number of cases[34] and the tendency for everything to be varying at once makes this difficult to ascertain, a more productive research strategy would seem to be to pass directly to multivariate, additive relationships.

MULTIVARIATE HYPOTHESES CONCERNING THE PRIMING CYCLE(S) ($T_{2..4}$)

1) The changes in national structures/values jointly influence the extent of variation in regional processes, but they do so in different respective proportions. Some, in other words, contribute more to our understanding or prediction of subsequent regional changes than others. Many of the more important of these changes have been discussed bivariately.

Moreover, as will be recalled from macrohypothesis number six, their specific marginal contributions will vary in different global settings (less and more developed countries).[35]

A great deal more work must be done on specific "additive" (and later, I am sure, "multiplicative") formulae for predicting the joint effect of changes at the level of national structures and values. A possible start might be to postdict on the basis of existing case studies, juxtaposing some crude ordinal or nominal indicator of regional process change to the series of independent national variables.

For example, it seems that in LDC settings (e.g., Central America) to predict the perception of equitable distribution of benefits (EDC_1) one must first check on changes in relative size/power (ΔRSP_2); second on rates of transaction (ΔROT_2); third on extraregional dependency, especially deliberate attempts by the hegemonic outsider to pay off perceivers of inequity, (ΔERD_2); fourth on respective elite values (ΔEVC_2); and, last and of little importance, on changes in member internal pluralism (ΔMIP_2). For more developed countries I would place the independent predictors in the following stepwise order according to their declining marginal importance: $\Delta ROT_2 > \Delta MIP_2 > \Delta EVC_2 > \Delta RSP_2 > \Delta ERD_2$. Joint evaluation by panels of scholars on the relative order and, perhaps, even magnitude of each of the national level changes upon each of the regional processes could set up a crude, "anticipated" multiple regression to guide simulation or to check against a "real"

[34] Leon Lindberg and Stuart Scheingold, in *Europe's Would-Be Polity: Patterns in the European Community* (Englewood Cliffs, N.J.: Prentice-Hall, 1970) argue that by treating each decision as a distinct unit "within system" comparisons can draw upon a much larger case base. Of course, this may not expand the ranges of variation very much since there is likely to be substantial autocorrelation in many variables.

[35] Jalloh, as mentioned in footnote 22, has argued the need for different variables and different weightings for the African context. I confess his case has not yet convinced me of the need for the former, but I can imagine a solution to the latter—namely, to subdivide the macrosettings further into three categories: 1) more developed countries; 2) intermediate developed countries; 3) less developed countries.

mutiple regression with coded and/or interval data independently gathered.

2) If no changes in the specific national structures/values are forthcoming (or, much more confusingly, if the scores are asynchronic and possibly self canceling), there should be no change in the regional processes and, subsequently, no inducement to change national actor strategies (except for the "throughputted," but probably futile, efforts at regional reform-mongering). The model would continue to cycle until this entropic condition stabilized (encapsulation) or until new values were generated sufficiently high to induce strategic redefinitions.

3) Asynchrony in rates of change at the national level sets up—due to their differing marginal impacts—asynchrony in rates of regional change. This, in turn, enhances the probability that less convergent, and possibly divergent, actor strategies will be promoted, making the adoption of a joint policy vector more and more difficult.

4) Also, asynchronic change at the regional level in particular enhances politicization—greater controversiality and the engagement of wider audiences. Particularly crucial to this is the generally very slow rate with which a distinctive regional identity emerges.

5) The "peculiar" configuration in the model of regional reform-mongering (RRM) introduces the possibility that anticipating, calculating *técnios* will promote a disparity between changes at the two levels—national and regional. During these priming cycles their activities are limited on the one hand by the reduced authority and resources of regional institutions and on the other by the relatively undifferentiated nature of national actors. Of course, as mentioned, they may be aided and abetted in their efforts by extraregional support.

6) During one of these priming cycles, i.e., early in the integration process, one should be able to discern the first signs of externalization—of conscious attempts by regional "partners" to bring the exogenously determined, extraregional dependence (ERD_1) under their, at least partial, negotiative control. The greater the initial scope and level and the more "progressive" the decisionmaking style, the more intensive will be the effect of regional decisions on ERD_2. The success or failure of these efforts will have an important impact on the international status of the movement (ISE_1).

7) The regional change processes "interdetermine" national actor strategies —or better, they set certain parameters within which alternative strategies are selected. Again, an inductive process similar to that suggested above in hypothesis number one may provide us with some crude estimates. Although the model is not constructed of phenotypical (actor-defined) conditions, a very useful adjunct to abstract deductivism would be to decompose the perceptions, motives, and factual assertions that actors disclose in justifying their changes in strategy. In short, they may just tip us off as to what were the relative con-

straints they experienced. I repeat that actor categories of analysis and evaluation may not be the same as the model's (they may not be aware of how a given process has limited or expanded their options), but I also admit that I would be concerned about the model's validity if actors never mentioned or explicitly discounted the importance of EDB, RGF, DRI, RRM, and ISE. If they kept citing some changes at the national levels as crucial, this might be a sign of possible throughputs, bypassing regional processes.

During the priming cycle(s) the probability that a given national actor will push a spillover policy is relatively slight. Subsequent changes are not likely to increase so rapidly; initial insecurity is likely to make all negotiators more cautious. A very convincing argument can be deduced from the model that the process scores in LDC settings are likely to be so low (except for negative EDB) and so asynchronic that they will never generate the "steam" for a simultaneous leap forward in level and scope.

Spill-around is a particularly attractive and easy strategy early in the process due to the ready availability of a large number of unexploited, noncontroversial adjacent policy areas.

Buildup is initially more difficult—despite the enthusiasm of regional reform-mongers for it—because of the "untried" capacity of newly formed RIs. It may prove attractive where a competent encapsulated one already exists and where units are strongly but unequally affected by regional change in a single sector.

Disintegrative strategies are, of course, less costly early in the process. Sunken costs are lower; patterns of benefits less entrenched; secondary and symbolic effects less widely felt. The most likely scenario for its use is by an actor weakly affected by RGF, DRI, RRM, or ISE but very sensitive to his perceived inequitable rate of return (EDB).

The most likely strategy—both individually and jointly—is for actors not too disfavored by the distribution of return, not too susceptible to the pleas (pro and con) of new nongovernmental organizations (NGOs), enjoying some satisfaction from their new regional "identity," moderately impervious to the machinations of regional *técnicos,* and mildly sensitive to their newly acquired status in the broader international community, to agree simply to continue the arrangement as is. This low-risk entropy will continue either until regional processes accumulate significantly or until some unforeseen exogenous crisis upsets the calculus.

8) The concatenation of national actors, each with different parameters and subsequent strategies, into some joint policy vector also deserves more deductive and inductive work. Clearly, *identical* strategies based on similar responses to regional processes are everywhere rare and likely to get rarer (due to asynchronies) as integration proceeds. On the other hand, if identity of aims and expectations sets in too early, it will be hard to find tradeoffs; bar-

gaining will jell on a fixed distribution of benefits of a restricted scope and encapsulation will set in quickly. Very sharp *divergences* across units should be picked up by the suggested indicators and should transmit the prediction that individual members or groups of members will drop the effort altogether or "hive off" to initiate another movement. The extent of tolerable spread in strategies which can be bridged by a *convergent* policy vector is difficult to determine a priori although it may increase over time with sunken costs and acquired institutional flexibility. In general I would venture the hypothesis that when strategies are convergent, the resultant policy will err on the conservative side since unanimity is usually necessary for "constitutional" revision or amendment. Nevertheless, the essence of package dealing is to incorporate side payments from other policy areas, and convergent objectives as well as multiple functions (i.e., wide scope) help this. In short, the more varied (but not radically divergent) the motives and expectations of negotiating parties, the greater the probability they will adopt a spill-around strategy during the priming cycle(s).

Most integration arrangements do not make it this far. Limited in initial scope to narrow policy areas or grudgingly conceded modest authoritative competence, the consequences of their activity have little impact. Some reciprocal distribution of benefits is eventually established (perhaps after a few decisional crises); a cluster of surrounding regional clients become satisfied with the existing level of services performed and grow wary of risking that for possibly greater but less certain future returns; socialization effects are confined to a small bureaucratic clique, itself devoted to avoiding change in established procedures; extraregional actors accommodate and come to regard the arrangement as an unobjectionable given. Large numbers of these encapsulated functionalist organizations persist in the international environment. By "doing their thing" and providing marginal, but often important, services to their clients, they tend to contribute more to maintaining than transforming the existing nation-state system.

As we look to the next cycle(s) in the integrative process, major structural changes in the nature and relative role of the actors occur. Therefore, I have labeled these the transforming cycles.

Rather than repeat past bivariate or multivariate hypotheses—most of which seem applicable to these cycles as well[36]—I will only introduce the qualitatively new elements of the model.

1) The first major innovation is an increase in the role of regional bureaucrats. Their capacity and resources augmented by previous (if positive) re-

---

[36] With the important caveat that the relative importance of independent and intervening variables is likely to change even if the direction of the effect and the basic structure of the model does not. Again, more speculative induction or postdiction is needed in order to specify which of the types of changes in national structures and values, for instance, decline in "potency" over time and which become increasingly better predictors of regional process.

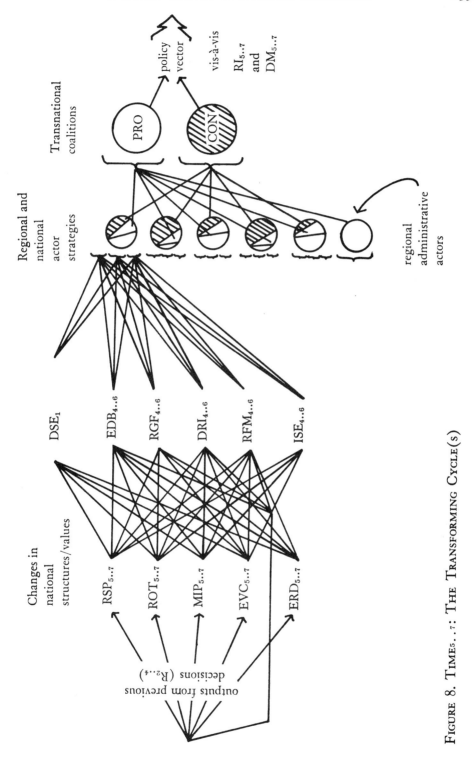

FIGURE 8. TIME$_{5..7}$: THE TRANSFORMING CYCLE(s)

definitions of scope and level, they are more likely to step up their efforts at directly influencing regional processes, bypassing intervening changes at the national levels. Negotiating directly with regional NGOs, inventing and promoting new symbols of regional identity, bargaining as representatives for the region as a whole with outsiders, they may begin to affect virtually all these processes rather than, as during the priming cycles, being confined to a single one.

2) The integrating units are most likely during these cycles to begin in earnest their attempts at externalization. The revised scope and level and the previously recorded and consolidated strength of regional change processes provide the internal basis for such an attempt; the impact of regional discrimination on nonparticipants is likely to provide an external stimulus. These outsiders are going to begin to insist on treating the movement as a new international bargaining unit.

3) As a consequence of one and two above, the regional institutions are likely to insist upon becoming recognized as actors in their own right, as formal participants with their own strategy in the concatenation which produces that *policy vector* which in turn redefines the scope and level of their authority.

4) A new regional process emerges: the domestic status effect (DSE$_1$). The redefined scope/level of regional institutions has begun to affect relative status and influence in domestic politics. Ministries, autonomous agencies, associations, and parties which have "gotten in on" the apparently successful earlier rounds of regional decisionmaking have thereby acquired more resources (proportion of the budget, international status, votes, etc.). This should cause other national institutions to try to "get in on" the operation although not necessarily in support of it. A good deal of this "fall-out," as I have called this process elsewhere,[37] may be purely symbolic—but at some point virtually all political and administrative organizations will have their respective "integration policies."

5) The most important transformation in the structure of the model during these stages occurs in the nature of national actors. Up to this point they have been treated as units with a single integrative or disintegrative strategy during any crisis. Now they appear as *differentiated* actors, a plurality of negotiating units (classes, status groups, subregions, *clientelas,* bureaucratic agencies, ideological clusters, etc.). This fragmentation depends, in large measure, upon the degree of prior change in regional group formation and the emergence of a new, superimposed wider identity.

6) These "subnational actors," each with their respective strategies, combine into stable "transnational coalitions" of support and opposition. The policy vector now becomes the product of alliances which cut across national boundaries (and, perhaps, historic national cleavages). National governmental ac-

---

[37] Schmitter, *Revista de la integración*, No. 5, pp. 131ff.

tors may continue to play the preponderant role in the concatenation of strategies, but they can be circumscribed, if not circumvented, by coalitions of other
governmental actors with subnational groups and regional *técnicos*.

7) The combination of increased activism by regional bureaucrats, their
attempt to gain full actor status, the spread of interest by "fall-out," the emerging differentiation or fragmentation of national actors, and the formation of
stable transnational coalitions makes the transforming cycles the most controversial and politicized point in the integration process. All these changes
are likely to be asynchronic. The bypassing of prior changes at the national
level (especially at the level of loyalty and legitimacy), the resistance to activism on the part of regional bureaucrats unaccountable to popular masses,
the reaction of governmental decisionmakers to the erosion of their monopolistic control over certain policy areas—all of this implies a period with an
enormous potential for conflict. This I would label "the integrative showdown"[38]; in the improbable event it is passed successfully, the movement will
find itself in yet another set of decisional cycles.

8) In terms of joint strategies, spillover seems increasingly likely to occur—
as the result of package deals designed to appeal to a broad transnational coalition of interests. Such a "solution" with its simultaneous payoffs in new arenas
and additional authority may, indeed, be the only "peaceful" voluntaristic
way to get beyond the showdown. Buildup is also a possible outcome where
national actor conflicts focus exclusively on a single sector. Spill-around, the
least costly of the "progressive" strategies, becomes less likely due to the rapid
exhaustion of easily accessible policy sectors and the growing need for the
adoption of "positive policies" which almost necessarily involve an increment
in the authoritative role of central institutions. Spill-back and the other disintegrative moves become less probable than during the priming cycles with
the rise in ensuing withdrawal costs. Encapsulation is still the most likely
"solution" of all, especially where the disparity between changes at the national and regional levels is great, the regional *técnicos* overstep their authority or resource base, and national actors adopt ever more divergent policies.
The following "transcending" cycles of the model are purely speculative. No
integration process in the contemporary setting has progressed this far—
through and beyond the initiation, priming, and transforming cycles. Therefore, my comments about hypothetical variable relationships will be brief.

1) The intervening role of changes in national structures and values declines in importance. It becomes more and more possible to predict changes
at the regional level as a direct, not mediated, consequence of regional decisions. Actors (now multiple and diverse) at the national level are less sensi-

---

[38] Amitai Etzioni has speculated about the necessity for the application of coercion in such circumstances. I have borrowed from him the concept of "showdown" but would disagree that it must necessarily involve the forceful imposition of one actor or coalition of actors over another, Amitai Etzioni,
pp. 87–88.

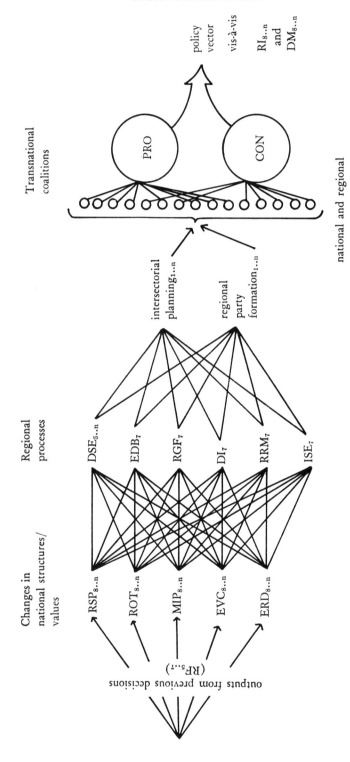

FIGURE 9. TIMES$_{8..n}$: THE TRANSCENDING CYCLES

tive to variation in relative size and power at the national level and have begun to calculate more in terms of transnational classes, status groups, subregions, etc. Transactions across national boundaries become less important than intersectoral flows of labor, capital, and management. The political role of regional NGO's begins to eclipse that of the national interest associations, the latter becoming subsections or branch offices of the former. Elite values are now more focused on regional symbols and loyalties although national ones are unlikely to wither away entirely.

2) Extraregional dependence becomes partly endogenous, no longer an exclusively exogenously determined variable. The region now bargains routinely across the whole range of issues with outsiders (full externalization) and, in return, it acquires and makes effective full recognition as a new actor in the global international system.

3) Two new regional processes appear coordinating the previous six: 1) intersectorial planning (ISP) which begins to impress upon previous autonomous efforts at regional policymaking some sense of priority and hierarchy of resource allocation; 2) regional party formation (RPF) which serves to aggregate different NGOs into a more unified system of representation, to provide a permanent intermediary focus for the diffuse sense of regional loyalty and identity, and, most importantly, to link the crisis issues to the broader concerns of the citizenry on a territorial, not functional, basis.

4) National actors with their unified single strategy for a given national unit disappear and are replaced by large transnational coalitions in favor of and opposed to diverse issues. The previous nations, as such, have lost their autonomous and monopolistic functions, and effective sovereignty has been devolved upon the new center.

5) In terms of strategies, spillover and spill-around are almost out—due to the virtual exhaustion of "untreated" issue areas (barring the creation of new ones). Buildup strategies aimed at increasing the authority of central (regional) decisionmakers seem more likely, especially in conjunction with the emerging emphasis on coordinated intersectorial planning. Encapsulation, however, is by far the most likely response. New initiatives in scope and level are likely to be very risky and contentious; internal organizational pressures may emerge for decentralization and the devolution of policymaking authority in "overextended" sectors; new regionally based political parties are likely to articulate citizen resistance to central management much more effectively. In short, during the transcending cycle(s) the institutional structure is likely to jell, to constitutionalize itself. This, of course, may involve a great variety of combinations of relative scope and level but all would be within that broad arc traced in the upper right-hand corner of Figure 4. For, once an integration movement has made it this far—through so many crisis-induced decisional cycles, it is very likely to have crossed that threshold into political

community status. Disintegrative "spill-back" strategies have become quite impracticable, if not unthinkable. A political community could then be defined as a decisionmaking system of sufficient authority that actors will predictably and peacefully resolve their conflicts without reducing either the scope or level of that authority.

Conclusion

This updated, revised "target" still has some rings missing and obviously lacks a consistent scoring system. Many linkages between variables and variable sets have yet to be specified hypothetically. The entire model is still far from quantification, and I remain ambiguous as to whether it should best move toward econometric techniques or simulation.

I am, however, convinced that we can waste a good deal of time and effort tracking down isolated bivariate relations, debating the relative merits of different (often equally arbitrary) measures, and rejecting macrotheories with single case studies and idiosyncratic variables. Understanding and explanation in this field of inquiry are, as in other fields such as political development, best served not by the dominance of a single "accepted" grand model or paradigm but by the simultaneous presence of antithetic and conflictive ones, which, while they may converge in certain aspects, diverge in so many others. If this sort of dialectic of incompleteness, unevenness, and partial frustration propels integration processes forward, why shouldn't it do the same for the scholarship that accompanies them?

7

Integration Logics:

A Review, Extension, and Critique

HAYWARD R. ALKER, JR.

COMPELLING as mathematical representations may seem to some interested in the "automaticity" of integration processes, to other empirical theorists they seem anything but obviously relevant. Yet there is a clear trend toward greater use of formal reasoning in both measurement and modeling work on integration processes.[1] Juxtaposing a variety of such inte-

HAYWARD R. ALKER, JR., chairman of the Mathematical Social Sciences Board, is a professor of political science and a senior staff member of the Center for International Studies at the Massachusetts Institute of Technology, Cambridge, Massachusetts. The research support of National Science Foundation Grant GS2429 to the center at M.I.T. is gratefully acknowledged.

[1] These studies, in addition to many of the articles in the present volume, can be grouped roughly in terms of their originating paradigms. One such is Karl W. Deutsch, and others, *Political Community and the North Atlantic Area: International Organization in the Light of Historical Experience* (Princeton, N.J: Princeton University Press, 1957). Deutsch, his associates, protégés, and critics have produced a number of works particularly relevant for our topic, including Bruce Russett, *Community and Contention: Britain and America in the Twentieth Century* (Cambridge, Mass: M.I.T. Press, 1963); Philip Jacob and James Toscano (ed.), *The Integration of Political Communities* (Philadelphia: J. B. Lippincott Co., 1964); Donald Puchala, "International Political Community Formation in Western Europe: Progress and Prospect" (Ph.D. dissertation, Yale University, 1966, being revised for publication); Karl W. Deutsch, "Integration and Arms Control in the European Political Environment: A Summary Report," *American Political Science Review*, June 1966 (Vol. 60, No. 2), pp. 354–365, and the several volumes written with Richard Merritt, Lewis Edinger, and Roy Macridis that this article summarizes; Hayward Alker and Donald J. Puchala, "Trends in Economic Partnership: The North Atlantic Area 1928–1963," in J. David Singer (ed.), *Quantitative International Politics: Insights and Evidence* (New York: Free Press, 1968); Ronald Inglehart, "An End to European Integration?," *American Political Science Review*, March 1967 (Vol. 61, No. 1), pp. 91–105; William E. Fisher, "An Analysis of the Deutsch Sociocausal Paradigm of Political Integration," *International Organization*, Spring 1969 (Vol. 23, No. 2), pp. 254–290.

The other major group of measurement and model-conscious regional integration studies take as their intellectual fount, the neo-functional approach of Ernst B. Haas in his *The Uniting of Europe: Political, Social, and Economic Forces, 1950–1957* (Stanford, Calif: Stanford University Press, 1958) and Ernst B. Haas and Philippe C. Schmitter, "Economics and Differential Patterns of Political Integration: Projections about Unity in Latin America," *International Organization*, Autumn 1964 (Vol. 18, No. 4), pp. 705–737. Important, in part derivative, measurement studies include Leon Lindberg, "The European Community as a Political System: Notes toward the Construction of a Model," in *Journal of Common Market Studies*, June 1967 (Vol. 5, No. 4), pp. 344–387; Per Olav Reinton, "International Structures and International Integration," *Journal of Peace Research*, 1967 (Vol. 4, No. 4), pp. 334–365; Joseph S.

gration logics—the mathematical formulae and conceptual abstractions incorporated in assessments of integration progress and regress—should help achieve the major purpose of this article: to introduce students to a variety of possible integration logics, some of their possible interrelationships, and the limitations of some of the simpler ones vis-à-vis current verbal theories of the integration process.

Once a rigorously specified integration logic has been clearly understood, we usually ask, "How valid is it?" At a more advanced, but still largely expository, level this article will also focus on some methodological implications of this question. Several attempts to validate integration logics, of either a descriptive or explanatory sort, will be noted; some as yet untried procedures will also be proposed. To some readers such discussions may seem to deflect their attention away from the primary review purposes of this article; but all should realize that critical appraisal of both simple and complex logical representations of some aspect of an integration process requires both the understanding and application of relevant validation procedures. More mathematically oriented scholars should also pay more attention to validating, i.e., attempting to falsify, their measurement and explanation logics. The record to date is at best a mixed one, and the appropriate degree of modesty has not always been forthcoming. If quantitative researchers are not willing to apply exacting scientific standards to their own measurement and explanation efforts, then by default their work is likely to become the subject of largely fruitless quantification versus nonquantification controversies.

A review of measurement and modeling logics that have been or might be validly applied to integration processes must rely on a number of organizing ideas. As argued at length elsewhere[2] the first of these is that most serious statistical measurement and explanation procedures do or should depend upon causally falsifiable theoretical assumptions. These assumptions or logics are of two basic sorts: measurement theories telling us how manifest observations are related to the underlying phenomena being measured, e.g., the degree of integration a system has achieved, and explanatory logics relating cause to effect, e.g., the ways in which background conditions facilitate or inhibit in-

Nye, "Comparative Regional Integration: Concept and Measurement," *International Organization,* Autumn 1968 (Vol. 22, No. 4), pp. 855–880; Mario Barrera and Ernst B. Haas, "The Operationalization of Some Variables Related to Regional Integration: A Research Note," *International Organization,* Winter 1969 (Vol. 23, No. 1), pp. 150–160; and Philippe C. Schmitter, "Further Notes on Operationalizing Some Variables Related to Regional Integration," *International Organization,* Spring 1969 (Vol. 23, No. 2), pp. 327–336.

A careful reading of these and other works by Deutsch, Haas, Lindberg, and Amitai Etzioni reprinted in *International Political Communities: An Anthology* (Garden City, N.J.: Anchor Books, Doubleday & Co., 1966) convinces me that the Deutsch and Haas groups overlap in too many ways to justify basically different labels for them.

[2] Hayward R. Alker, Jr., "Statistics and Politics: The Need for Causal Measurement," in Seymour M. Lipset (ed.), *Politics and the Social Sciences* (New York: Oxford University Press, 1969), pp. 244–314; and "Multivariate Data Analysis: Alternatives and Priorities," paper presented at the Australian UNESCO Seminar on Mathematics in the Social Sciences, May 24, 1968.

tegrative decisionmaking. Our second major organizing idea is that a rough, but instructive, ordering of integration logics is possible in terms of their formal complexity. The simplest of these, which to date have been most popular, are what will be called single-equation logics; typically they assume some kind of stimulus-subject-response relationship. Such equations are the natural building blocks of more complex, multiequation causal models. Somewhat more flexible and usually considerably more elaborate than causal models, computer simulations are the third general class of integration logics that we shall discuss.

It should not come as too much of a surprise that validation procedures for more complex computer simulations have not been fully developed, nor have any of those now available been applied to fully programmed simulations of integration processes. Although one is outlined below, no such models yet exist. Unfortunately, neither can one find any multiequation causal studies of regional integration despite the richness of the relevant validational methodology to be suggested below vis-à-vis a hypothetical causal model. Without making the frequently oversimplified or incorrect assumptions of single equation approaches, such logics can incorporate much of the conceptual richness of the best theoretical ideas in this volume and elsewhere. Thus the main desired consequence of this review is that it will soon become obsolete as complex, potentially more valid, integration logics begin to multiply.

I. Single-Equation Logics

Many apparently straightforward ways of measuring, explaining, or predicting regional integration exist. Some of these rely heavily on the logic of requisite conditions or functions; others more or less explicitly appeal to linear statistical models of the bivariate or multivariate sort. One can also distinguish efforts based heavily on judgmental assessments of the overall state of integration from approaches using more disaggregated, objective measures of certain aspects of the integrated or integrating process. Leon Lindberg's article in this volume makes clear, however, that judgmental procedures can also be applied to component aspects within a clearly articulated conception of the integration process. With an eye for logical assumptions, differing measurement procedures, and validity problems, we can group many recent efforts into five categories: linear logics, requisites analysis, the use of judgmental weights or indices, mixed models, and multiindicator approaches. The following discussion is intended to be a helpful, not merely a critical, review. Even though many flaws exist in single-equation procedures, much can be learned from them, and they may also serve to generate the components of more adequate multiequation approaches.

A. Linear Logics

The simplest linear logic is an additive one: just adding up the number of students exchanged, favorable attitudes, expenditures on joint services or national ministries affected to index integration. Similarly, one can count hostile incidents or incompleted negotiations to measure disintegration. Karl Deutsch, Ernst Haas, Leon Lindberg, Joseph Nye, and many others have used such indices, which can be represented in either absolute or relative terms in a number of simple ways. Thus, I_1 to I_3 are various integration or disintegration indices summed over times i within period t; these include:

$$I_1(t) = \sum_{\substack{i \\ \text{during} \\ t}} \text{integrative acts}_i \tag{1a}$$

$$I_2(t) = \sum_{\substack{i \\ \text{during} \\ t}} (\text{integrative acts}_i - \text{disintegrative acts}_i) \tag{1b}$$

$$I_3(t) = \frac{\sum\limits_{\substack{i \\ \text{during} \\ t}} (\text{integrative acts}_i)}{\sum\limits_{\substack{i \\ \text{during} \\ t}} \text{relevant acts}_i} \tag{1c}.$$

When, as in (1c), normalization of an index occurs through dividing the number of integrative (or already integrated) acts by their maximum possible total, the resulting index has a well-defined maximum and minimum value.

After deciding whether "integration" refers to the amount or level of already "integrated" acts or to "integrative" changes in that amount, one must still face other problems of conceptualization. Presumably, counting acts indicates a shared desire to focus on integrating or integrated practices rather than the potential for them. Which acts to include, with what weights, is of course both a definitional and a validity question.

But we need also to ask the more basic question: Are these indices true (and reliable) measures of the phenomenon we are interested in? Can integration ever adequately be measured as a weighted sum of integrated or integrative acts? Surely comparative studies of homogeneous cases are necessary before much confidence in an indicator's validity is warranted. Although it has been criticized as out of date, the work of Deutsch and his collaborators on the North Atlantic area remains methodologically very suggestive in this regard.[3]

[3] Karl Deutsch, and others. See pp. 72–80 in *International Political Communities* for the details of their procedure for evaluating the contribution of various political appeals and amalgamation strategies. Since actual classifications are not fully reported, the present reconstruction cannot be assumed precisely to be the one finally favored by Deutsch and his coauthors.

What these authors did was to agree first on a list of cases when political amalgamation did and did not successfully occur. The ratio of successful integration attempts to failures, call it $r_{s/f}$, was then calculated from these frequencies and used as a null or blind expectation of what was likely to happen in a particular case:

$$r_{s/f} = \frac{\text{number of integration successes}}{\text{number of integration failures}} = \frac{N_s}{N_f}$$

where $N_s + N_f = N$, the total number of integration attempts. Then for each political appeal or method (m) a ratio score $r(m)$ was calculated by dividing the frequency of a means being used with subsequent success (N_{sm}) by the frequency of its being used with subsequent integration failure (N_{fm}):

$$r_{s/f}(m) = \frac{\text{number of integration successes with m used}}{\text{number of integration failures with m used}} = \frac{N_{sm}}{N_{fm}}$$

where $N_{sm} + N_{fm} = N_m$, the number of times m was tried.

When each of these ratios exists, a decisiveness score $D(m)$ for any means or appeal m is given by

$$D(m) = \frac{r_{s/f}(m)}{r_{s/f}} \tag{2a}$$

or

$$D'(m) = \frac{r_{s/f}(m) - r_{s/f}}{r_{s/f}} \tag{2b}.$$

A slightly different approach would have used probability differences and produced decisiveness probabilities such as DP or DP':

$$DP(m) = \frac{N_{sm} - N_{fm}}{N_m} \tag{2c}$$

$$DP'(m) = \frac{N_{sm}}{N_m} - \left(\frac{N_s - N_{sm}}{N - N_m}\right) \tag{2d}.$$

It will be recalled that the most effective—not the most frequent—appeals were for more individual or group rights and liberties, and for more equality, with $D(m)$'s of about 3. As to amalgamation methods, popular participation in related movements and institutions and a pluralistic emphasis with promises of respect for national independence and sovereignty were most decisive.[4]

These decisiveness scores, in their probabilistic forms, can be used to predict integration success. To see why this is true, first let $I_m(m) = 1$ if means or appeal m is present, 0 if m is absent. If P_s is the probability of integration success, $p(s|\bar{m})$ is the probability of success when m was not used, and

---

[4] These findings are worth comparing with Haas's hypotheses or prescriptions in his *Beyond the Nation-State: Functionalism and International Organization* (Stanford, Calif: Stanford University Press, 1964), p. 115ff, as to the most efficient strategies usable by integration-prone supranational bureaucrats.

$p(s|m)$ is the conditional probability of s given that m was used, it logically follows from the exclusive and exhaustive nature of events $\overline{m}$ and m that

$$P_s = p(s|\overline{m}) + I_m(m) \cdot (p(s|m) - p(s|\overline{m})) \tag{3a}.$$

In words, the probability of success is equal to the probability of success not using m plus the increase in success probability that comes from m being used. Further manipulations of this result show how P_s and $DP'(m)$ are intertwined:

$$P_s = \frac{N_s - N_{sm}}{N - N_m} + I_m(m)DP'(m) \tag{3b}.$$

Note how in (3b) the revised decisiveness score $DP'(m)$ multiplies the observed dichotomous index $I_m(m)$ to predict an increase in success probability above what might otherwise be expected were m not to occur. Although a bivariate equation is not likely to be totally adequate in a multicausal world—the effects of other causal variables and relations affecting I_m and P_s have been omitted—this logic remains an insightful, causally suggestive empirical alternative.

When a deep explanation is not sought, for descriptive or predictive purposes one might measure integrating potential in terms of preexisting integration levels. To do so requires a differential or difference equation linking the two. Consider equations (4a) and (4b), where I is some hypothetical integration index, u a probabilistic error term, and the K's are constants:

$$\frac{d^2I}{dt} = K_1\frac{dI}{dt} + K_2I + K_3 \tag{4a}$$

$$I(t) = K_1I(t\text{-}1) + K_2I(t\text{-}2) + u \tag{4b}.$$

The first relates the second derivative or "acceleration" in integration to the current integration "velocity," $\frac{dI}{dt}$, and integration level, I; the second stochastically (probabilistically) suggests positive or negative "spillover" effects (depending whether K_1 and K_2 are positive or negative) from integration levels in two previous periods to the present.

$$P_j(t) = \sum_{i=1}^{n} P_{ji}P_i(t\text{-}1) \tag{4c}.$$

Equation (4c), the formula for a first order Markov process, requires a little more discussion. It assumes that integration has n different, possibly ordered, discrete states, indexed with i or j. Transition probabilities P_{ji} determine $P_j(t)$, the chances of being in state j at t given probabilities $P_i(t\text{-}1)$ for various i that the system of concern was in state i at $t\text{-}1$. As modeled here the transition probabilities P_{ji} are of first order, i.e., constant. A more complex representation, closer to (4b) in form, would assume second order transition probabilities that depend on both the last and the next to last state in which a system has been. For any version of equation (4), integration is questionably assumed mainly to depend on its own earlier values. The measurement of integrating predispositions, the K's or the P_{ji}'s, does not require that the model be causally realistic in this assumption if it is so regarding trend projections.

William Fisher in his recent reanalysis of the Deutsch sociocausal paradigm and Joseph Nye in his demonstration of the downward trend in hostile incidents within the Central American Common Market (CACM), 1952–1964,[5] have both used a linear functional form rather similar to that of equation (4b):

$$I_4(t) = a + bf(t) + u(t) \tag{5a}$$

Here $f(t)$ is some function of time, such as t, t^2, $t^{2/3}$, or c^t; a, b, and c are constants. Even though $f(t)$ may thus not have an exponent of unity, equation (4a) is still linear in the important sense that its unspecified coefficients, a and b, combine linearly and additively. Although (5a) has no direct explanatory power—at best it can show trends in conjunction with prior integration acts—it has proven a suggestive but imperfect index of their possible consequences. Nye, for example, showed a downward trend in violent acts among CACM members in the years after the market was formed.

A closely related linear logic would have I_4 (an integration index) explainable as well as measurable in terms of levels of a social assimilation index $A_s(t)$ and an error term $u(t)$:

$$I_4(t) = a + bf(A_s(t)) + u(t) \tag{5b}$$

Similarly, Nye has suggested that attitudinal integration ($PI_2(t)$) lags behind, but is caused by, policy integration ($PI_3(t)$) according to a curvilinear step effect:

$$PI_2(t) = f(PI_3(t')), \; (t' < t) \tag{5c}$$

In order to explain I_4 or PI_2—or to use $A_s(t)$ or PI_3 as indices of integration in cases where I_4 or PI_2 have not been measured—we need to validate the form and parameters of equations (5b) and (5c). To do this, it is clearly necessary to test these relationships by experimenting with other possible explanatory variables, formulae, and causal directions. Otherwise the attributed causal relations may well be spurious.[6]

---

[5] Fisher, *International Organization,* Vol. 23, No. 2, p. 265ff; Nye, *International Organization,* Vol. 22, No. 4, pp. 874–876.

[6] Nye himself has suggested some interesting alternatives. Recall his nonlinear restatement of key federalist, functionalist, and neo-functionalist single-equation, unidirectional, partly causal hypotheses in *International Organization,* Vol. 22, No. 4, p. 875:

Federalism: $(PI_2 \lor PI_3 \lor PI_4) \supset (PIB \geq K_1 \; \& \; PIJ \geq K_2)$ (6a).

In words, if either policy, attitudinal, or security integration (PI_2, PI_3, PI_4, respectively), is to occur,

Let us look at Fisher's major explanatory hypothesis from this perspective. In terms of the logic of equation (5b) Fisher argues convincingly that Deutsch is wrong about the positive causal impact of assimilation on integration because since the mid-fifties political integration among the countries of the European Economic Community (EEC) has increased but social assimilation has not. A number of alternate interpretations of such data, if correct, are plausible but have not been explored; thus what may have happened is "premature falsification" due to an inadequate specification of the relevant, perhaps ambiguous, verbal theory. First, it may well be that a more adequate formalization of the assimilation-integration relationship would state this link, using the differential calculus and a nonlinear logic. Perhaps integration levels increase at a varying rate $K_1(t)$ proportional to the absolute, not necessarily changing, level of assimilation above a certain threshold K_2:

$$\frac{dI}{dt} = K_1(t) \cdot (A_s(t) - K_2) + u(t) \tag{7}.$$

Notice how difficult it would be to estimate the nonlinear coefficient product $K_1(t)\,K_2$ from data on I and A_s alone; nonetheless, such a relationship would fit many of the curves that Fisher exhibits.

More complex, multiequation relationships taking into account such Deutschian variables as net elite prointegration appeal, $E(t)$, and the extent of value compatibility of prospective integration partners, $V_c(t)$, might also reflect the trends Fisher discovered. On reflection it is also quite plausible to

both bureaucratic and jurisdictional components of institutional integration (PIB, PIJ) have to be high (above thresholds K_1, K_2).

Functionalism: $PI_1 = f_1(PI_2, K_3)$,   (6b,c).

  e.g., $PI_1 = \text{sign } (PI_2 - K_3)$

Thus institutional (bureaucratic and jurisdictional) integration dichotomously defined (PI_1) is a function of the level of policy integration (PI_2) and a high threshold parameter K_3, e.g., PI_1 is one when PI_2 is as high as K_3, zero otherwise (here the sign function translates "+" and no sign into "i," "−" into "0" regardless of the levels of PI_3 and PI_4.

Neo-functionalism: $PI_3(t) = f_2(PI_2(t') - K_3,\ PI_1(t') - K_4,\ PI_3(t'))\ (t' < t)$ (6d).

Verbally, attitudinal integration (PI_3), defined now as a continuous variable, increases above its early level because policy integration and institutional integration at some previous point t' reached high and intermediate level threshold values, K_3 and K_4.

Taken together, equations (5c) and (6d) suggest multiequation, reciprocal, and lagged relations between policy and attitudinal integration. Moreover, Nye has further suggested that high PI_2 and intermediate PI_1 will *possibly* lead to high PI_4 and higher PI_1, further complicating variable interdependencies. Thus if we want to use policy integration PI_2 to explain or predict or index attitudinal integration at a later date, or vice versa, we cannot be sure of the validity of such measures until we have specified and estimated to our satisfaction valid versions of the *multiple* relations between them.

If such multiequation systems as this are "recursively" or "separably" structured, then highly suggestive quasi-experimental validation procedures for single equations like a discontinuous version of (5a,b, or c) or (6d), discussed in Donald T. Campbell, "Reforms as Experiments," *American Psychologist*, April 1969 (Vol. 24, No. 4), pp. 409–429, are relevant. Al Pelowski is now studying EEC innovations using such pretest-posttest research designs. I doubt, however, that such procedures could practicably be applied to simultaneously interdependent systems like (8a,b,c) below.

further interpret Deutsch's writings to imply the opposite causal relation from (5b), namely, that integration increases social assimilation. A plausible set of multiple interdependences between assimilation, integration, elite appeals, and community values is given in equations (8a,b,c):

$$\frac{dI(t)}{dt} = K_1 E(t) (A_s(t) - K_2) + u_1(t)$$

$$A_s(t) = K_3 \int_0^t e^{-a(t-\tau)} I(\tau)d\tau + K_4 \int_0^t e^{-b(t-\tau)} V_c(\tau)d\tau + u_2(t)$$

$$V_c(t) = K_5 A_s(t) + u_3(t) \qquad\qquad (8a,b,c).$$

In equation (8a) net elite integration appeal, $E(t)$, serves as the variable constant in (7), enhancing integration if assimilation is above a threshold K_2. Thus as Deutsch might well argue, a certain degree of assimilation is necessary, but is not in and of itself causally sufficient, for an increase in integration. Equation (8b) states that the assimilation level responds cumulatively, with decaying effects, to previous levels of integration and value compatibility (thus the use of an integral from the beginning of data collection [$t=0$] to the present (t) but with exponentially diminished effects from earlier periods; τ is the varying time parameter that the integral sums over). Like other dependent variables in equations (8a,b,c) in also being subject to a stochastic error term (u_3), value compatibility (V_c) is assumed mainly to respond fairly immediately to assimilation levels.

We have now reviewed over ten different linear integration logics and have raised questions about the validity of most of them. Only in a few cases—the early Deutschian work and more recent articles by Fisher and Nye—has a clear causal argument been presented. Upon careful inspection, however, most of the causal and the noncausal assumptions of these logics have been found to omit the effects of other plausible variables or relationships. *These remarks should suggest how inadequate it is to explain, estimate, or predict integration levels with bivariate linear relationships.* Rather than explore corrective possibilities further now, since a more extended illustration of multi-equation dynamic causal relations will follow, we turn to a review and critique of sociological arguments as to the necessary and sufficient conditions for integration.

B. Requisites Analysis

Requisites analysis is a venerable part of sociological analysis.[7] Its logical

[7] See Marion Levy, *The Structure of Society* (Princeton, N.J: Princeton University Press, 1952) and Ernst Haas, *Collective Security and the Future International System* (Denver, Col: Social Science Foundation and Graduate School of International Studies, 1967–1968), Vol. 5. These writings are clearly within the "functionalist" tradition of sociology, but even though Ernst Haas has suggested interesting links between sociological functionalism and integration-relevant neo-functionalism in his *Beyond the Nation-State*, part 1, I shall hereafter avoid the sociological phrase "functional analysis" for the sake of clarity.

emphasis on necessary and sufficient conditions, functions, and structures stands in marked contrast to the statistical formulae characteristic of most linear or nonlinear logics. Yet many of our reservations about linear logics also apply to such formulations.

We have already noted the exciting but incomplete use of logical relations in Joseph Nye's statement of a key federalist hypothesis, equation (6a). Perhaps the most widely cited use of necessity or sufficiency requisites in the regional integration literature is the list of necessary background conditions associated with either amalgamated or pluralistic security communities in *Political Community and the North Atlantic Area*. We can logically represent the claim there that compatibility of major values relevant to political decision-making, V_c, nonviolent intergovernmental responsiveness, R, and (perhaps) mutual predictability, *MP*, are essential (necessary) for pluralistic integration as follows:

$$I(t) \supset V_c(t')\&R(t')\&MP(t'), \ (t' < t) \tag{9a}.$$

This can be read, "If *I* (integration) is true at time *t*, then interunit value compatibility and responsiveness and predictability were also true at an earlier time *t'*." We have said that V_c, *R,* and *MP* should all occur together for at least one moment *t'*, prior to integration at *t*. Other temporal explications are of course possible and even appropriate. Unfortunately, ordinary English is rarely precise enough about the class of time relationships being considered.

As Deutsch and his associates readily admit, the major problem with many such efforts, including their own, is uncertainty as to whether, taken individually or collectively, the necessary conditions are themselves sufficient ones. If they are, we can say:

$$V_c(t')\&R(t')\&MP(t') \supset I(t) \tag{9b}$$

which reverses the "if . . . then . . . " language of (9a). Together propositions (9a) and (9b) can be written logically as $(t' < t)$:

$$I(t) \equiv V_c(t')\&R(t')\&MP(t') \tag{10a}$$

or

$$I(t) \equiv (V_c(t') \geq K_1)\&(R(t') \geq K_2)\&(MP(t') \geq K_3) \tag{10b}$$

which mean that *I* and the cooccurrence of V_c and *R* and *MP*, perhaps above threshold values of K_1, K_2, and K_3, are logically equivalent, i.e., constantly cooccurring. Some additional understanding is necessary between the mathematician and the reader, however, concerning the causal interpretability of such a constant cooccurrence; if the variables on the right-hand side of equations (10a) or (10b) or the left-hand side of (9b) are assumed to cause I(t), then both "$\supset$" and "$\equiv$" cannot be as freely manipulated as when they are considered merely logical or correlational connectors.[8]

***

[8] Note that (9a) is also not a completely adequate rendition of the necessity idea which may require a modal logic for adequate representation. E.g., "it is necessary that (Vc & . . .)" might be stated with

The easily falsifiable nature of necessary and/or sufficiency arguments—all that is required is a counterexample—is surely one of the most attractive features of requisites analysis from an empirical point of view. Some slippage usually occurs, however. There are, for example, other variables relevant to the development of a pluralistic security community, such as the continued existence of the parties concerned and the development of habitual patterns of intercourse appropriate to their propinquity; note how equations (10a) and (10b) assume these as part of a tacit *ceteris paribus*. What tends to result from an explication of such tacit assumptions is a linear logic, a multiplicative statistical assertion that the satisfaction of background conditions is neither necessary nor sufficient, but "extremely favorable" for integration.[9] Roughly, this translates into either

$$I(t) = K_1 C_1(t') \bullet C_2(t') \bullet C_3(t') + u(t) \tag{11a}$$

or

$$\frac{dI(t)}{dt} = K_2 C_1(t') \bullet C_2(t') \bullet C_3(t') + u(t) \quad (t' < t) \tag{11b}.$$

Here we use C_1 through C_3 to refer generally to "integration preconditions" defined intervally, with zero values considered as thresholds.

We have already discussed the explanatory weaknesses of such linear logics and the doubtful conclusiveness of falsification efforts directed against them. Certainly the suggestiveness of such multiplicative formulations has a lot to do with their continuing attractiveness as a way of representing necessity and sufficiency arguments within a richer variety of multiequation models. We turn now to a brief consideration of judgmental measures and explanations of regional integration phenomena.

C. Judgmental Procedures

Surely we are judgmental in any measurement or explanatory effort. The most frequent judgment made is of indicators of an underlying phenomenon or process. As psychologists have convincingly argued, such procedures usually

a modal predicate "N" as $N(Vc(t') \& \ldots)$; that such an approach would be appropriate here is also unclear, so we stick to a more conventional procedure of "overinterpreting" the proposition calculus and "$\supset$" and "$\equiv$" in causal terms. A brilliant but advanced discussion of the problems in causal attempts to interpret either ordinary propositional logic or various modal logics is found in Herbert Simon and Nicholas Rescher, "Cause and Counterfactual," in *Philosophy of Science*, December 1966 (Vol. 33, No. 4), pp. 323–332. It shows how the paradoxical counterfactual meaning of "$\supset$" in equation (9a), that false $I(t)$ is consistent with any V_c, R, MP combination, can be avoided in terms of a multiequation specification of linear or nonlinear causal relations between the variables involved. A similar argument holds for equation (9b) as well.

[9] Cf. Haas and Schmitter, *International Organization*, Vol. 18, No. 4, p. 712:

On the basis of previous work on the political implications of economic unions it was found that a high rate of previous transaction, a similarity in size and power, a high degree of pluralism, and marked elite complementarity were extremely favorable to the rapid politicization of economic relationships.

Presumably Deutsch, and others, would fall back on such a formulation when not sure of the necessity or sufficiency of a particular condition.

have only face validity.[10] The same must be said of the informed efforts of
Haas, Lindberg, Fisher, and Nye to rank collective decisionmaking activities
in terms of their spillover-prone bargaining modalities, their penetrativeness,
etc. These efforts often lead to equations like (1a,b,c) except that subjective
weights are also included. They contrast more or less sharply with the criterion validity of the decisiveness weights calculable from the data of *Political
Community in the North Atlantic Area* and the various versions of equation
(2). Until enough comparable evidence is collected, however, such weights
are not available; such is the situation of contemporary regional integration
research.

Two important developments do require our attention, however. The first
is the use of expert judges in scaling international acts or possibly transactions
or cooperation-conflict or integrative-disintegrative scales. Applied to new
data sets, these scores can be cumulated in various ways to derive integration-
relevant indices. When a variety of judges agree to the context-free coding of
international acts and can place them in ordered or even interval-scale categories, as does seem possible, useful indices are likely to result; subject to still
remaining vaguenesses in the conceptualization of integration, they can help
bridge the gap between current debatable objective indicators and the
criterion-validated measures of the future.[11]

One of the main emphases of several articles in this volume is that particular processes such as "politicization," transaction relationships, or the development of shared elite attitudes concerning integration can have both positive
and negative impacts on integration. It is not clear, for example, whether
Nye's stress on this point contradicts Lindberg's more context-free list of pre-

---

[10] The most relevant paper on alternate validation conceptions and procedures that I am aware of is
Charles Hermann, "Validation Problems in Games and Simulation with Special Reference to Models of
International Politics," in *Behavioral Science*, May 1967 (Vol. 12, No. 3), pp. 216–231. My own think-
ing has been considerably influenced by D. T. Campbell and Clyde Coombs; it will be elaborated in
Fred Greenstein and Nelson Polsby (ed.), *Handbook of Political Science* (Reading, Mass: Addison-Wes-
ley, forthcoming), Vol. 1. See the chapter on "quantitative methods."

[11] Donald Puchala's article in this volume is a significant contribution to the growing literature in
this regard, which cumulatively surely represents a measurement breakthrough. Edward Azar at Michigan State University is currently putting together a volume of relevant papers. Earlier relevant efforts
include Klingberg's use of judges from around the world in 1937 to estimate warlikeness among pairs of
great powers. These were then subjected to multidimensional scaling procedures that revealed configurations strikingly like those characterizing the antagonists of World War II: Frank Klingberg, "Studies in
Measurement of the Relations among Sovereign States," in James Rosenau (ed.), *International Politics
and Foreign Policy: A Reader in Research and Theory* (1st ed; New York: Free Press of Glencoe, 1961),
pp. 483–492. Also, applications by Holsti, Loomba, and North of Osgood's semantic differential to international data using the *General Inquirer:* Ole Holsti, with the collaboration of Joanne Loomba and
Robert North, "Content Analysis," in Gardner Lindzey and Elliot Aronson (ed.), *The Handbook of
Social Psychology*, Vol. 2: *Research Methods* (Reading, Mass: Addison-Wesley Publishing Co., 1968);
Charles McClelland's development of a set of categories for describing international transactions that
are both plausible and susceptible to high intercoder reliabilities: Charles McClelland, "Access to Berlin:
The Quantity and Variety of Events, 1948–1963," in J. David Singer, pp. 159–187; and the generalized
Q-sort procedures painstakingly tested by Lincoln E. Moses, and others, "Scaling Data on Inter-Nation
Action," in *Science*, May 26, 1967 (Vol. 156, No. 3778), pp. 1054–1059. The core of the Q-sort procedure is placing act descriptions in separate piles along a specified continuum with frequency approxi-
mating a normal (bell-shaped) curve. Corresponding quantitative standardized scores are then assigned.

sumably prointegration indices. Some difference of opinion may be due to a residual tendency to confuse integration variables, processes, and their properties. Nonetheless a clearly desirable step would be to use judges to code variable values, weights, or categories according to a Q-sort procedure. It could thus be discovered how much intersubjective agreement there is with Lindberg's categories.

A second judgmental procedure worth special attention is the use by Mario Barrera and Ernst Haas of a judges panel to estimate weights for a revised Haas-Schmitter model of the possible automatic politicization of a common market agreement. Rough averages were used to judge both the maximum possible importance for automatic politicization of the twelve explanatory variables and their actual importance in five particular cases.

To help clarify their procedure we quote Barrera and Haas as to the precise meaning of their maximum possible scores:

> In establishing across-the-board weights the judges were requested to ask themselves whether a given variable was both necessary *and* sufficient, just necessary, merely helpful, or plainly irrelevant. This judgment, in the case of background conditions, was made dependent on the answer to the question as to whether the variable was necessary and sufficient for the creation of interest among actors in having an economic union; for the period of negotiating the union the same question was phrased so as to determine whether the variable in question was necessary and sufficient for concluding the agreement and launching the organization; and for the process period the question was put in terms of the necessity or sufficiency of the variable for the triggering of automatic politization. The across-the-board rating of the relative importance of each of the twelve variables was as follows, with 400 representing the highest possible score, a score that would yield perfect automatic politization.[12]

The data in Table 1 represents judgments as to how high the twelve variables actually were in the two-year periods before and after the creation of an economic union, as well as during the negotiation process itself.

Perhaps the most interesting product of the Barrera-Haas study and of the refinements suggested by Philippe Schmitter is the considerable rank correspondence between various aggregate measures of levels of background variables and judges' scores as to their helpfulness for integration. For five common markets Kendall's rank order correlations *(taus)* of .83, .90, and .90 were found to exist between objective and subjective indices of the first three conditions in Table 1. The first three aggregate indices were 1) the normalized mean deviation in gross national products (GNPs) as a measure of homogeneity in the size of units, 2) the average over all future union members of the ratio of their bloc trade to their total trade as a measure of transaction level, and 3) a multidimensional, partly subjective combination of inter-

---

[12] Barrera and Haas, *International Organization*, Vol. 23, No. 1, p. 153.

TABLE 1. RESULTS OF THE BARRERA-HAAS JUDGES PANEL

Variables/Markets	EEC	EFTA	LAFTA	CACM	COMECON	Maximum Possible
1. Size of units (homogeneity)	3	2	1	4	1	5
2. Rate of transactions	8	5	5	3	8	10
3. Pluralism	22	23	10	10	15	25
4. Elite complementarity	30	25	10	20	30	40
5. External dependence	5	20	5	17	4	20
Total: background	68	75	31	54	58	100
6. Governmental purposes	40	25	10	35	30	50
7. External pressure	5	15	10	25	10	25
8. Powers of union	20	8	5	10	5	25
Total: time of union	65	48	25	70	45	100
9. Decisionmaking style	40	15	10	40	20	55
10. Rate of transactions	45	30	15	50	25	50
11. Adaptability of governments	50	40	10	50	35	75
12. External pressure	10	5	15	15	5	20
Total: process	145	90	50	155	85	200
Grand total	278	213	106	279	188	400

SOURCE: Barrera and Haas, *International Organization*, Vol. 23, No. 1, tables 1 and 2.

NOTE: The table lists the average judges' assessments of variable importance in a common market, rounded to whole numbers.

est articulation and socioeconomic modernization T-scores as a measure of pluralism. Thus some convergence between carefully chosen objective, aggregate indicators and more overall judgmental evaluations has been shown to occur.

D. Mixed Models

All formal procedures for measuring and explaining integration, however defined, mix judgmental and objective elements in some respects. In the choice of index components, category values, and aggregate weighting, coefficients judgmental needs are clear. When multiple judges are used, as in the Barrera-Haas study, and the results combined in terms of some nontrivial linear or requisite conditions logic, we are perhaps justified in treating such procedures as a whole under a rubric like "mixed models" or "synthetic approaches."

From such a holistic perspective, what more can we say about the Haas-Schmitter-Barrera effort? Consider the formula for arriving at the automatic politicization score at the bottom of Table 1 (call it integration index I_{ap}). Letting C_1, C_2, ... C_{12} represent the conditions for politicization at the various stages of the Haas-Schmitter paradigm, this formula amounts to

$$I_{ap} = C_1 + C_2 + \ldots + C_{12} \tag{12}$$

where $0 \leq C_1 \leq 5$, $0 \leq C_2 \leq 10$, $0 \leq C_3 \leq 25$, etc. I contend that it is impossible in a single index to combine values for C_1, C_2, ... C_{12} that are supposed, if high, to represent necessary and sufficient conditions for politicization, otherwise, just necessary conditions, helpful ones, or, if low enough, plainly irrelevant ones.

Recall the passage by Barrera and Haas cited above: $C_1 = 5$ or $C_2 = 10$ or $C_3 = 25$ means that one of these variables is at a high enough level for it to be "necessary *and* sufficient" for the creation of interest in negotiations for union (call NU a dichotomous, 0-1 measure of such a start). The resulting logic is hard to express in a single equation. "Sufficiency" of a single variable suggests a probability relation something like the form

$$\text{prob}(NU=1) = \max \left(\frac{C_1}{5}, \frac{C_2}{10}, \frac{C_3}{25} \right) \tag{12a}$$

Where any one variable reaches its maximum, then union negotiations ($NU = 1$) is certain. Perhaps a joint necessity-sufficiency notion was intended. In this case something like the product

$$\text{prob}(NU=1) = \frac{C_1}{5} \cdot \frac{C_2}{10} \cdot \frac{C_3}{25} \cdot \frac{C_4}{40} \cdot \frac{C_5}{20} \tag{12b}$$

would be more appropriate.

Just as straightforward is the following way of specifying how variables that are helpful, but not necessary or sufficient, might come into play:

$$\text{prob}(NU=1) = K_1 \left(\frac{C_1 + C_2 + C_3 + C_4 + C_5}{5 + 10 + 25 + 40 + 20} \right) \qquad (12c).$$

$$0 \leq K_1 \leq 1$$

If, as Barrera and Haas seem to imply, some conditions only reach the status of "necessary" when they exceed a threshold or when their maximum weight approaches 100, then none of the above three representations is appropriate; a still more complicated one is needed. But it seems clear that equation (12) misrepresents whatever logic Haas and his coauthors originally intended.

Is there some other way of stating (12) satisfactorily? If we define a dichotomous variable, U, to indicate the existence of an economic union and use PU to refer to union politicization, a reasonable causal paradigm is the following:

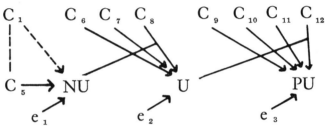

FIGURE I. A SIMPLIFIED CAUSAL DIAGRAM OF UNION POLITICIZATION. C_1–C_5 = background conditions, C_6–C_8 = union conditions, C_9–C_{12} = process conditions; $x \rightarrow y$ indicates a direct causal relation, x causes y; $x \not\!\!\rightarrow_w y$ indicates a multiplicative relation where x causes y contingent on w being nonzero.

Here only success at a previous stage is a necessary condition for progress to the next stage. Other necessity and sufficiency arguments do not apply, except when external influences e_1 to e_3 are vanishingly small and all conditions have their maximum values. This indeed seems quite close to what Haas and his associates intended to say. A simple multiequation representation responsive to this possibility would be

$$\text{prob}(PU=1) = \left(\frac{C_9 + C_{10} + C_{11} + C_{12}}{200} \right) U \qquad (12d)$$

and

$$\text{prob}(U=1) = \left(\frac{C_6 + C_7 + C_8}{100} \right) NU \qquad (12e)$$

together with (12c) and $K_1 = 1$. As a result, setting our automatic politicization index equal to the expected value of *PU* gives us a new equation, derivable from these three

$$
I_{ap} = \text{expected value of PU} = \left(\frac{C_9 + C_{10} + C_{11} + C_{12}}{200}\right)\left(\frac{C_6 + C_7 + C_8}{100}\right)
$$
$$
\left(\frac{C_1 + \ldots + C_5}{100}\right) \quad (13)
$$

which has the desired property of predicting automatic politicization with certainty only when all *C*'s attain their maximum value.

Having attempted to clarify the Haas-Schmitter-Barrera mixed model and Nye's revision of it in this volume, what can we now say about the validity of its estimates as derived either from equation (12) or (13)? Although considerable qualitative comparative research has gone into the development of the model, unfortunately not enough data has been collected on a year-to-year basis statistically to validate or falsify it. Perhaps the lack of logical clarity retarded such efforts. In any case, once variables and their temporal relations are clearly defined, a strategy complimentary to the use of judges seems possible. Just as Deutsch and his associates did, one could collect repeated measurements on politicization increments over a wide enough set of cases in order to be able statistically to estimate the ways in which various conditions influence integrative outcomes. These weights could be compared with panel judgments, such as those collected by Barrera and Haas, or individual a priori hypotheses as a way of testing such judgments for past cases. Predictions from judgments could then be much more reliably assessed in future cases where not all condition values and their consequences were yet visible. Until such an effort has been made, one must conclude that predictions derived by summing expert judgments according to a plausible explanatory schema do not yet have the characteristics of statistical validity that arise from the use of an operationally confirmed theoretical schema.

E. *The Use of Multiple Indicators*

The literature on measuring integration is too replete with references to the desirability of a "multiple indicator" approach to allow specific citations. When the indicators all concur, the validity of an argument is strengthened; otherwise an embarrassment of riches may develop. These problems apply both to measurement models and to explanatory ones. We shall look first at the variety of ways in which several indices can be combined into unidimensional measurements using single equation logics.

Among the several popular ways of responding to dilemmas of classificatory overabundance, Guttman scaling and factor analysis represent the most frequently used objective or "natural" quantifying or scaling procedures. In practice, these procedures can establish unidimensionality or disprove it and help quantify measures of the dimension or dimensions involved. As far as the validity of such dimensionalizing efforts is concerned, it is disconcerting, but appropriate, to report that they in many cases lead to different results.

This discrepancy occurs primarily because of the different measurement logics underlying their notions of dimensionality.[13] Factor analysis, for example, assumes manifest response variables V_{ji} reflect additively combined underlying unidimensional factors F according to

$$V_{ji} = \sum_{k=1}^{k=K} a_{jk}F_{ki} + U_{ji} \qquad (14)$$

j = variable index; $1 \leq j \leq m$
i = unit index; $1 \leq i \leq n$
k = factor index; $1 \leq k \leq K$.

The U_{ji} represent error terms; the a_{jk} are factor weights or loadings from K factors making up variable j. Usually additional assumptions, of varying plausibility, are made to ensure that the maximum number of factors K is small (hopefully one) and that many if not most of the a_{jk} are approximately zero. Statistical procedures exist for deriving explicit factor-score equations for the F_{ki} as linear combinations of the V_{ji} once the a_{jk} are known. Guttman scaling, on the other hand, assumes cumulative items, such that any one with at least as much of a certain property as an item conveys will respond positively to it. Well-known scaling algorithms and scalability criteria, if successfully applied, produce rankings of both nominal variables and responding actors.

The first step toward the valid use of such procedures is the development of an awareness of various alternatives for unidimensional measurement and their basic assumptions. Then a variety of tests of these assumptions needs to be devised and used, going considerably beyond ordinary goodness of fit measures. Assuming or even tentatively demonstrating that a measurement logic is valid, there is the additional problem that the indices chosen may not reflect, according to any demonstrable logic, the underlying integration phenomena of concern. Here again initial judgments of indicator relevance are extremely important, as are derivative subjective labels chosen for discovered empirical regularities. Criterion validation efforts, like those of the North Atlantic area study, are also appropriate for longer run or more comprehensive definitions of integration not conceived merely in terms of manifest behaviors.

As a simple but incomplete example of a multiindicator procedure employing different measurement assumptions of considerable plausibility, we shall briefly discuss the application of a nonmetric multidimensional "proximity" scaling procedure developed by Louis Guttman and James Lingoes to ordinal rankings by Leon Lindberg and Joseph Nye of EEC impact in 24 different

---

[13] A review of some of these alternatives is given in William Torgerson, *Theory and Methods of Scaling* (New York: John Wiley & Sons, 1962). See also Clyde Coombs, *A Theory of Data* (New York: John Wiley & Sons, 1964), and Alker, in Lipset, part 3.

Table 2. Lindberg-Nye Indices of Policy Integration

	EEC 1970	EEC 1966	Central America 1966	East Africa 1960	East Africa 1963	East Africa 1966	Aver- ages
1. External affairs	6	7	5	1	6	6	6.2
2. Public safety	7	7	7	4	7	7	7.8
3. Property rights	6	6	7	5	7	7	7.6
4. Civic rights	7	7	7	5	7	7	8.0
5. Morality	7	7	7	7	7	7	8.4
6. Patriotism	6	7	7	5	7	7	7.8
7. Education	6	7	6	4	4	5	6.4
8. Recreation	7	7	7	7	7	7	8.4
9. Knowledge	6	7	6	5	6	6	7.2
10. Health	6	6	6	6	6	6	7.2
11. Indigency	5	6	7	7	7	7	7.8
12. Energy	3	5	7	6	6	6	6.6
13. Water supply, sewerage	7	7	7	7	7	7	8.4
14. Currency	6	7	6	1	2	6	5.6
15. Domestic credit	5	7	7	3	3	6	6.2
16. Balance of payments	4	5	5	2	4	6	5.2
17. Current financing	6	6	7	4	5	6	5.8
18. Agriculture	3	3	6	6	6	6	6.0
19. Labor management	6	6	6	6	6	6	7.2
20. Industrial competition	4	5	6	6	6	6	6.6
21. Tariffs and quotas	1	2	3	1	1	3	2.2
22. Economic development	5	6	6	5	5	6	6.6
23. Transport and communication	4	6	6	3	3	4	5.2
24. Resources	6	6	7	7	7	7	8.0
Average	5.3	6.0	6.3	4.7	5.5	6.0	

Source: Lindberg, *Journal of Common Market Studies*, Vol. 5, No. 4, and Nye, *International Organization*, Vol. 22, No. 4, p. 870.

issue areas.[14] The data in Table 2 is obviously valuable, but it raises questions as to its unidimensionality and its further quantifiability. We shall use as a measurement logic the assumption that common markets and issues can be jointly plotted in a Euclidean space. Judgments of strong market impact in an issue area should lead to proximate spatial relations between the market and the issue concerned. In figures 2 and 2-A we have derived two such unidimensional summaries of Table 2.

What do the quantifications of ordinal common market properties in Figure 2 demonstrate? Most optimistically, Figure 2 produces a unidimensional repre-

[14] For a further discussion of the SSARI procedures, the coefficient of alienation, and $\emptyset$, see J. C. Lingoes, "Recent Computational Advances in Nonmetric Methodology for the Behavioral Sciences," Ann Arbor, Mich., 1966 (mimeographed) and Louis Guttman, "A General Nonmetric Technique for Finding the Smallest Coordinate Space for a Configuration of Points," in *Psychometrika*, December 1968 (Vol. 33, No. 4), pp. 469–506.

sentation that in terms of a goodness of fit criterion, the coefficient of alienation, explains something like three-quarters of the ordinal proximities of
markets and scope areas. Moreover, the measurement logic of treating such
policy scopes as proximities in Euclidean space given in Figure 2-A gives coordinates for the six temporally distinct common markets in Table 2 that are
remarkably similar to the intuitively appealing average policy integration
ranks suggested by Nye. In fact this similarity helps to validate our assumption of a Euclidean logic as underlying the data of Table 2.

On a quantitative scale, we can see the way and the extent to which the
East African Common Market (EACM) has disintegrated, and we can see
issue areas toward which or away from which the East African and the European markets have been moving. Thus tariff and quota regulation activities
seem to be closest on the average to all common markets; resource development to be more a characteristic of the European than of the East African
experience; agriculture, energy, and transport to be the next province of the
Europeans; economic development, currency regulation, and external affairs to
be the peculiar, lead items of the abortive 1960 East African experience. Patriotism, education, and property rights seem the most distant areas of EEC policy
impact, but seem closer matters of concern for the East Africans in 1960 and
even to some extent in 1963. A possible implication of these remarks, assuming
some continuity of movement by common markets and issue areas, is that for
a time common markets moving to the right on Figure 2-A would be getting
"more" integrated, at least until they reached the central point of the policy
areas; the farther the issue areas are from the concentration of markets, the
longer it will take or the harder it will be for them to become more integrated
policy sectors. In this regard, it can be shown that average impact ranks tend
to decrease as one moves away from the center of Figure 2-A.

Are these suggestions validated by the accompanying statistical mumbo
jumbo? No. But they are nonetheless a suggestive summary of contemporary
common market experience that has recognizable common elements despite
the considerable diversity of regional contexts within which the markets operate. Moreover, the time-series patterns of the EEC and the EACM do begin to
suggest some empirical tendencies of movement toward "appropriate" positions on a relatively widely shared ladder of integrative development. Considerably more time-series information and continued existence of a statistically
adequate unidimensional continuum need to be observed. And judgmental or
criterion validity as to the political "significance" of the various issue areas,
perhaps in terms of their likely contribution to transnational peaceful prob-
lem-solving capabilities, needs consideration: Both the simple average ranking
procedure and the smallest space analysis treat issue areas as statistically equal.
Fisher and Lindberg, for example, have tried ratings of 1, 2, and 3 for policy

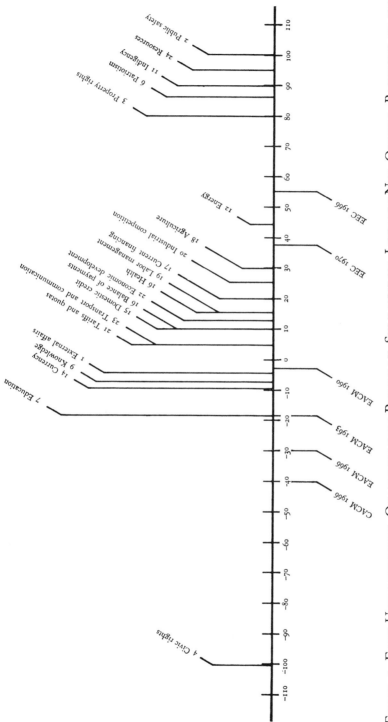

FIGURE 2. FIRST UNDIMENSIONAL QUANTIFICATION PARTIALLY SUMMARIZING LINDBERG-NYE ORDINAL RANKINGS OF THE EXTENT OF POLICY INTEGRATION. Coefficient of alienation = .252; rows 5, 8, and 13 omitted from Table 2.

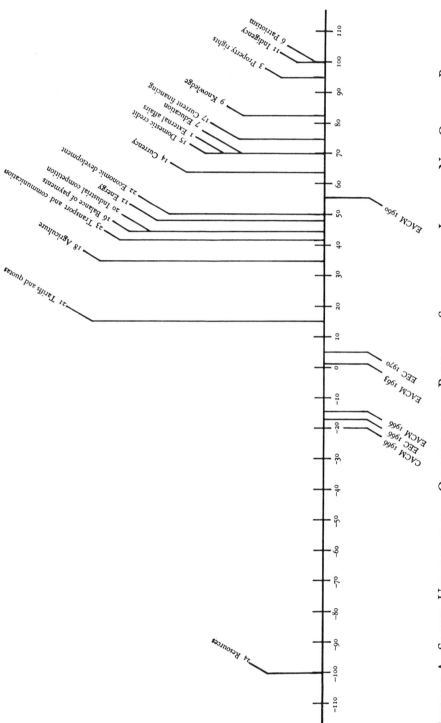

FIGURE 2-A. SECOND UNIDIMENSIONAL QUANTIFICATION PARTIALLY SUMMARIZING LINDBERG-NYE ORDINAL RANKINGS OF THE EXTENT OF POLICY INTEGRATION. Coefficient of alienation = .227; rows 2, 4, 5, 8, 10, 13, and 19 omitted. For figures 2 and 2-A data in Table 2 has been analyzed by the SSARI program of the Guttman-Lingoes series.

decisions or rulings within an issue area. Such a procedure could be subjected to panel judgments and extend across issue areas as well.

How satisfied should we be with the measurement logic and its implementation of the present case? There are several problems. Most serious, perhaps, is the sensitivity of nonmetric procedures to outlying or irrelevant variables. Rows 5, 8, and 13 in Table 2 have no comparative information: They produced extreme points which dominate the remaining configuration in a first scaling attempt. Leaving out these three rows produced Figure 2; leaving out four additional variables of low discriminating ability produced a configuration of considerable plausibility. But notice how issue area 24, resources, has flipped from being very close to issues 3, 6, and 11 to being very far from them, thus making a simple left-right interpretation very difficult; and note that Figure 2 gives a different picture of the similarity of the EEC and the other markets in their proximal clustering of impact areas. In addition to their rotational indeterminacies two-dimensional configurations relying only on ranked information are also very sensitive to extreme points; several different versions were tried, with the absence of any explicit market-to-market distance or proximity data leading to several possible, somewhat degenerate, clusterings of issues and markets that nonetheless had coefficients of alienation below 0.05. Also troublesome is the assumption used above that "policy impact equals proximity." For some issue-market configurations, it implies that a market moving toward some kinds of greater impact must move away from other areas of activities. The possibility that all markets could be on one side of a cluster of issue areas suggests, however, that proximity measurement logics can have some of the more nonzero-sum characteristics of cumulative measurement logics in this regard.

If some agreement on an overall index of (policy) integration can be reached, perhaps through the use of multidimensional scaling procedures, another look at the Haas-Schmitter-Barrera-Nye effort to judge the relevance of process conditions suggests a rather sophisticated use of multiple indicators for explanatory purposes. Thus either an individual or a panel is asked to assess the relative importance for integration of various process conditions. Assuming that necessity and sufficiency arguments have been restated in terms of an additive equation, this procedure amounts to asking for estimation of the weights W in an equation like (15):

$$I_{ap} = W_1 C_9 + W_2 C_{10} + W_3 C_{11} + W_4 C_{12} + u \tag{15}.$$

The W's may be interpretable as partial regression coefficients that measure the direct causal impact of C_9 through C_{12}, respectively. Such an interpretation might also be possible in extending the decisiveness scores of equations (2a,b,c) and (3a,b). Although Deutsch and his associates treated each explanatory indicator separately, bivariate decisiveness procedures ignore the possibilities of causal interdependence among independent variables. Regular multi-variate regression (or stepwise regression which does not have a clear causal interpretation but may prove predictively useful) on a meaningful dependent measure of integration would produce an appropriate extension of equation (3b) to something like

$$P_s = a_i + D_1 I_1 + D_2 I_2 + D_3 I_3 + u \tag{16}.[15]$$

Here P_s is again the probability of integration success, and the D's are partial decisiveness scores associated with various instrumentalities I. Except for the prospect of a more realistic multiequation theory being able to show how some of the D's are spurious, such a procedure seems rather exciting if a sufficient number of cases of (incremental) integration success or failure can be carefully measured. It is to some multiequation representations of integration processes that we now turn.[16]

II. MULTIEQUATION CAUSAL MODELS

We shall consider two kinds of multiequation causal models, systems of deterministic differential equations and stochastic finite difference relationships. In a highly abstract, operationally ambiguous, but relationally rigorous, way these models represent some early aggregative attempts to describe integration and disintegration possibilities arising out of interactions among several cooperating nation units. These are assumed to be relatively homogeneous and compatible in size, level of development, geographical propinquity, political and cultural values. As a consequence of this assumption, aggregation procedures should not be fundamentally misleading as to overall system trends; and other more stark mechanisms of international politico-economic adjustment than we shall discuss should not frequently come into play. Although each model is not necessarily limited to economic transactions between members of a common market—each is in fact transposed almost literally from the study of small group behavior—[17] we shall try to be more concrete and provocative by doing so.

[15] If one is serious about estimating equations like (16), where the dependent variable must be zero or one, transformation procedures exist that will ensure a corresponding range of predicted values; cf. the discussion of probit analysis and related techniques in Arthur S. Goldberger, *Econometric Theory* (New York: John Wiley & Sons, 1964).

[16] At this point I had originally intended to discuss integration measures based on transactional indicators, as in Alker and Puchala, in Singer. Puchala's excellent review of such approaches in the present volume makes my own remarks largely redundant. From the validity-conscious perspective of the present treatment, it is perhaps worth suggesting an as yet untried validation procedure. If it is assumed that large absolute or relative volumes of freely chosen, reciprocal transactions are rewarding, then some lagged index like (8b) could be used to predict to subsequent declines in violence or its expectation. I have in mind using Klingberg's remarkably accurate judgments around 1937 of the likely outbreak of war among a 100 or so nation pairs as an important criterion variable for at least a partial test of this assumption using trade data for the 1920's and the 1930's. See Klingberg, in Rosenau.

[17] Herbert Simon, "A Formal Theory of Interactions in Social Groups," chapter 6 of *Models of Man* (New York: John Wiley & Sons, 1957). (Simon formalizes a number of relations verbally de-

Each of the models to be defined below is defined in terms of four basic variables: T, transaction level; S, support; I, integration level; D, demand for integration.

Let $T(t)$ = the average *level of economically meaningful* (rewarding) *transactions* or interactions between common market members at time t. Operationally, either gross international economic transactions or a richer set of dyadic interactions including negotiating behavior could be signified by this term. An even more suggestive notion, in the Deutschian mode, would be to refer to I as the relative share of external or total transactions that pass through common market institutions. In any case, *T should be initialized (set to zero) at the level of international transactions expected to occur if a common market did not exist at all.*

Let $S(t)$ = the average level of *support* at time t by market members for common market trading and for its central decisionmaking activities. In primary group terms "friendship" might be a better label; in organizational theory Haas uses the phrase "authority-legitimacy sharing" to refer to a similar concept. Clearly support and compliance by subnational economic actors is also implied.

Let $I(t)$ = the *integration level* of the centrally coordinated institutions of the common market. Perhaps some measure of "collective decisionmaking activities" would be more appropriate: In some aggregate way this continuous variable refers to what Lindberg and Scheingold refer to as the scope and extent of task fulfillment by common market institutions (price regulations, competition facilitation, etc.). Presumably, the variable measures primarily within-market activities of these institutions. An increase in $I(t)$ may include either increasing task fulfillment or what Lindberg and Scheingold refer to as task extension.

Finally, let $D(t)$ relate to the task or *integration-related demands* directed toward central market institutions. These are generated primarily from within the national members of the common market. Although one may want to view these as exogenous to the market system we are grossly modeling, there is at least some pretheoretical correspondence between $D(t)$, $S(t)$, and the demand/support pairing of the Eastonian framework by Lindberg and Scheingold.

A. Four Deterministic Causal Models

We shall first consider four deterministic (causal) models stated in terms of these highly ambiguous, but hopefully evocative, concepts. No indeterminant error terms will be allowed; infinitesimal time differences and the differ-

scribed in George C. Homans, *The Human Group* [New York: Harcourt, Brace & World, 1950].) Most of the points we make in this section derive from Simon's analysis in the context of small group behavior.

ential calculus will be employed. Each model is made up of three or four basic dynamic relationships. The first of these we shall call the *international transaction production function,* considering two possible versions.

a) The level of intra-common market transactions $T(t)$ depends on, and increases within the year with, the level of support for (including compliance with) common market trading and institutional practices $S(t)$; it is similarly related to the level of integration of these practices $I(t)$. Briefly and plausibly, both integration and support independently produce high transaction levels (with weights a_1, $a_2 > 0$):

$$T(t) = a_1 S(t) + a_2 I(t) \tag{17a}.$$

The above transaction production function is completely linear. A somewhat more realistic version would perhaps use a nonlinear transaction production function of the sort frequently used in economic theory.

b) International transaction levels above what could be expected without a common market are multiplicatively produced by combinations of market support (e.g., compliance) and market integration activities:

$$T(t) = S(t)^{a_1} I(t)^{a_2} \tag{17b}.$$

If we were to take logarithms of both sides of this equation, a_1 and a_2 would again become linear coefficients susceptible to linear regression estimation procedures. These coefficients represent the effects of proportional changes in T and would normally be called elasticities. Note how nonzero levels of both S and I are necessary and sufficient causes of market-induced transaction levels.

Our second dynamic model element we shall call a *support-generating relationship.* The first version relies only on economically induced support. The second is more complex, more interesting, and perhaps more realistic. It involves a kind of indirect spillover relationship in that a large enough level of integrated decisionmaking activities will in and of itself "engineer" positive changes in its own support. This in turn can lead to further increases in integration.

a) A certain level of transactions between market members is "appropriate" to a given level of common market support in the sense that transactions above that level will gradually lead, through an adjustment process, to a higher level of support for the common market. Subjectively we will increase our support for the common market to the extent that it provides us with a gross transaction level greater than the one we "expected" would result from our present level of support, i.e., acceptance of its legitimacy and authority over our commercial relationships. With b a positive "speed of adjustment" or "learning rate" parameter and $\beta S(t)$ the level of "expected transactions," this becomes a differential equation:

$$\frac{dS(t)}{dt} = b_1 [T(t) - \beta S(t)] \tag{18a}.$$

b) A plausible variant of (18a) would add a term referring to some kind of induced change in support (with a positive coefficient b_2) due to integrated decisionmaking agents:

$$\frac{dS(t)}{dt} = b_1[T(t) - \beta S(t)] + b_2 I(t) \tag{18b}.$$

We shall consider only one *integration-producing relationship:*

a) In a somewhat Eastonian way the level of integration (collective decision-making or regulative activity) can be increased both by high enough common market support and by sufficient external member demands for such activity; similar relationships can also account for a decline in integration. Whether an increase or decrease will take place depends on how high the support level is vis-à-vis the level of support needed to maintain integration at such a level (an $S(t)$ of $\alpha I(t)$) and additively on how high the demand level is vis-à-vis current integration practice. With c_1 and c_2 as positive additive influence weights, the relevant deterministic differential equation is:[18]

$$\frac{dI(t)}{dt} = c_1[S(t) - \alpha I(t)] + c_2[D(t) - I(t)] \tag{19a}.$$

Simon's original model treats demand for integration as completely undetermined by the processes and variables so far modeled, i.e., as exogenous. Nonetheless, believing that demands for integrated activity should not be so treated, we suggest equation (20a). Using a mechanism like that of (18a) above gives the following *demand-generating relationship.*

a) Changes in demands for integration can be aggregatively stated in terms of disparities between the level of intra-common market transactions and an aggregate aspiration level for $T(t)$ of $D(t)$. The adjustment or "learning" rate is indicated by a parameter d (both δ and d should be > 0):

$$\frac{dD(t)}{dt} = d(\delta D(t) - T) \tag{20a}.$$

In various combinations, equations (17a–20a) give a number of suggestive models. Briefly we might represent some of these integration logics as follows:

Model I *(linear transaction production model with exogenous demand)* = (17a, 18a, 19a).

[18] It is of interest to compare this equation with a somewhat similar formula used by Leon Lindberg and Stuart Scheingold in *Europe's Would-Be Polity: Patterns of Change in the European Community* (Englewood Cliffs, N.J.: Prentice-Hall, 1970), p. 114:

$$dS = f[(S+Su)(dD+dL)] + e_n$$

where

dS = a change in the existing political system (its scope and institutional capacity)
Su = systematic support
D = demand
L = leadership
e_n = a general error term

This is the model that Simon originally analyzed.

Model II *(linear transaction production with induced support and endogenous demand)*

= (17a, 18b, 19a, 20a).

Model III *(multiplicative transaction production with exogenous demand)*

= (17b, 18a, 19a).

Since this is a direct nonlinear extension of Simon's model, his nonlinear generalizations should also apply to this case.

Model IV *(nonlinear transaction production with induced support and endogenous demand)*

= (17b, 18b, 19a, 20a).

Before discussing some of these models, let us go on to some probabilistic restatement of them.

B. Four Stochastic Causal Models

To the statistically trained,[19] it comes as no surprise that these are discrete probabilistic approximations to the above models with dynamic properties converging toward those of their deterministic counterpart. These stochastic variants, besides being more realistic and less deterministic, are also more readily estimated and tested with relevant data.

Before turning to the stochastic versions of models I and II (we shall call them I′ and II′) we note that stochastic versions of models III and IV (similarly called III′ and IV′) could just as easily be defined. Along with the discrete stochastic versions of (18a), (18b), (19a), or (20a), III′ or IV′ would include a multiplicative error term $u_1^{a_3}$ in an equation like:

$$T(t) = S(t)^{a_1} I(t)^{a_2} u_1^{a_3}$$

which is equivalent to the more manipulable

$$\log T(t) = a_1 \log S(t) + a_2 \log I(t) + a_3 \log u_1 \tag{17c}$$

where the a's are constants and $T, S, I,$ and u_1 have the same meaning as in (17a) and (17b).

Writing these new stochastic logics in discrete terms follows automatically with the approximation of derivatives by first differences divided by unitary time periods and the addition of a random error term. Thus *model I′ (linear stochastic transaction production with endogenous demand)* is

$$T(t) = a_1 S(t) + a_2 I(t) + u_1 \tag{17d}$$

$$S(t) = (1-b\beta) S(t\text{-}1) + bT(t\text{-}1) + u_2 \tag{18c}$$

$$I(t) = c_1 S(t\text{-}1) + (1-c_1\alpha-c_2)I(t\text{-}1) + c_2 D(t\text{-}1) + u_3 \tag{19b}, \text{ and}$$

[19] See, for example, the excellent parallel treatment of deterministic and stochastic dynamic models in Carl C. Christ, *Econometric Models and Methods* (New York: John Wiley & Sons, 1966).

model II' (linear stochastic transaction production with induced support and endogenous demand) is

$$T(t) = a_1S(t) + a_2I(t) + u_1(t) \tag{17d}$$

$$S(t) - S(t\text{-}1) = b_1(T(t\text{-}1) - \beta S(t\text{-}1)) + b_2I(t\text{-}1) + u_2(t) \tag{18d}$$

$$I(t) - I(t\text{-}1) = c_1(S(t\text{-}1) - \alpha I(t\text{-}1)) + c_2(D(t\text{-}1) - I(t\text{-}1)) + u_3(t) \tag{19b}$$

$$D(t) - D(t\text{-}1) = -d(T(t\text{-}1) - \delta D(t\text{-}1)) + u_4(t) \tag{20b}.$$

In order for us to work with either of these models, we need simplifying *ceteris paribus* error assumptions to complete them. The most elementary and drastic of these are to assume uncorrelated residuals and the absence of auto-correlation:

$$E\ (u_i(t)u_i(t+s)) = 0; \quad E(u_i(t)u_j(t)) = 0$$
$$s \neq 0 i \neq j$$

In other words we expect that repeated observations of residual causes (the *u*'s) of *T, S, I,* and *D* will show them not to be correlated with their own earlier or later values; moreover, simultaneous observations of these unspecified influences on *T, S, I,* and *D* would show them not to be related to each other. The underlying and falsifiable idea is not that there are no unmapped influences on the variables of the system of equations but that no such influence brings about coordinated changes in these variables that will seriously distort our estimation of the parameters linking them together.

C. *Estimation and Validation Strategies for Causal Models*

Those familiar with the Simon-Blalock tradition of causal modeling[20] should be able to see not only that models I'–IV' converge to models I–IV as observational time intervals become small and implicit error terms approach zero, but that model II' converges to model I' as b_2 and d approach zero. This is clear from the causal arrow diagram in Figure 3. Note how the figures become equivalent when the arrows on terms with d and b_2 are removed. Thus a frequently advocated strategy of choosing among causal models—in effect tending to validate one of them and falsify the other—is to estimate the coefficients of competing models and see whether those predicted to be zero by either model are in fact statistically insignificant. Choosing the model, if any, with correct predictions of absent links then follows. More generally, one can test for the absence of effects due to variables claimed not directly to cause one another. Such tests may lead to the rejection of *all* models being compared. Looking at model II', for example, one could add terms for all variables at time *t* and t = 1 not included in its equations. Theoretically, when all direct links are included in a regression estimate, all coefficients for these newly added

[20] Hubert M. Blalock, Jr., *Causal Inferences in Nonexperimental Research* (Chapel Hill: University of North Carolina Press, 1964).

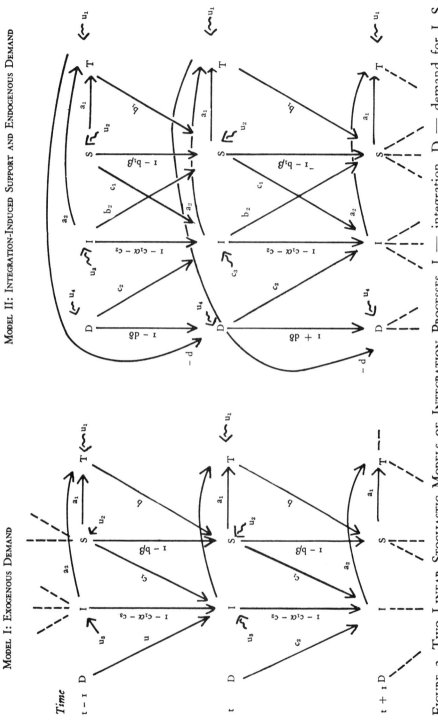

FIGURE 3. TWO LINEAR STOCHASTIC MODELS OF INTEGRATION PROCESSES. I = integration, S = support, T = intragroup transactions.

terms should vanish. Thus equation (17d) has no direct causal impacts on T(t) from D(t) or from D, I, S, or T at t–1. And (18d) claims that there is no direct impact of D(t), I(t), or T(t) on S(t).

The procedure is actually equivalent, it can be shown by simple derivations, to use of predictions derived from the models as to observable relations between correlations, covariances, or simple bivariate regression slopes. Thus using a regression version of path analysis developed by Sewell Wright and John Tukey,[21] from the figure we write down two different formulae for variable pairs differently related in model I' and model II' and a third relationship that should be true of both models. Although more laborious to articulate, these illustrative model tests are sometimes more suggestive than equivalent tests on supposedly absent multiple regression coefficient estimates. For example, tracing both the direct and indirect causal paths bringing variables together in the figure (where B's represent unstandardized bivariate regression slope estimates or path regressions) suggests at least the following (as yet not rigorously derived):

Model I'

$$B_{D(t)T(t-1)} = 0$$

$$
\begin{aligned}
B_{S(t)I(t)} = {} & C_1(1 - b\beta) + C_1 b B_{T(t-1)S(t-1)} \\
& + (1 - C_1\alpha - C_2) b B_{T(t-1)I(t-1)} \\
& + (1 - C_1\alpha - C_2)(1 - b\beta) B_{S(t-1)I(t-1)}
\end{aligned}
$$

$$
\begin{aligned}
B_{T(t)T(t-1)} = {} & a_1 b_1 + a_1^2 B_{S(t)S(t-1)} + a_2 B_{I(t)I(t-1)} \\
& + a_1 a_2 B_{S(t)I(t-1)} + a_2 a_1 B_{I(t)S(t-1)}
\end{aligned}
\qquad \text{(22a, b, c) etc.}
$$

Model II'

$$B_{D(t)T(t-1)} = -d + (1+d\delta)^2 c_2 a_2$$

$$
\begin{aligned}
B_{S(t)I(t)} = {} & C_1(1-b\beta) + C_1 b B_{T(t-1)S(t-1)} \\
& + (1-C_1\alpha-C_2) b B_{T(t-1)I(t-1)} \\
& + (1-C_1\alpha-C_2)(1-b\beta) B_{S(t-1)I(t-1)} \\
& + (1-C_1\alpha-C_2) b_2
\end{aligned}
$$

$$
\begin{aligned}
B_{T(t)T(t-1)} = {} & a_1 b_1 + a_1 B_{S(t)S(t-1)} + a_2^2 B_{I(t)I(t-1)} \\
& + a_a a_2 B_{S(t)I(t-1)} + a_2 a_1 B_{I(t)S(t-1)}
\end{aligned}
\qquad \text{(23a, b, c) etc.}
$$

Statistical estimation and validation efforts in political science have rarely gone beyond the systematic exploitation of either the "absence of coefficient" or "compound path analysis" procedures for overidentified models illustrated

---

[21] See the respective articles in Otto Kempthorne, *Multivariate Procedures in Biology* (Ames: State University Press of Iowa, 1954). The equivalence of present procedure to the more familiar Simon-Blalock procedure of deriving relations among correlations is briefly discussed at a number of points in my "Causal Inference and Political Analysis," in Joseph L. Bernd (ed.), *Mathematical Applications in Political Science* (Dallas, Tex: Southern Methodist University Press, 1966), Vol. 2, pp. 7–43.

above.[22] None of these procedures has yet been systematically applied to integration processes in part because of the absence of good time-series data, because of the lack of articulated relevant theory, and because of the lack of relevant statistical training possessed by the pioneers of empirical studies on integration. Yet this lack of development is also in part due to the absence of attention in political science to certain qualitative properties of complex models that can be used to test and validate some of their major assumptions. Rather than go on with an extended review of other statistical procedures relevant to the case of overidentified models with complete time-series data sets,[23] I would like briefly to suggest some such qualitative tests, based on Simon's earlier analysis of model I above.

Simon illustrates a number of qualitative properties of the dynamic system of model I as well as of nonlinear dynamic systems like model III and model IV. For simplicity of exposition purposes we shall work here only with models I (and briefly) II. The properties we shall look at are the existence of dynamic equilibrium, its stability, and the relationships between variables when perturbed away from equilibrium.[24]

Equilibrium occurs for model I "at infinity" when $\frac{ds}{dt}$ and $\frac{dI}{dt}$, as defined by equations (18a) and (19a), go to zero. Similarly for model I', when $S(t) = S(t\text{-}1)$ and $I(t) = I(t\text{-}1)$ in equations (18c) and (19b), the resulting equations can be solved for equilibrium values of T, S, and I, and D which we shall call $T\infty$, $S\infty$, and $I\infty$. In the deterministic case one finds the equilibrium relationships between the "at infinity" values of support, integration, transaction levels, and the driving exogenous demand to be

---

[22] The concept of overidentification is discussed in most econometric texts: in Blalock; in Alker, in Bernd; in Christ; and at length in Franklin Fisher, *The Identification Problem in Econometrics* (New York: McGraw-Hill, 1962). Briefly it refers to modes which constrain reality, whose coefficients can be uniquely estimated with less data than is actually available, where there are, roughly, more independent equations than there are unknowns requiring estimation.

[23] The last chapter of Christ is a revelation in this regard. One can test a priori hypotheses (and confidence intervals) concerning specific nonzero coefficient magnitudes; one can test and compare models as to the statistical properties (e.g., autocorrelation) of their error terms, their predictions of observable time series, their goodness of fit, etc.

Two more difficult validation problems that I shall not discuss further concern the problem of comparing predictions from different causal orders and different causal variables. Thus one has to be especially careful about the relative plausibility of a variety of causal models. Reliance on prior predictions as to animate magnitudes and signs of coefficients are useful procedures in this regard. But when variables in one model do not exist in another, comparability in terms other than gross goodness of fit and randomness of residual errors becomes difficult. In the case of equations (17c) and (17d), the problem is easier in that both the linear and the nonlinear relationships are readily comparable. But when totally different conceptualizations exist, unless variable-to-variable translations are possible, cumulative comparisons are difficult.

[24] Assuming positive coefficients and certain plausible directional relationships (such as for a given D, greater support will in the long run produce greater I) and saturation effects (as S increases, integration activities I increase at a slower rate) Simon's most novel derivation is the existence of a threshold level of demands below which group integrated activities will decrease and disappear even though demand levels move up again near to the threshold. This phenomenon corresponds rather closely to the verbal theories of both Deutsch, and others and Haas and Schmitter, *International Organization*, Vol. 18, No. 4.

$$S\infty = \frac{a_2}{\beta - a_1} \, I\infty$$

$$I\infty = \left[\frac{c_2(\beta - a_1)}{c_2(\beta - a_1) + c_1((\beta - a_1) - a_2)}\right] D\infty \qquad (24a, b, c).$$

$$T\infty = a_1 S\infty + a_2 I\infty$$

The fact that each of these can be stated through causally meaningful substitutions in terms of *D* shows an obvious testable property of the model: *If demands for integration remain constant over a sufficient period of time, so will integration and transaction levels. Moreover, in the long run, integration and higher-than-market-level transaction levels will disappear when demand has disappeared.*

Exploring the equilibrium relations, Simon suggestively defines what we shall call states of "surplus" and "deficit" integration depending on whether

$$I\infty > D\infty \qquad \text{or} \qquad I\infty < D\infty \qquad (25a, b).$$
$$\text{"integration surplus"} \qquad\qquad \text{"integration deficit"}$$

Under what conditions is a state of integration greater-than-demand levels likely to occur? Certainly this is a system property dear to supranationalists and of interest to all theorists. The nonobvious answer, derivable from equation (24b), is

$$\text{Integration surplus} <=> \alpha(\beta - a_1) < a_2 \qquad (26).$$

In this equation we can see three system properties that are of considerable theoretical interest and susceptible to qualitative verification or falsification. *In long-run situations of relatively constant demand, surplus integration will occur whenever the transaction-generating potency* (a_2) *of integration activity is sufficiently high, whenever integration-related support requirements* (αI) *are low, and whenever strong feedback relations exist from support levels to transactions back again to support* (as measured by $[\beta - a_1]$).

The last part of this assertion is nonobvious; it follows from a close look at the interrelations of β and a_1 in equations (17a) and (18a). Because all coefficients in this model are positive, including β, a_2, a_1, inequality (26) will hold whenever $\beta - a_1$ is a small enough positive or negative number, i.e., whenever β is small and a_1 is large. How does this give a strong feedback from *S* through *T* back to *S*? Equation (17a) shows how a big a_1 means that a little *S* produces lots of *T*; equation (18a) shows how a small β means a large *T* will have a further impact on increasing *S* as the above proposition claims.

Figure 3 shows the same thing for model *I′*, the discrete stochastic version of these equations. Notice how there are two paths linking S(t) to S(t+1):

$$S(t+1) = [a_1 b + (1 - b\beta)] \, S(t)$$
OR
$$\Delta S = S(t+1) - S(t) = b(a_1 - \beta) \, S(t) \qquad (27).$$

Thus here too a big a_1 and a small β means that S feeds back more strongly and positively on itself (since $b>0$).

This discussion raises the next qualitative question that Simon asks: whether or not any or all of the models presented have stable equilibria. Or are they like Richardson's unstable arms races leading either to orgies of integration or disintegration? As in the Richardson case,[25] there is a quantitative answer that can be derived from the model to this qualitative answer; it too is interpretable like equation (26) in qualitative terms:

$$\text{Stable Equilibrium of Model I} \quad <=> \quad \begin{matrix} \beta>a_1 \\ b\,[(\beta-a_1)(c_1\alpha+c_2)-a_2c_1]>0 \end{matrix} \qquad \text{(28a, b)}.$$

Drawing on Simon's careful analysis of the feedback properties of the model (recall the above discussion of $[\beta\text{-}a_1]$), we come to another rather powerful model derivation which might easily be used to falsify our model in certain common market contexts: *System stability will occur if and only if the amount of transactions ($\beta S\infty$) required to generate the equilibrium level of support is greater than the transaction level ($a_1 S\infty$) that would be generated by the equilibrium level of support in the absence of any integration activity; and similarly the feedback from I through S and T is not destabilizing.*

This brings us to the last testable qualitative property of this model that we shall mention, namely, its behavior when perturbed about its equilibrium by fluctuations in demand or in the strength of its coefficients. Although a number of such questions can be answered about models II–IV and I′–IV′, for the sake of brevity and simplicity we again limit ourselves to model I, characterized as it is by linear transaction production with transaction-induced support and endogenous demands.

Recall equations (24a,b,c) giving "at infinity" values of S, I, and T. Since $I\infty$ depended on $D\infty$, $S\infty$ on $I\infty$, and $T\infty$ on both $S\infty$ and $I\infty$, $D\infty$ is seen as the major long-run exogenous cause of these equilibrium values. Recalling that all coefficients are assumed positive (another testable model property), it follows that: *As equilibrium is reestablished, an increase in integration demands will increase the level of common market transactions, support, and integration; as demands decrease toward zero, other system variables will also.* This model clearly illustrates one of Lindberg's important emphases to the effect that demands provide the lifeblood of an integration process.

Contrived as such examples may seem, they have nonetheless suggested some important points about causal modeling integration processes: first, that a variety of both qualitative and quantitative validation procedures exists; second, that such theoretical statements can catch many of the more interest-

---

[25] Stability considerations are clearly exposited for the classic Richardson model (actually only one of many he discussed) in Anatol Rapoport, *Fights, Games and Debates* (Ann Arbor: University of Michigan Press, 1960), part I.

ing assertions in the integration literature and turn them into testable forms. Finally, the relative superiority of multiequation process models over single equation measuring or explanatory logics derives most importantly from their relative statistical adequacy vis-à-vis the spurious correlation problem.

III. Computer Simulations of Integration Processes

The causal models above deliberately aggregated over specific nations and multidimensional variables such as integration. Moreover, even though they dynamically elaborated upon the rather static logic of necessary, sufficient, helpful, or harmful conditions typical of the single-equation Haas-Schmitter tradition, these models inadequately handled the phase shift phenomena conspicuously discussed in the verbal theories of that tradition: changes in operative conditions from the prenegotiation to the postnegotiation process. In order to clarify how a simulation logic might further differ from a causal logic in modeling such processes we shall sketch several computer flow charts for a revised Haas-Schmitter-Nye simulation. Then we shall turn briefly to the problems and possibilities of validating such an approach.[26]

A. A Partial Haas-Schmitter-Barrera-Nye Simulation Design

Consider the computer programming flow chart of Figure 4. Although not completely specified, this figure should clearly convey an overview of what a Haas-Schmitter-Nye computer simulation would look like. The five diamonds are choice or turning points in the model; the five rectangular boxes refer to what might be thought of as model subprocesses or subroutines. The arrows to and from the clock and data update command ($t = t + 1$) do not imply causation; rather they convey sequencing instructions necessary for model operation. Trying logically to sketch in the relevant parts of the integration process, conceived in simulation modeling terms, helps clarify a number of theoretical issues. For example, the update requirement at the beginning of every time period demands clarification of what exogenous variables the model is sensitive to (e.g., external pressures) as well as the inertial processes within the system that require some or no updating, e.g., the memory of when a union was formed. And the embarrassing case where negotiating processes last longer than the data accumulation period (e.g., more than a year) means

---

[26] The most relevant introduction and bibliography for the present exercise are Robert Abelson, "Simulation of Social Behavior," in Lindzey and Aronson; William Coplin (ed.), *Simulation in the Study of Politics* (Chicago: Markham Press, 1968); Hermann, *Behavioral Science,* Vol. 12, No. 3; Harold Guetzkow, "Some Correspondences between Simulations and 'Realities' in International Relations," in Morton Kaplan (ed.), *New Approaches to International Relations* (New York: St. Martin's Press, 1968). My own thoughts on the metaphysics of process modeling in international relations/domestic politics are best elaborated in "Computer Simulations, Conceptual Frameworks and Coalition Behavior" in Sven Groennings, E. W. Kelley, and Michael Leiserson (ed.), *The Study of Coalition Behavior* (New York: Holt, Rinehart and Winston, forthcoming).

the flow chart must be more complicated to include the possibility of negotiations being in progress. Moreover, the question of missing links is very clear as one constructs such a figure with the intent of being completely explicit in terms of measurable variables and meaningful turning points. Thus it was felt that part of the Haas-Schmitter logic had to be extended to allow for separate attention to the conditions affecting politicization. In not including further model turning points we claim that preintegration conditions are in theory not necessary during later stages of the integration process.

Such discussions represent, however, but a minor part of the present exercise. Let us focus on the process of negotiating economic union, subprocess A in Figure 4, and its possible subsequent processes of union creation or negotiation termination. As modeled by Barrera and Haas, the relevant answers all come from a single equation in C_6, C_7, C_8; recall the variety of possibilities in our single-equation mixed model review. Although the attractiveness of the Barrera-Haas measurement procedure derives in part from the simplicity and tractability of the related theory, Figure 4 suggests just how large a burden they expect aggregate judgments and a single-equation model to bear. Must we assume that negotiations begin when five background conditions have been met for two years? No, but then Haas and Barrera do not yet have a determinate theory temporally speaking. A more probabilistic version of branch point 2 in Figure 4 might be desirable, but we need theoretical help in specifying it. Similarly, Figure 4 raises the questions whether conditions or variables $C_6 - C_8$, as defined in Table 1, are all we need to know in order to decide whether negotiations succeed. Barrera and Haas wisely limited their pioneering theorizing to predicting or explaining whether or not union or politicization occurred. But *if we are to go further, we need more complex theories as to the determinants of specific union characteristics and specific agents' actions in negotiation or politicization processes.*

If one wants to be theoretically explicit and to use operational concepts while at the same time desiring to manipulate theory assumptions so as to derive their causal or logical implications, simulational modeling is an attractive way of doing so. Note, for example, Nye's and Schmitter's interesting discussion in this volume as to how existing economic unions through a variety of subprocesses may become more or less integrated. Do we know when which of these processes occurs, and what effect it has on specific integration variables and actors? A major benefit of attempting to formalize the logic of such arguments is the sufficient clarification of process dynamics to answer such questions.

Model I' or a revision of it may be one useful way of elaborating the $C_9 - C_{12}$ politicization logic of the earlier Haas-Barrera scheme; it could even be treated as subroutine in the simulation of Figure 4! So could a more elaborate set of politicization subroutines closer in content to the new verbal theory of Nye

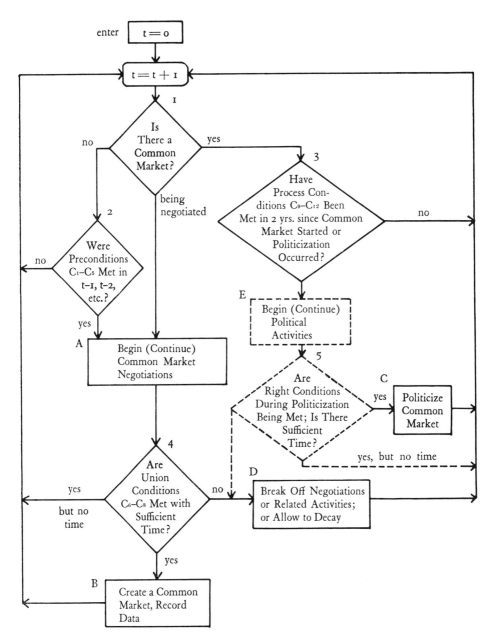

FIGURE 4. A SIMULATION FLOW CHART FOR A REVISED HAAS-SCHMITTER POLITI-
CIZATION MODEL. This figure derives in part from Barrera-Haas, *International
Organization,* Vol. 23, No. 1. See Table 1 for identification of C_1–C_{12}.

and Schmitter or to the negotiation routine suggested in the flow chart of Figure 5.

Referring not to the politicization process itself, but to negotiations for an economic union, Figure 5 suggests some ways of detailing how supranational actors can help out in an incremental, often bilateral, negotiation process. Note how specific actors and their value demands are exogenously put into the process, as in model I, but here on a disaggregated basis. In addition to quantitative predispositions, texts of tentative agreements become important also since these are important intermediate bargaining tokens as well as negotiation outcomes. Procedural sequences may be arbitrary, but they foreclose a number of possible agreements which supranational actors may help revive. Whether or not agreement occurs depends on the outcomes of a number of conscious and perhaps some unconscious turning points in the model (those that lead toward or away from the "sign an agreement" subroutine). In some, as yet not clearly specified, sense *the figure suggests measuring integrating capability in terms of what range of disparate actors and value demands can be accommodated through such a system of bargaining, innovation, and accommodation in forming an economic union with significant politicization potential.*

B. *Validation Possibilities with Simulation Models*

Given their greater realism one pays a considerable price in moving to the complexity of simulation modeling like that suggested by figures 4 and 5 taken together. Whether or not their many advantages of closer correspondence to verbal theories, explicitness, and manipulability are worth such efforts remains a debatable issue. Let us explore a few of the problems and possibilities associated with validating such models.

Perhaps the most important validation problem and prospect raised by such models concerns relevant data availability. Clearly subjective strategies and preferences, policy commitments, bureaucratic memories, irregular events, and textual materials are harder to gather and analyze than the aggregated variables typical of many causal models. That such data should be collected in at least some settings is an important implication of complex integration modeling efforts. But a related valid problem is the need to test theoretical models when not all relevant data is available.

Appropriate responses include testing some aggregate or qualitative response characteristics of a model vis-à-vis historical judgment. Many of our remarks on validating qualitative characteristics of causal models are thus by analogy useful in the present context. And there is also a clear need to rely strongly on a priori belief about what parts of a model are more vulnerable than others. Consider, for example, the commitment to success variables in Figure 5. A partial test of the relevant model mechanisms might have to rely

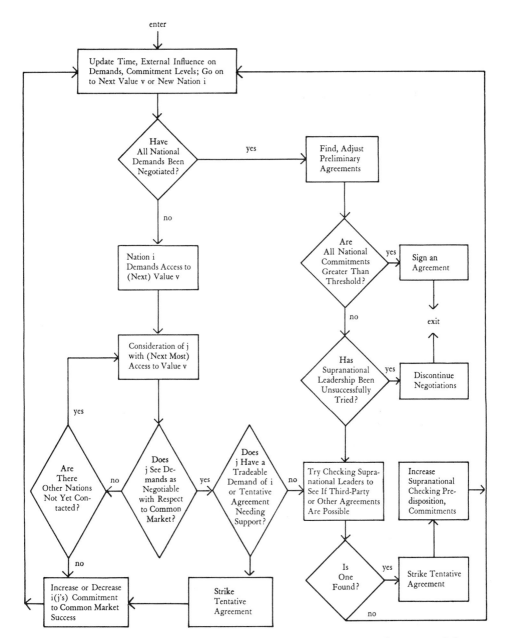

FIGURE 5. A PARTIALLY SPECIFIED FLOW CHART FOR A COMMON MARKET NEGOTIATION ROUTINE. This figure has been suggested by Barrera-Haas, *International Organization,* Vol. 23, No. 1, and Ronald Brunner, "Some Comments on Simulating Political Development," in Coplin.

upon before and after negotiation data averages. A close look at two or three specific deadlocks might be sufficient to falsify our suggestion as to supranational roles and actions in the negotiation process. Any such simple test assumes a priori, however, that other external and model phenomena are not causing any such behavioral links to be spurious.[27] Sophisticated uses of a priori knowledge in further testing international simulations remains a largely unmet challenge. It is nonetheless real because of the especially large number of parameters and small number of data points typically associated with such models.

A third validity problem and possibility concerns the testing of alternate theories using simulation. Simulation models often take a long time and a lot of work to develop. It becomes difficult but not impossible in such cases to construct alternate models using mostly different variables. Comparisons between such models—and this point refers to causal models as well—is much more difficult and sometimes more interesting than comparisons of different configurations of the same variables. Again reliance on qualitative differences in model properties, in aggregate output performance scores, and in substantial a priori judgmental inputs to validation efforts seems required.

IV. Comments and Conclusions

A reasonable strategy for integrating the major claims of this article is to first review what has been said about the variety of integration logics, then to discuss the implications of the newer and more sophisticated logics for empirical research, and finally to suggest how both the logical representations and empirical efforts help lead to a new conceptualization of integration practices and possibilities.

A. Toward Greater Realism in Integration Logics

Where should a potential integration theorist go in the search of greater realism in modeling and measurement assumptions? Clearly, almost every single-equation logic we have looked at suffered from specification problems, probably spurious relations, and/or the lack of adequate validation. Replies to our question will differ, however, depending among other things on rather deep intellectual differences as to the desirability or feasibility of parsimonious multiequation models.

---

[27] For a variety of intriguing statistical procedures for partially validating complex models see Thomas Naylor, Donald Burdick, and W. Earl Sasser, "Computer Simulation Experiments with Economic Systems: The Problem of Experimental Design," *Journal of the American Statistical Association*, December 1967 (Vol. 6, No. 320), pp. 1315–1337. My general proposal is that when only aggregate data time series is available, one can summarize simulation performance in terms of causal statistical models applied to their outputs for real or hypothetical input. These models are in turn testable vis-à-vis the poorer real-world data.

Thus among those articulating their logics of deduction and inference we can recommend and probably expect greater reliance on both multiequation dynamic causal models and computer simulations. For explanatory purposes, whichever approach is taken, it seems fair to expect that a new quality of theorizing is likely to develop. It is likely to pay more attention to a variety of clearly specifiable but not entirely linear formulations. The complexity cum consistency of such specifications makes for the advantage that deductions from them are likely to be both powerful, nonobvious, and falsifiable. These deductions will suggest not only probabilistic outcome predictions and observable patternings of behavior, such as the changing effectiveness of certain politicization processes, but also qualitative, dynamic properties of responses to external stresses. Most of the significant verbal explanatory concepts will be at least partially representable in such language, and new formal concepts will also emerge. If not realism, then certainly a much greater conceptual richness is possible with multiequation and simulation approaches.

The impetus for such development is partly an invisible college and an emerging consensus—an agreement within limits both to agree and to disagree—among integration theorists. There is considerable agreement as to appropriate conceptual apparatus, including an empirical "process theorizing" orientation. Many variables in different articles are conceptually related. Writers read and discuss the same works; data is shared. The strengths and weakness of a Deutschian, Haasian, or Eastonian theory are so richly interwoven that it no longer seems desirable or defensible to separate and isolate each theoretical tradition from the other.

B. New Directions in Empirical Research

What are some of the specific empirical questions we have commented on? Surely an obvious point has been the need for a revolution in data-collecting efforts. Among several reasons for the inadequacy of many earlier theorizing efforts was the lack of data both to estimate parameters and test modeling assumptions for possibly spurious relations. Closely related problems derived from the absence of time-series observations of great utility for sorting out controversial claims of causal priority. Relatively simple causal models will need new data through time in order for powerful tests to be made of their properties. Judgments of qualitative or quantitative variables or relationships need to be and can be more systematically gathered and checked for reliability and validity. Equally important, perhaps, is the implication of the revised Haas-Schmitter simulation sketch that textual or quantitative event data on how demands are generated and how they are responded to unevenly through time is vital for testing plausible theories of integration and disintegration processes. Of course, such data-collection efforts will have to be carefully focused in terms of prior theoretical development in order to be effective.

The need for such new data sets follows rather clearly from the strong emphasis in this article on validation problems and procedures. To falsify or validate complex models, a variety of data is obviously needed. But validity problems go beyond the often expensive need for data collection.

The intention of the discussion of how to validate or falsify the Simon integration model was to broaden in scope the usual validation procedures of political statistics to include qualitative as well as quantitative, cross-sectional as well as longitudinal, relationships. The need for similar estimation and validation procedures for complex simulation models, especially when the data is not complete, remains a major problem. A strong use of a priori theory and Bayesian reasoning will often be necessary to create sufficient overidentification in a multiparameter simulation model so that the model becomes falsifiable. As several of our examples showed, qualitative prediction from incompletely specified models and imperfect data sets should continue as an important validation procedure; so should the representation of some simulated model processes in summary, testable causal form. The costs of such data-collection efforts will surely not be as high as those for complete, disaggregated data sets.

C. Progress in Conceptualizing Integration Processes

The change in meanings associated with the phrase "integration" has been very great as we have moved through this article. We have left until now the chance for a more extended discussion.

Consider the following idealized historical sketch. In the mid-fifties European integration was progressing smoothly enough so that almost every part of the elephant grabbed by a myopic empiricist was moving pretty much in the same direction. These included decisional scopes, their penetrativeness, compliance rates, leadership styles, popular loyalties, relative and absolute transaction volumes, the development of new collective decisionmaking arenas and capabilities. Shortly thereafter, however, the indications stopped—all nicely covarying. As a result, a meaningful notion of integration became harder to define. Either a "retreat" to a single or weighted scope or penetrativeness or compliance score occurred, or integration was defined in a multiindicator way as something like a vector.

Much of the suggestibility of the old concept was lost. In a schedule sense,[28] however, several important notions of integration are still definable and are now becoming popular. As John Harsanyi did with the concept "social power," it is appropriate to ask what the schedule of possibilities is between resources, actions, outcomes and their opportunity costs. If the schedule of possibilities

---

[28] See Robert Axelrod, *Conflict of Interest* (Chicago: Markham Press, 1970) for measurement procedures.

is sufficiently restrictive, then for either compliance or penetrativeness a theoretical production function can be defined that draws the resource, action, and outcome variables together in a causally meaningful way. What more striking departure from more aggregation or unidimensional measurement can there be than Simon's astonishingly provocative definition (equation 24) of integration surplus in terms of a configuration of parameters of functional interdependence?

A related approach to measuring integration uses the theoretical model involved, such as the revised Haas-Schmitter model of figures 4 and 5 to derive outcome patterns from either hypothetical or actual input data. Just as we observed above about Figure 5, that it seemed natural to measure integration capabilities and practice in terms of the range of actual or potential demands that can be accommodated without minimum commitment levels being violated, consider:

$$I_1 = \frac{\text{collective demand processing success}}{} = \frac{\overset{N}{\underset{i}{\Sigma}} \gamma_i \overset{V}{\underset{}{\Sigma}} S_{vi} D_{vi} \quad \text{actors demands}}{\overset{N}{\underset{i}{\Sigma}} \gamma_i \overset{}{\underset{v}{\Sigma}} D_{vi}} \tag{29a}$$

where γ_i ($=$ the resource level of i) is a weighting factor, D_{vi} is the magnitude of i's demand for value V, and S_{vi} is a crucial 0–1 dichotomous variable equal to one if D_{vi} was satisfied or autonomously diminished in a way not associated with a decrease in common market commitment. S_{vi} is calculated by running the model or from real-world data. If we attempt to measure integration more in a capabilities sense, we need to sum over a range of hypothetical demands.

Let us assume that there is a finite integral range of D_{vi} values, from one to J, indexed by j. Then with slight modifications we have

$$I_2 = \frac{\text{collective demand processing success potential}}{} = \frac{\overset{J}{\underset{j=1}{\Sigma}} \overset{N}{\underset{i=1}{\Sigma}} \gamma_i \overset{V}{\underset{\gamma=1}{\Sigma}} P(D_{vi}=j) S_{vi} D_{vi}}{\overset{J}{\underset{j=1}{\Sigma}} \overset{N}{\underset{i=1}{\Sigma}} \gamma_i \overset{V}{\underset{\gamma=1}{\Sigma}} P(D_{vi}=j) D_{vi}} \tag{29b}$$

Where $P(D_{vi}=j)$ is the probability that $D_{vi}=j$ according to some plausible theory of demand structures, this gives us a normalized expectation on a zero to one scale of success potential.

If extremes of demand levels could be quantified on some scale and perhaps weighted by resources, a definition of integration potential in terms of the extreme levels of demand manageable (either responsively or repressively) by a system would be possible. Or one could study the extent to which salient demands with high conflicts of interest could be handled with system-commitment levels remaining above some critical threshold.

These examples of more novel ways of measuring integration are generalizations of the notion of "integration in a schedule sense" suggested above. They depend for their significance on the associated theoretical structure. Such theoretical schedules are implied by either implicit or explicit judgments of the "strength" of peaceful decisionmaking institutions within an area, or its collective decisionmaking "capabilities." Like Ronald Fisher's early definition of evolutionary fitness,[29] they integrate many of the components of a desirable answer to a complex question, "How is integration proceeding in the EEC?"

We have now come full circle in suggesting aggregate measures of demand satisfaction and institutional survivability. Others might refer to ratios of support or commitment summed over the interest groups or major actors whose demands form the basis of a simulation model. Although equation (29a) might be time-consuming to calculate, like other such aggregate measures it could be compared to the simplest empirical integration indices (summed over relevant actors), defined according to logics like equations (1), (2), or (3). Thus theory and data should converge through properly defined measurement.

If this discussion indicates some evolution of sophistication in conceptualizing integration, a concomitant growth in awareness of the role of pretheories in process models is also worth stating. Many linear logics carry none of the sophisticated neo-functionalist orientation of Haas and Nye, the Eastonian

---

[29] Although equations (29a,b) are but the beginning of an attempt to conceptualize integration in a synthetic way, the idea behind them is not new. Compare the somewhat analogous evolutionary concept of biological fitness. Biologists see this as involving various components: survival, longevity, time to age of first reproduction, and fertility. For bisexual populations, let x be the probability that an individual born at time o is still alive at time x, m_x be the number of female offspring born to a female during age x. If α is the age of first reproduction and w the age of last reproduction, then the net reproduction rate Ro is

$$Ro = \int_\alpha^w l_x m_x dx \tag{30a}.$$

Where T is the mean generation rate, we can describe the corresponding growth rate exponentially in terms of a fitness coefficient r for a specific ecology as:

$$Ro = e^{rT} \tag{30b}$$

A revealing interpretation of r is given by a formula taking into account all the components of fitness mentioned above:

$$1 = \int_\alpha^w l_x m_x e^{-rx} dx \tag{30c}.$$

Here r represents the attrition rate from hostile forces against which species growth can just reproduce one female child per mother.

In another context Noam Chomsky has similarly argued that linguistic behavior can better be understood in terms of its competences than its performance. See his *Aspects of the Theory of Syntax* (Cambridge, Mass: M.I.T. Press, 1969).

framework used by Lindberg, or the historical-sociological and cybernetic approaches of Deutsch. Is such pretheorizing excess baggage? Those used to relatively impoverished integration logics might think so. But those doing much work with multiequation, nonlinear causal models or computer simulations are probably less likely to agree. The Haas-Schmitter-Barrera model we have sketched needs concepts such as the demand conversion processes. Equations (29a and 29b) defined in terms of such a model in effect operationalize such a notion. Latent or uninspected functions are served by hierarchies of interdependent feedback loops such as those of the Simon-Homans model. Spillover or politicization is the key process idea of Figure 4. The realization that nothing therein allows for negative changes in politicization levels, e.g., spill-back, comes just as naturally from an educated hard look at the flow chart as from neo-functional critique of the original Haas-Schmitter article. Simulation modeling experience helps, moreover, clear up the fuzziness of many of the more complex concepts in the present literature. Many of the concepts of the earlier Haas literature and innovations in it, such as articles by Nye and Schmitter in this volume, contain process concepts that look suspiciously like big black boxes or substantive titles to the computer simulator. Related mechanisms need better specification.

A final comment on conceptual development concerns the hypothetical investigation of model properties. We have already mentioned how hypothetical variations in select model variables and their derivative consequences can be statistically analyzed to generate simple single or multiequation summaries of model properties that are illuminating in themselves and comparable for validity purposes to equivalent empirically derived logics. A second hypothetical model use is the exploration through such manipulations of parameters and variables related to important outcomes. Such sensitivity analysis can help pinpoint relationships worthy of especially careful empirical investigation.

In terms of hypothetical inputs, partly validated models can be used contingently to predict futures or to "try out" policy alternatives. But why not use models more imaginatively to evoke bolder conjecture? As Simon was able to demonstrate startling implications of certain feedback configurations for surplus integration, cannot the hypothetical or actual operation of complex simulations be part of a meditative and creative act?[30] One can play with radically different coefficient parameters to explore what their world would

30

    The impoverishment of education by the demands of methodism poses a threat not only to so-called normative or traditional theory, but to the scientific imagination as well. It threatens the meditative culture which nourishes all creativity . . . [and] is the source of the qualities crucial to theorizing: playfulness, concern, the juxtaposition of contraries, and astonishment at the variety and subtle interconnection of things.

Sheldon Wolin, "Political Theory as a Vocation," *American Political Science Review*, December 1969 (Vol. 63, No. 4), p. 1073.

or should be like; we can be astonished at the subtle implications of distant causes. Competing hypotheses, mechanisms, policies, demands, or political orders can be traced for their possible implications. Even the regularities of explicitly programmed regional integration models can be used as a touchstone for appreciating the spontaneous irregularities of life. Others might treat them as metaphorical utopias and contrast them with the tragic peace-forsaking failures of too many regional integration schemes in Honduras, Nigeria, nineteenth-century America, early twentieth-century Europe, and possibly in various futures as well.

III

NEW AREAS FOR
INVESTIGATION

8

Continuities and Discontinuities between Studies of National and International Political Integration:

Some Implications for Future Research Efforts

Fred M. Hayward

THE literature on integration has expanded tremendously during the last decade. This growing interest in the problems and processes of integration is particularly marked in two areas, studies of international regional integration and studies of national integration. On the whole, these efforts have been carried out with very little reference to each other. What is striking, nonetheless, is the similarity of much of the material and the relevance of work in one area for conceptualization and theory building in the other. As one who has been concerned primarily with national political integration I would like to delineate some of the major similarities and differences between the foci of national and regional integration studies, to suggest the utility of thinking in terms of a common conceptualization of political integration, and to discuss the relevance of some aspects of the work on national integration for regional theory and research.

This article is divided into three parts. In the first section some of the continuities and discontinuities between national and international studies are examined. I first look at the question of definition. In considering how scholars have defined the subject matter, does it appear that they are referring to the same phenomenon when delineating national and international integration, or are the two distinct phenomena? Second, I discuss briefly the subject

FRED M. HAYWARD is assistant professor of political science at the University of Wisconsin, Madison. The author is indebted to a number of individuals for their helpful comments and criticisms, in particular, Samuel Coleman, Victor Le Vine, Donald McCrone, Deane E. Neubauer, Stuart Scheingold, and James C. Scott.

matter of national and international studies. Do scholars seem to be looking at different processes? I note that the main focus of international studies has been on European efforts to establish and carry out a variety of integration projects while the major focus of national studies has been on problems of integration for developing nations. There are a number of features common to each area of study (national and international), but not to both areas, which are a consequence of the general foci of each. I discuss these similarities and differences in some detail. Finally, I suggest that the differences are not differences in kind, that they do not indicate that we are talking about two different phenomena.

In the second section of the article I suggest a conceptualization of integration which avoids some of the problems inherent in many formulations of integration. In the last section I note some of the contributions of national integration literature for studies of international integration and comment on several areas which warrant special focus in future research.

I.

When scholars examine integration within a single nation or among a group of nations, are they talking about the same kind of phenomena or is the common use of the term "integration" a misleading accident which confuses what are two quite different things?

In exploring this question it is worth looking at how scholars of national and international integration have defined the term integration. Do they seem to identify a common phenomenon? If they do not, are there areas of congruence?

In an examination of the literature of national and international integration one is quickly struck by the general lack of concern for conceptualization in national integration literature. With very few exceptions (most notably Karl Deutsch's early work) the literature on national integration has been remarkably lacking in conceptual and methodological rigor. In general the term political integration is used as an undefined predicate—that is, as a quality or characteristic which is affirmed or asserted (or sometimes denied). For example, the statement that "political parties are integrative" asserts integration as a quality, characteristic, or effect of political parties. It does not tell us much about what constitutes integration. For most writers the term integration generally remains undefined as such. When attempts at definition have been made, they have usually been incomplete and, in almost all cases, at variance with other definitions of the term.

Most scholars of international integration have been more self conscious about problems of definition and conceptualization. There have been major efforts to specify what constitutes integration, to identify the actions or end states involved (or both in some cases), to differentiate integration from other processes and conditions with which it might be confused, and to specify how one would identify integration empirically. This concern about conceptualization has not led to agreement about a definition of integration. We find, rather, that those who study international integration use an ever growing number of definitions of integration.[1] Where we find definitions at all in studies of national integration there is the same multiplicity of definitions, and many are fraught with conceptual problems which make them of questionable utility. Let us look at some of the definitions.

In studies of international regional integration scholars have defined integration in terms of the process of shifting loyalties from a national setting to a larger entity,[2] the ability to ensure peaceful change over time,[3] the establishment and maintenance of community,[4] the ability of a system to maintain itself,[5] and the collective capacity to make decisions.[6] Writers primarily con-

---

[1] A very useful effort at overcoming these difficulties for regional studies has been made by Joseph S. Nye, "Comparative Regional Integration: Concept and Measurement," *International Organization*, Autumn 1968 (Vol. 22, No. 4), pp. 855–880. Philip E. Jacob and Henry Teune have made an interesting, but less successful, attempt to synthesize all integration studies in "The Integrative Process: Guidelines for Analysis of the Bases of Political Community," in Philip E. Jacob and James Toscano (ed.), *The Integration of Political Communities* (Philadelphia: J. B. Lippincott, 1964). Myron Weiner suggests a synthesis at the national level and a categorization of types of integration in "Political Integration and Political Development," in Claude E. Welch, Jr. (ed.), *Political Modernization: A Reader in Comparative Political Change* (Belmont, Calif: Wadsworth Publishing Co., 1967), pp. 150–166.

[2] Ernst B. Haas defines integration as

> the process whereby political actors in several distinct national settings are persuaded to shift their loyalties, expectations, and political activities toward a new and larger center, whose institutions possess or demand jurisdiction over the preexisting national states.

The Uniting of Europe: Political, Social, and Economic Forces, 1950–1957 (Stanford, Calif: Stanford University Press, 1958), p. 16.

[3] Karl W. Deutsch, and others, describe integration as

> the attainment, within a territory, of a "sense of community" and of institutions and practices strong enough and widespread enough to assure, for a "long" time, dependable expectations of "peaceful change" among its population.

"Political Community and the North Atlantic Area," in *International Political Communities: An Anthology* (Garden City, N.Y: Doubleday & Co., 1966), p. 2.

[4] This conceptualization has been used by many individuals in studying regional integration. Joseph Nye has stated that integration is a

> process leading to political community—a condition in which a group of people recognizes mutual obligations and some notion of a common interest.

Pan-Africanism and East African Integration (Cambridge, Mass: Harvard University Press [under the auspices of the Center for International Affairs], 1965), p. 84.

Jacob and Teune define integration in a very similar fashion but suggest that such a definition is applicable to all types of integration, in Jacob and Toscano, p. 4.

[5] Amitai Etzioni defines integration as "the ability of a unit or system to maintain itself in the face of internal and external challenges" in his *Political Unification: A Comparative Study of Leaders and Forces* (New York: Holt, Rinehart and Winston, 1965), p. 330.

[6] Leon Lindberg suggests that integration be conceptualized as the

> process whereby a group of nations (or other political units) progressively takes on a collective capacity to make decisions which authoritatively allocates values for all their members

in his manuscript, "Europe as a Political System: Measuring Political Integration," Center for International Studies, Harvard University, April 1967, p. 2. (Mimeographed.)

cerned with national integration have defined integration as system cohesion,[7] adaptation to structures,[8] a bridging of the elite-mass gap,[9] the establishment of common norms and commitment to patterns of political behavior.[10]

A brief glance at these definitions gives us a "sense" that there is some commonality in all of them. There is a "sense" in which they all focus on what makes a system cohere. Yet the apparent differences are equally striking even among those who are interested in the same levels of integration—i.e., national integration or international integration. Furthermore, the differences in the definitions of integration between those studying either national or international integration are as great as the differences between the two areas of focus. While integration may be defined in an almost endless variety of ways without violating the limits of the criteria for scientific definition and while there are no "right" or "wrong" definitions, the multiplicity of definitions and the failure to agree on common conceptions makes useful comparison almost impossible. We will return to this particular problem in the second section of this article.

While an examination of definitions of national and international integration does not tell us much about the similarities and differences of the two areas of study, an analysis of what scholars do in the fields of international and national integration tells us a great deal. While any characterization of the literature is fraught with difficulties, an examination of the general areas of focus in national and international integration studies can help to demonstrate whether differences are a product of the focus or the distinct nature of the phenomena.

Most of the important early work on international integration focused on Europe, including its efforts at collective defense, political and economic unions of various sorts, proposals for federations of states, and so on. The nature of the material studied—i.e., the types of political actions occurring in Europe—set parameters for the research efforts. With a few exceptions (notably the study

---

[7] Myron Weiner describes integration as "referring to the generalized problem of holding a system together," in Welch, p. 153.

[8] Marion J. Levy, Jr., suggests that

the analytic structure of integration in a society or other concrete structure consists of those structures the operations of which make for the eufunctional adaptation of the members and/or members-to-be of the structure to the structure concerned

in his *The Structure of Society* (Princeton, N.J: Princeton University Press, 1952), p. 504.

[9] Coleman and Rosberg define political integration in terms of the

progressive bridging of the elite-mass gap on the vertical plane in the course of developing an integrated political process and a participant political community

in James S. Coleman and Carl G. Rosberg, Jr. (ed.), *Political Parties and National Integration in Tropical Africa* (Berkeley: University of California Press, 1964), p. 9.

[10]

A political system is integrated to the extent that the minimal units (individual political actors) develop in the course of political interaction a pool of commonly accepted norms regarding political behavior and a commitment to the political behavior patterns legitimized by these norms.

Claude Ake, *A Theory of Political Integration* (Homewood, Ill: Dorsey Press, 1967), p. 3.

of the Swiss federation)[11] research on international integration focused on cases which had a number of important common features:

1) The ends sought were functionally specific in intent: Cooperation was sought for mutual defense, tariff barriers were to be lowered on specific commodities, and certain kinds of external policies were to be established collectively. The nature of the commitment too was specified. It was relatively clear, at least initially, what one gave up and what one stood to gain.

2) The entities involved in the activity regard themselves as "autonomous" or "sovereign" states. In most cases the public posture of those who act in the name of these states is that the states are free agents and as such have the right (perhaps the duty) to decide their position in terms of their interests as they define them, free of external coercion or pressure. While no nation is completely autonomous—powerful ones may force weak ones to comply with their desires, the economic and political costs of nonparticipation may be too high, the common external threat may be too great to avoid common effort without peril to the nation—most of the cases of international integration which have been examined involve relationships voluntarily entered into by the nations involved. While the leaders of a nation may feel some compulsion to join in an agreement, they do make the decision to participate or not to participate. Each national government apparatus regards itself, and wishes to be regarded, as the major political entity within a specified geographic area. It is assumed that the national apparatus governs within this geographic entity. That is, it is assumed that the national government meets what I suggest are minimal conditions for governing—that it is generally recognized by the populace as setting rules which it is deemed able to enforce, which are conceived in the name of the society, and which deal at minimum with the allocation of power in the society.[12]

3) The basis of the relationships between the entities involved in efforts at integration is one of exchange. As a consequence of bargaining the actors make exchanges in terms of specific goods, promises, actions, and so on. In short, the agreement between the parties is predicated primarily upon the assumed utility of exchange relationships.

These three characteristics of the kinds of cases which have been studied have helped focus work in international integration in ways which have been particularly fruitful. The functionally specific nature of the efforts at integration have made it easier to identify and quantify those things which cohere. The relatively autonomous condition of the actors (states or, more correctly,

---

[11] Charlotte Muret, "The Swiss Pattern for a Federated Europe," in *International Political Communities*, pp. 149–174.

[12] There are cases in which more than one political entity claims to govern a defined territory (as in the Vietnam conflict). In such cases, however, decisions about which entity will be regarded as the "effective" governing authority are made by other states. Under most conditions the question of effective governing authority is assumed even though as scholars we might question it.

those who act in the name of the states) has made it easier to distinguish the nature of the relationship of the entities involved. The fact that most of the efforts at integration have dealt with exchanges has made it easier to specify the scope, extent, and consequences of integration.

The literature on national integration has focused primarily on the nature and extent of the individual's identification with the national entity, the extent and costs of compliance with directives of government, and the methods which affect the degree of national integration. Interest in national integration was heightened by the large number of states which became independent in the 1950's and 1960's. While national integration is not a phenomenon unique to any set of nations, the knowledge that most newly independent states were composed of a wide variety of quite different ethnic/cultural groupings led to emphasis on the problems involved in achieving it.

Fundamental to studies of national integration is the notion of national identity. What is the nature of individual identification with the nation as opposed to other units within the geographic entity? How uniform are conceptions of national identification? Do they differ on the basis of ethnicity, class, status, political position? How strong is the relationship between individuals and the state? On the whole, determination of the nature of national identity has been subjective. Since most research has dealt with nations which became independent during the last twenty years, it has been assumed that the level of national identity was low and the attachment to the national unit ambiguous. While I suspect that this is generally true, there have been few systematic attempts at verification.[13]

Another important aspect of national integration studies is the degree to which individuals comply with government directives. As in the case of national identity, assessments of the degree of compliance are largely subjective. The high levels of political instability in many nonmodernized societies emphasize the inability of many governments to effect compliance. For a variety of reasons the cost of enforcing compliance is beyond government capabilities.[14] This conclusion has led to a search for methods to achieve compliance and to relate individuals' expectations to some level of compliance with government directives.

[13] Some empirical work on national identity has followed Gabriel Almond's and Sidney Verba's study of political culture either utilizing data which they gathered on national identity or pursuing similar efforts. Particularly instructive in this respect is Joseph LaPalombara's analysis of the nonintegrative aspects of political identification in Italy. Italy is neither a newly independent state nor a stranger to modernization. The implications of the Italian case for what we are likely to find elsewhere should encourage further empirical efforts to specify the nature of political identification. Gabriel A. Almond and Sidney Verba, *The Civic Culture: Political Attitudes and Democracy in Five Nations* (Princeton, N.J: Princeton University Press, 1963). On national identity see Sidney Verba, "Conclusion: Comparative Political Culture," in Lucian W. Pye and Sidney Verba (ed.), *Political Culture and Political Development* (Princeton, N.J: Princeton University Press, 1965), pp. 512–560 and Joseph LaPalombara, "Italy: Fragmentation, Isolation, and Alienation," in Pye and Verba, pp. 282–329.

[14] See, for example, Samuel P. Huntington, "Political Development and Political Decay," and Weiner, in Welch, pp. 207–245 and 150–166, respectively.

Most works on national integration have explored questions of method. What types of structures, values, resources, and outputs facilitate or hinder national integration? Particular importance has been attributed to the role of special types of political parties and party systems (especially mass parties and single-party systems) as major instruments of national identity and thus national integration.[15] Others have argued that integration is dependent on the institutionalization of political participation and have sought to identify structures which will order participation.[16] Several writers have argued that integration is dependent on agreement on values for conflict resolution[17] and justice.[18] Government outputs, such as David Apter's "integrational integer,"[19] have been suggested as essential means for national integration.

The concentration of national integration research on nonmodernized societies has led to the identification of a number of common features:

1) The ends or benefits to be realized from national integration are primarily nonspecific and are usually couched in general, vague terms. With the exception of the brief preindependence and immediate postindependence period in some states (where national integration was to bring about the highly specific end of independence) the benefits of national integration have been the very general, long-term goals such as modernization and development. While these ends have some specific referents, they usually refer to vague notions such as "a better way of life" and are not expected to be realized immediately.

2) The allocation of political authority between national and subnational units is ambiguous. There is limited consensus about who has legitimate political authority and how political authority should be allocated among individuals in the geographic entity.

3) Political relationships between individual participants are not clearly defined. Civic rights and responsibilities are often undefined and are usually variable. The expectations of actors about and their experiences with the political process are highly unstable.

In order to understand some of the discontinuities between national and international studies it is useful to compare these features with those already mentioned for international integration studies.

Let us first examine the question of the functional specificity of the ends

[15] See, for example, Coleman and Rosberg, especially the introduction and conclusions; and Ruth Schachter Morgenthau, *Political Parties in French-Speaking West Africa* (Oxford: Clarendon Press, 1964), chapter 9.

[16] Samuel P. Huntington suggests that political parties are among these structures in his *Political Order in Changing Societies* (New Haven, Conn: Yale University Press, 1968), chapter 7.

[17] Weiner, in Welch, pp. 158–159.

[18] These values may be the simple rules for conflict resolution or represent a stratification system which express a justification for differential ranking judgments. See Bernard Barber, *Social Stratification: A Comparative Analysis of Structure and Process* (New York: Harcourt, Brace & World, 1957), p. 7.

[19] David E. Apter, *The Politics of Modernization* (Chicago: University of Chicago Press, 1965), pp. 240–243.

sought. On the whole, the areas of interaction between the national apparatus
of government and various subsectors of the society are functionally specific
only in the broadest sense of the term. For the most part the nature of the
relationship between the state and its citizens is not defined in great detail or
in terms of specific, well-delineated commitments where the costs and gains
are clearly spelled out. In most cases (including federations) the relationship
is functionally diffuse and vaguely defined within broad parameters. This fact
increases the problems for research, especially efforts to identify and quantify
"important" elements in the relationship.

The second factor identified as important for international integration was
the high degree of autonomy of the actors. Only in the formative stages are
some national entities established through the agreement of two or more
"sovereign," "autonomous," or nearly equal entities. Even when this has happened at the formative stage, it is assumed that the autonomy lapses once the
larger entity is established. Once the enlarged entity develops an effective government apparatus, such entities are in almost every case so functionally diffuse that it is very difficult, short of violence, to revert to the original units if
dissatisfaction occurs. One can think of federations which have broken up or
cases in which efforts have been made to dissolve a federation, but such actions have either preceded the establishment of an effective central governing
apparatus (e.g., Mali federation) or have been accompanied by a great deal
of bloodshed (e.g., United States). Since the state and its citizenry do not
interact as autonomous or nearly equal and independent actors, it is much
more difficult to determine the nature of the relationship between those who
act in the name of the government and the populace of the state.

Finally, I noted that international integration studies focused primarily on
exchange relationships—exchange of specific goods, promises of defense, concessions, and so on. National integration might also be conceived of as an exchange relationship, but that conception stretches the point a bit in most
cases.[20] There is an exchange, to be sure. One exchanges tax money for roads,
law and order, national defense, and so on. But it is not a clearly defined exchange in which the partners in the relationship bargain over the terms (although a less overt bargaining does occur). While compliance with rules and
directives is facilitated if the populace sees some benefits accruing from the
system, this relationship is better described and understood in terms of orientations of the populace about the propriety of government. In many states, individuals have little to exchange other than loyalty or some sort of identification with the national government. They are concerned, nonetheless, about
government outputs. It should be noted that as the scope of international in-

---

[20] A partial exception to this occurs in nations with a strong system of federalism. In these cases the
relation between the national government and the partners to the federation more closely approximates
a clear exchange relationship.

tegration increases between a given group of states, the nature of the exchange also becomes more ambiguous.

I suggest that the differences which are apparent between studies of national and international integration are primarily a consequence of focus and interest rather than being differences in kind. Most studies of national integration have concentrated on societies which were assumed to be relatively nonintegrated.[21] It was also assumed that there was a minimal, but undefined, level of integration which needed to be achieved. Studies of international integration have focused on national entities and what they gave up to international "communities." Given the possible range of interactions their "level of integration" was relatively low. If we look at national and international integration from the same perspective, that is in terms of the units which are being brought together, we can see the similarities in the process studied. From this perspective the differences in specificity of ends and autonomy of units and relationships between the entities cease to be as significant. We see that if we view national political integration from the perspective of the largest unit and international political integration from the perspective of the largest potential political unit (comprising existing actors) the processes involved begin to look amazingly similar. The fact that the largest potential international unit (e.g., a "United States of Europe" or a Mali federation) may never come into being does not alter the nature of the phenomenon.

As we begin to look in greater detail at cases of "international integration," in which the scope of action is extended and major political control for these units becomes the purview of a single entity, we will find that the process of integration at that level is quite like what scholars are trying to understand in the context of a single nation.

Throughout the literature on integration there appears to be a common concern with those factors which make individuals and groups within a particularly defined entity cohere and with the reasons why some do so more than others. The same entities seem to cohere more at certain times than at other times. Integration is a process of "ups" and "downs." We see this historically again and again. The United Kingdom developed a nation over several hundred years, bringing together a great number of disparate entities. Now there are strong demands for fragmentation, such as autonomy for Wales and parts of Northern Ireland. I suggest that we do not have a different phenomenon after each change in degree of integration—or at least that to conceptualize integration in that way is not very useful. At a low level there are units which have one or two ties of an occasional or transitory nature, perhaps a mutual friendship pact with cultural exchanges. At a high level there are units with a substantial degree of cooperation and shared authority in broad areas of mutual concern.

[21] We leave that term undefined for the moment.

Regional integration studies in general have dealt with integration at relatively low levels. That is, the areas of contact of units are limited. Studies of national integration are involved primarily with high levels of contact and coherence of units *or* with how one achieves such levels. This latter concern is primarily the focus of studies of underdeveloped states. How does a nation reach a "minimal level" of integration? It is the focus on higher levels of integration in national studies which has made them more difficult, but it also makes them instructive for international studies, especially since there are several examples in which the level of integration is increasing. It is here that we can most easily see areas where studies of national and regional integration converge. If we should see the efforts toward European integration realize the dreams of Jean Monnet and others for a united Europe, the entity so created will look very much like the nations studied or envisioned by those interested in national integration. In another area, federations have the functional specificity and defined areas of autonomy of many regional units. At a governmental level the relationships between the entities involved in a federation are exchange relationships. On the other hand, the relationship of the citizenry and the national entity in its spheres of authority is like any other nation.

I want to suggest that the discontinuities between studies of international and national integration are not a consequence of a fundamental difference in the process of national and international integration. Much of what appears to represent fundamental differences in process is a consequence of the focus of integration studies rather than a difference in kind.

There is no solid evidence which indicates that national integration is a fundamentally different phenomenon from international integration. There is a great deal of evidence which *suggests* that they are similar. Thus, as a strategy of comparative politics it would be useful to try to conceptualize integration in a way which is applicable to national and international studies. In short, I argue that thinking in terms of a single concept of integration will aid in the development of theory, will make our work comparable if not compatible, and might help move our efforts from an atomized pretheoretical level toward common efforts for understanding the phenomenon.

II.

How might one conceptualize "political integration" in a way that it is useful at any level of generalization—in the international sphere, on a regional basis, in a single nation, or in some subsection of a nation? What do we need to identify it? How would this affect existing definitions and paradigms?

Efforts at understanding integration and theorizing about it will be of little value if we cannot identify the phenomenon clearly. Despite the variety of subject matter and the differences in foci already mentioned between existing studies of national and international integration, we are better off—if only in terms of clarity—if we are always talking about the same thing when we refer to integration. We want a definition which is as precise as possible, which has referents which can be identified empirically, and which is useful in the formulation of hypotheses. It is very important that we do not confuse definition with explanation. Whatever characteristics we use to indicate integration by definition are true by definition. We want to be able to *identify* integration and distinguish various levels of integration (e.g., this is highly integrated, that is relatively marginally integrated). Having identified integration, we can try to explain why some systems have more or less of it (or none at all) and how these factors relate to other phenomena such as stability, capacity to modernize, and so on. In short, we do not want to confuse "causes" of integration or important explanatory elements with the definition. To do so would be to run the risk of circularity.

Drawing on some of the distinctions made and problems posed, coupled with some "primitive" research of my own on national integration,[22] I want to suggest some avenue for further work on political integration. I suggest a conceptualization of political integration which can be utilized for studies of national or international integration (or at any level of generalization involving two or more entities). This conceptualization is useful for identifying integration. It is not a synthesis of existing definitions, nor does it make all integration models, ideal types, and paradigms obsolete. Useful models, ideal types, paradigms, and, more importantly, propositions and theories might follow from such a definition. It is the search for a base for the latter that leads me to make this effort in addition to the fact that most conceptualizations of integration are directed at a particular level (national or international) of integration.[23]

I would like to suggest that it is useful to conceive of integration in terms of adaptation and orientation to a particular structure. I define political integration as *adaptation and orientation of actors to a political structure at a given level of generalization.* By adaptation I mean the response of individuals to directives to them made in the name of the political structure (i.e., do they comply?). By orientation I refer to actors' identification with and evaluation of the political structure. Actors include those individuals who are relevant at a given level of generalization—i.e., if we are looking at bureaucracy, the "members"; a nation, the populace; an international organization, the participants.[24] We might choose to examine integration in a city, a nation, or within

---

[22] This is expanded considerably in a forthcoming study of national integration in Ghana.

[23] There are a number of conceptual difficulties with existing general definitions which also lead me to undertake this effort. While this article is not the place for a detailed exegesis of the merits and demerits of definitions in the literature, the general problems of clarity, lack of stated empirical referents, circularity, and utility create serious difficulties for research based on existing general definitions of integration.

[24] In some cases it will be useful to conceptualize each nation participating as "an actor," in others it will be necessary to deal with the populace or some subgroup of the populace as actors.

an international grouping. The extent of integration (or nonintegration) is dependent on the degree to which individuals adapt to the directives of the political structure (or, more precisely, to those who act in the name of the structure) and the extent to which the actors are oriented toward and foster an orientation to the structure.

Activity becomes more highly integrative as it moves from acceptance (when necessary) of rules and directives toward active encouragement or support. That is, one catalogs responses to the structure on the basis of *both* behavioral and attitudinal characteristics. In terms of behavior we want to know: Did the actors comply to rules and directives made in the name of the structure? Did they try to avoid compliance? Did they resist or try to encourage others not to comply? In terms of attitudinal response we want to know whether the structure is felt to be proper and if the type of activity reflected in the directives is regarded as a proper sphere of activity for the structure. At one extreme, individuals may adapt to a rule or directive because they were coerced and/or feel that the cost of nonadaptive behavior is too high. At the other extreme, they comply and actively urge others to comply because they think the structure is proper and that it has legitimate authority in this sphere of activity.

There are, then, two indicators of integration which are important: 1) a behavioral one—the extent to which individuals adapt to rules and directives of the political structure; and 2) an attitudinal index—their orientation, that is, their identification with the structure and the degree to which they feel that they should or should not adapt to demands made in its name. Individuals may comply with directives given at gunpoint, but most of those complying will, I suspect, feel that one ought not to do that.

The level of integration in a structure (a society, a regional union, a village, and so on) at any one time can be indicated by the relationship of orientation and adaptation. We have at one extreme the probability that all actors will adapt and at the other the possibility that none will adapt. Similarly, in terms of orientations, possibilities range from cases in which all men think that they ought to adapt to ones in which all think that they should not adapt.

In assessing the importance of various levels of adaptation and orientation (including negative adaptation and negative orientations) we must remember that in very few structures is the political impact of all men equal. If, for example, in two cases 5 percent of the population exhibit negative adaptation, it matters very much with which particular 5 percent of the population we are dealing. If it is the armed forces, the consequences are likely to be far more serious than if it is rural herdsmen.

We might indicate the degree of integration on a graph in a rough way as the intersection between orientations and adaptation (subtracting negative adaptations or orientations from positive ones for a score, or vice versa, and listing the total in terms of a percentage of the total number of relevant actors or on some other basis).

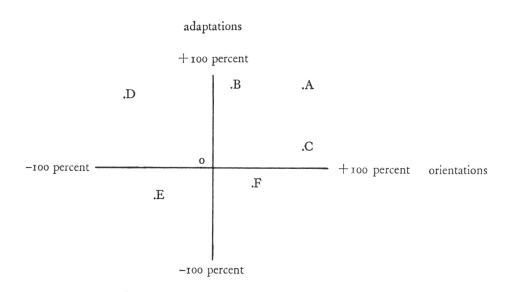

If the relationship or percentages of orientations to adaptation is 80 to 95 (A on the diagram above) we would regard the structure as highly integrated. We might assume that little coercion was used to gain compliance with directives if 80 percent of the actors felt that such compliance was proper. If the relationship, however, was 20 to 95 (B), we would assume that the structure was relatively nonintegrated and that adaptation to rules and directives was a function of the high cost of noncompliance. We would also suspect that the potential for a radical reduction in the percentage of adaptation was very likely. If the case was 95 to 20 (C), we might suspect that the performance of the structure was such that compliance was difficult. For example, 95 percent of the populace might agree that it was proper for government to tax all adults, but if there was no effective structure for collecting taxes, compliance would be difficult even for those "eager" to pay their taxes. If the predominant orientations were negative but adaptation still remained high (as in D), we would suspect that the high level of compliance resulted in the use of coercion and that the structure was potentially very unstable. Where both adaptations and orientations were negative (E), the structure involved clearly had no control —if this were a government we would expect either anarchy or control through some other competing structure. One might also find cases where positive orientations predominate but negative adaptations predominate (F). While I do not think that this is a very likely possibility, it is conceivable in a situation in which despite agreement on rules and principles, actors exhibited negative adaptation because of coercion from other quarters or when procedural problems made adaptation difficult or impossible.

In using a scale like this it is important to determine whether nonadaptation and/or nonorientation[25] are a consequence of ignorance about the political structure, a result of an inability to comply, or a representation of negative orientations or conscious efforts at negative adaptation. The first case would indicate the limits of penetration by the structure. The second would show a lack of means enabling adaptation. The third would indicate a feeling that some or all actions of the structure were not felt to be proper or that positive action was being taken to counter rules and directives. It is particularly important to differentiate these factors in cases where performance and penetration may be low, as in many underdeveloped nations where government penetration and influence is often limited. In such cases it is important to distinguish ignorance of government operations and inability to comply from negative adaptation and negative orientation toward the structure.

Indices need to be specified[26] in order to assess levels of adaptation and orientation. Do relevant actors generally obey rules and directives of the structure? For example, do members of the common market adjust their tariffs as scheduled? Or does the populace comply with directives of the national government?[27] In some cases the conclusions will be clear. Most people do (or do not) pay their taxes, carry out military obligations when asked, participate in national service, comply with rules about political activity, and so on. Most members of a regional body do (or do not) live up to the particulars of the agreements or treaties. Or most actors do feel that the structure *ought* to make such rules or issue such directives. In putting these tendencies in quantitative form we need to check responses to specific rules and directives or types of rules and directives.

In picking rules and directives for examination we need to include representative cases which will indicate responses to scope of authority of the political structure, methods used, and participants. What are the actors asked to do? How is it to be done? Who is to participate? Let us look at taxation as an example and consider orientations. Is taxation regarded as a legitimate activity of the political structure? Are the methods employed held to be proper? Is it felt that those who are directed to participate in paying taxes ought to par-

---

[25] I use the terms nonorientation and nonadaptation to refer to lack of orientations or adaptations toward a structure. This is distinct from the use of the word negative which refers to orientations and adaptations directed against or in opposition to the structure.

[26] I have not quantified indices of orientation or adaptation in this article, but I have suggested the types of things one would need to specify and identify in doing so.

[27] In some cases it may be easier to focus on nonadaptive behavior since in most nations most people comply with rules and directives where they know about them and can comply. Deane E. Neubauer and Lawrence D. Kastner have discussed the measurement of levels of compliance, in "The Study of Compliance Maintenance as a Strategy for Comparative Research," *World Politics*, July 1969 (Vol. 21, No. 4), pp. 629–640.

ticipate? We want to know about adaptation to directives about taxation. What percentage of the eligible actors pay their taxes? Is it done in the prescribed manner? How is nonadaptation manifested?

I have defined integration in terms of adaptation and orientation. Integration occurs when there is adaptation and orientation to a political structure. At any one time there is a level of integration which is likely to be different at another point in time or in another structure. Structure x at time t has a lower level of integration than structure y. Or structure x is more highly integrated at time t than at time t₁. In this sense the process of integration is indicated by the change in level of integration.[28]

Integration cannot be dealt with meaningfully except in terms of relative performance and this needs to be empirically exemplified. There is no "absolute" level of integration. This poses the question of cutoff or threshold. When is a structure integrated? This is a problem which I have not resolved. The easiest solution is to define a threshold—for example, all societies above the 60 percent level will be considered integrated. Or those who study integration might agree by convention that a structure is integrated when there are no negative orientations and nonadaptations. My own preference is to say that I do not know at what level it is meaningful to say that a structure is integrated. There is, no doubt, an empirical level of integration which is minimal for operation of political structures. I would prefer to set aside the delineation of threshold until a useful minimal level can be identified empirically on the basis of comparative study.

There are several advantages to formulating integration in terms of adaptation and orientation to a political structure, as opposed to some of the other possible conceptualizations. First, it helps us avoid confusing stability with integration, a confusion which is evident in much of the literature.[29] Yet it is very important that we be able to distinguish the two. For example, we might find two systems which are highly stable. In both cases individuals adapt to governmental rules and directives. In one system, however, the level of positive orientations is low while in the other it is high. The first system would be relatively nonintegrated although both systems were stable. We could presume that the system in which orientations were minimal or negative would have a high potential for instability.

The second advantage of this formulation of the term integration is that it lends itself to comparisons over time, at different levels of generalization, and between systems. The "unique" aspects of different types of political systems do not affect our ability to determine the extent of adaptation and orientation to that structure.

---

[28] This is not, however, the process of integration but a measure of it.

[29] We see this, for example, in work of Jacob and Teune, in Jacob and Toscano, pp. 4–8, and to some extent in the work of Huntington, in Welch.

Third, this definition gets away from the tendency to equate high levels of integration with high levels of modernization or industrialization. This is a particularly serious problem with many of the current conceptions of integration. One consequence of the emphasis in the literature on the extent of transactions, communications, and other exchanges as measures of integration has been the implication (at least) that integration was directly related to level of modernization.[30] While I suspect that these indices are useful in determining why integration occurs or is more likely to occur in one setting than in another, any highly modernized society or union of modernized structures will have a greater number of exchange relationships, a higher number of transactions between subunits, and a higher level of communication between units than a highly nonmodernized society or structure if only because of the requirements of the division of labor in highly modernized entities. While it is likely that these factors will be integrative in *many* cases, I would like to be able to deal with the case of a highly modernized entity which is not integrated or one which is in the process of becoming highly nonintegrated as well as the case of a nonmodernized entity (perhaps a traditional society) which is highly integrated. Focusing on the relationship of orientations to adaptations allows us to examine a variety of types of entities without confusing different levels of division of labor with levels of integration.

There are several difficulties related to this conceptualization of integration which should be noted. Any definition which involves orientations poses research problems. While it is not always necessary to do extensive (and expensive) survey research, as a variety of unobtrusive measures can often be used, some research on attitudes will usually be essential. When this requires interviews, the field worker faces serious difficulties in areas in which the research climate is hostile to interviews or the nature of the structure (e.g., military) precludes interviews. When large-scale interviewing is required, one may lack the human and technical capacities necessary for reliable interviews or surveys (as may be the case in many nonmodernized societies). These problems pose serious difficulties for some research interests. On the whole, however, I think they can be dealt with if one is self conscious about the limitations.

This formulation as it now stands does not take into consideration the question of the scope of integration. Using the present conceptualization, a system which gave only one directive that received 90 percent compliance and 85 percent positive orientation would be ranked at the same level as a society which had the same percentage of adaptations and orientations but gave 100 directives. While there is a point at which the question of number of directives and rules will be a function of the extent of division of labor, this is not al-

---

[30] This focus is exemplified in much of the work of Karl Deutsch. Most of those who focus on exchange relationships are dealing with relatively modernized societies and thus encounter this difficulty only if they make comparisons with nonmodernized societies.

ways the case. It is clear that one needs to differentiate between entities in which integration occurs within a limited scope and those in which the scope of action is very broad. One may also need to establish some minimal scope of actions if the relationship between orientations and adaptations is to be at all meaningful.

Related to the question of scope is another problem which is worth noting, regarding what, for want of a better term, I will call the "difficulty" of integration. Some directives will be harder than others and some changes in political structures will require substantial adjustments of individual orientations toward the structure while others will pose few difficulties. The present formulation does not lend itself to this distinction—e.g., how do we distinguish structures which have high levels of adaptation but are too timid to do things which those who govern the structures believe are essential (or draw back after directives have been given and do not enforce them because of public opposition) from structures which have equally high levels of adaptation but make greater demands or require more extensive adaptations. This problem does not pose serious definitional difficulties since, I suspect, its occurrence usually will be reflected in different levels or orientations or (in a few cases) adaptations. It is, however, a problem to which the researcher should be attuned in trying to understand both orientations and government capabilities.

The Congress Party in India has been timid in most of its demands on the populace. In general, it does not push because it wants to win the next election with a large margin. On the other hand, when a regime does insist that the populace carry out certain directives which it feels are essential to development, national defense, safeguarding the economy, we might find that the level of integration actually falls, at least in the short run. Long-run effects will depend in part on the success of the effort. In short, then, high levels of adaptation (and in some cases even orientations, although I think that is not usually the case) may illustrate a degree of failure in performance, an inability to induce (and convince) the populace that certain efforts are needed.

I have suggested that the conceptualization put forth here has utility for international as well as national studies and in some respects gets at an important factor often neglected by international studies—namely, orientations. The orientations of relevant actors provide clues to shifts in actions and make our measure of degree of integration more sensitive. Nations may maintain minimal adherence to the rules and directives of a regional union while their orientations toward the union shift radically. We saw this in the French posture toward the North Atlantic Treaty Organization (NATO) in the early and mid-1960's. For a time minimal compliance to agreements was maintained. A shift in attachment to NATO, however, was expressed initially through the growing number of attacks on NATO by President Charles de Gaulle and other French officials. This public expression of dissatisfaction with NATO preceded the French refusal to comply with many of the provisions of the NATO alliance.

I have devoted most of this section of the article to the conceptualization of integration and the determination of levels of integrations since this aspect of integration studies has been the basis for many of our problems and at the same time has often been seriously neglected. I have emphasized the need for a single conceptualization of integration since it is desirable that we be able to identify relative degrees of integration to allow us to go on to the *important questions* of *why* levels are different and *how* integration occurs. These questions can only be dealt with successfully if we know what we are talking about when we refer to integration. I am suggesting that a useful research strategy would be to say, "Let us call 'this' integration," and then proceed to determine levels of integration. Given different levels of integration, how did they get that way? I have suggested a conceptualization which might be used for both regional and national studies. Whether or not one accepts this definition as the "best" conceptualization, however, is less important than that we identify the process clearly so that we can profit from each other's efforts and move on to the more interesting problems.

III.

Having spelled out some rough notions about identifying integration and determining its level in a given context, I would like to suggest some areas for special focus based primarily on work on national integration and make some comments about several variables affecting level and extent of integration. How do societies become integrated? Why do some attempts fail? What factors account for the varying levels of integration? Can we be predictive about the future? Can we determine the direction of integration in a given case? Any success in answering these questions will depend on our ability to specify variables which affect integration. We have a good deal of material to draw from in the studies of national and international integration. This material is a good starting point for trying to isolate the important variables from the host of available possibilities—e.g., homogeneity, degree of political participation, goals, mobilization, proximity, exchange relationships, governmental effectiveness, autonomy, common experience, pluralism, size of units, style, ideological stances, degree of institutionalization, and so on. At this juncture the studies of national integration and my work to date are too subjective to substantiate authoritative judgments (although I have some guesses) about which are "key" variables or what additional variables might be more useful. I would like to make some comments on several variables for which there is some suggestive material in work on national integration, to note some areas for further research, and to discuss some of the ways in which this material may be useful for studies of international integration.

One of the fundamental concerns of studies of national integration (as noted in section I) has been the relationship between political structures and political integration. It has been asserted by both politicians and scholars[31] that there are certain types of political parties and structures of political competition which facilitate political integration (and usually other processes such as modernization). There is a great deal of evidence that "mass parties" have fostered integration, that they have created a new "ethnic definition"[32] with the nation representing the new community. As one author put it (perhaps a bit strongly in retrospect) when discussing mass parties in French-speaking West Africa,

> they and their affiliates were interested in everything from the cradle to the grave—in birth, initiation, religion, marriage, divorce, dancing, song, plays, feuds, debts, land, migration, death, public order—not only in electoral success.[33]

In fact most political parties (and their functional equivalents) in Africa have been integrative even when they have differed markedly in ideology. Disputes have seldom concerned the viability of the geographic entity but rather who should govern it.[34]

It is within the context of the one-party state that the greatest claims have been made for the integrative consequences of political structures. Those who would introduce one-party states argue that political competition fosters individual, regional, and ethnic tensions whereas a one-party state fosters unity.[35] The evidence is not at all clear on this point.[36] There have been a number of single-party or one-party dominant states, such as Liberia or Zanzibar (prior to 1954), in which the one-party state was not integrative but rather facilitated the perpetuation of privileges of a particular segment of the population. On the other hand, where the party has been effectively populist, as in Tanzania, in Mali under Modibo Keita, and to some extent in Guinea, the integrative consequences have been marked.

---

[31] Some of these assertions are summarized in the conclusions in Coleman and Rosberg.

[32] Apter, p. 375.

[33] Morgenthau, p. 341.

[34] See my "Predominantly Politically Oriented Organizations in Sierra Leone and Senegal" (Ph.D. dissertation, Princeton University, 1968), chapter 14.

[35] There are numerous government statements and "white papers" which make this point. Speaking on the need to introduce a "democratic one-party state" in Sierra Leone, the former prime minister, Albert Margai, argued:

> When you go to the Provinces, to some of the villages, you will find that the opposition is trying everywhere to divide the people. By a campaign of lies, they have put the people against the Chiefs and the Chiefs against the people. What benefit do we get from such disunity? When it comes to development and the people select a project, and A.P.C. comes and turns their minds from it by false propaganda. And so the country suffers.

"The Honourable Prime Minister's Address on the Introduction of a Democratic One-Party State in Sierra Leone," delivered at the Queen Elizabeth II Playing Field, January 28, 1966, mimeographed by Ministry of Information, pp. 7–8.

[36] For example, Myron Weiner argues that the competition of groups is a useful integrative force as long as no group predominates in his *The Politics of Scarcity: Public Pressure and Political Response in India* (Chicago: University of Chicago Press, 1962), chapter 3.

There is a related question regarding political structure and integration which is more directly applicable to the focus of most international studies—the effect of centralization (and decentralization) on integration. Implicit (or explicit) in most arguments supporting the notion that mass parties and one-party states foster integration is the assumption that their success as integrative mechanisms is due in part to the fact that they are (or can be) highly centralized political structures. It is assumed that centralized political structures break down parochial loyalties and lead to political integration. If this contention is verified (and there is a good deal of conventional wisdom which lends support) it has important implications for international integration. Some caution is in order, however, as, at least under some conditions, highly centralized political structures seem to have nonintegrative consequence,[37] as La-Palombara has suggested in the case of Italy.

Confusion about the effect of political structures on integration may indicate that the emphasis on the relationship between structures and integration is misplaced. Nonetheless, the nature of the evidence to date would suggest that it is a "relationship" which needs rethinking and that one should be aware of its implicit assumption in much of our "conventional wisdom."

One of the fundamental concerns of studies of national integration is the attitude of the populace toward the government. Do people conceive of themselves as members of the state? Do they identify with the government? One is concerned not only with attitudes of the populace as a whole toward the government[38] but with particular subsections of the populace.[39] If particular ethnic groups have negative orientations toward the government or major government policies, the consequences may radically affect the level of integration, as it did in Nigeria where the tensions between Ibos and non-Ibos led to civil war. A substantial level of low or negative orientations toward a political structure in the bureaucracy among traditional leaders or within the military will affect integration out of proportion to the numbers of individuals involved.

[37] LaPalombara, in Pye and Verba.

[38] An extensive effort to examine attitudes cross-nationally was made by Almond and Verba. More subjective assessments are found, however, in much of the literature on nationalism. See Thomas Hodgkin, *Nationalism in Colonial Africa* (New York: New York University Press, 1957); Rupert Emerson, *From Empire to Nation: The Rise to Self-Assertion of Asian and African Peoples* (Cambridge, Mass: Harvard University Press, 1960), who describes (p. 95) the emergence of the nation and the attitudes which this involves:

> The nation is a community of people who feel that they belong together in the double sense that they share deeply significant elements of a common heritage and that they have a common destiny for the future. In the contemporary world the nation is for great portions of mankind the community with which men most intensely and most unconditionally identify themselves, even to the extent of being prepared to lay down their lives for it, however deeply they may differ among themselves on other issues.

[39] Most of the literature on development has focused on political "elites." We see this in Coleman and Rosberg; David E. Apter, *The Political Kingdom in Uganda: A Study in Bureaucratic Nationalism* (Princeton, N.J: Princeton University Press, 1961); and Lucian W. Pye, *Politics, Personality, and Nation Building: Burma's Search for Identity* (New Haven, Conn: Yale University Press, 1962).

In studies of international integration scholars normally think in terms of "relevant" actors, that is, the state is often personified as the "relevant" actor or those who act for the state in official capacities are conceived of as the "relevant" actors. As the consequences of international agreements coordinating or merging certain aspects of policy affect the populace of one or more of the participating nations, the question of subsystem loyalty becomes more important. Similarly, the attitudes of larger percentages of the populations of each participating nation become relevant. Tariff adjustments, for example, in one nation will have different political costs than in another. Where domestic costs are deemed too high, regional integration will be affected. Policies of the European Economic Community (EEC) have sparked considerable popular discontent in some member nations, for example, with agricultural policy. Public hostility toward government plans for international integration, as expressed in the United Kingdom regarding the proposed entry into the Common Market, is indicative of the importance of subsystem loyalties to integration. While it may be useful to conceive of the "relevant" actors as those in the apparatus of government and to assume that politically significant subsystem preferences will be expressed in actions of the national actors, knowledge of subsystem preferences is important both to understanding international integration and predicting the future course of regional or international entities.

In examining both national and regional integration we need to do some rethinking about subsystem identity. We have generally assumed that it impeded integration, that ethnicity, caste, regional attachments, and other particularistic loyalties made integration more difficult.[40] Structures that were basically homogeneous were felt to have a greatly heightened potential for integration. There is a good deal of evidence that under certain conditions this is true. Highly particularistic loyalties exist, however, in most societies, federations, and unions. Many of these are highly integrated. Has this level of integration been achieved in spite of particularistic loyalties or have they facilitated integration? It seems to me that to argue that subnational integration at a high level is subversive to national integration, or the opposite, is to miss the import of the wide variation in cases on both sides. I think it is evident that there are examples of both. What is important is to try to isolate the reasons why these seemingly contradictory processes sometimes result in integration and sometimes in nonintegrative action.

Particularistic loyalties often aid the integrative process. Overt attempts to submerge particularistic loyalties will be likely to weaken adaptation and orientation toward government. Compliance with directives and orientations

---

[40] These assumptions are expressed by political leaders in resolutions on tribalism, religious separation, and traditional institutions passed at the close of the All African People's Conference in Accra, December 5–13, 1958. They are also discussed in Clifford Gertz, "The Integrative Revolution: Primordial Sentiments and Civil Politics in the New States," in Gertz (ed.), *Old Societies and New States* (London: Free Press, 1963).

toward a governmental structure need not conflict with subsystem loyalties. In fact, acceptance of directives by spokesmen for subsystems can strengthen adaptations and orientations where there are closer interactions in the subsystem than within the total system. The subsystem in such cases serves as a socializing agent.

Immanuel Wallerstein has found that ethnic loyalties facilitate integration into urban communities.[41] Myron Weiner has suggested that subnational loyalties are inevitable in diverse societies. The danger is not that these loyalties are subversive to the solution of national problems but that authoritarian efforts will be used to eliminate them.[42]

In African cities we find new types of "tribal" groupings being established. These can be important in aiding the integration of individuals into urban society. An individual still has a framework within which to work wherein his experience is somewhat in line with his expectations—e.g., the ethnic association, the *compin,* and so on. This grouping also serves to inculcate new ideas and values, to help him adjust to the new environment, its laws and its customs. The same types of integrative actions occur in many groupings. They serve as instruments aiding adaptation and orientation to a wide variety of rules and directives of the national government.

It is often argued that a higher level of national integration could be achieved if subsystem loyalties were eliminated. That is, one seeking a high level of integration may feel that it is "better" to destroy these loyalties despite some short-term costs. Historically, we have numerous examples of such efforts. I suggest, however, that in many cases the elimination of such loyalties and the enforcement of a broader adaptation to national authority cannot be realized short of civil war, if at all (e.g., the Nigerian conflict)—or at least not without a very high cost in repression. This would be equally true of the southern part of the United States. Furthermore, there is a good deal of evidence that these subsystem loyalties aid rather than hinder integration. The recent work by Richard Fox[43] concerning the integrative force of caste "*varna* schemes" is also suggestive in this vein.

The tensions between system and subsystem identity and loyalties need to be explored more fully. Some interesting related work has been done on congruence of authority,[44] and some suggestive material exists in the literature on federalism[45] and ethnicity.[46] It is becoming increasingly clear that integra-

[41] Immanuel Wallerstein, "Ethnicity and National Integration in West Africa," in Harry Eckstein and David Apter (ed.), *Comparative Politics* (Glencoe, Ill: Free Press, 1963), pp. 665–670.

[42] Myron Weiner, "India: Two Political Cultures," in Pye and Verba, pp. 199–244.

[43] Richard G. Fox, "*Varna* Schemes and Ideological Integration in Indian Society," *Comparative Studies in Society and History,* January 1969 (Vol. 11, No. 1), pp. 27–45.

[44] Harry Eckstein, "Theory of Stable Democracy," in Harry Eckstein, *Division and Cohesion in Democracy: A Study of Norway* (Princeton, N.J: Princeton University Press, 1966).

[45] See, for example, William H. Riker, *Federalism: Origin, Operation, Significance* (Boston: Little, Brown and Co., 1964).

tion within a particular geographic entity, in particular national or international integration, is the product of multiple attachments. The orientations and adaptations of individuals are affected by a variety of particularistic loyalties to other structures. In a large number of cases these foci reinforce one another. Where they conflict, the important factor becomes *which* predominate where the political structure in question is concerned.

Another major focus of national studies is governmental outputs. What benefits accrue to a population as a result of government action? What is the payoff for integration? Do these benefits affect the level of integration? While the relationships between integration and government outputs have not been clearly specified or systematically examined, a great deal of speculation has resulted from national studies.[47] Nonetheless, this relationship should also be an important one in regional studies. Some major steps have been taken recently to examine outputs in research on regional integration.[48] A more concerted effort to evaluate the impact of system outputs should greatly enhance the work on both national and international integration.

As structures become more complex, it is increasingly difficult to isolate the effect of individual outputs. It is much less difficult to evaluate the general outputs of the structure. National studies have mustered a great deal of evidence suggesting that there is a strong relationship between the benefits deemed to be outputs of a structure and integration. These may range from substantive outputs such as money, land, and health care to symbolic outputs such as prestige. Some outputs will be viewed as open-ended (e.g., maintaining order), others will be single-action outputs (e.g., independence). These distinctions are important. As one old villager in Ghana noted when asked about the benefits of national integration:

> it was useful for independence, but now that the tribes have come together to free the country from foreign domination, it is time to revert to the individual tribes as the fundamental authority.

This example also illustrates an important point, mentioned earlier, about direction of integration. Integration is not a one-way process. We have usually focused on those factors which strengthen integration (or sought to identify measures which would). We need to pay attention to the process of disintegration.

[46] See Pierre L. Van den Berghe (ed.), *Africa: Social Problems of Change and Conflict* (San Francisco, Calif: Chandler, 1965); Merran Fraenkel, *Tribe and Class in Monrovia* (London: Oxford University Press, 1964), Crawford Young, *Politics in the Congo* (Princeton, N.J: Princeton University Press, 1965).

[47] The political party literature assumes a high correspondence between promises, performance, and integration. See Coleman and Rosberg; Hodgkin; and Morgenthau. In several studies the limited success of national integration is asserted as a consequence of the ineffectiveness of government performance. See Aristide R. Zolberg, *Creating Political Order: The Party-States of West Africa* (Chicago: Rand McNally & Co., 1966) and Pye.

[48] Leon Lindberg and Stuart Scheingold, *Europe's Would-Be Polity: Patterns of Change in the European Community* (Englewood Cliffs, N.J: Prentice-Hall, 1970).

Another area in which more work is needed is in the examination of the relationship of types of political participation to integration. We have numerous examples of cases in which participation seems to have been nonintegrative, others in which it was integrative, and some in which not much seems to have changed as a result of participation. What we need to do is isolate the conditions which affect each type of case.

A few examples of the integrative consequences of participation and mobilization follow from some recent research I carried out in Senegal and Sierra Leone. In the process of seeking support political organizations carry out integrative functions as they recruit members and/or educate them. Both the All People's Congress and the Sierra Leone People's Party spent a great deal of time during the 1967 election campaign explaining voting procedures, methods of registration, the importance of putting the ballot in the box rather than on top of it, the significance of a vote for the party, and in the case of the All People's Congress in particular, warning supporters against illegal practices which would invalidate the results. All of the election speeches which I witnessed during the campaign devoted at least half of the time to explaining what the national government was, how the party fit into all this, how national government was related to local government, and what the rights, duties, and obligations of the men and women of Sierra Leone were.

What is particularly impressive in African politics, given the number of political organizations which have competed for power in the last 25 years, is that most of the organizations supported the existing political system despite a wide range of differences in goals.

Efforts at political mobilization had similar consequences. In Senegal and Sierra Leone, for example, from the late 1930's a growing discontent was expressed about the ability of the masses to participate in institutional structures. As more effective political organizations took up this cry, mobilized extensive and intensive support, and became part of the political structure, this sense of frustration began to diminish. Rapid mobilization can foster an intense commitment over a long period of time. While one must wait a number of years to see if this has in fact resulted in the institutionalization of these patterns, it is the fact that these organizations seem to be meeting needs deemed to be important by the masses rather than the speed with which it is done that results in the legitimation and acceptance of political organizations and the political system on grounds other than particularistic loyalties or as a consequence of coercion.

In this short piece I have suggested that there are many areas of congruence between studies of national and international integration and that, at least as a research strategy, it is useful to conceptualize integration in common terms. I have tried to show some of the areas in which the foci of national and international studies differ and to note areas of convergence. I have discussed some areas in which national studies are suggestive for work on regional integration. While we need to be aware of discontinuities in the foci of national and international studies, I suspect that we are more likely to develop a sound theoretical base for understanding integration through efforts which are easily translatable and thus build on our collective successes.

9

Theory and Practice of Regional Integration:

The Case of Comecon

ANDRZEJ KORBONSKI

I. INTRODUCTION

IT is generally recognized that the last decade or so witnessed a proliferation of studies dealing with different aspects of regional integration. While most of them discussed the origin and history of various international organizations, some, especially those of a more recent vintage, ventured into the thicket of theory building in an effort to engage eventually in some kind of comparative analysis.

Up to this time the focus of research on integration was clearly centered on Western Europe which offered not only a wealth of relevant data but also afforded the opportunity to test various hypotheses developed in the course of multifaceted attempts at theorizing. It was inevitable that sooner or later the deeply rooted yearning for comparative analysis would lead to research on regional integration in other parts of the world, mainly in Africa and Latin America. To be sure, this horizontal expansion was dictated by more considerations than merely simple desire for comparative study. The widespread dissatisfaction with the ethnocentric, Western Europe-oriented research which made its appearance earlier in the field of comparative politics was bound to spill over into other fields, including that of international relations. The same applied to the process of "model building" which utilized almost exclusively the Western European experience. Finally, the growing amount of available data forthcoming from other areas permitted the initiation of research in non-European integration processes similar to that done previously for Western Europe.

ANDRZEJ KORBONSKI is associate professor of political science at the University of California, Los Angeles.

One notable omission in this impressive array of integration studies was Eastern Europe, despite the fact that, formally at least, integration efforts there began twenty years ago and thus largely antedated similar attempts elsewhere. Whether one looks at the recently published anthologies of regional integration studies, at the volumes of periodicals devoted wholly or partially to research in that particular area, or at individual articles claiming to present a comprehensive picture of regional integration throughout the world, one is struck not only by the relative dearth of studies analyzing the Eastern European situation but also by the almost total lack of reference to that situation in works concerned with constructing a universalistic paradigm of integration processes. When and where such references do crop up they are usually either somewhat superficial or are treated as deviations from the norm due to the peculiar character of Communist politics.

There are, indeed, a number of reasons for treating Eastern Europe as a special case. First of all, it is probably correct to say that until very recently the so-called Communist studies could be described as parochial and traditional. Protected by the great wall of "special expertise" from the modernizing tendencies in various fields of social sciences and basking in the light of "expert knowledge" which implied that ordinary research methodology did not apply to their areas of interest, Sovietologists have been rapidly falling behind those of their counterparts in other fields of political science who did not claim such privileges. As a result, Communist studies, including those concerned with Eastern Europe, have over the years become cliché-ridden, stagnant, and plainly dull.

Within the subfield of Communist international relations the study of integration—political, economic, and military—was clearly the villain of the piece. It is true that various books and monographs devoted chapters to the problem of integration in Eastern Europe, but these were chiefly characterized by their concentration on historical analysis, on legal and institutional arrangements, and on policy "outputs," with little or no attention being paid to "inputs" and to decisionmaking processes. Above all, there was a total absence of even the slightest attempt at postulating working hypotheses which might lead to broader generalizations.

This absence of a theoretical bent could be excused on several grounds. To begin with, for a long time the concept of integration in Eastern Europe was firmly rooted in the "model" of the Stalinist monolith so ably presented by Zbigniew Brzezinski who applied to it the notion of "formal" and "informal" linkages.[1] Just as it took a number of years before political scientists began to question the validity of the totalitarian syndrome for the study of Communist internal politics, a similarly long interval elapsed before the idea of the mono-

---

[1] Zbigniew Brzezinski, *The Soviet Bloc: Unity and Conflict* (Rev. and enl. ed; Cambridge, Mass: Harvard University Press, 1967), pp. 107–124.

lith was replaced (with considerable hesitation) by the concept of the "Socialist commonwealth." It should be added, however, that conceptually the latter was never as fully elaborated as its predecessor, and the 1968 events in Eastern Europe, which threw a monkey wrench into a number of assumptions and near-dogmas, probably delayed indefinitely the task of creating a new model of interstate relations in Eastern Europe.

The transformation of the Moscow-controlled colonial empire into a much looser configuration necessitated the revival of the "formal" linkages which hitherto have been overshadowed by the "informal" ones. This meant that the Council of Mutual Economic Assistance (Comecon) had to be taken out of mothballs and elevated to the status of one of the major props supporting the new edifice. This rather sudden resurrection of the previously dormant Stalinist creation remained largely unnoticed until the early 1960's when its existence was finally rediscovered by both Western and Eastern social scientists. Paradoxically, it was precisely at that time that Comecon, having reached its apogee, entered a stage of crisis from which it has still not fully recovered.

The rediscovery of Comecon was followed shortly thereafter in both the East and the West by a number of monographs and studies. As was to be expected, Communist and particularly Soviet writers tended as a rule to glorify the achievements of the organization, pointing to various statistical indicators that showed the growth of intrabloc trade, industrial cooperation, and the like.[2] The Western studies were essentially historical monographs attempting for the first time to get a clear picture of what had been happening in the realm of East European economic integration.[3] As such they performed the indispensable task of accumulating basic factual economic data which filled a number of empty boxes then in existence. Once the boxes were filled they became transformed into an assemblage of building blocks ready to be used by someone either to construct some kind of a theoretical edifice or at least to come up with a series of hypotheses which might be empirically tested. It should be kept in mind, however, that the boxes and the blocks were of economic hue

---

[2] A. D. Stupov (ed.), *Ekonomicheskoe sotrudnichestvo i vzaiimopomoshch sotsialisticheskikh stran* (Moscow: Izdatelstvo Akademii nauk SSSR, 1962); N. Faddeev, *Sovet ekonomicheskoi vzaiimopomoshchi* (Moscow: Ekonomika, 1964); L. Ciamaga, *Od wspolpracy do integracji: Zarys organizacji i dzialalnosci RWPG w latach 1949–1964* (Warsaw: Ksiazka i wiedza, 1965); A. Bodnar, *Rozwoj gospodarczy krajow RWPG i problemy miedzynarodowego podzialu pracy* (Warsaw: Panstwowe wydawnictwo ekonomiczne, 1966); J. Novozamsky, *Vyrovnavani ekonomicke urovne zemi RVHP* (Prague: Nakladatelstvi politicke literatury, 1964); Bohuslav Maly, *Mezinarodni ekonomicke vztahy ve spolecenstvi RVHP* (Prague: Svoboda, 1968).

[3] Andrzej Korbonski, "Comecon," *International Conciliation,* September 1964 (No. 549); I. Agoston, *Le marché commun communiste: Principes et pratique du COMECON* (2nd ed; Geneva: Droz, 1965); Heinz Köhler, *Economic Integration in the Soviet Bloc* (New York: Frederick A. Praeger, 1965); Michael Kaser, *Comecon: Integration Problems of the Planned Economies* (2nd ed; London: Oxford University Press [under the auspices of the Royal Institute of International Affairs], 1967); Michael Kaser (ed.), *Economic Development for Eastern Europe: Proceedings of a Conference Held by the International Economics Association* (London: Macmillan & Co., 1968), pp. 125–159; P. J. D. Wiles, *Communist International Economics* (Oxford: Blackwell, 1968), pp. 306–342.

only. While they enlarged our horizon significantly, they still fell far short of the kind of data available in other regions.

Not that useful studies were totally absent. By and large, however, they were still confined mostly to the collection of facts—thus extending simply in time the work initiated in the early 1960's. As additional data became available, it was possible to probe more deeply into such problems as trade patterns, trade composition, price discrimination, balance-of-payments difficulties, and so on.[4] Despite these refinements the research was still predominantly descriptive. Relatively little effort was devoted to analyzing various processes connected with integration in the area and where such analysis made its infrequent appearance it was confined to a discussion of narrow, discrete problems such as currency convertibility or industrial specialization. All of these were analyzed in a vacuum created by the absence of even a rudimentary theoretical framework.

There was still another reason for the lack of progress in advancing the state of knowledge in this particular area. It is one which, interestingly enough, has up until now delayed such progress but is likely in the near future to advance it significantly. It appears that in the most recent period the emphasis in Communist studies began to shift in a twofold fashion: first, from the international to the domestic arena; and second, within the domestic sphere, from concentration on the "total" domestic system to an analysis of its component parts in both the static and the dynamic contexts. The first approach, as pointed out earlier, was due to the need to elaborate further the new concept of interstate relations in the bloc by starting, so to speak, from the bottom up. The second came about through the attempts to replace the totalitarian syndrome with other concepts.[5]

A similar change seems to have been occurring in the field of East European economics. On the one hand, after years of looking at the "total" process of economic development in the area, the economists began to pay greater attention to microeconomic problems. At roughly the same time the appearance of economic reforms in a number of East European countries forced the Western (and Eastern) economists to concentrate less on total performance of the entire system and more on its components and processes such as the behavior of enterprises, managerial and bureaucratic decisionmaking, interplay of economic groups, etc.[6]

Thus what we have been witnessing in the most recent period was a sort of

---

[4] For a good example see Alan A. Brown and Egan Neuberger (ed.), *International Trade and Central Planning: An Analysis of Economic Interactions* (Berkeley: University of California Press, 1968).

[5] A. G. Meyer, "USSR Incorporated," *Slavic Review*, October 1961 (Vol. 20, No. 3), pp. 369–376, and "The Comparative Study of Communist Political Systems," *Slavic Review*, March 1967 (Vol. 21, No. 1), pp. 3–12; H. G. Skilling, "Interest Groups and Communist Politics," *World Politics*, April 1966 (Vol. 18, No. 3), pp. 435–451.

[6] A recent example is Gregory Grossman (ed.), *Money and Plan: Financial Aspects of East European Economic Reforms* (Berkeley: University of California Press, 1968).

convergence between political scientists and economists in the field of East European studies and a move from "high" to "low" in politics and economics. Such an important step is sooner or later bound to make its impression on the study of East European integration, for it could provide the missing link without which it would be virtually impossible not only to utilize integration paradigms constructed earlier but also to formulate hypotheses that could be tested. Much remains to be done and many empty or half-empty boxes have yet to be filled, but there is little doubt that a threshold has been reached.

Thus for the first time since the beginning of integration efforts in Eastern Europe there are enough building blocks for us to erect if not a model then at least a paradigm which would explain and possibly even forecast integration processes in the area. In addition to statistical data and a considerable amount of macroeconomic information we are beginning to accumulate an impressive reservoir of micropolitical and economic data. At long last a kind of parity with other parts of the world is being reached.

II. The Concept of Integration: The Case of Eastern Europe

The confusion surrounding the concept of integration has been pointed out by a number of writers, including those in this volume.[7] Most of the generally accepted definitions run in terms of a process of bringing or combining parts into a whole, with the final product or dependent variable being gradually less and less rigidly determined. The three conventional pretheories of, or approaches to, integration—the federalist, the communications, and the neofunctionalist—have been rather thoroughly ventilated, amended, reformulated, and adjusted in the span of the last fifteen years or so. A number of models, paradigms, and syndromes have been constructed with varying degrees of explanatory and predictive success, always with an eye on their universal applicability to all systems.

As far as Eastern Europe is concerned, integration can be looked upon in a variety of ways. Since, as suggested by Philippe Schmitter, "the integration of formally independent political entities engages—in the contemporary world —basically the same variables and processes,"[8] the integrative processes in Eastern Europe should lend themselves to the kind of analysis practiced with regard to other regions. However, before such a task can be attempted one is compelled either to choose one of the available definitions of integration or to develop a new one in order to achieve the three major objectives: first, to be able to test the actual progress of integration with respect to the "ideal" final model; second, to be able to forecast the future of integration in the area; and third, to attempt some comparison with integration processes elsewhere in the world.

[7] Fred N. Hayward in this volume.
[8] Philippe C. Schmitter in this volume, p. 233.

At the risk of proliferating the number of definitions an adaptation of Morton Kaplan's definition of integration is suggested here as the most suitable and convenient for the East European context. Thus integration is defined as "a process by which separate systems develop a common framework which allows for the common pursuit of some goals and common implementation of some policies."[9]

Since "the real test of a definition is its utility for research and theorizing,"[10] it appears that there are several advantages associated with this particular definition. To begin with, it permits us to approach integration from a variety of viewpoints: political, economic, military, and ideological without creating a presumption favoring any one of them. It is also a "parsimonious" definition in the sense that it does not require the presence of such ambiguous concepts or conditions as "common behavioral norms," "sense of community," "mutual obligations," "collective capacity," or "authoritative allocation of values," all of which are subject to controversy and are difficult if not impossible to operationalize. This definition also seems "neutral" in the geographic and systemic sense, enabling us to compare integration processes in various regional subsystems regardless of location and regardless of respective levels of political and economic development. Finally, by being "low-key" it permits us to study integration processes in the absence of significant data which otherwise might reduce or even eliminate the chances of conducting meaningful research. Hence this definition appears particularly suitable for the study of integration in Eastern Europe.

The focus of this article is the economic integration in Communist Europe. Restricting the discussion to the economic sphere was to some extent motivated by the suggestion advanced recently by Joseph Nye who felt that the disaggregation of the concept of integration would avoid a number of pitfalls associated with many of the usages currently in vogue.[11] The point is well taken even though it carries some pitfalls of its own.

It is clear that the distinction between "economic" and "political" or between "economic" and "ideological" is nebulous in all systems and especially so in the Communist nations. The separation of economic from political integration in this case is therefore highly artificial and hence unsatisfactory. There are, however, at least two good reasons for limiting the discussion to the economic arena. First of all, there is the problem of data. While economic statistics are now not only relatively plentiful but also, by and large, reliable, the same does not hold true for the political sphere. Furthermore, it is much easier to gather information with respect to national economic policies or strategies of

---

[9] Morton A. Kaplan, *System and Process in International Politics* (New York: John Wiley & Sons, 1957), p. 98.

[10] Fred M. Hayward, draft revision of the paper prepared for the Conference on Regional Integration.

[11] Joseph S. Nye, "Comparative Regional Integration: Concept and Measurement," *International Organization,* Autumn 1968 (Vol. 22, No. 4), p. 858.

development than with regard to political decisionmaking on a national or bloc-wide basis. The perils of kremlinology are too well known to be discussed here. Finally, economic integration in Eastern Europe today can be studied more or less "rationally" with reference to the "objective" economic laws or theories whereas political integration in the area cannot be quite divorced from either the leading personalities or ideology, or both.

In a similar fashion political integration cannot be fully separated from military integration. Is the Warsaw Treaty Organization (WTO) mainly a political or a security community? Applying our definition to the military sector once again confirms the suitability of that definition for the study of various types of integration in Eastern Europe—viz., as a separate defense system developing a common framework (the Warsaw Treaty) for the common pursuit of at least one goal (defense against the West) and common implementation of some policies (training, weapons standardization, unified command structure). The fact that, as suggested elsewhere, the WTO cannot easily be conceived as either a political or a defense community, its greatest value being most likely a symbolic one, does not detract from the definition.[12]

Thus economic integration in Eastern Europe has been for all practical purposes a multidimensional process in which economics plays a major role but in which political, military, and ideological considerations intervene with varying intensity at various stages.

Here again the selected definition offers some advantages. The conventional definitions of economic integration as applied to Eastern Europe are clearly unsatisfactory. As pointed out by Nye, the textbook definition commonly in use has little relevance to planned economies.[13] According to J. M. Montias,

> few subjects of interest to economists are as soft, or "mushy," as the economics of East European integration; there is no recognized methodology for analyzing problems in this field; the problems themselves have not been rigorously formulated or put down in precise language.[14]

In order to get out of the definitional impasse and for the purpose of providing some standard for comparison with various integration systems, Nye postulated two subtypes of economic integration: trade integration measured by the proportion of intraregional exports to total exports of the region; and services integration measured by the share of the expenditure on jointly administered services in gross national product of the region.[15] Regarding the latter indicator, its usefulness for Eastern Europe is practically nil because of nonavailability of data. The former measure, though easily derived, can be highly misleading and can actually distort the real extent of integration.

---

[12] Andrzej Korbonski, "The Warsaw Pact," *International Conciliation*, May 1969 (No. 573), pp. 67–73.

[13] Nye, *International Organization*, Vol. 22, No. 4, p. 861.

[14] J. M. Montias, "Obstacles to the Economic Integration of Eastern Europe," *Studies in Comparative Communism*, July–October 1969 (Vol. 2, Nos. 3–4), p. 38.

[15] Nye, *International Organization*, Vol. 22, No. 4, p. 861.

If it could be assumed that the relative increase in the volume of Comecon trade was the outcome of the recommendations made by some common institutions, then that particular index could be considered as a more or less correct measure of economic integration in the region. It appears, however, that this was not quite the case. Montias has shown, for example, that the fluctuations in the volume of intra-Comecon trade hinged primarily on the changes in the rates of growth and the economic policies of member countries rather than on their mutually concerted actions.[16] It is also true that the strategic embargo imposed by the West at the outset of the Cold War was greatly responsible for the increase in intra-Comecon trade. The growing differentiation of the economic systems within Comecon clearly played a role as well. Consequently, the trade indicator as a true measure of economic integration must be considered as less than perfect, especially when treated in isolation.

In light of this, economic integration in Eastern Europe will be defined as a process by which separate economic systems have been developing a common framework—the Council of Mutual Economic Assistance—for the common pursuit of some economic goals (industrialization and a high rate of economic growth) and for the common implementation of some economic policies (coordination of national plans, specialization in production, and maximization of regional trade). Obviously, other goals and policies could be considered here but the history of Comecon seems to indicate that these were agreed upon if not by all then at least by the majority of the member states.[17]

What follows is an examination of various problems connected with the progress of economic integration in Eastern Europe since 1964. The choice of this year is not accidental. It coincides with the ouster of Premier Nikita Khrushchev whose fortunes seemed to be closely tied with those of Comecon. Khrushchev was, in a sense, an evil genius in the affairs of the organization, for it was he who in fact put Comecon on the map in the mid-1950's and it was also he who contributed largely to its decline in the early 1960's. The analysis that follows will concentrate on the reasons for that decline.

III. The Comecon Experience: Economic Factors

One possible way of analyzing the progress of economic integration in Eastern Europe would be to look at Comecon's performance in the implementation of the three major policies mentioned above: coordination of planning, production specialization, and intraregional trade.[18] It is suggested that this approach appears much more promising than the study of the volume of trans-

[16] J. M. Montias, "Problems of Integration," *World Politics,* July 1966 (Vol. 18, No. 4), p. 725.
[17] Cf. United Nations Document ST/CID/7.
[18] The section that follows is a revised version of a paper, "Recent Developments in the Comecon," presented at a meeting of the University of California Project on Comparative Study of Communist Societies, Berkeley, April 21, 1966.

actions, however defined, or the analysis of the legal-institutional development of the organization. Both of these were undoubtedly important and both had a bearing on the progress of integration. Nevertheless, it is felt that the three major functions spelled out above represented the heart of Comecon's activities and thus provided the major basis for the economic integration of the area.

Coordination of Planning

Coordination of national plans, especially in the field of industry, began in the mid-1950's. The actual coordination was attempted by a number of standing commissions for every major branch of economic activity. In the initial period the commissions examined the plans for the years 1956–1960 and 1961–1965 and made recommendations with regard to the allocation of outputs of selected commodities among the member countries. Currently, national plans for the period 1966–1970 and long-range (perspective) plans up to 1980 are being discussed by the commissions.

The coordination procedure, initiated in 1954 and continued without major changes for the last fifteen years, has been widely criticized by a number of member states. The major drawback of the whole process of coordination was the fact that the national plans have been examined post facto, i.e., after their approval by the party and government authorities in individual countries. This has meant that for all practical purposes it was next to impossible to make any adjustments in the plans without disrupting the whole precariously balanced economic edifice throughout the area. One remedy might be to compare draft plans rather than the final versions, but so far this suggestion has not made much headway.

As a result the coordination of plans existed mostly on paper and consisted basically of minor adjustments in nonessential sectors where the pressure of domestic requirements left room for some surpluses. For all practical purposes Comecon members continued preparing their annual and five-year plans very much as if Comecon did not exist, save for areas subject to specialization agreements endorsed by the organization. It was this lack of cooperation which apparently prompted Khrushchev in 1962 to come out with his proposal for a Comecon planning body with supranational powers to enforce coordination of plans and outputs.

Judging by the available evidence, Khrushchev's insistence on closer integration had, if anything, the opposite effect from that originally intended. If East European sources are to be believed, during the past several years coordination of plans has been conducted almost entirely along bilateral lines, even though lip service has been paid to the needs for, and advantages of, multilateral collaboration. The move to bilateral coordination which followed the shelving of Khrushchev's proposal received the official imprimatur of Comecon in 1963 and has not been challenged by Khrushchev's successors. Indeed the silence of both Leonid Brezhnev and Alexei Kosygin on the entire subject of Comecon until recently might be interpreted as still another sign of the lack of interest in the organization.

Up to now coordination of plans was conducted by bilateral commissions of economic cooperation set up by Comecon members and Yugoslavia to provide an instrument of mutual collaboration between themselves.[19] These commissions, which appear to have met fairly frequently, were entrusted primarily with comparison of individual plans covering both outputs and foreign trade. The mutually agreed-upon plans were then reported to the standing branch commissions which could make further recommendations for the purpose of achieving some degree of optimization of plans within the organization as a whole. What was involved here was a kind of successive approximation which, hopefully, might result in a mutually advantageous quasi-Comecon plan.

While the abandonment of multilateral coordination in 1962–1963 can be traced primarily to the refusal of the Comecon members to subject their own interests to the decisions of a supranational body, other factors contributed to the lack of progress in this area. One of them is that since 1964 various Comecon countries have been either undertaking or contemplating more or less comprehensive reforms of their economic systems. It is clear that the main focus of the reforms is to reduce the impact of central planning and of all its ramifications in favor of strengthening the market mechanism.

These reforms would clearly have a far-reaching effect on the future of Comecon. The availability of rational cost and price data would permit member states to engage in proper economic calculations. This, in turn, would make it possible for the various countries to improve the efficiency of their foreign trade, utilizing the principle of comparative cost. In this fashion some more rational, area-wide distribution of resources could theoretically be achieved.

At the end of the sixties all of this was still a long way off. The fact that various Comecon countries found themselves at different stages in their reformmaking meant that it was virtually impossible for them to engage in a meaningful cooperation. As long as any two countries maintained a highly centralized planning system, the least they could do was exercise some degree of control over the physical volume of output and, though considerably less so, over the volume of trade. Today and in the near future this may no longer be true. With the central planning machinery either scrapped or severely restricted, it would be difficult for the respective governments to force individual producers to deliver the quantities of exports agreed upon beforehand or to impose upon the industry a certain product-mix which the planners considered preferable when bilateral coordination was first initiated. It must be kept in mind that until now not only multilateral but also bilateral coopera-

[19] For a list of these commissions see Kaser, pp. 257–261.

tion has been conducted on an ad hoc basis. The yardstick of comparative advantage was taken into account only in the most obvious cases where it was hardly necessary to go through a process of complex calculation.[20] Otherwise there was a tendency to stick to the product-mix established in the past, often a long time ago, and any adjustments resulting from bilateral negotiations were of a marginal character.

The picture drawn so far is, however, incomplete. For the sake of focusing more sharply on the question of integrated planning in its narrowest sense, two rather interesting and important elements were left out: 1) specialization and 2) joint production and investment.

Product Specialization

Specialization in production, decreed some ten years ago, was eventually embodied in an agreement entitled "Principles of International Socialist Division of Labor."[21] The rationale here was essentially the same as in the case of coordination of plans—namely, to obtain a better allocation of resources by way of avoiding duplication of productive capacities; to expand the volume of output and thus gain benefits of internal and external economies; to increase intra-Comecon trade and to raise the economic level of the less developed member states. In this respect specialization agreements were likely to achieve much more than output coordination via the plan. The national plans were normally considered taboo and could not easily be tampered with. On the microeconomic level, however, there was usually some room left for maneuver, i.e., specialization. Thus some degree of international division of labor was agreed upon by at least the majority of the member states.

According to the opponents of rigid specialization, the decision to allocate outputs of individual commodities among member countries was based on purely static assumptions.[22] The fact that Czechoslovakia or the German Democratic Republic (East Germany) enjoyed comparative advantage in, say, the engineering industry, was to some extent a historical accident. There was no sound economic reason why other Comecon countries should not produce similar products just as, or even more, cheaply, given a chance to develop similar industrial capacity. The less developed countries were being deprived of that chance as long as Comecon was asked to retain the current profile of production. If one considers also the fact that it was the producer country which reaped the advantages of specialization (growth of monopoly power through restriction of the number of producers, economies of scale due to larger outputs, etc.) the opposition of the less developed countries becomes understandable.

[20] E. Neuberger, "International Division of Labor in CEMA: Limited Regret Strategy," *American Economic Review*, May 1964 (Vol. 54, No. 3), p. 515.

[21] Full text in *Pravda*, June 17, 1962.

[22] For an interesting Romanian exposition of this view see J. M. Montias, "Background and Origin of the Rumanian Dispute with Comecon," *Soviet Studies*, October 1964 (Vol. 16, No. 2), pp. 131–132.

Another type of opposition to specialization reflected the unwillingness of the member countries to scrap existing capacities for a number of reasons. First, many of the plants to be scrapped or adapted were of a fairly recent vintage, thus containing a sizeable amount of frozen resources. In general, various countries might perhaps be willing to abandon producing certain commodities—but not before recovering their investment.[23] The overall scarcity of investment funds meant also that the conversion of existing plants from one line of production to another could not easily be undertaken without some compensatory payment from the other member countries.

In the same context no country was likely to abandon a certain line of production unless it could be assured of obtaining sufficient supplies of a given commodity from outside sources.[24] It is common knowledge that foreign trade plans as well as output plans were seldom if ever fulfilled. This meant that individual importers were more often than not shortchanged. Once a rigid specialization agreement was reached, resulting in concentrating nearly the entire output of a particular commodity in one or, at most, two countries, the importers were at the mercy of the exporters and the only alternative was to turn to the capitalist world. The recent increase in East-West trade may be a partial reflection of this phenomenon.

The same applied to the problem of quality. Member countries asked to forsake the production of commodities in which they were efficient would consent to a specialization agreement only if in return they received goods of equal or higher quality. This, however, was not usually the case. The example of Hungary abandoning production of radios in favor of clearly inferior Bulgarian sets speaks for itself.[25] In addition, the growing competition and availability of higher quality West European imports has been making Comecon specialization less and less attractive.

Furthermore, closing down plants or switching to other branches of production was resented by countries with severe unemployment problems. While no Comecon member admitted it openly, there were indications that considerable slack in labor force did exist, particularly in the less industrialized countries. Yet these were the very countries which were expected to carry the main burden of specialization. Actually, opposition to rationalization was not confined to the less developed countries. Recent attempts to streamline certain industrial branches in Czechoslovakia by eliminating inefficient plants met with fierce resistance of the workers employed in the affected plants, and the attempt had to be temporarily abandoned.[26]

In a somewhat different vein the whole problem of allocation of industrial

[23] Personal interviews in Prague and Warsaw during the spring and summer of 1967.

[24] A. Bodnar, "Rok 1962—przełomowy w rozwoju RWPG," *Gospodarka planowa* (Warsaw), January 1963 (Vol. 18, No. 1), p. 15.

[25] Personal interviews in Prague and Warsaw during the spring and summer of 1967.

[26] Personal interviews in Prague during the spring of 1967.

outputs was still being solved largely on an ad hoc basis. Without proper cost accounting and meaningful exchange rates any distribution of particular outputs was still based, by and large, on the traditional or historical pattern of resource allocation which made it difficult to enforce adjustments. The Comecon countries stated openly that so far it had proved impossible to determine the economic efficiency of specialization for Comecon as a whole. All attempts either to work out an appropriate methodology or to calculate directly the most efficient allocation of outputs have met with failure.

Finally, one must not underestimate the strength of the perennial bias favoring maximum gross output regardless of cost. As long as national plans at various levels of activity were calculated in physical terms, there was likely to be a reluctance on the part of industry to close down inefficient plants and concentrate on the efficient ones. There were still abundant examples forthcoming from the Comecon countries which reflected general unwillingness to abandon unprofitable lines or to introduce technological progress if it meant a loss of bonus for both management and labor.[27] Though this argument is bound to lose its force once economic reforms are put into effect, for the time being it remained a significant obstacle on the road to specialization.

Some of the recent actual cases of specialization provide an example of the existing difficulties. Thus in the field of agriculture, Bulgaria was chosen as the major producer of oilseed, wool, and vegetables, supplying the northern members of Comecon. As it turned out, the increased Bulgarian output, thanks to the aid received from the other countries, was partly consumed at home and partly exported to the West, especially to the Federal Republic of Germany (West Germany). Bulgaria, on the other hand, resented the fact that it was obliged to export wool to countries which were in the process of reducing their own herds or to supply vegetables to countries such as Czechoslovakia which processed them and then reexported them also to the West.[28] The example of Bulgarian radios, mentioned above, fell into the same category.

There is little wonder then that specialization has progressed slowly with the participating countries much more preoccupied with reforms of their systems or with expanding trade with the West than with the allocation of specific types of output. Nevertheless, in the last five years some degree of specialization was achieved in engineering and shipbuilding industries and, according to official communiqués issued periodically by the Comecon Executive Committee, discussions are continuing with the aim of increasing the number of branches and products subject to specialization agreements.

The entire question of international specialization came under severe criticism at a conference of Comecon industrial experts held in Moscow in Febru-

[27] For an excellent treatment of this problem see Alec Nove, *The Soviet Economy: An Introduction* (Rev. ed; New York: Frederick A. Praeger, 1966), chapter 6.
[28] Personal interviews in Prague during the spring of 1967.

ary 1966. The conference represented a watershed in the long-standing discussions concerning industrial specialization within Comecon. Various members submitted far-reaching proposals aimed at a fairly fundamental departure from the current practice and reflecting a considerable difference of opinion on how to proceed.[29]

The proposals submitted by a majority of members at the Moscow conference and confirmed the following year called, first of all, for abandonment of the current practice of extending specialization agreements over the largest possible assortment of products. From now on specialization was to be restricted above all to goods which were either not produced at all within Comecon or which were in short supply. Even then specialization was not to be considered as permanent, and only short-term agreements were to be concluded.

The emphasis on specialization in the production of final products was to give way to stressing the need for enlarged international cooperation and subcontracting. This was not only to lead to a better utilization of capacity, greater technological progress, and higher quality but also to a closer and more permanent cooperation among enterprises in different countries. The new approach was intended also to solve the problem of a given country's being told to concentrate on the production of goods which were either expensive or without prospects for future growth. Specialization in the production of subassemblies and parts was to spread the cost more evenly among interested parties.

The majority of conferees agreed that the monopolistic tendencies resulting from allocating the output of a given commodity to a single country should be reduced by accepting the Hungarian suggestion which called for at least two countries producing a given commodity within Comecon. While suggestions concerning specialization might be made on a multilateral level, concrete specialization agreements were in general to be concluded bilaterally. The former "administrative" approach to specialization was to be replaced by an economic approach. This meant that agreements were to take into account all possible parameters in each of the interested countries.

In the final analysis each country was to be the ultimate judge of the benefits accruing from specialization. These benefits for both the producers (exporters) and buyers (importers) were to be calculated in world market prices. In anticipation of the changes to be introduced by the economic reforms, stress was laid on the economic rather than administrative character of specialization. The emphasis on the market as the final determinant of the product-mix produced in a given country spoke for itself, as did the concern with costs, profits, and prices. The need for flexibility, coupled with the assertion

[29] This summary is based on A. Bodnar, "Podzial pracy w przemysle maszynowym krajow RWPG," *Zycie gospodarcze* (Warsaw), 1966 (Vol. 9, No. 11), p. 8.

of the primacy of national over international interest, underlined the new approach.

The proposals also envisaged that specialization would be undertaken whenever at least three member states showed an interest in it. This meant that the principle of unanimity, long advertised as an example of Comecon's respect for its members' national sovereignty, was no longer to be adhered to. The emphasis on enterprises rather than governments as partners in specialization agreements spelled the further decline of Comecon as a coordinating agency.

It is clear that some of the proposals were not likely to generate much enthusiasm among the participants. The most controversial idea appeared to be that of specialization in the production of subassemblies and parts. Although economically justified the suggestion must have been approached with a healthy dose of skepticism, taking into account the perennial difficulties with subcontracting in the domestic economies throughout Comecon. To be dependent for essential parts on domestic producers was bad enough, and the extension of cooperation to foreign suppliers made the dependency worse still. On the other hand, the insistence on making individual enterprises signatories to specialization agreements attempted to eliminate one of the major drawbacks of the old system, namely, the total lack of interest on the part of individual producers in specialization. The involvement of enterprises combined with greater freedoms granted to managers was intended to make specialization mutually profitable.

There were other major differences of opinion among the member countries. Thus, there was disagreement concerning the duration and extent of specialization agreements. While Poland, and to some degree Romania, favored short-term agreements covering a narrow range of products, Czechoslovakia, East Germany, Hungary, and Yugoslavia called for a more permanent allocation of outputs.[30] To some extent the conflicting viewpoints reflected existing differences in the level and profile of the machine-building industries in individual countries. Poland and Romania had a less developed engineering industry than most of their opponents, and, in addition, Poland appeared to be most advanced in some of the most capital-intensive and slowest growing branches such as railroad equipment and shipbuilding. Neither country wanted to be permanently saddled with declining or slow-growing industries. On the other hand, countries such as Czechoslovakia and East Germany, currently enjoying supremacy over a wide range of engineering products, favored long-term arrangements which would permit them to retain their advantageous position for as long as possible.

For the same reason the more advanced countries called for the reintroduction of the market as the regulator of international exchange. The higher

[30] Ibid; Z. Keh, "Kierunki prac," *Zycie gospodarcze,* 1966 (Vol. 9, No. 17), p. 1.

level of productivity of their industries would guarantee them benefits of specialization based on purely economic criteria. Because of this at least one country, Bulgaria, voiced opposition to purely commercial specialization agreements between enterprises and demanded that main emphasis be put on intergovernmental agreements.[31] Such agreements would have the virtue of safeguarding Bulgaria's share in the Comecon division of labor.

Perhaps the only real progress in the entire field of economic cooperation in recent years was made in the area of joint production and investment. Here again, with few exceptions, most of the tangible results came into being prior to Khrushchev's ouster. Such joint projects as the "Friendship" pipeline, the freight car pool, and the electric power grid began operating prior to 1964. The only significant exceptions were the establishment of new joint enterprises in the field of metallurgy and chemicals under the names of *Intermetal* and *Interchem* and the creation of a ball-bearing cartel. Thus far these organizations have proved to be something less than successful. Their proclaimed purposes (full utilization of capacities, rationalization of production, coordination of investment, area-wide sales and purchasing agencies) were not achieved.[32] Once more the reason was the unwillingness of the members to commit their resources fully, thus risking further exposure to the vagaries of Comecon trade characterized by the persistent lack of sanctions for nonfulfillment of obligations.

This, then, was the way in which economic cooperation proceeded within Comecon in the past few years. The progress, with minor exceptions, was meager, and the future looked bleaker still. This picture, however, was not quite complete without taking into account intra-Comecon trade which was to have played a crucial role in the integration process.

Trade Policies within Comecon

Perhaps the major task which confronted the rejuvenated Comecon in 1956 was the need to expand intra-Comecon trade. During the first few years of the organization's existence trade among its members did not reach significant proportions for a variety of reasons. The most important among them were the belief in autarky and the distrust on the part of the planners who feared the consequences of possible import deficiency on the fulfillment of plans.

The emphasis put on the expansion of intra-Comecon trade went hand in hand with the new policy of coordination and specialization. It was trade which permitted the initial adjustments in national plans when available surpluses were exchanged among member countries, reducing pressure on existing capacities and releasing resources to other priority sectors. Moreover, the whole concept of international division of labor was based on the assumption

---

[31] Radio Prague, March 29, 1966; *Figyelo* (Budapest), May 11, 1966 (Radio Free Europe Hungarian Press Survey, No. 1714).

[32] Personal interviews in Prague and Warsaw during the spring and summer of 1967.

that intra-Comecon trade would play an ever-increasing role in relations among member countries.

As in the case of integration, the progress has been disappointing. Not that considerable expansion in turnover did not take place: Comecon statistics show a fairly high annual rate of growth and the share of Comecon countries in total value of trade of individual members remained high.[33] Nevertheless, judging by the tenor of various pronouncements, there was a good deal of dissatisfaction. The grounds for complaint may be treated under the headings of relatively narrow range of traded and tradable goods, incorrect prices, and payments difficulties.

Ever since the beginning, intra-Comecon trade has been a barter trade involving a bilateral exchange of goods, with prices serving mainly as units of account. It soon became clear that this procedure was not very successful in expanding trade. Despite the fact that the former autarkic bias has been severely restricted, the effects of the past policy have still been felt, meaning that with some exceptions the industrial outputs of individual Comecon countries reflected the same or similar system of priorities. Scarce commodities, whether raw materials or manufactured goods, were likely to be in high demand both in the producing country and in Comecon as a whole, and the opposite might well be true for the surplus goods. In other words, the range of commodities which have been surplus in some and in short supply in other Comecon countries tended to be narrow, limiting the possibility of trade. In the presence of fixed prices the trade consisted usually of exchanging raw materials for raw materials, machinery for machinery, and so on, always aiming to achieve as perfect a balance as possible, especially in the case of the so-called "hard" or deficit goods.[34]

The hard bargaining which usually accompanied trade negotiations among Comecon countries concerned also the quality of traded goods. As part of an agreement trading partners tried to sell to each other goods of inferior quality as a condition for the delivery of "hard" goods. Czechoslovakia, for example, was forced to acquire Hungarian trucks which had a tendency to overturn; this promptly earned them the sobriquet "Rakosi's revenge." Bulgarian radios and Romanian trucks came into the same category. Bulgarian battery-operated trucks were imported by Czechoslovakia principally as a means of obtaining the batteries which were then taken out and used elsewhere.[35]

This state of affairs was to be remedied by the specialization agreements. By concentrating on some lines of production and relinquishing others the Comecon countries were expected to expand trade rapidly, reaping the benefits of the division of labor. But, as shown, progress in specialization was pain-

[33] *Economic Survey of Europe 1966* (New York: United Nations, 1967), chapter 3, pp. 2–7.
[34] S. Ausch, "Mezinarodni delba prace a ekonomicky mechanismus," *Planovane hospodarstvi* (Prague), December 1965 (No. 12), p. 66.
[35] Personal interviews in Prague during the spring of 1967.

fully slow, and according to Comecon statistics even the volume of trade in categories of goods covered by specialization agreements did not look especially impressive.

It is not surprising, then, that one by-product of the slow expansion of intra-Comecon trade was a substantial increase in trade with the non-Communist world.[36] This trend, one must add, was provoked not only by the scarcity and low quality of available goods but also by the imperatives of an expanding economy throughout Comecon. These led to a growing demand for more sophisticated products which the member countries either did not produce at all or which were still in short supply. In time, member states were openly urged to acquire modern technology in the West instead of trying to develop it at home in order to accelerate the process of development.[37]

One of the two measures which might well contribute to the expansion of intra-Comecon trade would be a comprehensive reform of foreign trade and domestic prices. This was perhaps one of the most interesting, albeit most controversial, aspects of Comecon policy.[38]

Intra-Comecon trade, at least since 1956, is said to have been conducted at world market prices.[39] In fact most of the time there has been a sizable discrepancy between the "world prices" used by Comecon and the actual prices on the world market. No great difficulty has arisen so long as world prices did not exhibit any sudden and/or substantial movements. Once this happened, however, Comecon prices began to bear little resemblance to actual world prices except in name, and any attempt, however primitive, to calculate comparative advantage both between Comecon and the rest of the world, and within Comecon itself, was therefore made difficult, if not impossible.

One possible remedy, more frequent price adjustments, has not been applied in view of the attitude of the planners who have abhorred price changes and who have been essentially status quo oriented. Moreover, any price reform has had a tendency to drag itself into infinity and a number of years usually passed before the new price lists were ready. By that time the new prices would often have been again out of line with the actual world prices. Finally, were prices to have changed frequently, this would have affected the balance of payments, creating surpluses and deficits for the trading partners. The debtor countries in particular would have found themselves in a difficult position since inelastic supply conditions fixed by the plan would have made it next to impossible to eliminate the deficit by exporting additional quantities of goods.

[36] For a good discussion see *Economic Survey of Europe 1967* (New York: United Nations, 1968), chapter 2, pp. 71–79.

[37] W. Berger, "The Technological Revolution and Economic Cooperation among Socialist Countries," *World Marxist Review*, April 1965 (Vol. 8, No. 4), p. 17.

[38] B. Csikos-Nagy, "Currency and Price Problems in Socialist Economic Integration," *Gospodarka planowa*, August 1969 (Vol. 24, No. 8).

[39] For an excellent treatment of foreign trade pricing see United Nations, *Economic Bulletin for Europe*, 1964 (Vol. 16, No. 2), pp. 42–44.

The major drawback of fixed prices has been that they served to conserve the existing product-mix and the division between "hard" and "soft" goods. Comecon trade prices have not reflected the average cost of production within Comecon, nor the prices in the world market, nor supply-demand conditions in the Comecon market. For example, despite the chronic shortage of raw materials and relative abundance of certain categories of machinery within Comecon, the prices of raw materials in Comecon trade exceeded the level of world prices of raw materials much less than was the case with machinery.[40] Fixed prices also discouraged technological progress since producers received the same prices whether they introduced improvements or not.

It must be added, however, that in many instances the fixity of prices was more apparent than real. The "fixed" prices were, as a rule, adjusted during annual negotiations, with the result that one country was sometimes selling the same product to different countries at different prices. The annual price adjustments depended on the relative strengths of the negotiating partners and added more confusion to the already complex picture.

Interestingly enough the latest country to take issue with Comecon price policy was the Union of Soviet Socialist Republics, supported to some extent by Bulgaria.[41] Soviet complaints concerned the terms of trade within Comecon which apparently favored the smaller East European countries. The Soviet Union as the major supplier of raw materials to the member countries felt that the application of world market prices in intra-Comecon trade benefited the importers and penalized the exporters of raw materials. Since the real cost of developing new sources of raw materials in the Soviet Union has been going up, the Soviets felt that if the cost could not be shared by all members, then either the price level of raw materials should be raised or the ruble should be revalued.[42] At the same time the Soviet Union, which imports a large amount of engineering products from its East European partners, complained that the prices charged for machinery were too high, especially when quality was taken into consideration. Taking its cue from recent emphasis on the primacy of national interest, the Soviet Union implied that unless its terms of trade improved it may have to introduce some changes in its trade pattern.[43]

Thus far the response of the other countries has been mixed. Czecho-

---

[40] Ausch, *Planovane hospodarstvi*, No. 12, p. 66. See also P. Marer, *ASTE Bulletin*, Fall 1968 (Vol. 10, No. 2), p. 8.

[41] Cf. O. Bogomolov, "Khoziaistvovny reformy i ekonomicheskoe sotrudnichestvo sotsialisticheskikh stran," *Voprosy ekonomiki* (Moscow), 1966 (No. 2), pp. 76–86, and "Aktualne problemy ekonomicheskogo sotrudnichestva sotsialisticheskikh stran," *Mirovaia ekonomika i mezhdunarodnye otnoshenia* (Moscow), 1966 (No. 5), pp. 15–26; and V. Ladygin and Y. Shirayev, "Voprosy sovershenstvovania ekonomicheskogo sotrudnichestva stran SEV," *Voprosy ekonomiki*, 1966 (No. 5), pp. 81–89.

[42] *New York Times*, January 7, 1968; A. Shonfield, "Changing Commercial Policies in the Soviet Bloc," *International Affairs* (London), January 1968 (Vol. 44, No. 1), p. 11.

[43] Bogomolov, *Voprosy ekonomiki*, No. 2, p. 85; Wiles, pp. 248–250.

slovakia agreed to provide development capital while Hungary felt that the problem could be solved on a purely commercial (price and quality) basis. Hungarian spokesmen pointed out that no one had suggested that Italy, a major importer of Soviet oil (for which, by the way, it has been paying less than the Comecon countries), should help in developing Siberian oil fields.[44] Whatever the final result may be, this conflict represents another blow against Comecon.

The second measure which would likely result in the growth of intra-Comecon trade was the reform of the payments system. Until recently the payments system was based on bilateral settlements, with each partner trying hard to achieve balanced trade. Surpluses of deficits, if any, were not convertible into another currency. This lack of convertibility provided a powerful brake on trade expansion. In the final analysis it was the weaker of the two sides which determined the volume of trade. The creditor country found itself often at the mercy of the debtor and frequently had a long wait before the debt could be settled.

It was in order to introduce limited convertibility and thus contribute to an expansion of trade that the International Bank of Economic Cooperation began operating on January 1, 1964. The bank's main function was to provide an instrument for multilateral settlement of outstanding debts with the aid of the so-called "convertible rubles." Each of the eight member states was also required to put in a certain share of the bank's capital, thereby acquiring drawing rights on other members' currencies.

Even though on paper the bank represented an important step forward in the direction of facilitating trade expansion, it was a far cry from being a true bank of multilateral settlements comparable to the Bank of International Settlements which acted as a settlement agency within the European Payments Union. First of all, intra-Comecon trade was still conducted mainly along bilateral barter lines and there was little scope left for multilateral settlements which, moreover, had to be agreed upon by all interested parties. Furthermore, the penalty for nonsettlement of debts was so low as to make it almost worthwhile for the debtors to delay repayment, thus changing a short-term debt into a long-term credit. Since the creditor had to obtain the approval of the debtor before using the latter's debt in settling his own obligations, the whole procedure was slow and cumbersome, and there was no incentive to expand trade and build up surpluses which were essentially worthless.

As a result of strong criticism by certain countries, especially Poland, the bank's members have recently been required to contribute part of their shares in gold or convertible currencies.[45] Nevertheless, this alone is not likely to

[44] Personal interviews in Prague during the spring of 1967.

[45] E. Babitchev, "The International Bank for Economic Cooperation," in Grossman, pp. 148–152.

Since the completion of this article there were further developments in the Comecon banking field. Following a series of discussions regarding the ways and means of strengthening the organization, cul-

result in significant trade expansion. On the contrary, intra-Comecon trade may in fact decline still further since member countries would not want to be caught with deficits which would have to be settled in dollars or gold and would be likely to limit their trade to the amounts that could be balanced.

It was difficult to be optimistic about the future of multilateral payments within Comecon. The payments question formed a link in the vicious circle which included intra-Comecon trade, specialization, and coordination of production. Any change in one of them had to affect the others, and the prospects in each were slim. Some East European sources saw great potential for improvement of the payments problem in the economic reforms under discussion at the present time. While in the long run they might very well be right, the uncertainty surrounding the reforms and the confusion which inevitably would follow them (as well as the need for lengthy period of adjustment) might be expected to make the hoped-for solution an uncertain prospect. In the meantime, the tug-of-war was likely to continue between debtors and creditors and true multilateralism might be a long way off.

IV. THE COMECON MILIEU: REGIONAL AND INTERNATIONAL ENVIRONMENTS

The preceding discussion concentrated almost entirely on economic factors hindering economic integration in Eastern Europe. While clearly important, they alone could not fully explain the difficulties encountered in the integration process in the area. The analysis of the situation would not be complete without some discussion of the political changes in the individual member states and, to borrow James Rosenau's terms, in the "regional" and "cold-war" environments.[46]

The three major changes in individual polities were: the persistence of factionalism within ruling oligarchies, the emergence of new political elites, and the growing importance of pressure groups. The extent of these changes varied from one national system to another but elements of each of them were present in every country and all of them undoubtedly had an impact on integration processes.

The last six years witnessed a change in top leadership in three member

minating in a Comecon "summit" meeting in April 1969, a Comecon investment bank was formally established in July 1970. Its basic purpose is to finance investment projects in the various member countries which would benefit the organization as a whole. The bank is to start operating in 1971. Henry Schaefer, "What Role for Comecon?" *Radio Free Europe Research Reports in Economics,* April 1970 (No. 1), and "Recent Developments Involving the Comecon Investment Bank," ibid., July 30, 1970 (No. 5); Harry Trend, "The Comecon Investment Bank," ibid., June 15, 1970 (No. 2); Hertha W. Heiss, "The Council for Mutual Economic Assistance—Developments since the Mid-1960's," in United States Congress, Joint Economic Committee, *Economic Developments in Countries of Eastern Europe* (Washington: Govenment Printing Office, 1970), pp. 528–542.

[46] James Rosenau (ed.), *Linkage Politics: Essays on the Convergence of National and International Systems* (New York: Free Press, 1969), pp. 49–56.

countries (the Soviet Union, Czechoslovakia, and Romania) and a major challenge to the existing leadership in a fourth country (Poland). Everywhere, with the possible exception of the Soviet Union, the ruling elite was subjected to increasing pressure from below which in some cases necessitated major reshuffling in the highest echelons of the party and government bureaucracy. Only in the Soviet Union did the ruling gerontocracy manage to escape unscathed.

In addition to personnel changes it was becoming increasingly clear that most of the member countries have been undergoing a crisis in their decision-making apparatus. The process of the disintegration of the decisionmaking structures had been under way for some time and it became accelerated some six years ago, following the ouster of Khrushchev. As far as the Soviet Union alone was concerned,

> the fragmentation of the decisionmaking process combined with the erosion of Soviet ideology has produced a new element of both instability and uncertainty in Soviet behavior, an institutionalized irrationality, particularly in crisis situations.[47]

The erratic Soviet behavior in the months preceding the intervention in Czechoslovakia is a case in point. Except in emergencies Soviet actions are likely to be rational and cautious and characterized by a persistent immobilisme. The latter appears to be the result of a precarious interfactional consensus on the basis of the lowest common denominator.

There is evidence that junior Comecon partners have experienced similar difficulties. The split within the Czechoslovak leadership which antedated the "Prague spring" of 1968 has continued ever since, even after the ouster of Alexander Dubcek and the return of conservatives to power in the spring of 1969. The right-wing challenge to Wladyslaw Gomulka in Poland, accompanied by the virulent antisemitic campaign and temporarily deflected by the events in Czechoslovakia, has not been fully eliminated. In East Germany Walter Ulbricht, forced to admit some young technocrats to the party's top leadership, has been under pressure to abandon his traditional policies, as, for example, in the case of negotiations with West Germany. Only in Romania, and to some extent in Bulgaria and Hungary, has the leadership been united.

The inertia resulting from continuing factionalism among top national elites did not augur well for the future of integration in Eastern Europe. The tendency to sweep problems under the rug, the inclination to postpone decisionmaking for as long as possible, and the propensity to avoid making drastic solutions, so characteristic of the current regimes, were not likely to speed up the process of integration.

Another factor contributing to either the slowdown or to the maintenance

---

[47] Vernon V. Aspaturian, "Soviet Foreign Policy at the Crossroads: Conflict and/or Collaboration?" *International Organization*, Summer 1969 (Vol. 23, No. 3), p. 598.

of the status quo was the emergence of the "new middle class" in each of the member states, but especially in the smaller East European countries.[48] The new elite, better educated, more pragmatic, and, above all, often highly nationalistic, appeared to be much more interested in establishing closer economic links with the West than in fostering integration in their region. The young technocrats, especially the economists, were increasingly concerned with the growing technological gap between East and West, the gap which Comecon was simply unable to narrow. Their pragmatism was further reflected in greater emphasis on rational economic calculation at the expense of ideological considerations. Their nationalism which burst out in the late 1950's continued unabated, also militating against closer ties with their immediate neighbors.

The emergence of the "new middle class" was tied in with the growing influence of pressure groups. The problem of pluralism in Eastern Europe has not been dealt with in the literature until recently, and there is today still no agreement on such issues as the actual presence, power, influence, and scope of activity of interest groups.[49] Additional research is needed before anything definite can be said about the role of groups in the integrative processes. Judging from fragmentary data on group behavior in at least two Comecon countries, Czechoslovakia and Poland, one important group, the managers of the nationalized enterprises, has been divided on the issue of intrabloc economic relations. While some members of this group were strongly opposed to the continuation of close links with other Comecon countries, others favored it since this type of trade guaranteed them a more or less steady market for their low quality products which otherwise could not be sold elsewhere.[50] On the other hand, there is also evidence that various groups have been participating more and more frequently in major policy formulation in an advisory capacity for some time. Their influence was particularly visible in the preparation and implementation of economic reforms which, as suggested earlier, were hardly conducive to improved chances of successful integration.[51] Moreover, the leadership of the groups shared similar characteristics with the new political elites. Both exhibited a healthy dose of pragmatism and nationalism, and both were relatively well educated even by Western standards.

The changes in the "regional environment" have been ably analyzed elsewhere and need not be discussed here.[52] Suffice it to say that disintegration rather than integration characterized the developments in Comecon and the

---

[48] K. Jowitt, "Revolutionary Breakthroughs and National Development: The Case of Romania 1944–1965" (unpublished Ph.D. dissertation, University of California, Berkeley, 1970), pp. 231–240.

[49] Skilling, *World Politics*, Vol. 18, No. 3; and A. Korbonski, "Bureaucracy and Interest Groups in Communist Societies: The Case of Czechoslovakia," *Studies in Comparative Communism* (forthcoming).

[50] Personal interviews in Prague and Warsaw during the spring and summer of 1967.

[51] See p. 359 above.

[52] Brzezinski, pp. 433–455.

Warsaw Treaty Organization during the period under discussion. The top elites, although still meeting periodically if only to maintain a facade of unity for outside consumption, have been known to be frequently divided on a variety of issues, be it the Sino-Soviet conflict, the Middle East crisis, the situation in Czechoslovakia, or the rapprochement with West Germany.

The "new middle class" in individual countries felt it progressively harder to find a common language with their counterparts elsewhere in Comecon which made communication more and more difficult. Elite complementarity, fairly strong until the early 1960's and considered crucial for the success of integration, has been eroding rapidly. Even if the national political elites in Communist Party leadership strata and high-level bureaucracies occasionally tended to think and act alike, the same did not hold true for the economic elites. In the early days of Comecon the economists from different countries, educated with the aid of Soviet textbooks and speaking the same pseudo-Marxist economic jargon, had at least a common standard of reference.

Today the situation is quite different. The economic reforms in various countries were in some cases accompanied by reforms in the curriculum, especially in the field of economics. As a result the young economists in Czechoslovakia and Hungary began to pay more attention to John Maynard Keynes, Paul Samuelson, and Milton Friedman than to Marx while their counterparts elsewhere probably considered Yevsei Liberman the greatest innovator since Adam Smith. While the Czechs and the Hungarians spoke in terms of value-added, free price formation, and comparative costs, others still adhered to the old concepts of central plan, price control, and gross output regardless of cost. It can only be presumed that in many instances the partners in trade negotiations simply talked past, rather than to, each other.

The lack of a common standard of reference negatively influenced the chances of integration by making it difficult to agree on an objective yardstick with which to measure and distribute the benefits accruing from integration. As pointed out earlier, none of the Comecon countries has been able to calculate real benefits derived from international transactions. All such calculations have been hitherto conducted on an ad hoc basis without real grounding in both static and dynamic cost analysis. Of course, what mattered here was the *perceived* rather than *real* benefits. Thus the Romanian policymakers saw the various specialization agreements as detrimental to their country's economic future even though, at least in the long run, some type of a division of labor in Comecon would be beneficial to all countries.[53] Similarly, the Soviet Union saw itself being "exploited" by the smaller East European countries without actually being able to prove it satisfactorily.[54] Similar

[53] For the best treatment of Romania's attitude see J. M. Montias, *Economic Development in Communist Rumania* (Cambridge, Mass: M.I.T. Press, 1967), pp. 187–230.

[54] See p. 356 above.

problems have been encountered with regard to the distribution of real or alleged benefits, thus hurting the chances of integration.

The changes in the "cold-war environment" also had an impact on East European economic integration. Here again the developments have been discussed in some detail and the main arguments are generally familiar.[55] The chief factor was the decline in the intensity of the Cold War, followed by the change in the attitudes of the two superpowers and their respective clienteles. The idea of "peaceful coexistence" began to compete with that of "peaceful engagement" and the outcome was a rapprochement between the two camps which showed no signs of diminishing despite occasional lapses.

In practical terms the consequences of the détente proved almost identical on both sides. Perhaps the most striking were the parallel developments in the two military alliances—the North Atlantic Treaty Organization (NATO) and the WTO. Initially established as defense measures against an outside threat—imaginary rather than real—both organizations lost their raison d'être once the danger was perceived as rapidly disappearing. France's behavior was matched by that of Romania and there was a good chance that if the restiveness, particularly among the junior members, was permitted to continue unabated, both alliances would be reduced to the role of talking shops. For Eastern Europe the weakening of the cohesion of the WTO meant that one major prop capable of sustaining and justifying economic integration was showing signs of fatigue.

Perhaps a more important consequence of the continuing détente was the rapid expansion of East-West economic contacts which reinforced rapprochement through a snowballing effect. The impact of the growing East-West trade on integration was discussed earlier. Here one may venture a prediction that in the final analysis the revival of the traditional economic links in Europe, spearheaded by West Germany and aided and abetted by other countries in the European Economic Community (EEC) and by the United Kingdom, may mean a kiss of death for the chances of integration in the East. The realization of the growing technological gap between Eastern and Western Europe appeared to convince even the most die-hard champions of Comecon that the only way of overcoming the persistent economic difficulties in the area was to import modern technology and know-how from the West.[56]

To a large extent it was a reversal of the situation that existed twenty years before. There is little doubt that Comecon, created in 1949 for the purpose of laying the foundations for economic integration of the Communist camp, was the stepchild of the Cold War. The embargo imposed by the West at that time was largely responsible for the increase in the intra-Comecon trade which in turn had a spillover effect in other areas of common interest, thus contrib-

---

[55] Korbonski, *International Conciliation*, No. 573, pp. 71–73.
[56] *Economic Survey of Europe 1967*, chapter 2, pp. 79–84.

uting greatly to the progress of economic integration at least until the early 1960's. It was only when the trade barriers were lowered once again that the process of integration began to show signs of slowing down.

It may also be speculated that the difficulties encountered by the Common Market in the most recent period had some repercussions on Comecon although their magnitude cannot be easily ascertained. The whole question of the "demonstration effect" of the EEC on Comecon is a moot one. It can be presumed that the early successes of the Common Market, realized rather late by Comecon leaders, affected East European integration in at least two ways: First, the genuine fear of the effects of a common EEC tariff, especially on agricultural products and raw materials, might have forced Comecon countries to seek common solutions; second, the impressive performance of the EEC might have helped to reduce the resistance to closer cooperation. To say this, however, is not to imply, as Marshall Shulman seems to do, that the success of the EEC was *the* factor responsible for the noticeable increase in Comecon activities in the early 1960's.[57] It can be assumed that closer integration in the bloc would have taken (or not taken) place regardless of the success or failure of the Common Market. If, on the other hand, the atmosphere of early successes in the EEC did in fact prove contagious east of the Elbe, the present impasse in the West might have some impact on the developments in Eastern Europe.

In the light of the foregoing discussion the question should now be raised about the extent of economic integration in Eastern Europe 21 years after the first step was made in that direction. Keeping in mind our original definition it can be said that the common framework managed to maintain itself in one form or another throughout the entire period and that it did provide for the mutual pursuit of some goals and common implementation of some policies. However, it can also be said that the past six years or so showed hardly any progress in the three variables. On the contrary, some of them reflected growing decay.

The institutional framework has remained roughly unchanged since 1964 even though the creation of the Comecon bank and the establishment of some cooperative ventures might be interpreted as a functional expansion of the organization. On the other hand, there has been a visible decline in the area of common pursuit of goals and execution of policies. While the ultimate goal of every polity remained industrialization, there was much less agreement regarding the other goals such as the achievement of the maximum rate of growth, rapid development of heavy industry, or full (or overfull) employment. While some countries (Soviet Union, Poland, Bulgaria) still seemed to adhere to these goals, others preferred to think in terms of optimum allo-

---

[57] Marshall D. Shulman, "The Communist States and Western Integration," *Problems of Communism*, September–October 1963 (Vol. 12, No. 5), pp. 47–54.

cation of resources and/or improvement in consumption patterns of the population (Czechoslovakia and Hungary), in terms of expanding commercial ties with the West (Romania), or in terms of improving the old economic system by eliminating its worst features (East Germany).

There seems to be also little agreement on the implementation of economic policies. Growing differentiation in the national economic systems made it virtually impossible to coordinate domestic and foreign economic policies, and competition rather than cooperation seemed to become the prevailing form of intra-Comecon relations.

Departing for a moment from a strictly definitional standpoint, it can be stated that Comecon as an instrument of integration in 1970 was a far cry from what it was ten years earlier. Stripped of its function as a coordinating agency, Comecon also appeared to be deprived of its role as an instrument of allocation. Its competence as a promoter of intra-Comecon trade was also seriously challenged not only by the continuing stress on bilateral agreements but also by the increase in East-West trade and growing demands for participation in the worldwide rather than the Comecon division of labor. More and more, Comecon seemed to act primarily as a clearing house for ideas and suggestions, providing an institutional umbrella for bilateral and occasionally multilateral agreements; serving as a forum for the exchange of economic and technical information; conducting research; and acting as an arbiter in cases of disagreement or nonfulfillment of contracts. However important and useful, all these functions could be seen as a terminal rather than an initial stage in the East European integration process.

V. COMECON WITHIN THE THEORETICAL ENVIRONMENT

Until now the question of integration in Eastern Europe was discussed in largely nontheoretical terms. It was also limited to the analysis of the various factors hindering economic integration in the area. Such a discussion, however interesting and enlightening, has one major drawback in that it does not permit meaningful comparisons with integration processes in other parts of the world. As suggested above, the absence of any theoretical studies of East European integration was a reflection of the peculiar character of the so-called Communist area studies which until now abhorred theorizing, considering it inappropriate and downright harmful.

It is thus not without some irony that the first systematic attempt at including Comecon in a broader theoretical framework was made by scholars whose interest lay well beyond the boundaries of the area. In their pioneering 1964 article Ernst Haas and Philippe Schmitter included Comecon among the seven integration schemes they tested, and on the basis of their investigation they concluded that the "chances of automatic politicization" of Comecon, i.e., the chances of the economic union being transformed into a political one, were "possible-doubtful."[58]

This is not the place to discuss in detail the ranking assigned to Comecon by the authors. My own verdict, based on the Haas-Schmitter paradigm, would have been considerably less optimistic. Nevertheless, keeping in mind the fact that the above-mentioned article was written in 1964 when no one else even attempted to present a comprehensive *factual* history of Comecon, the courage and imagination of the authors in undertaking this task can only be admired, even if today their interpretation has lost some of its earlier glitter.

The criticism of the Haas-Schmitter paradigm induced Joseph Nye to construct what he calls "a revised neo-functionalist model," intended to remedy the major deficiencies of the earlier approach.[59] There is no doubt that Nye's model represents a significant advance in the field of comparative integration studies. From a parochial East European point of view it appears to overcome a number of problems associated with the Haas-Schmitter model even though it still leaves some issues unresolved. Space does not permit a full discussion of the various "process forces" and "integrative conditions" which form the core of the model, especially as some of them were mentioned earlier. Thus only a few variables will be briefly commented upon.

Perhaps the two most important or strategic variables are the *involvement of external actors in the process* and the *perception of external compelling-ness*. The peculiarity of the Comecon situation lies in the position of the Soviet Union. Although a founding member of Comecon, the Soviet Union easily could (and perhaps should) be treated as an external actor since its influence upon and involvement in the affairs of the organization are of paramount importance.

It is probably correct to say that the Soviet attitude toward Comecon has been highly ambiguous over the years. As mentioned below, the reasons for creating Comecon in the first place are still obscure. It also appears that the Soviet Union, or more correctly Stalin, effectively destroyed the chances of an economic union in Eastern Europe by permitting the then satellites to retain a semblance of political independence and control over their economies. There is also little doubt that a political union could have been formed with the use of force. No such attempt was made, however, and instead Comecon never got off the ground as long as Stalin was alive.

It is also clear that the perception by the national decisionmakers of the Soviet attitude vis-à-vis Comecon was (and is) of considerable importance for at least some of the junior partners. Thus a strong Soviet commitment to the

[58] Ernst B. Haas and Philippe C. Schmitter, "Economics and Differential Patterns of Political Integration: Projections about Unity in Latin America," *International Organization*, Autumn 1964 (Vol. 18, No. 4), p. 720.
[59] J. S. Nye in this volume.

organization would most likely induce the smaller members to move in the same direction, and vice versa. The decline in Comecon activities after 1963 could be attributed to a reduction of Soviet interest in East European economic integration which was correctly interpreted as such by some of the countries.[60] On the other hand, a revival of Soviet concern about integration might also influence some of the member countries in the opposite direction, as witnessed by Romania's resistance to closer integration in 1963 and after.

The sheer economic size of the Soviet Union does not in itself present any inherent problems.[61] In the case of Comecon the huge size of the Soviet economy might actually be considered as a catalyst which, *ceteris paribus,* could be instrumental in maintaining and expanding the scope of integration. The presence of an immense market for manufactured goods as well as the existence of large raw material reserves puts the Soviet Union in a highly favorable role as the potential economic federalizer. Once the *ceteris paribus* clause is removed, however, the importance of this particular factor is considerably reduced.

Another condition to be commented upon, *low (or exportable) costs of integration,* is of some relevance to the Comecon situation. To be sure, even the limited degree of East European integration was said to be quite costly in terms of foregone alternatives. Seen in this light the process of economic integration in the area might have already gone too far.[62] While there was clearly a diminution in the welfare on the part of the East European population, it was much larger than a corresponding decline outside the region due to trade diversion, as the share of East European trade in the total volume of trade in the non-Communist world was much smaller than the share of Western trade in total Comecon trade.[63]

There is, however, another aspect of the exportability of costs within Comecon. It concerns the problem of the so-called "exploitation" in intrabloc trade. Space does not permit a full discussion of this interesting question but it appears that a number if not all of the Comecon members have been engaged in exploiting each other by charging higher prices for their exports than those paid by non-Communist buyers of identical commodities and by being forced to pay similarly higher prices for their imports from other Comecon countries.[64] The extent of this "exploitation" varies in time and between different partners in the exchanges, and the fact that all members participate in this

---

[60] For a somewhat different interpretation of the role of the Soviet Union see Karl Kaiser, "The Integration of Regional Subsystems: Some Preliminary Notes on Recurrent Patterns and the Role of the Superpowers," *World Politics,* October 1968 (Vol. 21, No. 1), pp. 99ff.

[61] Kaser, pp. 202–205.

[62] J. M. Montias, "Obstacles to the Economic Integration of Eastern Europe," paper prepared for the Semaine de Bruges, College of Europe, Bruges, Belgium, 1969, p. 5.

[63] For details see *Economic Survey of Europe 1966,* chapter 3, sections 2 and 4.

[64] Cf. F. Holzman, "More on Soviet Bloc Trade Discrimination," *Soviet Studies,* July 1965 (Vol. 17, No. 1); Wiles, pp. 222–248; Marer, *ASTE Bulletin,* Vol. 10, No. 2, pp. 6–7; and Kaser, pp. 182–185.

"beggar my neighbor" policy goes a long way in sweetening the potentially bitter pill of integration.

When the "exploitation" becomes too one-sided or when it persists for a long period of time, it may develop into a threat to the integrative process. In the last few years, for example, there were several indications that the Soviet Union was less than happy with the conduct of intra-Comecon trade, claiming among other things that it had to pay too high a price for the low quality manufactured products imported from its junior partners while at the same time the prices it received for its exports of raw materials were below world market prices.[65] In other words, the Soviet Union de facto charged price discrimination on the part of the other Comecon members, and it demanded some sort of compensation for its worsening terms of trade. It is quite possible that these charges and the lack of enthusiastic response to them by the rest of the membership were responsible for the lack of progress in Comecon in recent years.

Nye's "expected national response" in the case of Comecon is the maintenance of status quo. This could be perceived as the most likely outcome in the short run although the possibility of disintegration cannot be completely ruled out. My own judgment of the strength of process forces and favorability of integrative conditions is somewhat less sanguine than that of Nye, and my own verdict as to the chances of integration in Eastern Europe would be even less optimistic.

Another interesting attempt at defining the scope of integration in the area was made by Michael Gehlen who utilized the communications approach for that purpose.[66] Gehlen tested the progress of integration in Eastern Europe with reference to ten types of transactions of which the most important seemed to be the interpersonal contacts among top national elites, bilateral and multilateral treaties, other interpersonal contacts such as educational exchanges and tourism, and finally trade. On that basis Gehlen then proceeded to rank the seven East European countries in terms of high, medium, and low levels of integrative activity and in terms of their dependence on the Soviet Union. The two divisions did not parallel each other so that in a number of cases countries which showed a low degree of integrative behavior had a high level of dependence on the Soviet Union. Gehlen saw this discrepancy as the result of the lack of agreement by the partners to establish a regulatory, coordinating mechanism and of the different appreciation of the intraregional relationships by the Soviet Union and its junior partners. Thus,

for the latter they are economically vital but for the former such relationships

---

[65] See p. 356 above.

[66] Michael Gehlen, "The Integrative Process in East Europe: A Theoretical Framework," *The Journal of Politics*, February 1968 (Vol. 30, No. 1), pp. 90–113.

seem to be largely a question of commercial partnership enabling the USSR to obtain certain resources for its own advantage.[67]

The appropriateness and usefulness of the communications model for the study of integration has been debated for a long time and there is no need to restate the arguments here. In Gehlen's case it appears that in the final analysis the overall judgement regarding integration in Eastern Europe hinges on the volume of intra-Comecon trade. This, as was suggested above, is not a very useful index of integrative process, especially when considered in isolation. Moreover, Gehlen's explanation of the discrepancy between each country's integrative behavior and its dependency on the Soviet Union is not convincing. It can be argued that with the exception of Bulgaria, by far the least economically developed member of Comecon, for no country including the Soviet Union were the intraregional relationships "economically vital," especially in the second half of the last decade.

In the end Gehlen appears to discard the communications approach and explains the meager results of integration processes in Eastern Europe with reference to "operational problems within the system making it difficult for a resolution of conflict over goals to be attained within the official organs of Comecon."[68] This seems to be the crux of the matter and confirms the judgment that emerged from the earlier discussion in this article.

Two other recent articles by David Finley and R. J. Mitchell also deal with theoretical aspects of integration in Eastern Europe.[69] Neither of them attempts to explain its progress or predict its future, but both seek rather to develop a theoretical framework for study and research. Thus Finley uses four indices of integration—scope, institutional structure, authority, and extent—to compare three supranational institutions in Communist Europe: Comecon, the Warsaw Pact, and the Joint Institute for Nuclear Research. His conclusion is that while the latter two organizations appeared to reach a higher plateau of integration, Comecon had a better chance to maintain itself in the long run mainly because it relied more on consensus than on coercion. This may well be true although one could argue that a comparison between the three organizations is not very meaningful in view of the striking differences in their respective areas of concern, institutional structures, and sheer volume of transactions.

Mitchell in turn applied both coalition theory and organization theory to the study of Comecon, claiming that each of the theories taken separately has only partial explanatory, and no predictive, value. He concludes by saying that

it seems beyond question that quantification and other behavioral study can

[67] Ibid., p. 112.

[68] Ibid.

[69] D. Finley, "Integration among the Communist Party-States: Comparative Case Studies," and R. Mitchell, "A Theoretical Approach to the Study of Communist International Organizations," in J. Triska (ed.), *Communist Party States: Comparative and International Studies* (Indianapolis, Ind: Bobbs-Merrill Co., 1969), pp. 57–105.

yield predictions with far greater accuracy than any guesswork based upon impressionistic conclusions about the communist system.[70]

This statement is as vague as it is meaningless. Mitchell does not make clear what kind of "quantification" he has in mind and thus it is difficult to say anything about his conclusion. Not every piece of statistical data necessarily improves our understanding of integrative processes; and Mitchell's effort, while suggestive, does not contribute much to advancing the theory of integration.

Another recent effort to discuss obstacles to economic integration in Eastern Europe was that of J. M. Montias.[71] Looking at Comecon as an integrative vehicle, Montias distinguishes four factors which played (and continue to play) a major role in obstructing the path toward closer integration in the area. The four factors are: political restrictions on the movement of labor and other resources, obstacles due to the strategy of development of individual member states, impediments to trade inherent in the economic mechanism of member states, and obstacles arising from the institutional arrangements for trade in goods and services among members.

It can be seen that Montias's discussion runs in terms comparable to those used in the analysis of economic factors hindering integration in part II above. The only major difference between the two discussions lies in the varying interpretations of the importance of political restraints on integration.

In discussing the political and strategic restrictions on integration in Eastern Europe, Montias emphasizes the point that it was in effect the Soviet Union which lost its chance of integrating the area economically in the early postwar years when it had the power to do so. By retaining, at least formally, the system of independent East European states, Stalin "laid the foundations of economic nationalism" which has since haunted the Soviet leadership.[72] In Montias's view the reasons for the formation of Comecon in 1949 are still shrouded in obscurity, and it is not at all certain that Comecon was ever seriously intended as an instrument of genuine economic integration of the Soviet bloc.

There is nothing basically wrong with this interpretation except that it seems to provide only a partial explanation of the lack of progress in East European integration. To be sure, Stalin appeared opposed to any form of international cooperation in this area as evidenced by his criticism of the attempted Balkan federation of the late forties, and it may be assumed that he did not seriously contemplate Comecon becoming an efficient tool of integration. But why limit the discussion to Stalin?

Undoubtedly, by not insisting on total absorption of individual countries

[70] Mitchell, in Triska, p. 103.
[71] J. M. Montias, *Studies in Comparative Communism*, Vol. 2, Nos. 3–4, pp. 38–60.
[72] Ibid., p. 41.

into the Soviet Union Stalin allowed the former to retain a modicum of sovereignty and notion of national interest as well as some control over the movement and utilization of resources. Montias might conceivably be right in claiming that this single act destroyed any chances of meaningful economic integration, yet one may wonder whether this was really the case. Comecon was clearly imposed on Eastern Europe from above and had little chance of success as long as it remained part and parcel of the Stalinist system. Yet there are strong indications that after Stalin's death and Khrushchev's accession to power, Comecon did have some chance of success. Thus, as suggested elsewhere,

> the main reason for its failure in the early sixties was the inability or unwillingness of the Soviet leadership to make the final break with the Stalinist *modus operandi,* and its determination to continue imposing its own preferences on Comecon.[73]

Also, while in the initial stages of Comecon's existence the Soviet Union was guilty of a lack of commitment, in the latter stages it tried to do too many things too fast without realizing that its earlier inaction did little to prepare the junior members for what was to come later.

Montias's conclusion is that the key role in the liberalization and expansion of exchanges, i.e., integration, will be played by the economic reforms now under way in some of the countries. He also feels, however, that chances of such a liberalization are slim until and unless the Soviet Union abandons its policy of high-cost autarky in raw materials and agricultural products which would lead the relative scarcities (and prices) of commodities in Comecon to coincide with those in the world market. Only then will the individual countries be able to depart from irrational trading practices and to expand multilateral trade. Furthermore, the uneven pace in reformmaking is not likely to bring about that expansion for reasons spelled out earlier in the article. Thus, according to Montias, the overall prospects for closer economic integration in Eastern Europe are not very bright.

Montias feels, however, that the so-called "Brezhnev Doctrine," justifying the Soviet intervention in Czechoslovakia, might be used by the Soviet leadership to impose "integration from above."

> Putting teeth into Comecon by fiat would, as a matter of fact, be much simpler and more consonant with the working style of communist bureaucrats than the patient search for solutions agreeable to every member of the organization in the framework of liberalized institutions.[74]

While Montias's prognosis concerning the economic obstacles to East European integration is highly plausible, the same cannot be said about the possi-

---

[73] A. Korbonski, "Some Random Thoughts on Economic Integration of Eastern Europe," paper prepared for the Conference on Regional Integration, Madison, Wisconsin, April 1969, p. 13.

[74] Montias, p. 60.

bility of politically inspired and Moscow-enforced integration. The meaning of the "Brezhnev Doctrine" is still a subject of controversy and its full impact on the future of Eastern Europe cannot be easily predicted.[75] Moreover, there is no evidence that the Soviet Union is strongly interested in the speed-up of integration and in the revival of Comecon as an instrument of Moscow's control. With overall Soviet foreign policy becoming gradually more pragmatic and conventional, Russia's interest and involvement in Comecon are becoming more and more a function of the short- and long-run usefulness of the organization for the achievement of Soviet policy objectives. As long as Comecon proved helpful in providing an instrument of control over Eastern Europe, the Soviet Union was actively concerned with maintaining and even strengthening it. Today, however, it is clear that Comecon's performance in that particular sphere was and is a disappointment. As long as the organization served as a channel for economic exploitation and regulation it did perform a useful task. At the present time, however, Comecon may have already become an economic burden for Moscow and this would tend to explain a decline in Soviet involvement manifested, for example, in the lukewarm support for the East European convertibility scheme.

To be sure, the events preceding the invasion of Czechoslovakia seemed to confirm Montias's hypothesis. References to Comecon cropped up with increasing frequency in the various Soviet-sponsored official statements made public during that period. The need for continuing close mutual economic relations, reaffirmed in the Dresden declaration of March, in the Warsaw letter in July, and the Cierna and Bratislava communiqués in August 1968, underscored the seeming importance of this particular problem. It apparently reflected the apprehension on the part of Czechoslovakia's partners within Comecon that that country might in the near future reduce its participation in that organization and turn instead to the West, following the path chosen by Romania. The evidence of Czechoslovakia's intention to withdraw from Comecon is hard to come by, however, and in the final analysis it is hard to imagine that the intervention of August 1968 was undertaken in order to keep the country in Comecon. Moreover, the large expansion in East-West contacts following the invasion would indicate that economic rapprochement with the West was no longer considered anathema by Moscow.

Except for sporadic attempts to breathe some new life into the Warsaw Pact, Soviet international behavior seems to reflect continuing interest in maintaining political détente with the West, as evidenced by the recent revival of the idea of the conference on European security. As a rule, political rapprochement tends to sustain and expand economic rapprochement. Thus Montias's prediction about the possibility of "integration from above" does not appear to be well founded, at least not at present. On the other hand, the erratic behavior

[75] Aspaturian, *International Organization*, Vol. 23, No. 3, p. 595.

of the Soviet oligarchy so well demonstrated during the events of 1968 may yet manifest itself in some sudden tightening of the reins of economic control in Eastern Europe.

What then is the future of integration in Communist Europe? The overall consensus that emerges from the writings of Nye, Gehlen, and Montias would indicate that the most likely tendency, at least in the short run, is going to be the maintenance of the status quo. My own feeling is that while the latter appears plausible there is also a good chance of economic disintegration in the area. In the final analysis the outcome will be dictated by the combination of endogenous and exogenous factors. Changes in the political, social, and economic systems, as well as developments in the regional and "cold-war environments" which are hardly predictable, cannot help but make any hypothesis highly tentative.

VI. East European Integration: Prospects for Future Research

The final issue to be considered is the agenda for future research in the area of East European integration.

The priority should be assigned above all to microtheories in both the political and economic arenas. Western scholars seem to have a pretty good knowledge of the workings of the national economic and political systems. What is needed is a switch in emphasis from the macro- to the microtype of analysis. We still know relatively little about the behavior of some key individuals and groups such as party and government bureaucrats, managers, and planners. We have even less knowledge about the processing of "inputs" and the process of decisionmaking in Comecon countries. The same applies to such problems as negotiating techniques and style, ways and means of solving disputes, formal and informal arrangements for consultations among strategic actors, and so on.

As far as a more general type of theorizing is concerned, one possible approach might be the linkage theory made popular recently by Rosenau.[76] The concept of direct and indirect linkages and of policy and environmental inputs and outputs may well be applied to the study of integration in Eastern Europe. To be sure, the concept of linkages per se has been used by Nye and other students of integration but only as one of the variables in the model. On the East European scene the linkage analysis was applied by R. V. Burks to the study of leadership selection, policy formulation and implementation, and ideological community.[77]

What might be done in the case of Eastern Europe is to utilize more extensively the matrix of national-international linkages developed by Rosenau.

[76] Rosenau, pp. 44–63.
[77] R. V. Burks, "The Communist Polities of Eastern Europe," in Rosenau, pp. 275–303.

This may permit us to establish a linkage network which, in turn, might bring to the surface some unfamiliar (latent) linkages that heretofore played little or no role in the process of integration. Also linkage research might bring into focus other interesting problems such as the duration, flexibility and stability of various linkages, linkages between various environments, fused linkages, and others. To quote Rosenau,

> such research would focus on the interdependence of polities and their environments, and would thus be of special interest to students of international institutions and to those concerned with the prospects of supranational integration.[78]

The point is well taken and it is worth pursuing.

---

[78] Rosenau, p. 59.

10

Domestic and International Consequences of Regional Integration

STUART A. SCHEINGOLD

I. INTRODUCTION

THE purpose of this article is to suggest that the perspective of scholars studying regional integration be broadened to include research expressly concerned with the consequences of integration and to indicate the directions that such efforts might take. To date, the students of integration have been mainly describing, analyzing, and measuring the integration process. This is true of research on the European Communities as well as of studies of integration elsewhere in Europe and on other continents. In our quest for political community we have utilized a number of different research strategies and focused on a broad range of indicators, but our primary concern has been with regional capacities for aggregating political authority.

What has been missing from all this work is some attention to the difference it makes whether or not such regional entities are created. As a result, after more than a decade of research we have only a very limited understanding of the costs and benefits of integration.[1]

Economists who have studied integration provide the major exception to the above generalization. They have tended, right from the outset, to be sensitive to the repercussions of regional integration on world trade and total welfare.[2] The internal consequences of integration for patterns of consumption

STUART A. SCHEINGOLD is an associate professor of political science at the University of Washington, Seattle.

The author's intellectual debt extends beyond the contributors to this special issue, to his colleague Professor Kenneth M. Dolbeare who first interested him in this article's most basic concerns. He is also grateful to Professor Jack Dennis for his assistance with data analysis.

[1] This article will draw almost exclusively on the experience of the European Communities in specifying the limits of current research efforts and in discussing the kinds of problems that remain to be tackled. Nevertheless, the underlying argument for research on the consequences of integration should be relevant to other regions.

[2] See, for example, one of the standard works: Bela Balassa, *The Theory of Economic Integration* (Homewood, Ill: Richard D. Irwin, 1961), chapter 1.

and competition have also been matters of concern for economists.[3] Their focus on consequences in general and concern with welfare in particular stands in sharp contrast to the perspectives of most political scientists. It should, nevertheless, be pointed out that the economists have been more inclined to theory and commentary than to empirical research.[4]

To a limited extent a portion of the work done by political scientists also sheds some light on the consequences of integration. In particular, political scientists working with Karl W. Deutsch have systematically collected and analyzed data which gives us a sense of the changes in attitudes and aggregate behavior (trade, mail, student travel, and tourism) which have accompanied integration. Indeed, they began to study changes in trading patterns well before serious empirical research by the economists was initiated. (Donald Puchala's article in this volume is the latest in a series of such studies.) Similarly, studies by Ernst Haas and Leon Lindberg, among others, have indicated how integration has given rise to community-wide organization of pressure groups and unprecedented cooperation between national and community bureaucrats, not to speak of the institutional innovations that characterize the integrative system.

One might reasonably think of all these changes as the consequences of integration. They are, however, confined to a relatively narrow range of problems. To those who study them these changes are not consequences but *indicators* of integration. Researchers use such data to determine whether or not integration is taking place. For Deutsch, the indicators of social community—transaction flows and elite and mass attitudes—are the defining characteristics of integration while to Haas, the growth of a pluralist political arena in the context of effective community institutions indicates successful integration. In other words, while this research does yield as a by-product information on the consequences of integration, these consequences are indistinguishable from process concerns having to do with the aggregation of political authority at the regional level.

In contrast, this article will focus squarely on consequences of integration and will broaden the inquiry beyond those considerations which are identifiable with the integration process. Two distinct sets of research questions will be pursued.

The first is to consider the results of integration in terms of the *original incentives* for creating a European community. The integrative process was expected to alter dramatically the relationships between the nation-states of

---

[3] This was probably first explored by Tibor Scitovsky, *Economic Theory and Western European Integration* (Stanford, Calif: Stanford University Press, 1958).

[4] An obvious exception is Lawrence B. Krause's excellent empirical study, *European Economic Integration and the United States* (Washington: Brookings Institution, 1968). Krause's book is certainly a big step in the direction favored in this article and will be discussed below. Ingo Walter has also collected a good deal of data in *The European Common Market: Growth and Patterns of Trade* (New York: Frederick A. Praeger, 1967).

Europe, transform faltering economic systems, and even change continental life-styles. While it is true that the development of the European Communities has been associated with peace, economic growth, and an apparent "Americanization" of life-style, we have little understanding about the extent to which integration is promoting or undermining these trends.[5]

There is also a second set of questions which directs our attention to a range of *distributional issues* transcending the original aspirations of the founders. How is integration affecting the distribution of influence and material well-being among the peoples of the European Communities and what is its impact on other regions of the world?

One can only speculate on the reasons for the rather limited research attention to the consequences of integration. But such speculation is useful if it makes us more sensitive to our own preconceptions and more self-conscious about the limitations of our research paradigms. The preconception in this case was, I believe, that integration was good by definition[6] since it was directed at economic reconstruction and permanent reconciliation between nations whose bloody conflicts had led to major wars engulfing significant portions of the world. A "United States of Europe" seemed almost by definition likely to serve the cause of a peaceful and prosperous future. Under these circumstances the more challenging research problem for social scientists was to describe, explain, and forecast the course of the integrative process. The result has been increasingly subtle paradigms and some very revealing findings, as other articles in this volume indicate.

At the same time, we have learned very little about the costs and benefits of integration. Europe is prosperous and peaceful, but we do not really know whether, or to what extent, this can be traced to the European Communities. The march toward federal union has been slowed and perhaps arrested. What has emerged is a relatively stable complex of European and national institutions, and the impact of this partially integrated regional system on the European economy—let alone on politics and diplomacy—is not at all clear. Moreover, peace and prosperity do not seem to have insured domestic tranquility. Partisan political conflict over the distribution of wealth and influence seems to be increasing despite affluence—or perhaps because of it. Should we not consider how the growth of the community feeds into these distributional issues? And what of the impact of integration on the rest of the world? What is good for the communities may not be good for nonmembers. Perhaps internal economic growth is being attained at the expense of developing areas.

[5] The recent outbreak of hostilities between two members of the relatively stable Central American Common Market (CACM) is a case in point—particularly since the conflict seems to have been due at least in part to the absence of regional policies on the free movement of labor.

[6] Again, my reference is primarily to political scientists who have been doing empirical studies of integration.

How does peaceful resolution of regional conflict relate to international politics?

In sum, what I am suggesting is a kind of dual perspective for investigating the consequences of integration: 1) actor incentive analysis (to what extent have the initial goals of the European Communities been attained?) and 2) distributional issues (how are the costs and benefits of integration shared within the community and with the world at large?). There is no elaborate rationale for this approach; it has the merit, however, of first allowing us to evaluate the European Communities on their own terms—that is, with respect to the problems which necessarily occupied Europeans at the close of World War II. We will then broaden the investigation to consider issues which do not seem to have figured directly in the plans of the founders. There is a way in which the first line of analysis relates to the communities' recent past while the second has to do with their proximate future. Certainly, the who-gets-what questions seem likely to intrude themselves with greater insistence into domestic European politics and also into the role of European states in world affairs. To raise questions about the way in which integration impinges upon these problems may then be to focus on issues which will determine the future of the European Communities.

To ask who wins and who loses as a result of integration is also to suggest that we as students of integration should be sensitive to value questions and willing to confront them directly in our research. Such studies could take the form of rigorous critiques of the value premises of integration theory in the classical tradition of political theory. This kind of work would make us more aware of the implications of our own research and would, as well, enhance our understanding of the range of potential consequences of integration. What I have in mind in this article, however, is not exercises in political theory but simply value-sensitive *empirical* research aimed at determining what difference it makes, in fact, whether or not Europe integrates. This kind of work may well be anchored in normative goals and could provide the basis for making informed judgments on the desirability of integration or on future directions that it should take. Nevertheless, personal value preferences are not preconditions to impact research, nor are they obstacles to empirical analysis; and, of course, impact research cannot in any case resolve value conflicts. Thus, my goal in this article is simply to explore an inviting void in the empirical analysis of regional integration and make some tentative suggestions on how it might be filled.

II. The Incentives to Integrate

There are at least two reasons why it is relatively easy to identify with some assurance the original goals—economic, political, and diplomatic—of the European Communities.[7] In the first place, the enormous common problems of postwar Europe suggested a set of obvious priorities. Economic reconstruction and growth, political stability and republican regimes, and peace within Europe, perhaps with restoration of European diplomatic influence, were clearly the goals to be sought—at least by the moderate, governing mainstream parties. Second, political leadership in the nations that were to become members of the community was in the hands of a relatively small and homogeneous group of primarily Christian-Democratic politicians and technocrats. This resulted in a significant agreement on means and ends and, therefore, a relatively coherent set of reasons for choosing integration as a way of coping with postwar problems.[8] The founders tended to see regional integration as the solution to all problems that were pressing in on the states of Western Europe in the decade after World War II. This was an idea rooted in lessons drawn from the thirties by men who were committed to both the productive and consensual capacities of welfare capitalism and pluralist democracy. The communities were to occupy a kind of middle ground which has been characterized as a "pragmatic synthesis of capitalism and socialism in the form of democratic planning."[9] In fact, despite exceptions (in agriculture and regional development, for instance), the treaties—particularly the Treaty Establishing the European Coal and Steel Community—lean more toward a market economy than toward planning. The basic orientation of the communities is toward changing practices by adjustments in the incentives available to entrepreneurs. Planning is to be used only in combination with such adjustments or when the inadequacy of the market is patently clear; hence the exceptions for agriculture and regional development.

This "pragmatic synthesis" was certainly not common ground at the outset of integration. The European Coal and Steel Community (ECSC) was, for example, established in the face of significant distrust on the part of working class parties and major portions of the trade union movement. The consensus that the founders perceived in the ECSC lay in the future. Their economic goal was not simply to utilize integration as an agent of economic reconstruction but also to exploit a single continental-sized market to increase the rate of

[7] The argument here is admittedly simplified with a great many other contributory factors excluded. For a more systematic consideration which places the communities within the general postwar context in Europe see Leon N. Lindberg and Stuart A. Scheingold, *Europe's Would-Be Polity: Patterns of Change in the European Community* (Englewood Cliffs, N.J: Prentice-Hall, 1970), chapter 1. See also Stanley Hoffmann's analysis, "Obstinate or Obsolete? The Fate of the Nation-State and the Case of Western Europe," reprinted in Joseph S. Nye, Jr. (ed.), *International Regionalism: Readings* (Boston: Little, Brown and Co., 1968), in particular, pp. 185–198.

[8] It is interesting to note that where other parties were in power and/or the effects of the war did not seem so crushing, the integration option was not so appealing—in particular, in the United Kingdom and Scandinavia.

[9] Ernst B. Haas, "Technocracy, Pluralism and the New Europe," in Stephen R. Graubard (ed.), *A New Europe?* (Boston: Houghton Mifflin, 1964), p. 68.

economic growth which had sagged badly during the interwar period—particularly in relation to the United States.[10] Affluence, in its turn, was to undermine the appeal of extremist ideologies, thus simultaneously insuring political stability and reducing the constituencies of those parties on the Right and Left with expansionist international programs.

Scholars developed the socioeconomic logic of this political program. It involves a kind of chain reaction from the larger market through changes in business practice to new life-styles and political orientations. One of the earliest economic studies of integration developed this line of reasoning:

> Economic union may be expected to change methods of production in two ways. First, it would provide marginal producers with a powerful stimulus to mend their ways and lower their costs; second, it would provide manufacturing industry at large—at least in the competitive markets—with some inducements and new opportunities for the greater use of mass-production methods.[11]

Standardization and mass production would replace the old pattern of product differentiation which would, in turn, bring "a typical middle class item of consumption within the reach of working-class budgets."[12] The logical conclusion of this argument is that to bring the item within reach is tantamount —with some judicious promotion—to establishing a market for it. This, of course, implies that the working class will readily adopt the values and the life-style of the middle class and presumably their moderate political preferences as well.

One can thus think of the purposes to be served by integration on two rather distinct levels. Most obviously and directly, integration was to be an agent of economic reconstruction and a vehicle for creating among the member states permanent institutional ties. At another level integration was related to a general social theory which saw productivity and affluence as a kind of universal problem solvent. There is considerable dispute about the contribution of integration, if any, to either of these objectives. Given the paucity of data and the divergent speculations about the impact of the communities there is no way in which these differences can be resolved in this article. What can be done is to present the available findings together with some of the questions which have been raised and in this way indicate the most promising possibilities for further research.

Economic growth was perhaps the most generally accepted immediate goal of the founders, at least those of the ECSC and of the EEC. Professional economists, however, differed about the effects of integration on growth: Would it induce growth at all? If so, would growth stem from the economies of scale,

[10] See Angus Maddison, *Economic Growth in the West: Comparative Experience in Europe and North America* (New York: Twentieth Century Fund, 1964), p. 37.

[11] Scitovsky, pp. 31–32.

[12] Ibid., pp. 27ff.

specialization, competition, etc?[13] The impressive growth rates of member states, particularly since 1958, have not really stilled the controversy since it has been argued that the spurt in growth rates was under way prior to integration.[14] The implication of this line of thought is that the progress of integration is more a consequence than a cause of economic growth.[15]

In this setting of controversy we must be grateful for Lawrence Krause's efforts to cut to the heart of the matter with actual measurement of the impact of integration on the income levels of the member states. It is beyond the scope of this article to consider his measurement techniques or even his results in detail. Krause concluded that the "income of member countries has been stimulated" by integration.[16] He calculated the increment with precision, determined the portion attributable to increases in efficiency and investment, and supported his findings with reasoned argument. All told, this surely adds up to the most impressive effort to come to grips with the consequences of integration.[17]

Still, it is not clear just what the implications of the Krause study are, since the growth attributable to integration seems to be rather modest. The compound annual rate of growth in gross domestic products varied between 5.1 percent and 7.1 percent for the member countries of the EEC during the period between 1958–1959 and 1964 (see Table 1), but the annual income increments induced by economic integration during the transitional period varied between .18 percent and .22 percent.[18] Integration would thus seem to be responsible for only 2 to 3 percent of the annual increase.[19]

What can we conclude from a comparison of the income impact of the relatively well-integrated Common Market with that of the European Free Trade Association (EFTA)? According to Krause:

> The median increase for the Common Market was at a compound annual rate of 0.19 percent (Netherlands and France) while the median for EFTA was 0.16 percent (Switzerland and the United Kingdom). The lowest estimate for an EEC country was above the EFTA median.[20]

---

[13] See Balassa, chapters 5–8.

[14] One of the most persistent skeptics has been Alexandre Lamfalussy. See his *The United Kingdom and the Six* (London: Macmillan & Co., 1963).

[15] For a rejoinder see Richard Mayne, "Economic Integration in the New Europe," in Graubard, pp. 174–199.

[16] Krause, p. 73.

[17] Ibid., see particularly pp. 35–45. The book ranges well beyond a consideration of these income effects for the member states. Indeed, the basic concern is, as the title suggests, with the impact on the United States. Incidentally, the above conclusions on income are based on manufactured products. Agriculture is treated separately since it has been subjected to a program which has tended to promote self-sufficiency rather than the most efficient allocation of resources. See chapter 3.

[18] Krause, p. 44.

[19] This rough estimate would presumably have to be adjusted for the exclusion of agricultural products from Krause's calculation of annual income increments attributable to integration, but this adjustment would not seem likely to change the total picture appreciably.

[20] Krause, p. 44.

TABLE I. GROWTH OF GROSS DOMESTIC PRODUCT

| | Compound Annual Rate of Increase in Percentages | | |
Country	1953 to 1958–1959	1958–1959 to 1964	Change in Growth Rates
EEC			
Belgium-Luxembourg	2.7	5.1	2.4
France[a]	4.7	5.6	0.9
Germany	6.9	7.1	0.2
Italy	5.2	6.0	0.8
Netherlands	4.5	5.6	1.1
EFTA			
Austria	6.7	4.8	⁻1.9
Denmark	2.9	5.8	2.9
Norway	2.9	5.3	2.4
Portugal	4.0	6.7	2.7
Sweden	3.9	5.1	1.2
Switzerland	4.6[b]	5.7	1.1
United Kingdom	2.4	3.8	1.4
United States	2.1	4.1	2.0

SOURCE: Krause, p. 37.

NOTE: This table lists gross domestic product growth for each country in the EEC and EFTA, plus the United States, before and after integration in terms of 1958 prices at factor costs.

[a] At market prices.

[b] 1954 to 1958–1959.

The differences may be distinct and measurable but do they not amount to a rather small return for the heavier commitments made by the member states to the European community? Krause may have demonstrated generally that integration can serve as an agent of economic growth. His analysis still raises questions about whether the constraints imposed by membership in the EEC can be justified on economic grounds alone.

This theme is explored by J. J. Servan-Schreiber in his provocative study, *The American Challenge*.[21] Servan-Schreiber's thesis is that the only meaningful gauge of European economic performance is the United States, and he argues that European firms have not made the necessary changes in general business practice which are required if the European corporate culture is ever to compete technologically and financially with its American counterpart. His is not a study heavy in data, but the information which is presented suggests weaknesses in scale, research expenditure, and profit margins. The direction of change is positive; the scale of European business does show signs of increasing, for example. But either the American firms are moving ahead at a

[21] J. J. Servan-Schreiber, *The American Challenge*, trans. by Ronald Steel (New York: Atheneum, 1968).

better pace or else the European gain is too small to promise any significant narrowing of the gap in the near future.

Servan-Schreiber's case for using American performance as a standard of European achievements is compellingly simple:

> Fifteen years from now it is quite possible that the world's third greatest industrial power, just after the United States and Russia, will not be Europe, but *American industry in Europe*. Already, in the ninth year of the Common Market, this European market is basically American in organization.[22]

It is not just that America continues to offer an object lesson in technocracy and affluence as it did to the founders of the European Communities. Now, the influx of American investment threatens the independent existence of European industry. Servan-Schreiber's conclusion is that the European Economic Community which he characterizes as a "tariff union" can never be expected to induce the changes which are prerequisites to really dynamic growth. Only a European federal system with its own "industrial policy" can stimulate the necessary commitments to research, flexible management, and large-scale production, Servan-Schreiber argues.

Both the problems and the solutions, in all likelihood, are a good deal more complex than are implied in *The American Challenge*. Take the issue of American investment, for example. Is it really an obstacle to growth and innovation among European firms? Krause suggests that this capital may be inducing just the kind of changes that Servan-Schreiber advocates:

> The implications of the growing opposition to American direct investment could be far-reaching. The immediate reaction of European business has been a movement towards mergers among companies in order to reach a scale of operation closer to that of the American firms with which they compete. . . . Mergers in the past have been mainly among firms of the same nationality or between national firms and the large international firms—usually American based. But recently with the Common Market there have been some faint signs that the transnational mergers that have long been expected are finally beginning.[23]

Indeed, one might wonder whether the influx of American capital is not responsible at least indirectly for a portion of the income increment which Krause attributes to integration. It is true that the total flow has been relatively small, but these investments have been concentrated in the most dynamic "research-intensive" sectors.[24] Were Servan-Schreiber's federal system to answer the American challenge by reducing or reversing the flow of American capital, the results might be counterproductive—at least in the short run.

---

[22] Ibid., p. 3.
[23] Krause, p. 146.
[24] Ibid., pp. 144–145. See also Christopher Layton, *Trans-Atlantic Investment* (The Atlantic Papers) (Boulogne-sur-Seine: Atlantic Institute, 1966).

But all this is mere speculation. What Servan-Schreiber does is direct our attention to handicaps that *may* be inherent in operating through what can be termed a partial political system. At present we *know* very little, if anything, about the extent to which weaknesses in the community political system have stood in the way of an industrial policy and/or the projected transformation in business practice. This problem takes on added importance since— Servan-Schreiber's plea to the contrary notwithstanding—dramatic changes in the character of the current system are unlikely in the foreseeable future. Here then is a neglected area where further research might pay significant dividends.

A European community was to bring peace as well as prosperity to Europe. Certainly, the relationships between the nations of Western Europe have been peaceful in the two decades since World War II. It is, of course, particularly satisfying that Franco-German relations have been so free of conflict. But again we may well ask whether integration is a cause or primarily a consequence of this relatively tranquil period. And how do the communities relate to the continuing tensions with Eastern Europe? Obviously, these are questions of more than passing importance, yet we are without any answers. Or perhaps it is more accurate to say that a number of answers have been proposed but none of them has been validated. Indeed, those who have commented on the impact of regional integration on questions of peace and war have tended to use quite different styles of analysis and often have raised the issues rather obliquely. While I sense competing hypotheses in the various positions taken, they are rather like arguments passing in the night.

David Mitrany asserts that the EEC is increasingly a "closed" system that pursues exclusivist policies and is likely to generate a parochial brand of regional patriotism.[25] It is, he contends, aggregating economic power and diplomatic influence, and consequently its exclusivist policies tend to increase tensions and conflict in Europe and elsewhere. For evidence in support of Mitrany's argument we need look no further than the division in Western Europe between EFTA and the EEC. That the EEC is still composed of six members is not due to a lack of applicants. The failure of the United Kingdom's bid for membership so far is due, at least in part, to a fear of watering down that which has already been achieved, just as Mitrany suggests.[26] More-

[25] David Mitrany, "The Prospect of Integration: Federal or Functional?" as reprinted in Nye, pp. 43–74.

[26] "The more fields of activity it actively enters, e.g., agriculture, the more acquisitive it tends to become; and in the degree to which it is rounded out it also hardens into a segregated entity." Mitrany, in Nye, p. 69. Of course, Mitrany's concern is not with the EFTA/EEC split, per se, which he sees as symptomatic of the federalist approach to integration. The confusion of terminology among students of integration is suggested by this characterization of the community. Servan-Schreiber, of course, stigmatizes the community for its failure to adopt a federalist approach. One way out of this confusion is to distinguish between the neo-functional approach of the European Communities and Mitrany's functional ideas—both separable from federal schemes. For details see Lindberg and Scheingold, chapter 1. Chapter 7 of the same study analyzes the problem of British entry.

over, Krause provides us with quantitative evidence of the trade-diverting effects of commercial competition between the blocs.[27]

While the conflict between EFTA and the EEC is real, there are those who doubt that the resultant tensions are likely to ripen into anything approaching armed struggles. Raymond Aron, for example, considers the differences between the EEC and EFTA as

> a conflict of internal policy more than a dispute between sovereign states. By the fact of being allied for better or worse, the adversaries were deprived of the supreme recourse. . . . None was in a position to employ military force; none could employ the threat of commercial war: such threats were resented by public opinion because the reprisals would not be in accord with the spirit of the fundamental alliance among the adversaries and because no violation of the GATT charter by the Six would have justified it. The foils had to remain buttoned. The fencers were debaters, the winners more skillful and determined.[28]

For Aron, the North Atlantic alliance of sovereign states is the relevant policy arena for "political questions." In his analysis of the blocs the European Communities are discussed as "economic organizations" and hardly enter at all into the subsequent consideration of "intra-bloc conflicts."

Aron's assertion could be taken at face value as a kind of empirical observation: The European Communities have been preoccupied with their economic mission and have thus not been a factor in major foreign policy problems.[29] The recent announcement that the foreign ministers of the six had agreed to work toward a joint foreign policy would then suggest that a change was imminent.[30] The communities' marginal role in matters of war and peace can, however, be seen as inherent in their economic orientation. The root assumption is that there are significant discontinuities between economic and political problems—or between what Stanley Hoffmann refers to as "high" and "low" politics."[31] Functional theorists resist such distinctions and see major foreign policy implications in the operations of the European Communities. Haas, for example, has argued that German reunification is inconsistent with a viable European community.[32] Similarly, there is a body of opinion, which by all accounts included President Charles de Gaulle, that believed British membership would in all likelihood entail a radical realignment of relations within

---

[27] Krause concludes, somewhat surprisingly, that "the loss inflicted on the EEC by EFTA is almost twice as great as the reverse loss." Krause, p. 72.

[28] Raymond Aron, *Peace and War* (New York: Frederick A. Praeger, 1967), pp. 462–463.

[29] On the basis of a very unsystematic sampling it is reasonable to conclude that the policymakers share this view. See, for example, Dean Acheson, "Europe: Decision or Drift," *Foreign Affairs*, January 1966 (Vol. 44, No. 2), pp. 198–205, or an earlier piece in the same journal: Heinrich von Brentano, "Goals and Means of the Western Alliance," *Foreign Affairs*, April 1961 (Vol. 39, No. 3), pp. 416–429.

[30] *New York Times*, March 7, 1970, p. 3.

[31] Stanley Hoffmann, *Gulliver's Troubles, or the Setting of American Foreign Policy* (Atlantic Policy Studies) (New York: McGraw-Hill, 1968), chapter 11.

[32] Haas, in Graubard, p. 78.

the North Atlantic area. According to functional theorists the potential linkages for building a foreign policy inhere in problems generated by the communities as now constituted. Hoffmann, on the other hand, sees little if any likelihood of a common will emerging in matters which fall outside the realm of economic policy and, of course, does not find the notion of intrinsic linkages very convincing.

The matter at issue is, of course, not whether the communities as presently constituted have a foreign policy; clearly they do not. On this all the commentators cited would presumably agree. The problem is rather whether there is any way in which the economic tasks of the communities impinge on the more general issues of diplomacy and security within the North Atlantic area or beyond it. Aron and Hoffmann argue in somewhat different ways that integration has no such effects while Haas and Mitrany imply that it does—albeit, perhaps in a covert or indirect fashion. No matter, for the extent to which the communities relate to "high politics" and whether they are increasing or easing political tensions is in the final analysis an empirical question. Yet it is a question that has not been confronted directly in research on integration. We have theories and commentary but very little in the way of empirical research.

There is, on the other hand, some suggestive data which bears on Mitrany's concern that the EEC is nurturing a parochial brand of patriotism. Attitudinal data indicates increasingly favorable orientations toward the goals and institutions of the European Communities.[33] Donald Puchala, writing in this volume, sees in French and German attitudes "evidence of mutual identification—i.e., some hint of a 'we feeling'" characteristic of community.[34] Of particular relevance to Mitrany's argument is his finding that Frenchmen tend to see the six current members of the European Communities as those which in the long run "must participate."[35]

Puchala's findings are not conclusive, however, since other data suggests that the shifts in loyalty that would seem to be a precondition to regional chauvinism are not developing. Among elites in the Federal Republic of Germany (West Germany) and France there is a strong ad hoc or expediential element in the support for integration. As Robert Weissberg writes,

> among the elite sampled here there are "internationalists" (or integrationists), "nationalists," and many who may lean one way on one issue and another way on a different issue.[36]

Moreover, preliminary analysis of a recent study of European youth in France and West Germany does not indicate that those committed to a single Euro-

---

[33] See Lindberg and Scheingold, chapter 2; also Ronald Inglehart in this volume.

[34] Donald Puchala in this volume, p. 140.

[35] Ibid., Table 2, part 3, p. 142.

[36] Robert Weissberg, "Nationalism, Integration, and French and German Elites," in *International Organization*, Spring 1969 (Vol. 23, No. 2), p. 347. The data considered by Weissberg is that collected by Karl Deutsch, and others. See Karl Deutsch, and others, *France, Germany and the Western Alliance: A Study of Elite Attitudes on European Integration and World Politics* (New York: Charles Scribner's Sons, 1967).

pean government are more strongly attached to the present Europe of the six than are those young people who favor looser forms of cooperation or integration (see Table 2).[37]

TABLE 2. ATTITUDES OF GERMAN AND FRENCH YOUTH ABOUT A
UNITED STATES OF EUROPE

Type of European System[a]	Size of the European System[b]					
	Europe of Six	Six and Great Britain	All Western Europe	All Europe Except the Soviet Union	All Europe Including the Soviet Union	Total
No European government, regular cooperation among national governments	6	27	18	18	30	99
European government dealing with the most important questions, national governments handling particular problems	6	13	26	26	29	101
European government, no national government	4	12	4	32	48	100

SOURCE: European Youth Study conducted by Jacques-René Rabier, director of information for the European Economic Community, together with Jack Dennis, Ronald Inglehart, Leon Lindberg, and Stuart Scheingold.

NOTE: The attitudes polled are on the countries to be included in a United States of Europe according to preference for the type of European system. Undertaken in 1969, the results are expressed in percentage figures and N = 184, with sixteen respondents in the sample failing to respond to one or both (of the following) questions:

a. As far as bringing about the unification of Europe is concerned, which of the following three formulae would you prefer?

   A. "There is no government at European level, but the governments of each country meet regularly to try to adopt a common policy."
   B. "There is a European government which deals with the most important questions, but each country retains a government to handle its own particular problems."
   C. "There is a European government which deals with all questions and the member countries no longer have a national government."

b. Which countries in your opinion must form part of a United States of Europe. I mean the United States of Europe which has been proposed. Would you choose a statement from this list to tell me how you feel about this?

   Statement A: Europe of the Six
   Statement B: The Six plus Great Britain
   Statement C: All Western Europe
   Statement D: All Europe except Russia
   Statement E: All Europe including Russia

[37] Given the rather small number in the sample and the uneven distribution, the German and French figures have been combined. Consideration of each country individually would not, however, alter the above conclusion.

Trying to draw general conclusions on the basis of the rather meager data which is available is hardly an inviting task. Some of the objectives of integration have been realized at least in part. A Franco-German rapprochement certainly seems to have been effected, and West European economic growth has been impressive. But whether all this adds up to peace and prosperity within Western Europe is more difficult to determine, as is the role of integration in whatever developments are taking place. Krause assures us that at least a portion of the economic gains of the postwar period are attributable to integration, but Servan-Schreiber warns that these gains are rather modest and that the EEC as it is now constituted is an obstacle to more dynamic and dependable patterns of growth. Opinion data does not indicate clearly whether or not committed "Europeans" are turning inward, but the European Communities do seem to have engendered conflicts and schisms within Western Europe. In any case, much more work must be done if we are to answer even these relatively straightforward questions.

Oddly enough, it is easier to speak with conviction about the more grandiose aspirations of the integrators: the communities' mission to promote beneficent and stabilizing trends. These were to be the fruits of an affluent continental-sized economic union. It now seems clear, however, that the association of affluence with moderation and stability which initially inspired the European Communities is, at the very least, too simplistic a perspective to guide policymakers or to describe adequately current trends. This essentially nonpolitical, no-conflict, technocratic model does not explain the world we see around us in which political conflict coexists with affluence and in which the old problems of redistributing material welfare and influence remain salient. Nowadays, it seems just as reasonable to expect the changes that community was supposed to generate to breed dislocation, discontent, and instability—at least in the short run. What we need then are some orienting concepts and researchable questions which will aid us in discovering how the communities relate to the changing patterns of demands that seem to be emerging in postindustrial societies.

III. THE NEW POLITICS

Let us begin by trying to get some idea of the dimensions and nature of this new pattern of demands. I have already referred to them as distributive, and Haas elsewhere in this volume uses the term consummatory. Insofar as these words suggest concern with the way in which material welfare and political influence are shared, they are appropriate but somehow too narrow. The diffuse, eclectic, and value-sensitive spirit of the "new politics" is better captured in the following assertion from the European review, *Agenor:*

NEW POLITICS

—critical and continuing education, self management, the right to information, and the problems of our natural and man-made environment

—these themes are more immediately relevant to the quality of the life of the individual citizen than tranditional (sic) political issues

—and they are going to be increasingly the object of citizen and political action throughout Europe.[38]

At the very least, the lesson of the new politics is that affluence is no longer its own justification. Affluence perhaps—but for what, for whom, and at what cost?

To read *Agenor* is to be constantly confronted with the full range of objectives to which the European Communities might aspire. It is not the kind or reading likely to evoke complacency among the supporters of European integration. *Agenor* differs from other critiques in that its emphasis is less on the failure to aggregate authority than on the inability to relate to the emerging problems of the latter decades of the twentieth century. The journal is, then, rather like the conscience of European community; if its forecasting is accurate, a failure to relate to these issues may imperil the integrative process. As Haas sees it,

> new national stimuli stressing demands for change with a consummatory quality strike Brussels while the national arena continues to be struck with EEC outputs that correspond to the earlier incremental-instrumental style.[39]

Such developments undermine the initial congruence between the European and the national systems. They also suggest that the European system will be increasingly vulnerable either because it is an obstacle to changes being pressed upon the national systems or simply because it slips further outside the political mainstream and thus becomes quite dispensable.

The demands of the new politics, therefore, provide standards for assessing the consequences of integration—standards which are much broader than those implied by the initial incentives to integrate and which at the same time may reveal a great deal about the future success of European integration. Although we once again have a good many theories about the way in which the communities do now or will in the future relate to the new politics, there is not much data. Moreover, even the theories do not really cover the full range of problems to be found in the pages of *Agenor*. The discussion which follows will, therefore, be introductory and illustrative and will focus on those aspects of the new politics which are entangled, albeit marginally, with the work of the European Communities. With respect to the member states let us consider whether the communities are likely to promote, or be responsive to, demands

---

[38] *Agenor*, October 1969 (No. 12), p. 34.
[39] Ernst B. Haas in this volume, p. 37.

for more egalitarian and participatory systems. Internationally, let us consider briefly the impact of integration within Western Europe upon developing areas.

One student of integration, Amitai Etzioni, argues that regional integration in general and the European Economic Community in particular may well be the agent of a participatory or "active society."[40] Etzioni sees regional systems as one of a number of possible "new action units" for transforming unresponsive societies. The active society is, in his words, "a society in charge of itself rather than unstructured or restructured to suit the logic of instruments and the interplay of forces that they generate."[41] The secret of the "active society" is that it is responsive to the needs of all its members, and this calls for a sustained and concerted effort to induce these members to articulate their needs and to mobilize for their realization. In particular, it requires the authorities to enhance "the political power of collectivities whose social power is rising."[42] Were it true that European integration is responding to these ideals, the new consummatory demands would certainly be met: Indeed, there would be no noncongruence problem. But can we realistically expect the communities as they are now constituted even to move in the consummatory direction?

The available evidence, while once again inconclusive, suggests that the European Communities are not presently structured to promote a more active society. Their technocratic orientation and indirect institutions imply limited participation. It is not simply that these institutions are dependent on elites; it is difficult to imagine a political system of any size that is not dependent on elites. Nor can it be said that the communities have not been instrumental in mobilizing or activating societal groups. The more fundamental problems are that: 1) the institutions are designed to minimize rather than maximize participation; 2) integration has been associated primarily with *established* elites; and 3) such mobilization which has occurred has been confined largely to already influential groups.

All of these tendencies are, it seems to me, closely associated with certain aspects of the integrative process. In the first place technocratic decisions designed to maximize wealth call for expertise, not participation. Andrew Shonfield argues that the technocrat

is normally called in to deal with the type of problem whose solution cannot

---

[40] Amitai Etzioni, *The Active Society: A Theory of Societal and Political Processes* (New York: Free Press, 1968). Regional integration is, it should be pointed out, at most tangential to the concerns of this elaborate and imposing tome.

[41] Ibid., p. 6. The precise role of regional communities is that of "a 'middle' tier in an evolving world-community consensus-formation structure." Not all regional schemes are suitable, but integrative projects along the lines of the European Communities have significant potential. They serve "central" rather than "marginal" societal functions; they are not directed at "countervailing" other regional bodies as are the North Atlantic Treaty Organization (NATO) and the Warsaw Pact; and finally they are "welfare" communities rather than defensive trading blocs like the European Free Trade Association. See p. 596.

[42] Ibid., p. 514.

be precisely defined in advance, and where the area of administrative discretion is therefore recognized as being very large. In practice such a person combines a large part of the lawmaking function with the executive function. He is the embodiment of the principle which is the opposite of classical separation of powers.[43]

Second, resources for generating consent are relatively limited. The result is a heavy dependence on established governmental elites with efforts to mobilize groups restricted to influential collectivities which are in a position to thwart integrative schemes. Jean Monnet's Action Committee for a United States of Europe is prototypical: It is the most unique mobilizing agent associated with integration, and it draws entirely upon established elites. The committee seldom if ever goes outside the mainstream and prides itself on the collection of notables that it has assembled. Consider also the following rather typical assessment of the European Parliament:

> But the European Parliament is not the mother of parliaments. It makes no policies, passes no legislation, appropriates no money, brings down no governments. Nor does it even represent, as the treaty intended it should. None of the appointive delegations has thus far included a communist, even though the French and Italian communist parties have regularly polled 20 and 25 percent of the total vote.[44]

In sum, these nonparticipatory tendencies may be more than peculiarities of the process that has unfolded in Europe; indeed, they may be among the predictable costs of regional integration. At the very least, if Etzioni's vision of a "middle tier action unit" is to take shape at the regional level, these obstacles to participation will have to be overcome.

Of course, the "active society" is not necessarily an end in itself. Were the community committed to the equal distribution of the benefits of integration and to other goals of the new politics, then participatory values might be less important. But the materialistic orientations of the communities are suspect, and given the nature of integration it seems clear that certain groups will be disadvantaged:

> Not all groups are destined to participate in prosperity. As a matter of fact, the process by which prosperity is being created is squeezing some groups viciously —mostly the self-employed and those at the bottom of the service class. The former group include most notably small farmers, artisans, and shopkeepers, who are destined to be replaced by their large-scale counterparts. The emergent new society does not have a high tolerance for inefficiency.[45]

[43] Andrew Shonfield, *Modern Capitalism: The Changing Balance of Public and Private Power* (New York: Oxford University Press, 1965), p. 408. For a discussion of the participatory implications of technocracy within the European community see Lindberg and Scheingold, pp. 266–269.

[44] J. L. Zaring, *Decision for Europe: The Necessity of Britain's Engagement* (Baltimore, Md: Johns Hopkins Press, 1969), p. 70. Zaring's discussion extends well beyond the parliament and devotes considerable attention to the problem of representation. For a consideration of the community's rather limited and uneven contribution to mobilization see Lindberg and Scheingold, pp. 75–80.

[45] Lindberg and Scheingold, p. 273.

Even the established ideology of the communities is that of the modified market economy with no real commitment to egalitarian values.

This problem of distribution is raised more concretely by the French left-wing intellectual, André Gorz, in his book *Strategy for Labor: A Radical Proposal*. Gorz believes, contrary to Servan-Schreiber, that the EEC has been successful in promoting the changes in business practices that both authors see as prerequisites to more effective growth. That is to say, he believes that European corporations have been willing and able to take advantage of the opportunities for expansion provided by the Common Market. Gorz, however, denies that corporate initiative can promote balanced economic growth. His argument is for planning and his fear is that the market approach to growth will cause as many problems as it will cure; he predicts a failure to develop depressed regions and a growing disparity between these regions and those which are better endowed. More specifically, he argues that the agricultural policy of the EEC will promote overproduction and irrational population shifts which will depopulate agricultural areas "below the threshold of economic viability."[46] Gorz thus challenges the theory of welfare capitalism on which the communities are based and foresees major dislocations stemming directly from their modified laissez faire, *laissez innover* orientation. This is, of course, a neo-Marxist critique, but its relevance and interest lie not so much in its Marxist implications as in its reintroduction of political conflict—whether among groups, classes, or parties—into the analytic framework. Gorz, in other words, directs our attention to the possibility that affluence, technology, and the acquisitive instinct will not necessarily sublimate political conflict. Moderate two-party or multiparty systems may yet emerge, but clearly there is ferment, and Gorz directs us toward the impact of regional integration on the politics of the member states. He argues that integration may catalyze a major realignment of political forces—specifically, that community policies will tend to generate three distinctive political coalitions:

1) The Atlantic coalition: This would be the neo-liberal or free trade bloc which he identifies as a declining group, composed of a significant portion of European bankers and West German and Dutch (and ultimately British) big business, with tactical support of American corporate enterprise throughout the Common Market.

2) The nationalist coalition: This would be based on precapitalist and what he refers to as "paleo-capitalist" enterprises (in other words: family business, small shopkeepers, medium and small peasants) and perhaps portions of the labor movement.

3) The European coalition: Included in this grouping would be the Euro-

46 André Gorz, *Strategy for Labor: A Radical Proposal* (Boston: Beacon Press, 1967), p. 162.

pean technocracy, the Social-Democrats, and what he refers to as neo-capitalist big business.[47]

One may well have doubts as to whether the communities will soon become such a pivotal factor in domestic politics, but since community policies are so integrally linked to the future of such key groups as the farmers and corporate enterprise, is it unreasonable to assume that integration will have an impact on the patterns of political conflict?

If the patterns of party conflict change and new coalitions form while others break up, it stands to reason that the quality of political life will be affected. One could argue, for example, that the divisions that Gorz foresees might promote reactionary politics by splitting the forces of liberal capitalism between Atlantic and European blocs. This is, of course, entirely speculative and would in any case depend on whether or not these divisions tended to congeal into long-term alliances. The fact remains that variations in parliamentary coalitions may well facilitate certain tendencies and undermine others, thus significantly affecting the kind of policy outputs that emerge from the national political systems.

Finally, let us consider a distributional issue relating to the international consequences of regional integration in Europe—the impact of integration on the developing areas. Once again questions can be posed, but data bearing on these questions is not really available. Another echo from the earlier analysis is the significant potential for discontinuity between initial expectation and actual impact. Recall that, to the extent that general international relations were considered, regional integration in Europe was perceived as part of a generally expansive trend in world trading patterns—an expansion from which all would gain, if not necessarily in equal shares. This seems to remain the official position of the European Communities which stresses their trade with developing areas, the special concessions granted to those less developed countries (LDCs) that are linked by agreements of association, etc. But if we do not accept at face value the notion that a general expansion in world trade necessarily represents a net gain for all or that what advances the interest of certain LDCs necessarily advances the interest of all, then we might want to probe more deeply and ask some additional questions.

The basic grounds for concern about the impact of European integration on the economic growth and diplomatic influence of developing nations were discussed some years ago by Ellen Frey-Wouters.

---

[47] Ibid., p. 149. These coalitions are not, it should be pointed out, perceived to be the normal and necessary consequence of integration, per se, but rather part of a scenario which stems directly from Gorz's mistrust of the communities' essentially market approach to integration. Thus the coalitions will form in periods of recession, brought on by the overproduction which Gorz does perceive as a necessary consequence of integration. As such recessions become the salient political issue, the above groups would tend to crystallize around distinctive solutions: The Atlantic coalition would choose an Atlantic free-trade response; the Nationalist coalition would opt for dismantling the European Communities; and the European coalition would put their faith in planning, intervention, and stabilization at the supranational level.

1. Do the association agreements indicate a new willingness on the part of European states to assume part of the burden and responsibility for the welfare of developing nations or is it simply a subtle new version of the old colonial relationship?

2. Do the association agreements benefit the associated states at the expense of the other developing areas, thereby reducing the chances of coordinated development and dividing the developing nations against one another?[48]

As she sees it, the answer to the first question is to be found in whether or not the association agreements promote indigenous industrial development by permitting the developing states to protect their infant industries, restrict the entrée of European corporations, encourage the establishment of processing facilities for raw materials in the developing nations, etc. The crucial facets of the second question are more difficult to specify. Certainly, they would include an investigation of trade- and aid-diverting effects which would permit certain developing states to benefit at the expense of others and might at the same time not really encourage development since protected access would not be likely to stimulate industrial efficiency. It would also be significant to learn whether the association agreements were obstacles to regional plans in Africa or whether, in world trading conferences, the associated states regularly broke with the developing states on EEC-relevant issues.

These are the kinds of problems that must be explored if we are to assess the impact of the European Economic Community on developing nations and, more generally, if we are to begin to evaluate the likelihood of regional integration as an agent of upward transfer in the process of world community consensus building. Even without research we can be reasonably sure from statements made that association agreements are perceived as a threat by non-associated states in both Africa and Latin America.[49] Similarly, efforts have been made within the General Agreement on Tariffs and Trade (GATT) and the United Nations Conference on Trade and Development (UNCTAD) to unite the developing nations in defense of such principles as the most-favored-nation clause.[50] But while there is some rather impressionistic evidence that the EEC is often perceived as disruptive rather than as an agent of development and welfare, more evidence is obviously necessary if we are to assess the accuracy of that perception.

The foregoing analysis raises a good many questions about the way in which the European Communities relate to the demands and values of the new politics. My own impression is that the communities, at least as they are now con-

[48] Ellen Frey-Wouters, "The Progress of European Integration," *World Politics*, April 1965 (Vol. 17, No. 3), pp. 472–476.

[49] See, for example, Ali A. Mazrui, "The Common Market and Non-Member Countries: African Attitudes to the European Economic Community," in Lawrence B. Krause (ed.), *The Common Market: Progress and Controversy* (Englewood Cliffs, N.J.: Prentice-Hall, 1964), and Sidney Dell, *Trade Blocs and Common Markets* (New York: Alfred A. Knopf, 1963), pp. 186–193.

[50] Frey-Wouters, *World Politics*, Vol. 17, No. 3, p. 476.

stituted, entail a significant sacrifice of participatory and egalitarian values. Etzioni would apparently disagree. Again, what is needed is empirical research directed at determining just how integration feeds into national political processes and impinges upon relations with the third world. Such research would be useful in assessing the future prospects of the European Communities—particularly if it focused on the way in which the costs and benefits of integration are tabulated within nation-states.[51] But above and beyond what this work would reveal about the future, it would add an important dimension to our understanding of regional integration by making us sensitive to both its burdens and its benefits.

IV. ALTERNATIVE RESEARCH STRATEGIES

The simple sum of the arguments presented in this article is that our understanding of what is at stake in integration tends to be confined to the member states as such. I am, of course, not arguing that research on integration has focused exclusively or primarily on national units. On the contrary, the tendency to conceptualize integration in terms of interpenetration of the national and the supranational units has directed attention to the attitudes and/or behavior of bureaucrats, politicians, trade unionists, etc. But what *cost-benefit analysis* there has been has focused primarily on the national units. Political science research on the aggregation of authority, for example, sheds some light on what, if anything, the member states have to lose in terms of legitimacy and independence of action. Similarly, economists tell us how the material gains are being distributed among nation-states.[52] What I am suggesting is that the calculation of gains and losses be extended in a number of ways. Within the communities let us ask about distribution among groups and social classes and let us also consider the costs of increased consumption and technological advance in terms of the quality of life in an affluent society. In addition, more attention should be devoted to the impact of integration on outsiders: Are regional peace and material satisfaction being purchased at the expense of "third countries" in general and developing areas in particular?

At this juncture, given the paucity of empirical information bearing on these issues, I would propose a rather eclectic approach to research. The initial goal should be to accumulate detailed information on individual policy areas or on discrete problems. Rather than attempting, right at the outset, to answer

[51] Without research we can only speculate about the costing process. It seems safe to say, however, that it is a good deal more complex now than it was when Europe lay in ruins at the close of World War II and when there were fundamental doubts about the economic potential and political viability of the European state system. Bargains which have to take into account the kinds of expectations voiced in the new politics will surely be more intricate and perhaps more delicately balanced than those of the 1950's in which peace and affluence were the controlling values.

[52] In addition to Krause, see on this point Bernard Heidelberger, "La ventilation des dépenses communautaire," unpublished manuscript.

sweeping questions about the impact of integration per se, let us try to understand the variety of ways in which integrative processes impinge on national policies and world politics. Such pilot projects could, like Haas's study of the European Coal and Steel Community, generate tenable hypotheses based on a solid empirical foundation.

It should be noted in passing that my priorities would tend to exclude, for the present, survey research and aggregate data projects. The survey data currently available offers, at best, only some clues to the kinds of problems which will have to be investigated—whether or not, for example, a parochial regional loyalty is to be one of the costs of integration. New data to serve these purposes directly will have to be collected, and this raises questions of time and money. Aggregate data on income, employment, and regional discontinuities is, no doubt, available, but projects to determine whether lifestyles are changing or patterns of mobility and stratification are being altered would require large-scale data processing. Moreover, these projects would be best carried out, it seems to me, by sociologists, political scientists, and economists working together. Such interdisciplinary possibilities are attractive and should be encouraged but will take time to develop and could be rather costly. In any case, it is difficult to get at causal relationships or account for opportunity costs with survey and aggregate data. We would, that is, not be likely to get beyond uncovering correlations between general trends and would not be able to determine what would have happened without integration. For all these reasons—time, expense, causal problems, and opportunity costs—I would suggest deferring more elaborate studies until we were better prepared to make these heavier investments wisely.

Accordingly, in the discussion that follows, the emphasis will be on rather modest research strategies that can be undertaken by individual scholars with limited research support. Moreover, since it would, in my judgment, be premature to hypothesize on the basis of the meager data now available, the discussion will be discursive rather than analytical. That is to say, no attempt will be made to conceptualize and operationalize variables or to develop formal propositions. Instead, I shall, within the context of two possible strategies, offer some concrete suggestions about just which policies and processes warrant investigation. In this inquiry we need no longer be concerned with the distinction between the original objectives of the communities and the aspirations suggested by the new politics since the important thing is that we remain sensitive to the full range of costs and benefits as well as to the manner in which they are distributed.

The first strategy calls for an assessment of the impact of given community policies in areas like agriculture, antitrust, medium-term planning, regional development, association agreements, and general commercial policy. The goal of such studies would not be to determine whether or not policies were emerging but rather to evaluate these policies in terms of the changes they are making in the distribution of, for example, welfare and influence. Are antitrust policies frustrating increases in the scale of production or stimulating competition? Are regional development policies effectively attracting private capital to depressed areas or is more extensive planning necessary to avoid increasing disparities between regions? Is medium-term planning effectively coordinating investments or is European economic space, as Gorz charges, increasingly laced together by a "multiplicity of private plans" engineered by transnational mergers, cartels, subsidiary arrangements, etc., which are too broad to be confined by national plans and too powerful to be affected by the community's incipient programs?[53] What kinds of displacements are being wrought by the EEC's agricultural policies in terms of unemployment, migration, and regional disparities? Are some people being put out of work? Who are they and what are their prospects for reemployment? We must also learn more in these terms about the process itself: Which groups have effective access and which are excluded? In dealings with nonmembers on questions of commercial policy, for example, we might want to learn about the relative influence and avenues of access of the developing nations, the United States, the associated territories, the states of Eastern Europe, etc. It is not important which policy area is chosen since we know virtually nothing about channels of influence and/or the impact of any of them. What counts is the making of a thoroughgoing intensive investigation of the manner in which burdens and benefits are distributed so that we will understand more about the nature of the change that can be attributed to European integration.

The second line of inquiry would be to begin with interesting changes and recognized problems which appear as if they might be related to the growth of the European Communities and then attempt to determine whether or not this is, in fact, the case. Thus, one could work backward, so to speak, from worker discontent in the German Ruhr; from the long-standing complaints of certain groups of French farmers; from regional problems in Belgium or Italy; or from the rise of extremist-nationalist parties like the National Partei Deutschland. Picking up on Gorz's thesis about changing coalitions, one could check parliamentary votes and debates bearing on community questions and seek to determine whether or not "normal" political alignments are altered on some or all of them, not necessarily to test Gorz's idea, but simply to spot signs of significant political shifts, assess the role of integration, and evaluate the significance for the quality of political life. The goal would once again be to assess the gains and losses of various political groupings and the impact of these changes on the character of political activities. Investigations of this sort could also be made by individual scholars with relatively limited re-

[53] Gorz, pp. 144–153.

sources, and they could be sufficiently detailed so as to reduce the difficulty of identifying causal relationships.

All the approaches that I have suggested are basically inductive and atheoretical, and the root assumption of this strategy is that it is just as well to avoid theorizing until more data has been accumulated. It is possible, however, that some of the questions posed in this article will not be answered without theory. How, for example, are we to assess Mitrany's thesis that supranational systems (or federal systems, as he terms the European Communities) tend to heighten conflict and endanger world peace? We can uncover some relevant information and probably gain partial insights with a pragmatic approach which raises certain obvious questions. Do the European Communities regularly resolve internal quarrels at the expense of outsiders? Do outsiders have an opportunity to influence decisions which affect them? Such questions would lead to the study of negotiating sequences with outsiders and to multilateral arenas in which the communities are involved. In this way we might be able to learn whether the communities were exerting a moderating influence on interbloc relations or contributing to the creation of an international environment which was more responsive to the needs of developing areas. While useful, the information obtained from this ad hoc agenda would fall short of providing a calculus for assessing the net impact of the European Communities on world security. Obviously, imaginative theorizing would be more likely to permit us to design research projects which would answer the big questions posed by Mitrany, Gorz, Etzioni, and others and should be encouraged along with the kind of intensive field research which I am inclined to believe constitutes the most sensible first step.

V. CONCLUSIONS

Regional integration in Europe is a complex process linking nations together through mutual involvement in collective decisionmaking mechanisms and institutions. It is potentially of great significance to both domestic and international politics. In professional terms it thus defies or straddles the standard divisions of the field of political science, in particular, those of comparative politics and international relations. It presumably has implications for both. The fact remains that most members of the profession probably perceive it primarily as a significant subfield within international organization. One of the consequences of this relative isolation is an intensive and highly rewarding pattern of collegial relationships which, as this volume suggests, is beginning to yield the kinds of cumulative research findings which seem likely to result in a real understanding of the nature and the many possible permutations of the process of regional integration. On the other hand, it is difficult to engage the attention and energies of students of comparative politics and international relations whose knowledge of domestic politics and the international system might add a great deal to our understanding of the integrative phenomenon. In other words, the consequence of isolation may be the sacrifice of breadth for depth.

One way to break out of this circle is to develop analytical techniques which by their sophistication and analytic power command the attention of researchers in other areas like organization theory and political behavior. Clearly, this process has already begun, but one of the purposes of this article is to suggest that, in addition, attention to the consequences of integration will make integration more meaningful to other political scientists.[54] These consequences are, after all, the inputs into "their systems" and the obvious point where our interests converge. As Joseph Nye's article in this volume indicates, as we move away from the simpler neo-functionalist model, it becomes increasingly clear that whether feedback is positive or negative depends more on the state of the national systems than on the character of regional outputs per se.[55] Haas alludes to the same point in stressing the importance of non-congruence models whereby "we sensitize ourselves to a two-way flow of inputs and outputs. . . ."[56]

I have done little more than scratch the surface with my proposals. If, however, these and other leads are followed, if a systematic set of propositions is formulated, and if data collection and testing begin, will we not necessarily be dealing with problems which will be relevant to comparative politics and international relations? In this way we can increase the chances of enlisting the expertise and understanding which are vital to grasping the domestic and international implications of the process of regional integration. To date, we have very little concrete evidence on which to stake a claim to such general relevance.

In closing let me simply underscore the gains that can be expected from a full consideration of the consequences of integration. These gains include: 1) challenging research opportunities; 2) the possibility of engaging more political scientists in our inquiry; and 3) through feedback analysis, a better understanding of the determinants of the success of regional integration. I would not, however, rest my case on any or all of these grounds. The more fundamental justification for this kind of research is that it turns our attention to the product of politics and makes us sensitive to the values by which this product must be judged. More specifically, in the case of the European Communities we are led to ask what difference it makes whether Europe integrates. And in answering that question we cease taking for granted either the goodness of integration or the desirability of the communities' initial goals.

---

[54] That portion of Leon Lindberg's article in this volume which is concerned with outputs and feedback opens the same kinds of opportunities.

[55] Joseph S. Nye in this volume.

[56] Haas in this volume, p. 37.

Selected Bibliography

COMPILED BY MUKUND UNTAWALE AND ERNST B. HAAS

1. THEORY AND METHOD

MAJOR BOOKS OF READINGS

International Political Communities: An Anthology. Garden City, N.Y: Anchor Books, Doubleday & Co., 1966. 512 pp.

Kelman, Herbert C. *International Behavior: A Social-Psychological Analysis.* New York: Holt, Rinehart & Winston [for the Society for the Psychological Study of Social Issues], 1965. xiv + 626 pp.

Kriesberg, Louis (ed.). *Social Processes in International Relations: A Reader.* New York: John Wiley & Sons, 1968. xi + 577 pp.

McNeil, Elton B. (ed.) *The Nature of Human Conflict.* Englewood Cliffs, N.J: Prentice-Hall, 1965. xvi + 315 pp.

Nye, Joseph S., Jr. (ed.) *International Regionalism: Readings.* Boston: Little, Brown and Co. [under the auspices of the Center for International Affairs, Harvard University], 1968. xiii + 432 pp.

Rosenau, James N. (ed.) *International Politics and Foreign Policy: A Reader in Research and Theory.* Rev. ed. Glencoe, Ill: Free Press, 1969. xii + 511 pp.

Singer, J. David (ed.). *Quantitative International Politics: Insights and Evidence.* (International Yearbook of Political Behavioral Research, No. 6.) New York: Free Press, 1968. xiii + 394 pp.

BASIC THEORIES OF INTERNATIONAL INTEGRATION

Beloff, Max. "International Integration and the Modern State." *Journal of Common Market Studies* (Oxford), 1963 (Vol. 2, No. 1), pp. 52–62.

Brenner, Michael J. *Technocratic Politics and the Functionalist Theory of European Integration.* (Cornell Research Papers in International Studies, No. 7.) Ithaca, N.Y: Cornell University Press, 1969. 164 pp.

Deutsch, Karl W. *Nationalism and Its Alternatives.* New York: Alfred A. Knopf, 1969. Chapters 4 and 5.

———. *Political Community at the International Level: Problems of Definition and Measurement.* Garden City, N.Y: Doubleday & Co., 1954. x + 70 pp.

Deutsch, Karl W., and others. *Political Community and the North Atlantic Area: International Organization in the Light of Historical Experience.* Princeton, N.J: Princeton University Press, 1968. xiii + 227 pp.

Etzioni, Amitai. *Political Unification: A Comparative Study of Leaders and Forces.* New York: Holt, Rinehart & Winston, 1965. xx + 346 pp.

Franck, Thomas M. (ed.) *Why Federations Fail: An Inquiry into the Requisites for Successful Federalism.* (Studies in Peaceful Change, No. 1.) New York: New York University Press, 1968. xv + 213 pp.

———. *Man and His Government: An Empirical Theory of Politics.* New York: McGraw-Hill, 1963. xiii + 737 pp.

Friedrich, Carl J. *Trends of Federalism in Theory and Practice.* New York: Frederick A. Praeger, 1968. xii + 193 pp.

Haas, Ernst B. *Beyond the Nation-State: Functionalism and International Organization.* Stanford, Calif: Stanford University Press, 1964. x + 595 pp.

———. "International Integration: The European and the Universal Process." *International Organization,* Summer 1961 (Vol. 15, No. 3), pp. 366–392; also in *International Political Communities,* pp. 93–129.

———. *The Uniting of Europe: Political, Social, and Economic Forces, 1950–1957.* Stanford, Calif: Stanford University Press, 1958. xx + 552 pp.

———. "*The Uniting of Europe* and the Uniting of Latin America." *Journal of Common Market Studies* (Oxford), June 1967 (Vol. 5, No. 4), pp. 315–343.

Haas, Ernst B., and Philippe C. Schmitter. "Economics and Differential Patterns of Political Integration: Projections about Unity in Latin America." *International Organization,* Autumn 1964 (Vol. 18, No. 4), pp. 705–737; also in *International Political Communities,* pp. 259–299.

Hansen, Roger D. "Regional Integration: Reflections on a Decade of Theoretical Efforts." *World Politics,* January 1969 (Vol. 21, No. 2), pp. 242–271.

Jacob, Philip E., and James V. Toscano (ed.). *The Integration of Political Communities.* Philadelphia: J. B. Lippincott Co., 1964. x + 314 pp.

Lindberg, Leon N., and Stuart A. Scheingold. *Europe's Would-Be Polity: Patterns of Change in the European Community.* Englewood Cliffs, N.J: Prentice-Hall, 1970. vi + 314 pp.

Mitrany, David. *A Working Peace System.* Chicago: Quadrangle Books [in cooperation with The Society for a World Service Federation], 1966. 221 pp.

Monnet, Jean. "A Ferment of Change." *The Common Market: Progress and Controversy.* Edited by Lawrence B. Krause. Englewood Cliffs, N.J: Prentice-Hall, 1968. pp. 40–50.

Nye, Joseph S. "Patterns and Catalysts in Regional Integration." *International Organization,* Autumn 1965 (Vol. 19, No. 4), pp. 870–884; also in Nye, pp. 333–349.

Schmitter, Philippe C. "Three Neo-Functional Hypotheses about International Integration." *International Organization,* Winter 1969 (Vol. 23, No. 1), pp. 161–166.

Taylor, Paul. "The Concept of Community and the European Integration Process." *Journal of Common Market Studies* (Oxford), December 1968 (Vol. 7, No. 2), pp. 83–101.

The Concept of Transaction in Integration Theory

Alker, Hayward, Jr., and Donald Puchala. "Trends in Economic Partnership: The North Atlantic Area, 1928–1963." In Singer, pp. 287–316.

Andrén, Nils. "Nordic Integration: Aspects and Problems." *Cooperation and Conflict* (Stockholm), 1967 (No. 1), pp. 1–25.

Angell, Robert C. "The Growth of Transnational Participation." In Kriesberg, pp. 226–245.

Deutsch, Karl W. "The Propensity to International Transactions." In Kriesberg, pp. 246–254.

Feldstein, Helen S. "A Study of Transaction and Political Integration: Transnational Labour Flow within the European Economic Community." *Journal of Common Market Studies* (Oxford), September 1967 (Vol. 6, No. 1), pp. 24–55.

Fisher, William E. "An Analysis of the Deutsch Sociocausal Paradigm of Political Integration." *International Organization,* Spring 1969 (Vol. 23, No. 2), pp. 259–290.

Galtung, Johan. "East-West Interaction Patterns." In Kriesberg, pp. 272–307.

Gehlen, Michael P. "The Integrative Process in East Europe: A Theoretical Framework." *Journal of Politics,* February 1968 (Vol. 30, No. 1), pp. 90–113.

Hall, Edward T., and William Foote Whyte. "Intercultural Communication: A Guide to Men of Action." In Kriesberg, pp. 255–271.

Puchala, Donald J. "The Pattern of Contemporary Regional Integration." *International Studies Quarterly,* March 1968 (Vol. 12, No. 1), pp. 38–64.

Reinton, Per Olav. "International Structure and International Integration." *Journal of Peace Research* (Oslo), 1967 (Vol. 4, No. 4), pp. 334–365.

Russett, Bruce M. *Community and Contention: Britain and America in the Twentieth Century.* Cambridge, Mass: M.I.T. Press, 1963. xii + 252 pp.

The Concept of Structure and Task in Integration Theory

Galtung, Johan. "A Structural Theory of Integration." *Journal of Peace Research* (Oslo), 1968 (Vol. 5, No. 4), pp. 375–395.

Haas, Michael. "A Functional Approach to International Organization." *Journal of Politics,* August 1965 (Vol. 27, No. 3), pp. 498–517; also in Rosenau, pp. 131–141.

Lagos, Gustavo. *International Stratification and Underdeveloped Countries.* Chapel Hill: University of North Carolina Press, 1963. 302 pp.

The Concept of Learning in Integration Theory

Alger, Chadwick F. "Personal Contact in Intergovernmental Organizations." In Kelman, pp. 521–547.
————. "Interaction and Negotiation in a Committee of the U.N. General Assembly." In Rosenau, pp. 483–497 and Singer, pp. 51–84.

Deutsch, Karl W., and others. *France, Germany and the Western Alliance: A Study of Elite Attitudes on European Integration and World Politics.* New York: Charles Scribner's Sons, 1967. xi + 324 pp.

Guetzkow, Harold Steere. *Multiple Loyalties: Theoretical Approach to a Problem in International Organization.* (Center for Research on World Political Institutions, Publication 4.) Princeton, N.J: Princeton University, 1955. 62 pp.

Harsanyi, John C. "Rational-Choice Models of Political Behavior vs. Functionalist and Conformist Theories." *World Politics,* July 1969 (Vol. 21, No. 4), pp. 513–538.

The Study of Regional Integration Methodology

Barrera, Mario, and Ernst B. Haas. "The Operationalization of Some Variables Related to Regional Integration: A Research Note." *International Organization,* Winter 1969 (Vol. 23, No. 1), pp. 150–160.

Etzioni, Amitai. "Epigenesis of Political Communities at the International Level." In Kriesberg, pp. 446–466.

Nye, Joseph S. "Comparative Regional Integration: Concept and Measurement." *International Organization,* Autumn 1968 (Vol. 22, No. 4), pp. 855–880.

Russett, Bruce M. *International Regions and the International System: A Study in Political Ecology.* (Series in Comparative Government and International Politics.) Chicago: Rand McNally & Co., 1967. xvi + 252 pp.

Schmitter, Philippe C. "Further Notes on Operationalizing Some Variables Related to Regional Integration." *International Organization,* Spring 1969 (Vol. 23, No. 2), pp. 327–336.

Weissberg, Robert. "Nationalism, Integration, and French and German Elites." *International Organization,* Spring 1969 (Vol. 23, No. 2), pp. 337–347.

The Study of the International System in General

"The Actions and Interactions of States: Research Techniques and Orientations." Part V in Rosenau, pp. 457–724.

Alger, Chadwick F. "United Nations Participation as a Learning Experience." In Kriesberg, pp. 505–521.

Alker, Hayward R., Jr. "Supernationalism in the United Nations." In Kriesberg, pp. 522–539.

Brecher, Michael. "The Middle East Subordinate System and Its Impact on Israel's Foreign Policy." *International Studies Quarterly,* June 1969 (Vol. 13, No. 2), pp. 117–139.

Brecher, Michael, Blema Steinberg, and Janice Stein. "A Framework for Research on Foreign Policy Behavior." *Journal of Conflict Resolution,* March 1969 (Vol. 13, No. 1), pp. 75–101.

Dahl, Karl Nordrup. "The Rôle of I.L.O. Standards in the Global Integration Process." *Journal of Peace Research* (Oslo), 1968 (Vol. 5, No. 4), pp. 309–351.

Etzioni, Amitai. "The Kennedy Experiment." In Kriesberg, pp. 415–438.

Farrell, John C., and Asa P. Smith (ed.). *Image and Reality in World Politics.* New York: Columbia University Press, 1967. ix + 140 pp.

Haas, Ernst B. "Collective Security and the Future International System." *International Law and Organization: An Introductory Reader.* Edited by Richard A. Falk and Wolfram F. Hanreider. Philadelphia: J. B. Lippincott Co., 1968. Pp. 299–344; also in Richard A. Falk and Cyril E. Black (ed.). *The Future of the International Legal Order.* Princeton, N.J: Princeton University Press, 1969. Vol. 1, pp. 226–316.

Haas, Michael. "Social Change and National Aggressiveness, 1900–1960." In Singer, pp. 215–244.

Hanrieder, Wolfram F. "International Organizations and International Systems." *Journal of Conflict Resolution,* September 1966 (Vol. 10, No. 3), pp. 297–313; also in Richard A. Falk and Wolfram F. Hanreider (ed.). *International Law and Organization: An Introductory Reader.* Philadelphia: J. B. Lippincott Co., 1968. Pp. 277–298.

Holsti, K. J. "Resolving International Conflict: A Taxonomy of Behavior and Some Figures on Procedures." In Kriesberg, pp. 540–564.

Holsti, Ole R., Richard A. Brody, and Robert C. North. "Measuring Affect and Action in International Reaction Models: Empirical Materials from the 1962 Cuban Crisis." In Kriesberg, pp. 390–414.

Iklé, Fred C. *How Nations Negotiate.* New York: Harper & Row, 1964. xii + 274 pp.

Iklé, Fred Charles, and Nathan Leites. "Political Negotiation as a Process of Modifying Utilities." *Journal of Conflict Resolution,* March 1962 (Vol. 6, No. 1), pp. 19–28.

Jervis, Robert. "Hypotheses on Misperception." *World Politics,* April 1968 (Vol. 20, No. 3), pp. 454–479; also in Rosenau, pp. 239–254.

Katz, Daniel. "Nationalism and Strategies of International Conflict Resolution." In Kelman, pp. 354–390.

Kriesberg, Louis. "U.S. and U.S.S.R. Participation in International Non-Governmental Organizations." In Kriesberg, pp. 466–485.

Lasswell, Harold D. "The Climate of International Action." In Kelman, pp. 337–353.

Lieberman, Bernhard. "i-Trust . . . : A Notion of Trust in Three Person Games and International Affairs." In Kriesberg, pp. 359–371.

Mueller, John E. (ed.) *Approaches to Measurement in International Relations: A Non-Evangelical Survey.* New York: Appleton-Century-Crofts, 1969. vi + 311 pp.

Pruitt, Dean G. "Definition of the Situation as a Determinant of International Action." In Kelman, pp. 391–432.

Raser, John R., and Wayman J. Crow. "A Simulation Study of Deterrence Theories." In Kriesberg, pp. 372–389.

Riggs, Fred W. "The Nation-State and Other Actors." In Rosenau, pp. 90–92.

Robinson, James A., and Richard C. Snyder. "Decision-Making in International Politics." In Kelman, pp. 433–463.

Sawyer, Jack, and Harold Guetzkow. "Bargaining and Negotiation in International Relations." In Kelman, pp. 446–482.

Smoker, Paul. "Nation-State Escalation and International Integration." In Kriesberg, pp. 486–504.

Vellut, Jean-Luc. "Smaller States and the Problem of War and Peace: Some Consequences of the Emergence of Smaller States in Africa." *Journal of Peace Research* (Oslo), 1967 (Vol. 4, No. 3), pp. 252–269.

Verba, Sidney. "Assumptions of Rationality and Non-Rationality in Models of the International System." In Rosenau, pp. 217–231.

Wright, Quincy. "The Mode of Financing Unions of States as a Measure of Their Degree of Integration." *International Organization,* Winter 1957 (Vol. 11, No. 1), pp. 30–40.

Devices and Approaches Suggested by Other Disciplines

Alger, Chadwick F. "Decision-Making Theory and Human Conflict." In McNeil, pp. 274–292.

Blau, Peter M., and W. Richard Scott. *Formal Organizations: A Comparative Approach.* San Francisco, Calif: Chandler Publishing Co., 1962. x + 312 pp.

Boulding, Kenneth E. "The Economics of Human Conflict." In McNeil, pp. 172–194.

Braybrooke, David, and Charles E. Lindblom. "Types of Decision-Making." In Rosenau, pp. 207–216.

Cooper, W. W., and others (ed.). *New Perspectives in Organization Research.* New York: John Wiley & Sons, 1964. xxii + 606 pp.

Etzioni, Amitai. *Modern Organizations.* (Foundations of Modern Sociology Series.) Englewood Cliffs, N.J.: Prentice-Hall, 1964. vii + 120 pp.

Katz, Daniel. "Group Process and Social Integration: A System Analysis of Two Movements of Social Protest." *Journal of Social Issues,* January 1967 (Vol. 23, No. 1), pp. 3–22.

Lawrence, Paul R., and Jay W. Lorsch. *Organization and Environment: Managing Differentiation and Integration.* Boston: Division of Research, Graduate School of Business Administration, Harvard University, 1967. xv + 279 pp.

Singer, J. David. "The Political Science of Human Conflict." In McNeil, pp. 139–154.

Tanaka, Yasumasa. "Cross-Cultural Compatibility of the Affective Meaning System." *Journal of Social Issues,* January 1967 (Vol. 23, No. 1), pp. 27–46.

Terreberry, Shirley. "The Evolution of Organizational Environments." *Administrative Science Quarterly,* March 1968 (Vol. 12, No. 4), pp. 590–613.

Thompson, James D. (ed.) *Approaches to Organizational Design.* Pittsburgh, Pa: University of Pittsburgh Press, 1966. vi + 223 pp.

———. *Organizations in Action: Social Science Bases of Administrative Theory.* New York: McGraw-Hill, 1967. xi + 192 pp.

Whithey, Stephen, and Daniel Katz. "The Social Psychology of Human Conflict." In McNeil, pp. 69–90.

2. ORGANIZATIONS: GENERAL

Balassa, Bela. *The Theory of Economic Integration.* London: George Allen & Unwin, 1961. 304 pp.

———. *Economic Development and Integration.* Mexico City: Centro de estudios monetarios latino-americanos, 1965. 157 pp.

Dell, Sidney Samuel. *Trade Blocs and Common Markets.* New York: Alfred A. Knopf, 1963. pp. 37–93.

Eide, Asbjørn. "Peace-Keeping and Enforcement by Regional Organizations." *Journal of Peace Research* (Oslo), 1966 (Vol. 3, No. 2), pp. 125–145.

Gordon, Lincoln. "Economic Regionalism Reconsidered." In *International Political Communities,* pp. 233–259.

Griffin, Keith, and Ricardo Ffrench-Davis. "Customs Unions and Latin American Integration." *Journal of Common Market Studies* (Oxford), October 1965 (Vol. 4, No. 1), pp. 1–21.

Kaiser, Karl. "The Interaction of Regional Subsystems: Some Preliminary Notes on Recurrent Patterns and the Role of the Superpowers." *World Politics,* October 1968 (Vol. 21, No. 1), pp. 84–107.

Lawson, Ruth C. (ed.) *International Regional Organization: Constitutional Foundations.* New York: Frederick A. Praeger, 1962. xiii + 387 pp.

Miller, Linda B. "Regional Organizations and the Regulation of Internal Conflict." In Nye, pp. 77–96.

Nye, Joseph S. "United States Policy toward Regional Organization," *International Organization,* Summer 1969 (Vol. 23, No. 3), pp. 719–740.

Russett, Bruce M. "The Ecology of Future International Politics." In Rosenau, pp. 93–103.

Schmitt, Hans O. "Integration and Conflict in the World Economy." *Journal of Common Market Studies* (Oxford), September 1969 (Vol. 8, No. 1), pp. 1–18.

Vanek, Jaroslav. "Payments Unions among the Less Developed Countries and Their Economic Integration," *Journal of Common Market Studies* (Oxford), December 1966 (Vol. 5, No. 2), pp. 187–191.

Wionczek, Miguel S. (ed.) *Economic Cooperation in Latin America, Africa, and Asia.* Cambridge, Mass: M.I.T. Press, 1969. xi + 566 pp.

Yalem, Ronald J. *Regionalism and World Order.* Washington: Public Affairs Press, 1965. xi + 160 pp.

3. ORGANIZATIONS: SPECIFIC REGIONS AND ACTIVITIES

WESTERN EUROPE
POLITICAL

Alting von Geusau, Frans A. M. *European Organizations and Foreign Relations of States: A Comparative Analysis of Decision-Making.* Leiden: A. W. Sijthoff, 1964. xiii + 290 pp.

Anderson, Stanley V. *The Nordic Council: A Study of Scandinavian Regionalism.* Seattle: University of Washington Press, 1967. xvi + 194 pp.

Bell, Coral (ed.). *Europe without Britain: Six Studies of Britain's Application to Join the Common Market and Its Breakdown.* Melbourne: Chesire [for the Australian Institute of International Affairs], 1963. 120 pp.

Bodenheimer, Susanne J. "The 'Political Union' Debate in Europe: A Case Study in Intergovernmental Diplomacy." *International Organization,* Winter 1967 (Vol. 21, No. 1), pp. 24–54.

Camps, Miriam. *Britain and the European Community, 1955–1963.* Princeton, N.J: Princeton University Press, 1964. x + 547 pp.

———. *European Unification in the 60's: From the Veto to the Crisis.* New York: McGraw-Hill [for the Council on Foreign Relations], 1966. Pp. 196–235.

Cartou, Louis. *Précis des organisations européennes.* Paris: Dalloz, 1965. li + 476 pp.

Curtis, Michael. *Western European Integration.* New York: Harper & Row, 1965. x + 262 pp.

Deutsch, Karl W. "Integration and Arms Control in the European Political Environment: A Summary Report." *American Political Science Review*, June 1966 (Vol. 60, No. 2), pp. 354–365.

Feld, Werner. *The European Common Market and the World*. Englewood Cliffs, N.J: Prentice-Hall, 1967. viii + 184 pp.

Fisher, Sydney Nettleton. *France and the European Community*. Columbus: Ohio State University Press, 1965. viii + 176 pp.

Graubard, Stephen R. (ed.) *A New Europe?* Boston: Houghton Mifflin Co., 1964. x + 691 pp.

Haas, Ernst B. "Technocracy, Pluralism and the New Europe." In Nye, pp. 149–176.

——. *The Uniting of Europe: Political, Social, and Economic Forces, 1950–1957*. Stanford, Calif: Stanford University Press, 1958. xx + 552 pp.

Hallstein, Walter. *United Europe: Challenge and Opportunity*. (William L. Clayton Lectures on International Economic Affairs and Foreign Policy, Fletcher School of Law and Diplomacy, 1962.) Cambridge, Mass: Harvard University Press, 1962. x + 109 pp.

Hay, Peter H. *Federalism and Supranational Organizations: Patterns for New Legal Structures*. Urbana: University of Illinois Press, 1966. 335 pp.

Heathcote, Nina. "The Crisis of European Supranationality." *Journal of Common Market Studies* (Oxford), December 1966 (Vol. 5, No. 2), pp. 140–171.

Hoffmann, Stanley. "Obstinate or Obsolete? The Fate of the Nation-State and the Case of Western Europe." In Nye, pp. 177–230.

Inglehart, Ronald. "An End to European Integration?" *American Political Science Review*, March 1967 (Vol. 61, No. 1), pp. 91–105.

Kitzinger, Uwe W. *The Politics and Economics of European Integration: Britain, Europe, and the United States*. New York: Frederick A. Praeger, 1963. 246 pp.

Kohnstamm, Max. *The European Community and Its Role in the World*. (John Findley Green Foundation Lectures, 1963.) Columbia: University of Missouri Press, 1964. xi + 82 pp.

Lichtheim, George. *The New Europe: Today, and Tomorrow*. New York: Frederick A. Praeger, 1963. xv + 232 pp.

Lindberg, Leon N. "Decision Making and Integration in the European Community." In *International Political Communities*, pp. 199–231.

——. "Integration as a Source of Stress on the European Community System." In Nye, pp. 231–268.

——. *The Political Dynamics of European Economic Integration*. Stanford, Calif: Stanford University Press, 1963. xiv + 367 pp.

——. "The European Community as a Political System: Notes toward the Construction of a Model." *Journal of Common Market Studies* (Oxford), June 1967 (Vol. 5, No. 4), pp. 344–387.

Lindgren, Raymond E. *Norway-Sweden: Union, Disunion and Scandinavian Integration*. Princeton, N.J: Princeton University Press, 1959. ix + 298 pp.

Liska, George. *Europe Ascendant: The International Politics of Unification*. Baltimore, Md: Johns Hopkins Press, 1964. x + 182 pp.

Mayne, Richard J. *The Community of Europe*. New York: W. W. Norton & Co., 1963. 192 pp.

Scheinman, Lawrence. "Some Preliminary Notes on Bureaucratic Relationships in the European Economic Community." *International Organization*, Autumn 1966 (Vol. 20, No. 4), pp. 750–773.

Silj, Alessandro. *Europe's Political Puzzle: A Study of the Fouchet Negotiations and the 1963 Veto*. (Occasional Papers in International Affairs, No. 17.) Cambridge, Mass: Center for International Affairs, Harvard University, 1967. v + 178 pp.

Spinelli, Altiero. *The Eurocrats: Conflict and Crisis in the European Community*. Translated by C. Grove Haines. Baltimore, Md: Johns Hopkins Press, 1966. xi + 229 pp.

Stein, Eric. "Assimilation of National Laws as a Function of European Integration." *American Journal of International Law*, January 1964 (Vol. 58, No. 1), pp. 1–40.

Willis, F. Roy. *France, Germany and the New Europe: 1945–1967*. Revised and expanded edition. Stanford, Calif: Stanford University Press, 1968. xiv + 431 pp.

Yondorf, Walter. "Monnet and the Action Committee: The Formative Period of the European Communities." *International Organization*, Autumn 1965 (Vol. 19, No. 4), pp. 885–912.

ECONOMIC

Clark, W. Hartley. *The Politics of the Common Market.* Englewood Cliffs, N.J: Prentice-Hall, 1967. xi + 180 pp.

Denton, Geoffrey. *Planning in the EEC: The Medium-Term Economic Policy Programme of the European Economic Community.* (European Series, No. 5.) London: Chatham House, September 1967. 54 pp.

Diebold, William. *The Schuman Plan: A Study in Economic Cooperation, 1950–1959.* New York: Frederick A. Praeger [for the Council on Foreign Relations], 1959. xviii + 755 pp.

Feld, Werner. "External Relations of the Common Market and Group Leadership Attitudes in the Member States. *Orbis,* Summer 1966 (Vol. 10, No. 2), pp. 564–587.

——. "The Association Agreements of the European Communities: A Comparative Analysis." *International Organization,* Spring 1965 (Vol. 19, No. 2), pp. 223–249.

Feldstein, Helen S. "A Study of Transaction and Political Integration: Transnational Labour Flow within the European Economic Community." *Journal of Common Market Studies* (Oxford), September 1967 (Vol. 6, No. 1), pp. 24–55.

Geneva Graduate Institute of International Studies. *The European Free Trade Association and the Crisis of European Integration; An Aspect of the Atlantic Crisis?* New York: Humanities Press, 1968. 323 pp.

Gregg, Robert W. "The UN Regional Economic Commissions and Integration in the Underdeveloped Regions." *International Organization,* Spring 1966 (Vol. 20, No. 2), pp. 208–232.

Houben, P.-H. J. M. *Les Conseils de ministres des Communautés européennes.* Leiden: A. W. Sijthoff, 1964. 259 pp.

Jensen, Finn B., and Ingo Walter. *The Common Market: Economic Integration in Europe.* Philadelphia: J. B. Lippincott Co., 1965. vii + 278 pp.

Krause, Lawrence B. (ed.) *The Common Market: Progress and Controversy.* Englewood Cliffs, N.J: Prentice-Hall, 1964. x + 182 pp.

Lambrinidis, John S. *The Structure, Function, and Law of a Free Trade Area: The European Free Trade Association.* New York: Frederick A. Praeger, 1965. xxii + 303 pp.

Lister, L. *Europe's Coal and Steel Community: An Experiment in Economic Union.* New York: Twentieth Century Fund, 1960. 495 pp.

Meade, J. E., H. H. Liesner, and S. J. Wells. *Case Studies in European Economic Union: The Mechanics of Integration.* New York: Oxford University Press, 1962. vii + 424 pp.

Meade, J. E. *Negotiations for Benelux: An Annotated Chronicle.* (Princeton Studies in International Finance, No. 6.) Princeton, N.J: International Finance Section, Department of Economics and Sociology, Princeton University, 1967. 89 pp.

Plessow, Utta. *Neutralität und Assoziation mit der EWG: Dargestellt am Beispiel der Schweiz, Schwedens und Österreichs.* (Kölner Schriftenzum Europarecht, Vol. 8.) Cologne: C. Heymanns, 1967. xiv + 288 pp.

Riesenfeld, Stefan A. "The Decisions of the Court of Justice of the European Communities, 1961–1963." *American Journal of International Law,* April 1965 (Vol. 59, No. 2), pp. 325–334.

Scheingold, Stuart A. *The Rule of Law in European Integration: The Path of the Schuman Plan.* New Haven, Conn: Yale University Press, 1965. xii + 331 pp.

Shoup, Carl S. (ed.) *Fiscal Harmonization in Common Markets.* Vol. I: *Theory,* Vol. II: *Practice.* New York: Columbia University Press, 1967. xx + 468 pp., xxi + 674 pp., respectively.

Siotis, Jean. "The Secretariat of the United Nations Economic Commission for Europe and European Economic Integration: The First Ten Years." *International Organization,* Spring 1965 (Vol. 19, No. 2), pp. 177–202.

——. "ECE in the Emerging European System." *International Conciliation,* January 1967 (No. 561), 72 pp.

Triffin, Robert. *Gold and the Dollar Crisis: The Future of Convertibility.* New Haven, Conn: Yale University Press, 1960. xii + 195 pp.

——. *Europe and the Money Muddle: From Bilateralism to Near-Convertibility, 1947–1956.* (Yale Studies in Economics, No. 7.) New Haven, Conn: Yale University Press, 1957. xxvii + 351 pp.

Walsh, A. E., and John Paxton. *The Structure and Development of the Common Market.* London: Hutchinson, 1968. viii + 232 pp.

MILITARY

Deutsch, Karl W. "Integration and Arms Control in the European Political Environment: A Summary Report." *American Political Science Review,* June 1966 (Vol. 60, No. 2), pp. 354–365.

Imbert, Armand. *L'Union de l'Europe occidentale.* Paris: Librairie générale de droit et de jurisprudence, 1968. iii + 238 pp.

Örvik, Nils. "Scandinavia, NATO, and Northern Security." *International Organization,* Summer 1966 (Vol. 20, No. 3), pp. 380–396.

Rothstein, Robert L. *Alliances and Small Powers.* New York: Columbia University Press, 1968. x + 331 pp.

Ten Years of Seven-Power Europe. Paris: Assembly of the Western European Union, 1964. 149 pp.

IDEATIONAL

Beever, R. Colin. *European Unity and the Trade Union Movements.* (European Aspects, Series D: Social Science, No. 2.) Leiden: A. W. Sijthoff, 1960. 303 pp.

Borcier, Paul. *The Political Rôle of the Assembly of WEU.* Strasbourg: n.p., 1963. xiii + 50 pp.

Feld, Werner J. "National-International Linkage Theory: The East European Communist System and the EEC." *Journal of International Affairs,* 1968 (Vol. 22, No. 1), pp. 107–120.

Haas, Ernst B. *Consensus Formation in the Council of Europe.* (University of California Publications in Political Science, Vol. 11.) Berkeley: University of California Press, 1960. 70 pp.

Haas, Ernst B., and Peter H. Merkl. "Parliamentarians against Ministers: The Case of Western European Union." *International Organization,* Winter 1960 (Vol. 14, No. 1), pp. 37–59.

McCreary, Edward A. *The Americanization of Europe: The Impact of Americans and American Business on the Uncommon Market.* Garden City, N.Y: Doubleday & Co., 1964. xiv + 295 pp.

Mélanges offerts à Polys Modinos: Problèmes des droits de l'homme et de l'unification européenne. Paris: Editions A. Pedrone, 1968. xxi + 498 pp.

Merkl, Peter H. "European Assembly Parties and National Delegations." *Journal of Conflict Resolution,* March 1964 (Vol. 8, No. 1), pp. 50–64.

Robertson, Arthur Henry. *The Council of Europe: Its Structure, Functions and Achievements.* (Library of World Affairs, No. 32.) London: Stevens, 1961. xv + 288 pp.

———. *Human Rights in Europe.* Manchester, England: Manchester University Press, 1963. ix + 280 pp.

———. *The Law of International Institutions of Europe, An Account of Some Recent Developments in the Field of International Law.* Dobbs Ferry, N.Y: Oceana Publications, 1961. ix + 140 pp.

Salter, Noël. "Western European Union—The Role of the Assembly 1954–1963." *International Affairs* (London), January 1964 (Vol. 40, No. 1), pp. 34–46.

Schwelb, Egon. "On the Operation of the European Convention on Human Rights." *International Organization,* Summer 1964 (Vol. 18, No. 3), pp. 558–585.

Stein, Eric. "The European Parliamentary Assembly: Techniques of Emerging 'Political Control'." *International Organization,* Spring 1959 (Vol. 13, No. 2), pp. 233–254.

Van Oudenhove, Guy. *The Political Parties in the European Parliament: The First Ten Years (September 1952–September 1962).* (European Aspects, Series C: Studies on Politics, No. 18.) Leiden: A. W. Sijthoff, 1965. xv + 268 pp.

Weil, Gordon L. *The European Convention on Human Rights: Background Development, and Prospects.* (European Aspects, Section II, College of Europe, Series C: Politics, No. 12.) Leiden: A. W. Sijthoff, 1962. 260 pp.

Wendt, Frantz. *The Nordic Council and Cooperation in Scandinavia.* Translated by A. A. Anslev. Copenhagen: Munksgaard, 1959. 247 pp.

TECHNICAL

Myrdal, Gunnar. "Twenty Years of the United Nations Economic Commission for Europe." *International Organization,* Summer 1968 (Vol. 22, No. 3), pp. 617–628.

Pfaltzgraff, Robert L., Jr., and James L. Deghand. "European Technological Collaboration: The Experience of the European Launcher Development Organization." *Journal of Common Market Studies* (Oxford), September 1968 (Vol. 7, No. 1), pp. 22–34.

Polach, Jaroslav G. *Euratom: Its Background Issues and Economic Implications.* Dobbs Ferry, N.Y: Oceana Publications, 1964. xxiv + 232 pp.

Scheinman, Lawrence. "Euratom: Nuclear Integration in Europe." In Nye, pp. 269–281.

Von Bonsdorff, Göran. "Regional Cooperation of the Nordic Countries." *Cooperation and Conflict* (Stockholm), 1965 (Vol. 1), pp. 32–38.

EASTERN EUROPE

POLITICAL

Brzezinski, Zbigniew K. *The Soviet Bloc: Unity and Conflict.* Revised and enlarged edition. (Russian Research Center Study, No. 37.) Cambridge, Mass: Harvard University Press, 1960. xxii + 470 pp.

——. "The Organization of the Communist Camp." *World Politics,* January 1961 (Vol. 18, No. 2), pp. 175–209.

Cattell, David T. "Multilateral Co-operation and Integration in East Europe." *Western Political Quarterly,* March 1960 (Vol. 13, No. 1), pp. 64–69.

Dallin, Alexander, and others (ed.). *Diversity in International Communism: A Documentary Record, 1961–1963.* New York: Columbia University Press [for the Research Institute on Communist Affairs, Columbia University], 1963. xliv + 867 pp.

Grzybowski, Kazimierz. *The Socialist Commonwealth of Nations: Organizations and Institutions.* New Haven, Conn: Yale University Press, 1964. xvii + 300 pp.

Modelski, George A. *The Communist International System.* (Center of International Studies, Princeton University. Research Monograph No. 9.) Princeton, N.J: Princeton University Press [for the Woodrow Wilson School of Public and International Affairs], 1961. 78 pp.

ECONOMIC

Agoston, Istvan. *Le Marché commun communiste: Principes et pratique du COMECON.* Geneva: Librairie Droz, 1965. xii + 353 pp.

Arsić, Dragina. "Certain Problems of Economic Development and Cooperation within the COMECON." *International Problems* (Belgrade), 1967 (8th Year), pp. 133–162.

Finley, David D. "A Political Perspective of Economic Relations in the Communist Camp." *Western Political Quarterly,* June 1964 (Vol. 17, No. 2), pp. 294–316.

Kaser, Michael. *COMECON: Integration Problems of the Planned Economies.* London: Oxford University Press, 1965. vi + 215 pp.

Korbonski, Andrzej. "COMECON." In *International Political Communities,* pp. 351–403.

Pryor, Frederic L. *The Communist Foreign Trade System.* Cambridge, Mass: M.I.T. Press, 1963. 269 pp.

Soldaczuk, Józef. "Regional Integration and East-West Trade." *Polish Perspectives* (Warsaw), January 1966 (Vol. 9, No. 1), pp. 10–17.

MILITARY

Clemens, Walter C., Jr. "The Future of the Warsaw Pact." *Orbis,* Winter 1968 (Vol. 11, No. 4), pp. 996–1033.

IDEATIONAL

Burks, R. V. *The Dynamics of Communism in Eastern Europe.* Princeton, N.J: Princeton University Press, 1961. xii + 244 pp.

TECHNICAL

Ginsburgs, George. "Soviet Atomic Energy Agreements." *International Organization,* Winter 1961 (Vol. 15, No. 1), pp. 49–65.

ATLANTIC

POLITICAL

The Atlantic Nations: Converging or Diverging? Prospects for 1975, Report of the Transatlantic Colloquium at Royaumont, France, July 7–10, 1966. Boulogne-sur-Seine: Atlantic Institute, 1967. 104 pp.

Beer, Francis A. *Integration and Disintegration in NATO: Processes of Alliance Cohesion and Prospects for Atlantic Community.* Columbus: Ohio University Press, 1969. xiii + 330 pp.

Cerny, Karl H., and Henry W. Briefs (ed.). *NATO in Quest of Cohesion: A Confrontation of Viewpoints at the Center for Strategic Studies.* New York: Frederick A. Praeger [for the Hoover Institution on War, Revolution, and Peace], 1965. xii + 476 pp.

Cottrell, Alvin J., and James E. Dougherty. *The Politics of the Atlantic Alliance.* New York: Frederick A. Praeger, 1964. 264 pp.

Dickey, John Sloan (ed.). *The United States and Canada.* (American Assembly, No. 12.) Englewood Cliffs, N.J: Prentice-Hall, 1964. viii + 184 pp.

Fox, William T. R., and Annette Baker Fox. *NATO and the Range of American Choice.* (Institute of War and Peace Studies of the School of International Affairs.) New York: Columbia University Press, 1967. xii + 352 pp.

Furniss, Edgar S., Jr. "De Gaulle's France and NATO: An Interpretation." *International Organization,* Summer 1961 (Vol. 15, No. 3), pp. 349–365.

Hartley, Livingston. *Atlantic Challenge.* Dobbs Ferry, N.Y: Oceana Publications, 1965. xii + 111 pp.

Kaiser, Karl. "The U.S. and EEC in the Atlantic System: The Problem of Theory." *Journal of Common Market Studies* (Oxford), June 1967 (Vol. 5, No. 4), pp. 388–425.

Kissinger, Henry A. *The Troubled Partnership: A Re-Appraisal of the Atlantic Alliance.* New York: McGraw-Hill [for the Council on Foreign Relations], 1965. xiv + 266 pp.

Örvik, Nils. "NATO—The Role of the Small Members." *Atlantic Community Quarterly,* Spring 1966 (Vol. 4, No. 1), pp. 92–103.

Ries, John C. "NATO Reorganization: A Critique and Analysis." *Western Political Quarterly,* March 1965 (Vol. 18, No. 1), pp. 64–72.

Spaak, Paul-Henri. *The Crisis of the Atlantic Alliance.* (Mershon Center Pamphlet Series, No. 5.) Columbus: Ohio University Press, 1967. 24 pp.

Stanley, Timothy W. *NATO in Transition: The Future of the Atlantic Alliance.* New York: Frederick A. Praeger [for the Council on Foreign Relations], 1965. xii + 417 pp.

Van B. Cleveland, Harold. *The Atlantic Idea and Its European Rivals.* New York: McGraw-Hill [for the Council on Foreign Relations], 1966. xxxi + 186 pp.

Van der Beugel, Ernst H. *From Marshall Aid to Atlantic Partnership: European Integration as a Concern of American Foreign Policy.* New York: Elsevier Publishing Co., 1966. xxi + 480 pp.

White, Dorothy Shipley. *Seeds of Discord: De Gaulle, Free France, and the Allies.* Syracuse, N.Y: Syracuse University Press, 1964. xi + 471 pp.

ECONOMIC

Aubrey, Henry G. *Atlantic Economic Cooperation: The Case of the OECD.* New York: Frederick A. Praeger, 1967. x + 214 pp.

Cooper, Richard N. *The Economics of Interdependence: Economic Policy in the Atlantic Community.* (Atlantic Policy Study.) New York: McGraw-Hill [for the Council on Foreign Relations], 1968. xiv + 302 pp.

Coppock, John O. *Atlantic Agricultural Unity: Is It Possible?* (Atlantic Policy Study.) New York: McGraw-Hill [for the Council on Foreign Relations in cooperation with the Food Research Institute, Stanford University], 1966. xvi + 238 pp.

Drummond, Roscoe. "From European to Atlantic Common Market." *Freedom and Union,* September 1961 (Vol. 16, No. 9), p. 5.

English, H. Edward. "Prospects for the North Atlantic Economic Community." *Atlantic Community Quarterly,* Winter 1966–1967 (Vol. 4, No. 4), pp. 573–580.

Esman, Milton J., and Daniel S. Cheever. *The Common Aid Effort: The Development Assistance Activities of the Organization for Economic Co-operation and Development.* Columbus: Ohio University Press, 1967. xiv + 421 pp.

Franck, Thomas M., and Edward Weisband (ed.). *A Free Trade Association.* New York: New York University Press, 1968. xv + 239 pp.

Hinshaw, Randall. "European Integration and American Trade Policy." *Atlantic Community Quarterly,* Spring 1965 (Vol. 3, No. 1), pp. 64–75.

Humphrey, Don D. *The United States and the Common Market: A Background Study.* (Books that Matter.) New York: Frederick A. Praeger, 1963. 176 pp.

Johnson, Harry G., and others. *Harmonization of National Economic Policies under Free Trade*. (Canada in the Atlantic Economy, No. 3.) Toronto: University of Toronto Press [for the Private Planning Association of Canada], 1968. 84 pp.

Krause, Lawrence B. *European Economic Integration and the United States*. Washington: Brookings Institution, 1968. xiv + 265 pp.

Ohlin, Goran. "The Organization for Economic Cooperation and Development." *International Organization*, Winter 1968 (Vol. 22, No. 1), pp. 231–243.

Rubin, Seymour J. *The Conscience of the Rich Nations: The Development Assistance Committee and the Common Aid Effort*. New York: Harper & Row [for the Council on Foreign Relations], 1966. x + 164 pp.

Uri, Pierre. *Partnership for Progress: A Program for Transatlantic Action*. New York: Harper & Row [for the Atlantic Institute], 1963. 126 pp.

Wonnacott, Ronald J., and Paul Wonnacott. *Free Trade between the United States and Canada: The Potential Economic Effects*. Cambridge, Mass: Harvard University Press, 1967. xx + 430 pp.

MILITARY

Ailleret, Charles. "The Strategic Theory of 'Flexible Response'." *Atlantic Community Quarterly*, Fall 1964 (Vol. 2, No. 3), pp. 413–428.

Birrenbach, Kurt. *The Future of the Atlantic Community: Toward European-American Partnership*. New York: Frederick A. Praeger, 1963. xii + 94 pp.

———. "Partnership and Consultation in NATO." *Atlantic Community Quarterly*, Spring 1964 (Vol. 2, No. 1), pp. 62–71.

Buchan, Alastair. *NATO in the 1960's: The Implications of Interdependence*. London: Wiedenfeld and Nicolson [for the Institute for Strategic Studies], 1960. xii + 131 pp.

———. "The Multilateral Force—A Study in Alliance Politics." *International Affairs* (London), October 1964 (Vol. 40, No. 4), pp. 619–637.

Buchan, Alastair, and Philip Windsor. *Arms and Stability in Europe: A British-French-German Enquiry*. New York: Frederick A. Praeger, 1963. x + 236 pp.

Kaplan, Lawrence S. (ed.) *NATO and the Policy of Containment*. Boston: D. C. Heath & Co., 1968. xiv + 114 pp.

Osgood, Robert Endicott. *NATO: The Entangling Alliance*. Chicago: University of Chicago Press, 1962. x + 416 pp.

Richardson, James Longden. *Germany and the Atlantic Alliance: The Interaction of Strategy and Politics*. Cambridge, Mass: Harvard University Press, 1966. vii + 403 pp.

Vandevanter, E., Jr. *Coordinated Weapons Productions in NATO: A Study of Alliance Processes*. (Research Memorandum RM-4169-PR.) Santa Monica, Calif: RAND Corporation, 1964. xi + 99 pp.

IDEATIONAL

Hovey, J. Allen. *The Superparliaments: Interparliamentary Consultation and Atlantic Cooperation*. New York: Frederick A. Praeger, 1966. xiv + 202 pp.

Szent-Miklósy, István. *The Atlantic Union Movement; Its Significance in World Politics*. New York: Fountainhead Publications, 1965. xix + 264 pp.

TECHNICAL

Foch, René. "An Example of Atlantic Partnership: EURATOM." *Atlantic Community Quarterly*, Spring 1964 (Vol. 2, No. 1), pp. 72–80.

MIDDLE EAST

POLITICAL

Boutros-Ghali, B. Y. "The Arab League." *International Conciliation*, May 1954 (No. 498), pp. 387–448.

Khalil, Muhammad. *The Arab States and the Arab League: A Documentary Record*. Vols. I and II. Beirut: Khayats, 1962.

Lenczowski, George. *The Middle East in World Affairs*. Ithaca, N.Y: Cornell University Press, 1953. xx + 459 pp.

MacDonald, Robert W. *The League of Arab States: A Study in the Dynamics of Regional Organization*. Princeton, N.J: Princeton University Press, 1965. xiii + 407 pp.

ECONOMIC

Diab, Muhammad A. *Inter-Arab Economic Cooperation, 1951–1960.* Beirut: American University Economic Research Institute, 1964. viii + 319 pp.

———. "The Arab Common Market." *Journal of Common Market Studies* (Oxford), May 1966 (Vol. 4, No. 3), pp. 238–250.

Islam, Nurul. "Regional Co-operation for Development: Pakistan, Iran and Turkey." *Journal of Common Market Studies* (Oxford), March 1967 (Vol. 5, No. 3), pp. 283–301.

Kanovsky, E. "Arab Economic Unity." In Nye, pp. 350–376.

Regional Cooperation for Development. *Regional Trade Directory: Iran, Pakistan, Turkey.* Karachi: Madatali Karamali, 1968.

IDEATIONAL

Anabtawi, M. F. *Arab Unity in Terms of Law.* The Hague: Martinus Nijhoff, 1963. xiv + 263 pp.

Foda, Ezzeldin. *The Projected Arab Court of Justice: A Study of Regional Jurisdiction with Specific Reference to the Muslim Law of Nations.* The Hague: Martinus Nijhoff, 1957. xii + 258 pp.

TECHNICAL

Islam, Nurul. "Regional Co-operation for Development: Pakistan, Iran and Turkey." *Journal of Common Market Studies* (Oxford), March 1967 (Vol. 5, No. 3), pp. 283–301.

Kashefi, R. (ed.) *Report on First Two Years of R.C.D.* Teheran: Regional Cooperation for Development, Information Department, July 1966.

R.C.D. Anniversary Publication. Teheran: Regional Cooperation for Development Secretariat, 1965.

Regional Cooperation for Development. *Regional Trade Directory: Iran, Pakistan, Turkey.* Karachi: Madatali Karamali, 1968.

AFRICA

POLITICAL

Azikiwe, Nnamdi. "The Future of Pan-Africanism." An address given by the Governor-General of the Federation of Nigeria in London, August 1961. London: Nigeria High Commission, 1961.

Boutros-Ghali, Boutros. "The Addis Ababa Charter." *International Conciliation,* January 1964 (No. 546), 62 pp.

Carter, Gwendolen M. (ed.) *National Unity and Regionalism in Eight African States: Nigeria, Niger, the Congo, Gabon, Central African Republic, Chad, Uganda, Ethiopia.* Ithaca, N.Y: Cornell University Press, 1966. xiii + 565 pp.

Cox, Richard. *Pan-Africanism in Practice: An East African Study, PANAFMECSA 1958–1964.* New York: Oxford University Press, 1964. viii + 95 pp.

Emerson, Rupert. "Pan-Africanism." In *International Political Communities,* pp. 437–456.

Hamilton, W. B., and others (ed.). *A Decade of the Commonwealth, 1955–1964.* (Commonwealth Study Center, Duke University, Publication 25.) Durham, N.C: Duke University Press, 1966. xx + 567 pp.

Harvey, Heather J. *Consultation and Co-operation in the Commonwealth: A Handbook on Methods and Practices.* London: Oxford University Press [under the auspices of the Royal Institute of International Affairs], 1952. 411 pp.

Hazlewood, Arthur (ed.). *African Integration and Disintegration: Case Studies in Economic and Political Union.* New York: Oxford University Press [under the auspices of the Oxford University Institute of Economics and Statistics and the Royal Institute of International Affairs], 1967. Pp. 3–68.

Ingram, Derek. *Commonwealth for a Colour-Blind World.* London: George Allen & Unwin, 1965. 224 pp.

Kloman, Erasmus H., Jr. "African Unification Movements." *International Organization,* Spring 1962 (Vol. 16, No. 2), pp. 387–404.

Legum, Colin. *Pan-Africanism: A Short Political Guide.* New York: Frederick A. Praeger, 1962. 296 pp.

Lewis, I. M. "Pan-Africanism and Pan-Somalism." *Journal of Modern African Studies* (Cambridge), June 1963 (Vol. 1, No. 2), pp. 147–162.

Markakis, John. "The Organization of African Unity: A Progress Report." *Journal of Modern African Studies* (Cambridge), October 1966 (Vol. 4, No. 2), pp. 135–153.

Mazrui, Ali A. *Towards a Pax Africana: A Study of Ideology and Ambition.* Chicago: University of Chicago Press, 1967, pp. 74–96.

Mezu, Sebastian Okechukwu (ed.). *The Philosophy of Pan-Africanism: A Collection of Papers on the Theory and Practice of the African Unity Movement.* Washington: Georgetown University Press, 1965. 142 pp.

Nyerere, Julius K. "A United States of Africa." *Journal of Modern African Studies* (Cambridge), March 1963 (Vol. 1, No. 1), pp. 1–6.

Padelford, Norman J. "The Organization of African Unity." *International Organization,* Summer 1964 (Vol. 18, No. 3), pp. 521–542.

Padelford, Norman J., and Rupert Emerson (ed.). *Africa and World Order.* New York: Frederick A. Praeger, 1963. 152 pp.

Quaison-Sackey, Alex. *Africa Unbound: Reflections of an African Statesman.* New York: Frederick A. Praeger, 1963. 174 pp.

Rothchild, Donald S. *Toward Unity in Africa: A Study of Federalism in British Africa.* (Books that Matter.) Washington: Public Affairs Press, 1960. 224 pp.

Touval, Saadia [Saadia Weltmann]. "The Organization of African Unity and African Borders." *International Organization,* Winter 1967 (Vol. 21, No. 1), pp. 102–127.

Wallerstein, Immanuel. "The Early Years of the OAU: The Search for Organizational Preeminence." *International Organization,* Autumn 1966 (Vol. 20, No. 4), pp. 774–787.

Zartman, I. William. *International Relations in the New Africa.* (A Spectrum Book.) Englewood Cliffs, N.J.: Prentice-Hall, 1966. xi + 175 pp.

ECONOMIC

Green, Reginald Herbold, and K. G. V. Krishna. *Economic Co-operation in Africa: Retrospect and Prospect.* London: Oxford University Press [for University College, Nairobi], 1967. x + 160 pp.

Gregg, Robert W. "The UN Regional Economic Commissions and Integration in the Underdeveloped Regions." *International Organization,* Spring 1966 (Vol. 20, No. 2), pp. 208–232.

Karefa-Smart, John (ed.). *Africa: Progress Through Cooperation.* New York: Dodd, Meade & Co., 1966. xvi + 288 pp.

Okigbo, P. N. C. *Africa and the Common Market.* Evanston, Ill: Northwestern University Press, 1967. xv + 183 pp.

Rivkin, Arnold. *Africa and the European Common Market: A Perspective.* (Monograph Series in World Affairs, Monograph No. 2.) Denver, Colo: Social Science Foundation and the Department of International Relations, University of Denver, 1963–1964. iii + 61 pp.

Robson, Peter. *Economic Integration in Africa.* London: George Allen & Unwin, 1968. 320 pp.

MILITARY

Wild, Patricia Berko. "The Organization of African Unity and the Algerian-Moroccan Border Conflict: A Study of New Machinery for Peacekeeping and for the Peaceful Settlement of Disputes among African States." *International Organization,* Winter 1966 (Vol. 20, No. 1), pp. 18–36.

WEST AFRICA

POLITICAL

Gareau, Frederick H. "Bloc Politics in West Africa." *Orbis,* Winter 1962 (Vol. 8, No. 4), pp. 470–488.

Newbury, Colin W. *The West African Commonwealth.* (Duke University Commonwealth Studies Center, Publication No. 22.) Durham, N.C: Duke University Press, 1964. xiv + 106 pp.

Tevoedjre, Albert. *Pan-Africanism in Action: An Account of the UAM.* (Occasional Papers in International Affairs, No. 11.) Cambridge, Mass: Center for International Affairs, Harvard University, 1965. 88 pp.

Welch, Claude E., Jr. *Dream of Unity: Pan-Africanism and Political Unification in West Africa.* Ithaca, N.Y: Cornell University Press, 1966. xv + 396 pp.

ECONOMIC

Plessz, Nicholas G. *Problems and Prospects of Economic Integration in West Africa.* (Keith Callard Lectures, Series 2.) Montreal: McGill University Press [for the Center for Developing-Area Studies], 1968. x + 91 pp.

POLITICAL   EAST AFRICA

Leys, Colin, and Peter Robson (ed.). *Federation in East Africa: Opportunities and Problems*. London: Oxford University Press, 1968. viii + 244 pp.

Ndegwa, Philip. *The Common Market Development in East Africa*. (East African Studies, No. 22.) Nairobi: East African Publishing House [for the East African Institute of Social Research], 1965. 150 pp.

Nye, Joseph S., Jr. "East African Economic Integration." In *International Political Communities*, pp. 405–436.

ECONOMIC   NORTH AFRICA

Zartman, I. William. "North Africa and the EEC: Negotiations." *Middle East Journal*, Winter 1968 (Vol. 22, No. 1), pp. 1–16.

POLITICAL   WESTERN HEMISPHERE

Castañeda, Jorge. "Panamericanism and Regionalism: A Mexican View." *International Organization*, August 1956 (Vol. 10, No. 3), pp. 373–389.

Dreier, John C. *The Organization of American States and the Hemisphere Crisis*. (Council on Foreign Relations, Policy Book.) New York: Harper & Row, 1962. xii + 147 pp.

———. "New Wine and Old Bottles: The Changing Inter-American System." *International Organization*, Spring 1968 (Vol. 22, No. 2), pp. 477–493.

Fenwick, Charles G. *The Organization of American States: The Inter-American Legal System*. Washington: Kaufman Printing, 1963. xxxiii + 601 pp.

Gregg, Robert W. (ed.) *International Organization in the Western Hemisphere*. (Papers presented at the Third Maxwell Institute on the United Nations, 1966.) Syracuse, N.Y: Syracuse University Press, 1968. viii + 262 pp.

Morrison, de Lesseps S. *Latin American Mission: An Adventure in Hemispheric Diplomacy*. New York: Simon & Schuster, 1965. 288 pp.

Plaza, Galo. "New Horizons for the OAS." n.p: Organization of American States, May 18, 1968.

Ronning, C. Neale. *Law and Politics in Inter-American Diplomacy*. New York: John Wiley & Sons, 1963. 167 pp.

———. *Punta del Este: The Limits of Collective Security in a Troubled Hemisphere*. (Occasional Paper No. 3.) New York: Carnegie Endowment for International Peace, 1962. 31 pp.

Slater, Jerome. *The OAS and United States Foreign Policy*. Columbus: Ohio State University Press, 1967. viii + 315 pp.

ECONOMIC

Gregg, Robert W. "The UN Regional Economic Commissions and Integration in the Underdeveloped Regions," *International Organization*, Spring 1966 (Vol. 20, No. 2), pp. 208–232.

Maritano, Nino, and Antonio H. Obaid. *An Alliance for Progress: The Challenge and the Problem*. Minneapolis, Minn: T. S. Denison & Co., 1964. 205 pp.

Sáez S., Raúl. "The Nine Wise Men and the Alliance for Progress," *International Organization*, Winter 1968 (Vol. 22, No. 1), pp. 244–269.

MILITARY

Slater, Jerome. *A Revaluation of Collective Security: The OAS in Action*. (Social Science Program of the Mershon Center for Education in National Security, Ohio State University, Pamphlet No. 1.) Columbus: Ohio State University Press, 1965. 56 pp.

———. "The United States, the Organization of American States, and the Dominican Republic." *International Organization*, Spring 1964 (Vol. 18, No. 2), pp. 268–291.

IDEATIONAL

Ball, M. Margaret. "Issue for the Americas: Non-Intervention v. Human Rights and the Preservation of Democratic Institutions." *International Organization*, Winter 1961 (Vol. 15, No. 1), pp. 21–37.

Cabranes, José A. "The Protection of Human Rights by the Organization of American States." *American Journal of International Law,* October 1968 (Vol. 62, No. 4), pp. 889–908.

Scheman, L. Ronald. "The Inter-American Commission on Human Rights." *American Journal of International Law,* April 1965 (Vol. 59, No. 2), pp. 335–343.

Schreiber, Anna P., and Philippe S. E. Schreiber. "The Inter-American Commission on Human Rights in the Dominican Crisis." *International Organization,* Spring 1968 (Vol. 22, No. 2), pp. 508–528.

Thomas, A. van Wynen, and A. J. Thomas, Jr. *Non-Intervention: The Law and Its Import in the Americas.* Dallas, Tex: Southern Methodist University Press, 1956. xvi + 476 pp.

Wells, Henry. "The OAS and the Dominican Elections." *Orbis,* Spring 1963 (Vol. 7, No. 1), pp. 150–163.

Whitaker, Arthur P. *The Western Hemisphere Idea: Its Rise and Decline.* Ithaca, N.Y: Cornell University Press, 1954. x + 194 pp.

CENTRAL AMERICA

POLITICAL

Busey, James L. "Central American Union: The Latest Attempt." *Western Political Quarterly,* March 1961 (Vol. 14, No. 1, Part 1), pp. 49–63.

Karnes, Thomas L. *The Failure of Union: Central America, 1824–1960.* Chapel Hill: University of North Carolina Press, 1961. Pp. 174–203, 243–254.

Nye, Joseph S. "Central American Regional Integration." *International Conciliation,* March 1967 (No. 562), 66 pp.; also in Nye, pp. 377–428.

Padelford, N. J. "Cooperation in the Central American Region: The Organization of American States." *International Organization,* Winter 1957 (Vol. 11, No. 1), pp. 41–54.

Sidjanski, Dusan. *Dimensiones institucionales de la integración latinoamericana.* Buenos Aires: Instituto para la Integración de América Latina, 1967. 164 pp.

Villagrán-Kramer, Francisco. *Integración económica centroamericana: Aspectos sociales y políticos.* (Estudios universitarios, Vol. 4.) Guatemala: Universidad de San Carlos, 1967. 374 pp.

ECONOMIC

Castillo, Carlos M. *Growth and Integration in Central America.* (Praeger Special Studies in International Economics and Development.) New York: Frederick A. Praeger, 1966. x + 188 pp.

Cochrane, James D. *Politics of Regional Integration: The Central American Case.* (Tulane Studies in Political Science, No. 12.) New Orleans, La: Tulane University, 1969. viii + 225 pp.

Hansen, Roger D. *Central America: Regional Integration and Economic Development.* (Studies in Development Progress, No. 1.) Washington: National Planning Association, 1967. pp. 1–65, 92–102.

Pincus, Joseph. *The Central American Common Market.* Washington: Regional Office for Central America and Panama Affairs, Agency for International Development, Department of State, 1962. 231 pp.

Wionczek, Miguel S. (ed.) *Latin American Economic Integration: Experiences and Prospects.* (Praeger Series on International Economics and Development.) Revised edition of original Spanish. New York: Frederick A. Praeger, 1966. pp. 263–306.

CARIBBEAN

POLITICAL

Lewis, S., and T. G. Matthews (ed.). *Caribbean Integration: Papers on Social, Political, and Economic Integration.* Rio Piedras: Institute of Caribbean Studies, University of Puerto Rico, 1967. 258 pp.

Lowenthal, David (ed.). *The West Indies Federation: Perspectives on a New Nation.* (American Geographical Society, Research Series, No. 23.) New York: Columbia University Press, 1961. 142 pp.

Springer, Hugh W. *Reflections on the Failure of the First West Indian Federation.* (Occasional Papers in International Affairs, No. 4.) Cambridge, Mass: Center for International Affairs, Harvard University, 1962. 66 pp.

ECONOMIC

Andic, Fuat M. "The Development Impact of the EEC on the French and Dutch Caribbean." *Journal of Common Market Studies* (Oxford), September 1969 (Vol. 8, No. 1), pp. 19–49.

Brewster, Havelock, and Clive Y. Thomas. *The Dynamics of West Indian Economic Integration.* (Studies in Regional Economic Integration, Vol. 1.) Jamaica: Institute of Social and Economic Research, University of the West Indies, 1967. xx + 335 pp.

Segal, Aaron. *The Politics of Caribbean Economic Integration.* (Institute of Caribbean Studies, Special Study No. 6.) Rio Piedras: University of Puerto Rico, 1968. vii + 186 pp.

TECHNICAL

Corkran, Herbert. *From Formal to Informal International Cooperation in the Caribbean.* (Arnold Foundation Monograph, No. 17.) Dallas, Tex: Southern Methodist University Press, 1966. 34 pp.

Poole, Bernard L. *The Caribbean Commission: Background of Cooperation in the West Indies.* Columbia: South Carolina University Press, 1951. xix + 303 pp.

SOUTH AMERICA

POLITICAL

Connell-Smith, Gordon. *The Inter-American System.* New York: Oxford University Press [under the auspices of the Royal Institute of International Affairs], 1966. xix + 376 pp.

Denham, Robert Edwin. "The Role of the U.S. as an External Actor in the Integration of Latin America." *Journal of Common Market Studies* (Oxford), March 1969 (Vol. 7, No. 3), pp. 199–216.

Herrera, Felipe. *América Latina integrada.* Buenos Aires: Editorial Losada, 1964. 249 pp.

———. *Nacionalismo latinoamericano.* (Colección imagen de América Latina, Vol. 1.) Santiago: Editorial universitaria, 1967. 224 pp.

Hirschman, Albert O. *Latin American Issues: Essays and Comments.* New York: Twentieth Century Fund, 1961. 201 pp.

Migone, Raúl C. "Inter-American Co-operation and Western Europe." *Internationale Spectator* (The Hague), March 22, 1966 (20th Year, No. 6), pp. 386–401.

Sidjanski, Dusan. *Dimensiones institucionales de la integración latinoamericana.* Buenos Aires: Instituto para la Integración de América Latina, 1967. 164 pp.

ECONOMIC

Baerresen, Donald W., and others. *Latin American Trade Patterns.* Washington: Brookings Institution, 1965. xix + 329 pp.

Brown, Robert Tennant. *Transport and the Economic Integration of Latin America.* (Transport Research Program.) Washington: Brookings Institution, 1966. xiii + 288 pp.

Cevallos, Gonzalo. *L'Integration économique de l'Amérique latine.* Ambilly-Annemasse, France: Presses de Savoie, 1968. 276 pp.

Dell, Sidney. *A Latin American Common Market?* New York: Oxford University Press [under the auspices of the Royal Institute of International Affairs], 1966. xi + 336 pp.

Fuentas, Irurozqui, Manuel. *La integración económica de América Latina.* Madrid: Ediciones cultura hispánica, 1967. 280 pp.

Garcia-Amador, F. V. *Instruments Relating to the Economic Integration of Latin America.* Dobbs Ferry, N Y: Oceana Publications, 1968. 464 pp.

Haas, Ernst B., and Philippe C. Schmitter. *The Politics of Economics in Latin America: The Latin American Free Trade Association after Four Years of Operation.* (Monograph Series in World Affairs, Vol. 3, Monograph No. 2.) Denver, Colo: Social Science Foundation and Graduate School of International Studies, University of Denver, 1965–1966. 78 pp.

Herrera, Felipe. "The Inter-American Development Bank and the Latin American Integration Movement." *Journal of Common Market Studies* (Oxford), December 1966 (Vol. 5, No. 2), pp. 172–180.

Herrera, Felipe, and others. "Document: Proposals for the Creation of the Latin-American Common Market." *Journal of Common Market Studies* (Oxford), September 1966 (Vol. 5, No. 1), pp. 83–110.

The Inter-American Development Bank and the Economic Integration of Latin America. Washington: Inter-American Development Bank, November 1967. (Mimeographed.)

Multinational Investment, Public and Private, in the Economic Development and Integration of Latin America. Washington: Inter-American Development Bank, 1968. viii + 381 pp.

Pruque, Armando. *Siete años de acción de la ALALC.* Buenos Aires: Instituto para la Integración de América Latina, 1968. 167 pp.

Schmitter, Philippe C., and Ernst B. Haas. *Mexico and Latin American Economic Integration.* (Research Series, No. 5.) Berkeley: Institute of International Studies, University of California, 1964. 43 pp.

Triffin, Robert. "International Monetary Arrangements, Capital Markets and Economic Integration in Latin America." *Journal of Common Market Studies* (Oxford), October 1965 (Vol. 4, No. 1), pp. 70–104.

Urquidi, Victor L. *Free Trade and Economic Integration in Latin America: The Evolution of a Common Market Policy.* Translated by Marjory M. Urquidi. Berkeley: University of California Press, 1962. 190 pp.

Wilkinson, Joe R. *Latin America and the European Economic Community: An Appraisal.* (Monograph Series in World Affairs, No. 4.) Denver, Colo: Social Science Foundation and Graduate School of International Studies, University of Denver, 1964–1965. i + 65 pp.

Wionczek, Miguel S. "Latin American Free Trade Association." *International Conciliation,* January 1965 (No. 551), 80 pp.

————. (ed.) *Latin American Economic Integration: Experiences and Prospects.* (Praeger Series on International Economics and Development.) Revised edition of original Spanish. New York: Frederick A. Praeger, 1966.

IDEATIONAL

Lagos, Gustavo. "El rol político de las organizaciones económicas regionales en América Latina." *Revista de la integración* (Buenos Aires), November 1967 (No. 1), pp. 76–104.

Mitchell, Christopher. "The Role of Technocrats in Latin American Integration." *Inter-American Economic Affairs,* Summer 1967 (Vol. 21, No. 1), pp. 3–29.

POLITICAL   AUSTRALASIA AND THE PACIFIC

Gelber, H. G. *Australia, Britain and the EEC, 1961–1963.* New York: Oxford University Press, 1966. xii + 296 pp.

MILITARY

Starke, Joseph Gabriel. *The ANZUS Treaty Alliance.* London: Melbourne University Press, 1965. xiv + 315 pp.

POLITICAL   SOUTHEAST AND EAST ASIA

Bull, Hedley. "What is the Commonwealth?" *World Politics,* July 1959 (Vol. 11, No. 4), pp. 577–587; also in *International Political Communities,* pp. 457–468.

Gordon, Bernard K. "Regionalism and Instability in Southeast Asia." In Nye, pp. 106–125.

————. "Problems of Regional Cooperation in Southeast Asia." *World Politics,* January 1964 (Vol. 16, No. 2), pp. 222–253.

Grant, Margaret (ed.). *South Asia Pacific Crisis: National Development and the World Community.* New York: Dodd, Meade & Co., 1964. xiv + 314 pp.

Hanna, Willard A. *The Formation of Malaysia: New Factor in World Politics.* New York: American Universities Field Staff, 1964. 247 pp.

Joyaux, François. "L'Association des etats asiatiques." *Politique étrangère* (Paris), 1965 (30th Year, No. 1), pp. 98–107.

McHenry, Dean E. "Regionalism in the South Pacific." *World Affairs Quarterly,* January 1956 (Vol. 26, No. 4), pp. 378–386.

Shizuo, Maruyama. "Asian Regionalism." *Japan Quarterly* (Tokyo), January–March 1968 (Vol. 15), pp. 53–61.

ECONOMIC

Gupta, Sisir. *India and Regional Integration in Asia.* Bombay: Asia Publishing House, 1964. 155 pp.

Gregg, Robert W. "The UN Regional Economic Commissions and Integration in the Underdeveloped Regions." *International Organization,* Spring 1966 (Vol. 20, No. 2), pp. 208–232.

Institute of Asian Economic Affairs. *Intra-regional Cooperation and Aid in Asian Countries.* Tokyo: Asian Economic Press, 1968. 188 pp.

Ikramullah, Mohammad. "The Commonwealth Economic Committee and Its Work." *Pakistan Horizon* (Karachi), 1st quarter 1963 (Vol. 16, No. 1), pp. 15–21.

Kang, Shin Joe, in collaboration with Klaus Boeck. *Economic Integration in Asia.* (Publications of the Hamburg Institute for International Economics.) Hamburg: Weltarchiv Publishers, 1969. 90 pp.

Singh, Lalita Prasad. *The Politics of Economic Cooperation in Asia: A Study of Asian International Organizations.* Columbia: University of Missouri Press, 1966. xiii + 271 pp.

———. *The Colombo Plan: Some Political Aspects.* (Working Paper No. 3.) Canberra: Department of International Relations, Research School of Pacific Studies, Australian National University, 1963. iv + 57 pp.

Stonham, P. E. "Intra-Regional Trade Co-operation in Developing Asia." *Journal of Common Market Studies* (Oxford), December 1967 (Vol. 6, No. 2), pp. 197–210.

Wightman, David. *Toward Economic Cooperation in Asia: The United Nations Commission for Asia and the Far East.* New Haven, Conn: Yale University Press [for the Carnegie Endowment for International Peace], 1963. xii + 400 pp.

MILITARY

Kennedy, D. E. "The Scope for Collective Security in Southern Asia." *World Today* (London), October 1964 (Vol. 20, No. 10), pp. 440–447.

Modelski, George Alexander (ed.). *SEATO: Six Studies.* Melbourne: Cheshire [for the Australian National University], 1962. xxxiii + 302 pp.

TECHNICAL

Padelford, Norman J. "Regional Cooperation in the South Pacific: Twelve Years of the South Pacific Commission." *International Organization,* Summer 1959 (Vol. 13, No. 3), pp. 380–393.

Sewell, W. R. Derrick, and Gilbert F. White. "The Lower Mekong: An Experiment in International River Development." *International Conciliation,* May 1966 (No. 588), 63 pp.

INDEX

Action Committee for a United States of Europe, 203, 390
Actors, 56, 243
  national, 23, 97–98, 256–258, 263, 317
    regional integration and, 248, 249
    autonomy, importance of, 320
    decisions on, 240
    perception of, 254
    strategies of, 253, 254
  political integration, role in, 323–324, 326–328
  regional integration and, 23, 24, 195–199, 207–208, 333
  supranational, 23, 84, 85, 97–98
Adenauer, Konrad, 198
Africa
  federalism and, 20, 21
  regional integration in, 14–15, 36
    politicization, 219
  trade in, 23
  tribal groupings in, 334
  See also East Africa; East African Common Market; East African Common Services Organization; Joint African and Malagasy Organization
Age
  France, factor in voting in, 176
  nationalism, western European, as factor in, 164
  Western European integration, as factor in attitudes toward, 182–187, 189, 385–386
Agency for International Development, 207
Agriculture
  Eastern European, 350
  EEC policy on, 333, 391
  public policy decisions regarding, 68
  regional integration and, 34
  Western European, 200, 201
Alker, Hayward R., Jr., 313–337
  on collective demand processing success, 120, 126
  on integration logics, xi
  on political integration, 46
Andean Group, 15
Anderson, Charles, on LAFTA, 206
Argentina, LAFTA, role in, 11

Aron, Raymond, on EEC and EFTA, 384, 385
Asia
  economic union in, 16
  regional integration in, 231
  See also Economic Commission for Asia and the Far East
Asymmetrical overlapping, 30, 31
Austria, EFTA and gross domestic product, 381
Authority-legitimacy transfer, 34

Balassa, Bela, on European Communities, 112
Bank of International Settlements, 357
Bargaining, 34, 276, 317
Barrera, Mario
  on politicization
    computer simulation for, 299–302, 305, 307
    judges panel for, 277–281
Bavaria, national movement in, 41–42
Behrman, Jack, on LAFTA, benefits under, redistribution of, 221
Belgium
  EEC and
    gross domestic product, growth of, 381
    trade with, 133
  regional organizations, frequency of mutual membership, in, 154
  regional problems in, 397
  Western European integration, public opinion on, 172
    age as factor in, 183, 184, 186, 187, 189
Benelux, collective decisionmaking in, 73
Biafra, national movement in, 41–42
Bismarck, Otto von, 3
Blalock, Hubert M., Jr., on causal models, 293
Blough, Roy, on LAFTA, benefits under, redistribution of, 221
Bolívar, Simón, 3
Bonaparte, Napoleon, 3
Brazil, LAFTA, role in, 11
Bretagne, national movement in, 41–42
Brezhnev, Leonid, 347
  Brezhnev Doctrine, 370, 371
Brzezinski, Zbigniew, on Soviet bloc, 339
Buchanan, James, on game theory, 100

Build-up, 242, 243, 257, 261, 263
Bulgaria
  agriculture in, 350
  Comecon and, 349, 353, 354, 356
  leadership in, 359
  product specialization, policy on, 349, 353, 354
Burks, R. V., on Eastern Europe, 372
Butler, David, on Labor Party, 163

Campbell, Angus, on Democratic Party, 163
Cavour, Camillo, 3
Central America
  policy integration in, indices of, 283–288 *passim*
  regional integration in, 213, 229, 256
    government contributions to, 201–202
  regional nongovernmental organizations in, 205, 206
  tariffs in, 200–201, 216
  trade in, 210
  See also Central American Common Market
Central American Common Market, 11, 16, 207, 211, 218
  beginnings of, 198
  collective decisionmaking in, 73
  cooperation in, 213
  creation of, 203
  crises in, 27
  elite complementarity in, 15
  Guatemala and, 227
  Honduras and, 214
  hostilities in, 376
  Nicaragua and, 202
  political integration, attitude toward, 56
  trade in, 23
Coalition formation, 202–203
Coalition theory, 100
Cognitive mobilization, 179–182
Cold war, détente in, 362
Coleman, James, on socialization, 103
Collective decisionmaking, 236–237, 276
  aggregate measurement of, 120–127
    system autonomy-dependency, 121–124
    system capabilities, 124–127
  bargaining modalities, 99–104
  collective arena, relative decisiveness of, 68–75
  collective leadership, 53–54, 93–98
    national actors, 97–98
    supranational actors, 97–98
  decisions, compliance with, 108–109
  decision stages, range of, 64–67
  demand flow, 75–78
  distributive consequences, 109–113
  functional scope of, 59–64
    issue areas
      economic, 60
      external relations, 60
      political-constitutional, 60
      salience of, 61–64
      social-cultural, 60

neo-functionalism and, 23
penetrativeness of, 104–108
properties of, 47–58
  animators, 53–54
  comparisons of, 115–120
  consequences, 54–58
  level, 51–53
  resources, 53–54, 78–93
    decisionmaking norms, 81–82
    financial resources, 87
    prior agreement, 80–81
    support resources, 87–93
    supranational structures, 82–87
  restrictions on, 248
  style of, 248, 249
  utility function, 54
  See also Actors
Comité des organisations professionelles agricoles, 205
Common market
  effects of commitment to create, 12
Communications approach in regional integration, 18, 19, 22–23, 24–26
Community
  security community, 210
    Scandinavia as, 56
  Western European, formation of, 140–149
Computer simulation. *See* Simulation (computer)
Conflict resolution, 319
Congress Party, 329
Congruence, national-regional, 36–37
Conseil de l'entente, 16, 207
Converse, Philip, on Democratic Party, 163
Costa Rica, CACM and, 206
Council for Mutual Economic Assistance, 13, 201, 213, 218, 230–231
  collective decisionmaking in, 73
  economic factors operating in
    planning, coordination of, 346–348
    product specialization, 348–353
    trade policies, 353–358
  EEC and, 363
  elites in, 358, 359–360
  factionalism within ruling oligarchies, 358–359
  inequality in, 11
  Khrushchev, Nikita, and, 345, 346–347
  milieu of, 358–364
  payments system of, 357–358
  pressure groups in, 358, 360
  price policy of, 355–357
  research on, 340–342
  Soviet Union and, 11, 361, 365–366, 371
  theoretical environment of, 364–373
  trade in, 345, 353–358, 366, 370
Council of Europe, collective decisionmaking in, 73
Cutler, Neal H., on public opinion and age, 185
Czechoslovakia
  leadership in, 359

on product specialization, 349, 352, 354
on Soviet Union, development capital for, 356–357
pressure groups in, 360
Soviet intervention in, 359, 370, 371

Dahl, Robert A., on power, 120
Decisionmaking. *See* Collective decisionmaking; National decisionmaking
Defense policy, retraction and, 34
de Gaspari, Alcide, 198
de Gaulle, Charles
NATO, attacks on, 329
on regional integration, 23, 26
on Western European integration, 161, 173–178, 195
Democratic Party, 163
Denmark
EFTA and gross domestic product, growth of, 381
regional organizations, frequency of mutual membership in, 154
Deutsch, Karl W.
on arms control, French elite attitude toward, 175
on core area, 210
on EEC, 52
sociocausal paradigm for, 271, 272, 273
on political integration, relative acceptance index for, 111
on regional integration
definition of, 7
indices of, 268, 375
on transaction flows and community, 137–139
on Western European integration, 22–23
elite attitudes toward, 171, 173

East Africa, 27, 204
currency of, 201
elites in, 213
industry in, 212
policy integration in, indices of, 283–288 *passim*
regional integration in, 229
road transport in, 201
trade in, 202
trade unions in, 206
See also Africa; East African Common Market; East African Common Services Organization; Joint African and Malagasy Organization
East African Common Market, 16, 206, 213, 218
disintegration of, 284
process mechanisms in, 217, 218
trade in, 23
East African Common Services Organization, 56, 204–205
Eastern Europe
agriculture in, 350
elites in, 360

politicization and, 364–365
regional integration in, xi
concept of, 342–345
research on, 339–342
future of, 372–373
Soviet Union and, 365, 369–370
trade in, 366, 370
See also Council for Mutual Economic Assistance; Warsaw Treaty Organization
Easton, David
on demand flow, 75, 76
on European Communities, leadership of, 97
on political regimes, 82, 90, 93
on systems analysis of political life, 48, 51, 54
Economic Commission for Asia and the Far East, 231
Economic Commission for Latin America, 204, 207
Education, political skills and, 180–181
Elites, x–xi, 15, 175
Comecon, emergence in, 358, 359–360
East European, 360
elite value complementarity, 247–248, 249, 252
European Communities and, 66, 389, 390
public opinion and, 165, 166, 167
regional integration and
attitudes toward, 107, 276
role in, 199
responsiveness of, 33, 34
socialization of, 203–205
Western European integration, attitudes toward, 171, 173, 175, 385
Encapsulation, 11, 12, 14, 121, 238, 240, 242, 243, 251, 254, 258, 261, 263
Engrenage, 195, 198, 216, 221, 236, 250
Envy, 236, 250
Equity, 236
Ethnic loyalties, 334
Etzioni, Amitai
on collective decisionmaking, 78–79
on egalitarian vs. elite unions, 211
on regional integration, 389
definition of, 6
on transactions, rise in, 201
Europe. *See* Eastern Europe; Western Europe
European Atomic Energy Community, 29
transactions concerning, 157
European Coal and Steel Community, 198
coal crisis in, 201
founding of, 378–379
transactions concerning, 157
European Communities
agriculture in, proposed research on, 395, 396
antitrust, proposed research on, 395, 396
association agreements, proposed research on, 395
benefits from, 66
distribution of, 376, 390–391, 394
collective decisionmaking in

collective leadership, 93
    issue areas subject to, 61–62
    locus of, 68–73
    resources, 84–85, 91
commercial policy, proposed research on, 395,
    396
Commission, 84–85, 200
creation of, original incentives for, 375–376,
    377–379
egalitarian values in, 390–391, 394
elites in, 66, 389, 390
goals of, 377–379
leadership of, 97, 98
new politics in, 387–394
North Atlantic area and, 384, 385
planning, medium-term, proposed research on,
    395, 396
political integration in, attitude toward, 65–66
problems in, 396
regional development, proposed research on,
    395, 396
regional integration in, consequences of, 112,
    113, 374–398 passim
research strategies for, 394–397
society in, participatory vs. nonparticipatory
    nature of, 389–390
technocracy in, 389–390, 394
transactions concerning, 157
European Economic Community, 11, 17, 29, 52,
    207, 218
agriculture in, 200, 333, 391
benefits from, distribution of, 111
bureaucrats in, 203
coalition formation in, 202–203
collective decisionmaking in, 73, 106
    bargaining and, 99
Comecon and, 363
EFTA vs., 383–384
establishment of, 379
gross domestic product, growth in, because of,
    381
income levels in, 380
integration under, pace of, 14
less developed countries, effect on, 392–393, 394
national-regional congruence, 36, 37
policy integration in, indices of, 282–288 passim
political community, possible formation of, 27
political integration in, 56, 292
politicians in, 203
social assimilation in, 272
spillover in, 200
tariffs in, 200, 202
trade in, 23, 111, 133
transactions and, 147–149, 157
United Kingdom and
    entry into, 187–191, 333, 383, 384–385
        public opinion on, 160, 161, 177, 183
    transactions with, 148, 149
United States, transactions with, 148, 149

European Free Trade Association, 17, 218
collective decisionmaking in, 73
EEC vs., 383–384
gross domestic product, growth in, because of,
    381
income levels in, 380
integration under, 14
Portugal in, 212
transactions concerning, 157
European integration, See Western Europe, region-
    al integration in
European Parliament, 179, 183, 390
European Payments Union, 357
Extension, 34
Externalization, 236, 244, 250, 260

Federalism, 18–19, 20–21, 26, 150, 225, 274, 334
Finley, David, on Eastern European integration,
    368
Fisher, William
on collective decisionmaking, 88, 276
on Deutsch sociocausal paradigm, 271, 272
on European Communities, 88, 107–108
on policy integration, 284, 285
on Western European political vs. social integra-
    tion, 52
France
age as factor in voting in, 176–177
agriculture in, 201
    farmers' complaints, 396
balance of payments of, 200
EEC and, 200, 204, 216
    benefits from, 111
    gross domestic product, growth of, 381
    trade with, 133
elite attitudes in, 175, 385
Germany, Federal Republic of, relations with,
    103–104, 140–145, 147, 153, 155, 157,
    158
NATO, attitude toward, 329–330
political parties in, 176–178
regional organizations, frequency of mutual
    membership in, 154
United Kingdom, relations with, 145–147, 153,
    156, 157
Western European integration
    elite attitudes toward, 385
    public opinion on, 169–179, 181–182, 189
        age as factor in, 183, 184, 186, 187, 189
Frey-Wouters, Ellen, on less developed countries,
    and European integration, 392–393
Friedrich, Carl J., on federalism, 21
Fulfillment, 34
Functionalism, 235, 236, 237
    See also Neo-functionalism

Game theory and political integration, 100–103
Gehlen, Michael, on Eastern European integration,
    367–368, 372

General Agreement on Tariffs and Trade, 393
German reunification, 384
Germany, Democratic Republic of
  Germany, Federal Republic of, negotiations with, 359
  leadership in, 359
  product specialization, policy on, 352
Germany, Federal Republic of
  agriculture in, 201
  EEC and, 149, 200, 216
    gross domestic product, growth of, 381
  elite attitudes in, 175, 385
  France, relations with, 103–104, 140–145, 147, 153, 155, 157, 158
  Germany, Democratic Republic of, negotiations with, 359
  National Partei Deutschland, 396
  regional organizations, frequency of mutual membership in, 154
  Ruhr, workers' discontent in, 396
  Western European integration
    elite attitudes toward, 385
    public opinion on, 169–173, 181–182, 189
      age as factor in, 182, 183–187
      youth's attitudes toward, 385–386
Gomulka, Wladyslaw, 359
Gorden, Morton, on Western European integration, elite attitudes toward, 173, 175
Gorz, Andre
  on EEC, 391–392
  on European Communities, 396
  on political integration, 112–113
Greenstein, Fred, on de Gaulle and Western European integration, 174
Guatemala, CACM and, 203, 227
Guttman, Louis, scaling procedure of, 282

Haas, Ernst B., 3–42
  on authority legitimacy transfer, 19–20
  on bargaining modalities, 99
  on collective decisionmaking, 276
  on collective leadership, 94–95
  on Comecon, 364–365
  on European Communities and North Atlantic area, 385
  on German reunification, 384
  on neo-functionalism, 193, 194, 234
  on political integration, theory vs. operationalization concerning, 114–115
  on politicization
    computer simulation for, 299–302, 305, 307
    judges panel for, 277–281
  on regional integration, ix, x, 375
    indices for, 268
    integrative potential of a region, 208, 210
    non-congruence models, 398
    structural conditions for, 214
    variables to be used in study of, 46
  on spillover, 200

on Western European integration, actors in, 195
Hallstein, Walter, 23, 200
  Hallstein commission, 206
Hansen, Roger, on regional integration and less developed countries, 215
Harsanyi, on power, 124, 126
Hayward, Fred M., 313–337
  on national political integration and relevance for international integration, xi
Hitler, Adolf, 3
Hoffman, Stanley, on EEC, 385, 388
Honduras, 203
  CACM and, 203, 206, 214
Human rights
  encapsulation and, 11, 12
  regional arrangements for, 12
Hungary
  leadership in, 359
  on Soviet Union, development capital for, 356–357
  product specialization, policy, toward, 349, 351, 352, 354

Iceland, regional organizations, frequency of mutual membership in, 154
Ideological-identitive appeal, 206
India, Congress Party in, 329
Inglehart, Ronald, 160–191
  on Western European integration and publics and elites, x–xi
Institute for Latin American Integration, 204
Institutionalization, 29–30, 33, 34
Integration. See Asia, regional integration in; East Africa, regional integration in; Eastern Europe, regional integration in; Latin America, regional integration in; Political integration; Regional integration; Western Europe, regional integration in
Integration logics. See subheading under Regional integration
Inter-American Development Bank, 204
Interest groups, 107
International Bank of Economic Cooperation, 357
International integration. See Regional integration
International Monetary Fund, 216
International status effect, 253, 254
International trade, 22–23
  among Comecon members, 345, 353–358
  Eastern European, 366, 370
  EEC and, 111
  See also International transactions
International transactions, 38–40, 128–159, 276
  analytical and operational attributes, 129–136
    absolute transaction volumes, 131
    foreign-to-domestic ratios, 135
    Michaely concentration index, 135
    percentage and proportion transformations, 131, 134

rate measures, 135–136
relative acceptance transformations, 134–135
transaction indices, varieties of, 132–133
attitude change and, 38–40
common market transactions, level of, 289–293
  passim
less developed countries and, 23, 208, 210
rates of, 246–247, 252, 253
  regional integration and communications approach, 22–23
rise in, 201–202, 222
transactionalists, 32
transaction analysis
  political amalgamation and, 149–152
    Western Europe and, 152–158
  regional integration, causal dynamics of, 158–159
  transaction patterns and regional integration, 136–158
    community formation and, 137–139
    Western Europe and community formation in, 140–149

Intersectorial planning, 263
Italy
  EEC and
    benefits from, 111
    gross domestic product, growth of, 381
  regional organizations, frequency of mutual membership in, 154
  regional problems in, 396
  Soviet oil, as importer of, 357
  unification of, 210
  Western European integration, public opinion toward, 169–172, 189
    age as factor in, 183, 184, 186, 187, 189

Jacob, Philip, on regional integration, definition of, 6–7
Johnson, Harry, on economic nationalism, 216
Johnson, Lyndon, 160
Joint African and Malagasy Organization, 207

Kaplan, Morton, integration, definition of, 343
Kenya
  industry in, 212, 229
  trade by, 202
Khrushchev, Nikita, Comecon, role in, 345, 346–347
Korbonski, Andrzej, 338–373
  on Eastern Europe and economic integration, xi
Kosygian, Alexei, 347
Krause, Lawrence
  on EEC
    EFTA and, 384
    income levels of, integration's impact on, 380
    trade in, 111
  on market integration, 226
  on Western Europe

economic gains in, and integration, 387
United States investment in, 382

Labor Party, 161, 163
Lasswell, Harold D., on decisionmaking, 64, 66
Late developing nations. *See* Less developed countries
Latin America
  regional integration in, 15, 36, 215, 228
  See also Central America; Central American Common Market; Latin American Free Trade Association; Organization of American States
Latin American Free Trade Association, 16, 204, 206, 207, 210, 211, 218
  beginnings of, 198
  benefits under, redistribution of, 221
  collective decisionmaking in, 73
  elites in, 15
  inequality in, 11, 212
  tariffs and, 216
  trade in, 23
Leadership. *See* Actors; Collective decisionmaking; National decisionmaking
Learning, 33, 39–40
Lecanuet, Jean, 23
Lerner, Daniel, on Western European integration, elite attitudes on, 173, 175
Less developed countries
  product specialization in, opposition to, 348
  regional integration among, 16, 213, 226–230, 245, 246, 247, 257
    benefits under, distribution of, 255
    empirical generalizations concerning, 14–15, 16
    interest in, 215
  transactions by, 23, 208, 210
  Western European integration, effects on, 392–393, 394
Lindberg, Leon N., ix–xi, 45–63
  on collective decisionmaking, 276
  on EEC, politicians and bureaucrats in, 203
  on European Community, 29
  on market integration, 226
  on neo-functionalism, 193
  on policy integration, 284, 285
    indices of, 282–288
  on political integration, x
  on regional integration, 375
    benefits from, distribution of, 197
    indices of, 268, 276–277
    judgmental procedures and, 267
  on Western European integration, 221
Lingoes, James, scaling procedure of, 282
Linkage theory, 372, 373
Literacy
  political skills and, 180, 181
Lowi, Theodore, on redistributive and distributive policies, 63

Luxembourg
  EEC and
    benefits from, 111
    gross domestic product, growth of, 381
    trade with, 133
    regional organizations, frequency of mutual membership in, 154

McClelland, Charles
  on coding interactions and influence attempts, 77–78
  on event interaction analysis techniques, 104
Mansholt, Sicco, 23
Mazrui, Ali, on EACM, 206
Mexico, LAFTA, role in, 11
Military strategy and procurement, encapsulation and, 11
Miller, Warren, on Democratic Party, 163
Mitchell, R. J., on Eastern European integration, 368–369
Mitrany, David
  on EEC, 383
  on European Communities, 397
    and North Atlantic area, 385
Mitterrand, François, 176
Monnet, Jean, 23, 322
  Action Committee for a United States of Europe, 203, 390
Montias, J. M., on Eastern European integration, 344, 345, 369–372
Moscow, Comecon conference at, 350–351
Muddle-about, 242

Nagaland, national movement in, 41–42
Nash, John, on zero-sum vs. cooperative rationality, 100
National actors. See Actors, national
National decisionmaking, 213, 222, 243
  Communist, 359
  global insecurity of decisionmakers, 246
  institutions of, structure of, 161–162
  neo-functionalism and, 23
  political skills within society and, 162–163
  public opinion and, 160–169
  public's values and, 163–169
  regional integration and, 195, 240–242
    perceptions of, 215
  restrictions on, 248
  Soviet Union and, 359
  style of, 248, 249
  Western European integration, public opinion on, 169–179
  See also Actors, national
National identity, 163–164, 188, 318
National integration
  centralization, effect of, 332
  government directives, compliance with, 318
  international integration and, xi, 313–337
    literature on, 314–322
  variables affecting, 330–337

Nationalism
  community formation and transaction flows, 137–139
  Western European integration and, 184, 189
Nationality, 163–164
National movements, 41–42
Neo-functionalism, 18, 19, 23–26, 32, 192–231 passim, 233, 234
  Communications approach, overlap with, 24–26
Netherlands
  EEC and, 204
    gross domestic product, growth of, 381
    regional organizations, frequency of mutual membership in, 154
    Western European integration, public opinion on, 170, 172, 189
      age as factor in, 183, 184, 186, 187, 189
Nicaragua, CACM and, 202
Nongovernmental organizations (regional), 205–206
Nordic Common Market, 16
Nordic Council
  collective decisionmaking in, 73
  encapsulation and, 14
North Atlantic area
  European Communities and, 384, 385
  integration in, 268, 274, 276
  See also North Atlantic Treaty Organization
North Atlantic Treaty Organization
  decline of, 362
  French attitude toward, 329–330
  inequality in, 11
  transactions concerning, 157
Northern Ireland, autonomy in, demand for, 321
Norway
  EFTA and gross domestic product, growth of, 381
  regional organizations, frequency of mutual membership in, 154
Nye, Joseph S., 192–231
  on CACM, 271
  on collective decisionmaking, 276
  on Comecon, 372
  on Eastern Europe, 365
  on federalism, 274
  on international organizations, resources of, 83–84
  on policy integration, indices for, 282–288
  on political integration, 30
    governmental expenditure as salience measure, 62
  on politicization, 281, 299
  on regional integration, 398
    causal paradigm for, xi
    concept of, disaggregation of, 343
    definition of, 46, 344
    indices for, 268, 276-277
    schedules for measuring, 126
    variables used by, 33, 36, 37

Ogaden desert, national movement in, 41–42
Organization for Economic Cooperation and Development
  collective decisionmaking in, 73
  transactions concerning, 157
Organization for European Economic Cooperation
  collective decisionmaking in, 73
  transactions concerning, 157
Organization of African Unity, 211
Organization of American States, 11

Parent-child comparisons in attitudes toward Western European integration, 186, 187
Penã, Felix, on decisionmakers, 245–246
Piaget, Jean, on nationality, 163–164
Pinder, John, on economic integration, 194
Pluralism, 213, 247, 252, 253
Poher, Alain, 178, 215
Poland
  International Bank of Economic Cooperation and, 357
  leadership in, 359
  pressure groups in, 360
  product specialization within Comecon, policy on, 352
Policy integration
  indices of, 282–288
  transaction analysis and, 149–152
    Western Europe and, 152–158
Political integration, x, xi
  aggregation, 115
  benefits from, 112
  collective decisionmaking and. See Collective decisionmaking
  conceptualization of, 322–330
  definition of, 45–46
    as adaptation and orientation of actors, 323–324, 326–328
  exogenous linkages, 123
  game theory and, 100–103
  multivariate description of, 58–113
  multivariate measurement of, 113–127
  political parties and, 331–332
  relative acceptance index for, 111
Political parties
  national integration, role in, 319
  party identification, 188
  political integration and, 331–332
  regional integration and, 107, 263
Political skills, 162–163
  changing balance of, 179–182
  literacy and, 180, 181
Politicization, 218–220, 276, 277–281
  automatic, 193–194
  Eastern Europe and, 364–365
Pompidou, Georges, 177–178, 215
Portugal
  EFTA and, 212

gross domestic product, growth in, because of, 381
Prebisch, Raúl, 23
Pressure groups, Eastern European, 358, 360
Process mechanisms in regional organizations. See subheading under Regional organizations
Pryor, Frederick, on Comecon, 201
Public health, encapsulation and, 11
Public opinion
  national decisionmaking and, 160–169
  regional integration and, 107, 160–191
  salience of, 167–168
  stability of, 167–168
Puchala, Donald J., 37, 128–159
  on European Communities
    French and German attitudes toward, 385
  on Franco-German relations, 88, 103–104
  on international institutionalization, 84
  on regional integration
    indicators of, 374
    measurement of, x
  variables used by, 33

Quebec, national movement in, 41–42

Rapoport, Anatol, on game theory, 100, 103
Regional bureaucrats, 258–260
Regional commune, 30, 31
Regional cooperation, 230
  definition of, 7
Regional Cooperation for Development, 230
Regional decisionmaking. See Collective decisionmaking
Regional development banks, 217, 229–230
Regional group formation, 252
Regional identity, development of, 252, 254
Regional integration
  alternatives, reduction of, 221–222
  benefits under, distribution of, 252
  causal paradigm for, xi
  conference on, ix–x
  consequences of, xi, 374–398
  core areas, 210
  definition of, 343
  disintegration, vs., 335
  empirical generalizations concerning, 9–18
    external world, 16–17
    gaps, 17–18
    global, 10–12
    industrialized-pluralistic nations, 13–14
    late developing nations, 14–15
    socialist groupings, 12–13
  externalization, 222–224
  extraregional dependence, 248, 249, 254, 263
  federation and, 225
  inequality as hindrance to, 11
  integration logics, xi

computer simulations of integration processes, 299–304
  Haas-Schmitter-Barrera-Nye simulation design, 299–302
  validation possibilities with simulation models, 302–304
conceptualizing integration processes, progress in, 306–309
empirical research in, 305–306
multiequation causal models, 288–299
  deterministic models, 289–292
  estimation and validation strategies for, 293–299
  stochastic models, 292–293
realism in, 304–305
single-equation logics, 267–288
  judgmental procedures, 275–279
  linear logics, 268–273
  mixed models, 279–281
  multiple indicators, use of, 281–288
  requisites analysis, 273–275
integrative potential, 208–218
  perceptual conditions, 214–218
  structural conditions, 210–214
international transactions and, 128–159
  transaction patterns and, 136–158
member internal pluralism, 247, 252
national actors and, 248
national decisionmaking and, 240–242
national integration, compared with, 313–337
  literature on, 314–322
political participation and, 336
political parties and, 107, 263
politicization, 218–220
pretheories of, 18–26
public opinion and, 160–191
redistribution, 220–221
relative size-power, 252
research on, gaps in, 17–18
scales for measurement of, 27–30
scope of, 328–329
social learning and, 39–40
study of
  definition of, 6–7
  reasons for, 3–9
transaction analysis and causal dynamics of, 158–159
variables used to study, 32–34, 37
See also Actors; Political integration
Regionalism, definition of, 8
Regional organizations
  membership (mutual) in, frequency of, 154
  nongovernmental, 205–206
  process mechanisms in, 199–208
    actors (external), 207–208
    deliberate linkages and coalition formation, 202–203
    elite socialization, 203–205
    functional linkage of tasks, 200–201

ideological-identitive appeal, 206
regional group formation, 205–206
transactions, rise in, 201–202
study of, 7–8
Regional party formation, 263
Regional reform-mongering, 253, 254
Regional state, 30, 31
Regional subsystems
  definition of, 8
Regional systems, definition of, 8
Retraction, 34
Retrenchment, 242
Romania
  leadership in, 359
  on Eastern European integration, 366
  on product specialization within Comecon, 354, 361
Rosenau, James
  on linkage theory, 372, 373
  on public opinion, 162
Russett, Bruce, on integration, 210

Sardinia, 210
Savage, I. Richard, on political integration, relative acceptance index for, 111
Scandinavia
  .EEC, transactions with, 148–149
  political integration, attitude toward, 56, 65–66
Scheingold, Stuart A., ix–xi, 374–398
  on European Community, 29
  on integration
    benefits from, distribution of, 197
    consequences of, xi, 104, 105, 113
  on Western European integration, benefits of, redistribution of, 221
Scheinman, Lawrence, on EEC, politicians and bureaucrats in, 203
Schmitt, Hans, on European Communities, 113
Schmitter, Philippe C., 232–264
  on Comecon, 364–365
  on neo-functionalism, 193, 194
  on politicization, 277–281
    computer simulation for, 299–302, 305, 307
  on regional integration
    externalization and, 222, 224
    integration processes, causal paradigm for, xi
    integrative potential of a region, 208, 210
    less developed countries' interest in, 215
    schedules for measurement of, 126
    structural conditions for, 208, 210, 212–213, 214
  variables used by, 33, 36, 37
Schuman, Robert, 198
Schuman Plan, 169
Scotland, national movement in, 41–42
Self-encapsulation. See Encapsulation
Senegal, political participation in, 336
Servan-Shreiber, J. J.
  on Western Europe, 194

economic performance and United States, 381–383, 387
Sierra Leone, political participation in, 336
Simon, Herbert, on small group behavior, 288–299 *passim*
Simulation (computer), 40–42, 299–304
Socialist states, regional integration and, 12–13
Socialization, 33
Social learning, regional integration and, 39–40
Soviet Socialist Republics, Union of
　Comecon and, 11, 356, 361, 365–366, 371
　Czechoslovakia, intervention in, 359, 370, 371
　decisionmaking in, 359
　Eastern Europe and, 365, 369–370
　monolithic nature of, 339–340
　WTO and, 371
Spill-around, 11, 33, 151, 242, 243, 257, 261, 263
Spill-back, 121, 151, 201, 242, 243, 261, 264
Spillover, 12, 17, 24, 33, 34, 121, 151, 200, 201, 202, 242, 243, 257, 261, 263, 290, 362
Stability, integration, confusion with, 327
Stalin, Josef, Eastern Europe and, 365, 369–370
Stinchcombe, Arthur
　on equifinality, 243
　on functionalism, 235
Stokes, Donald
　on Democratic Party, 163
　on Labor Party, 163
Subsystems, 333, 334
Sweden
　EFTA and gross domestic product, growth in, 381
　regional organizations, frequency of mutual membership in, 154
Switzerland
　EFTA and gross domestic product, growth in, 381
　regional organizations, frequency of mutual membership in, 154
Systems analysis, collective decisionmaking processes, as tool in studying, 48–49

Tanzania
　industry in, 212
　trade policy of, 202
Tariffs, 34, 216
　Central American, reduction of, 200–201
　EEC and, 200, 202
　Western European, reduction of, 200
Taxation, 326–327
Technocracy, European Communities and, 389–390, 394
Telecommunications, encapsulation and, 11
Teune, Henry, on regional integration, definition of, 6–7
Tojo, Hideki, 3
Transactions, international. *See* International transactions
Transcendence, 236

Transnational coalitions, 263
Tukey, John, on path analysis, 295
Tullock, Gordon, on game theory, 100

Uganda, industry in, 212
Ulbricht, Walter, 359
Underdeveloped countries. *See* Less developed countries
Union des industries de la Communauté européenne, 205
Union douanière et économique de l'Afrique centrale, 16, 211
　trade in, 23
Union of Soviet Socialist Republics. *See* Soviet Socialist Republics, Union of
United Kingdom
　EEC and
　　entry into, 333, 383, 384–385
　　　public opinion on, 160, 161, 177, 183, 187–191
　　transactions with, 148, 149
　EFTA and gross domestic product, growth in, 381
　elite attitudes in, 175
　France, relations with, 145–147, 153, 156, 157
　national integration in, 321
　regional organization, frequency of mutual membership in, 154
　Western European integration, public opinion on, 169–173, 189
　age as factor in, 183–190 *passim*
United Nations Conference on Trade and Development, 393
United States
　CACM, relations with, 16
　EEC, transactions with, 148, 149
　LAFTA, relations with, 16
　NATO, unequal role in, 11
　Western Europe, investment in, 381–382
University of Wisconsin
　regional integration, conference on, ix–x

Wales, national movement in, 41–42, 321
Wallerstein, Immanuel, on ethnic loyalties, 334
Warsaw Treaty Organization
　concept of, 344
　decline of, 361, 362
　Soviet Union and, 371
Weiner, Myron, on loyalties, 334
Western Europe
　agriculture in, 200, 201
　federalism and, 20, 21
　national-regional congruence, 36
　neo-functionalism in, 24, 213
　political amalgamation in
　　transaction analysis and, 152–158
　regional integration in, 13–14, 216
　　Action Committee for a United States of Europe, 390

benefits from, distribution of, 220, 221, 376
cognitive mobilization and, 181
elite attitudes toward, 385
initiation of, 198
peace, relation to, 383
political vs. social, 52
politicization of, 219
public opinion on, x–xi, 169–179, 181–191
   age as factor in, 182–187, 189, 385–386
   parent-child comparisons in attitudes toward, 186, 187
   research on, 338
   youth's attitudes toward, 385–386
socialization in, 164
tariffs, reduction of, 200–201
United States investment in, 381–382
See also Council of Europe; European Atomic Energy Community; European Coal and Steel Community; European Communities; European Free Trade Association; North Atlantic Treaty Organization; Organization for Economic Cooperation and Development; Organization for European Economic Cooperation
West Irian, national movement in, 41–42
Wilson, Harold, 160
Wionczek, Miguel, on Latin America, 214
Wright, Sewell, on path analysis, 295

Youth, Western European, attitudes of, 164, 385–386
Yugoslavia
   Eastern European countries, economic cooperation with, 347
   product specialization within Comecon, policy on, 352